CONFESSIONAL LUTHERAN DOGMATICS

Gifford A. Grobien, Editor

III

The Holy Trinity

by

Carl L. Beckwith

Published by
The Luther Academy
Ft. Wayne, Indiana

Jennifer H. Maxfield, Technical Editor

© 2016 by The Luther Academy, 6600 North Clinton St., Ft. Wayne, IN 46825
To order copies of Luther Academy books contact Logia Books at P.O. Box 81, Northville, SD 57465

All rights reserved. Except where cited for the purposes of review, no part of this publication may be reproduced, stored in a retrieval system, or transmitted in any form or by any means, electronic, mechanical, photocopying, recording, or otherwise, without the prior permission of The Luther Academy.

Biblical references, except where noted, are from the English Standard Version of the Bible, copyright © 2000, 2001 by Crossway Bibles, a division of Good News Publishers, 1300 Crescent Street, Wheaton, IL 60187, USA. All rights reserved.
Library of Congress Catalog Number: 89-84112

ISBN: 978-1-935035-18-3   (Volume III, paperback)
       978-0-9622791-0-2   (13-Volume Set)

Printed in the United States of America

For Julie, Paige, and Madeleine

CONTENTS

Preface to the General Introduction vii
General Introduction viii
Preface xi
Abbreviations xvi

Part One: On God 1

   1. The Problem of Modernity 3
   2. Seeing in a Mirror Dimly: The Fathers and Knowledge of God 22
   3. Proving God: Medieval Ambitions and Knowledge of God 42
   4. The Centrality of Christ: The Lutheran Approach to the Trinity......... 62
   5. Rightly Speaking about God 89

Part Two: On the Trinity 113

   6. Trinity and the Bible 115
   7. The Trinity and the Old Testament: YHWH, Our Elohim 132
   8. Father and Son: The Ordinary Language of the New Testament 162
   9. Father and Son: The Dogmatic Commitments
      of the New Testament 193
  10. The Holy Spirit 218
  11. The Procession of the Holy Spirit 244

Part Three: Dogmatic Reflection of the Church 265

  12. Distinguishing the Persons: Patristic Insights 267
  13. Distinguishing the Persons: Medieval and
      Reformation Reflections 289
  14. Unity in Trinity: *Opera ad Extra* 310
  15. Unity in Trinity: Appropriation, Attributes,
      and Divine Simplicity 336

Conclusion: Modern Trinitarianism 359

Select Bibliography 367
Indices 376

PREFACE TO THE GENERAL INTRODUCTION
by Robert H. Bennett, Executive Director
The Luther Academy

This book is the seventh to be produced in the thirteen-volume Confessional Lutheran Dogmatics series. Each volume is written with the objective of presenting Lutheran doctrine faithfully and in a fresh way. Carl Beckwith's volume on *The Holy Trinity* continues to meet the high standard established by the earlier volumes in the series. This volume provides a thorough systematic, historical, and exegetical treatment of the Holy Trinity. Beckwith accomplishes this goal by first demonstrating the identity of the Holy Trinity through an extensive exegesis of both the Old and New Testaments. He then progresses to the church fathers and finally to the reformers.

This addition to the Confessional Lutheran Dogmatics series is sure to take its place next to previous volumes as a dear addition to many pastors' libraries and seminary curriculums. Luther Academy remains committed to completing the entire series.

GENERAL INTRODUCTION
by
Robert D. Preus, General Editor, 1984–95
Confessional Lutheran Dogmatics

For some time now those of us in the Lutheran church who have interested ourselves in the Lutheran Confessions, taught from them, and conducted research in these great symbolic writings have recognized the need for a dogmatics resource based upon the outline and thought pattern of the Lutheran Confessions. Such a resource, heretofore available only in Leonard Hutter's little *Compendium Locorum Theologicorum*, would address theologians of our day with a truly confessional answer to the theological issues we are facing in Christianity and in our Lutheran Zion today. We were in no way interested in replacing as a textbook in our Lutheran Church—Missouri Synod Francis Pieper's monumental *Christian Dogmatics*, which has served students in our church body and others for three generations. Such an endeavor would have been unnecessary and unproductive. The authors of the various monographs in this Confessional Lutheran Dogmatics series come at their respective subjects from somewhat different vantage points and backgrounds and personal predilections as they practice dogmatics. It was decided, therefore, to issue a series of dogmatics treatises on the primary articles of faith usually taken up in traditional dogmatics since the sixteenth century—the Augsburg Confession, Phillip Melanchthon's *Loci Communes*, and Martin Chemnitz's *Loci Theologici*, for example.

But why the approach from the Lutheran Confessions? Are not these musty old creeds and symbols irrelevant to our day, and would not a series of monographs written from the point of view of confessional Lutheran theology be equally irrelevant to the theological issues presently confronting the church? It is because we must respond to such a question with an emphatic *No* that we presume to issue the forthcoming volumes. The Confessions, whose theology is taken directly from the Scriptures, are indeed relevant to our day, just as are the Scriptures themselves which are always "profitable for doctrine, for reproof, for correction, for instruction in righteousness" (2 Tm 3:16). There has been a real call and need for just the kind of dogmatics series here proposed, that is, a confessional Lutheran dogmatics. First of all, no dogmatics book of any kind has been published by orthodox confessional Lutheran theologians (along the lines of Elert, Pieper, Hoenecke, and Hove) within the last generation. During the same time, however, there has been a renewed interest in the Lutheran Confessions, in their function in giving form to our Lutheran presentation of doctrine, and to some extent even in norming that doctrine: note the excellent studies of Edmund Schlink, Holsten Fagerberg, Leif Grane, Peter Brunner, Wilhelm Maurer, Friedrich Mildenberger, Hermann Sasse, and others as well as the many recent books and studies written in connection with anniversary observances of the Book of Concord, the Augsburg Confession, etc. Thus, it would appear that there is need not only for a dogmatics resource in our day, but one that is strictly and consciously confessional in its presentation of doctrine and its assessment and analysis of modern theological trends throughout the Christian church. This series, of which the present volume is a part, is written to fill this need, and it is the hope and prayer of the editors that the present volume will to some extent accomplish this aim.

The volumes making up Confessional Lutheran Dogmatics are not a theology of the Lutheran Confessions; they are rather a series in dogmatics. They differ from other dogmatics books in that they are patterned strictly after the theology of the Book of Concord as they address the issues of today. They follow not only the theology of the Book of Concord, as the texts of Francis Pieper and Adolf Hoenecke and other confessional Lutheran dogmaticians have done, but, unlike these dogmaticians, the authors of the present volumes follow the actual pattern of thought (*forma et quasi typus*, ὑποτύπωσις) of the Lutheran Confessions. Such a procedure is according to the principle of the Confessions themselves; creeds and confessions are indeed a pattern and norm according to which all other books and writings are to be accepted and judged.[1] This fact will account for the agreement in both doctrine and formulation that the reader will observe within the present entire dogmatics series; the authors bind themselves not only generally to the theology of the Book of Concord, but to its content and terminology (*rebus et phrasibus*).[2]

There is another reason for the doctrinal agreement which will be apparent among the authors of the Confessional Lutheran Dogmatics. It is this: all the authors share the concept of doctrine, unity of doctrine, consensus in doctrine, and purity of doctrine consistently articulated in our Confessions. All of the Lutheran Confessions see doctrine as a singular, organic whole. Christian doctrine is like a body (*corpus doctrinae*) with parts (*partes*) or joints (*articuli*) and ligaments and members (*membra*). The plural "doctrines" is rarely used in the Confessions, as in Scripture, but rather the singular "doctrine." In the church, if one member suffers the whole body suffers; according to the organic, unitary nature of Christian doctrine, if one article or member fails, the whole body of doctrine is adversely affected. Luther said, "One article is all the articles, and all articles are one."[3]

As a confessional Lutheran dogmatics, the present volume will consciously and scrupulously draw its doctrine from Scripture. All the Confessions, beginning with the creeds and concluding with the Formula of Concord, claim

---

1. See SD RN.10.
2. Preface, *The Book of Concord: The Confessions of the Evangelical Lutheran Church*, trans. and ed. Theodore G. Tappert (Philadelphia: Fortress Press, 1959), 13.
3. *Lectures on Galatians*, 1535 (AE 27:38; WA 40.3:47.32–33).

to be and are direct explications of Sacred Scripture. As such, their purpose is never to lead us away from Scripture, nor to summarize the Scriptures in such a way as to make their further study unnecessary. They are written to lead us *into* the Scriptures. This is exactly what their function has been in the history of the church, whether we think of the many commentaries written on the early creeds by the church fathers or the expositions of our Confessions by the reformers and their successors. The reader will therefore notice that the present work in dogmatics engages in much more direct and extensive exegesis than other works in dogmatic theology of our day, except the immense *Church Dogmatics* by Karl Barth. This is altogether proper and called for in a confessional Lutheran dogmatics text.

The present work is a kind of *loci communes*, the recapitulation of the main themes of Scripture on the basis of the confessional Lutheran outline and pattern of thought. The Lutheran Confessions themselves never claim to be the final work on the understanding and exegesis of the Scriptures; we recall Luther's statement on *oratio, meditatio, tentatio*[4] with its blasts against theological know-it-alls and how often this statement of Luther's was repeated by the post-Reformation theologians in their dogmatics works. The Confessions always lead deeper into the Scriptures, especially as new issues arise in new cultures and succeeding generations which must be faced only with theology drawn from the Scriptures and patterned after the Lutheran Confessions.

The volumes in this series are dedicated to Francis Pieper, a great confessional Lutheran dogmatician of our church, in the hope and prayer that they will help to achieve what he did so much to accomplish in his day—namely, doctrinal unity and consensus in the doctrine of the Gospel and all its articles among all Lutherans and a firm confessional Lutheran identity so sorely needed in our day.

---

4. *Preface to the Wittenberg Edition of Luther's German Writings*, 1539 (AE 34:285; WA 50:659.4).

PREFACE

Hermann Sasse once remarked, "There is, thank God, no specific Lutheran doctrine on the Trinity . . ."[1] On more than one occasion Martin Luther made the same point.[2] Although Luther criticized the speculative interests of the medieval schoolmen on the Trinity, he never questioned the orthodoxy of the doctrine among them or among his Roman contemporaries. In Luther's day the threats to the doctrine of the Trinity came from the Protestant side. Luther responded to these challenges by emphasizing the importance of the church's trinitarian language for guarding Scripture's teaching on the coequality and coeternity of the Father, Son, and Holy Spirit. His classroom teaching, published works, and hymn translations from 1530 onward show his increasing concern for the Trinity.[3]

One of the more subtle and dangerous challenges faced by Luther dealt with the church's Christological and trinitarian reading of the Old Testament. The renewed study of Hebrew during the sixteenth century led some, including Luther for a time, to read the Old Testament too strictly, after the manner of the rabbis, undermining the Christian reading of the Old Testament. Luther responded to this trend by showing how the New Testament allows us to look the Old Testament "straight into the eye" (*recht unter die Augen*) and see Christ and the Trinity.[4] The new Hebraists, as Luther dubbed them, undermined the Christian reading of the Old Testament by setting aside Christ. Luther reminded them that Jesus points us to the Old Testament—to the Law, Prophets, and Writings—for they are about Him (Lk 24:25-27, 44-45). Moses wrote about Jesus (Jn 5:46), but the new Hebraists were not so sure. This kind of exegete needs to stay away from the Bible. Luther writes, "Whoever does not have or want

---

1. Hermann Sasse, "Tradition and Confession: A Response to Jaroslav Pelikan," *Lutheran World* 4:1 (June 1957): 78.
2. SA I.4: "These articles [i.e., Trinity and incarnation as expressed in the creeds] are not matters of dispute or contention, for both parties confess them" (Tappert, 292). In his treatise *On the Last Words of David* (1543) Luther writes, "And this article of faith [i.e., Trinity] remained pure in the papacy and among the scholastic theologians, and we have no quarrel with them on that score" (AE 15:310; WA 54:64.19-21).
3. In 1531 Luther wrote a preface to Johann Bugenhagen's edition of the trinitarian works of Athanasius. Bugenhagen published this edition because of Luther's concern over the antitrinitarian teachings of the radicals. Carolyn Schneider, "Luther's Preface to Bugenhagen's Edition of Athanasius," *Lutheran Quarterly* 17 (2003): 226-30. Recent scholarship has drawn attention particularly to the trinitarian emphasis in the doctoral disputations of 1543-45. We will make use of these disputations in part 3. Cf. Dennis Bielfeldt, Mickey L. Mattox, and Paul R. Hinlicky, *The Substance of the Faith: Luther's Doctrinal Theology for Today* (Minneapolis: Fortress Press, 2008). Finally, Luther's last hymn was a translation of Ambrose's trinitarian hymn *O lux beata Trinitas* (WA 35:473; AE 53:308). For Luther's rendering of this hymn see "Thou Who Art Three in Unity" in *Evangelical Lutheran Hymn-Book* (St. Louis: Concordia Publishing House, 1931), #266.
4. *On the Last Words of David*, 1543 (AE 15:287; WA 54:45.13-14).

to have this Man properly and truly who is called Jesus Christ, God's Son, whom we Christians proclaim, must keep his hands off the Bible—that I advise."[5]

Luther knew that many in his day did not agree with his strong Christological and trinitarian reading of the Old Testament. To them he simply responded: "If it [my exegesis] pleases no one else, it is sufficient that it pleases me."[6] Luther's exegetical instincts and dogmatic insights guided the robust works on the Trinity by our Lutheran dogmaticians. Johann Gerhard demonstrates at length the scriptural identity of the Trinity in the Old and New Testaments and further shows how the church, both early and medieval, expressed and guarded this scriptural witness with technical terminology and proper patterns of speech.[7] Gerhard is not alone. Abraham Calov and Johann Andreas Quenstedt, the bookkeeper of Lutheran orthodoxy, offer similarly robust dogmatic treatments of the Trinity.[8] Although the Trinity fared well during the Reformation and among the subsequent generations of orthodox Lutheran dogmaticians, something changed over the course of the seventeenth and eighteenth centuries that made the church's confession of the Trinity more and more difficult. That change affects us in significant ways today.

The major thinkers of the Enlightenment had little interest in anything inaccessible to reason. Natural theology made sense to these thinkers, and elaborate philosophies about God and ethics emerged. Among these figures an orthodox understanding of the Trinity was set aside, even if the name Trinity and a rationalization of something termed Trinity was embraced. In the centuries that followed, philosophers and theologians dealt with this marginalization of the Trinity in different ways. Some simply ignored it, but many others sought to recover some semblance of the Trinity. The twentieth century often is heralded as a period of renewed interest in trinitarian thought. We must not, however, confuse renewed interest with orthodoxy. Many writers of the twentieth century, despite their strong interest in the Trinity, continue to labor under the greatest problem of modernity: the loss of faith in the historical reliability of the Scriptures, in the truth of the Bible as God's Word, and in the providentially ordered language of faith. Lutherans are no strangers to this problem.

---

5. *On the Last Words of David*, 1543 (AE 15:268; WA 54:29.10–12).

6. *On the Last Words of David*, 1543 (AE 15:320; WA 54:73.2–3).

7. Gerhard's three works on the Trinity are available only in Latin: *De Tribus Elohim* (Locus 4/1, ed. Cotta, 185–223), *De Deo Patre et Aeterno Eius Filio* (Locus 4/2, ed. Cotta, 223–96), and *De Spiritu Sancto* (Locus 4/3, ed. Cotta, 296–342). I have found no clearer presentation of the Trinity among the dogmaticians than these three works by Gerhard. These works offer extensive interpretation of the Old and New Testaments and present the best insights of the Fathers and medieval theologians on the Trinity.

8. Isaac Dorner bestowed this oft-repeated nickname upon Quenstedt. Dorner, *Geschichte der protestantischen Theologie* (Munich: J. G. Cotta, 1867), 530; Dorner, *History of Protestant Theology*, trans. George Robson and Sophia Taylor (Edinburgh: T & T Clark, 1871), 2:109.

Gotthold Lessing (1729–81) famously declared that "contingent truths of history can never become the proof of necessary truths of reason."[9] Lessing states this in a discussion of Jesus' miracles and His resurrection. The historical reports about these events lack the certainty required for one to confess further that this Jesus is the Son of God, of the same essence with the Father. For Lessing and the other rationalists of his day, all historical accounts, whether about Jesus or Alexander the Great, could never be more than probable. It will not do for Lessing to be told that these biblical writers were inspired, were carried along by the Holy Spirit, and cannot err. To leap from the diverse accounts of the historical Jesus in the Scriptures to the church's faith in the Trinity and the two natures of Christ is too much for Lessing: "This, this is the broad and ugly ditch which I cannot get across, no matter how often and earnestly I have tried to make the leap."[10] When modernity lost faith in the Scriptures, it created an impassable ditch between the historical accounts of Jesus and the confession of His divinity by the faithful. Lessing's problem remains for many of the people writing on the Trinity in the twentieth century.

Gotthold Lessing's father was a devout Lutheran pastor. His father sent him to the universities of Leipzig and Wittenberg. Lessing knew his catechism well and throughout his life, especially toward the end, would be embroiled in controversy with conservative Lutheran pastors. As with all those who abandon Lutheranism for the allure of something more freeing and tolerant, Lessing claimed Luther as his own: "You [Luther] redeemed us from the yoke of tradition; but who will redeem us from the more intolerable yoke of the letter? Who will at last bring us a Christianity as you would teach it *now*, as Christ himself would teach it?"[11] Lessing may have claimed the name Christian, perhaps even the name Lutheran, but his religion had nothing to do with the Bible, the intolerable yoke of the letter, or the great creeds of the church. It had nothing to do with the Lutheranism preached by his father and taught in his catechism. And yet, Lessing remained convinced that if only Luther, or even Jesus, could be around in his day they would side with his views on Scripture and embrace the relativism and religious pluralism that made sense to him.[12]

Lessing could not believe the Bible. He was convinced nearly all Christians shared his doubts and uncertainties with Scripture. Those who are truly Christians shared these doubts but not, Lessing insists, those "Wittenbergian Lutheran Christians, or Christians by the grace of Calov . . ."[13] Abraham Calov insisted on the inerrancy of Scripture. Like Gerhard before him, he

---

9. Gotthold Lessing, "On the Proof of the Spirit and of Power," *Philosophical and Theological Writings*, ed. Hugh Barr Nisbet (Cambridge: Cambridge University Press, 2005), 85.
10. Lessing, "On the Proof of the Spirit and of Power," 87.
11. Lessing, "A Parable," *Philosophical and Theological Writings*, 118. Luther anticipated this false claim by Lessing (and others) in *Confession concerning Christ's Supper*, 1528 (AE 37:360–61; WA 26:499.15–26).
12. Lessing, "Introduction," *Philosophical and Theological Writings*, 5.
13. Lessing, "Axioms," *Philosophical and Theological Writings*, 125.

demonstrated at length the scriptural identity of the Trinity. Lessing stood for something radically opposed to Calov and set himself apart from theologians like him. We have many Lessings in our day but too few Calovs, and this is seen especially when it comes to the Trinity.

The Trinity has a tenuous hold on the identity of Christians today. Although Christians affirm the doctrine of the Trinity, pray the Nicene or Athanasian Creed, and sing the common doxology without much hesitation, they struggle to explain how the Trinity informs their Christian life. This struggle often has less to do with the presumed difficulty of talking about the Trinity than with the place of Scripture in our day. When modernity marginalized the Scriptures and labeled the exegetical labors of the Fathers and the reformers "premodern" or "precritical," they also marginalized the history of exegesis that confessed the Trinity. The voice of the church, the way in which the faithful have always read the Scriptures, was silenced, and all that remained were the creeds. We live in a peculiar time. We embrace the tradition of a doctrine but not the doctrine's tradition of exegesis.

There is no specific Lutheran doctrine of the Trinity, but there is most certainly a Lutheran approach to the doctrine of God and the Trinity. This Lutheran approach makes no easy distinctions between doctrine, liturgy, and what Luther called the *vita passiva*, the life of receiving and suffering the work of God. Liturgy, the divine service, stands decisively at the center of a Lutheran way of doing theology. God serves, we receive; God condescends and comes to us; God's Word creates and determines faith. For the reformers, like the Fathers before them, doctrine and life, theology and faith always remain together. The idea that they could be separated was the invention of modernity.[14] This book reflects this Lutheran approach. Further, we will not detach our efforts from those who have gone before us. Throughout we will present the teaching of the church by looking closely at the Fathers and the reformers, their scriptural insights and pious reasoning, but always from the perspective of the difficulties bequeathed to us by modernity. Our questions derive from the challenges of modernity, and our answers are informed by the great theologians of the church. We join our voices to theirs as we answer the difficult questions of our day on knowledge of God (part 1), the scriptural witness to the Trinity (part 2), and the proper patterns of speech for responsibly confessing and guarding that scriptural witness (part 3).

NOTE TO READER

The translation of the Bible used throughout is the English Standard Version (ESV). When I depart from the ESV, I indicate in the citation of the text the

---

14. Oswald Bayer, *Theology the Lutheran Way*, trans. Jeffrey Silcock and Mark Mattes (Grand Rapids: Eerdmans, 2007), 83. Bayer elsewhere states, as we have here, "Theology begins and ends with the divine service" (xxiv, 88–96).

translation used. On some occasions I use my own translation and indicate this in the footnote. I also have taken two liberties with my quotations from the ESV. I have left untranslated YHWH and Elohim in most of the quotations from the Old Testament. My reasons for doing this will become evident in the chapters on the scriptural witness to the Trinity. I also have changed the capitalization of certain words. The way we capitalize words indicates how we understand them. Most readers know there is a difference between writing God or god. Although context would determine what we meant in either case, the capitalizing of God normally indicates we are discussing the one made known to us in Scripture. The numerous titles used for Christ in the Old Testament often are not capitalized in the ESV. In my discussion of these titles, I capitalize them in order to indicate better that I am talking about the Second Person of the Trinity. The same applies to the Holy Spirit and the different titles used for the Spirit in Scripture.

Carl L. Beckwith
Birmingham, Alabama
Feast of St. Athanasius of Alexandria, 2016

ABBREVIATIONS

References to versions of the Bible:

LXX	Septuagint
Vulg.	Vulgate
KJV	King James (Authorized) Version
NKJV	New King James Version
NRSV	New Revised Standard Version
ESV	English Standard Version

References to the Book of Concord:

AC	Augsburg Confession
Ap.	Apology of the Augsburg Confession
SA	Smalcald Articles
Tr.	Treatise on the Power and Primacy of the Pope
SC	Small Catechism
LC	Large Catechism
FC	Formula of Concord
	Ep. Epitome of the Formula of Concord
	SD Solid Declaration of the Formula of Concord
	RN Rule and Norm of the Ep. or SD

References to the editions and translations of the Book of Concord:

Bente   *Concordia Triglotta. The Symbolical Books of the Ev. Lutheran Church.* Edited by F. Bente. St. Louis: Concordia Publishing House, 1921.

BSLK   *Die Bekenntnisschriften der evangelisch-lutherischen Kirche.* 12th ed. Göttingen: Vandenhoeck & Ruprecht, 1998.

Tappert   *The Book of Concord: The Confessions of the Evangelical Lutheran Church.* Translated and edited by Theodore G. Tappert. Philadelphia: Fortress Press, 1959.

References to the Book of Concord are to the confession, article, and paragraph number.

References to Luther's works:

St. L.   *D. Martin Luthers Sämmtliche Schriften,* ed. Johann Georg Walch. St. Louis: Concordia Publishing House, 1890.

WA   *D. Martin Luthers Werke. Kritische Gesamtausgabe.* 69 vols. Weimar: Hermann Böhlaus Nachfolger, 1883–1993.
WADB   *D. Martin Luthers Werke. Deutsche Bibel.* 12 vols. Weimar: Hermann Böhlaus Nachfolger, 1906–61.
AE   *Luther's Works.* American Edition. 82 vols. Edited by Jaroslav Jan Pelikan, Hilton C. Oswald, Helmut T. Lehmann, and Christopher Boyd Brown. St. Louis: Concordia Publishing House, 1955–.

Other references:

ACW   Ancient Christian Writers series. Mahwah, NJ: Paulist Press.
ANF   *The Ante-Nicene Fathers.* Grand Rapids: Eerdmans, reprint.
CCSL   *Corpus christianorum.* Series Latina. Turnhout: Brepols, 1953–.
CR   *Corpus Reformatorum.* Halle and Brunswick: C. A. Schwetschke and Sons.
CSEL   *Corpus scriptorum ecclesiasticorum latinorum.* Vienna: Österreichische Akademie der Wissenschaften.
ELH   *Evangelical Lutheran Hymnary.* Mankato, MN: Evangelical Lutheran Synod, 1996.
Fathers of the Church   Fathers of the Church series, Washington, D.C.: Catholic University of America Press.
GNO   *Gregorii Nysseni Opera,* ed. Werner Jaeger. Leiden: Brill.
LCL   *Loeb Classical Library.* Cambridge, MA: Harvard University Press.
NPNF   *Nicene and Post-Nicene Fathers.* Grand Rapids: Eerdmans, reprint.
PG   Migne, J. P., ed. *Patrologia Cursus Completus.* Series graeca. 161 vols. Paris: Garnier Fraher, 1844–.
PL   Migne, J. P., ed. *Patrologia Cursus Completus.* Series latina. 221 vols. Paris: Garnier Fraher, 1844–.
PPS   Popular Patristics Series. Crestwood, NY: St. Vladimir's Seminary Press.
SC   *Sources chrétiennes.* Paris: Éditions du Cerf.
ST   Thomas Aquinas. *Summa Theologiae.* Translated by Laurence Shapcote. Latin/English edition, 8 vols. Lander, WY: The Aquinas Institute for the Study of Sacred Doctrine, 2012.
TLH   *The Lutheran Hymnal.* Evangelical Lutheran Synodical Conference of North America. St. Louis: Concordia Publishing House, 1941.
WSA   Works of Saint Augustine. Hyde Park, NY: New City Press.

PART ONE

ON GOD

Statements about God abound in our world. The philosopher seeks to demonstrate the necessary existence of God. The theologian talks at length about the essence and attributes of God. The politician invokes God's blessing upon our nation. Interfaith events involving Jews, Christians, and Muslims claim to worship the God of Abraham, Isaac, and Jacob. Still others profane the name of God and, when misfortune befalls our world, ask where God is. Do these various figures refer to the same God or simply use the same word, God, to designate someone or something? How do they know what they claim to know about this God? Part 1 examines at length how we rightly know God and how we properly speak about Him.

We begin with a chapter on the problem of modernity in order to orient ourselves to the challenges we face today when confessing the Trinity. We then turn back to the history of the church. Two different ways of thinking about God have come down to us in the church's tradition. There are those who think we may begin with nature, with natural knowledge of God, and arrive at a partial but true understanding of God. For these thinkers Scripture complements and perfects the knowledge we gain through a reasonable consideration of nature. Scripture adds the Trinity to this initial understanding of God. This approach may be seen in the early church with figures like Justin Martyr and Tertullian, and during the medieval period with Thomas Aquinas and John Duns Scotus. It is an approach that appeals to many today. A second group agrees that God reveals His existence through nature but that this knowledge is never sufficient and always susceptible to idolatry. Our sinful nature, our fallen intellect, cannot avoid positing a "God" that answers our greatest fears and anxieties and affirms our basest desires. Natural knowledge left to its own best ideas leads to idolatry. Rather than building on this initial knowledge we repent of it. This is the view of the fourth-century Greek theologians, Luther, and the Book of Concord.

Finally, how we think we think about God affects our language for God. Part 1 ends by looking closely at language and how our words refer to God. Although this discussion is technical, it is necessary to understand what our words mean when we talk about God. Our conclusions will inform our reading of Scripture in part 2. We will also see in part 3 that these semantic concerns were part of Luther's own teaching on the Trinity at the University of Wittenberg and remained a significant issue for the Lutheran dogmaticians.

1

THE PROBLEM OF MODERNITY

The doctrine of the Trinity presents problems for the church today. For too many the Trinity is known only by abstract formulations that are unsuitable for preaching and far removed from the spiritual life of the church. This way of thinking about the Trinity renders it little more than an article of faith, a difficult doctrine, burdened with technical terminology. Out of fear that we might say the wrong thing about the Trinity we declare it a mystery that eludes human reason and words. This seemingly pious move frees us to focus on the more practical concerns for the life of the church. Unfortunately, this sort of piety also places the Trinity on the margins of Christian identity. We keep the doctrine of the Trinity because we know we must, but in reality we have little to say about it.

Despite the above difficulties, no one claiming orthodox Christianity would deny the pervasive trinitarian language of God as Father, Son, and Holy Spirit in the liturgy, lectionaries, and prayers of the church. Few are willing to admit that God has left us unable to speak about Him; we rightly confess that God's self-communication is trinitarian. This divine address, preserved for us in the canonical Scriptures, declares unequivocally God's triune identity and how we are to confess and worship Him. Herein lies the problem: according to Scripture, the triune identity and life of God is foundational to Christian self-understanding, and yet in our day it remains beyond the grasp of most Christians to explain how our trinitarian confession identifies the God we worship and confess, and in whom we live.

Some might argue that it is enough to name the God of the Bible as Father, Son, and Holy Spirit. Must we also wade into those difficult trinitarian questions discussed by the Fathers and reformers? If we switched the issue from the Trinity to the gospel, most Lutherans would see immediately the urgency of clarifying what is meant by the word "gospel." The gospel has always and will always remain susceptible to misunderstanding and distortion. Ambiguity in expression will neither deliver us from our sins nor comfort our consciences. The purity of the gospel must always be guarded diligently and proclaimed clearly by the faithful; the same applies to the Trinity. Naming God as Father, Son, and Holy Spirit will not free a person from modalism, subordinationism, or tritheism. We cannot just confess God's identity narratively but must also explain God's identity dogmatically; we must show how our confession is scripturally Nicene and how it rejects all other possibilities.

Confession requires doctrine; doctrine produces confession. The ancient trinitarian heresies and their modern counterparts show us the necessity of marking off what we mean when we confess the triune God. The mere existence of creeds and rules of faith assumes the presence of misunderstanding and distortion. To make confession is both to affirm and to deny. The Fathers established normative patterns of speech to convey what they meant by such confession and to anathematize what they did not mean. It is this normative speech that orthodox Christians continue to receive and appropriate as their own. Yet for this patristic doctrine to be our confession it must proceed from a life of prayer (*oratio*) and scriptural meditation (*meditatio*), and it must resonate with our Christian lives (*tentatio*) to such an extent that explanation seems redundant.[1] To put this more pointedly, Lutherans need to be able to confess the Trinity as clearly and persuasively as they do justification by faith alone.

The dissonance between confession and doctrine in our day appears when a parishioner asks a pastor how the Father, Son, and Holy Spirit are all three God and yet only one God. Any explanation that begins with creedal formulas, retreats to contradictory arithmetic, or diverts the conversation with imaginative analogies will remain unsatisfying to the parishioner asking what the Bible has to say about this.[2] The issue is exacerbated by the liturgical peculiarity of having a Trinity Sunday that occasions a sermon on the Trinity—something unknown to the early church.[3] What about all of those other Sundays and sermons? Were they less trinitarian? Were they a-trinitarian in the sense that the scriptural identity of God was obscured or even ignored in the very act of preaching about the creative and redemptive work of Father, Son, and Holy Spirit?

If the Trinity serves only as a doctrine for us, it is necessary to ask what effect this has on the shape of our Christian lives. If Christian conversion is, at a basic level, the move from a self-centered love to a God-centered love, and the God who saves us from the sin that curves us in upon ourselves is Father, Son, and Holy Spirit, then this God-centered love must be Trinity-centered love. If it is not, then we risk confessing one God and loving another.[4] We risk being trinitarian in doctrine but something else in life.[5] It is precisely at this point that the sharp difference between the church's tradition and our day is seen with

---

1. For an example of how Luther's *oratio, meditatio,* and *tentatio* structures Lutheran dogmatics, see Matthias Hafenreffer, *Loci Theologici* (Tübingen, 1603), 1–23 (Prolegomena).

2. Basil of Caesarea *On the Holy Spirit* 18.44 (PPS, 71): "When the Lord taught us the doctrine of Father, Son, and Holy Spirit, He did not make arithmetic a part of this gift!"

3. Trinity Sunday was introduced, with controversy, during the fourteenth century.

4. Johann Gerhard, *Theological Commonplaces: On the Nature of God and on the Trinity*, trans. Richard J. Dinda (St. Louis: Concordia Publishing House, 2007), Exegesis III, §7, 269: "If we are ignorant of or deny the mystery of the Trinity, we are ignorant of or deny the entire economy of salvation."

5. Karl Rahner, *The Trinity*, trans. Joseph Donceel (New York: Crossroad, 1997), 10: "Despite their orthodox confession of the Trinity, Christians are, in their practical life, almost mere 'monotheists'."

respect to the Trinity. With some labor we may rightly confess the Trinity and expound it in a dogmatically satisfying manner. But can we without maximal effort live a Christ-centered life that is trinitarian and not just rhetorically so?

Consider the following two examples. In the Small Catechism Luther offers a brief description of what a Christian is to do each day of his life: "In the morning, when you rise, make the sign of the cross and say, 'In the name of God, the Father, the Son, and the Holy Spirit. Amen.'" Likewise, Luther continues, "In the evening, when you retire, make the sign of the cross and say, 'In the name of God, the Father, the Son, and the Holy Spirit. Amen'" (SC VII.1, 4). The same sign of the cross and the same confession of the Trinity made upon you at your baptism is acted out and spoken again by you as you rise to start your day and as you retire at the end of your day. By framing the Christian life in this way, Luther places before the believer a daily remembrance of baptism and its benefits, and furthermore construes daily living according to the saving work of the Trinity.[6] This is not mere remembrance but daily participation in the saving event of baptism.[7] Both aspects of the believer are united in the trinitarian confession of baptism and baptismal living: "I am baptized, instructed with the word alone, absolved, and partake of the Lord's Supper. But with the word and through the word the Holy Spirit is present, and the whole Trinity works salvation, as the words of baptism declare."[8] In another work Luther envisions the Christian day as one of unceasing prayer in which believers faithfully fulfill their divinely appointed vocations. To do this, explains Luther, is to glorify our triune God.[9] For Luther, Christian salvation, identity, and ethics find their coherence and grammar in the Trinity and our trinitarian confession. We live in Christ by the Holy Spirit to the delight of the Father.

Basil the Great, the fourth-century bishop of Caesarea, and his brother, Gregory of Nyssa, offer similar visions for the Christian life. For Basil and Gregory, and indeed all of the normative writers from the patristic period, the Trinity is the central mystery of the Christian faith that illumines the entirety of the Christian life. Basil writes:

> As we are baptized, so also do we believe; as we believe, so also do we give glory. Since, then, baptism has been given to us by our Savior in the name of the Father and of the Son and of the Holy Spirit, we offer the confession of our faith in accordance with our baptism, and also the doxology in accordance with our faith, glorifying the Holy Spirit with the Father and the Son.[10]

---

6. *Lectures on Genesis*, 1535–45 (AE 8:145; WA 44:685.32): "In Baptism the voice of the Trinity is heard."

7. Cf. Gerhard von Rad, *Old Testament Theology*, trans. D. M. G. Stalker (New York: Harper, 1965), 2:104: "When Israel ate the Passover . . . she was manifestly doing more than merely remembering the Exodus: she was entering into the saving event of the Exodus itself and participating in it in a quite 'actual' way."

8. *Lectures on Genesis*, 1535–45 (AE 8:264; WA 44:773.4–6).

9. *A Simple Way to Pray*, 1535 (AE 43:193–94; WA 38:358.11–17).

10. Basil of Caesarea *Letter* 159 (LCL 2:395–97), translation slightly altered. For similar language see also Basil *Letters* 91, 125, and 210.

Gregory of Nyssa likewise construes the faith he confesses and the worship he offers with baptism. Gregory writes:

> Hence we are baptized as it has been handed down to us, into *Father and Son and Holy Spirit*, and we believe as we are baptized—for it is fitting that our confession be of one voice with our faith—and we give glory as we believe, for it is not natural that worship make war against faith, but as we believe, so also we give glory. Now since our faith is in *Father and Son and Holy Spirit*, faith, worship, and baptism accord with each other.[11]

Can we join Gregory, Basil, and Luther in confessing the trinitarian character and grammar of our Christian lives? Is our daily Christian living, our faith and worship, in accord with our baptism? Does our baptism, our faith, make war with our worship? Does our dogmatic confession of the Trinity stand apart from our practical lives as Christians? If that is the case, only with great imagination could such a life be considered Christian according to the Scriptures.

NAMING GOD

Some may argue that the persistent use of the word "God" in our prayers, worship, and devotional life protects us from the concerns noted above. Is it sufficient to speak only of God and mean by that pronouncement the triune God of the Bible? The answer depends in large measure on the context in which the word is used. To speak of God in the public square or at a civic event is presumably different than speaking of God in a sermon on the Nativity of our Lord. Similarly, to speak of God at a synagogue is presumably different than speaking of God at a mosque. Both are different from a sermon on the Nativity. In a religiously indifferent and pluralistic society, the propositional content of the term "God" is always disputed and necessarily ambiguous. The term is equivocal.[12] Luther warned about this: "Therefore everyone who does not want to be deceived must learn and note with all diligence not to listen and agree when God is merely named or mentioned, even though men exalt and praise His name as greatly as possible and act ever so gloriously and majestically."[13] Context must be used to restrict the meaning of the word. The word alone cannot do this.

---

11. Gregory of Nyssa *Letter* 24.8 in *Gregory of Nyssa: The Letters*, trans. Anna M. Silvas (Leiden: Brill, 2007), 194.

12. Thomas Aquinas *ST* I.13.10c: "No one can signify what he does not know. But the heathen does not know the divine nature. So when he says an idol is God, he does not signify the true Deity. On the other hand, a Catholic signifies the true Deity when he says that there is one God. Therefore this name *God* is not applied univocally, but equivocally to the true God, and to God according to opinion."

13. *Sermons on the Gospel of St. John*, 1537–38 (AE 24:71; WA 45:526.1–4). Also *Sermons on the Gospel of St. John*, 1530–32 (AE 23:288; WA 33:460a.31–37): "The term 'god,' for example, is given the most manifold meanings. I suppose there are a thousand different gods. . . . Everybody has his own particular god. Therefore you must be wary."

Theologians have made a point of clarifying crucial terms throughout the history of the church lest ambiguity prevail. Luther's addition of *allein* to Rom 3:28 is a well-known example.[14] At the Council of Nicaea (325), *hypostasis* and *ousia* were synonymous. To say that the Son's *hypostasis* was eternally distinct from the Father's *hypostasis* was anathema; following the Council of Constantinople (381), not to say this was anathema. Theologians during the fourth century clarified the meaning of these words to reflect more appropriately the witness of Scripture. Something similar occurs in the Scriptures. What does "love" mean for a Christian? How are we to understand brotherly love? John limits the range of this term by locating a proper understanding of it in the saving work of Christ (1 Jn 3:16) and in God Himself (1 Jn 3:1). Love obviously means something different to a Christian than a non-Christian (2 Tm 3:2). The same holds for the term "peace" (1 Thes 5:3; 2 Thes 3:16). Peace comes from above, from the Lord of peace, and is found among those justified by faith (Rom 5:1), those who are in Christ (1 Thes 5:23; 2 Thes 3:16; 1 Pt 5:14; et passim). We are "called" to this peace by God (1 Cor 7:15), which is far different than that deceitfully spoken by the world (Jer 6:14; 8:11, et passim). Jesus declares, "Peace I leave with you; my peace I give to you. Not as the world gives do I give to you" (Jn 14:27). Both love and peace are fruits of the Spirit, gifts from God (Gal 5:22). These words receive their proper meaning not from the prevailing culture, where ambiguity reigns, but from Scripture, where the Spirit determines their proper meaning for us.

The method exhibited in the previous paragraph and used by the Lutheran dogmaticians is that Scripture is its own interpreter (*Scriptura sacra sui ipsius interpres*).[15] Peace means different things based on the cultural or socio-political context of the discourse. According to Scripture, even religious insiders mean different things by the word (Jer 9:8). When politicians and pundits devise plans for peace in the Middle East, they are not calling for the peace of Christ that passes all understanding but for a cessation of the violence and hostility that disrupts the stability of the region. Christians are not confused by the use of the term in this way and are able to translate it according to the political context in which it is spoken. What about the term "God"? When a politician ends a speech with the words "God bless America," have we any idea what is meant by the term God? We are not able to consider what this blessing is and what it would amount to until we can determine who or what is providing the blessing. The same holds for "interfaith" events masquerading as joint worship of *the same* God. Worship of which God, we must ask. The content of the term is unclear in our day. By no means does the term secure a Christian understanding

---

14. *On Translating: An Open Letter*, 1530 (AE 35:188; WA 30/2:636.31–34).
15. Chemnitz, *Examen* (Frankfurt, 1596), 3:31; Abraham Calov, *Systema Locorum Theologicorum* (Wittenberg, 1655), 1:318, 425, 639. Calov explicitly links this axiom to 2 Pt 1:21. See also *Assertio omnium articulorum M. Lutheri per bullam Leonis X. novissimam damnatorum*, 1520 (WA 7:97). For an extended discussion see Quenstedt, *Systema Theologicum* I, 4 (Wittenberg, 1691), 137–48.

of the triune God. Why? Because the term is equivocal. It is used by various individuals with contradictory understandings of the term. Again, Scripture alerts us to this. YHWH is a proper name, unique to the God of Israel; Elohim is generic and used by other nations. These nations have their Elohim but Israel's Elohim is YHWH. For this reason God begins the Decalogue by declaring, "I am YHWH, your Elohim" (Ex 20:2; Dt 6:1). Similarly, *Theos* was appropriated by Judaism and Christianity from the Greeks. Plato can speak of god (ὁ θεὸς) but not the God of Israel (ὁ θεὸς τοῦ Ἰσραηλ), not Jesus Christ, the Son of God (ὁ τοῦ θεοῦ υἱὸς). The Athenians had an altar with the inscription "To the unknown god" (Acts 17:23). Paul took the common term, *theos*, and gave it Christian meaning. The "god" named by them as unknown is the God who made the heavens and the earth and who is Lord over all. The predicate specifies or marks out the subject. Which "god" are we talking about? Paul's answer is the God who creates, the God from whom we have breath and by whom we are called to repent. These activities serve as narrative markers to identify dogmatically the true God.

Abraham Calov writes, "Those who fail to mention the three persons in their description of God convey in no way a genuine or complete description, which, absent these three, corresponds in no way with who the true God is."[16] As Christians speaking in a Christian context, can we name the triune God as God? Certainly we can as the Scriptures have also patterned our speech in this way.[17] But Scripture has narrowed the semantic range of the term "God" and distinguished it from all other competing uses, ancient and modern. The God encountered in the Scriptures, the one true God of Israel, YHWH, is triune and is named Father, Son, and Holy Spirit. We are taught to pray "Our Father, who art in heaven," not "Our God, who art in heaven." We pray *our Father*, through the Son by the Holy Spirit. We baptize not in the name of God but in the name of God the Father, God the Son, and God the Holy Spirit.[18] These names are not just scripturally warranted but scripturally mandated. It is not for us to alter the name of God, and therefore it is not for us to speak ambiguously about the God we worship and come to know only as Father, Son, and Holy Spirit.[19]

TRINITY AS TASK

Robert Jenson describes the doctrine of the Trinity as more a task than a homogeneous body of timeless propositions.[20] The task involved is the

---

16. Calov, *Systema Locorum Theologicorum* 2:182.

17. Cf. Gregory of Nazianzus *Or.* 38.8 in *Festal Orations* (PPS, 66): "When I say 'God,' I mean Father, Son, and Holy Spirit."

18. Cf. Athanasius *Orations Against the Arians* 1.34 and *De Decretis* 31; Basil of Caesarea *Against Eunomius* 1.5.

19. Johann Gerhard, *Theological Commonplaces*, Exegesis III, §2, 268: "For the catholic faith, which is necessary for all who are to be saved, there must be *not a confused and implicit* but a *distinct and explicit* knowledge and confession of the three persons of the Godhead."

20. Robert Jenson, *Systematic Theology* (Oxford: Oxford University Press, 1997), 1:90.

continuing effort by the church to acknowledge and adhere to the scriptural identity of God. Jenson's point is straightforward enough but easily overlooked. The doctrine of the Trinity, expressed as "three irreducible persons inseparably united in one undivided nature," is a dogmatic proposition drafted and deployed by the Fathers during a particular historical course of scriptural reflection and ecclesial controversy. That historical context decisively shaped the dogmatic propositions put forward by the Fathers. For this reason, observes Jenson, talking about the Trinity, confessing the Trinity, may not simply be reduced to restating propositions.[21] Right confession of the Trinity, indeed of any article of faith, is always an exegetical task that falls to each generation of the church. Scripture norms our faith; tradition shows us appropriate patterns of speech for expressing and guarding that faith. If we dislodge the patterns of speech used by the church from the source of those speech patterns, we not only pursue a task alien to that of the church's best theologians but also a task contrary to our scriptural convictions.

Jenson's comment is crucial to any discussion of the Trinity, as it prevents us from reflexively reducing the central doctrine of our faith to metaphysical propositions embedded in a culture removed from our own. Too often we elect to teach and preach the doctrine of the Trinity by recourse to the technical vocabulary of the patristic debates and the concluding formulae embraced by the decisive councils of the fourth and fifth centuries. There are a few problems with this. One is the failure to recognize that the questions addressed in the ancient church are not necessarily the same questions being asked today. If the questions are not quite the same, then recourse to their answers will either confuse or remain unsatisfying; this is not to say the answers are unhelpful or untrue but only that they may fail to address the question at hand. The philosophical questions confronted by the Fathers in the early church tended to be about metaphysics and the relationship between creator and creation. For example, a real problem for thinkers as diverse as neo-Platonists, Gnostics, and Arians was the need to protect the transcendent one, Bythos, or the true God (*ho theos* as opposed to the anarthrous *theos*) from contact with creation. All assumed the necessity of having a mediator or mediators of God's creative agency.[22] The Fathers rejected the chain of intervening being found in neo-Platonism and Gnosticism and the subordinate mediation of the Son in Arianism by pointing to the scriptural confession of the Son's condescension. The explanation of how the Son related to the Father and also the Holy Spirit

---

21. The historical background, or philosophical context, in which these patristic pronouncements were made is referred to by Jenson as the theology of Mediterranean antiquity. He specifically has in mind Greek paganism's construal of deity as timelessness and impassibility. My sympathy with Jenson's comment lies not with these contested issues but with his observation that Trinity talk is not simply restating propositions. See also Robert Jenson, "Ipse Pater Non Est Impassiblis," *Divine Impassibility and the Mystery of Human Suffering*, ed. James F. Keating and Thomas Joseph White (Grand Rapids: Eerdmans, 2009), 117–26.

22. Athanasius conflates the thinking of the Gnostics, Greeks, and Arians on this very point at *Orations Against the Arians* 2.21–24.

is what we refer to today as the doctrine of the Trinity. The terms they used for their explanation derived from the context of the debate. These metaphysical terms remain an indispensable resource for the church today when answering metaphysical questions about the Trinity.

Too often the Fathers are accused of hellenizing the Christian faith because they operated within the philosophical idiom of their day. This thesis has outlived its usefulness. A more accurate expression would be the Christianization of Hellenism.[23] The Fathers addressed the issues of their day by using the philosophical idiom available to them. It is not the case that the Fathers delighted in metaphysical speculation and wished to construe God's being according to the ontological and rational norms of their day.[24] Indeed, for the most part they avoided such arguments and routinely accused their opponents of engaging in such behavior (e.g., Arius, Aetius, Eunomius). At the same time, to talk of the essence, being, or nature of God was to do nothing other than express their scriptural faith in the language of the day and to use the best possible words available to them to clarify and guard the witness of Scripture. And yet in using this shared philosophical idiom the Fathers critiqued and revised it according to the demands of Scripture.[25] Their faith in Scripture constrained them to talk in ways their contemporaries found contradictory.

Another problem of approaching the Trinity by recourse to the technical vocabulary of the patristic debates and their concluding formulae is that we begin with tradition and theological conclusions, whereas the Fathers began with Scripture and exegesis. In other words, we begin where they ended. Their propositions sought to make sense of Scripture's narrative about the tri-unity of God, a trinitarian logic confessed throughout Scripture but lacking precise dogmatic language. The task that fell to the church's earliest theologians was to provide a level of coherence and intelligibility to the Bible's trinitarianism in response to antiquity's philosophical presuppositions on what it meant to be divine. Our task is not one of simple repristination, of repeating authoritative names and conclusions, thinking this secures for us a right confession of the Trinity; our task is to relearn their exegesis in order to grasp the intelligibility of their conclusions, as seen for example in the technical grammar used to express their scriptural convictions and in the creedal summaries of those convictions.

If we elect not to begin with the harder task of exegesis and instead take the seemingly easier path, namely the history of the doctrine in the theological reflection of the church, we reverse the order of our convictions as Lutherans. Such a course would mean that we begin with theological argumentation on the being and persons of the Trinity rather than the scriptural foundation of

---

23. Robert Louis Wilken, *The Spirit of Early Christianity* (New Haven, CT: Yale University Press, 2003), xvi.

24. Augustine famously remarks that he uses this technical language only to avoid saying nothing. See Augustine *The Trinity* 5.10 (WSA I/5, 196).

25. R. P. C. Hanson, *The Search for the Christian Doctrine of God* (Grand Rapids: Baker Academic, 2005), 870–71.

those theological arguments. Pitfalls abound. We remove our confession of the Trinity from the chief source of our knowledge about who God is, the Scriptures (*norma normans*), and mistakenly assign it to the creedal history of the church (*norma normata*). We also end up complicating our confession of the Trinity as we tie it to formal terminology that eludes the ordinary Christian and pastor and likely answers questions not being asked. The consequences are disastrous: the Trinity is approached and discussed only as "the doctrine" of the Trinity rather than confessed as the horizon of our reality and the source of our life, joy, and hope.

When the Trinity is reduced to creedal propositions, the church's trinitarian exegesis is set aside and eventually forgotten. The difficulty of the doctrine of the Trinity in our day has less to do with the subject matter and more to do with the approach we have taken. We are now forced to master a tremendous body of information: the history and theology of the debates on the Trinity from the early church to our day. What we have forgotten is the very thing our parishioners seek, the trinitarian exegesis of the church. When we recover this exegesis, the voice of the church, we will achieve more than just a trinitarian understanding of the Scriptures. Indeed, we will begin to glimpse, as Luther, Basil, and Gregory did, the trinitarian shape and meaning of the Christian life.

A BRIEF HISTORY OF THE PROBLEM OF MODERNITY

The standard narrative of the problem inherited by the twentieth century normally begins with the eighteenth-century marginalization of the Trinity by Immanuel Kant (1724–1804) and the nineteenth-century response by Friedrich Schleiermacher (1768–1834).[26] Kant thought the doctrine of the Trinity was an unintelligible mystery without practical or moral value. Not only was the doctrine irrelevant for Christianity but even potentially detrimental to a truly religious disposition.[27] For these reasons Kant marginalized the doctrine and gave it the status of adiaphora.[28] Kant's thinking was very much in step with the broader, ambivalent attitude toward the Trinity in the eighteenth century. His dismissal of the Trinity rested upon the doctrine's relevance for the individual's practical and moral life. Judgment proceeds from the thinking subject; the Trinity is here viewed as object. Kant declared this object unintelligible and therefore unnecessary for us in our own construction of reality.

The neo-Protestant response of the nineteenth century should be seen as a reaction against the eighteenth century and the grand claims of the Enlightenment. Although both Schleiermacher and Hegel (1770–1831) attempted to recover the "symbol" of the Trinity, their trinitarian proposals

---

26. Cf. Robert Jenson, *The Triune Identity* (Philadelphia: Fortress Press, 1982), 131–38.
27. Immanuel Kant, *Religion and Rational Theology* (Cambridge: Cambridge University Press, 1996), 167, 264.
28. Cyril O'Regan, "The Trinity in Kant, Hegel, and Schelling," *The Oxford Handbook of the Trinity* (Oxford: Oxford University Press, 2011), 254.

were far removed from orthodox Christianity. Schleiermacher considered the orthodox doctrine of the Trinity conceptually incoherent and forever burdened with the difficulty of relating the unity of essence to the trinity of persons. The doctrine was simply unnecessary for the Christian self-consciousness. Schleiermacher and Hegel both rejected the notion of an eternal distinction of persons in God as essential to Christian teaching and advanced a view of the Trinity more akin to an eschatologically fulfilled modalism.[29]

The marginalization of the Trinity did not mean a rejection of God by these thinkers. Schleiermacher's view of God focused on the union of the divine essence with human nature, "both in the personality of Christ and in the common Spirit of the church."[30] In this sense the church was correct in emphasizing redemption through Christ and the communication of this redemption to the world through the church. These emphases occur only if God's own being is genuinely present in both Christ and the common Spirit of the church.[31] These are the "essential elements" in the doctrine of the Trinity.[32] Although Schleiermacher understands that the doctrine of the Trinity aims to predicate something of God's being, he empties the doctrine of any reference to God's intrinsic being, which ends up separating "the meaning of the doctrine from the doctrine itself."[33] Schleiermacher writes, "Hence it is important to make the point that the main pivots of the ecclesiastical doctrine—the being of God in Christ and in the Christian church—are independent of the doctrine of the Trinity."[34] In other words, what occupies the center of the ecclesiastical doctrine, the orthodox teaching of the Trinity, is independent of what Schleiermacher and Christian self-consciousness, as he would have it, know of God. We cannot offer a viable doctrine of the Trinity that is speculative and removed from history: God is known, for Schleiermacher, through His redemptive activity in history and my experience of Him.[35] Although stated quite differently, Schleiermacher's proposal remains in the subjective orbit of Kant. Both constructions of God proceed from my construal of reality and the space I create for that which is termed "God." The term is equivocal.

How could Kant and Schleiermacher be so dismissive of the traditional doctrine of the Trinity? The questions have changed and therefore the old answers don't always work. In the case of Schleiermacher, if the old answers

---

29. Friedrich Schleiermacher, *The Christian Faith* (Edinburgh: T & T Clark, 1986), 738–51 (§170–72). Schleiermacher even asks if the conceptual idiom of Sabellianism might not be as useful in expressing the church's awareness of God as the "Athanasian hypothesis" (750, §172.3). For a brief summary of Hegel's trinitarian thought, see Cyril O'Regan, "The Trinity in Kant, Hegel, and Schelling," 257–62.

30. Schleiermacher, *The Christian Faith*, 738 (§170.1).

31. Bruce Marshall, "Trinity," *The Blackwell Companion to Theology*, ed. Gareth Jones (Oxford: Blackwell, 2004), 183.

32. Schleiermacher, *The Christian Faith*, 738–39 (§170.1).

33. Khaled Anatolios, *Retrieving Nicaea* (Grand Rapids: Baker Academic, 2011), 3.

34. Schleiermacher, *The Christian Faith*, 741 (§170.3).

35. Samuel M. Powell, "Nineteenth-Century Protestant Doctrines of the Trinity," *The Oxford Handbook of the Trinity* (Oxford: Oxford University Press, 2011), 271.

The Problem of Modernity

cannot be "known" by the religious consciousness of the Christian, it cannot be a genuine Christian doctrine.[36] Indeed, posits Schleiermacher, if not for the church telling us about the eternal hypostatic distinctions in the doctrine of the Trinity, it would have remained unknown to us.[37] Schleiermacher's concern is knowledge and how we "know" God. If the philosophical questions confronting the Fathers in the fourth century concerned "being" (metaphysics) and the questions debated among the Nicenes and the anti-Nicenes were about what sort of being the Son is in relation to the Father, the philosophical questions confronting Schleiermacher and modernity concerned "knowledge" (epistemology) and how a universal knowledge of God could be achieved through human reason or Christian experience.[38]

The significance of Kant lies in his effort to resolve the difficulties presented by the rationalists and empiricists of the seventeenth and eighteenth centuries. Both the rationalists and the empiricists sought to achieve knowledge of reality as it is. The problem, as Kant saw it, was that they credited the human mind with far more than it could achieve. Reason has its limits, he argued. We cannot know reality in itself (*noumena*), but we can know our experience of the world (*phenomena*). By placing our experiences of the objects around us into their proper categories, our minds produce meaning. When we arrive at Schleiermacher, the source of truth is located in Christian self-consciousness and experience. The move from metaphysical to epistemological questions also moved human beings from objects of God's creation to the center of the discussion as thinking subjects. Both Kant and Schleiermacher constructed their views of reality and of God in response to the various modern proposals produced since the beginning of the seventeenth century.

Modernity did not just pursue different questions; it changed the way we ask questions and answer them. In his lectures on the history of philosophy Hegel wrote that the philosophy of the modern period begins with Descartes (1596–1650): "Now we come for the first time to what is properly the philosophy of the modern world. . . . Here, we may say, we are at home and, like the sailor after a long voyage, we can at last shout, 'Land ho.'"[39] What seemed so at home to Hegel in Descartes was at the same time a decisive break from his spiritual home in the Lutheranism of Luther (despite Hegel's repeated avowals of his Lutheranism).[40] Hegel's judgment about Descartes is correct: with his famous "I

---

36. Bruce Marshall summarizes Schleiermacher's objection this way: "We know God only as we are experientially related to him in various ways, and these relations give us no basis for speculation about the being of God in himself, independently of the varieties of his presence to us in time (see §172, 1; also 170, postscript)." Marshall, "Trinity," 184.

37. Schleiermacher, *The Christian Faith*, 739–42 (§170.2–postscript).

38. This move from ancient to modern questions should be seen as a shift in emphasis. Questions of being (metaphysics) always involve structures of knowing (epistemology).

39. G. W. F. Hegel, *Lectures on the History of Philosophy*, trans. R. F. Brown et al. (Berkeley: University of California Press, 1990), 3:108. Quoted in William Placher, *The Triune God: An Essay in Postliberal Theology* (Louisville, KY: Westminster John Knox Press, 2007), 3.

40. Cyril O'Regan, "The Trinity in Kant, Hegel, and Schelling," 258. O'Regan shows how

think, therefore I am" (*cogito, ergo sum*), theology moves from the premodern to the modern period, from God at the center of reality to me at the center of reality. If God is to have a place in my construction of reality, I will be the one to give it to Him. Further, any construction of reality, any sense of truth, will proceed from my own inward turn and reflection upon the self.

DESCARTES AND HIS GOD

Although Descartes departed from the traditional authorities for arriving at knowledge of God and His saving works, he did not, so he argues, want to distance himself from the traditional dogmatic positions of the church; he only wished to arrive at them differently.[41] If Scripture could not resolve the competing truth claims advanced by the various groups asserting scriptural authority, could human reason be of service? Human reason already had shown remarkable promise in the scientific discoveries of Copernicus (1473–1543), Kepler (1571–1630), and Galileo (1564–1642), among others. Reason also had created a good deal of angst. Although heliocentrism is a truth we have lived with for many centuries, we should not underestimate the emotional and intellectual impact this discovery had on the world of the seventeenth century. No longer were humans at the center of the universe, with everything revolving around them. If we are not at the center, perhaps the universe doesn't exist for us. Perhaps we aren't the reason for *its* existence. These concerns led in all sorts of directions. Our focus will be on the emergence of unaided reason as the means by which truth and reality could be constructed and the means whereby we could secure our precarious hold on being at the center of reality—a position that led to the marginalization of the Trinity.

Descartes's pursuit of an indubitable foundation on which to base truth and reality led him to the discovery of his own undeniable existence: *cogito, ergo sum*. His emphasis on the thinking subject (the *ego* and *res cogitans*) established subjectivity as the modern approach to truth. This move marked the entrance

---

Hegel's version of Lutheranism was indebted to Jacob Boehme (1575–1624). Hegel mentions Boehme in his 1827 *Lectures on the Philosophy of Religion* as providing the template for the dynamic trinitarianism he advocates. O'Regan comments, "As a precursor [to Hegel's thought], Boehme is not only in select company, he is in strange company. The other two figures Hegel routinely mentions as providing precedents for the symbol of the Trinity are the Jewish Platonist, Philo of Alexandria, and the Gnostic Valentinus" (260).

41. William Placher asks if Descartes's bow to the authority of revelation was less out of conviction and more out of a concern to avoid the fate of Galileo. Placher, *The Triune God*, 4. Gottfried Leibnitz was not so hesitant in his judgment. He thought Descartes's description of God leads only to atheism. Leibnitz, *Philosophical Works of Leibnitz*, ed. George Martin Duncan (New Haven, CT: The Tuttle, Morehouse, and Taylor Company, 1890), 1. Cf. Michael Buckley, *At the Origins of Modern Atheism* (New Haven, CT: Yale University Press, 1987), 37–38: "It would be false to tax the Enlightenment with indifference to religion. It would be more discerning to say that is was obsessed with it.... Whatever the individual histories of Diderot and d'Holbach, by and large the Enlightenment did not countenance atheism; it rejected it. But in this repudiation, its major figures counted the Church and confessional religion not as allies, but as adversaries."

into modernity and meant that knowledge of God would be achieved through the medium of human subjectivity. In his *Meditations on First Philosophy*, Descartes argued that we must question and doubt everything in order to arrive at those ideas that are so clear and distinct that they cannot be doubted. Those unable-to-be-doubted ideas serve as the foundation of his philosophy and understanding of reality. For Descartes everything can be doubted except the self as a thinking thing, a doubting subject. After an extended exercise in doubting the world, the sky, the earth, the mind, and even his own body, Descartes ventures to ask if he himself exists. And in such a question he finds his breakthrough: "At last I have discovered it—thought; this alone is inseparable from me. I am, I exist—that is certain."[42] Descartes could doubt everything derived from the senses; he could not doubt that he is a thinking thing.

From the certainty of his own existence as a thinking thing, Descartes proceeded in his *Meditations* to present two arguments for the existence of God: an argument from causality and an argument from the being of God (what Kant dubbed the ontological argument).[43] Descartes's causal argument for the existence of God begins with his innate idea that there is such a being who is eternal, infinite, immutable, omniscient, omnipotent, and the creator of all things that exist apart from Him. Descartes then states a crucial cause and effect axiom: "Now it is manifest by the natural light that there must be at least as much <reality> in the efficient and total cause as in the effect of that cause. For where, I ask, could the effect get its reality from, if not from the cause? And how could the cause give it to the effect unless it possessed it?"[44] From this it follows, argues Descartes, that something cannot arise from nothing (every effect must have a preceding cause), and that which is more perfect, meaning that which contains more reality in itself, cannot arise from what is less perfect (an effect cannot enjoy a greater state of being than its cause). Descartes gives the example of a stone. A stone (effect) must be produced by something (cause) which contains either formally or eminently everything to be found in the stone. To possess "stoneness" formally means to possess it literally; to possess "stoneness" eminently means to possess it in some higher form. Moreover, continues Descartes, even if the stone does not exist, the idea of stone could only exist in the human mind if some cause possessing at least as much reality as conceived to be in the stone put it there.[45]

After an extended consideration of corporeal, finite reality, Descartes concludes that all of his ideas of such things as stone or any other finite

---

42. René Descartes, "Meditations on First Philosophy," *Philosophical Writings*, trans. John Cottingham (Cambridge: Cambridge University Press, 1984), 2:18.
43. The arguments in *Meditations* III and V are found also in *Discourse*, part IV, and *Principles*, part 1, §§14–21. In this latter work Descartes reverses the order of the arguments, beginning with the ontological argument.
44. Descartes "Meditations" 2:28. Descartes added the bracketed text in later editions of his work.
45. Descartes "Meditations" 2:28.

substances are contained in him eminently, which is to say that in the order of being Descartes ranks higher than the stone and any other idea he has of a finite substance.⁴⁶ At this point Descartes turns to the idea of God.

> So there remains only the idea of God; and I must consider whether there is anything in the idea which could not have originated in myself. By the word 'God' I understand a substance that is infinite, <eternal, immutable,> independent, supremely intelligent, supremely powerful, and which created both myself and everything else (if anything else there be) that exists. All these attributes are such that, the more carefully I concentrate on them, the less possible it seems that they could have originated from me alone. So from what has been said it must be concluded that God necessarily exists.⁴⁷

God must exist because there is no way for Descartes, as a finite substance, to account for the existence of an infinite substance, whose reality is formally and eminently greater than he. For Descartes, the causal argument, when rightly considered, demonstrates the necessary existence of an infinite, eternal, immutable, independent, supremely intelligent, supremely powerful being that created all things. He calls this non-personal being God.

Descartes's second argument for the existence of God is the familiar ontological argument. He begins by rehearsing the various ideas produced by his mind. If he has in his mind the idea of shape and number, among other things, and can prove things about them, can he not likewise demonstrate the necessary existence of God from the mere fact that he has the idea of God in his mind? For example, Descartes not only has the idea of a triangle in his mind but he also knows clear and distinct things about the triangle: its three angles equal two right angles; its hypotenuse subtends its greatest angle. Surely, he asserts, by a similar endeavor the existence of God may be known with "the same level of certainty as I have hitherto attributed to the truths of mathematics."⁴⁸ The measure of truth and certainty is mathematics, and Descartes aims to achieve an argument for God's existence on at least the same plane of certainty.⁴⁹

He proceeds with his argument by considering what is proper to the essence or being of God. He writes,

> It is quite evident that existence can no more be separated from the essence of God than the fact that its three angles equal two right angles can be separated from the essence of a triangle, or than the idea of a mountain can be separated from the idea of a valley. Hence it is just as much of a contradiction to think of God (that

---

46. Descartes "Meditations" 2:31.
47. Descartes "Meditations" 2:31. Descartes added the bracketed text in later editions of his work.
48. Descartes "Meditations" 2:45.
49. Augustine says something similar in the *Confessions*. He writes, "I wanted to be as certain about things I could not see as I am certain that seven and three are ten" (VI.6). Augustine has this thought before his conversion to Christianity. He goes on to critique this idea of knowing truth with mathematical certainty and emphasizes instead the need for faith in Scripture. Augustine, *Confessions*, trans. Henry Chadwick (Oxford: Oxford University Press, 1992), 95–96.

is, a supremely perfect being) lacking existence (that is, lacking a perfection), as it is to think of a mountain without a valley.[50]

Descartes acknowledges that his thoughts cannot impose necessity on things. In other words, just because he has these thoughts about God's essence and existence, this alone does not account for God's necessary existence. The same holds true for a mountain and valley. Descartes revises his statement in the light of this and concludes that his thoughts reveal the inseparability of God's essence and existence and the inseparability of a mountain and a valley. What accounts for this inseparability is not the necessity imposed by his thoughts but rather the necessity of the thing itself. Mountain, as a projecting landmass, is defined only in relation to a valley, such that if there were no valley, there would be no mountain, *per definitionem*. The same holds true for God's essence and existence. Therefore, we are not free, argues Descartes, to think of God without existence. If God is a "supremely perfect being," He cannot be conceived without a "supreme perfection." And for Descartes existence is one of the perfections.[51] Therefore God necessarily exists.

The significance of the above has very little to do with the success of Descartes's arguments for the existence of God and everything to do with the way he goes about these arguments and why he offers them in the first place. We should be troubled by the role played by God in Descartes's construction of reality. He embraces a dualism between mind and body—what he refers to as the "real distinction."[52] For Descartes the most basic characteristic of "matter" is extension. Two substances exist for him: the mind, the thinking faculty, which does not extend physically, and non-thinking matter, which does extend. The body is matter, it extends physically, and therefore a real distinction exists between mind and body. Descartes explains,

> Thus, simply by knowing that I exist and seeing at the same time that absolutely nothing else belongs to my nature or essence except that I am a thinking thing, I can infer correctly that my essence consists solely in the fact that I am a thinking thing. It is true that I may have (or, to anticipate, that I certainly have) a body that is very closely joined to me. But nevertheless, on the one hand I have a clear and distinct idea of myself, in so far as I am simply a thinking, non-extended thing; and on the other hand I have a distinct idea of body, in so far as this is simply an extended, non-thinking thing. And accordingly, it is certain that I am really distinct from my body, and can exist without it.[53]

---

50. Descartes "Meditations" 2:46.
51. This is the point critiqued by Kant. He argued that existence is not a predicate and therefore not one of the perfections. A predicate is an attribute of something, and every attribute presupposes the "existence" of that something. Cancel existence and you cancel the thing itself with all its predicates. According to Kant, when Descartes posits "existence" as a predicate and one of the perfections, he advances nothing more than a tautology. Kant, *Critique of Pure Reason*, 563–69.
52. Descartes "Meditations" 2:50. The phrase comes from the heading of Descartes's Sixth Meditation and is used throughout his treatise to refer to the distinction between the mind and the body.
53. Descartes "Meditations" 2:54.

ON GOD

Here we begin to understand the function of Descartes's doctrine of God and the sort of "God" this is. He began his treatise with doubt, questioning everything in order to arrive at that which is clear and distinct. He concluded that the only thing he knew with certainty was his own existence as a thinking thing. From here his search continued, questioning the existence of every other idea he had. He could not be certain of the existence of the external world or indeed even the existence of his own body. Something needed to reconcile these two things: the thinking subject and the possibility of the external world. For Descartes that thing was God. His attention turned to the idea of God and proceeded with a causal and ontological argument to demonstrate God's necessary existence. Descartes's God is a supremely perfect being, possessing every perfection, which means, importantly, that He is a non-deceiving God. Therefore these ideas of the external world, including Descartes's body, are true and exist, because the non-deceiving, supremely perfect God would not have given him these innate ideas if they were not true.[54] Descartes's final move is significant. Michael Buckley comments, "This is a revolutionary moment in Western philosophy. It is not the sensible universe that is the evidence for god, but the nature of god that is the warrant for the sensible universe."[55] For Descartes the nature of God meets his philosophical needs: God is what He is so Descartes's world can be what he thinks it is. God is a means to an end—the hallmark of all modern arguments for God.

Although Descartes does not formally reject the Trinity, his view on God proved unsatisfactory to many in the seventeenth century. Leibnitz thought his concept of God closely approximated Spinoza's concept of God, and no one should desire such a God as that.[56] For Leibnitz, Descartes's God plays such a meaningless role in his construction of reality that it leads only to atheism. Leibnitz is right. The divine being constructed by Descartes is a product of his own reasoning. Every fitting perfection is assigned this God, but what do these perfections amount to? Far removed is this non-personal philosophical theism from the confession of Paul's crucified Christ, whose power is perfected in weakness, and in whom the faithful confess by the Holy Spirit the power and wisdom of God. Descartes's philosophical construction of omnipotence is the power greater than and extending far beyond our strength and might; it is not the sort of power that embraces condescension, suffering, and the cross.

When viewing Descartes's divine being—and the list could include numerous other figures of modernity—it is hard not to agree with Ludwig Feuerbach's estimation that "man makes a god of what he is not but would like to be."[57] The sort of theology advanced by Descartes and others throughout the modern period is the projection and objectification of man's own needs

---

54. Descartes "Meditations" 2:48–49.
55. Buckley, *At the Origins of Modern Atheism*, 92.
56. Leibnitz, *Philosophical Works of Leibnitz*, 8–10.
57. Feuerbach, *Lectures on the Essence of Religion*, trans. R. Manheim (New York: Harper and Row, 1967), 234.

to secure the truth of reality constructed by the human mind. God becomes the answer to our anxieties and deficiencies. When we reach the limit of our control, our power over our self-constructed reality, when we can go no further, when fear and impotence converge, there we place God. For example, Descartes's system needs a non-deceiving God, but as we have seen this has less to do with God and more to do with Descartes's epistemological demands. Similarly, Kant needs God as a basis of human morality to avoid moral anarchy or relativism. Kant's system of ethics, in keeping with the subjectivism of the modern period and its concern for freedom, departs from the classical Christian tradition, which argues that our ethical behavior succeeds when our wills are conformed by grace to God's will. Kant sees this as external coercion and instead emphasizes the autonomy of the moral agent. In order for him to ground his ethics in an absolute and universal principle (the categorical imperative), maintain the freedom of the moral agent acting out his own self-imposed duty, and insist upon a *telos* for the ethical commonwealth, he needed to posit God.[58] For both Descartes and Kant God is an intellectual tool needed to bring coherence to their respective projects. Again, it is hard to see how these modern uses of God are not susceptible to Feuerbach's criticism: "God is the manifested inward nature, the expressed self of a man—religion the solemn unveiling of a man's hidden treasures, the revelation of his intimate thoughts, the open confession of his love-secrets."[59] When God is the mere product of human thinking, when revelation is displaced by the hubris of rationalism, what other God could possibly emerge than "the mirror of man"?[60] Scripture warns of this: "Those who make [idols] become like them; so do all who trust in them" (Ps 115:8). Descartes's God achieves what Descartes the man could not but what he desperately desired: a certain foundation of truth and reality. But how did his God achieve this? Did the achievement have anything to do with this God? No. The achievement comes from Descartes, who assigns perfections to this non-personal being and concludes that since this being is in possession of such perfections, it therefore guarantees the rest of reality.

Descartes stands at the beginning of the turn toward modernity. He is a representative of rationalism, but by no means the only one. Although admired for the trajectory he set, his conclusions proved unsatisfactory to many in his day. Blaise Pascal, known for his wit, declared him to be both "useless and uncertain."[61] Leibniz, who preferred to mix praise and criticism when discussing Descartes, labeled his philosophy the "ante-chamber" of true philosophy.[62] This

---

58. For a concise summary of Kant's ethics see James M. Byrne, *Religion and the Enlightenment* (Louisville, KY: Westminster John Knox Press, 1996), 214–26.

59. Feuerbach, *The Essence of Christianity*, trans. George Eliot (New York: Torchbook, 1967), 12–13. For a further discussion of Feuerbach see Walter Kasper, *The God of Jesus Christ* (New York: Crossroad, 1986), 28–30, and Kevin J. Vanhoozer, *Remythologizing Theology: Divine Action, Passion, and Authorship* (Cambridge: Cambridge University Press, 2010), 18–21.

60. Feuerbach, *Essence of Christianity*, 63.

61. Pascal, *Pensées*, 887; Blaise Pascal, *Pensées* (New York: Penguin Books, 1995), 275.

62. Leibniz, *Philosophical Works of Leibniz*, 1–2, 108.

meant, that one needed to "pass through" Descartes to arrive at the truth, but also that one should not linger too long if the goal is truth.[63] Locke mocked Descartes's exercise in doubting his own existence and body: "If any one pretends to be so skeptical, as to deny his own existence (for really to doubt of it is manifestly impossible) let him for me enjoy his beloved happiness of being nothing, until hunger or some other pain convince him of the contrary."[64] None of this should surprise us. The world was moving fast. Modernity was here to stay, and Descartes's name would assume an iconic place in the narrative of modernity's rise.

CONCLUSION: KNOWING AND SPEAKING ABOUT GOD TODAY

If we are to speak rightly about our triune God in the twenty-first century, we need to understand the problems inherited from modernity. Descartes's pursuit of clear and distinct ideas on which to construct truth and reality became a hallmark of the modern period. Every serious thinker of the day participated in this effort, even if they departed from one another, often in significant ways, in achieving these "clear and distinct" ideas. For many this pursuit entailed abandoning the God of the Bible. By the time we reach Kant, the doctrine of the Trinity is declared irrelevant and potentially harmful. When figures like Schleiermacher and Hegel attempt to retrieve the Trinity, it is only ever the symbol of the Trinity. The residue of modernity remains with the equivocal place of God-talk in our own day and the subjectivist constructions of reality that have moved from the subjectivism of modernity (universalist in point of view) to subjectivity (particularist in point of view). The mixing of these two perspectives yields personal spiritualities or theologies haphazardly constructed from borrowed iconography and pagan spiritual impulses.

We should think of modernity as a cultural revolution and not merely as a period characterized by the emergence of reason and remarkable scientific discovery. The whole person was reconceived during the Enlightenment. The problems outlined at the beginning of this chapter are our problems because we are all children of modernity. Of course that does not mean we embrace the canons of modernity or all of the critiques of postmodernity, but we deceive ourselves if we think our unexamined assumptions are those of Basil of Caesarea, Gregory of Nyssa, or Martin Luther. They are not. The same holds for those in the pews. The people visiting our churches bring with them intellectual baggage. Equivocal talk of God in our preaching, singing, and praying will further their doctrinal and spiritual confusion. Language that yields

---

63. Leibnitz, *Philosophical Works of Leibnitz*, 7–8, 107. In his day Leibnitz was accused of trying to ruin Descartes's reputation in an effort to establish his own importance. See Leibnitz, *Philosophical Works of Leibnitz*, 107–11.

64. Locke, *An Essay Concerning Human Understanding*, IV.X.2 (Oxford: Oxford University Press, 1979), 619–20.

too much to culture too easily becomes unmoored from the Spirit's normative telling of God's triune identity, Christ's peace, or *Christian* love, and succumbs to intellectual and cultural idols. Freedom for twenty-first century Americans means freedom from moral constraints, "freedom as an opportunity for the flesh" (Gal 5:13); true freedom, as Paul tells us, is to be freed "in Christ" to love and serve the neighbors God has given us in our vocations. Our language and our doctrine need to be grounded in the Scriptures; our confession needs to speak that doctrine in the historical and cultural location in which we live. We can avoid great frustration when doing this only if we have a sense of the disillusionment and misguided assumptions of the places we inhabit.

In the next few chapters we take up the issue briefly sketched above with Descartes: how may we know and speak about God? Discussions about God today often proceed with the traditional distinction between natural and revealed knowledge of God. In what sense, however, is this distinction traditional? In what way is it scriptural? Nearly all theologians throughout the history of the church have acknowledged the legitimacy of natural knowledge of God. The more significant question, and the one pursued in the next four chapters, is what this knowledge amounts to and how it is related—if at all—to revealed knowledge. In other words, what use, what purpose, does natural knowledge of God serve? Does it aid our knowing and speaking about God? Further, what is the relationship between our faith and the faculty of reason? Modernity's turn to the subject distorted faith in two ways. The rationalists placed faith in reason; the pietists placed faith in faith. Both alternatives are treacherous: both imperil the scriptural identity of God and a right understanding of ourselves.

Closely related to the question of how we know God is how we speak about God. When we say that God is wise and Socrates is wise, how do we understand the term "wise"? In this example we have two distinct subjects, God and Socrates, but one predicate, wise. In the domain of natural knowledge of God, unaided reason, it is fair to ask what a person means when he declares that God is wise, good, loving, and so on. Either these words which are commonly used of both God and man mean something or they do not. If they have no meaning, then there is no point in talking about God. If they mean something, which all engaged in such discussions acknowledge they do, then the question is, what do they mean? Are they used univocally or analogically? Chapter 5 takes up this question in detail. Although the discussion is technical, it is necessary for a proper understanding of what our words can and cannot mean when used to talk about God.

2

SEEING IN A MIRROR DIMLY:
THE FATHERS AND KNOWLEDGE OF GOD

Theologians distinguish between natural and revealed knowledge of God. The question that underlies this distinction is whether human reason possesses the capacity to know, apart from Scripture, God's existence and something about His essence. Two basic strategies have been deployed throughout the history of the church to respond affirmatively to this question. Theologians advance arguments for the necessary existence of God either by looking to the works and order of creation to deduce the existence of an intelligent creator, architect, and designer, or by looking inward at their own troubled soul and its innate awareness of virtue, vice, and mortality. Both approaches find their warrant in Paul's epistle to the Romans. Paul states in the first chapter that God's invisible attributes and divine power have been revealed to the Gentiles since the creation of the world in the things that have been made (Rom 1:19-20). Paul further argues in the second chapter that the Gentiles have the law written upon their hearts and therefore are accused by their consciences and thoughts (Rom 2:15).

Far more is at stake in this discussion of natural knowledge than whether or not God has made Himself known to us through nature and conscience. All the writers discussed in the next few chapters share this basic conviction. The more pressing issue, the one that informs our theological vision and therefore affects our understanding of such things as the gospel and the Christian life, the question that lies behind so many of our theological judgments today, concerns what this knowledge amounts to and its role in dogmatic reflection.[1] In other words, how do we use natural knowledge? What do our conclusions on natural knowledge tell us about ourselves and about the necessity of God's revelation? When we privilege these questions, the discussion of natural knowledge is less about asserting some awareness of the divine by unaided reason and more about theological vision, structures of thought, and commitments on such topics as Scripture, faith, reason, and the gospel, among other things.

The church has not been of one voice on these questions. The fourth-century fathers and the medieval theologians think differently about natural

---

1. Robert Preus calls this the apologetic problem with natural knowledge; the second issue identified below he terms the semantic problem (*The Theology of Post-Reformation Lutheranism* [St. Louis: Concordia Publishing House, 1972], 2:34-45). Preus also asserts a third problem with natural knowledge, the conceptual problem, which asks if God's essence can be defined (45-51), and responds, "Lutheran theology makes no attempt to define God and His essence" (45). I will not pursue this third problem separately but will include it in the discussion throughout.

knowledge of God. The fourth-century fathers, writing during a time of heated debate on the scriptural identity of God, use Paul's affirmation of natural knowledge of God to show the deficiencies of such knowledge apart from Christ. For these writers, the incarnation makes possible our right knowing of God. Natural and revealed knowledge are not complementary in the sense that one prepares for the other: the Trinity never supplements a generic and impersonal notion of divinity achieved by reason. Natural knowledge prepares us for a proper discussion on the scriptural identity of God only in the sense of exposing our creaturely limitations to rise to any knowledge of God apart from God's own descent to us in the incarnation. For these fourth-century fathers, natural knowledge serves the important purpose of humbling our exalted opinion of unaided reason. The medieval theologians, on the other hand, pursue something quite different. The question about natural knowledge of God has changed: these theologians ask if the existence of God can be shown from rational proofs apart from Scripture. These a priori and a posteriori proofs aim to establish the logical necessity of God's existence, or at the very least the necessary existence of something to which people ordinarily ascribe the name "God." Scripture subsequently complements this natural knowledge with the Trinity. This medieval theological vision establishes a meeting point between God and man in the acquisition of legitimate knowledge about God. We become coworkers with God in coming to know Him.

The next few chapters answer the above questions by looking closely at the Fathers, the medieval theologians, and the Lutheran reformers. Two trajectories exist in the history of the church. One group exalts human reason apart from faith and the other locates reason as faith's servant. When faith and reason become separated both suffer; when faith no longer orders and directs reason, irrationality and anarchy follow. The separation of faith and reason belongs to modernity and especially to our day. For the fourth-century fathers, particularly Athanasius and Gregory of Nazianzus, and for our Lutheran reformers, we depend on faith to know God. Gregory writes, "Faith rather than reason shall lead us, if, that is, you have learned the feebleness of reason to deal with matters quite close at hand and have acquired enough knowledge of reason to recognize things which surpass reason."[2] In the next few chapters we will focus on the question of natural and revealed knowledge. Only after establishing how we rightly know and confess God may we turn fruitfully to the scriptural identity of the Trinity in the Old and New Testaments.

THE ARGUMENT FROM SCRIPTURE

In the first chapter of his letter to the Romans, Paul briefly discusses the knowledge of God as creator. This discussion occurs amidst Paul's broader reflection on the universality of sin (1:18–3:20). All have sinned, both Jew and

---

2. Gregory of Nazianzus *Or.* 28.28 (PPS, 60).

Greek. There is no distinction. All lack the righteousness of God. They are both without excuse and their condemnation is just. No complaint can be lodged against God. No one, particularly the Gentile, can claim that God was unknown to them because, as Paul emphasizes, what can be known about God has been shown to them by God (1:19). They cannot deny this natural revelation and therefore cannot lodge a complaint against God for the wrath that has come upon them (1:18).

What has God revealed to the Gentiles? Paul writes, "For his invisible attributes, namely, his eternal power and divine nature, have been clearly perceived, ever since the creation of the world, in the things that have been made. So they are without excuse" (1:20). God's invisible things (τὰ ἀόρατα αὐτοῦ), which Paul identifies as God's eternal power, acts, and attributes (ἥ τε ἀΐδιος αὐτοῦ δύναμις καὶ θειότης),[3] have been made visible from the creation of the world "in the things that have been made" (τοῖς ποιήμασιν). This fact, insists Paul, leaves them without excuse. God graciously has made His invisible power and attributes known through His visible creation, in the so-called ποιήματα. From the abundance of the visible and temporal evidence surrounding the Gentiles, they should have concluded at the very least that there is *a* God, unlike all the so-called pagan gods, who is not visible, but who has made the visible, and therefore who stands apart from creation as the one who created all things. They should have deduced that this God was far different from their pagan notions and idolatries.[4] This revelation, however, was rejected by the Gentiles (1:21). Their rejection of these rays of light left them in darkness (1:21). Although they claimed wisdom, they were fools (1:22) and exchanged the glory of God for an idolatry of their own making (1:23). They rejected the Creator and worshipped the created; they exchanged the truth for a lie. False knowledge of God always leads to false worship and perverted ethics (1:24–32).

It is worth emphasizing what is and is not here revealed by God to the Gentiles, who are lost in their own constructed idolatries, rejecting the truth and clinging to the darkness of their own falsehood. To put this in traditional dogmatic categories, we may ask three questions about God: *An sit Deus? Quid sit Deus? Qualis sit Deus?* The first question (Is there a God?) concerns the existence of God; the second (What is God?) His nature; and the third (What sort of God is this?) His attributes. We confess the coeternity and coequality of Father, Son, and Holy Spirit as one God by answering the second question. Only in knowing our triune God in this way do we come to know of His righteousness and the salvation made available to us in Jesus Christ and delivered by the Holy Spirit. This sort of knowledge is saving knowledge because

---

3. Paul uses θειότης instead of θεότης, which he uses at Col 2:9, "For in him the whole fullness of the deity dwells bodily." θειότης refers more specifically to the acts and attributes of God (cf. τὰ θεῖα). August Graebner, "Doctrinal Theology: Theology," *Theological Quarterly* 2/1 (1898).

4. Roland Ziegler, "Natural Knowledge of God and the Trinity," *Concordia Theological Quarterly* 69/2 (2005): 145–46.

it is centered in Christ's person and work. This knowledge is trinitarian as it is the revelation of the Father in the Son by the Holy Spirit, who was sent in turn by the Father and the Son to point us always to the Son, who alone makes the Father and Spirit known to us.

The knowledge described by Paul in Romans 1 is not answering the question *Quid sit Deus?* and is for that reason a non-trinitarian knowledge of God. But what sort of knowledge is that? It is by no means a saving knowledge. Indeed, it is not the righteousness of God that is revealed to the heathen but rather the wrath of God (ὀργὴ θεοῦ): "For the wrath of God is revealed [ἀποκαλύπτεται] from heaven against all ungodliness and unrighteousness of men, who by their unrighteousness suppress the truth" (Rom 1:18). What God reveals here is a knowledge that brings low, that condemns and crushes. This revelation makes absolutely clear that God exists (*An sit Deus?*) and that this is a God whose power is eternal, who gives life and sustains it, and indeed whose wrath stands against all unrighteousness (*Qualis sit Deus?*). To see God outside of Christ, which comes only in knowing *Quid sit Deus*, is to see wrath. Once such knowledge takes hold despair follows. There is no escape from the one whose eternal power made all things and whose wrath stands against unrighteousness. For such a person, the words of the psalmist become intensely unbearable: Whither shall I flee from Thy presence?

Although theologians refer to the knowledge of God described by Paul in Romans 1 as natural knowledge of God, it would be more accurate to call it natural revelation. This knowledge of God comes not from within man—it is not innate—but from outside of man, from God Himself. He is the one doing the revealing (1:18) and the making known (1:19) through the things that He Himself and none other has made (1:20). For this reason, the Gentiles' ignorance and ungodliness is without excuse. They fail to know what the heavens declare and the sky above proclaims (Ps 19:1); they remain ignorant of what the beasts of the field, the birds of heaven, the fish of the sea, and even the bushes of the earth reveal (Jb 12:7–10). If such knowledge depended upon us, we would advance all sorts of excuses for our ignorance. God's point, however, is that all are without excuse, both Jew and Greek, because God has made Himself known through nature and through the law. In both cases, He is the revealer and He here declares to us the sufficiency of His natural revelation to make Himself known to us. To seek an excuse at this point is to accuse God of deceit—to exchange truth for a lie (1:25).

God's revelation of Himself through creation confronts the individual in every place at every moment. As created beings we cannot flee creation; it is as close and inescapable as the created air we breathe (Jb 12:10; Dn 5:23; Ps 150:6). The testimony of God can never be avoided. What if, however, we were to close our eyes? What if we could somehow shut ourselves off from this revealed, natural knowledge? Are those born blind unaware of God's existence? Almost as if anticipating such a devilish ploy, Paul directs his attention in Romans 2 to our innate knowledge of God's law. The Gentiles did not possess the written tablets of the law but nevertheless did "by nature" (φύσει) things required by the law (2:14). They were a law unto themselves. For the Gentiles, this awareness of the law or morality is "written on their hearts" and their "conscience bears witness" to this (2:15).

Does this mean that there are or were virtuous pagans who followed their hearts by serving and loving God and their neighbors? Could this mean, as Zwingli surmised, that such virtuous pagans were saved?[5] No. Such a conclusion bears no resemblance to Paul's argument (especially 1:24–32) or the mind of Scripture (Gn 6:5; Jer 17:9; Rom 14:23). The kind of works done by the Gentiles, who have the law written upon their hearts, belongs to civil righteousness and to the first use of the law. To love God and neighbor belongs to the third use of the law as this sort of love proceeds only from faith. The Apology states this plainly: "The law cannot be kept without Christ, and that if civil works are done without Christ they do not please God."[6] Paul's point in Romans 2 is that the Gentiles possess an awareness of the law written on their hearts. This knowledge comes not from without but from within. He goes on to emphasize that they possess not only this law in their hearts but also a conscience that judges the things they do as known from their heart. These judgments are the "thoughts" that either accuse or excuse (2:15). They accuse when the conscience judges against the immoral works done; they excuse when moral successes are exaggerated in an effort to lessen the awareness of failures.

Paul uses the two arguments above to show the pervasiveness of God's presence in the lives of all. Gentiles unfamiliar with the Scriptures confront the knowledge of God externally in God's revelation of Himself through the things He made and internally through the testimony of their own consciences.[7] They are without excuse. There is nowhere to go, nowhere to flee from God's created works and the voice of one's own conscience. They may close their eyes to the abundance of God's testimony around them, but cannot flee from the

---

5. Martin Chemnitz, *Loci Theologici*, trans. J. A. O. Preus (St. Louis: Concordia Publishing House, 2008), 1:63, 67; Johann Gerhard, *Theological Commonplaces: On the Nature of God and On the Trinity*, trans. Richard Dinda (St. Louis: Concordia Publishing House, 2007), Exegesis II, §81–87, 82–90; Francis Pieper, *Christian Dogmatics* (St. Louis: Concordia Publishing House, 1950), 1:376 n. 7. Gerhard quotes the joke from Veit Winsheim: "My listeners, beware of the heaven of the Zwinglians. I would not want to live there, for I would be afraid of Hercules' club" (83).

6. Ap. IV.184 (Tappert, 132). Cf. George Stoeckhardt, *Commentary on the Epistle to the Romans*, trans. Erwin W. Koehlinger (Ft. Wayne: Concordia Theological Seminary Press, n.d.), 26: "But even if the conscience once excuses man, even if the heathen once do what is demanded by the law, this civil righteousness permits no exception from the general rule: because of Adam's fall human nature and essence are altogether corrupt. Civil righteousness is no true fulfillment of the law, no obedience of the heart, but only an outward work, which is also found where man is barren of all fear and love of God. In no way does civil righteousness make the individual well-pleasing before God."

7. Gerhard refers to these two types of knowledge as the book of nature (acquired knowledge) and the book of conscience (inherent knowledge). Gerhard, *Theological Commonplaces*, Exegesis II, §88, 91.

accusations of the conscience. As Augustine puts it, "You [God] are closer to me than my inmost self."[8] Only the most perverted person can deny the existence of God. Only the "fool" can say in his heart, "There is no God" (Ps 14:1). The fool, the person bereft of all wisdom, utters a lie and dwells in the darkness of that lie, all the while *believing* the darkness to be light (Is 5:20). Abominable deeds follow (Ps 14:1; Rom 1:24–32).

And yet Paul wishes to emphasize that the Gentiles did not know God through this external revelation and internal testimony. Roland Ziegler explains,

> Man has not effectively known God through this revelation, not because of the deficiencies of the revelation, but because of his sinful, warped nature. In the hands of man, the natural revelation of the true God is turned into an idolatrous concept of god and gods. The problem of man is therefore not simply an intellectual one, but it is sin. The remedy for this is not a return to a purer, better natural theology but the proclamation of Christ.[9]

Lutherans never lose sight of the destructive presence of sin. August Graebner emphasizes this very point:

> The same Apostle who says that the invisible things of God are beheld by the vision of the mind (Rom 1:20) also teaches that the mind of natural man is vain (Eph 4:17), his understanding darkened (Eph 4:18), his heart hardened, insensible to impressions (Eph 4:18), that the god of this world has blinded the minds of them which believe not (2 Cor 4:4). God's handwriting still covers every inch of the universe; but man's defective mental vision prevents him from making out, even with his telescopes and microscopes, what the heavens as well as the mustard seeds declare.[10]

When natural revelation of God is thought to be more than it is, the result is natural theology. The rise of such a discipline, wrongly extrapolated from what Paul describes in these two chapters, has led to ambitious rational demonstrations of God's existence that prepare the way for a fuller account of God through Scripture. Modern accounts of God have preferred to start with a non-trinitarian concept of absolute being or absolute subject—philosophical theism—that is thought to anticipate constructively the biblical revelation of the triune God or perhaps even eclipse this revelation altogether, rendering the orthodox and scriptural teaching of the Trinity superfluous.

Two points must be stressed. First, the warrant for the natural revelation of God is Scripture. The scriptural understanding of this knowledge amounts to little more than an apprehension of God through the revelation of nature or the prick of the conscience. This apprehension is just that—a feeling, a suspicion, a hazy idea that there is something more to this world than ourselves, that there

---

8. Augustine *Confessions* III.6.11.
9. Ziegler, "Natural Knowledge of God," 156.
10. Graebner, "Doctrinal Theology." Graebner continues by emphasizing that all our knowledge about God, even if available through nature, is to come from Scripture. He writes, "We look upon Scripture as the only source of Christian theology also in the article *de Deo*, and define theology proper as the doctrine of holy Scripture concerning the true God."

is someone or something greater than us. This apprehension prevents many from believing with certainty their self-constructed atheism but rarely moves them beyond crudely expressed agnosticism. This seems to me in keeping with Scripture. The Bible never suggests that this natural knowledge prepares the way for the gospel or that the scriptural revelation of the triune God complements and completes the work achieved by our rational endowments. Paul argues emphatically that natural knowledge results in idolatry.

And here we arrive at our second point. Despite what Paul says, some in the history of the church have attempted to place natural knowledge on a surer foundation. The ambitious use of human reason by the various medieval theologians, Descartes's avowal to believe only what his intellect achieves with certainty—these theological judgments, so appealing in our day, need a non-scriptural foundation for truth, and this they achieve by positing God as a passive object of the thinking subject. When natural knowledge of God is thought of in these terms, God becomes no more than the imaginative limits of the human thinking subject. Revealed knowledge of God works in just the opposite direction: God remains subject and revealer of His own identity, and we are the recipients of God's gracious and loving revelation of Himself to us. For this reason, Luther in his own colorful way declared that those delighting in natural knowledge dream idle dreams and are "the devil's mocking birds."[11] These two very different approaches are present already in the early church.

THE FATHERS

As early as the second century the Fathers appealed, with varying levels of enthusiasm, to the distinction between natural and revealed knowledge of God. Justin Martyr and Tertullian eagerly exploited the shared ideas or common notions (*communes sensus*) between the poets and philosophers of antiquity and the canonical Scriptures.[12] Few Christians today would be comfortable with their ambitious efforts to locate all the central teachings of Christianity and particularly the work of Christ in the pagan literature of the ancient world. And yet there are many who would not resist Tertullian's equally problematic argument that we know God first through natural knowledge, through creation and His created works, and then through Scripture: "We maintain that God must first be known by nature (*natura*) and afterwards known further by doctrine (*doctrina*), from nature by works, from doctrine by official teaching."[13] Not everybody in the early church agreed with Tertullian's assignment of priority to nature in our knowing God. The author of the *Epistle*

---

11. *The Gospel for the Festival of the Epiphany, Matthew 2:1–12*, 1522 (AE 52:162; WA 10/1:563.9).

12. Johann Gerhard offers a brief discussion of the similarity between Christian doctrine and pagan ideas on the Trinity at *Theological Commonplaces*, Exegesis III, §30, 287–89.

13. Tertullian *Against Marcion* 1.18, ed. Ernest Evans (Oxford: Oxford University Press, 1972), 46.

to *Diognetus*, about whom we know nothing other than that he was roughly Tertullian's contemporary, declares unequivocally that outside of Christ there is no knowledge of God.[14] The author's emphasis on the priority of Christ for knowing God appears in a discussion of Greek and Jewish claims about God.[15] In other words, he makes this statement against those claiming to know God apart from Christ. To know God is to know Him as Father, and this we know only through the Son by the Holy Spirit.

The divergent paths taken by Justin and Tertullian on the one hand and the author of the *Epistle of Diognetus* on the other wind through the entire history of Christian thought. What accounts for such difference? Why such radically different answers to the question of how we know God? More to the point, does it matter which path we choose to follow? Two issues stand out and inform one another. For a Lutheran, the most notable difference between Justin and Tertullian and the author of the *Epistle to Diognetus* is not their different thoughts on knowledge of God but rather their thoughts on the gospel. The author of the *Epistle to Diognetus* assigns priority to the gospel in our theological reflections. He highlights the great exchange between Christ and the sinner, and emphasizes that Christ alone accomplishes our salvation through His substitutionary atonement.[16] For this author there is no common ground to be exploited, no continuity between the gospel and paganism. Whatever salutary

---

14. The *Epistle to Diognetus* has survived against great odds. The manuscript containing the *Epistle* was being used in 1436 to wrap fish at a market in Constantinople. A young clergyman from Italy thankfully saw the value of the manuscript and purchased it without the fish. The *Epistle* was part of a larger codex containing twenty-one other early Christian writings and was grouped with works by pseudo-Justin Martyr. Cardinal Johannes of Ragusa acquired the manuscript and brought it to Basel. Upon the cardinal's death in 1442, Johannes Reuchlin, Philipp Melanchthon's uncle, came into possession of the manuscript. Eventually the manuscript ended up in the national library of Strasbourg and was destroyed during the Prussian siege in 1870. Although the original manuscript no longer survives, careful copies of it had been made. On the history of the manuscript, see Anders Klostergaard Petersen, "Heavenborne in the World: A Study of the *Letter to Diognetus*," in *In Defence of Christianity: Early Christian Apologists*, ed. Jakob Engberg, Anders-Christian Jabobsen, and Jörg Ulrich (Frankfurt am Main: Peter Lang, 2014), 125–38.

15. A similar example is found in the fourth-century *Life of Antony*, one of the works read most widely in the early church. Athanasius describes for us the visit of Greek philosophers to Antony in the desert. The philosophers want "proofs" and rational demonstrations of God from Antony. He rejects such a pursuit. Faith in Christ is sufficient in itself and does not seek proofs through arguments. Athanasius, *Life of Antony*, trans. Robert Gregg (New York: Paulist Press, 1979), 89.

16. *Epistle to Diognetus* in *The Apostolic Fathers*, 2d ed., ed. Michael Holmes (Grand Rapids: Baker Academic, 1989), 302: "In his mercy he took upon himself our sins; he himself gave up his own Son as a ransom for us, the holy one for the lawless, the guiltless for the guilty, 'the just for the unjust' (1 Pet 3:18), the incorruptible for the corruptible, the immortal for the mortal. For what else but his righteousness could have covered our sins? In whom was it possible for us, the lawless and ungodly, to be justified, except in the Son of God alone? O the sweet exchange, O the incomprehensible work of God, O the unexpected blessings, that the sinfulness of many should be hidden in one righteous man, while the righteousness of one should justify many sinners!" This text is cited frequently by the dogmaticians. Cf. Johann Gerhard, *De Justificatione*, Locus 19, §8 (Jena, 1613), 3:439 and §213, 3:696; Calov, *Systema Locorum Theologicorum* (Wittenberg, 1677), 6:503.

things may have been known through nature have all been corrupted and entangled in idolatry. Nature's role is secondary, never primary; for the faithful, nature reveals God's creative activity and mercy. It is the faithful who marvel at this creation and sing forth, "The earth is the Lord's and the fullness thereof, the world and those who dwell therein" (Ps 24:1). Justin and Tertullian, on the other hand, fail to appreciate the gospel. Justin's heaven is not unlike Zwingli's: they both have a place for Socrates. Justin and Tertullian locate Christian salvation in virtuous living, in good works, in our moral striving. They share with the philosophers not only ideas about God gathered from nature but also a commitment to reward for virtuous living. For Justin in particular, Christianity becomes the clearest and best expression of the philosophy sought by all those concerned with wisdom and virtue. Knowledge of God and the gospel always involve and inform one another.

The second issue is the place of philosophy in Christian theology. The pursuit of the *communes sensus* by Justin and Tertullian derives from the Epicureans and Stoics. It is not scripturally warranted but proceeds from the best ideas of the surrounding culture. Shared here are not just similar ideas but similar commitments to how knowledge is facilitated, justified, and acted upon. The philosophers of the ancient world argued at length over the unassailable starting-points of knowledge and belief?[17] Plato and Aristotle labeled these first principles hypotheses.[18] Aristotle further contended that it was not possible to demonstrate a first principle.[19] If such could be demonstrated, it would depend on something prior, something more fundamental, and therefore would not be a first principle. Establishing first principles became necessary for any rightly ordered presentation of a person's philosophy. For Epicurus and the Epicureans, these first principles, these hypotheses, became the necessary "criteria" or "concepts" for establishing and examining truth.[20] The Stoics took over this Epicurean theory and distinguished between "concepts" and "preconceptions." The former are formed through instruction; the latter come to us naturally.[21] Without these fundamental preconceptions, these innate ideas or common notions, imprinted upon us from nature, knowledge could not be pursued.

---

17. For a fuller discussion of what follows, see the various articles collected in *Doubt and Dogmatism: Studies in Hellenistic Epistemology*, ed. M. Schofield, M. Burnyeat, and J. Barnes (Oxford: Oxford University Press, 1980), especially Malcolm Schofield, "Preconception, Argument, and God," 283–308; *Epistemology*, ed. Stephen Everson (Cambridge: Cambridge University Press, 1990), chapters 7 to 9; and John Behr, *The Way to Nicaea* (Crestwood, NY: St. Vladimir's Seminary Press, 2001), 30–35.

18. Cf. Plato *Republic* VI (510–11), trans. G. M. A. Graube (Indianapolis: Hackett Publishing, 1992), 183–85.

19. Aristotle *Metaphysics* 5.1.2 (1013a) and 4.4.2 (1006a). For Plato hypotheses are confirmed not by prior demonstration but by the persuasiveness of their explanatory power. Gail Fine, "Knowledge and Belief in Republic V–VII," in Everson, *Epistemology*, 109.

20. Diogenes Laertius *Lives of Eminent Philosophers* X.33; Schofield, "Preconception, Argument, and God," 291–93, 296.

21. H. von Arnim, *Stoicorum Veterum Fragmenta* (Leipzig, 1903–24), II, 28:19–22, quoted in Schofield, "Preconception, Argument, and God," 294.

Related to this commitment was the Stoic appeal to the *consensus omnium*. We should expect to find these common notions, unevenly expressed of course, among all people. For the Stoics, this consensus serves as the guarantee for the truth of these preconceptions.

Skeptics aside, truth for these ancient philosophers was reasonable. Philosophical dogmatism emerged when these reasonable truths were thought to be innate. Rejecting an innate truth violated nature. It meant you embraced the unnatural and unreasonable. No better example of this can be seen than the Stoic method for demonstrating the existence and nature of the gods. Sextus Empiricus, himself a skeptic, describes the Stoic method as proceeding in four ways: "arguing first from the agreement among all men, second from the orderly arrangement of the universe, third from the absurd consequences of rejecting the divine, fourth and last by undermining the opposing arguments."[22] Sextus's description of the Stoics fits Justin and Tertullian just as well. Sextus, of course, did not agree with the Stoics. He was persuaded neither by their appeal to *consensus omnium* nor by their appeal to *communes sensus*. Although the great philosophical debates of the ancient world sought to secure the unassailable first principles or hypotheses that would facilitate knowledge and justify truth claims, they could not agree on what was innate, natural, and reasonable. The further problem with these arguments and their appeal to Christians both ancient and modern is the place they assign to our own intellectual accomplishments in determining who God is and what this means for human living. The high price paid by Christians embracing this philosophical approach almost always involves the corruption of the gospel. First principles, it seems, always account for two things: an explanation for the beginning of all things and the purpose of human life. If we can answer the first without God, we can answer the second without Him too.

Many of the second- and third century theologians participated in the great debates of antiquity by highlighting the points of continuity and discontinuity between Christianity and the philosophers. The Apologists especially exploited the *communes sensus*. The path travelled by the Epicureans and Stoics looks very similar to the path taken by Justin and Tertullian, and it is a path that appealed especially to the later theologians of the West.[23] Hilary of Poitiers, for example, recounts his intellectual journey in terms reminiscent of Justin but rejects the shared ideas approach. He recalls how he overcame the philosophical confusion among the schools by reposing in Scripture and God's revelation

---

22. Sextus Empiricus *Adversus Mathematicos* IX.60, quoted in Schofield, "Preconception, Argument, and God," 299.

23. For example, for the Epicureans God was eternal, blessed, immortal, and imperishable. For the Stoics God was immanent, providential, rational, and active. They knew these attributes by reason and nature. Many later Christian theologians would agree. For a lengthy list of Epicurean and Stoic sources on this point, see Basil of Caesarea *Against Eunomius* I.12 (Fathers of the Church, 108 n. 77). Basil's *Against Eunomius* offers a good example of how Christians should think about the common notions held by many and how they relate to Scripture.

of Himself. In this regard Hilary proves the exception among the Latin theologians.[24] Augustine stands closer to Tertullian than Hilary on this issue. He more favorably recounts in the *Confessions* his journey from Platonism to Christianity, highlighting the points of agreement and disagreement. Augustine would continue to maintain the complementarity between nature and Scripture for knowledge of God in his later works.[25] Thomas Aquinas, a figure explored in detail in the next chapter, travels this same path but under the banner of new terminology: preambles to the articles of faith (nature) and articles of faith (Scripture). For Thomas, like Tertullian, Scripture completes and perfects what we learn from nature.

The Greek theologians of the fourth century took a different path. The debate between the Nicenes and the various parties opposed to Nicaea concerned the identity of God. The Nicene theologians used natural knowledge of God arguments to make a crucial epistemological point: knowledge of God outside of Scripture and apart from Christ was necessarily insufficient and problematic. Although scripturally correct statements could be made by non-Christians about God, these were always mixed with false and idolatrous sentiments. For this reason they did not think of natural knowledge of God as a neutral starting point upon which the doctrine of God could be built. That cursory and distorted knowledge needed to be replaced, not augmented, with the right knowledge of the Trinity made known in and by the incarnate Son of God. Athanasius and Gregory of Nazianzus make this point well. Amidst great difficulties these two Fathers imparted to the faithful a proper scriptural understanding of the first two ecumenical councils, the Council of Nicaea (325) and the Council of Constantinople (381). Moreover, Athanasius and Gregory offer us an alternative theological vision than the one embraced by Justin and Tertullian and by the later medieval schoolmen. The larger question, of course, is whether it matters which theological vision we embrace. This chapter and the next few argue it does.

Athanasius of Alexandria

De Incarnatione (*On the Incarnation*) by Athanasius (c. 298–373) comprises only the second half of a much longer treatise written by him. The first half of Athanasius's work, *Contra Gentes*, is a thoroughgoing defense of Christianity against the irrationality of paganism and idolatry. *Contra Gentes* is not simply an apologetic for the reasonableness of Christianity: its larger purpose is to invite the reader to continue with *De Incarnatione*, which lays out the salvation we have in Christ, who is the true source of our wisdom and proper knowledge of God. *Contra Gentes* begins with a consideration of the question of evil—what it

---

24. Carl Beckwith, *Hilary of Poitiers on the Trinity* (Oxford: Oxford University Press, 2008), 151–70.

25. Augustine *On the City of God* 8.10, trans. R. W. Dyson (Cambridge: Cambridge University Press, 1998), 325–27.

is and who is responsible for it. Athanasius uses this question as an opportunity to present the church's understanding of sin and humanity's rejection of God. The rejection of God is at the same time a pursuit of falsehood and unreality which ends in idolatry and immorality. For Athanasius, idolatry is irrational, pagan worship is madness, and therefore their works are immoral. Knowledge of God (true and false) informs worship and ethics (Romans 1). All three go together and all three determine the identity of the believer. Knowledge has moral value. To know rightly entails living rightly; conversely, immorality always stems from false knowing.

After establishing what evil and sin are, how false knowledge of God leads to false worship and behavior, Athanasius turns to the question of how God may be known rightly. At first glance his treatise seems to conform to our expectations of a discussion on natural knowledge of God. He begins with a psychological argument: a proper consideration of the self shows that we are rational creatures capable of abstract thinking and analytical reasoning. By means of such thinking we arrive at thoughts of immortality and the determination that the soul is self-moving.[26] For Athanasius, these two observations lead to the conclusion of an innate immortality in us, and this should set us on the correct path to knowing God.[27] A second argument, and probably more persuasive to many, is the argument from creation. A proper consideration of the world yields the conclusion that God is a perfect governor of the world,[28] that He brings order, unity, and symmetry to creation,[29] and that this order and rationality proceed from one source: the Father of Christ, who through His Wisdom and Word, our Lord and Savior, guides and orders the universe.[30] Athanasius's surprising conclusion seems obtrusive and threatens to undermine his entire project. After all, if his goal is to demonstrate the necessary existence of God from a consideration of the soul and creation, something available to all thinking people whether they know the Bible or not, then his conclusion seems to have missed the mark. Surely nobody ponders the soul or observes the order of creation and from this concludes the necessary existence of the Trinity and Christ as Lord and Savior.

Athanasius's conclusion indicates that his treatise is not a demonstration of the natural knowledge of God apart from Scripture. Indeed, Scripture interrupts the argument throughout *Contra Gentes*. Athanasius ends with a discussion of the unity and distinction between the Father and the Son and an emphasis on the salvation we have in Christ, who is the Door, the Shepherd, the Way, the King, the Guide, and the Savior of all—all titles taken from Scripture.[31]

---

26. Athanasius, *Contra Gentes* and *De Incarnatione*, trans. Robert Thompson (Oxford: Oxford University Press, 1971), 91.
27. Athanasius *Contra Gentes* 85–94.
28. Athanasius *Contra Gentes* 99.
29. Athanasius *Contra Gentes* 101.
30. Athanasius *Contra Gentes* 111.
31. Athanasius *Contra Gentes* 131.

Did Athanasius fail? Only if we place upon his work modern expectations of what constitutes a proper discussion of natural knowledge of God. Athanasius never promises to tie one arm behind his back in the contest with paganism. Reason is not a faculty abstracted from faith. Reason and faith coexist without the conjunction. It is only ever faith's reason or reason's faith. For Athanasius, faith informs reason and not the other way around; or, as we will see below with Gregory of Nazianzus, faith gives fullness to reason. Athanasius makes this point clear in *De Incarnatione*, the second part of his treatise. Apart from Christ knowledge of God eludes us. The Son of God, the Word made flesh, enters into our life that we might share in the life of the Trinity. This He does by conquering death for us and restoring our knowledge of God. And yet Athanasius was not offering empty promises in *Contra Gentes* with his two arguments for the existence of God; He really can be known by a meditation upon the soul or contemplation of creation, but this general knowledge falls far short of anything salutary. In the end this kind of argument for Athanasius falls into the category of apologetics. He is dismantling the irrationality of paganism/idolatry and preparing the way for the reasonableness of Christianity. He builds or constructs a proper knowledge of the Father only through the Son, who is the Word and Reason, the Logos, the ground of our knowing as *logikoi*.

Gregory of Nazianzus

In the year 380 Gregory of Nazianzus (c. 330–90) delivered a series of sermons to his small pro-Nicene congregation in Constantinople. He later revised and polished these sermons, publishing them as *Orations* 27–31 in his literary corpus. These five orations are known more simply today as Gregory's *Theological Orations*. Gregory's opponents are the second-generation Arians, the so-called neo-Arians, the radical Arians. Gregory's polemic especially targets Eunomius of Cyzicus, a brazen rationalist who succumbs to intellectual idolatry. To the horror and shock of the Cappadocians, Eunomius insisted that the human mind could comprehend and express with precision and completeness the very essence of God. Eunomius writes, "God does not know anything more about his own essence than we do, nor is that essence better known to him and less to us. Rather, whatever we know about it is exactly what he knows, and conversely, what he knows is what you will find without change in us."[32] Eunomius defined God's essence with the term "unbegotten," and further declared that since the Son is "begotten" He must not be *per definitionem* God. Eunomius presented a number of rational puzzles that sought to undermine the orthodox confession of the Trinity; these mental teasers appealed to the masses and were repeated in casual debates at the public baths, the market place, and other popular gatherings. As Gregory describes it, these "verbal tricksters" and

---

32. Richard Vaggione, *Eunomius: The Extant Works* (Oxford: Oxford University Press, 1987), 178.

"word-gamesters" turned a discussion of God into an irreverent intellectual game of one-upmanship.³³

In his first two theological orations Gregory articulates a theological vision that embraces humility and reverence in speaking about the Trinity, that emphasizes the necessity of God coming to us to make Himself known, and that shows the priority of faith in apprehending and speaking the truths of God. Gregory warns his congregation that the subject of the Trinity is not for every occasion or every audience. We should not discuss the eternal generation of the Son from the Father at the bath house or with those who seek only to mock Christianity. Gregory writes, "Let us not 'sing the song of the Lord in a foreign land,' by which I mean before any and every audience, heathen or Christian, friend or foe, sympathetic or hostile."³⁴ Gregory exhorts his hearers to understand the limits of such discussions. There are aspects of the Trinity not open to inquiry.³⁵ Those who seek to pursue the hidden things of God and ascend to the heights beyond what God has made known are those ignorant of their own ignorance. They are like those who stare at the sun, rendering themselves blind by their own foolishness.

To argue that theology is not for everyone or to urge caution in our discussions (audience, occasion, content) does not entail limiting our thoughts about God. Gregory writes, "It is more important that we should remember God than that we should breathe: indeed, if one may say so, we should do nothing else besides."³⁶ The entirety of our lives should be given to the contemplation and awareness of God. The Scriptures direct us to "meditate day and night," to call upon the Lord "evening and morning and at noon." We are to "bless the Lord at all times," and this we are to do "when we lie down, when we rise up, and when we walk by the way."³⁷ The person who meditates upon God's Word day and night and who calls upon the Lord and blesses the Lord at all times is a person properly freed from the distractions and whirl of life. God declares in the psalms, "Be still, and know that I am God" (Ps 46:10).³⁸ Gregory seizes upon this verse. The person rightly prepared to talk about God possesses "inner stillness."³⁹ No longer eager to win a verbal skirmish or prevail over an opponent with a mental teaser, such a person reverently contemplates the triune God as a lover of truth and seeks to share this God with others. Such a person, concludes Gregory, rightly understands that God must enlighten if we are to know and worship the Father, Son, and Holy Spirit, as three irreducible persons in one undivided Godhead.⁴⁰

---

33. Gregory of Nazianzus *Or.* 27.1 (PPS, 25).
34. Gregory of Nazianzus *Or.* 27.5 (PPS, 28); Ps 137:4.
35. Gregory of Nazianzus *Or.* 27.3 (PPS, 27).
36. Gregory of Nazianzus *Or.* 27.4 (PPS, 27–28).
37. Gregory of Nazianzus *Or.* 27.4 (PPS, 28); Ps 1:2; Ps 55:17; Ps 34:1; Dt 6:7.
38. Gregory of Nazianzus *Or.* 27.3 (PPS, 27).
39. Gregory of Nazianzus *Or.* 28.1 (PPS, 37).
40. Gregory of Nazianzus *Or.* 28.1 (PPS, 37); *Or.* 31.28 (PPS, 139).

Gregory turns next to an extended and lengthy consideration of the created works of God. Such a move was hardly novel in the early church and can be found in nearly all discussions of God in the history of the church.[41] And yet Gregory does something quite unexpected: he uses this reflection on nature to impress upon us not only the incomprehensibility of God outside of Scripture but also our own limited understanding of the creaturely realities around and within us. It is in the very awareness of our unknowing that we are overcome with wonder and awe at the one who does know, at the one true Knower who created and governs all that is unknown to us. This awareness humbly disposes us to confess rightly, to speak rightly, and to worship rightly the true God. Gregory's remarkable hymn of creation renders us reverently silent and in the position of stillness needed to know God. Our mouths are agape in wonder and our souls thirst for more: "If our hymn has been worthy of its theme, it is the grace of the Trinity, of the Godhead one in three; if desire remains incompletely satisfied, that way too my argument can claim success."[42]

When we gaze at the created things of God, we are like Moses in the cleft of the rock, seeing only, as Gregory describes it, the "averted figure," the back parts of God.[43] We must be like Moses. In the *Oration*, it is Gregory who is in the cleft of the rock. He sees God's averted figure *because* he is in the cleft of the rock, which, as Paul tells us, is Christ, "God the Word Incarnate for us."[44] Gregory's intertextual exegesis leads him to a fundamental point: we see only when we are in Christ. Gregory will make this point with earnestness in his subsequent orations. For the time being, he is more interested in discussing how God mediates knowledge of Himself through creaturely realities. The splendor and majesty of God have been disclosed to us "in the created things he has brought forth and governs."[45] These vestiges of God that *He* has left behind for us are God's averted figure. They are like shadowy reflections of the sun in water accommodated to weak eyes too impotent to gaze directly upon the sun. If we seek more than our bodily eyes are able to accomplish by staring directly at the sun, which is no different than pursuing the hidden things of God by our bodily reason, we render ourselves blind, physically and spiritually. As the sun mediates its brilliance by the reflection in the pond, so too God mediates His presence through created realities, averted figures. This God has done for us and our benefit.

Gregory, like so many of the Fathers, emphasizes the incomprehensibility of God.[46] Since we are corporeal and even our most exalted language is

---

41. See for example Cyril of Jerusalem *Catechetical Lectures* IX; Basil of Caesarea *Homilies on the Hexaemeron* 7 (on fish), 8 (on birds), and 9 (on land animals); Augustine *On Christian Teaching* Book 1.
42. Gregory of Nazianzus *Or.* 28.31 (PPS, 63).
43. Gregory of Nazianzus *Or.* 28.3 (PPS, 39); Ex 33:21–23.
44. Gregory of Nazianzus *Or.* 28.3 (PPS, 39).
45. Gregory of Nazianzus *Or.* 28.3 (PPS, 39).
46. Gregory of Nazianzus *Or.* 28.4 (PPS, 39).

conditioned by elements of corporeality, by time and space, it is impossible to know fully the reality or essence of God in thought or communicate it in speech. We are no more capable of exact knowledge of God's essence than we are of God's creation.[47] Here an analogy emerges for Gregory. Our knowledge of nature is but an outline of its reality. There will come a time, however, when we will know these things more fully. And yet even with this partial understanding we know that creation exists. A distinction is to be made between existence and essence: "[knowing] a thing's existence is quite different from knowledge of *what* it is."[48] The same applies to God: "That God, the creative and sustaining cause of all, exists, sight and instinctive law inform us—sight, which lights upon things seen as nobly fixed in their courses, borne along in, so to say, motionless movement; instinctive law, which infers their author through the things seen in their orderliness."[49] Knowing the existence of God by sight and instinctive law is far removed from knowing the "reality" of God in His fullness.

Gregory turns to a reflection on language. When we say God is incorporeal, we say far less than we think. When we use terms like incorporeal, ingenerate, immutable, immortal, we are not speaking of what God's essential being is. Rather by circumlocution we state what God is not. And yet comprehending any object of knowledge requires more than negation. Positive assertion of "what a thing is" is far easier to state than numerous statements of "what a thing is not." Gregory explains:

> A person who tells you what God is not but fails to tell you what he is, is rather like someone who, asked what twice five are, answers "not two, not three, not four, not five, not twenty, not thirty, no number, in short, under ten or over ten." He does not deny it *is* ten, but he is also not settling the questioner's mind with a firm answer. It is much simpler, much briefer, to indicate all that something is *not* by indicating what it *is*, than to reveal what it *is* by denying what it is *not*.[50]

When we use apophatic terms to describe God, we say only what He is not, not what He is. Strictly speaking these terms reveal more about our relation to God than His essence. To say God is immortal is to say that He is not mortal *like us*. To say God is incorporeal is to say that He is not bodily *like us*. We are the point of reference for these terms; all they assert is that God is not like us. When we deceive ourselves into thinking we are talking about the reality and essence of God by using these terms, we succumb to the grand rationalist claims made by Descartes and the charges of self-projection leveled by Feuerbach: "man makes a god of what he is not but would like to be."[51]

Gregory's digression on language undermines the laughable argument of his opponents who claim to know God's essence by human reason. But more

---

47. Gregory of Nazianzus *Or.* 28.4–5 (PPS, 39–40).
48. Gregory of Nazianzus *Or.* 28.5 (PPS, 40).
49. Gregory of Nazianzus *Or.* 28.6 (PPS, 40–41).
50. Gregory of Nazianzus *Or.* 28.10 (PPS, 43–44).
51. Ludwig Feuerbach, *Essence of Religion*, trans. R. Manheim (New York: Harper and Row, 1967), 234. This issue of language is taken up again in chapter 5 below.

than that, he explains, "I wanted to make plain the point my sermon began with, which was this: the incomprehensibility of deity to the human mind and its totally unimaginable grandeur."[52] These two things work together for Gregory. This is, as I said above, the unexpected turn in Gregory's argument. By confessing the incomprehensibility of God and creation we arrive at a proper stillness and humble place of knowing. Gregory's interest here is not radical apophaticism, it is not to argue that we know nothing of God. His interest is to clear away the intellectual idolatries that claim to know the full reality of who God is. His conclusion, as we will see, is that God is always greater than our understanding.[53]

Before turning to his hymn on the beauty of creation, Gregory emphasizes one more time the limitation of language and its metaphorical character when speaking of God.[54] Because we are corporeal, our minds, our thoughts, express themselves always through the medium of corporeality. Gregory explains:

> Let those whose business it is discuss the matter, let them take their philosophical investigation as high as they can. Yet we "prisoners of the earth," in divine Jeremiah's phrase (Lam 3:34), pent in this gross portion of flesh, know this: you cannot cross your own shadow however much you haste—it is always exactly ahead of your grasp. Sight cannot approach its objects without the medium of light and atmosphere; fish cannot swim out of water; and no more can embodied beings keep incorporeal company with things ideal. Some corporeal factor of ours will always intrude itself, even if the mind be most fully detached from the visible world and at its most recollected when it attempts to engage with its invisible kin.[55]

The mind tires of transcending these bodily conditions; it gazes in impotence. Although the thinking subject longs for God, it is powerless to grasp Him.[56] Frustrated by these efforts, the mind tries another route. It looks upon creation, taking in the visible, and declaring either these things to be divine, succumbing to crass idolatry, or discovering here beauty and order, "using sight as a guide to what transcends sight without losing God through the grandeur of what it sees."[57] This latter approach led on by the beauty and order of created things arrives at "their designer."[58] Such beauty and order could not be ascribed to mere chance but rather to something else, to a designer, to God. In this way reason, though burdened with thoughts that are corporeal—"our earthly shackles," as

---

52. Gregory of Nazianzus *Or.* 28.11 (PPS, 45).
53. Cf. Christopher Beeley, *Gregory of Nazianzus on the Trinity and the Knowledge of God* (Oxford: Oxford University Press, 2008), 99: "For Gregory God is ineffable not because we cannot say anything about him or express his nature with any certainty, but because we could never possibly express *all* of what God is."
54. On this point see especially *Or.* 31.7 (PPS, 121–22) and *Or.* 30.17–21 (PPS, 107–12).
55. Gregory of Nazianzus *Or.* 28.12 (PPS, 46).
56. Gregory of Nazianzus *Or.* 28.13 (PPS, 47).
57. Gregory of Nazianzus *Or.* 28.13 (PPS, 47).
58. Gregory of Nazianzus *Or.* 28.16 (PPS, 49).

Gregory elsewhere describes it—discovers through corporeal things the maker and preserver of such things, God.[59]

Gregory ends his oration with a lengthy hymn of creation.[60] Here his eloquence and rhetorical craft soar to their greatest height. He marvels over the soul and body, why children resemble parents in their appearance, how our bodily parts work so harmoniously together. Speech and hearing fascinate Gregory. How are sounds produced by our vocal organs and received by ears? How does sound travel through the air? He wonders at the speed of our eyes joining what they see to thoughts in our mind. Turning to animals, he wonders at their diversity of habitats, behaviors, and diets. Some animals are swift, strong, and beautiful; others are slow, weak, and hideous. Why do some take pride in their appearance and others do not? Why do some crawl and some go upright? Fish are a constant source of amazement. They glide through water as if in air. They breathe in water. Their diversity in size and color is pure wonderment. Similarly, the birds of the air possess an array of design and color. Their songs and sounds are beautiful and striking. Where did they get such music? Nothing captures the imagination more than the industriousness of bees, spiders, and ants. Their work is ingenious; the spider's web beyond explanation. What about plants? Their scents and medicinal qualities make them dearer than gems. Who can explain the geography of the earth, the movements of the seas, the origin and destination of the winds? What about the rotation and movement of heavenly bodies? Who put the stars in order? Gregory marvels over the unhalting course of the sun and its consistent kindnesses. The even imbalance of night and day, the orderly arrival and disciplined departure of the seasons, are all necessary for us, and yet who can explain such mysteries?

Gregory moves from contemplating creation to the heavenly beings above. Scripture encourages us to bend our gaze upon holy things. But even here, notes Gregory, we see not in a manner free of bodily description. We know angels to be incorporeal or very near it, and yet Scripture says, "He makes his angels winds, and his ministers a flame of fire" (Heb 1:7).[61] We become dizzy by our contemplation of angels, archangels, thrones, dominions, princedoms, and powers. We know that they are but can go no further than this. At this point Gregory brings his hymn to a close: "If our hymn has been worthy of its theme, it is the grace of the Trinity, of the Godhead one in three; if desire remains incompletely satisfied, that way too my argument can claim success."[62]

Gregory's hymn serves a twofold purpose. On the one hand he creates an insurmountable intellectual burden for his readers. If we are unable to answer every question we may ask of creation, how much more unable are we to define the very nature of God. Gregory's hymn makes this point well. We cannot boast

---

59. Gregory of Nazianzus *Or.* 30.17 (PPS, 107).
60. Gregory of Nazianzus *Or.* 28.22–31 (PPS, 53–64).
61. Gregory of Nazianzus *Or.* 28.31 (PPS, 63).
62. Gregory of Nazianzus *Or.* 28.31 (PPS, 63).

of our knowledge of God when we know so little about ourselves, our own body and soul. We cannot boast of things spiritual when questions remain about the fish in the sea and the web of a spider. The person who does this, argues Gregory, is ignorant of his own ignorance. He spends his day trying to cross his own shadow or groping after mist.[63] Gregory's hymn also leads a person to wonder and awe at the beauty, order, and grandeur of creation. If pride was the mark of the person who ends in intellectual idolatry, humility is the mark of this person. It is in the very awareness of our unknowing that we are brought to a position of stillness. Our speaking ceases as we are now humbly disposed to receive God's speaking, His Word by His Spirit. God grants illumination, He guides and safeguards our right thinking, speaking, and worshipping. Our knowing proceeds from His gift of faith and this faith gives fullness to our reason.

CONCLUSION

The Fathers were not of one voice on the question of natural knowledge of God. For the most part the Latin or Western theologians demonstrate greater sympathy for natural knowledge arguments than their Greek counterparts. The issue is not whether there is such a thing as natural knowledge of God; all of the writers discussed above share this conviction. The issue is what a theologian does with this knowledge. What role does he assign it in our coming to know God? Justin and Tertullian think our knowledge of God begins with nature and then we turn to Scripture. God's revelation complements what reason discovers through nature. Athanasius and Gregory of Nazianzus, the great voices of the Councils of Nicaea and Constantinople, both uncompromising in their confession of the Trinity, assign a modest and humble role to natural knowledge. For them knowing the God of the Bible always begins with the incarnation, the Word made flesh, God coming to us. When we repose in the Word by faith, we rightly order our reason. As we will see in chapter 4, Luther and the Lutheran Confessions stand very close to the theological vision expressed by Athanasius and Gregory.

Perhaps it is overly simple to put it this way, but for those theologians who emphasize the radical work of the gospel, of the surprising salvation achieved for us in the person of Jesus Christ, the very Son of God, there is also a great emphasis placed upon God's revelation of Himself in Christ—"All other ground is sinking sand" (TLH 370). For those who seek a greater role for human striving and achievement in our salvation, there is on the other hand a greater emphasis upon natural reason and the shared ideas of the world in our coming to know God. The former think the key or right hypothesis to knowing the identity of God must begin with Christ and His cross; the latter think we may begin

---

63. Gregory of Nazianzus *De rebus suis*, II/I/I.92 (Fathers of the Church, 28); cf. *De vita sua* II/I/XI.1774–75 (Fathers of the Church, 126).

first with nature and then proceed to Scripture. The former are deeply suspect of reason unguided by faith; the latter speak optimistically about a reason supplemented by faith. The difference between these approaches may not be reduced to a matter of emphasis; they are qualitatively different, of a different order altogether, as they each envision a radically different gospel and doctrine of God.

3

PROVING GOD: MEDIEVAL AMBITIONS AND KNOWLEDGE OF GOD

It is no mere coincidence of history that the triumph of Gothic architecture coincided with the rise of scholasticism.[1] The same world, the same human dreams and aspirations, produced both. Encountering one of the great medieval summas was not at all unlike encountering the Gothic cathedral. Something extraordinary was before you, something new and unimagined by previous generations. A person both delights and exhausts when taking in the cathedral's soaring verticality, its never-ending towers and spires, dynamic arches, flying buttresses, and delicate rose windows. The completeness, the grandeur, and the mental rigor of scholasticism finds its analogue in the Gothic cathedral.[2] Both aimed at the ideal; both were considered the pinnacle of human achievement; both left their audiences marveling.

Theology, like architecture, never takes place in a vacuum. These two marvels of the Middle Ages coincided with remarkable demographic, agricultural, and commercial advances.[3] The world was changing. To use the poetic designations of the old textbooks, the Dark Ages were over and a future of endless possibility lay ahead. People lived longer and there were more of them. Europe's population boomed from forty-two million to seventy-three million between the years 1000 and 1300. The rapid increase in population significantly altered the social, economic, and intellectual landscape of Europe. Learning also changed: it was no longer a private affair to be pursued by the reclusive monk. Learning went public and found a home in the new universities. Instruction was offered in theology, philosophy, law, and medicine. In this world of growing urban centers, remarkable achievements in architecture, and expanding horizons of human learning, scholars and scholarship emerged.[4]

---

1. On the relationship between medieval architecture and scholasticism see Erwin Panofsky, *Gothic Architecture and Scholasticism* (New York: Meridian Books, 1957). For a less ambitious construal of architecture and theology see Charles Radding and William W. Clark, *Medieval Architecture, Medieval Learning: Builders and Masters in the Age of Romanesque and Gothic* (New Haven, CT: Yale University Press, 1992).

2. James Snyder, *Medieval Art* (Englewood Cliffs, NJ: Prentice Hall, 1989), 343–49.

3. For a fuller discussion of these different aspects of medieval culture see John Baldwin, *The Scholastic Culture of the Middle Ages, 1000–1300* (Project Heights, IL: Waveland Press, 1997).

4. The excitement for knowledge and discovery during the thirteenth century is seen in the ambitious production of encyclopedias. Mary Franklin-Brown, *Reading the World: Encylopedic Writing in the Scholastic Age* (Chicago: University of Chicago Press, 2012).

No person affected learning in the medieval period more than Aristotle. His texts on logic, ethics, metaphysics, and the physical sciences transformed the way people thought about God, ethics, and the natural world. When Aristotle's influence surpassed that of Plato, the question of how knowledge is brokered shifted from recollection and divine illumination to the world of the senses, from a priori to a posteriori arguments. The epistemological movement from Anselm to Aquinas reflects this change. For Anselm the question of God's existence is a mental exercise, "thinking" of that which nothing greater can be conceived. For Thomas the question of God's existence begins with the senses, the experience of the physical world, and proceeds from there to the mind. Aristotle opened up new ways (*viae*) of thinking for schoolmen as diverse as Thomas Aquinas and William of Ockham.

The period between Thomas and Luther is marked by struggle over which Aristotle to privilege—either Thomas's Christian Aristotle or the pagan Aristotle favored by the nominalists—and the consequences for both theology and philosophy. All parties were convinced of Aristotle's importance. The charm he exerted reached such a height that Lambertus de Monte Domini, a fifteenth-century Thomist professor in Cologne, proposed beatification for the pagan philosopher.[5] The bishop of Erfurt, John Bonemilch von Lasphe, who likely ordained Luther to the priesthood in 1507, echoed a common sentiment of the day when he told Luther and his peers "without Aristotle no one could be a theologian."[6] From this context issues Luther's famous declaration in 1517 that Aristotle is to theology as darkness is to light.[7] A decisive part of Luther's breakthrough was an abandonment of this way of thinking: "It is an error to say that no one can become a theologian without Aristotle. This is in opposition to common opinion."[8] The problem exposed by Luther had less to do with the philosopher than with how his philosophy was used by the schoolmen, who failed to comprehend "the correct meaning of Aristotle."[9] Luther's statements against Aristotle, unthinkable not only for a figure like Thomas Aquinas but also for many in Luther's own day, gets to the heart of the intellectual struggle inherited by the Reformers between an older way (*via antiqua*) and a newer way of thinking (*via moderna*).

Textbooks often describe these two medieval *viae* according to the epistemological struggle over universals and particulars. Realists like Thomas

---

5. Heiko Oberman, "*Via Antiqua* and *Via Moderna*: Late Medieval Prolegomena to Early Reformation Thought," *Journal of the History of Ideas* 48:1 (1987): 27.

6. *Nachwort zur Epistola Theologorum Parisiensium*, 1534 (WA 60:125.40): "Absque Aristotele nemo potest theologus fieri." Text referenced in Bernard Lohse, *Martin Luther's Theology*, trans. Roy A. Harrisville (Minneapolis: Fortress Press, 1999), 26.

7. *Disputation against Scholastic Theology*, 1517 (AE 31:12, thesis 50; WA 1:226.26). For a summary of Luther's objections to the continued use of Aristotle in the Wittenberg curriculum from 1517 to 1520 see Steven Ozment, *The Age of Reform 1250–1550* (New Haven, CT: Yale University Press, 1980), 310–11.

8. *Disputation against Scholastic Theology*, 1517 (AE 31:12, thesis 43; WA 1:226.14).

9. *Disputation against Scholastic Theology*, 1517 (AE 31:12, thesis 51; WA 1:226.28).

Aquinas were opposed by William of Ockham and the nominalists or terminists of the late medieval period. It would be hard to imagine a thornier question than the one that occupied these medieval thinkers on the acquisition of knowledge. Although this issue of universals exposes an important point of departure for these thinkers, restricting their disagreement to this finer point of epistemology obscures larger differences on the substantive questions of how God is known and the prevailing relationship between God's truth and the natural world. Their differing epistemologies are important not because of what they say or think about the relationship between universals and particulars but because their respective theories on knowledge necessarily inform their respective views of reality. How we *think* we think informs how we talk about reality and how we understand it.

In part 1 of this book we have been pursuing the question of epistemology (theory) under the topic of natural and revealed knowledge of God (practice). The reason, as just suggested, is that whatever conclusions we reach on the theological question of natural knowledge proceeds from our epistemological commitments. We ought to wonder why Thomas Aquinas begins his treatise on God with a natural knowledge demonstration of God's necessary existence (*ST* I.2). Why does Thomas first discuss *what* God is as God (*ST* I.3–26) before talking about *who* God is as Trinity (*ST* 1.27–43)? Does the distinction even matter?[10] If we say yes, then how does it matter? Should the order be reversed? Should there even be such a distinction? We likewise ought to wonder why Luther shows little interest in natural knowledge demonstrations of God's existence. It is not the case that he rejects natural knowledge—indeed it could be argued that his Large Catechism provides the most radical argument for it. Why then the stark difference between Thomas's approach and the one taken by Luther? Why does Luther choose to approach the Trinity by way of the person and work of Christ and the delivery of that saving work by the Holy Spirit through Word and sacrament? Does that not seem disorderly and unnecessarily confused with the other articles of faith?[11] These different theological judgments proceed from different epistemological commitments and have significant consequences for our construal of reality, our understanding of God, our confession of the gospel, and our newness of life lived according to the gospel.

---

10. The older response to this question was, yes, it matters a great deal and shows the Latin or Western preference for talking about the essence before the persons. This was meant as criticism and an apologetic for the Greek or Eastern approach which almost always follows such criticism. More recently it has been fashionable to alleviate the reader's concerns with Thomas's approach by pointing out that any scriptural presentation of God's identity must show both unity and diversity. It matters very little, it is implied, which we do first. My interest with this question lies elsewhere.

11. If you find that you cannot talk about the Trinity without also talking about baptism, then you will be at home in the thought world of the Fathers and Lutheran reformers. If you find that you can talk about the Trinity without ever mentioning your baptism, then you will be at home in the thought world of the schoolmen.

To appreciate the alternative theological vision given by the medieval writers, a vision not followed by Lutheranism, we will look at three significant figures on the question of the knowledge of God in the medieval period: John of Damascus, Anselm of Canterbury, and Thomas Aquinas. Thomas will occupy most of the discussion as he bequeaths a greater influence to subsequent generations and remains the medieval figure studied most widely by theologians today. Before discussing Thomas we will chart the emergence of natural knowledge as a distinct pursuit by human reason in John of Damascus. John bridges the patristic and medieval period and exercises considerable influence on Western trinitarian thought. Both Melanchthon and Chemnitz censure John for departing from the theological vision of the Fathers, straying from the Scriptures into the realm of speculative theology, and introducing new ways of speaking (*novimodi loquendi*).[12]

Following John we will look at two of the most ambitious and adventurous efforts to demonstrate God's necessary existence. Anselm's *Proslogion* will be discussed because of its prevalence today in philosophical and apologetic musings on the existence of God. Thomas's distinction between preambles of faith and articles of faith and his five ways of proving God's existence will then be considered. Thomas's distinction and proofs provide two discrete ways of knowing God that complement one another. The first way begins with our rational judgments about who God must be, and the second way adds God's revelation of Himself as Trinity to our rational efforts. I will argue below that this move by Thomas amounts to an epistemological *facere quod*.[13] The chapter ends with a brief description of the nominalist alternative to Thomas's synthesis of revelation and reason, an alternative known by Luther and in part embraced by him.

JOHN OF DAMASCUS

John of Damascus (d. 749), living at the periphery of a disintegrating Roman world, wrote an epitome of patristic theology, *On the Orthodox Faith* (*De Orthodoxa Fide*), that would make his name and work known among all the great centers of learning in the Christian West. His summary served as the principal resource for patristic trinitarian and Christological thought

---

12. Philipp Melanchthon, *Loci Communes* (1521), CR 21:82–84; Martin Chemnitz, "On the Use and Value of Theological Topics," in *Loci Theologici*, trans. J. A. O. Preus (St. Louis: Concordia Publishing House, 2008), 1:42–43; Chemnitz, *Loci Theologici* (Wittenberg, 1653), 11.

13. *Facere quod* is the shortened form of the late medieval axiom *facientibus quod in se est, Deus non denegat gratiam* (God will not deny grace to those who do what is in them). Figures such as Ockham and Gabriel Biel taught that God would respond graciously to our initial and minimal act of good toward Him. Luther rightly assails this position as Pelagianism and often broadly assigns it to the whole of scholasticism. See *Disputation against Scholastic Theology*, 1517 (AE 31:9, theses 5–7, 33; WA 1:224.15–19, 225.35–36). Cf. *Heidelberg Disputation*, 1518 (AE 31:40, thesis 16; WA 1.354.11–12); *Preface to the Epistle of St. Paul to the Romans*, 1522/1546 (AE 35:367–68; WADB 7:6.7–11).

for the medieval schoolmen, the reformers, and the seventeenth-century dogmaticians.[14] John was not an original thinker, and in keeping with his Byzantine culture disavowed the very idea of originality. He provided careful summaries of the best insights from the Fathers on diverse theological issues and questions. His contribution lies less with substance and more with style. New with John is the manner in which he organizes and presents his material, and how he frames it with his own exegetical instincts and technical terminology. For these reasons he is best seen, as Melanchthon and Chemnitz argue, standing not at the end of the patristic period but at the beginning of a decidedly different time in the history of Christian thought, the medieval period.

The first part of John's treatise, "On God and Trinity," emphasizes the necessity of God for knowledge about God: "No one has ever known God unless God Himself revealed it to him—not only no man, but not even any of the supramundane powers: the very Cherubim and Seraphim, I mean."[15] And yet, he notes, God has not left us in complete ignorance, for "through nature" the knowledge of God's existence "has been revealed by Him to all men."[16] The harmony and ordering of creation proclaim God's existence. John says nothing more than this about natural knowledge. He turns next to God's proper revelation and the knowledge we have through the Scriptures and through Jesus Christ. In the second chapter he introduces the Greek patristic distinction between theology proper and divine economy, reflects on the limitations of human language, and offers a brief exposition of the Creed. John ends this chapter in a manner similar to the first. Since there are many things we cannot understand (God's essence, the incarnation, the virgin birth, Christ walking on water), we are to abide in the Scriptures: "It is impossible either to say or fully to understand anything about God beyond what has been divinely proclaimed to us, whether told or revealed, by the sacred declarations of the Old and New Testaments."[17]

John's first two chapters provide a good summary of the patristic presentation given in the previous chapter. Melanchthon himself follows the spirit of these first two chapters in his *Loci Communes* (1521).[18] Had John stopped here all would be well. The problem appears in the third chapter, where he aims to demonstrate the existence of God. Although what he says in this chapter has patristic support, the manner in which he presents this material moves him decidedly in the direction of Anselm and Aquinas. For John the existence of God is neither doubted by those who accept the Scriptures nor by the majority

---

14. Andrew Louth, *St. John Damascene: Tradition and Originality* (Oxford: Oxford University Press, 2005), 3.
15. John of Damascus, *An Exact Exposition of the Orthodox Faith*, in *Writings*, trans. Frederic H. Chase, Jr. (Washington, D.C.: Catholic University of America Press, 1958), I.1 (Fathers of the Church, 165).
16. John of Damascus, *An Exact Exposition of the Orthodox Faith* I.1 (Fathers of the Church, 166).
17. John of Damascus, *An Exact Exposition of the Orthodox Faith* I.2 (Fathers of the Church, 168).
18. Philipp Melanchthon, *Loci Communes* (1521), preface (CR 21:83–85).

of Greeks, since the knowledge of God's existence has been revealed through nature. However, the wickedness of the devil has led some to say there is no God. The Scriptures record, notes John, that "the fool hath said in his heart: 'There is no God'" (Ps 14:1). The apostles performed miracles by the power of the Holy Spirit to show people the existence of God. Similarly, the shepherds and teachers who followed the apostles performed miracles and sought by the grace of the Spirit to enlighten those in darkness. Since by his own admission John does not have this gift of miracles or teaching, he proposes to pass along two arguments that have been handed down in the history of the church to demonstrate God's existence.

John's first argument begins with the premise that all things are either created or uncreated. Whatever is created is subject to change by corruption or will; whatever is uncreated is not subject to change. Everything that falls within our range of experience is subject to change and to being moved in various ways. Intellectual beings (angels, souls, and demons) change by free choice; the rest change by corruption. John further argues that all changeable beings must have been created by something. Even if we admit that something is created by another who was also created, we eventually will arrive at something or someone that has not been created. Therefore "the creator is an uncreated and entirely unchangeable being. And what else would that be but God?"[19]

John's second argument focuses on the harmony of creation and its preservation. When we observe such things, we learn that there is a being who put all things together and preserves them. John proceeds with a litany of questions. What is it that ordered the things of heaven and earth? What is it that arranged all things? What is it that set them in motion and continues to move them? Could it be that there is no architect behind all of this? Could such things be attributed to spontaneity? Could mere chance so perfectly arrange such things? No, concludes John, there must be an architect to account for all of this. What else is this if not God?[20]

A lingering problem with these sorts of demonstrations has to do with their purpose and audience. Christians certainly appreciate the logical force of John's arguments because they already believe God created the heavens and the earth and never tire of meditating on His wondrous works (Psalms 8, 104, 111). Scripture makes this certain for them. Believers rarely wonder about the logic of such arguments and what must be true for these arguments to be true. Here we encounter thorny questions about the predictability of God's being and *necessary* actions. John hardly could have anticipated these fiercely disputed medieval questions. Setting these questions aside, we can ask at the very least what has been proved by these arguments. Although the fool may say in his heart that there is no God, John thinks his two logical arguments make clear to any reasonable person the necessary existence of something that must be

---

19. John of Damascus, *An Exact Exposition of the Orthodox Faith* I.3 (Fathers of the Church, 169).
20. John of Damascus, *An Exact Exposition of the Orthodox Faith* I.3 (Fathers of the Church, 170).

"God." Indeed, as he timidly puts it, if this thing isn't God, what else could it be? Whatever it might be, we can fairly well say that neither the Greek nor the Muslim, John's principal audience, would find it foolish or a stumbling block. The term is equivocal.

John's arguments clearly offer very little to believers. What about the fool? Scripture tells us the fool not only denies God (Ps 14:1; Ps 53:1) but also fails to understand the works of God (Ps 92:6). It could be argued that the unbeliever hears these arguments and is left more stupefied than when he began: he started by saying that there is no god and yet now must admit how unreasonable his faith in the non-existence of the divine is. The apologetic use of such arguments may silence or frustrate unbelievers, but this will hardly lead them to anything remotely similar to what John means when he concludes, "What else is this, if it is not God?" What does John mean by God? He seems to mean the God made known to us in Scripture. He could hardly mean otherwise (cf. Ps 96:5). And this is precisely the problem. As soon as we assign a constructive or complementary role to this sort of natural knowledge, it is difficult to see how we avoid the intellectual idols argued against by Gregory of Nazianzus. In such a scenario, the foundation for any claim to belief in God always will have started with the rational arguments of the individual. The existence of God will no longer be an object of faith but will belong to reason and nature. Admittedly this may be a harsh and unfair reading of John's modest attempt to demonstrate the existence of God. His argument, however, directly informs Thomas's proofs and leads Thomas to state that the existence of God is not an article of faith but rather a preamble to the articles of faith. Scripture, of course, says otherwise. The existence of God belongs to faith not reason: "Whoever would draw near to God must believe that he exists [ὅτι ἔστιν]" (Heb 11:6). The Lutheran dogmaticians repeatedly cite this verse against Thomas and his contemporaries. Whether John intended the dire consequences suggested here we need not decide. Melanchthon and Chemnitz rightly detect with John a new way of speaking about God and a new theological vision.

ANSELM OF CANTERBURY

Anselm (1033–1109), a Benedictine monk and the eventual abbot of the famous monastery at Bec, spent thirty years of his life teaching the monks entrusted to him (1063–93). He later would serve as archbishop of Canterbury (1093–1109). Anselm attempted to show in his works that no contradiction existed between the truth of Scripture and reason. His so-called proof for the existence of God, referred to since Kant as the ontological argument, often is seen as one of the boldest attempts in the history of the church to demonstrate the necessary existence of God by appeal to reason alone.[21] Such characterization, as shown

---

21. Anselm follows this method at length in his *Monologion*, an exposition of the divine being. In the prologue he explains how he was asked to proceed in this meditation by the monks

by Jean-Luc Marion, is not only misleading but obscures the argument put forth by Anselm.²²

In chapters 2 and 3 of his *Proslogion* Anselm argues that God is "something" (*aliquid*) than which nothing greater can be thought.²³ This "something" is what is meant when we use the name God—a fact that would be admitted readily by even the fool who has said in his heart that there is no God. Whether the fool grants the existence of this "something" is the question; that the fool understands the meaning of the words and therefore that this "something" exists in the understanding is beyond dispute for Anselm. We could quibble with this point by noting a number of possible reasons for the fool's misunderstanding, anything from semiotic failure (the lexeme or linguistic sign is unknown) to semantic failure (the meaning of the utterance is equivocal or obscure). In some measure Anselm anticipates these sorts of concerns. Because *Scripture* declares that the fool "said in his heart" (Ps 14:1), a contradiction would arise if we concluded that the fool could not think something he already has "said in his heart." For Anselm these are synonymous expressions. Therefore he can confidently assert that the fool understands the meaning of the words.²⁴

Another quibble, certainly more to the point for our inquiry, has to do with Anselm's epistemology.²⁵ Most of us no longer embrace the Platonic assumptions he held concerning the intellect, ideas, and reality. In that tradition, mediated as it was through centuries of Christian reflection, what is in the intellect, in idea, is more real than what is measurable by the senses.²⁶ That an innate idea, as it were, corresponds to reality is far different than how we often articulate this sort of Platonic position. We suggest that any "best possible" or "greater than" idea we might have must then correspond to reality. This was the approach taken by Gaunilo of Marmoutiers and his perfect island.²⁷ Since this is obviously absurd, we discount Anselm's way of thinking and assume we have found its weakness. We have not; we have only misunderstood his argument and imposed on him an extreme position that would appear as strange to him as it does to us.

---

at Bec: "They specified . . . the following form for this written meditation: nothing whatsoever to be argued on the basis of the authority of Scripture, but the constraints of reason concisely to prove, and the clarity of truth clearly to show, in the plain style, with everyday arguments, and down-to-earth dialectic, the conclusions of distinct investigations." *Anselm of Canterbury: The Major Works*, ed. Brian Davies and G. R. Evans (Oxford: Oxford University Press, 1998), 5.

22. Jean-Luc Marion, "Is the Ontological Argument Ontological? The Argument According to Anselm and Its Metaphysical Interpretation According to Kant," in *Flight of the Gods: Philosophical Perspectives on Negative Theology*, ed. Ilse Bulhof and Laurens ten Kate (New York: Fordham University Press, 2000), 78–99.

23. Anselm *Proslogion* II; *St. Anselm's Proslogion*, ed. and trans. M. J. Charlesworth (Notre Dame, IN: University of Notre Dame Press, 1979), 116.

24. Anselm *Proslogion* IV; Charlesworth, 119–21.

25. Etienne Gilson, "The Meaning and Nature of St. Anselm's Argument," *Medieval Essays*, trans. James Colbert (Eugene, OR: Cascade Books, 2011), 39–41.

26. Davies and Evans, "Introduction," *Anselm of Canterbury*, xii.

27. Anselm *Pro Insipiente* 6; Charlesworth, 162–65.

In *Proslogion*, Anselm exposes a looming contradiction for the fool. All must acknowledge that "something" that exists in reality and in the understanding is greater (*maius*) than "something" that exists only in the mind. But this "something" than which nothing greater can be thought *cannot* exist in the mind alone and not also in reality and remain that than which nothing greater can be thought: for such to occur would be a contradiction. Therefore, concludes Anselm, this "something" exists in both the mind and in reality, and this "something" we call God. Further, this "something" cannot even be thought not to exist. This "something" that necessarily exists is God: "And You, Lord our God, are this [*hoc*]."

Anselm identifies three degrees of existence in his brief argument.[28] Before concluding that the "something" in the intellect must also be in reality, he gives the example of a painter. When the painter plans to create something, he has this thing in his mind but it does not yet exist because it is only in his mind. This is the lowest degree: the item is in the understanding but not in reality. The second degree is the move made to avoid the contradiction stated above: the "something" must be both in the understanding and in reality (*in intellectu et in re*). The final degree of existence is what Anselm suggests in chapter 3 and states plainly in the short chapter 15 of *Proslogion*, which is entitled "How He is greater than can be thought." He writes, "Therefore, Lord, not only are You that than which a greater cannot be thought, but You are also something greater than can be thought."[29] Anselm calls upon the reader who has travelled with him through *Proslogion* to confess that *this* God exists precisely because He remains beyond our understanding. Jean-Luc Marion writes, "Therefore, God exists *in re* in a very special way—not because He is in understanding, but despite the fact that He is not. Further, He is in reality *because* He is not in understanding."[30] This is the third and highest degree of existence for Anselm.

If we fail to recognize Anselm's three degrees of existence, we risk confusing his efforts with those of Descartes, who posited God's necessary existence in the second degree listed above. God does not transcend our human thoughts and conceptions. Although Descartes's language is exalted (God is the Supreme Being possessing every supreme perfection), God is nonetheless a determinate being within the reach of the thinking subject. This is not the case for Anselm. Indeed, to acknowledge that God in His fullness cannot be grasped by the human mind, which means, as Anselm rightly concludes, that *this* God is the *aliquid*, is a humble bow to Scripture. After establishing this third degree of being Anselm turns immediately to Scripture: "Truly, Lord, this is the inaccessible light in which You dwell" (1 Tm 6:16), and yet it is only through this Light that we see light (Ps 36:9).[31] It should be clear, as it was with Athanasius,

---

28. Marion, "Ontological Argument," 91.
29. Anselm *Proslogion* XV; Charlesworth, 137: "Ergo domine, non solum es quo maius cogitari nequit, sed es quiddam maius quam cogitari possit."
30. Marion, "Ontological Argument," 92.
31. Anselm *Proslogion* XVI; Charlesworth, 137.

that what Anselm is doing with this "proof" is far from a philosophical demonstration of the existence of God. That kind of demonstration belongs to Descartes and his successors. Anselm is seeking something of a higher order, something that transcends human knowing, something that can be known only when that something reveals Himself to us and brings us to understanding through faith. Anselm's argument leads not to victory for human reason but to its defeat apart from faith.

The syntagm Anselm uses throughout his argument is sometimes rendered "a being than which nothing greater can be thought/conceived." Anselm, however, uses such words as *aliquid, id, quiddam*—all indefinite words—to refer to the "thing" or the "that" under consideration. It is significant that he begins with something that is indeterminate. He does not begin with a determined concept of being, as Descartes does, and proceed to demonstrate the concept's necessary existence. Rather, for Anselm the "that" being conceived *cannot* be conceived; it cannot be grasped, conceptualized, or determined by the thinking subject. Jean-Luc Marion refers to this as Anselm's non-conceptual starting point. The *aliquid*, if such a thing exists, we cannot conceive; if we can conceive it, then it isn't God because God transcends all definitions and dwells in light inaccessible. And yet for Anselm this does not mean God escapes our thoughts. As Marion explains, God is met by thought under two conditions: first, thought experiences the maximum of the conceivable; second, that same thought acknowledges that it cannot surpass, conquer, or rule the *aliquid* because of its finiteness. In other words, God begins where we exhaust our attempts to determine Him and where we yield in humility to faith. It begins when we arrive, as Gregory put it, at stillness (Ps 46:10). Marion concludes:

> [Anselm's syntagm] claims neither to define God by a concept, even in a negative way, nor to give access to any transcendental item or being. It only indicates the limits felt by all possible efforts toward any conception of God, that is, all efforts to think beyond the limits of our power of thinking. This syntagm deals more with our finitude than with the conception of God, as it reveals the essential finitude of our thoughts, whatever progress they may indefinitely achieve.[32]

Anselm's argument, whatever success we are persuaded to assign it, proceeds with far more restraint and humility than the one offered by Descartes.[33] We

---

32. Marion, "Ontological Argument," 88.
33. Cf. Kevin Vanhoozer, *Remythologizing Theology: Divine Action, Passion, and Authorship* (Cambridge: Cambridge University Press, 2012), 93–94: "For the so-called 'perfect being' theology associated with Anselm had a second coming as it were with Descartes, with one important difference: the Anselmian approach deployed the concept in a ministerial way and with an intratextual aim, with an intention to exposit the logic of the biblical account of God. It may therefore be helpful to distinguish the biblical-theological theism of the patristic, medieval, and Reformation eras from the more properly philosophical theism of the modern era during which the concept of a being 'than which nothing greater can be thought' sets out on a career of its own, independent of the biblical narrative and the three-personed God of the gospel. Modern philosophical theism takes its marching orders not from the canon but from the concept of a being of infinite perfection."

see this especially in the manner in which Anselm begins and ends his *Proslogion*.

In the Preface to *Proslogion* Anselm tells us that he will write from the point of view "of one seeking to understand what he believes."[34] For this reason he appended a subtitle to his work: *fides quaerens intellectum*, faith seeking understanding.[35] We see the earnestness of this subtitle in the way Anselm begins his allocution: Come now, insignificant man (*homuncio*), lay aside your affairs, abandon yourself, and rest in God. Anselm next turns to prayer, imploring God to teach him and show him the way, "for we can avail nothing without You."[36] He continues, "Teach me to seek You, and reveal Yourself to me as I seek, because I can neither seek You if You do not teach me how, nor find You unless You reveal Yourself."[37] The beginning point for Anselm is faith and prayer; it is this faith that allows him to seek understanding. More to the point, since faith is the beginning, it is God Himself who must come to Anselm, who must reveal Himself by raising him up, if He is to be known. Anselm continues,

> I do not try, Lord, to attain Your lofty heights, because my understanding is in no way equal to it. But I do desire to understand Your truth a little, that truth that my heart believes and loves. For I do not seek to understand so that I may believe; but I believe so that I may understand. For I believe this also, that "unless I believe, I shall not understand." (Is. 7:9)[38]

When we bear in mind that Anselm begins *Proslogion* with prayer, that he consistently seeks the Lord's help in understanding, and that such understanding proceeds from the faith he confesses, the beginning of his proof for the existence of God takes on a wholly different character. For this reason it would be a mistake to rush too quickly over the manner in which he begins his proof in chapter 2: "Well then, Lord, You who give understanding to faith, grant me that I may understand, as much as You see fit, that You exist as we believe."[39] These prayerful petitions interrupt the *Proslogion* throughout. When you read the work in its entirety, you cannot help but see that it is a work of devotion, filled with prayer, always beginning with faith, pursuing philosophical rigor and clarity, that the "free gift" of faith may be understood through God's "illumination."[40] When read in this way, the reader ends the work as Anselm does:

> I pray, O God, that I may know You and love You, so that I may rejoice in You. And if I cannot do so fully in this life may I progress gradually until it comes to fullness.... Until then let my mind meditate on [Your truth], let my tongue speak of it, let my heart love it, let my mouth preach it. Let my soul hunger for it, let my

---

34. Anselm *Proslogion* Preface; Charlesworth, 102.
35. Anselm *Proslogion* Preface; Charlesworth, 104.
36. Anselm *Proslogion* I; Charlesworth, 115.
37. Anselm *Proslogion* I; Charlesworth, 115.
38. Anselm *Proslogion* I; Charlesworth, 115.
39. Anselm *Proslogion* II; Charlesworth, 117.
40. Anselm *Proslogion* IV; Charlesworth, 121.

flesh thirst for it, my whole being desire it, until I enter into the "joy of the Lord" [Matt. 25:21], who is God, Three in One, "blessed forever. Amen" [Rom. 1:25].[41]

Two basic points should be made with Anselm. On the one hand, he still operates very much within the patristic model of faith seeking understanding (Augustine) or faith giving fullness to reason (Gregory of Nazianzus). His priorities are right; his instinct to begin and end with the humility of prayer is worthy of imitation. At the same time, his task, his purpose, and his confidence in human reason, albeit ultimately regarded as insufficient and deployed within his hermeneutic of piety, are clearly something new, something decidedly medieval and not patristic. This point was not lost on the Lutheran dogmaticians. Rare is any interest in the Anselmian project. Rather they pass in silence over such arguments and proofs in their own consideration of natural knowledge. Their silence is their judgment, not on Anselm's theological method but certainly on this sort of theological enterprise.

THOMAS AQUINAS

The most significant theologian of the medieval period was Thomas Aquinas (1224–74). He performed his tasks chiefly in the context of the medieval university, a fact which sets him apart from the Fathers whose lives and theological labors were expended for the most part in the church as bishops. Not only has the setting for theological exchange and reflection changed, but also and perhaps most significantly a new method has emerged for expressing theological truths. The scholastic method that would come to dominate the medieval period found its best representative in the rigorously precise mind of Thomas Aquinas. His most significant work, *Summa Theologiae*, is an attempt to present the truths of the Christian faith in their most orderly and logical way. Thomas wrote this work at the end of his life. He began writing in 1266 and stopped abruptly after a mystical experience while saying mass on 6 December 1273. He died three months later.

At the beginning of the *Summa Theologiae*, Thomas establishes an important distinction between articles of faith (*articuli fidei*) and preambles to the articles (*praeambula ad articulos*).[42] Articles of faith transcend human reason and are revealed by God through Scripture.[43] Preambles to the articles of faith are known to reason apart from Scripture. The doctrine of the Trinity is an article of faith requiring revelation; the existence of God is a preamble to the articles because it can be known by human reason apart from revelation. Although the Lutheran dogmaticians exhibit a great debt to Thomas's trinitarian theology, something we will show at length in part 3, they criticized him for

---

41. Anselm *Proslogion* XXVI; Charlesworth, 153, 155.
42. Thomas Aquinas *ST* I.2.2 ad 1.
43. Thomas Aquinas *ST* I.1.1c.

assigning the existence of God to the preambles of faith.[44] As noted above, Scripture says otherwise: "Whoever would draw near to God must believe that he exists [ὅτι ἔστιν] and that he rewards those who seek him" (Heb 11:6). Although the dogmaticians rightly criticized Thomas on this point, we must note his conservatism. Many during the medieval period also thought reason could know the trinity of persons. Abelard argued that Plato taught all that is essential for knowing the Trinity.[45] Raymond Lully declared that the mystery of the Trinity can be demonstrated "solely by the natural power of the intellect without revelation."[46] Thomas labored against these ambitious pursuits in his *Summa*, explicitly rejecting Abelard's position.[47]

After establishing the distinction between articles of faith and preambles of faith, Thomas explores at length "the unity of divine essence" (I.2–26) and "the Trinity of the persons in God" (I.27–43).[48] Two discussions of God follow. The first, *de deo uno*, approaches God abstractly and philosophically through the preambles of faith. The second, *de deo trino*, discusses God as Trinity as an article of faith. Thomas's proofs for God's existence belong to this first division. Although it is not self-evident that God exists, the existence of God can be demonstrated.[49] Thomas cites Romans 1 as his warrant. Two types of demonstration may be used: a priori demonstration, which was pursued by Anselm, and a posteriori demonstration. Thomas favors the second kind of demonstration, which deduces pre-existent causes from observable effects. It is at this

---

44. See for example Johann Gerhard, *Theological Commonplaces: On the Nature of God and on the Trinity*, trans. Richard J. Dinda (St. Louis: Concordia Publishing House, 2007), Exegesis II, §58, 57; and Abraham Calov, *Systema Locorum Theologicorum* (Wittenberg, 1655), 2:140. Calov makes the same point at *Systema* 2:110 and 130. Although Gerhard raises the issue, as far as I can determine Calov is the first Lutheran theologian to discuss Thomas's distinction between articles of faith and preambles to the articles.

45. Abelard *Theologia Summi Boni* 1.36, in *Petri Abaelardi opera theologica, Corpus christianorum continuation mediaevalis*, vol. 13 (Turnhout: Brepols, 1987), 98–99. Abelard ends his work on the Trinity by declaring that all people—Christians, Jews, and Gentiles—may know through reason God as power, wisdom, and goodness. Abelard *Theologia Summi Boni* 3.100, 200–201. Similarly, Hugh of St. Victor writes, "We say that reason, through the light <of truth> naturally implanted in it, could first know that God exists, next that God is one, and afterwards that God is triune." See Hugh of St. Victor, *Sentences on Divinity*, part 3 in *Trinity and Creation: A Selection of Works of Hugh, Richard, and Adam of St. Victor*, ed. Boyd Taylor Coolman and Dale M. Coulter (Hyde Park, NY: New City Press, 2011), 157.

46. For Lully's comment and others like it see Gerhard, *Theological Commonplaces: On the Trinity*, Exegesis III, §27, 283. Similarly, Gerhard quotes the Reformed theologian Bartholomew Keckerman, who places reason over Scripture. Keckerman writes, "We shall make it clear to the Antitrinitarians that the trinity of persons flows forth from the very essence of God and that God cannot be God without having three different modes of existing, as persons. When we have shown this, we shall also produce testimonies from Holy Writ" (Gerhard, §27, 283–84). Francis Pieper quotes Quenstedt's rejection of Keckerman. See Francis Pieper, *Christian Dogmatics* (St. Louis: Concordia Publishing House, 1950), 1:400.

47. Thomas Aquinas *ST* I.32.1.

48. Thomas uses these phrases for the division he has made in the preface to *ST* I.27.

49. Thomas Aquinas *ST* I.2.1–2.

point that Thomas proceeds with his "five ways" of "proving" the existence of God.⁵⁰

The first way uses the argument from motion. Whatever is in motion is put in motion by another. Since everything that moves, either actually or potentially, is moved by another and this exchange of mover and moved cannot go on into infinity, it is necessary to arrive at a first mover, put in motion by no other. "This," Thomas ends, "everyone understands to be God."

The second way is based on the order of efficient causes. In the world of sense there is an order of causes and there is no example of anything that is the efficient cause of itself (*causa efficiens sui ipsius*). If such a thing existed it would necessarily be prior to itself, which is impossible. Since every effect has a prior cause and it is not reasonable to go on into infinity, there must be a first efficient cause. To this first cause, ends Thomas, "everyone gives the name of God."

The third way is taken from possibility and necessity. When we consider the things existing around us, we discover that they were created and that they become corrupt. Therefore they have the possibility to be or not to be. If everything has the possibility not to be, then there could have been a time when nothing existed. But this presents a problem: if there was a time when nothing existed, there could not now be a time when things exist, since everything that exists only begins to exist by something already existing. This means there must exist "something" whose existence is necessary. Now every necessary thing either has its necessity caused by another or not. Since we cannot go on to infinity, we must posit the existence of some being possessing its own necessity and causing in others their necessity. "This," concludes Thomas, "all men speak of as God."

The fourth way is taken from the gradation of things. Among things some are more or less good, true, noble, etc. More or less is predicated of different things according to the manner in which they relate to a maximum. Something is said to be more or less hot the more nearly it resembles that which is hottest. The argument works similarly for what is truest, best, noblest, and what is maximal being (*maxime ens*). Moreover, the maximum in any genus is the cause of all in that genus. Fire, which is the maximum of heat, is the cause of all hot things. The same argument holds for being: there must be something which is to all beings the cause of their being. And this, concludes Thomas, "we call God."

The fifth way is taken from the governance of the world. We can observe that things lacking intelligence, such as material objects in nature, act for an end. This is clear in that they "usually" act in the same way and achieve their end by purpose, not chance. Something without intelligence may achieve its goal only if it is directed by something with intelligence, as the arrow reaches its mark because of an archer. Therefore, concludes Thomas, there is a being with intelligence that directs all natural things to ends. And this "we call God."

---

50. The following summary, expressed largely in Thomas's own words, is taken from Thomas Aquinas *ST* I.2.3c.

After presenting these proofs for God's existence, Thomas puts them to work. He turns to a lengthy discussion of God's simplicity and attributes in order to show the difficulty of rightly speaking about God. Here we see with clarity his own understanding of what natural reason accomplishes and its relationship to revealed knowledge of God. Thomas appeals to all five ways to show God's absolute simplicity.[51]

Thomas regularly returns to these five ways in his discussion of God. At one point he pauses to clarify the relationship between the knowledge gleaned by reason and that received by faith in Scripture. He begins, as he so often does, with Romans 1. God can be known by us through His created effects.[52] Although reason may not know the complete essence of God, the quiddity of God, something that eludes faith as well, it may know whether God exists and what necessarily belongs to Him because of such existence.[53] For example, by reflecting on the effects of created reality the mind moves to a consideration of causes and concludes that God is the first cause of all things. Further, this first cause must exceed all things caused by Him.[54] At this point Thomas asks if a higher knowledge of God is available through grace. The answer is yes. Grace produces a more perfect (*perfectior*) knowledge of God.[55] When we turn to Scripture we come to have a fuller or more complete (*plenior*) knowledge of the God who is "Three and One."[56]

Thomas's use of comparatives to describe the relationship between natural and revealed knowledge, between reason and faith, underscores their complementarity. Here we encounter another problem. Michael Buckley explains, "Aquinas' problematic method and reflexive principles distinguish two ways to religious awareness and conviction."[57] The first is philosophical (preambles) and agrees with the second, which is theological and based on revelation (articles). Whatever we wish to say about natural knowledge, its limitations and inadequacies, for Thomas it nonetheless contributes to our understanding of God. Rather than seeing a disjunction between philosophical theism and biblical trinitarianism, he sees complementarity. This first type of knowledge, which begins with us and our rational efforts, which pertains to the preambles of faith, is built upon by faith and God's revelation. God makes Himself known first by nature through reason and then by Scripture through faith. God takes our initial effort through reason and perfects it, completes it, by adding to it His eternal identity as three irreducible persons in one undivided essence. We might call this an epistemological *facere quod*.[58]

---

51. Thomas Aquinas *ST* I.3.7c.
52. Thomas Aquinas *ST* I.12.12.
53. Thomas Aquinas *ST* I.12.13 ad 1.
54. Thomas Aquinas *ST* I.12.12c.
55. Thomas Aquinas *ST* I.12.13c.
56. Thomas Aquinas *ST* I.12.13 ad 1.
57. Michael J. Buckley, *At the Origins of Modern Atheism* (New Haven, CT: Yale University Press, 1987), 55.
58. Hermann Sasse describes Thomas's five ways as "the theology of glory of the half-

Perhaps some relief comes by distinguishing between essence and existence. Does not Thomas simply grant knowledge of God's existence? The answer to who God is and what sort of God this is belongs to the articles of faith and therefore to Scripture, right? Unlike the Greek Fathers in the previous chapter, Thomas, like Tertullian, assigns positive value to natural knowledge of God and to his arguments for God's existence. These arguments do not lead us to humility but contribute to our doctrine of God. To achieve an understanding of a thing's existence is to know something about that thing. No matter how indefinite or abstract a person wishes to make that "thing" under consideration, it is still some *thing* and not another. Assigning existence to something means you have at minimum a rudimentary understanding of how the thing that exists exists, and this tells you what sort of thing it is. Put simply, to be is to be something or other.[59] Thomas states this plainly: "The existence of God is His essence itself, which can be said of no other."[60] Thomas's supporters and commentators emphasize this point. Etienne Gilson explains:

> To posit God in this way is to affirm an act of existing which needs no cause of its own existence. Such would not be the case were His essence distinguished, in so far as it is, from His existence.... Like whatever exists, God is by His own act-of-being; but, in His case alone, we have to say that *what* His being is is nothing else than that by which He exists, namely, the pure act of existing.
>
> Any one of the proofs for the existence of God would lead to the same conclusion precisely because they all set out from contingent existences in order to reach the first *esse* which causes them. As St. Thomas himself says of this thesis: it can be shown in many ways. God is the first cause; He has therefore no cause; now God would have a cause if His essence were distinct from His existence, because then it would not be enough, in order to exist, to be what He is. It is therefore impossible that God's essence be anything other than His act-of-being.... Such is the God whom the five proofs of St. Thomas seek and finally attain by five different ways.[61]

Since our existence is contingent, we must conclude that what a man is (*quod quid est homo*) and that a man is (*esse hominem*) are different.[62] This is the case for all contingent beings because they possess being by participation. As Thomas puts it, existence (*esse*) and essence (*quidditas entis*)

---

heathen proofs for the existence of God." Hermann Sasse, *We Confess Anthology* (St. Louis: Concordia Publishing House, 1999), 1:45.

59. Ralph McInerny, *Praeambula Fidei: Thomism and the God of the Philosophers* (Washington, D.C.: Catholic University of America Press, 2006), 296.

60. Thomas Aquinas *ST* I.13.11.c.

61. Etienne Gilson, *The Christian Philosophy of St. Thomas Aquinas* (Notre Dame, IN: Notre Dame University Press, 1956), 91–92.

62. This celebrated remark by Aristotle distinguishing essence and existence gave rise to numerous commentaries in the Middle Ages (*Posterior Analytics*, II, 7, 92b, 10–11). For a discussion of the text and its reception see Gilson, *St. Thomas Aquinas*, 89–95.

differ for us. This is not the case with God, who is essentially being.⁶³ For God alone "existence and quiddity are one and the same."⁶⁴

Thomas understands that to prove God's existence is necessarily to say something minimal about God's quiddity or essence. There are no mere demonstrations of necessary existence apart from essence. At some point we reach the limit of our human reason and must give way to faith and God's revelation. Etienne Gilson explains the process: "To prove God is to re-climb by reason from any finite act-of-being whatsoever, to the pure Act-of-Being which causes it. Here the knowledge of man reaches its ultimate terminus. When God has been established as the supreme Act-of-Being, philosophy ends and mystical theology begins."⁶⁵ What begins with us, God completes. The combination of our natural efforts by human reason and God's completion of those efforts with the gift of faith in His revelation yields an understanding of God as Father, Son, and Holy Spirit. The movement is from God as object of our thoughts and rational expectations to God as subject. For Thomas this move must happen: God must assume His rightful place as revealer of His triune identity. Reason must be perfected and completed by revelation. Otherwise the synthesis collapses. This approach looks far different when modernity insists upon keeping God as object and ourselves as subject. In this sense, as Steven Ozment observes, "Aquinas himself may have unwittingly sown the seeds for the dissolution of his own synthesis of reason and revelation and prepared the way for the rationalism of the modern world."⁶⁶

WILLIAM OF OCKHAM

Thomas's approach to knowledge and his understanding of the relationship between God and the world found its harshest critic in William of Ockham (c. 1287–1347) and his intellectual heirs, the so-called nominalists or terminists. Ockham's logic has few rivals in the history of the church. For Ockham, attempts to demonstrate, to prove, the existence of God were hopelessly flawed and never amounted to more than the first cause of a cosmological argument. At best reason may show the probability of God's existence but reason's God, insists Ockham, is never the God of the Bible.

The epistemological commitments of Thomas and Ockham are completely opposed to one another. We see this especially with the question of knowledge of God. Truth for Thomas could be found in both revelation and the world. Some things were made known to faith (articles of faith), and other things were made known to reason (preambles to the articles of faith). Neither could contradict the other as both found their source, their foundation, in the very being of

---
63. Thomas Aquinas *ST* I.3.4c.
64. Thomas Aquinas, *Expositio Posteriorum Analyticorum*, II, lectio 6 n. 3: "Ipsum esse et quidditas eius est unum et idem." Text quoted in McInerny, *Praeambula Fidei*, 297.
65. Gilson, *St. Thomas Aquinas*, 372.
66. Ozment, *Age of Reform*, 52.

God. In this way Thomas and his contemporaries had a great appreciation for the interconnectedness of all reality. Everything God had done in creation and redemption was before them to be explained. The complementarity of natural and revealed knowledge of God made sense. They both aimed at the same thing. Thomas explains, "Since natural reason ascends to knowledge of God through creatures and, conversely, the knowledge of faith descends from God to us by a divine revelation—since the way of ascent and descent is still the same (*eadem*)—we must proceed in the same way in the things above reason which are believed as we proceeded . . . with the investigation of God by reason."[67]

During the medieval period, theologians distinguished between God's absolute power (*potentia absoluta*) and ordered power (*potentia ordinata*).[68] What is God able to do? Why did He do the things He did? For Thomas things are the way they are because it was most fitting for them to be this way. God, who is the source and cause of all created reality, does all things according to His wisdom. Therefore how things are reflects God's wisdom, and this we refer to as God's eternal law. As seen above with Thomas's five ways, our knowledge of things begins with God's created effects. From a consideration of these effects we may arrive at an understanding of a first mover, first cause, necessary being, who is pure act. Our access to God's eternal law, that overarching order of things, starts with natural law and natural reason, which is common to all people and shared by all humanity. From such a commitment the synthesis between revelation and reason finds traction and begins the work of demonstrating the reasonableness of things as we know them. Natural law, like natural reason, makes a promising start but in itself is insufficient. Natural law must be perfected and completed by divine law, both of which are aspects of God's eternal law.[69] Thomas plots his discussion of natural and divine law along coordinates similar to those discussed above: as grace "perfects" nature and revelation "perfects" natural knowledge, so too divine law "perfects" natural law. Here again we see Thomas's emphasis upon the interconnectedness of all reality. Whether we travel by reason or faith, we travel the same path.

William of Ockham sought to undermine the predictability of Thomas's construction of reality by arguing that God could have done things differently. There was no inherent necessity in what God did. Things are the way they are because this is what God *has willed*. Although we might think it fitting and reasonable that God accomplishes our salvation through the incarnation, suffering, death, and resurrection of His Son, He could have done things differently according to His *potentia absoluta*. Ockham offers extreme examples to show this. His opponents charged him with positing an uncertain

---

67. Thomas Aquinas, *Summa Contra Gentiles* IV.1.11, trans. Charles J. O'Neill (Notre Dame, IN: University of Notre Dame Press, 1975), 39.
68. Heiko Oberman, *The Harvest of Medieval Theology* (Grand Rapids: Baker Academic, 2000), 36.
69. Joseph Wawrykow, *The Westminster Handbook to Thomas Aquinas* (Louisville, KY: Westminster John Knox Press, 2005), 85–90.

and arbitrary God, but they missed Ockham's point. The force of his dialectic between what God has done (*potentia ordinata*) and what He could have done (*potentia absoluta*) freed the God of revelation from the predictability of human reason. Luther echoes this sentiment throughout his works when he declares, "Let God be God."[70]

Heiko Oberman argues that there is a twofold yield to Ockham's critique. God is no longer tied to creation by causation but related to it by volition. Therefore all metaphysical arguments based on "necessary causal links" lose their cogency and credibility.[71] Further, metaphysics becomes sheer speculation when it stands apart from God's self-revelation. There is no possibility of reasoning back to God through natural phenomena because there is no causal link. Thomas's way of ascent and descent will not work. Things are the way they are because God willed them to be this way and not another possible way. If we are to understand God's will, we must direct ourselves to His revelation. For Ockham, the schoolmen assign too much to human reason and natural knowledge and too little to faith and revelation. They domesticate God and force faith into the harness of natural reason.[72]

CONCLUSION

There are two distinct trajectories in the history of the church on the relationship between natural knowledge of God and revealed knowledge of God. One trajectory, charted in the previous chapter with Athanasius and Gregory of Nazianzus, emphasizes the disjunction between natural and revealed knowledge. We do not first start with ourselves, our natural reason, and seek out God. Rather we look to the Word made flesh, to the incarnation, and to our baptism for our knowledge of God. For these writers a consideration of nature brings about knowledge of a divine architect, but this awareness is not meant to become the foundation of our knowledge of the triune God. Rather the consideration of nature is to lead us to humility as we realize all we do not know of created reality, a humility meant to check our intellectual hubris and idolatries. Our consideration of nature does not construct a Jacob's ladder, ascending from effect to cause, from lower being to higher being, in order to arrive at God.[73]

A second trajectory, stretching back to the second century but flowering with the schoolmen, places great confidence in natural reason's ability to

---

70. Cf. *Sermons on the Gospel of John*, 1537–38 (AE 24:72; WA 45:526.26); *Sermon on Preparing to Die*, 1519 (AE 42:105; WA 2:690.16–17); *Disputation against Scholastic Theology*, 1517 (AE 31:10, thesis 17; WA 1:225.1).
71. Oberman, "*Via Antiqua* and *Via Moderna*," 28.
72. Oberman, "*Via Antiqua* and *Via Moderna*," 31.
73. Cf. *Lectures on Hebrews*, 1517–18 (AE 29:111; WA 57:99.3–4): "For the humanity [of Christ] is that holy ladder of ours, mentioned in Gen. 28:12, by which we ascend to the knowledge of God."

construct arguments for the necessary existence of God. This was done unevenly during the medieval period. Although many think of Anselm as offering the most ambitious use of reason in service of "proving" God's existence, a fuller reading of his *Proslogion* creates some discomfort with such a characterization. The real problem is the complementarity between natural and revealed knowledge as suggested by John of Damascus and insisted upon by Thomas Aquinas. It is Thomas who claims he has "proved" God's existence, and he who asserts that this knowledge is "presupposed" by faith, preparing the way for a more perfect and complete knowledge of God as revealed in Scripture. His synthesis met its strongest opponent in William of Ockham. The distinction between God's *potentia absoluta* and *potentia ordinata* freed God from the predictability of human reason and from our fitting arguments for His being and will. Luther and the Lutheran dogmaticians, guided by the Scriptures, made use of the best insights of the Greek fathers and the best ideas of those critiquing the Thomistic synthesis to argue that knowledge of God and our salvation are found in the same place: in Christ Jesus, crucified and risen for us.

4

THE CENTRALITY OF CHRIST:
THE LUTHERAN APPROACH TO THE TRINITY

The Augsburg Confession begins, "We unanimously hold and teach, in accordance with the decree of the Council of Nicaea, that there is one divine essence, which is called and which is truly God, and that there are three persons in this one divine essence, equal in power and alike eternal: God the Father, God the Son, God the Holy Spirit."[1] The final words of the Formula of Concord are directed against the "new Arians" and the "new anti-Trinitarians."[2] Our Lutheran Confessions begin and end with an affirmation of the central doctrine of the Christian faith, the doctrine of the Trinity. There is no part of our faith, no aspect of our worship, no expression of our piety outside the confession of our triune God.

The guiding question throughout part 1 of this book is how we rightly know and speak about our triune God, and how this understanding informs our theological vision, directs our doctrinal judgments, and structures our liturgy and prayers. The Book of Concord answers this question from the start both structurally and dogmatically. Before we arrive at the Augsburg Confession we encounter the three ecumenical creeds of the church catholic: the Apostles' Creed, the Nicene Creed, and the Athanasian Creed. By beginning with these three creeds our Lutheran fathers privileged both the normative, catholic confession of the doctrine of the Trinity as the first article of Christian theology, and further the liturgical life of the church as the proper location for knowing and confessing the Trinity. These three creeds address the salvation of sinful humanity by our triune God. The context for knowing, confessing, worshipping, and glorifying the Trinity is the salvation wrought by the Son through the cross and delivered to us by the Holy Spirit through Word and sacrament. Viewed in this way, these three creeds are the words of the Christian faithful. They are our response to the Word of God, our answer to what Scripture says about the Father, Son, and Holy Spirit. These words proceed from faith and are concerned chiefly with the right speaking of that faith. Lutherans emphasize that God and faith always belong together; they permit no scholastic abstraction of God and faith. This means the doctrine of God may never stand apart from justification by faith.

---

1. AC I.1–3 (Tappert, 27).
2. SD XII.36–38 (Tappert, 635–36).

Both the Apostles' Creed and Nicene Creed begin with the baptismal affirmation "I believe." The Athanasian Creed begins more explicitly: "Whoever wishes to be saved must, above all else, hold the true Christian (catholic) faith. Whoever does not keep it whole and undefiled will without doubt perish for eternity."[3] What is the faith that must be held undefiled? The Creed continues, "This is the true Christian faith, that we worship one God in three persons and three persons in one God without confusing the persons or dividing the divine substance." The faith that must be kept undefiled is the Trinity, which comprehends all the articles of faith, and this trinitarian faith is known and confessed in worship. The Apostles' Creed proved useful in the early church, argues Martin Chemnitz, because those who knew it were able to recognize "those who truly preach Christ" according to the Scriptures.[4] For Chemnitz, preaching Christ crucified is necessary for a right confession of the Trinity. Remove Christ from the center of the Scriptures or from the center of your worship, and your confession of the Trinity suffers.

As Lutherans we are accustomed to saying the church stands or falls on the article of justification by faith alone. While certainly true, that article proceeds from our confession of the coequality and coeternity of the Father, Son, and Holy Spirit. In this sense, explains Robert Preus, "the doctrine of the Trinity is the basis of all Christian doctrine." The Trinity governs all Christian teaching. Preus continues, "Christian doctrine cannot be rightly understood or taught, neither can Law and Gospel be rightly divided, apart from the doctrine of the Trinity."[5] Preaching the gospel is preaching the Trinity. The reverse is necessarily true: to fail to preach the Trinity is to fail to preach the gospel. We cannot preach about salvation apart from the divine persons who accomplish that salvation for us. No generic god, no philosophically safe divinity will work here. As Luther succinctly reminds us, "The whole Trinity works salvation."[6] Such a claim means not only that the Father, Son, and Holy Spirit are the starting and ending point of every article of faith but also that a right understanding of God as Trinity and ourselves as sinners gives content and weight to everything we say about our Christian faith. To teach or preach Christian doctrine without a proper understanding of and reference to the doctrine's author is to do something other than Christian theology. For this reason the doctrine of the Trinity is the

---

3. Athanasian Creed, 1–2 (Tappert, 18–19).

4. Martin Chemnitz, *Loci Theologici*, trans. J. A. O. Preus (St. Louis: Concordia Publishing House, 2008), 1:39. Chemnitz's statement comes from Rufinus's commentary on the Apostles' Creed (*Expositio Fidei*). He goes on to offer a similar comment from Irenaeus.

5. Robert Preus, *The Theology of Post-Reformation Lutheranism* (St. Louis: Concordia Publishing House, 1972), 2:15. Cf. Holsten Fagerberg, *A New Look at the Lutheran Confessions 1529–1537*, trans. Gene J. Lund (St. Louis: Concordia Publishing House, 1972), 114: "To confess the Triune God is the common basis of all Christian faith. Those who do not do so have placed themselves outside the church of Christ (AC I.2). . . . One cannot stress strongly enough that the doctrine of the Trinity is the foundation of Reformation theology."

6. *Lectures on Genesis*, 1535–45 (AE 8:264; WA 44:773.4–6).

basis of all Christian theology and informs our speaking, singing, and praying as Christians.[7]

Hermann Sasse once said, "There is, thank God, no specific Lutheran doctrine on the Trinity."[8] On more than one occasion Luther made the same point.[9] Although Lutherans do not, as Sasse observes and Luther insists, have a parochial doctrine of the Trinity, the same cannot be said for the manner in which Lutherans think about and discuss the doctrine of God. This can be seen in a number of ways. Luther, for example, nowhere offers a doctrine of God apart from the Trinity; he nowhere posits a natural knowledge of God that constructively anticipates our revealed knowledge of God. Although natural knowledge knows what revealed knowledge knows, these two types of knowledge are of an entirely different character, qualitatively different. There is no complementarity between them as argued by figures as diverse as Tertullian and Thomas. Assigning positive value to a knowledge of God apart from Christ and His cross belongs to scholasticism, not Lutheranism.[10] Two important points proceed from this for Luther. First, if you are to know God rightly you must know yourself as a sinner and God's will for the sinner. The issue is never whether a person may arrive by nature or reason at an awareness of God: Luther firmly believes the philosopher achieves this. The problem for Luther is what the philosopher fails to know: God's attitude toward him, God's will toward him. If you fail to know God's will for you, His promises for you, you are no better off than a cow who stares at a new gate.[11] True knowledge always involves God's attitude toward me. Luther writes, "This, then, is the true knowledge of God: to know His nature and will, which He reveals in the Word, where He promises that He will be my Lord and God and orders me to take hold of this will in faith."[12] When God becomes subject, I become object,

---

7. Edmund Schlink writes, "*The doctrine of the Trinity is the basis for all statements of the Lutheran Confessions.* This must be said with all definiteness over against the manifold attempts of neo-Protestantism to give a new interpretation of the ancient church's doctrine of the Trinity as contained in the Confessions, or to explain it away from the Confessions. No article in the Confessions can be understood apart from the doctrine of the Trinity." *Theology of the Lutheran Confessions*, trans. Paul F. Koehneke and Herbert J. A. Bouman (St. Louis: Concordia Publishing House, 1961), 62 (emphasis original).

8. Hermann Sasse, "Tradition and Confession: A Response to Jaroslav Pelikan," *Lutheran World* 4:1 (June 1957): 78.

9. SA I.4: "These articles [i.e., Trinity and incarnation as expressed in the creeds] are not matters of dispute or contention, for both parties confess them" (Tappert, 292). In his treatise *On the Last Words of David* Luther writes, "And this article of faith [i.e., Trinity] remained pure in the papacy and among the scholastic theologians, and we have no quarrel with them on that score" (AE 15:310; WA 54:64.19-21).

10. *Lectures on Hebrews*, 1517-18 (AE 29:111; WA 57:99.5-11): "Therefore he who wants to ascend advantageously to the love and knowledge of God should abandon the human metaphysical rules concerning knowledge of the divinity and apply himself first to the humanity of Christ. For it is exceedingly godless temerity that, where God has humiliated Himself in order to become recognizable, man seeks for himself another way by following the counsels of his own natural capacity."

11. *Lectures on Genesis*, 1535-45 (AE 8:17; WA 44:591.38-39).

12. *Lectures on Genesis*, 1535-45 (AE 8:17; WA 44:592.6-8).

and my concern shifts from speculative thoughts about God to God's concrete promises *pro me* (for me). Although Luther believed the schoolmen endorsed an orthodox understanding of the Trinity, he also thought they were poor theologians because they failed to know God's will for them.[13] He writes, "By their own natural reason, they speculate about attributes and distinctions that are *extra deum* and apart from the Word. They are unaware of what God wills toward them."[14]

To use the scholastic distinctions introduced in previous chapters, Lutherans, like the Greek fathers, refuse to approach the question *An sit Deus?* apart from *Quid sit Deus?* The triune God of Scripture, the one and only true God, is not rightly known in the abstract, in theory, in the neutral space of scholastic endeavor, but always and only through a person, Jesus Christ, the one crucified and risen, and this by the working of the Holy Spirit through Word and sacrament. There is no mere doctrine of God for Lutherans but only ever the faithful confession of a sinner's salvation by the Father, Son, and Holy Spirit. Bernard Lohse writes:

> What is unique about [Luther's] speaking of God is that it is never theoretical. It is always clear that where God is concerned we have to do with the Lord of world and history, thus of our own life. There is thus an incomparable concreteness and directness about Luther's speaking of God. There is no mere doctrine of God, but a statement of faith in ever-new variations to the effect that God calls to life, that he judges and pardons his creatures, and takes them again to himself. This fact has extraordinary significance for the way in which Luther adopted trinitarian dogma.[15]

Luther and the Book of Concord stand apart from the scholastic vision described in the previous chapter and charted in the next with John Duns Scotus.

KNOWING AND SPEAKING ABOUT THE TRINITY

How does a Lutheran discuss the Trinity? The Lutheran approach returns to the scriptural and pastoral commitments of the Fathers. Lutherans know the Trinity, as Athanasius and Gregory of Nazianzus did, through the economy of salvation. We follow the pattern set by Scripture. In his explanation of the Apostles' Creed, Luther explains, "Neither you nor I could ever know anything of Christ, or believe in him and take him as our Lord, unless these were first offered to us and bestowed on our hearts through the preaching of the Gospel by the Holy Spirit."[16] Again Luther states, "We could never come to recognize the Father's favor and grace were it not for the Lord Christ, who is a mirror of the

---

13. "Psalm 122" in *Vorlesungen über die Stufenpsalmen*, 1532–33 (WA 40/3:79.3). Luther uses Erasmus's adage *asinus ad lyram* to describe such theologians.
14. "Psalm 122" in *Vorlesungen über die Stufenpsalmen*, 1532–33 (WA 40/3:78.14–16).
15. Bernhard Lohse, *Martin Luther's Theology* (Minneapolis: Fortress Press, 1999), 209.
16. LC II.38 (Tappert, 415).

Father's heart. Apart from Him we see nothing but an angry and terrible Judge. But neither could we know anything of Christ, had it not been revealed by the Spirit."[17] It is the Second Article of the Creed that opens and makes possible our right understanding of the First Article; it is by means of the Third Article that we come to know and confess the Second. At the center lies the gospel—no gospel, no Trinity; no Trinity, no gospel.

Luther's backward approach follows the order of Scripture, privileging Christ, the true Son of God, as the center of Scripture and the one through whom alone we know God the Father. Likewise, no one knows the Son, confessing Him as Lord, except by the Holy Spirit, whom the Father and Son send to work faith through the means of grace. Person and work go together. To know the Son, or the Father and the Spirit, is to know both the person and the work. Thus to know the Son always involves His identity—He is the Christ, the Son of the living God, Emmanuel, David's son and Lord—and His work—He is the world's Redeemer, Propitiator, and Justifier, especially of those who believe (1 Tm 4:10). Luther's approach to God's revelation of Himself to us as Father, Son, and Holy Spirit mirrors that of the Greek fathers, who understood and confessed the Trinity according to the divine economy. Gregory of Nyssa, anticipating the points made by Luther, writes:

> We are not to think of the Father as ever parted from the Son, nor to look for the Son as separate from the Holy Spirit. As it is impossible to mount to the Father, unless our thoughts are exalted thither through the Son, so it is impossible also to say that Jesus is Lord except by the Holy Spirit. Therefore, Father, Son, and Holy Spirit are to be known only in a perfect Trinity, in closest consequence and union with each other, before all creation, before all the ages, before anything whatever of which we can form an idea. The Father is always Father, and in Him the Son, and with the Son the Holy Spirit.[18]

Our right knowing and speaking about the Father, according to Scripture, may be only through the Son by the Holy Spirit. The center of our trinitarian thought is always and necessarily Christological and evangelical. To know the Son is to know the Father and the Holy Spirit; apart from the Son there is no knowledge of the Trinity. The Father will not be known apart from His Son; the Son will not be known apart from the Holy Spirit, who speaks only of the Son, taking what belongs to the Son and declaring it to us. Luther writes, "Where this God, Jesus Christ, is, there is the whole God or the whole divinity. There the Father and the Holy Spirit are to be found. Beyond this Christ God nowhere can be found."[19]

By pursuing the identity of our triune God through Christ, we begin at the cross where this becomes possible. At this unexpected place we not only come to know the Son most clearly and rightly but also the Father and the Spirit (cf. Mt 16:16–23; Lk 18:31–34), and this knowledge never stands apart from an

---

17. LC II.65 (Tappert, 419).
18. Gregory of Nyssa, *On the Holy Spirit*, NPNF, second series, 5:319.
19. "Psalm 130" in *Vorlesungen über die Stufenpsalmen*, 1532–33 (WA 40/3:338.35–339.14).

understanding of who I am and the work of the cross *pro me*. Here the Son bears my sins and the Father removes His condemnation from me. This accomplished and perfect reconciliation becomes ours through the sacramental working of the Holy Spirit, who convinces the world of sin and righteousness, and by whose power we as adopted sons and therefore heirs confess Christ as Lord and pray to God as *our* Father. It is the cross that reveals most vividly, most strikingly, the love of God the Father, Son, and Holy Spirit. For this reason, David Scaer declares, "the crucifixion . . . is the greatest manifestation of God's essence."[20]

To approach the question of how we know the triune God in this manner is to emphasize the priority of the gospel and justification by faith for rightly knowing and confessing the Trinity. Proper knowledge of our triune God is thus by grace through faith, and that sort of faith, saving faith, cannot be known apart from Christ's righteousness by which we are reconciled to the Father. The opposite of this truth necessarily follows: to know God apart from Christ's righteousness is to know a misleading and ultimately contrived God. It is by justifying faith that we rightly know the Son, who alone reveals to us the Father, becoming, as Luther puts it, "a mirror of the Father's heart," and all this by the grace and working of the Holy Spirit. Since this is the case, knowing God rightly demands that God make Himself known to us. And this He does in surprising places. The creator of the heavens and the earth is worshipped as king by wise men in a small corner of creation as He lies as a babe in a manger; the same creator who upholds all of creation by the word of His power sends forth a cry of dereliction from Calvary's cross. In the estimation of human reason, the manger and cross are unlikely places to find the Lord of glory, and yet it is in these places that faith rightly beholds God. Luther writes, "Let us go to the child lying in the lap of His mother Mary and to the sacrificial victim suspended on the cross; there we shall really behold God, and there we shall look into His very heart."[21] Scripture allows no wedge between knowing the triune God and being clothed in the righteousness of Christ. If knowing the Father is knowing His glory, and His glory is known only through the peace brought about by the saving work of the Son and delivered by the Holy Spirit through the means of grace, then knowing the Father rightly always entails knowing the salvation wrought by Christ through His incarnation, suffering, death, and resurrection. The theologian seeking to know the triune God of Scripture must find himself in humble places.

LUTHER'S REFORMATION BREAKTHROUGH

Why does Luther approach the Trinity by beginning with Christ and the cross? Why not begin with proofs for the existence of God, as Thomas Aquinas did?

---

20. David Scaer, *Christology*, vol. 6 of Confessional Lutheran Dogmatics (St. Louis: Luther Academy, 1989), 75.
21. *Lectures on Genesis*, 1535–45 (AE 3:276–77; WA 43:73.4–6).

ON GOD

Why not first establish what we know by reason and nature and then proceed to Scripture? The simple answer to this is Luther does not think it possible to say something about God by unaided reason that does not fall inevitably into idolatry. Although reason may say something true about God (He creates the heavens and the earth), reason fails to know many other things. Rather than reposing in humility, reason presses on and asserts all sorts of reasonable things about God. In this process reason fashions for itself a god and a world that conforms to its best ideas and reasonable assumptions. These insights stand at the heart of Luther's Reformation breakthrough and inform the whole of his theology.

In 1545 Luther looked back upon his breakthrough and remembered how he had come to distinguish between active and passive righteousness, between the imperfect righteousness we have in ourselves, which is never sufficient for salvation, and the perfect righteousness of Christ, which is outside of us and ours by faith alone.[22] Luther famously admits that he was "angry" with God and "hated" the righteous God. It is too easy to dismiss Luther's comments as a pious wrestling with God. The God that angered Luther was not the God of the Bible. Luther, the monk without reproach, sought to placate this "God" with his works, and yet the sting of the law kept accusing Luther, making his sins ever apparent to him. Two things were at war: the "God" of Luther's imagination who demanded perfection and satisfaction, and the Word of God, particularly the law, which crushed Luther's conscience by exposing his sin to him. The more Luther sought to placate this imagined "God" with good works the more the law exposed his sin and the angrier he became. Luther's breakthrough came when he allowed God's Word to show him the true God, the God who imputes His righteousness to us, and who mercifully justifies us by faith apart from our works. Luther stopped thinking about God as he had been taught to do, as an object of human speculation apart from His Word and promises.

Luther's Reformation breakthrough freed God from our best ideas about Him. It allowed God to be God. Further, it freed us from ourselves, allowing us to repose by faith in the certain promises of God, in the completed salvation of Jesus Christ, and to live joyfully and freely in loving and serving our neighbor. At the heart of Luther's breakthrough was freedom—freedom for God from the constraints of human reason and freedom for us from self-constructed pieties. In 1517, two months prior to posting the Ninety-five Theses, Luther wrote, "Man is by nature unable to want God to be God. Indeed, he himself wants to be God, and does not want God to be God."[23] This programmatic thesis informs the whole of his theology. Luther describes us all as by nature unable to free God from ourselves, from our best ideas, and from the bright light of human reason. Therefore we are also unable to free ourselves from ourselves. Our self-constructed pieties proceed from our self-constructed view of God.

---

22. *Preface to Latin Writings*, 1545 (AE 34:336–38; WA 54:185.12–186.13).
23. *Disputation on Scholastic Theology*, 1517 (AE 31:10, thesis 17; WA 1:225.1–2).

In 1532, during his lectures on Psalm 51, Luther again reflected on his breakthrough and specifically highlighted the close relationship between the gospel and the doctrine of God. As a young man he would shudder when he heard someone mention "the righteous God" and "hated" this name for God.[24] Luther was taught that God is righteous in such a way that He righteously punishes according to our deeds. Since we are all sinners, this sort of God devours us. Our deeds can never be good enough. When God's Word of law exposes our sins (Rom 3:20; 7:7) and presses heavy upon our conscience, we can do nothing other than hate this sort of God who punishes according to our deeds. This way of thinking about God's righteousness posits a false god and forces us to create a false understanding of the Christian life. It holds God in bondage to our ideas of who the righteous God must be, and it holds us in bondage to a made-up idea of how to appease this God. The only way to bear such an idea of God is to diminish the reality of sin, to say that something is not sin that is sin, to call evil good and good evil. Moreover, good works need to be created that will be above and beyond what God asks—works of supererogation, as they were called. New institutions and new rules will follow: monasticism instead of marriage, celibacy instead of children. In other words, to sustain this false view of God we must recreate the world, its order, and our place in it. All of this happens contrary to the world and order established by God and declared to us in His Word.

Luther blames the cleverness of sinful human reason for this false view of God and the Christian life, which in his opinion proceeds from scholasticism. For Luther, scholasticism is both a theological method and a theological attitude that places high value on the ability of human reason to organize and harmonize matters of faith, to figure things out and to bring order to God and our chaotic world. Scholasticism cannot let God be God but must determine what is appropriate to the being and work of God. Scholasticism is the temptation that lurks in the shadows for all who take up the task of theology, for all who think that theology is something we do. It is the temptation to remove God from the world, to abstract Him as a concept, and to busy ourselves with things beyond or apart from Christ and His cross. Scholasticism reposes in reasonable and fitting arguments about

---

24. *Lectures on Psalm 51*, 1532 (AE 12:313–14; WA 40/2:331.26–34): "So it happened to me when I was a young man that I hated this name for God, and from this deep habit I still shudder today when I hear someone say, 'the righteous God.' So great is the power of wicked teaching if the mind is imbued with it from childhood. Yet almost all the early theologians expound it this way. But if God is righteous in such a way that He righteously punishes according to deserts, who can stand before this righteous God? For we are all sinners and bring before God a righteous reason for Him to inflict punishment. Out of here with such a righteousness and such a righteous God! He will devour us all like a consuming fire (Dt 4:24). Because God sent Christ as Savior, He certainly does not want to be righteous in punishing according to deserts. He wants to be righteous and to be called righteous in justifying and having mercy on those who acknowledge their sins."

how things ought to be one way and not another.²⁵ The consequences are disastrous.

Scholasticism produces a theology insulated from the reality lived by the believer. For Luther, faith occupies a world filled with suffering, anguish, injustice, and death. Faith does not look to reason to make sense of the evil of life. Faith remains steadfast in the promises of God even when the world is one way and God's promises another. Faith trusts and clings to God's promises, not to fitting and reasonable arguments. Luther writes, "Faith is the true substance of the heart; that is, the firm and certain trust in God's promise of mercy and help."²⁶ Whatever the world presents to us, we trust in God's certain promises. Luther gives the following examples: despite the wicked plot to kill her, Susanna "trusted in the Lord" (Dn 13:35 Vulg.). Although Daniel was cast into the lions' den, he "trusted in his God" (Dn 6:23).²⁷ God promises us life and yet we are surrounded by death. Faith lives in the contradictions of the world. Reason smoothes these out. Faith trusts in God's promises despite *tentatio*. Reason must make sense of suffering in order to render the unbearable bearable. As Oswald Bayer puts it, *tentatio* does not authenticate faith: *tentatio* shows the Word of God to be credible and mighty amidst struggle.²⁸

Luther's Reformation breakthrough, allowing God to be God, freeing God from our idolatries, entailed not just rejecting a scholastic attitude but pursuing an entirely different path to knowing God. The young Luther, of course, belonged mentally to the scholastic world. He studied their works; he wrote a commentary on Peter Lombard's *Sentences*, as had Thomas Aquinas, Bonaventure, and all the other great theologians of the medieval period. Luther knew what he was rejecting and why he was rejecting it. At the risk of oversimplification, the chief thing Luther rejected was the attempt to think and talk about God apart from the cross. When we think of God in terms of the cross, we can do so only with regard to ourselves and the reason the creator of the heavens and earth would be upon that cross. For Luther, this means any discussion of God involves creation and redemption, sin and grace, man and justification. Luther's Reformation breakthrough was never merely about justification by faith. His breakthrough necessitated a decisive break with the way theology was done, the way Scripture was read, and the way the Christian life was lived. Justification by faith stands at the center and belongs both to Luther's understanding of God and our salvation.

---

25. Luther's attitude toward reasonable and fitting arguments is best seen in his works on the Lord's Supper. See for example *The Sacrament of the Body and Blood of Christ*, 1526 (AE 36:338, 343–45; WA 19:500, 494–97).

26. *Contra Satanam et Synagogam ipsius*, 1542 (WA 59:722.15–16).

27. *Contra Satanam et Synagogam ipsius*, 1542 (WA 59:722.9–12). For Daniel 13, see *The Apocrypha: The Lutheran Edition with Notes* (St. Louis: Concordia Publishing House, 2012), 244.

28. Oswald Bayer, *Martin Luther's Theology: A Contemporary Interpretation*, trans. Thomas Trapp (Grand Rapids: Eerdmans, 2008), 37. On this topic see Bayer's full discussion (1–43).

LUTHER ON KNOWING GOD

Luther was not a systematic theologian. He did not order his theology according to the norms of his day. He offers no doctrine of God apart from the Trinity. He does not start with natural knowledge and proceed to revealed knowledge. It is of no use for a person "to recognize God in his glory and majesty, unless he also recognizes him in the humility and shame of the cross."[29] Talk of God's power and glory requires talk of God's weakness on the cross. Such talk makes sense only to the person of faith, to the one justified by God and clothed in the righteousness of Christ. God and faith always belong together for Luther.[30]

In Luther's commentary on Psalm 51 he writes, "The proper subject of theology is man guilty of sin and condemned, and God the Justifier and Savior of man the sinner."[31] Luther's approach to knowing God pivots on the relationship between these two things. We cannot know God rightly if we fail to know ourselves; we cannot know ourselves rightly if we fail to know God. Both inform one another, and both are revealed to us. God declares to us that we are sinners and that He justifies the sinner. We receive this declaration by faith, and in prayer and confession speak it back to Him, acknowledging ourselves as sinners and God as the justifier of sinners. David confesses: "Against You, You only, have I sinned and done what is evil in Your sight, so that You may be justified in Your words and blameless in Your judgment" (Ps 51:4). David's confession is the confession of all believers. When we confess this we acknowledge that we are sinners and that our sin is against God. When we speak this confession in faith we justify God in His words, acknowledging that He is right in what He has declared about us.

Luther provocatively asserts that "faith makes God" and that we as believers must justify God.[32] He means by this that God is known properly in His Word and promises as the one who created and justified me "without any merit or worthiness in me."[33] Faith makes God, and believers justify God by acknowledging that His words are true. When David says, "God is justified in His words" (Ps 51:4), this happens for us when we believe and accept God's words as true and just.[34] Unbelief does not justify God in His words but condemns Him and judges Him. The unbeliever further regards his own understanding, which stands contrary to God's words, to be true and just. For this person, God is not justified but regarded as and declared a liar. This of course does not mean

---

29. *Heidelberg Disputation*, 1520 (AE 31:52–53; WA 1:362.11–13).
30. *Lectures on Hebrews*, 1517–18 (AE 29:110–11; WA 57:99.2). For Luther Heb 1:2 establishes "the well-known rule that one learns to know God in faith."
31. *Lectures on Psalm 51*, 1532 (AE 12:311; WA 40/2:328.17–18): "Nam Theologiae proprium subiectum est homo peccati reus ac perditus et Deus iustificans ac salvator hominis peccatoris."
32. *Lectures on Galatians*, 1535 (AE 26:227; WA 40/1:360.24–25): "Ea consummat divinitatem et, ut ita dicam, creatrix est divinitatis, non in substantia Dei, sed in nobis."
33. SC II.2 (BSLK, 511, "Sine ullis meis meritis aut ulla dignitate").
34. *Lectures on Romans*, 1515–16 (AE 25:210; WA 56:225.15–226.6).

that God *is* a liar, only that the unbeliever regards Him as one. Luther explains: "This justification and judgment of God [spoken about by David] are outside of God and His Word, that is, in men. For intrinsically both God and His words are righteous and true. But they have not as yet become such in us until our wisdom yields to them and in faith gives them a place and accepts them."[35] When the believer confesses "Against Thee have I sinned," he forsakes his own human wisdom and righteousness. He "frees God" and himself, confessing himself a sinner and unrighteous and God as the justifier of sinners. The believer makes God's words, which are true in themselves, true for him. For Luther this is the faith that justifies. That is to say, the faith that justifies God in His words is the faith God imputes with the righteousness of Christ. Luther explains: "When [God] is justified, He justifies, and when He justifies, He is justified."[36] These two things occur simultaneously, as it is one and the same faith. Luther's point underscores the relational aspect of justification: we are not righteous formally or according to substance but according to relation, our relation toward God in Christ. God stands justified in His words in relation to us, and we stand justified before the Father, imputed with Christ's righteousness and the free forgiveness of our sins by the work of the Holy Spirit through the gift of faith.[37]

Although we may without much difficulty understand what Luther means when he says faith justifies God by believing His words to be true, what does he mean when he says faith makes God? Here we must be careful lest we misunderstand Luther's point. He uses this sort of expression throughout his writings. In his commentary on Ps 90:1 ("Lord, You have been our dwelling place in all generations"), Luther writes, "If you believe that God is your Dwelling Place, He is truly a Dwelling Place for you. If you do not believe this, He is not."[38] Just as God's words are true and just in themselves but only become true and just for us when we by faith acknowledge them to be true and just, so likewise God is our Dwelling Place apart from faith but known to be this only by faith. Similarly, when we pray "Hallowed be Thy name" in the Lord's Prayer, we pray that God's name which is holy in itself (*per se*) may be holy among us also.[39]

Luther discusses the distinction between what God is in Himself and what He is for us by faith or unbelief in his great commentary on Galatians. Faith is the supreme worship of God because faith and not reason properly attributes

---

35. *Lectures on Romans*, 1515–16 (AE 25:210–11; WA 56:226.12–16).
36. *Lectures on Romans*, 1515–16 (AE 25:211; WA 56:227.7–8).
37. *Lectures on Psalm 51*, 1532 (AE 12:329; WA 40/2:353.36–354.19): "Therefore the Christian is not formally righteous, he is not righteous according to substance or quality—I use these words for instruction's sake. He is righteous according to his relation to something: namely, only in respect to divine grace and the free forgiveness of sins, which comes to those who acknowledge their sin and believe that God is gracious and forgiving for Christ's sake, who was delivered for our sins (Rom 4:25) and is believed in by us."
38. *Lectures on Psalm 90*, 1534 (AE 13:88; WA 40/3:503.26–27).
39. SC III.4 (BSLK, 512): "Nomen Dei per se quidem sanctum est, verum nos oramus hac petitione, ut apud nos quoque sanctificetur."

glory to God, regarding Him as truthful, wise, righteous, merciful, and almighty.[40] The attributes of God belong to a discussion of the Trinity, not an abstract doctrine of God. Luther continues provocatively, "[Faith] consummates the Deity; and, if I may put it this way, it is the creator of Deity, not in the substance of God but in us."[41] The relational aspect of knowing God according to the Scriptures becomes most evident here. Although God is God apart from me, in His substance, He is only my God and my Lord when I acknowledge Him to be so by faith.[42] Apart from faith I can neither know Him nor trust Him. Faith "attributes" to God His glory, wisdom, righteousness, truthfulness, mercy, etc., when it believes God's Word to be true and just. Apart from faith or apart from God's Word none of this can be said of God. Luther writes, "Faith justifies because it renders to God what is due Him."[43] When the person of faith attributes such things to God, he does so only because he has come to know himself as sinner and God as the one who justifies the sinner. This he knows because he has clothed God in His Word and promises.

Once again we see that faith and God belong together. The person of faith justifies God in His words and allows God to be God for himself as a believer. The person without faith fails to justify God and makes another "god" of his own liking. This is why unbelief is such a great sin: it denies to God who He is and creates a different god, an idol, and calls that the true god.[44] True knowledge always involves God's attitude toward me and my faith accepting that God's words about Himself and about me as sinner are true and just. I justify God in His words when I free God from my own reasonable ideas. Luther writes: "And this is the reason why our theology is certain: it snatches us away from ourselves and places us outside ourselves, so that we do not depend on our own strength, conscience, experience, person, or works but depend on that which is outside ourselves, that is, on the promise and truth of God, which cannot deceive."[45] Freedom for God means freedom from ourselves. Scholasticism, in Luther's estimation, domesticates God and His Word through reasonable and fitting assertions about how things ought to be one way and not another. Scholasticism does not justify God in His words, but rather justifies itself in its attempt to conceptualize God according to its best ideas.

---

40. *Lectures on Galatians*, 1535 (AE 26:227; WA 40/1:360.21–23).

41. *Lectures on Galatians*, 1535 (AE 26:227; WA 40/1:360.24–25): "Ea consummat divinitatem et, ut ita dicam, creatrix est divinitatis, non in substantia Dei, sed in nobis."

42. Cf. *Commentary on Psalm 68*, 1521 (AE 13:26; WA 8:25.18–23): "No one can say 'My God and my King' unless he regards God with the eyes of faith, not only as a God, not only as a King, but as *his* God and *his* King, as the God and King of his salvation. Neither is it possible to recognize the ways and works of God in the absence of that faith. Faith renders Him my God and my King, and brings me to a realization that all my works are, after all, not mine but God's."

43. *Lectures on Galatians*, 1535 (AE 26:227; WA 40/1:361.12).

44. *Lectures on Galatians*, 1535 (AE 26:228; WA 40/1:361.28–362.14).

45. *Lectures on Galatians*, 1535 (AE 26:387; WA 40/1:589.25–28).

ON GOD

Natural Knowledge and Idolatry

Luther insists that all people possess a natural knowledge of God. And yet, just as Luther's understanding of how we know God proceeds differently than it did for the schoolmen, so too his understanding of natural knowledge accomplishes something quite different than it did for the schoolmen. For Luther, natural knowledge—because it relies upon reason—necessarily leads to false understandings of God, false worship, and false forms of the Christian life. This is so because reason can never justify God in His words and therefore desperately seeks to establish its own order for God and the world.

Luther distinguishes between general and particular knowledge of God in his 1535 *Lectures on Galatians*. All men have a general knowledge that there is a "god."[46] The numerous religions and forms of worship that have littered human civilization throughout its history evidence this truth. General knowledge has a severe limitation, however: it knows only the existence of God, "that God is," answering affirmatively the question *An sit Deus?* For Luther this general knowledge reveals to a person that the God who exists created all things, is just, and punishes the wicked.[47] This sort of knowledge does not tell us what God thinks of us, what He wants to give us or do for us. Reason achieves no more than the absolute God or naked God without His Word and promises.[48]

---

46. *Lectures on Galatians*, 1535 (AE 26:399; WA 40/1:607.19–20).

47. Luther makes a similar point in his early *Lectures on Romans*: "All those who set up idols and worship them and call them 'gods,' or even 'God,' believing that God is immortal, that is, eternal, powerful, and able to render help, clearly indicate that they have a knowledge of divinity in their hearts. . . . This was their error, that they did not worship this divinity untouched but changed and adjusted it to their desires and needs. Everyone wanted to see the divinity in the one who appealed to him, and so they changed the truth of God into a lie" (AE 25:157; WA 56:176.29–177.11).

48. *Lectures on Psalm 51*, 1532 (AE 12:312; WA 40/2:329.17–330.21): "David mentions God [in the first verse of Psalm 51] and makes no reference to Christ. Here at the very beginning you should be reminded of something so that you do not think that David is talking about God like a Mohammedan or like some other Gentile. David is talking with the God of his fathers, with the God who promised. The people of Israel did not have a God who was viewed 'absolutely,' to use the expression, the way the inexperienced monks rise into heaven with their speculations and think about God as He is in Himself. From this absolute God everyone should flee who does not want to perish, because human nature and the absolute God—for the sake of teaching we use this familiar term—are the bitterest of enemies. Human weakness cannot help being crushed by such majesty, as Scripture reminds us over and over. Let no one, therefore, interpret David as speaking with the absolute God. He is speaking with God as He is dressed and clothed in His Word and promises, so that from the name 'God' we cannot exclude Christ, whom God promised to Adam and the other patriarchs. We must take hold of this God, not naked but clothed and revealed in His Word; otherwise certain despair will crush us. This distinction must always be made between the Prophets who speak with God, and the Gentiles. The Gentiles speak with God outside His Word and promises, according to the thoughts of their own hearts; but the Prophets speak with God as He is clothed and revealed in His promises and Word. This God, clothed in such a kind appearance and, so to speak, in such a pleasant mask, that is to say, dressed in His promises—this God we can grasp and look at with joy and trust. The absolute God, on the other hand, is like an iron wall, against which we cannot bump without destroying ourselves. Therefore Satan is busy day and night, making us run to the naked God so that we forget His promises and blessings shown in Christ and think about God and the judgment of God. When this happens, we perish utterly and fall into despair."

If Luther had stopped here, he merely would have repeated what so many advocates of natural knowledge have said throughout the history of the church. Luther pushes on. Although we may discern God's existence through reason, we cannot know something exists without also knowing something about that thing. Existence assumes essence. Luther goes yet one step further: God's essence or being never can be abstracted from His will. Luther asks, "What good does it do you to know that God exists if you do not know what His will is toward you?"[49] Gone are all the scholastic distinctions that made possible an abstract notion or concept of God that Scripture could complement and perfect. And with that move problems lurk. Since all people have a general knowledge of God but know not God's will and what He wants, they necessarily fall back upon reason to make up the deficit. The result is idolatry. These people "become futile in their thinking" (Rom 1:21). Luther explains, "Not knowing what is pleasing to God and what is displeasing to Him, they adore the imaginations of their own heart as though these were true God by nature, when by nature these are nothing at all."[50] Not knowing the will of God necessarily leads to false worship and false constructions of "beings that by nature are no gods."[51] Reason promotes an idea of God that is not God by nature, justifying its idea of God as God and rejecting the true God. Luther explains:

> From the acceptance of this major premise, "There is a God," there came all the idolatry of men, which would have been unknown in the world without the knowledge of the Deity. But because men had this natural knowledge about God, they conceived vain and wicked thoughts about God apart from and contrary to the Word; they embraced these as the very truth, and on the basis of these they imagined God otherwise than He is by nature.[52]

Luther gives the example of a monk in his day, an example that recurs throughout his writings, and one that reminds us of Luther the monk before his Reformation breakthrough. This monk "imagines" a God who forgives sins and grants eternal life in exchange for our good works. This is the order the monk has imposed upon God and the world through his reason, and this is the order he justifies, he believes, as God and from God. Luther states plainly, "That God does not exist anywhere." The monk serves and worships "one who by nature is no god" but rather a "figment and idol of his own heart, his own false and empty notion about God, which he supposes to be the surest truth."[53]

---

49. *Lectures on Galatians*, 1535 (AE 26:400; WA 40/1:608.15–16).
50. *Lectures on Galatians*, 1535 (AE 26:400; WA 40/1:608.19–21).
51. *Lectures on Galatians*, 1535 (AE 26:400; WA 40/1:608.23).
52. *Lectures on Galatians*, 1535 (AE 26:400; WA 40/1:608.25–30).
53. *Lectures on Galatians*, 1535 (AE 26:400; WA 40/1:608.30–609.11). Cf. Ap. IV.203-5 (Tappert, 135). See also Francis Pieper, *Christian Dogmatics* (St. Louis: Concordia Publishing House, 1950), 1:430: "A god who justifies sinners not by grace but on the basis of His remunerative righteousness does not exist. All who deny Christ's vicarious atonement have painted a caricature of God and, like the heathen, who know not God, worship an idol."

Luther knows of no neutral territory between grace and wrath; so too he knows of no neutral idea of God that exists for reason. No one has a static notion of God to which he does not at the same time offer worship and seek reward. A commitment to God—whether the Father as revealed through the Son by the Holy Spirit, a general knowledge derived from nature, or the monk's absolute and naked God—always entails faith. Further faith justifies the words of God and receives justification from God. If the God we believe in is derived from our reason, then the justification we seek and the worship we offer will be according to our reason. And in every case it is an idea of God and justification contrary to the gospel.

Jonah and the Mariners

The book of Jonah illustrates well Luther's understanding of natural knowledge of God. After Jonah boarded the ship for Tarshish a mighty tempest arose, threatening the ship and its crew. At this point the mariners became afraid and "each cried out to his god" (Jon 1:5).[54] Here we find the scriptural demonstration of Paul's point in Romans 1. Although the mariners lack true faith and a proper understanding of God, they hold at the very least that there is a God who helps in times of need.[55] If this God can help in times of need, then reason further concludes that all that is good comes from this God. Thus the God who saves from misfortune also grants all that is good.[56] At this point reason reaches its limit: it knows nothing more about God than that He exists and that He is kind, gracious, merciful, and benevolent. Although a "bright light," as Luther puts it, this insight of reason is never content with this limitation and succumbs to two serious defects. The first defect is reason's lack of certainty. As Luther puts it, you may know by reason that God is able to help but not if He is willing to help you. The second defect is that reason cannot identify God properly. Reason knows that there is a god but not who or which is the true God. Again, problems lurk. Reason abhors uncertainty and refuses to allow these questions to remain unanswered. When reason asserts itself it reaches beyond its ability, beyond the possibilities assigned this faculty, and manufactures idols and idolatry. Luther explains:

> Thus reason also plays blindman's buff with God; it consistently gropes in the dark and misses the mark. It calls that God which is not God and fails to call Him God who really is God. Reason would do neither the one nor the other if

---

54. The following discussion follows Luther's exposition closely (AE 19:53–57). Cf. Lohse, *Martin Luther's Theology*, 210–12; and Roland Ziegler, "Natural Knowledge of God and the Trinity," *Concordia Theological Quarterly* 69:2 (2005): 153–54.

55. Gregory of Nazianzus recounts how he was once caught in a terrifying storm at sea. The ship seemed lost and at that time everyone aboard cried out to Christ, even those, notes Gregory, who formerly knew not God. Gregory of Nazianzus *De vita sua* II/I/XI.139–43 (Fathers of the Church, 81). Gregory notes that fear is an opportune teacher.

56. Oswald Bayer rightly shows how provocative Luther's insight is. Both reason and faith know the same things about God but know these things in radically different ways. Bayer, *Martin Luther's Theology*, 130–35.

it were not conscious of the existence of God or if it really knew who and what God is. Therefore it rushes in clumsily and assigns the name God and ascribes divine honor to its own idea of God. Thus reason never finds the true God, but it finds the devil or its own concept of God, ruled by the devil. *So there is a vast difference between knowing that there is a God and knowing who or what God is.* Nature knows the former—it is inscribed in everybody's heart; the latter is taught only by the Holy Spirit.[57]

Luther demonstrates this with a few examples. The papists labor under the delusion that God is a being "moved and satisfied by good works."[58] Therefore they order their entire way of life around the idea of serving and pleasing God in order to merit His benevolence. Luther writes:

> Now tell me, what are these people worshiping as God if there is no God whose mind and will conforms to theirs? Is it not true that they are honoring their own delusion and their own fancy as God? For in truth there is no God who is of one mind with them. Therefore they go awry with their illusion. They miss the true God, and nothing remains but their own false notion. That is their god. To him they assign the name and honor of God. Of course, no one but the devil can be behind this delusion, for he inspires and governs these thoughts. Thus their delusion is their idol; it is the image of the devil they hold in their hearts. For the real and the true God is He who is properly served not with works but with the true faith and with sincerity of heart, who gives and bestows mercy and benefactions entirely gratis and without our works and merits. That they do not believe, and therefore they do not know God but are bound to blunder and to miss the mark.[59]

The same pattern is seen in Scripture. King Ahab knew there was a god and imagined this god was pleased with the sort of worship given to Baal: "Thus he called God Baal, and Baal God, as is evident from Hos. 2:16."[60] King Jeroboam asserted that his god was pleased with the worship of golden calves: "And therefore calves had to be called the God of Israel, and, again, God has to be called a calf (1 Kings 12:28)."[61] This pattern also is seen with the mariners in the ship with Jonah. They all know that there is a god, but have no definite god. Jonah tells us that each person called upon his own concept of God, and when that did not work they asked Jonah to call upon his God. Therefore, concludes Luther, the mariners each call upon an idol and honor this idol with their idolatry, and this is the evidence and fruit of the natural knowledge of God (Rom 1:19–23).

What about St. John?

Most discussions of natural knowledge of God focus on Paul's argument in Romans. Luther also wonders about John. Luther writes, "On the one hand, St. Paul says that man can know God; one the other hand, St. John clearly states that

---

57. *Lectures on Jonah*, 1525 (AE 19:55; WA 19:207.3–13), emphasis added.
58. *Lectures on Jonah*, 1525 (AE 19:55; WA 19:207.16).
59. *Lectures on Jonah*, 1525 (AE 19:55–56; WA 19:207.18–30).
60. *Lectures on Jonah*, 1525 (AE 19:56; WA 19:208.7–8).
61. *Lectures on Jonah*, 1525 (AE 19:56; WA 19:208.10–11).

no one has seen God, be he ever so wise, clever, and smart, except the Son of God, who revealed Him to us."[62] Before attempting an answer, Luther raises the stakes even higher, paraphrasing Jesus' words to the Pharisees in John 8, "You claim to know God, but you do not know Him; you call Him your Father but do not know who He is."[63] As Luther puts it, Christ was not rebuking Epicureans or godless people, who are uninterested in God, but the Pharisees, who were concerned about God and were seeking Him. Luther prophetically declares, "Someday this question is going to cause trouble."[64]

Luther's reconciliation of Paul and John proceeds according to law and gospel, and clarifies especially well his thoughts on natural knowledge of God. There are two kinds of knowledge of God: "The one is the knowledge of the Law; the other the knowledge of the Gospel."[65] Reason's knowledge of God is based on law, and this law is written on our hearts (Rom 2:15). All rational beings know the natural law stated by Moses in the Ten Commandments. Although there is a degree of understanding here, although reason has, as Luther puts it, "sniffed God," this "legal knowledge of God . . . derived from the Law is not the true knowledge of Him, whether it be the Law of Moses or the Law instilled in our hearts."[66] Here is Luther's point of departure from the schoolmen. Knowledge is never passive. We act upon what we know. There is no abstract knowledge of God that stands apart from our heart and our actions. Luther illustrates this point, as he did above, by appealing to the monk and his understanding of God. The monk imagines a God after his own image. By conforming to this image of God the monk claims to merit salvation for himself and others. Luther exclaims, "This is blindness beyond all blindness, as must be apparent to all."[67] This twisted knowledge of God falls below what even the heathen imagine who conform their lives to the natural law. In either case, however, both groups are only sniffing the existence of God.[68]

The other sort of knowledge of God proceeds from the gospel. From this knowledge we learn that we are by nature an abomination before God, subject to His wrath, and eternally damned. Our only remedy lies with the Son, who rests in the bosom of the Father, who became man, died, and rose again from the dead, conquering sin, death, and the devil.[69] Luther writes,

> This is the true and thorough knowledge and way of thinking about God; it is called the knowledge of grace and truth, the evangelical knowledge of God. But this knowledge does not grow up in our garden, and nature knows nothing at all about it. Reason has only a left-handed and partial knowledge of God, based on

---

62. *Sermons on the Gospel of John*, 1537–38 (AE 22:150; WA 46:666.32–35). We could extend Luther's question to Matthew (11:27) and Luke (10:22) too.
63. *Sermons on the Gospel of John*, 1537–38 (AE 22:150; WA 46:666.35–37).
64. *Sermons on the Gospel of John*, 1537–38 (AE 22:150; WA 46:667.7).
65. *Sermons on the Gospel of John*, 1537–38 (AE 22:150; WA 46:667.8–9).
66. *Sermons on the Gospel of John*, 1537–38 (AE 22:151; WA 46:668.9–13).
67. *Sermons on the Gospel of John*, 1537–38 (AE 22:152; WA 46:668.25–26).
68. *Sermons on the Gospel of John*, 1537–38 (AE 22:152; WA 46:668.33–34).
69. *Sermons on the Gospel of John*, 1537–38 (AE 22:152; WA 46:669.1–6).

the law of nature and of Moses; for the Law is inscribed in our hearts. But the depth of divine wisdom and of the divine purpose, the profundity of God's grace and mercy, and what eternal life is like—of these matters reason is totally ignorant. This is hidden from reason's view.[70]

Proper knowledge of God requires knowledge of God's will, His Word and promises, and faith which justifies God in His words and receives the imputation of Christ's righteousness.

What accounts for the vast difference between the two ways of knowing God? Luther's answer is sin. Christian knowledge of God requires an understanding of sin and the all-sufficient salvation purchased for us by the Son. Human reason has no inkling of this knowledge.[71] Luther explains, "To summarize, we have been so abominably corrupted by sin that we not only know nothing about our first and natural knowledge of God any longer, but we have also defected from the righteousness of the Law and fallen into lies."[72] Sin has effaced whatever natural knowledge may have been available through the law. Luther explains:

> It is indeed true . . . that there are some things outside of Christ which are true and pleasing, as the natural light, which teaches that three and two are five, that God should be honored, and the like. But this light never accomplishes its end; for as soon as reason is to act, and make use of its light, and exercise it, it confuses everything, calls that which is good bad, and that which is bad good; calls that the honor of God which is his dishonor, and vice versa. Therefore man is only a liar (Ps 116:11) and vain (Ps 39:5), and unable to make use of this natural light except against God, as we have already said.[73]

In the Smalcald Articles Luther states that original sin is such a deep corruption of nature that reason cannot understand it. It must be believed according to the revelation of Scripture.[74] Here we arrive at the heart of the disagreement between Luther and the schoolmen. It is vain for the schoolmen to magnify the light of nature and think it comparable to the light of grace.[75] We are by nature curved in on the self.[76] Our natural faculties are corrupted by sin. There is no light but rather darkness. Luther concludes, "Therefore, this wisdom is not a light, but it can much better be called darkness . . . [A]s it turns all knowledge in upon itself, it is the most complete darkness."[77]

How do we reconcile Paul and John? We acknowledge that God has revealed Himself to all men through nature and law but all men have corrupted this natural revelation. Outside of Christ there is no proper knowledge of God.

---

70. *Sermons on the Gospel of John*, 1537–38 (AE 22:152–53; WA 46:669.7–15).
71. *Sermons on the Gospel of John*, 1537–38 (AE 22:153; WA 46:669.33–39).
72. *Sermons on the Gospel of John*, 1537–38 (AE 22:155; WA 46:671.22–25).
73. *Complete Sermons of Martin Luther*, trans. John Nicholas Lenker (Grand Rapids: Baker Books, 2000), 1.1:223.
74. SA III.i.3 (Tappert, 302). Cf. Augustine *Confessions* 10, 7.
75. *Lectures on Romans*, 1515–16 (AE 25:345–46; WA 56.356.18–19).
76. *Lectures on Romans*, 1515–16 (AE 25:345; WA 56:356.7).
77. *Lectures on Romans*, 1515–16 (AE 25:346; WA 56:357.13–16).

More to the point, revelation never supplements our natural knowledge of God because there is no such thing as static or passive knowledge of God.[78] Natural man acts upon the knowledge he achieves, and in every case apart from Christ it results in idolatry. As Luther puts it, "All this must die, be committed to the grave, and interred."[79] We do not build upon idolatry, we repent of it. Thomas's grand effort to coordinate reason and revelation is thoroughly rejected by Luther, and with it the grand efforts at demonstrating natural knowledge of God.

THE BOOK OF CONCORD

The Book of Concord devotes no section exclusively to the natural knowledge of God. Instead it offers comments on the topic in connection with other teachings. Although Luther's distinction between general and particular knowledge of God is not found in the Confessions, the basic outline of his above argument is. The Confessions emphasize two points. First, natural knowledge of God exists and is derived from creation (Romans 1) and the law written upon human hearts (Romans 2). Second, sin has so marred such knowledge that it leads only to a perverse understanding of God and the worship owed Him. Although the tradition, as we have seen, consistently affirms that such knowledge exists and is not saving knowledge, our Confessions make this point with force by bringing together knowledge and worship. By consistently reflecting upon the knowledge of God as something not only possessed in the head but also used by the heart, which is to say as something that guides, directs, and informs human behavior, the Book of Concord resists conceiving of the knowledge of God as a static and abstract thing accessed and analyzed by human reason. Knowledge acts in the way that faith works.

When we consider natural knowledge of God in this broader context, we discover far more in the Book of Concord addressing this question. What is God? Luther famously responds to this question in the Large Catechism:

> A god is that to which we look for all good and in which we find refuge in every time of need. To have a god is nothing else than to trust and believe him with our whole heart. As I have often said, the trust and faith of the heart alone make both God and an idol. If your faith and trust are right, then your God is the true God. On the other hand, if your trust is false and wrong, then you have not the true God. For these two belong together, faith and God. That to which your heart clings and entrusts itself is, I say, really your God.[80]

Philosophical or scholastic abstraction is of little interest here. Luther begins not with the intellect but with the heart. A god is not a carefully constructed

---

78. Cf. Bernhard Lohse, "Reason and Revelation in Luther," *Scottish Journal of Theology* 13:4 (1960): 347–48: "Revelation therefore means the end of any human attempt to get a knowledge of God. Reason and revelation differ not only quantitatively but qualitatively."

79. *Sermons on the Gospel of John*, 1537–38 (AE 22:158; WA 46:673.17–18).

80. LC I.2–3 (Tappert, 365).

definition or concept to which we give intellectual assent; a god is that to which our heart clings, that which we fear and love, that which we trust and believe, that which we justify as "our" god.

That a natural knowledge of God exists among all people is seen in the fact that all maintain some sort of worship. This false worship, this idolatry, is the expression of the heart. Luther writes, "There has never been a people so wicked that it did not establish and maintain some sort of worship. Everyone has set up a god of his own, to which he looked for blessings, help, and comfort."[81] Luther insists that idolatry is not just a matter of erecting an image and praying to it. It primarily concerns the heart. In every case, rather than clinging to the true God it clings to "creatures, saints, or devils."[82] Even the heathen agree that to have a god means to trust and believe. All people have something to say about God, and all people trust and believe in whatever "god" this is and worship this same "god" or "gods." Christians know and worship the true God—Father, Son, and Holy Spirit—and the rest, who possess only a "dim spark" (*obscuram scintillulam*) of the natural knowledge of God, have an understanding that is "so ignorant, blind, and perverse" that their worship is perverted and their trust is false and wrong.[83]

Law and Gospel

By following closely Paul's construal of natural knowledge of God with false worship (Rom 1:21), the Book of Concord presents its discussion of knowledge of God according to law and gospel. In the Large Catechism, the counterpart to Luther's reflection on the Ten Commandments "which are inscribed in the hearts of all men" is the Apostles' Creed, in which we have "the entire essence of God, his will, and his work exquisitely depicted in very short but rich words."[84] The gospel as presented in the creed surpasses all the wisdom, understanding, and reason of men. Whatever knowledge of God the natural man has, it can never be the basis for true faith and worship: "Although the whole world has sought painstakingly to learn what God is and what he thinks and does, yet it has never succeeded in the least."[85] The world knows nothing of the profound and unutterable love of God for us. It knows not that He wishes to redeem and sanctify us. It is only through the Lord Christ that we know the Father's favor and grace, and it is only by the Holy Spirit that we know and call upon Christ as our Lord. To claim knowledge of God apart from Christ is to know nothing but "an angry and terrible Judge."[86]

The world knows nothing of God's grace and love because the world's knowledge is based entirely on law. Luther explains, "Now you see that the

---

81. LC I.17 (Tappert, 367).
82. LC I.21 (Tappert, 367).
83. SD II.9 (Tappert, 521); LC I.18–23 (Tappert, 367).
84. LC II.63–69 (Tappert, 419–20).
85. LC II.63 (Tappert, 419).
86. LC II.65 (Tappert, 419).

Creed is a very different teaching from the Ten Commandments. The latter teach us what we ought to do; the Creed tells what God does for us and gives to us."[87] Natural knowledge of God, which leads to false trust and false worship, also leads to self-justification. This latter form of false worship, according to Luther, is "the greatest idolatry" as its places God in our debt and makes us His liege lords.[88] The gospel alone reveals true knowledge of God, His grace and love, His work of creation, redemption, and sanctification for us. The Trinity and justification by faith are intimately connected. Holsten Fagerberg explains:

> Since the doctrine of the Trinity is thus connected to justification by faith, it also stands in an inner, organic relationship to the distinction between Law and Gospel. Reason apart from the Gospel cannot bring man true knowledge of God. Law and reason go together, but through them we see only a caricature of God. What God actually thinks of us we learn through the Gospel, and the Gospel has to do with Father, Son, and Spirit.[89]

The gospel grants both a proper knowledge of the Trinity and their gifts for us.[90] By insisting upon this point our Confessions present knowledge of God according to law and gospel. The law, which for Luther is seen in the Ten Commandments, teaches us what we ought to do; the gospel, expressed in the Apostles' Creed, tells us what God does for us and gives to us. Luther explains:

> The Ten Commandments, moreover, are inscribed in the hearts of all men. No human wisdom can comprehend the Creed; it must be taught by the Holy Spirit alone. Therefore the Ten Commandments do not by themselves make us Christians, for God's wrath and displeasure still remain on us because we cannot fulfill his demands. But the Creed brings pure grace and makes us upright and pleasing to God. Through this knowledge we come to love and delight in all the commandments of God because we see that God gives himself completely to us, with all his gifts and his power, to help us keep the Ten Commandments: the Father gives us all creation, Christ all his works, the Holy Spirit all his gifts.[91]

Natural knowledge of God and natural law not only do not make us Christians, but even more cannot make us Christians. God cannot be rightly known apart from the saving gifts He imparts. The knowledge of God that exists apart from the gift of salvation is rightly characterized by our Confessions as ignorant, blind, and perverse.[92] Natural knowledge of God, whatever it amounts to, is never Christian knowledge of God.

When we know the gift of salvation—the Father's act of justification, accomplished through the life, death, and resurrection of the Son, and delivered

---

87. LC II.67 (Tappert, 419). A similar distinction can be seen in Augustine *On the Spirit and the Letter* 22 (WSA I/23), 164.
88. LC I.22-23 (Tappert, 367).
89. Fagerberg, *A New Look at the Lutheran Confessions, 1529–1537*, 115.
90. Cf. Schlink, *Theology of the Lutheran Confessions*, 62: "The triune God reveals himself in the Gospel through which he grants us the merit of Christ and gives us the Holy Spirit who in us takes hold of Christ's work."
91. LC II.67-69 (Tappert, 419-20).
92. SD II.9 (Tappert, 521).

by the Holy Spirit's creation of faith in Christ through the means of grace—we rightly know ourselves and our God. There is no partial knowledge, no shadowy insight that the natural man builds upon, making it more complete and perfect (Thomas's *perfectior* and *plenior*). Why? Because there is no static and abstract concept of God possessed by people.[93] The Formula states this plainly:

> The Word of God testifies that in divine matters the intellect, heart, and will of a natural, unregenerated man is not only totally turned away from God, but is also turned and perverted against God and toward all evil. Again, that man is not only weak, impotent, incapable, and dead to good, but also that by original sin he is so miserably perverted, poisoned, and corrupted that by disposition and nature he is thoroughly wicked, opposed and hostile to God, and all too mighty, alive, and active for everything which is displeasing to God and contrary to his will.[94]

Natural knowledge never remains in the head alone but always informs the heart. It always expresses itself in act and in worship, in dishonorable passions (Rom 1:26) and idolatry (Rom 1:23). Such things are works of the flesh (Gal 5:19–20), and works of the flesh are against the Holy Spirit (Gal 5:17) and hostile to God (Rom 8:7). Although the natural man knows that there is a god, he is a stranger to the true love, fear, and trust of God. Again, no neutral position exists because of the natural knowledge that there is a god. This shadow of knowledge for the natural man results in idolatry and hostility. As the Apology puts it, the chief flaws of human nature because of original sin are "ignorance of God, contempt of God, lack of the fear of God and of trust in him, inability to love him."[95] A proper understanding of sin means that the natural man has no true knowledge of God—no trust, no fear, no love of God.[96] For this reason the natural man must despair of his own dim light or natural "ignorance of God" (*ignoratio Dei*) and be enlightened, converted, and regenerated by the Spirit through the Word.[97]

By refusing to abstract knowledge of God from worship of God, which is to say theory from practice, Luther and our Lutheran Confessions present the topic of natural and revealed knowledge of God according to two types of knowledge about God. In this sense our Lutheran fathers better capture the truth that all people are theologians in that all people have something to say about God and the worship given to Him. As Luther insists, all people, even

---

93. Lohse, *Martin Luther's Theology*, 211: "The knowledge of God through reason as well as through revelation cannot be linked in merely supplementary fashion. Between the two there is the question of the true God. In Luther's terms, we must say that reason knows something of God as well as that it knows nothing of God. It possesses no 'neutral' knowledge of God."
94. SD II.17 (Tappert, 523–24).
95. Ap. II.14 (Tappert, 102). See also Ap. II.8 (Tappert, 101).
96. Ap. II.23 (Tappert, 103). The Apology consistently links knowledge of God with fear of God, love of God, and hope. These all belong to our rebirth by the Holy Spirit in baptism. True knowledge of God enables us to truly fear, love, and trust God. See Ap. IV.351 (Tappert, 161) and Ap. II.17–18, 23 (Tappert, 102–3). Cf. SD II.16 (Tappert, 523).
97. On the relationship between the Formula's "dim spark" and the Apology's *ignoratio Dei* see Schlink, *Theology of the Lutheran Confessions*, 49–52.

the heathen, teach that to have a god means to trust, believe, and worship that god. This distinction is also made in the Formula of Concord: "There is a vast difference between the knowledge of God which comes from the Gospel and that which is taught by and learned from the law, since from the natural law even the heathen had to some extent a knowledge of God, although they neither understood nor honored him rightly (Rom 1:21)."[98] The false worship of God is evidence of the general knowledge of God possessed by all people and at the same time the perversion of that dim spark. True knowledge of God comes only from the gospel. This is why our Confessions insist that "the chief worship of God is the preaching of the Gospel."[99]

The Problem of Sin

Sin is the chief problem with natural knowledge of God. Scholastic notions of natural knowledge proceed on the basis that sin has affected the human will and our capacity to know God only marginally. Adam and Eve lost the *donum superadditum*, but their natural faculties remained unhindered.[100] The Confessions depart from Rome on this crucial point.[101] Both believers and unbelievers bear the effects of original sin, a sin that darkens the mind and the will. In the article on free will in the Formula of Concord these two items are brought together. The chief issue pursued in the article on free will is the state of unregenerated man's intellect and will, and whether he can do anything to bring about his conversion. Since conversion requires both the intellect and will insofar as the natural man must "know" what it is he assents to by his will, the issue involved concerns both knowledge of God and His saving works on our behalf. These two issues, theology proper and soteriology, Trinity and gospel, must remain together, as the pattern of Scripture shows us, lest "knowledge of God" be abstracted from God's revelation of Himself and His works.

According to the Formula, man by nature not only cannot understand the Word of God but considers it foolishness.[102] The Formula states its position plainly: "We believe that in spiritual and divine things the intellect, heart, and

---

98. SD V.22 (Tappert, 562).

99. Ap. XV.42 (Tappert, 221). The Triglot adds: "Now, if this worship is omitted, how can there be knowledge of God, the doctrine of Christ, or the Gospel?" (Bente, 327).

100. The schoolmen disagreed on whether the *donum superadditum* could be regained (i.e., merited) after the Fall. Thomas said no. Adam and Eve received this gift by grace and therefore it could not be merited. John Duns Scotus and William of Ockham thought we could merit this gift by our natural abilities (*ex puris naturalibus*). The Lutheran reformers rejected the theological anthropology that lies behind both of these views.

101. Cf. Johann Andreas Quenstedt, *Systema Theologicum*, I, 6 (Wittenberg, 1691), 254. Quenstedt shows that natural knowledge of God must be considered from two perspectives. On the one hand we may consider it from the perspective of its original integrity before the Fall. This was a perfect knowledge bestowed upon Adam and Eve by God's grace. After the Fall, however, this knowledge has been corrupted significantly. Although it remains, it never amounts to more than "a small spark of that original light, a meager little drop of water from the vast ocean, or a small piece of ash from the ruins of a splendid house."

102. SD II.5 (Tappert, 521).

will of unregenerated man cannot by any native or natural powers in any way understand, believe, accept, imagine, will, begin, accomplish, do, effect, or cooperate, but that man is entirely and completely dead and corrupted as far as anything good is concerned."[103] After the Fall and prior to our conversion, "not a spark of spiritual powers has remained or exists" by which a person could in any way apply himself toward conversion, not even "in the tiniest or smallest degree."[104] Everything done by our natural free will in spiritual and divine things is without qualification always "in the direction of that which is displeasing and contrary to God."[105] All of this is said especially against John Duns Scotus and those sympathetic to his theology.

At this point the Formula raises the question of natural knowledge of God. There is "not a spark" of spiritual powers in us but there is a "dim spark" of knowledge that "a" god exists (Romans 1). To what does this dim spark amount? The Formula seems to leave the question unanswered. Rather than addressing the question of knowledge of God (theology proper), the Formula qualifies the "dim spark" comment by turning to the gospel (soteriology).

> In the first place, although man's reason or natural intellect still has a dim spark of the knowledge that there is a God, as well as the teaching of the law (Rom 1:19–21, 28, 32), *nevertheless*, it is so ignorant, blind, and perverse that when even the most gifted and the most educated people on earth read or hear the Gospel of the Son of God and the promise of eternal salvation, they cannot by their own powers perceive this, comprehend it, understand it, or believe and accept it as the truth.[106]

The "nevertheless" that qualifies the "dim spark" addresses not knowledge of God but rather the knowledge of what God has done, His saving works, the gospel. This the natural man can no more accept than he can comprehend it. The Formula reverses Luther's insight. Luther knows with certainty that there is a natural knowledge of God (Romans 1) because of the presence of idolatry among all the peoples of the world. Their false worship proceeds from their natural knowledge that there is a god. When they act upon their natural knowledge according to the natural intellect and will, they construct false religions opposed to the true God and the true gospel. When the Formula addresses the issue of the "dim spark" of natural knowledge, it characterizes it as "darkness."[107] Although a dim spark remains that a god exists, it is entirely in the dark concerning the true Light which enlightens everyone. Only the grace of the Holy Spirit through Word and sacrament can bring such Light to our darkness. The Formula ends this section by pointing the reader to baptism.

> We should thank God from our hearts for having liberated us from the darkness of ignorance and the bondage of sin and death through his Son, and for having

---

103. SD II.7 (Tappert, 521).
104. SD II.7 (Tappert, 521).
105. SD II.7 (Tappert, 521).
106. SD II.9 (Tappert, 521–22).
107. SD II.10 (Tappert, 522).

regenerated and illuminated us through Baptism and the Holy Spirit. And after God, through the Holy Spirit in Baptism, has kindled and wrought a beginning of true knowledge of God and faith, we ought to petition him incessantly that by the same Spirit and grace, through daily exercise in reading his Word and putting it into practice, he would preserve faith and his heavenly gifts in us and strengthen us daily until our end. Unless God himself is our teacher, we cannot study and learn anything pleasing to him and beneficial to us and others.[108]

The Formula unmistakably shows the pernicious effects of sin on the unregenerated intellect, heart, and will. More significantly the Formula reminds us of the relationship between knowledge of God and baptism. The Bible consistently describes the unregenerated state as darkness and the regenerated one as light. Believers are those who have been "enlightened" (Heb 6:4 and 10:32). Prior to this they were in darkness. God finds us not in a neutral place where we somehow possess natural knowledge of God by our natural abilities but have yet to act upon such knowledge with our hearts and will. Peter tells us that God called us "out of darkness into his marvelous light" (1 Pt 2:9). This light is Jesus (Jn 8:12). He is the "true light, which enlightens everyone" (Jn 1:9). This Light came into the world but "the people loved darkness rather than light because their deeds were evil" (Jn 3:19). Those who are perishing do not know this Light because "the god of this world has blinded the minds of the unbelievers, to keep them from seeing the light of the gospel of the glory of Christ, who is the image of God" (2 Cor 4:4). This enlightenment, this move from darkness to light, belongs to our new birth, our regeneration and renewal, which is the work of the Holy Spirit through baptism (Ti 3:5–7). For this reason Jesus tells Nicodemus he must be reborn by water and the Spirit (Jn 3:5). Prior to the working of the Holy Spirit in baptism we are unenlightened, dwelling in darkness, and our minds are blinded and so too our deeds. Although we may have general knowledge of a god, it remains darkness because it does not know Jesus Christ, the true Light, who alone makes known to us the Father and who makes Himself known by the sending of the Holy Spirit. As Paul asks, "What fellowship has light with darkness? What accord has Christ with Belial?" (2 Cor 6:14–15). Whatever knowledge of God precedes the means of grace, it is never more than "darkness" which has no fellowship with the true God. This is what the Confessions term *ignoratio Dei*.

CONCLUSION

In his lecture on Psalm 121 Luther emphasizes where God is to be found and not found. The answer is Christ and always Christ: "Thus in Christ you will find God but outside of him you will not find God, not even in heaven."[109] If we wish to have a right knowledge of the Trinity we must place our gaze upon Christ,

---

108. SD II.15–16 (Tappert, 523).
109. "Psalm 121" in *Vorlesungen über die Stufenpsalmen*, 1532–33 (WA 40/3:56.11–12): "Sic in Christo invenies deum, extra eum ne in coelo eum invenies."

who alone reveals the Father to us by the Holy Spirit. This means that God must come to us if we are to know Him; we cannot ascend to Him by means of reason, good works, or spiritual exercises. The decisive event in our coming to know God is the incarnation.[110] The Son came to us that we might come to know the Father. No one has ever seen the Father, and yet all who see the Son have seen the Father (Jn 12:45; 14:9). Herein lies the key to knowing and speaking about God rightly. If we seek the Father apart from the man Jesus Christ, whatever our motivations or zeal for such a pursuit, it is "not according to knowledge" but ignorance (Rom 10:2; cf. Jn 16:2–3). Luther writes: "Just as after God revealed himself in Christ, the man, we properly say and believe that all those who do not grasp this man born of Mary simply cannot grasp God. Even if they say they believe in God, the creator of heaven and earth, nevertheless they believe in an idol fashioned by their own hearts, because apart from Christ there is no true God."[111] To seek God apart from Christ is to seek God on our own terms and according to our own philosophical constructions and analogies. Those who proceed in this way are theologians of glory, seeking to ascend to God through human wisdom and shrewdness. A true theologian is one who seeks God where God has clothed Himself and has promised to be.

The question of natural knowledge of God is one of the most vexing for the church today. If any constructive space is given natural revelation, it becomes natural theology and the consequences are dire for the scriptural doctrine of the Trinity and our confession of the pure gospel. God no more needs our help in constructing His eternal triune identity than He does in bringing about our creation or salvation. We should be on our guard not only against the encroachment of philosophical theism, no matter the pious guise in which it is presented or pursued, but also against an ambitious use of apologetics that aims to construct a positive starting place, the so-called common ground, into which to speak the Scriptures and the gospel. As Roland Ziegler insists, we cannot think of natural knowledge of God "as a welcome point of contact for the proclamation of the gospel."[112] Apologetics tears down false statements and characterizations of Christianity; it exposes the foolish faith of the unbeliever; it does not advance persuasive arguments upon which faith may later repose. Again as Roland Ziegler puts it, "The faith into which one can be reasoned is nonetheless not faith in the triune God."[113]

The idea that there is a neutral space occupied by people possessing natural knowledge of God must always be resisted. No such neutral space or people

---

110. *Lectures on Hebrews*, 1517–18 (AE 29:111; WA 57:99.3–4): "For the humanity [of Christ] is that holy ladder of ours, mentioned in Gen. 28:12, by which we ascend to the knowledge of God."

111. "Psalm 121" in *Vorlesungen über die Stufenpsalmen*, 1532–33 (WA 40/3:56.31–57.21). Quoted in Robert Kolb, "Luther's Theology of the Cross Fifteen Years after Heidelberg: Lectures on the Psalms of Ascent," *Journal of Ecclesiastical History* 61 no. 1 (2010): 76. Translation modified.

112. Ziegler, "Natural Knowledge of God," 146.

113. Ziegler, "Natural Knowledge of God," 158.

exist. Paul certainly did not envision such people. Their general knowledge of God through creation or the accusation of their conscience was only ever enough to condemn them because of the false and idolatrous ideas they added to the natural light of their reason. When we are brought to faith by the Holy Spirit through the means of grace, we are not asked by God to build upon our own efforts at achieving a partial knowledge of Him and His will. We are called to repent, and that repentance includes not only our sins but our sinful thoughts, our intellectual idolatries, and our false worship. Scripture teaches us to confess that apart from Christ and His promises there is no knowledge of the blessed Trinity. It is through the Son alone that the Father is made known to us, and it is by the mutual sending of their Spirit that we know the Son, the man Jesus, born of the Virgin, crucified and risen for us and our salvation.

5

RIGHTLY SPEAKING ABOUT GOD

The Franciscan masters began their public disputations, their *quodlibets*, with a verse from Ecclesiastes: "All things are difficult because man's language is inadequate to explain them" (Eccl 1:8, Vulg.).[1] If this is true of the ordinary matters of life, how much more must it be for theology? To what extent, we must ask, are our words sufficient for speaking rightly about God? All of our words are conditioned by space and time. They are tensed; God is not. Furthermore, the way we think of the world around us necessarily informs the words we use to talk about God, whether we use positive (*cataphatic*) or negative (*apophatic*) terms. Although a distinction exists between natural and revealed knowledge of God, the same words are used for both. Reason and faith share a vocabulary. There is, however, a difference. The question that guides natural knowledge of God is whether *we* can speak responsibly and rightly about God by unaided reason. The question that guides revealed knowledge is whether *God* has spoken responsibly and rightly about Himself.

God's revelation of Himself has occurred historically. He spoke through the prophets of old by His Spirit (2 Pt 1:20–21), and in these latter days through His Son, Jesus Christ (Heb 1:1–2). The prophets, guided by the Spirit of Christ, pointed to Christ's suffering and glory for us (1 Pt 1:10–12). The same Spirit who moved the prophets and apostles to record God's revelation continues to guide the reader of Scripture today. The Holy Spirit, the Spirit of Truth, sent by the Father and the Son to us, takes the words of Christ and declares them to us (Jn 16:12–15). By this same Holy Spirit we confess Christ as Lord (1 Cor 12:3) and preach the good news to others (1 Pt 1:12). For these reasons the language of faith, as opposed to the language of reason, is always maximally Christological in both doctrine and worship. This is especially true when discussing the Trinity. We know the Father only through the Son by the Holy Spirit. Any speaking or worshipping of God in which it is possible for the person to indicate what is meant by God and to specify things known of God without reference to Jesus is contrary to the pattern of Scripture and unavoidably susceptible to idolatry. Here doctrine and confession unite. Doctrine, as argued in chapter 1, protects our right speaking and worship of God; it disciplines, as Nicholas Lash puts it, "our propensity toward idolatry." Lash continues, "Idolatry is a matter of getting the reference wrong: of taking that to be God which is not

---

1. John Duns Scotus, *God and Creatures: The Quodlibetal Questions*, trans. Felix Alluntis and Allan B. Wolter (Princeton: Princeton University Press, 2015), 3.

God."[2] This happens when we attempt to speak of God apart from the man Jesus, and therefore apart from the way in which God spoke to us.[3]

In the *Heidelberg Disputation* Luther identifies two types of theologians, the theologian of the cross (*theologus crucis*) and the theologian of glory (*theologus gloriae*). Behind this distinction lies the question of how a person arrives at authentic knowledge of God. The *theologus crucis* speaks according to God's self-communication in Jesus Christ, which means that God's revelation sets the terms for the discussion—both its possibility and its limits. The *theologus gloriae*, on the other hand, speaks according to natural knowledge and the created effects of God. Problems arise for the *theologus gloriae* when it comes to the cross and suffering, and this, according to Luther, further entails works righteousness and idolatry. Our previous chapters have established the fact that no neutral doctrine of God exists apart from worship and ethics. The question we need to pursue here is how we rightly know God and speak about Him.

How does the *theologus gloriae* achieve knowledge of God? According to Luther this theologian relies upon human reason to arrive at reasonable conclusions about God and man. The *theologus gloriae* observes that man possesses such attributes as being, love, goodness, and justice among other things, and that reasonable people assign similar attributes to God (e.g., God is, God loves, God is good and just, etc.). How are these things predicated of God and man? Two issues are at work here. First, how do we know and name things (term, definition, instance)? For example, what does "love" mean? How do we define it? Why do we define it the way we do? Second, in what sense do God and man share these attributes? When we say God loves or I love, are we using the term in the same way? The *theologus gloriae* reasonably assumes that humans resemble God After all, we are made in the image and likeness of God.[4] Therefore, concludes the *theologus gloriae*, every perfection we possess finds its source and cause in God, in whom all of our perfections exist in a more eminent way (*via eminentiae*). The task before such a theologian is to ascend from what is known of creation to God. This is done by use of analogy which asserts that a similarity prevails between the "love" God is and our "love," or between the "being" God is and our "being." Piety constrains such a theologian to speak of this similarity in terms of an always greater dissimilarity (*maior dissimilitudo*), maintaining

---

2. Nicholas Lash, "When Did the Theologians Lose Interest in Theology?" in *The Beginning and End of 'Religion'* (Cambridge: Cambridge University Press, 1996), 133.

3. The liturgy serves as our corrective. In the liturgy we speak back to God His words and promises. When theological discourse moves away from the sound pattern of words found in the liturgy, from the doxology of the faithful, from baptism, trouble always lurks.

4. The alternative theological anthropologies underlying medieval theology and Lutheran theology depart significantly on how to understand the terms "image and likeness" and the debilitating effects of sin upon our "image and likeness." These alternative anthropologies lead to divergent understandings of grace and justification. Despite the efforts of many, you cannot reconcile Lutheranism and scholasticism without doing harm to both.

the distinction between God and creation, between the infinite and the finite.[5]

Most theologians acknowledge the need for analogy to speak and think about God. Moreover, Scripture plainly asserts that God and man possess attributes under the same name.[6] The problem with the *theologus gloriae* lies not with his appeal to analogy but with the poor manner in which he uses it. The proper use of analogy stands behind Luther's description of a *theologus gloriae* who looks to the *invisibilia* of creation to deduce an understanding of God. Luther only suggests how this happens in the *Heidelberg Disputation*. In Thesis 19 he states, "That person does not deserve to be a theologian who looks upon the invisible things of God as though they were clearly perceptible through those things that have been made" (*per ea, quae facta sunt*).[7] The Latin at the end of Thesis 19 indicates that Luther has in mind Rom 1:20 and natural knowledge of God.[8] Those who concentrate their efforts on the invisible things of God, which Luther identifies as power, godliness, wisdom, and goodness, do not deserve the name theologian. These individuals are not wise but foolish because they claim to see the invisible.

The foolishness of those who gaze upon the *invisibilia* is seen in how they construct a doctrine of God. They look upon the visible creation and assert by analogy all sorts of things that must be fitting for the invisible God. These analogies always begin with us as subject and proceed to God as object. The formula is always the same: whatever quality or virtue we identify among rational creatures that we think it good to have, we assign to God with one important qualification—God must have this more eminently than we do. God becomes just like us, only greater: we are wise, God is eminently wise (omniscient); we are powerful, God is eminently powerful (omnipotent), etc. God becomes the biggest thing around. The problem with this way of thinking is not the assertion that God is supremely wise or powerful, but that our wisdom and power is the measure of God's wisdom and power.[9] Our wisdom knows

---

5. Fourth Lateran, 1215, canon 2: "Quia inter creatorem et creaturam non potest tanta similitudo notari, quin inter eos maior sit dissimilitudo notanda" ("For between creator and creature there can be noted no similarity so great that a greater dissimilarity cannot be seen between them"). *Decrees of the Ecumenical Councils*, ed. Norman P. Tanner (Washington, D.C.: Georgetown University Press, 1990), 1:232.34–35.

6. Francis Pieper gives the following list: "Being (God is, Is 48:12; men are, Acts 17:28); life (God lives, Ez 14:16; man lives, Gn 3:20); love (God loves, Jn 3:16; man loves, 1 Kgs 5:1); justice (God is just, Rom 3:26; man is just, Mt 1:19); sight (God sees, Gn 1:31; man sees, Dt 32:52); etc." Pieper, *Christian Dogmatics* (St. Louis: Concordia Publishing House, 1950), 1:431.

7. *Heidelberg Disputation*, 1520 (WA 1:354.17; cf. AE 31:40); my translation.

8. Thesis 19 reads, "Non ille digne Theologus dicitur, qui invisibilia Dei per ea, quae facta sunt, intellecta conspicit" (WA 1:354.17). Romans 1:20 (Vulg.) reads, "Invisibilia enim ipsius a creatura mundi per ea, quae facta sunt intellecta conspiciuntur" ("For the invisible things of [God] are seen from the creation of the world, understood through those things that have been made").

9. Cf. Irenaeus of Lyons, *Against Heresies*, 2.13.4 (ACW, 43): "He may well and correctly be called a Mind that comprehends all things; but his Mind is not like the mind of men and women. He may most correctly be called Light, but he is nothing like our light. In the same manner

nothing of the Lord of Glory being crucified (1 Cor 2:8); our understanding of power has nothing to do with weakness and suffering (2 Cor 12:9). Reason cannot look upon the crucified Christ and see the wisdom and power of God (1 Cor 1:18, 24, 30). While the human wisdom of the *theologus gloriae* may sound reasonable enough to the philosopher, the scriptural theologian cannot proceed in this way. According to Scripture, it is this sort of human wisdom that God "destroys" and "thwarts" by His unexpected saving acts (1 Cor 1:19).

How did the medieval schoolmen understand our language for God? This is the question we will pursue in the rest of the chapter. We begin with Thomas and his formal description of analogy, and then look in detail at the alternative understanding of human language by John Duns Scotus. It is not misleading to say that these two distinct views of language explain the radical differences in how people talk about God in our day. Following our discussion of analogy part 1 concludes by returning to the Fathers to show the Lutheran approach to knowledge of God, how we responsibly discuss the scriptural identity of the Trinity, and the proper location of such discussions. In what follows we will mostly agree with Thomas Aquinas. Given our critique of him in chapter 3, this moment of agreement many confuse the reader. We agree with him because not everything he wrote stands opposed to Scripture. Our Lutheran dogmaticians leaned heavily upon Thomas in their discussions of the Trinity; they did not follow him blindly. At times they criticized him; more often they praised him. It would be much easier for us if everything Thomas said was wrong: we could dismiss him and move on—but this is not the case. The dogmaticians did not think so, and neither should we. Thomas fascinates because he says many things that are in agreement with Scripture; he frustrates because he departs from Scripture at critical points. That fact should be a lesson for us all: the greatest human minds are still fallen and sinful minds—a point Thomas himself makes.[10]

TYPES OF PREDICATION

There are three ways to account for our shared language about God and man. When we use terms such as "being," "love," "justice," etc. for God and for man, our language is either univocal, equivocal, or analogical.[11] Univocal predication means that when the same term is used of God and man that term is used in a common way. When we say the building is tall and the man is tall, we use "tall" to refer to the same thing, even if the building and the man are in obvious ways quite different. So too when we say God loves and man loves, or God is

---

in regard to all the other points, the Father of all things is in no way similar to humankind's littleness."

10. Thomas Aquinas *ST* I.1.8 ad 2.
11. Aristotle was the first to offer a technical discussion of analogy in his *Metaphysics*. This discussion was again taken up during the medieval period. Thomas Aquinas's commentary on the *Metaphysics* and his discussion of analogy in his *Summa Theologiae* (I.12–13) have been the chief statements on analogy engaged by friend and foe since.

and man is, we would be using "love" and "being" to refer to the same thing or concept, even if the subjects of those predicates differ significantly. The language of tallness, like that of love and being, is used univocally. The chief difficulty with univocity, a difficulty that will require explanation by anyone maintaining such a position, is how to avoid reducing God to that of His creation. Univocal predication always threatens God's transcendence and immanence.[12]

Equivocal predication asserts inequality and dissimilarity between God and His creation. God "is," but in a manner totally unlike man; God "loves," but in a manner totally unlike man. The meaning is equivocal, even if the same term is used. The word "bark" can describe the sound a dog makes or that which covers the outside of a tree. The word bears two unrelated meanings, referring either to dog or to tree. And yet neither reference captures what we mean when we sing, "Thou art my Anchor when by woe / My bark is driven to and fro / On trouble's surging billows" (TLH 142:5). In all three cases the context determines the meaning of bark. We know that a dog, a tree, and a small boat are not the same thing and do not confuse the use of the word "bark" in reference to them. Although on the surface this way of talking about God may seem appealing to a *theologus crucis*, it is really just the opposite. Equivocal predication retreats to a self-constructed radical apophaticism, a perverse form of a *theologia gloriae*, by undermining and neglecting the fact that God has revealed Himself to us through the certain words of Scripture.[13] God has made use of human language to communicate to us who He is as Father, Son, and Holy Spirit and what He has done for us. The pattern here is not all that different from God making use of water, bread, and wine to convey forgiveness of sins and eternal life. Equivocal predication, despite its pious posture, accuses God of deception by rendering His scriptural revelation insufficient and therefore meaningless.[14] It spiritualizes everything and retreats to its own self-made Gnosticism.

The final option, analogical predication, seeks an alternative way of speaking that neither collapses the meaning of terms (univocity) nor renders them meaningless (equivocity). Moreover, analogical predication neither reduces God to the level of creation (univocity) nor removes Him altogether

---

12. Cf. John Theodore Mueller, *Christian Dogmatics* (St. Louis: Concordia Publishing House, 1934), 162: "If we ascribe the essence and attributes to God and creatures univocally (Duns Scotus, d. 1308), the essential difference between God and the creatures is denied, and the creatures are coordinated with God and made divine (pantheism)."

13. Thomas Aquinas *ST* I.13.5c: "Neither, on the other hand, are names applied to God and creatures in a purely equivocal sense, as some have said. Because if that were so, it follows that from creatures nothing could be known or demonstrated about God at all; for the reasoning would always be exposed to the fallacy of equivocation." Our Lutheran dogmaticians frequently quote this statement from Thomas. See for example Abraham Calov, *Systema Locorum Theologicorum* (Wittenberg, 1655), 2:196–97; Johann Andreas Quenstedt, *Systema Theologicum*, I, 8 (Wittenberg, 1691), 295; David Hollaz, *Examen Theologicum Acroamaticum*, I, 1, Q. 18 (Leipzig, 1763), 231.

14. Cf. Mueller, *Christian Dogmatics*, 162: "If we ascribe the essence and attributes to God and creatures equivocally (Peter Aureolos, d. 1321; the Franciscans), it is impossible for us to know God (agnosticism), since then we cannot tell what really the attributes in God mean."

from it (equivocity).¹⁵ The way we understand and use language in reference to God has important theological consequences. During the medieval period Thomas Aquinas set forth a clear argument for analogical predication, and John Duns Scotus for univocal predication.¹⁶

Thomas Aquinas

Thomas Aquinas (1225-74) explains the mechanics of analogy toward the beginning of his *Summa Theologiae*. In the treatise on God he asks how God is known by us (*ST* I.12) and how He is named by us (*ST* I.13).¹⁷ The names

---

15. Cf. Mueller, *Christian Dogmatics*, 162: "If we ascribe the essence and attributes to God by way of analogy, or resemblance, then in our contemplation of God we rise from the imperfection of the human attributes to the absolute perfection of the divine, Is. 49, 15."

16. The clearest discussion of this issue among the Lutheran dogmaticians can be found with Abraham Calov, Johann Andreas Quenstedt, and David Hollaz. See Calov, *Systema Locorum Theologicorum* (Wittenberg, 1655), 2:195-98; Johann Andreas Quenstedt, *Systema Theologicum*, I, 8 (Wittenberg, 1691), 293-96; David Hollaz, *Examen Theologicum Acroamaticum*, I, 1, Q. 18 (Leipzig, 1763), 231-32. The Lutheran dogmaticians express their agreement with Thomas Aquinas and distance themselves from Scotus's univocity and the Reformed equivocity (e.g., Polanus, *Syntagmatis Theologiae Christianiae*, II, 3 [Hanoviae, 1610], col. 859). Quenstedt states the question clearly: "Whether essence, substance, spirit, and any other [shared] attribute of God and rational creatures ought to be predicated univocally, equivocally, or analogically" (293). Quenstedt states his position: "Essence, substance, spirit, and the remaining attributes ascribed to God and creatures alike are neither predicated univocally nor equivocally but analogically such that they are applied to God primarily and absolutely and to creatures secondarily and dependently" (293). At this point Quenstedt and the other dogmaticians engage in the history of interpretation on Thomas Aquinas, showing a particular awareness of the work by Thomas de Vio (Cardinal Cajetan) and Francisco Suárez. Immediately following the above quote from Quenstedt he writes, "Thus the analogy (*analogia*) is properly said to be of intrinsic attribution (*attributionis intrinsecae*)" (293). Quenstedt offers a brief summary of Cajetan's three types of analogies: the *analogia inaequalitatis*, *analogia proportionalitatis*, and *analogia attributionis* (294). Cajetan rejected *analogia inaequalitatis* as nothing more than equivocity, and *analogia attributionis* as not really being an analogy. The example he gives to demonstrate *analogia attributionis* is the one below from Aristotle that Thomas Aquinas uses to show what analogy is and how it works. In that sense Cajetan rejects Thomas's understanding of analogy and embraces *analogia proportionalitatis*. Quenstedt affirms only *analogia attributionis* which may be either intrinsic or extrinsic (294). It is said to be intrinsic when the analogy applies both to God and the creature inwardly or intrinsically. It is said of God properly but of the creature secondarily and derivatively in the sense that the creature is wholly dependent upon God (294). Quenstedt's distinction between intrinsic and extrinsic attribution comes from Suárez and the Jesuits from the University of Coimbra, the *Conimbricenses* as he calls them.

The Lutheran dogmaticians aligned themselves with Thomas's understanding of analogy over against Scotus's univocity and the Reformed equivocity. Whether they departed unwittingly from Thomas in engaging in the discussions of analogy by Cajetan and Suárez, something everyone in the seventeenth century did, falls outside our purpose here. Our aim in this chapter is to return to Thomas and Scotus to understand what they were saying and how they understood the reference of our words in talking about God and His creation.

For a helpful discussion of Quenstedt and Hollaz on analogy see Robert Preus, *The Theology of Post-Reformation Lutheranism* (St. Louis: Concordia Publishing House, 1972), 2:39-45.

17. For a more detailed discussion of Thomas and analogy see Bruce Marshall, "Christ the End of Analogy," *The Analogy of Being*, ed. Thomas Joseph White (Grand Rapids: Eerdmans, 2011), 280-313.

predicated of both God and His creatures are to be understood analogically.[18] Thomas uses the Aristotelian example of "healthy" (*sanus*) to demonstrate what analogy is and is not. Healthy is said of a person as the subject of health, of medicine as cause, and of urine as sign. Although the term does not have the same meaning for all three (thus not univocal), it retains "an ordered dependence" in its various uses and is therefore analogous (thus not equivocal).[19] In each case the referent for the term is the person and that person's health. Therefore, healthy is predicated of medicine and urine "in relation and proportion" to the person.[20] What gives conceptual content to the term? It is the health *of the person*. Remove the person from the discussion and the reader has no idea "for what or for whom" medicine is healthy as cause and urine is healthy as sign. Thomas explains, "In names predicated of many in an analogical sense, all are predicated because they have reference to some one thing; and this one thing must be placed in the definition of them all."[21] Remove the "one thing," the point of reference, and the terms lack meaning.

Analogies have three parts: the *ratio* or conceptual content, a subject who possesses the *ratio* primarily or "in a prior way" (*per prius*), and an object who possesses the *ratio* secondarily or "in a posterior way" (*per posterius*).[22] In the example before us, healthy is the *ratio* said primarily of the person and secondarily of medicine and urine. The point that must be stressed here is that the *ratio* of an analogous term applied *per posterius* depends upon the *per prius* for its particular meaning. The reason is that health "exists" only in the person, not in medicine or urine. Further, as the present example makes clear, not all analogies involve a causal or ontological relationship. The person is not the cause of health for medicine and medicine does not possess health as part of its being.

Furthermore, the order of naming does not necessarily correspond to the order of being. Bruce Marshall explains, "As a cause of health, medicine is ontologically prior to its effect, namely, health in an animal. But we put 'animal health' in the definition of 'medicine,' in this case naming the cause from the effect."[23] The reason for this naming of the cause from the effect is that we "name" as we "know." Thomas explains, "We can give a name to anything in as far as we can understand it."[24] This means that "the thing known is in the knower according to the mode of the knower."[25] It follows that the knowledge

---

18. Thomas Aquinas *ST* I.13.5c.
19. Marshall, "Christ the End of Analogy," 286.
20. Thomas Aquinas *ST* I.13.5c.
21. Thomas Aquinas *ST* I.13.6c.
22. Thomas Aquinas *ST* I.13.6c: "Et quia *ratio* quam significat nomen, est definitio, ut dicitur in IV Metaphys., necesse est quod illud nomen *per prius* dicatur de eo quod ponitur in definitione aliorum, et *per posterius* de aliis, secundum ordinem quo appropinquant ad illud primum vel magis vel minus."
23. Marshall, "Christ the End of Analogy," 291.
24. Thomas Aquinas *ST* I.13.1c.
25. Thomas Aquinas *ST* I.12.4c.

of every knower is according to the knower's nature. For this reason, explains Marshall, we know and name things (both material and divine) "in a manner different from that in which they actually exist."[26] This pattern is seen with medicine. In the order of being, as a cause of health, medicine is prior; in the order of naming and knowing the order is reversed: the cause follows its effect. For example, there likely exists a medicinal plant today that is yet unknown to us and therefore is not yet named by us as a cause of health. It is simply a plant that has no medicinal significance *for me*. My lack of knowing and naming does not, however, change the character of that plant as a cause of health. Until the effect is known the cause will not be known and named.

At this point we are better able to assess what a *theologus gloriae* means when he seeks to correlate attributes between God and man. To say that God is good or God is wise is to say something about God's goodness and wisdom, and therefore to assert something about God's essence or reality. The attributes assigned to God belong to Him by nature and to us through His gracious gift of them.[27] Marshall explains,

> In the order of being, that is, these perfections belong first to God, and only derivatively to creatures. But we can name God only from creatures. When we seek to know God analogically, the terms we use inevitably apply, in the order of naming, primarily to creatures and derivatively to God. In Thomas' vocabulary for analogy, we apply perfection *terms* to creatures *per prius* and to God *per posterius*, even though the *perfections* we are referring to exist first of all in God, and only derivatively in creatures.[28]

The creaturely limitations of our knowing and naming mean that when we speak of God with unaided human reason, which is only to say apart from Scripture, God's attributes can be understood only ever in terms of our own possession and experience of such attributes. We may piously assert that God possesses these attributes "truly" or "more eminently," but this linguistic maneuver only masks the truth that our point of reference for who God is in His essence is ourselves. The technical term used by Thomas to describe this point of reference for analogy is "mode of signification" (*modus significandi*). Every "ratio" has a mode of signification. When we use "good" and "wise" to describe God and man analogically, we say that the "rationes" are diverse (not univocal) but ordered to one (analogical and not equivocal).[29] This means that when we name something in God (wise, good, powerful, etc.), we can do so only ever from a creaturely mode of signification. The only way a *theologus gloriae* can say God is wise or powerful is from the vantage point of his own creaturely wisdom or power. God's wisdom can be envisioned only ever in terms of created wisdom; God's power can be envisioned only ever in terms of created power.

---

26. Marshall, "Christ the End of Analogy," 291.
27. Thomas Aquinas *ST* I.13.5c.
28. Marshall, "Christ the End of Analogy," 295.
29. Thomas Aquinas *ST* I.13.5c; Marshall, "Christ the End of Analogy," 296.

Thomas states this plainly: "No name can be applied to God according to its mode of signification."[30] Marshall explains,

> The mode of signifying of any *per posterius* use of an analogous term consists in some specific relation to the primary *ratio*, or meaning. So when we say "God is good" *per posterius*—the only way we can—we have to include in what we mean by "good" a reference to some sort of created goodness, as caused, exemplified, or perfected by God. Even when we intend to leave creatures and their derivative goodness behind and speak only of God's goodness, we cannot. Whatever meaning "good" has for us when applied to God depends on its reference to a specific *per prius*: created goodness. The same goes for all other perfection terms, that is, for any term we can apply to God *proprie*, rather than in a simply metaphorical way.[31]

All of this means that when the natural man, the *theologus gloriae*, attempts to ascend to God through the *invisibilia*, he can do so only ever by knowing and naming God according to his own created reality. God becomes greater than what we think and know of ourselves. The end result is a constructed idolatry. The *theologus gloriae* of course would deny such a charge and would suggest that he is talking about God's love or God's justice. As desirable as such a move might be, it cannot be done by means of analogy. When the point of reference, the mode of signification, is man or any other created reality, we are talking not about God properly but about ourselves and our world.

Thomas's understanding of language and the incomprehensibility of God's essence was contested and emended by both friend and foe. John Duns Scotus, who offers a different theological vision than that of Thomas and subsequent Thomism, is best known for his univocal understanding of being. It is with Scotus that an alternative trajectory to talking about God finds a firm foundation—which does not mean that Scotus is the first to claim that the words used of God and man are univocal. As seen in chapter 2, Eunomius of Cyzicus asserted that we know as much about God's essence as He does, which is something that could be true only if the same words used of God and of man were univocal. It also should be said that the path set by Scotus was traversed by a variety of thinkers, many of whom would not have thought of themselves as indebted in any way to Scotism. For our purposes here it will be sufficient to show what this alternative theological vision is and how it elevates the significance of human speech and thought about God in a way that makes possible the philosophical theism of modernity.

John Duns Scotus

John Duns Scotus (c. 1265–1308) was a Franciscan friar who received his education at Oxford. He subsequently taught at both Oxford and Paris. Reading Scotus is not easy. His contemporaries dubbed him *doctor subtilis*, subtle

---

30. Thomas Aquinas *ST* I.13.12, ad 1.
31. Marshall, "Christ the End of Analogy," 297. A similar point is made in Ralph McInerny, *Aquinas and Analogy* (Washington, D.C.: Catholic University of America Press, 1996), 160–61.

doctor, because of the complexity of his thought. Richard Cross remarks that understanding Scotus is always a provisional matter.[32] Those opaque and obscure passages that litter his writings can suddenly, upon further consideration, yield meanings that force an interpreter to revise earlier conclusions. This is also what makes a figure like Scotus such a fascinating person to read, the difficulties and subtleties notwithstanding. Scotus is without question the most significant medieval theologian after Thomas Aquinas. Although he has a good deal in common with Thomas, he also advances his own particular theological vision that moves in a decidedly different direction.[33] The places of disagreement evoke the most interest.

We see Scotus's subtlety and complexity especially in his discussion of God. That God is Trinity cannot be known by natural reason.[34] We can know, however, God's existence and something about His essence by natural reason. It is in his explanation of how we know this or why we know this that we begin to appreciate the distinctiveness of his thinking. God's existence is not known in the a priori manner pursued by Anselm. Scotus favored Thomas's method, which is itself a shared commitment to Aristotelian empiricism, that God's existence can be known through a posteriori arguments. The difficulty faced by all of these medieval thinkers, and indeed anyone pursuing these questions of how we know God, is how finite creatures, limited by their own creaturely realities, attain knowledge of a transcendent God through the medium of their own creaturely patterns of thought and speech. Thomas resolved this difficulty by arguing that natural reason knows the existence of God as a preamble of the articles of faith but not what God is positively, only what He is not. Scotus, on the other hand, wished to say more than this: he wanted to argue that some positive knowledge of God's essence could be known by natural reason.[35]

Scotus was far more indebted to Aristotle on the acquisition of human knowledge than Thomas. For Scotus all people acquire knowledge through sense experience by forming concepts of the material substances or essences around us (quiddities). The problem we face is how our human concepts can arrive at knowledge of a supernatural or transcendent being. Scotus argued that the only way we can do this is by having a concept that is not restricted to the material world of creation but is common to the infinite and finite, the immaterial and material. And we do. The concept is "being," and it is univocal when used of God and of man. Without this concept, argues Scotus, we would be unable to achieve any knowledge of God in this life.

---

32. Richard Cross, *Duns Scotus* (Oxford: Oxford University Press, 1999), xi.

33. Although Scotus's thought often is placed in distinction to his most significant predecessors (Anselm, Bonaventure, and Thomas Aquinas), his work is concerned mostly with a lesser known contemporary, Henry of Ghent. See Stephen Dumont, "Henry of Ghent and Duns Scotus," in *Medieval Philosophy: Routledge History of Philosophy*, ed. John Merenbon (London: Routledge, 1998), 3:291–328.

34. Others in Scotus's day thought the Trinity could be known by natural reason. His denial is no mere formality but a stern rebuke of their ambitious efforts.

35. Dumont, "Henry of Ghent," 298.

Scotus arrives at this conclusion after much work. He asks "whether the intellect of man in this life is able to know God naturally."[36] Before answering this question he makes a number of preliminary observations. There is no need to make the distinction that we cannot know what God is, only what He is not. Scotus explains, "Every denial is intelligible only in terms of some affirmation." In order to deny something of God we must first know something of Him. He continues, "If we deny anything of God, it is because we wish to do away with something inconsistent with what we have already affirmed."[37] Likewise, there is no reason to distinguish between knowledge of God's essence and knowledge of His existence. Scotus follows a similar logic as above. In the same way that denial of something assumes some prior affirmation of that thing, existence assumes essence. He explains, "I intend to seek a simple concept (*conceptum simplicem*) of which existence may be affirmed or denied by a judgment of the intellect. For I never know anything to exist unless I first have some concept (*aliquem conceptum*) of that of which existence is affirmed."[38] Existence must be predicated of a subject, therefore distinguishing between existence and essence is misleading. To know the existence of something requires some positive knowledge of that subject of which existence is predicated. After making these two points, Scotus narrows his initial question about natural knowledge of God. He writes, "The meaning of the question, then, is this: 'Is it possible by natural means for man's intellect in the present life to have a simple concept in which concept God is grasped?'"[39] The narrowing of the initial question raises the stakes considerably for Scotus.[40] Since he already established that negation (saying what God is not) depends upon prior affirmation (what God is), he must now find something to affirm about God that is a positive concept. If he fails to do this, then according to the demands of his own argument he would render any natural knowledge of God impossible.[41]

Scotus turns next to the issue of language and predication. For starters Scotus maintains that it is possible to have a concept in which God is known not only accidentally (for instance, under the aspect of an attribute) but also essentially (*per se et quidditative*).[42] He uses the example of "wise" to make his point. When we say God is wise, we must have some prior notion of the subject to which we predicate wise. It is this prior notion, this quidditative concept, to which "wise" is attributed that we must seek.[43] When we use the word "wise,"

---

36. *Opus oxnoniense*, I, d. 3, pars I, q. I, trans. Allan Wolter, *Duns Scotus: Philosophical Writings* (Indianapolis: Hackett, 1987), 14. Wolter provides both English and Latin; all Latin references are to the same book.
37. Wolter, *Duns Scotus*, 15.
38. Wolter, *Duns Scotus*, 16.
39. Wolter, *Duns Scotus*, 17.
40. William Mann, "Duns Scotus on Natural and Supernatural Knowledge of God," in *Cambridge Companion to Duns Scotus* (Cambridge: Cambridge University Press, 2002), 240.
41. Cf. Wolter, *Duns Scotus*, 20.
42. Wolter, *Duns Scotus*, 19.
43. In this section Scotus further distinguishes between attribute and quasi-attribute. The

we take it from the world around us. We observe wisdom in some people and declare that that person is wise. Moreover, we find this attribute desirable. It is better to be wise than foolish. We further observe that there are degrees to wisdom. Some people are more wise than others in the same way that some are more foolish than others. From this we conclude that God too is wise, but in a manner that is in part both different and similar. It is different in that wise people arrive at wisdom through deliberation. It is a temporal process. God's wisdom works differently. He knows without deliberation, without time. Furthermore, although we observe degrees of wisdom among different people, indeed a wise person even theoretically can become wiser, God's wisdom is perfect.

As emphasized above, Thomas resolved this way of talking by appealing to analogy. When we ascribe "wise" to God, drawn as it is from our creaturely experiences, we do so only analogically. Scotus found this way of thinking and speaking confusing. He proceeds by arguing that a concept is either univocal or equivocal. When we identify a person as wise and God as wise, we are using "wise" either univocally or equivocally. Why not also analogically? Here we have to be careful or we will miss Scotus's nuance. Terms may be used analogically to refer to God but not in a sense that excludes univocity. Scotus writes, "I say that God is conceived not only in a concept analogous to the concept of a creature, that is, one which is wholly other than that which is predicated of creatures, but even in some concept univocal to himself and to a creature (*in conceptu aliquo univoco sibi et creaturae*)."[44] Scotus does not deny analogical predication but rather denies that analogical predication works without some prior univocal concept. If we exclude the prior univocal concept, then analogical predication is simply equivocation.[45] The example used by Scotus is "being." He explains,

> Every intellect that is certain about one concept, but dubious about others has, in addition to the concepts about which it is in doubt, another concept of which it is certain. (The subject includes the predicate). Now, in this life already, a man can be certain in his mind that God is a being and still be in doubt whether he is a finite or an infinite being, a created or an uncreated being. Consequently, the concept of "being" as affirmed of God is different from the other two concepts but is included in both of them and therefore is univocal.[46]

The two alternatives given by Scotus, being and infinite/finite being, represent two distinct things: being and the degree to which that being is infinite. Certainty rests with the concept of being, uncertainty with whether God is infinite or finite. In this example the concept "being" grounds the intrinsic mode of that being as either infinite or finite. Scotus here labors to prevent the idea that infinite being corresponds to substance and accident. Infinity is not

---

distinction is subtle, and although quite important for appreciating all that Scotus has to say here, it is beyond our present purpose to pursue it. See Mann, "Duns Scotus," 243–45.

44. Wolter, *Duns Scotus*, 19.
45. Mann, "Duns Scotus," 246–47.
46. Wolter, *Duns Scotus*, 20.

an attribute or property of being or of that of which it is predicated. Scotus explains, "Rather it signifies an intrinsic mode of that entity, so that when I say 'Infinite Being,' I do not have a concept composed accidentally, as it were, of a subject and its attribute. What I do have is a concept of what is essentially one, namely of a subject with a certain grade of perfection (*in certo gradu perfectionis*)—infinity."[47] The idea of grades of perfection informs the way Scotus thinks about the other "pure perfections" attributed to God. He follows Anselm on this point, and writes, "With regard to everything except relations, whatever is unconditionally better than something which is not it, must be attributed to God, even as everything not of this kind must be denied of him. According to Anselm, then, we first know something to be a pure perfection and secondly we attribute this perfection to God."[48]

When natural reason thinks about God, it proceeds first with the formal notion of something, such as wisdom or power. All creaturely imperfections are removed from the notion and the ultimate degree of perfection ascribed to it. We then attribute the notion to God. Richard Cross calls this Scotus's "divine modification."[49] This move depends upon the intellect having "the same univocal concept which it obtained from creatures."[50] Through the exercise of natural reason we take the concept of "wise," remove all creaturely imperfections, give it the highest degree of perfection which we call omniscience, and then assign this to God. The same procedure applies to all the other perfections, all the other things we identify as better to have than not to have. Cross concludes, "The difference between God and creatures, at least with regard to God's possession of the pure perfections, is ultimately one of degree. Specifically, the perfections exist in an infinite degree in God, and in a finite degree in creatures."[51]

There is a further consequence to note with Scotus's theory of univocity. In one of his last writings he takes up the question "whether it is the essential or the notional that is more immediate to the divine essence."[52] Scotus begins with definitions. When applied to God, the essential includes those things common to all three persons because of the shared divine essence; the notional are those characteristic only of one or two of the persons, such as generation or procession.[53] Following this distinction Scotus raises the issue of pure perfections as observed above. He again appeals to Anselm to state that God must be, absolutely speaking, whatever it is better to be than not to be.[54] He

---

47. Wolter, *Duns Scotus*, 27.
48. Wolter, *Duns Scotus*, 24. Anselm, *Monoslogion*, 15 in Davies and Evans, *Anselm of Canterbury*, 28. On Scotus's somewhat ambivalent use of Anselm on this point throughout his whole corpus see Richard Cross, *Duns Scotus on God* (Burlington, VT: Ashgate, 2005), 50–51.
49. Cross, *Duns Scotus* (1999), 32.
50. Wolter, *Duns Scotus*, 25.
51. Cross, *Duns Scotus* (1999), 39.
52. Scotus, *God and Creatures*, 5–30.
53. Scotus, *God and Creatures*, 9–10. This is a helpful distinction with scriptural warrant and one used throughout the tradition. More will be said about this distinction in part 3.
54. Scotus, *God and Creatures*, 12.

then appeals to the distinction between essential and notional features in God in order to limit the pure perfections to those things that do not involve relation.[55] After making this move, he concludes that the essential features are prior to the notional in a logical sense. He writes, "Now the first notional element (at least that which includes the first positive relation to a person) is that of speaking [the Word]." The speaking of the Word, the generation of the Word, is a notional element referring only to the Son. The question Scotus is pursuing is whether there is something more immediate to the divine essence than this first notional element. He believes there is, and continues, "Therefore, something essential . . . is more immediate to the essence than is the first notional element, and hence is more immediate than any notional element whatsoever."[56] Scotus's conclusion proceeds from a logical distinction between what belongs to all three persons and what is particular to one or two of the persons. This distinction allows him to speak far more positively about the essential features of the divine essence apart from the personal relations that avail between the Father, Son, and Holy Spirit. By abstracting the pure perfections from relations, explicitly excluding anything that involves relation, and by insisting upon a theory of univocity, Scotus has made possible the philosophical theism that will flower fully during the seventeenth century and that continues to plague our discussions of God today. He has given Luther's *theologus gloriae* philosophical credibility and warrant.

Although Scotus consistently reminds his readers that there are things that human reason cannot know about God (that He is Trinity), natural reason is nonetheless able to know that God is a maximally excellent, perfect being, and that when we attribute such traits as wise, true, good, powerful, and so forth to both God and man we do so univocally. Stephen Dumont describes the effect of Scotus's argument: "By admitting a simple and univocal concept of being, Scotus provided a true conceptual community between God and creature and placed the project of natural knowledge of the divine nature on a firm epistemological footing."[57] That firm footing was the ability for Scotus to "conceptualize" God. Despite the subtle qualifications of his argument, Scotus brought the transcendent God within the confines of creation. As Robert Barron puts it, Scotus's way of thinking allowed God to be "mappable" along the same coordinates as creatures.[58]

Consequences of Univocity

Scotus's insistence on univocity has shaped the modern discussion of God in two significant ways. First, since something positive could be said of God's

---

55. This move follows the logic put forward by Anselm, *Monoslogion*, 15, in Davies and Evans, *Anselm of Canterbury*, 26–28.
56. Scotus, *God and Creatures*, 22.
57. Dumont, "Henry of Ghent," 313.
58. Robert Barron, *Priority of Christ: Toward a Postliberal Catholicism* (Grand Rapids: Brazos, 1997), 193.

essence by unaided reason, a way of talking about God emerged for Scotus that has been dubbed "perfect-being theology."[59] This way of talking proceeds from the distinction noted above between the essential and notional features of God. Since the essential features are logically prior to the notional, a person is able to speak of that which belongs to God's essence without reference to the persons. Although for Scotus this is only a logical distinction, and in his theological vision a useful way of talking about what pertains to God *qua* God and God *qua* Trinity, this distinction in less capable hands becomes the hallmark of modern philosophical theism—the abstraction of "God" from the scriptural revelation of God as three coequal and coeternal persons, Father, Son, and Holy Spirit. This way of talking suggests that the divine essence is anterior to the persons. The essential and notional, however, are not to be distinguished as primary and secondary. The divine persons are not a Sabellian addition to the divine essence but the irreducible reality of that essence. William Weinrich makes this point with great clarity: "There is no reality that we might call 'God' that is prior to God *as God the Father*; there is no reality that we might call 'God' that is prior to God *as God the Son*."[60] The persons are inseparable from the indivisible essence, and the essence is inseparable from the irreducible persons. Augustine expresses this point with grammatical precision: "Pater et filius et spiritus sanctus unus deus est" ("Father and Son and Holy Spirit *is* the one God").[61]

The second major consequence of Scotus's univocity of being concerns our thinking about God and where we locate Him in our formal theological judgments. This consequence, raised at the beginning of chapter 2 and momentous for understanding the soteriological difficulties attending so much of contemporary Christianity, is seen with the example of creation. Following the lead of the Fathers, Thomas Aquinas emphasized both difference and similarity between God as creator and His creation. He rejected any attempt to assign creator and creation univocally to the same philosophical category of being. God is not comparatively different but absolutely different. And yet amidst this radical difference there is similarity between God and creatures. How are we to express this difference and similarity? Thomas, like the Fathers, expresses this concept in terms of borrowed existence. God is *ipsum esse*, existence itself, and *esse subsistens*, His existence and essence necessarily coincide.[62] For God alone, writes Thomas, "existence and quiddity are one and the same."[63] Creatures are not beings that exist in their own right. Essence and existence do not coincide for us. We are not, as David Bentley Hart puts it, timeless essences that demand

---

59. Cross, *Duns Scotus* (1999), 31–32; Cross, *Duns Scotus on God* (2005), 49–54.
60. William Weinrich, "Trinitarian Reality as Christian Truth: Reflections on Greek Patristic Discussion," *Concordia Theological Quarterly* 67 no. 3/4 (2003): 338.
61. Augustine *The Trinity* I.12 (WSA I/5), 72.
62. Thomas Aquinas *ST* I.44.1c: "Deus est ipsum esse per se subsistens." Cf. Augustine *Confessions* 1, vi.10, trans. Henry Chadwick (Oxford: Oxford University Press, 1992), 8: "In you (God) it is not one thing to be and another to live: the supreme degree of being and the supreme degree of life are one and the same thing."
63. Thomas Aquinas *ST* I.44.1c: "Deus est ipsum esse per se subsistens."

existence.⁶⁴ We possess no actuality of our own. The synthesis of our essence and existence is pure gratuity from God. This means we have no natural claim to existence; we exist according to relation (*secundum relationem*).⁶⁵ That relation is toward God, our creator, who is the principle and cause of all things.⁶⁶ Only in Him do we live and move and have our being. This means for Thomas that God not only creates all things but sustains all things in existence. As God's creatures, our very existence, our being, depends upon our relation to God.⁶⁷ We do not exist of ourselves; we have no independent ground on which to claim existence. All existence is borrowed existence, as all that exists does so only in relation to the giver of life, Father, Son, and Holy Spirit.⁶⁸ Our very existence serves as a constant reminder of God's continued grace, mercy, and activity in our lives; indeed, it serves as a constant reminder of the pervasive dependence of all creation upon the Trinity.⁶⁹

Despite Thomas's preference to think of God in terms of causality, which involves him in other difficulties, as we have seen, it has the virtue of distancing him from the onto-theology that plagues Scotus and his intellectual heirs.⁷⁰ Scotus's insistence that the term "being" applies univocally to both God and creatures allowed people to talk differently about God and our borrowed existence or our dependence upon Him. Scotus's flattening of the category of "being" to include both God and man meant that man's being no longer required God for its definition. The insistence upon univocity effectively rends the dependence of the created order from God. It becomes possible to say that the created order exists in its own right, as much as God exists. This sort of

---

64. David Bentley Hart, "The Destiny of Christian Metaphysics: Reflections on the *Analogia Entis*," in *The Analogy of Being: Invention of the Antichrist or the Wisdom of God?* ed. Thomas Joseph White (Grand Rapids: Eerdmans, 2011), 397-99.

65. Thomas Aquinas *ST* I.45.3c. Augustine famously begins his *Confessions* with this very theme. See Augustine *Confessions* 1, ii.2.

66. Thomas Aquinas *ST* I.44.1c; *ST* I.13.6c.

67. Thomas Aquinas *ST* I.45.3 ad 1 and *ST* I.46.1.

68. Cf. Martin Luther, commenting on Jn 1:4 ("In him was the life"), says: "There is nothing here about a philosophical interpretation of the life of creatures in God; rather these words speak only of how God lives in us and makes us partakers of his life, and how we live through him and from him and in him. For it cannot be denied, that through him natural life exists, which even unbelievers have from him, as St. Paul says in Acts 17[:28]: 'In him we live and move and have our being and are of his kind.' Indeed, natural life is a part of eternal life and its beginning, but it ends through death because it does not acknowledge nor honor him from whom it comes. Sin cuts it off, so that it must die eternally. On the other hand, those who believe in him, and acknowledge him from whom they have their being never die. Their natural life will be stretched out into life eternal, so that they never taste death, as he says in John 8[:52]: 'He who keeps my words, will never taste death,' and in John 11[:25]: 'He who believes in me, even if he dies, will live.'" *Sermon on the Gospel for the Main Christmas Service*, 1522 (AE 52:55; WA 10/1.199.24-200.10).

69. For further discussion of this point see David Burrell, "Analogy, Creation, and Theological Language," *Proceedings of the American Catholic Philosophical Association* 74 (2000): 35-52.

70. For a thorough discussion of this issue see Jean-Luc Marion, "Thomas Aquinas and Onto-Theo-Logy," in *God Without Being*, 2d ed., trans. Thomas Carlson (Chicago: University of Chicago Press, 2012), 199-236.

thinking leads to the rupture between God and nature and the emergence of the natural sciences as an independent field of inquiry. The result is an autonomous, secular order divorced from God and His creative agency.

Modernity's rendering of God as an object of *our* intellective activity works because God and man belong to the same category of being. A pious retreat at this point to the claim that God is eminently more than we in the great chain of being offers very little. No longer is our being, our personhood and our freedom, understood only in relation to the Trinity and the gratuitous sharing of God's life with us in Christ by the Holy Spirit, but now God's essence and existence are mapped according to the way we understand ourselves. The result is God after our image, according to our sensibilities, and on our terms. God becomes the biggest thing around. A return to Thomism will not solve the problem; indeed the problems of Thomism gave rise to Scotus's critique. The answer rests with Luther and our Lutheran dogmaticians, which is in itself a return to the best insights of the Fathers.

THE NECESSITY OF UNLEARNING

Grand claims about what we know of God arose not with Scotus or with those who would exploit the epistemological foundation he secured. This problem emerged especially during the fourth-century Arian controversy. Eunomius of Cyzicus insisted that the human mind could comprehend and express with precision and completeness the very essence of God. Eunomius famously asserted, "God does not know anything more about his own essence than we do, nor is that essence better known to him and less to us. Rather, whatever we know about it is exactly what he knows, and conversely, what he knows is what you will find without change in us."[71] Basil of Caesarea disagreed: "Comprehension of God's substance transcends not only human beings, but also every rational nature."[72] Basil wonders how Eunomius can boast of knowing God's essence when Scripture tells us that "the peace of God passes all understanding" (Phil 4:7). How is it that God's peace passes understanding but not His essence? Basil returns to Scripture and declares, "No one knows the Father except the Son" (Mt 11:27), and "The Spirit searches everything, even the depths of God. For no one knows what belongs to a man except the spirit that is in him, and no one knows what belongs to God except the Spirit that is from God" (1 Cor 2:10–11).[73] According to the Scriptures the Father is known through the Son by the Holy Spirit. We do not supplement our best ideas about God with His revelation to us. Whatever we think we know, we must unlearn, repent of, that

---

71. Richard Vaggione, *Eunomius: The Extant Works* (Oxford: Oxford University Press, 1987), 178.

72. Basil of Caesarea *Against Eunomius* 1.14 (Fathers of the Church, 112).

73. Basil of Caesarea *Against Eunomius* 1.14 (Fathers of the Church, 112). Basil conflates 1 Cor 2:12 and 1 Cor 2:10. Rather than saying "except the Spirit of God," he has "except the Spirit that is from God."

we would rightly confess, according to our baptism, the Blessed Trinity.[74] For Basil, we must give up the knowledge derived from human teaching in order to receive divine instruction. He explains, "And making the heart ready for this means the unlearning of the teachings which already possess it, derived from evil habits. For it is no more possible to write in wax without first smoothing away the letters previously written thereon, than it is to supply the soul with divine teachings without first removing its preconceptions derived from habit."[75] We must know both the limit of our knowing and the necessity of Scripture, of God's revelation of Himself, for proper thinking, speaking, and praying.

We cannot cling to concepts of God derived from reason and build upon them. This is why the Fathers insisted that God was beyond being, which meant quite simply beyond definition, beyond the limits of our human concepts, transcending every category available to us. Gregory of Nyssa regards it idle speculation to assign any discrete conception to what is above all conception.[76] Augustine makes the same point: "We are talking about God; so why be surprised if you cannot grasp it? I mean, if you can grasp it, it isn't God. Let us rather make a devout confession of ignorance, instead of a brash profession of knowledge."[77] Again Augustine writes, "So what are we to say, brothers, about God? For if you have fully grasped what you want to say, it isn't God. If you have been able to comprehend it, you have comprehended something else instead of God. If you think you have been able to comprehend, your thoughts have deceived you."[78] Gregory of Nazianzus pursues a similar line of argument. He declares, "To tell of God is not possible," and "To know him is even less possible."[79] To suggest otherwise, for Gregory, is "to boast over infinity."[80] For Gregory, we are no more capable of exact knowledge of God's essence than we are of God's creation. Echoing Basil, Gregory writes, "For our part, not only does God's peace pass all thought and understanding with all the things stored up in promise for the righteous—things unseen by the eye, unheard by the ear (1 Cor 2:9), unthought, or at least but glimpsed by the mind—but so does exact

---

74. Basil of Caesarea *Letter* 91 (LCC, 2:131).
75. Basil of Caesarea *Letter* 2 (LCC, 1:11). Cf. Gregory of Nazianzus *Or.* 2.43 (NPNF, ii, 7, 443): "Accordingly, to impress the truth upon a soul when it is still fresh, like wax not yet subjected to the seal, is an easier task than inscribing pious doctrine on the top of inscriptions—I mean wrong doctrines and dogmas—with the result that the former are confused and thrown into disorder by the latter. It is better indeed to tread a road which is smooth and well trodden than one which is untrodden and rough, or to plough land which has often been cleft and broken up by the plough: but a soul to be written upon should be free from the inscription of harmful doctrines, or the deeply cut marks of vice: otherwise the pious inscriber would have a twofold task, the erasure of the former impressions and the substitution of others which are more excellent, and more worthy to abide."
76. Gregory of Nyssa *Letter* 35.3e in *Gregory of Nyssa: The Letters*, trans. Anna M. Silvas (Leiden: Brill, 2007), 252. Cf. *Letter* 24.5: "But their substance, whatever this is—for it is inexpressible in words and cannot be grasped in thought" (193).
77. Augustine *Sermon* 117.5 (WSA III/4, 211).
78. Augustine *Sermon* 52.6 (WSA III/3, 57).
79. Gregory of Nazianzus *Or.* 28.4 (PPS, 39).
80. Gregory of Nazianzus *Or.* 28.7 (PPS, 41).

knowledge of the creation as well."⁸¹ We know that nature exists, but possess only a bare outline of its reality.

When it comes to knowing who God is, two issues must be rightly understood. We must have a proper understanding of faith and reason, and a proper understanding of human language. Because we are corporeal creatures, even our most exalted language remains conditioned by elements of time and space. The very nature of our rational faculty excludes the possibility of ever knowing or speaking the full reality or essence of God. This is why no common notions or concepts derived from reason ever achieve a knowledge of God's very nature or the fullness of His reality. Gregory emphasizes two points throughout his discussion: "The Divine cannot be grasped by human understanding and the entirety of its greatness cannot even be imagined."⁸² God exceeds the grasp of our intellect because He surpasses our level of existence.⁸³ As Thomas emphasized above, the knowledge of every knower corresponds to the knower's nature. As finite creatures we measure and think in finite categories; God is not finite. He exceeds our creaturely abilities, our creaturely existence. He is beyond category. For this reason the language we use to talk of God, language drawn from our creaturely reality, is always provisional, always analogical. That point has been made above sufficiently with Thomas and Scotus. At this point we need to say something more about faith and reason and the proper location for authentic knowledge of the Trinity. Since Gregory's thought has been discussed at length in chapter 2 and the reader already has some familiarity with him, we will make use of him here as well.

Gregory's discussion of faith and reason is placed within a larger reflection on God's magnitude and greatness. Christopher Beeley explains, "For Gregory the incomprehensibility of God is the necessary result of the infinitude of God's being and the finitude of creaturely existence, including human thought."⁸⁴ Incomprehensibility results because of who God is and who we are. He is the creator and we the created. He necessarily surpasses all things in magnitude and greatness. And yet, as Beeley continues, "God is not merely greater than all things by degree, he is *infinitely* great, entirely transcending creation."⁸⁵ Gregory's point would be misunderstood if we thought this meant that God is known only vaguely because of His metaphysical otherness. God has made Himself known to us in Christ through the words of Scripture. Although these words proceed from our creaturely existence, although they correspond to our creaturely world, the Holy Spirit reassigns the content of these terms for faith. Meaning proceeds from God. The Scriptures declare, for example, that nothing

---

81. Gregory of Nazianzus *Or.* 28.5 (PPS, 40).
82. Gregory of Nazianzus *Or.* 28.11; translation from Christopher Beeley, *Gregory of Nazianzus on the Trinity and the Knowledge of God* (Oxford: Oxford University Press, 2008), 94.
83. Gregory of Nazianzus *Or.* 18.16.
84. Beeley, *Gregory of Nazianzus*, 94.
85. Beeley, *Gregory of Nazianzus*, 95; cf. Gregory of Nazianzus *Or.* 6.12 (Fathers of the Church, 12).

can separate us from the love of God in Christ Jesus (Rom 8:39), and this love which we know by the Holy Spirit (Rom 5:5) was made known in that Christ laid down His life for us (1 Jn 3:16). This love "surpasses knowledge" (Eph 3:19). This love has a depth known only by the Spirit of God (1 Cor 2:10–11). To be sure, we come to know this love that surpasses knowledge by faith, but since by faith only in part, in a mirror dimly.[86] These two points must remain together. First, we know this love with certainty and yet only in part. Second, our knowing proceeds from God's revelation. Scripture both makes possible our knowing and speaking and norms that very knowing and speaking.

For Gregory, we learn from Scripture what belongs to God's nature by hearing and seeing what God declares and does. Gregory writes, "We use facts connected with him to outline qualities that correspond with him, collecting a faint and feeble mental image from various quarters. Our noblest theologian is not one who has discovered the whole—our earthly shackles do not permit us the whole—but one whose mental image is by comparison fuller, who has gathered in his mind a richer picture, outline, or whatever we call it, of the truth."[87] In the same way that we cannot breathe in all the air there is to breathe in, a person cannot comprehend entirely in the mind or express completely in speech the being of God. The noble theologian seeks not the impossible but the possible. He receives from Scripture the truth about God, and this truth is fuller and richer than anything else that could be known. And yet this truth, grasped by faith, conveying that which is real through creaturely language, is still only partial. A greater depth remains. When we confess that we know in part, in a mirror dimly, or through a glass darkly, however we wish to express it, we are not confessing uncertainty. Nor are we confessing that "the more" that awaits our understanding when we shed our earthly shackles in anyway contradicts or undermines "the part" we know with certainty by faith. This is the truth we sing, in the words of Paul Gerhardt, "For God will show thee things above / Which here 'tis only given to hear of, and see darkly" (ELH 405:5; ELHB 264:5).

That there are things we cannot bear to know in full when we wish to know them is made plain by Christ. There are things the disciples needed to know but could not bear them before the crucifixion and resurrection. They knew in part but would know more when the Spirit came upon them (Jn 16:12–13). The

---

86. Francis Pieper makes a very similar point. He writes, "It is indeed a foolish and blasphemous undertaking when we men on an a priori basis (i.e., independent of God's self-revelation in His Word) presume to determine what God according to His love or righteousness can or ought to do, or what is or is not compatible with God's love or justice. This attempt rests on the false premise that finite man can comprehend the infinite God. The fact is that as God is infinite, so also His attributes are infinite and are therefore beyond our comprehension" (*Christian Dogmatics* 1:430–31). Pieper underscores the incomprehensibility of God and the necessity of analogical language. Again Pieper explains, "Every Scripture theologian desires to remain in agreement with St. Paul, who expressly describes the knowledge of God in Scripture as partial, fragmentary, piecemeal (1 Cor 13:9: 'We know in part, and we prophesy in part')" (*Christian Dogmatics* 1:430).

87. Gregory of Nazianzus *Or.* 30.17 (PPS, 107–8).

same is true for us as sojourners whose citizenship is in heaven. Here we know in part but there we will know in full. Paul experienced this in a way that no one else has: "I know a man in Christ who fourteen years ago was caught up to the third heaven—whether in the body or out of the body I do not know, God knows. And I know that this man was caught up into paradise—whether in the body or out of the body I do not know, God knows—and he heard things that cannot be told, which man may not utter" (2 Cor 12:2-4). Paul experienced something true and real but beyond description. He heard things that he could not put into words. Paul was caught up into a place—whether in the body or out of the body, whether a place defined by corporeality or not, a place of space and dimension as we *know* it, he did not know. Paul is not just struggling here to know if he was taken bodily to this "place" or taken by vision only. There is real confusion and uncertainty on Paul's part. Whatever it was, it was real in a sense beyond what he knows here, and therefore words fail. He heard things that were inexpressible, unspeakable, too sacred to speak (ἤκουσεν ἄρρητα ῥήματα). These things cannot be told, cannot be uttered, not because we are not permitted to know them, such that Paul knew something contrary to what the Scriptures elsewhere declare. No, he was not able to speak these words, to say these things, because it was "not possible" (οὐκ ἐξὸν) for them to be uttered by man.[88] It was beyond his creaturely ability, beyond the nature of the knower and speaker.

Failure to understand who we are as creatures and therefore the creaturely limitations of our faculties results in idolatry. Eunomius fails to understand the limitations of human nature, and specifically the faculty of human reason. Reason itself is a gift from God, a tremendous blessing that sets us apart as rational creatures from the rest of God's creation. It is this faculty that allows us to meditate upon the Scriptures, to proclaim the wonders of our God, and to share with others the joys of life. This gift of reason is from God, and He properly suited it to us as finite human beings. This means that our reason functions in spatial and temporal terms—in terms that correspond to our finite existence. To suggest that reason could comprehend the essence of God is to claim something utterly impossible. Our finite reason cannot perfectly grasp the infinite essence of God.[89]

Gregory draws a helpful analogy. How are we able to see the sun? The answer is our faculty of sight. This is what makes possible our seeing. What happens when we use this faculty of sight to stare directly at the brightness of the sun? We abuse our faculty, seeking to do more with it than is possible, and

---

88. Cf. Paul Kretzmann, *Popular Commentary of the Bible* (St. Louis: Concordia Publishing House, n.d.), New Testament, 2:219: "Paul had had a taste of that bliss and glory in this vision. And he had heard words which were unutterable for any mere human tongue."

89. Gregory of Nazianzus *Or.* 38.7-8. Again Pieper, *Christian Dogmatics* 1:431, "This attempt [to determine God's attributes by reason] rests on the false premise that finite man can comprehend the infinite God. The fact is that as God is infinite, so also His attributes are infinite and are therefore beyond our comprehension."

the end result is we blind ourselves. By abusing the faculty of sight to see things beyond our ability to see, we render ourselves sightless. Eunomius abuses his faculty of reason by reaching for something that is beyond the nature of reason to grasp. By doing this, he abuses his faculty and succumbs to ignorance. He is no different than the person standing before the vastness of the ocean, water stretching as far as the eye can see, who declares he has taken in the whole of the waters before him. For him the horizon is the end, the limit, rather than merely the beginning of a vastness yet unknown. He thinks he has grasped the whole; we know that he sees only in part.[90]

CONCLUSION TO PART ONE

A recurring theme in conservative catholic theology today is that the disintegration of the Thomistic synthesis by John Duns Scotus, William of Ockham, and the late medieval nominalists secularized the world, divorcing it from the being of God, and this path, the *via moderna*, gave rise to all the evils of modernity that we observe in our day.[91] This Thomistic interpretation of history further believes nominalism to be anti-catholic, or at the very least non-catholic.[92] Since Luther received his formative theological training at Erfurt in the nominalist tradition, from the perspective of this Thomistic narrative, the Reformation was unwittingly doomed from the start. For Roman Catholics this accounts for the misguided and heretical nature of Luther's efforts;[93] for those Protestants championing this Thomistic narrative, of which there are not a few, the Reformation is cause for lament.[94]

To get at the heart of this issue of knowledge of God and the manner in which we speak about Him, we must acknowledge that simplistic judgments proceeding from grand historical narratives will never suffice. For this reason we have focused in part 1 as much as possible on actual texts by actual theologians. Our conclusions proceeded from these texts. Although our approach was necessarily selective in the theologians and texts used, at the very least we avoided couching theological insights in ambiguous terms and reducing theologians to generalized categories of thought. All theologians are eclectic. Luther is a classic example. He was an Augustinian monk who received his formative theological training from a faculty committed to a certain type

---

90. Gregory of Nazianzus *Or.* 28.3; cf. Gregory of Nazianzus *De rebus suis*, II/I/I.92 (Fathers of the Church, 28); cf. *De vita sua*, II/I/XI.1774–75 (Fathers of the Church, 126); Basil of Caesarea *Against Eunomius* 1.16 (Fathers of the Church, 115).

91. For a recent example see Brian Gregory, *The Unintended Reformation: How a Religious Revolution Secularized Society* (Cambridge, MA: Harvard University Press, 2012).

92. Heiko Oberman, *The Harvest of Medieval Theology* (Grand Rapids: Baker Academic, 2000), 1–3.

93. Joseph Lortz, *The Reformation in Germany*, 2 vols. (New York: Herder and Herder, 1968).

94. Hans Boursma, *Heavenly Participation: The Weaving of a Sacramental Tapestry* (Grand Rapids: Eerdmans, 2011). Boursma writes, "We, as evangelicals, only do justice to our past if we regard the Reformation not as something to be celebrated but as something to be lamented" (85).

Rightly Speaking about God

of nominalism. However we wish to think of Luther's nominalism and the diverse thinkers who influenced him, we miss the importance of his scriptural insights if we seek only to label him. We must struggle through his works, his sharp dialectic, and sometimes confusing rhetoric. The same holds for Thomas Aquinas, John Duns Scotus, and all the other writers we have explored.

The previous chapters plotted two distinct approaches to how we rightly know and speak about God. One the one hand, several thinkers placed great emphasis on knowledge of God gained by unaided human reason that was then perfected and completed by Scripture. Despite their considerable differences on other matters, Tertullian and Thomas Aquinas, the former guided by Stoicism, the latter by Aristotelianism, both thought knowledge of God began with nature, with the preambles to the articles of faith. Extreme examples of this philosophical approach were seen in different ways with Eunomius, Scotus, and Descartes. These figures and their intellectual heirs placed a high value on the intellect in thinking about God and in expressing Him in human language. Their different approaches reduced God to an object of human intellective activity by determining which divine attribute suitably defines God and by proceeding to construct a concept of God from there. God stands apart from us as we analyze and construct the sort of ontological and moral being He most fittingly ought to be. To approach God in this way is to be guided by hubris, constructing intellectual idolatries upon which faith might repose. More often than not God becomes the answer to our human anxieties and deficiencies. This is the way of the *theologus gloriae*.

Athanasius, Gregory of Nazianzus, and the Lutheran reformers embraced an alternative theological vision, characterized by humility, persistently interested in the Christological and soteriological center of trinitarian thought. For these figures Scripture and specifically the saving work of Christ occupy the central place for authentic knowledge of God, not because of any great insight on their part but because this is how the triune God has determined things for us. For this reason, whatever knowledge of God we might have prior to faith and apart from Christ must be unlearned and turned from. Right knowledge of the Trinity for the Fathers and reformers never occurs in the lofty places of scholastic endeavor but in the humble actions of the church's liturgy. It is not any particular attribute that reveals God to us but rather the event of the cross. The shift from attribute to event is significant and informs our liturgy. Here we come to know, worship, and glorify our triune God, not merely by speaking *about* Him but also by speaking *to* Him. It was no coincidence that Luther structured the Christian's day around baptism in the Small Catechism. It was no coincidence that Basil of Caesarea wrote a treatise on the Holy Spirit by focusing on liturgy and prayer. It was no coincidence that the fourth-century trinitarian creeds were taken from the baptismal liturgies of the church. The patristic debates on the Trinity had to do with our salvation in Christ and the praise and glory given to the Father and the Son and the Holy Spirit in the divine liturgy. At stake for them was not just the heart of the Christian faith but the core of who they understood themselves to be as baptized children of God. To defend the Trinity was to defend their baptism; to safeguard their confession of the Trinity was to safeguard their liturgy. When baptism loses meaning, when liturgy gives way to the trends of the day, the ground on which the Trinity is known and confessed disappears.

The Fathers and the Lutheran reformers confessed the triune identity of God because of their commitment to Scripture alone. Part 2 of this book will proceed with this same commitment. We will present the scriptural identity of God as revealed by God in the Old and New Testaments. Following these chapters we will turn to the dogmatic reflections of the church in part 3. Here we will encounter the technical terminology and grammar used by the faithful to confess, clarify, and guard the scriptural doctrine of the Blessed Trinity.

PART TWO

ON THE TRINITY

When the people in the pew ask the pastor to explain the Trinity, they do not want clever analogies or carefully worded creeds. They want to know what Scripture says about the Trinity. Part 2 demonstrates the scriptural identity of the Trinity. We begin with a short chapter on the Trinity and the Bible. Many scholars today think the Trinity belongs to the history of the church and not to the authors of Scripture. After addressing the state of scriptural interpretation in our day and the false assumptions embraced by many biblical scholars, we examine at length the Bible's presentation of the Father, Son, and Holy Spirit. The New Testament consistently points us to the law and the prophets, to the Old Testament, to understand rightly the identity of Jesus Christ, the true Son of God. He is the one sent by the Father, who in turn, with the Father, sends the Holy Spirit, as promised by the prophets. The conviction of the apostles is that the triune identity of God is known according to the Old Testament. Therefore we begin with the Trinity in the Old Testament.

YHWH, our Elohim, is triune. The Old Testament makes clear that YHWH alone creates all things, governs His creation, redeems His people, and alone receives worship. These divine prerogatives belong only to YHWH and none other. And yet the Old Testament assigns these prerogatives, these identity markers, to the Father, the one who speaks forth His Word in the beginning, to the Son, who is the Word of YHWH, spoken in the beginning, who creates all things, and to the Spirit of YHWH, the breath of the Almighty, who also created all things. The Old Testament makes clear that the Father, Word, and Spirit are intrinsic to the identity, reality, being, and essence of YHWH. A faithful and careful reading of the Scriptures demands the confession that YHWH, our Elohim, is triune: He is Father, Word, and Spirit, three who are one, coequal and coeternal, inseparably united as one and yet eternally distinct as three.

The rest of part 2 focuses on the New Testament's presentation of the divine identity of the Father, Son, and Holy Spirit. The New Testament marks out the divine identity of the Son and the Holy Spirit through careful exegesis of the Old Testament. The divine name and the unique characteristics belonging to YHWH are assigned to both the Son and the Holy Spirit. We end part 2 with a discussion of the eternal origin of the Holy Spirit from the Father and the Son (*filioque*). Lutherans teach and confess the *filioque* because of Scripture, not because of creeds, and therefore our commitments demand that we take up this issue in the chapters on the scriptural identity of the Trinity. The exegesis offered throughout these chapters follows the insights of the Fathers and reformers and aims to recover the voice of the church in our reading of Scripture and theological practice.

6

TRINITY AND THE BIBLE

Does the Trinity have a place in responsible and authentic exegesis of the Bible? That such a strange question could be asked indicates something dire about the times in which we live.[1] Critical scholars of the Bible claim that the Trinity belongs to the church's history and to theologians interested in that history but has no place in the New Testament, let alone the "Hebrew" Scriptures, as the Old Testament is now designated in the academy.[2] The difficulty facing the church today is how we retain our confession in the scriptural identity of God when many exegetes, both liberal and evangelical, no longer regard this as proper exegesis. The theological contrast between our day and that of the Fathers and reformers can be explained almost entirely by our strikingly different views of Scripture—what it is and how it ought to be interpreted. The following chapters aim to recover the Bible for our understanding of the Trinity. They aim to return us to the exegetical instincts and scriptural commitments of the Fathers and reformers.

Since the issue of the Trinity and the Bible occupies such contested terrain, this chapter will address the state of scriptural interpretation in our day, particularly with reference to the Trinity, before turning to the chapters on the scriptural identity of our triune God. We will begin by briefly showing the difference between the Fathers and ourselves in terms of where we locate the Trinity in our academic literature. The Trinity has been forced to move over the years, and its relocation in our day indicates the challenge we face in demonstrating the scriptural identity of God. Next we turn to the modern presuppositions for scriptural interpretation and how these presuppositions lead either to the rejection of the Trinity or its marginalization. The academic reading of Scripture in our day, among both liberals and evangelicals, has

---

1. Robert Jenson, "The Bible and the Trinity," *Pro Ecclesia* 11/3 (2002): 329: "The usual supposition is that the doctrine of the Trinity, and the Chalcedonian Christology which follows from it, are not in the Bible, and certainly not in that bulk of the Bible we call the Old Testament." Cf. Donald Juel, "The Trinity in the New Testament," *Theology Today* 54 (1997): 313: "The New Testament contains no doctrine of the Trinity."

2. There is the further problem that some of the most influential theologians of the twentieth century also denied that Scripture taught the Trinity. See for example Emil Brunner, *The Christian Doctrine of God: Dogmatics*, trans. Olive Wyon (Philadelphia: The Westminster Press, 1950), 1:205: "We must honestly admit that the doctrine of the Trinity did not form part of the early Christian—New Testament—message, nor has it ever been a central article of faith in the religious life of the Christian church as a whole, at any period in its history." Again, Brunner, 236: "The doctrine of the Trinity itself, however, is not a Biblical doctrine, and this indeed not by accident but of necessity."

entangled itself in modern presuppositions on history and meaning that derive not from Scripture but, like natural theology, from the best ideas of the day. These best ideas have become the agreed-upon rules for constructing authentic meaning. Although the academic scholars committed to this way of reading the Bible differ significantly in terms of theological commitments, particularly on the historicity of the Bible, they share a common approach to the Scriptures, an approach far removed from the traditional exegesis of the Fathers and reformers. Although this modern way of reading typically presents itself as more critical, more advanced, or more sophisticated than premodern readings, it proceeds from theological judgments. The exegesis of the Fathers and reformers proceeded from theological judgments too. The issue is not whether we can read the Scriptures apart from theological judgments; rather the issue is which theological judgments proceed from Scripture and which stand apart from it. To reject modern exegetical commitments is to reject their faulty and misguided theological judgments.

THE TRINITY'S RELOCATION

Before Augustine wrote his influential work on the Trinity, he started, as all writers ought to do, with research. Augustine explains:

> The purpose of all the Catholic commentators I have been able to read on the divine books of both testaments, who have written before me on the Trinity which God is [*trinitatis qui est Deus*], has been to teach that according to the scriptures Father and Son and Holy Spirit in the inseparable equality of one substance present a divine unity and therefore there are not three gods but one God.[3]

When Augustine wanted to read what those theologians before him had written on the Trinity, he looked to their commentaries on the Old and New Testaments. In Augustine's world, to write a commentary on either testament meant you wrote on the identity of the one who acted in and authored those books. Augustine and his contemporaries engaged Scripture, God's Word, to understand the identity of the one God who is Father, Son, and Holy Spirit, eternally distinct in person, yet indivisibly one in essence. Hilary of Poitiers, writing during the height of the fourth-century trinitarian controversy, repeatedly emphasized in his treatise on the Trinity that God is a fitting witness of Himself, and therefore we know Him rightly through His own perfect revelation.[4] Luther echoes this sentiment: "God wants to be acknowledged as he reveals himself."[5] Similarly, Martin Chemnitz states, "We must think about

---

3. Augustine *The Trinity* 1.7 (WSA I/5, 69).
4. Hilary of Poitiers *De Trinitate* 1.18; see also *De Trinitate* 2.6–7, 3.9, 4.1, 4.14, 5.20, 8.43, 9.40, 9.69.
5. *On the Last Words of David*, 1543 (AE 15:338; WA 54:88.9): "Sondern wil erkand sein, wie er sich uns offenbart."

God as he has revealed himself."[6] According to the Fathers and the reformers, if we wish to know God, to speak properly about Him and His work on our behalf, we must look to the Scriptures and faithfully expound them. The instinct exhibited by Augustine—to read the available commentaries in his day—is an instinct shared by all the orthodox writers on the Trinity from the early church and also by our Lutheran fathers.[7]

The pressing question for us is to what extent we share Augustine's instinct. Would we begin with the numerous commentaries produced in our day to learn about the Trinity? Even if we were inclined to do so, our efforts would be frustrated quickly. As things stand in our day, the doctrine of the Trinity finds a home not in commentaries on Scripture but in systematic theologies. In these sorts of books we learn about the various formulae used to express the doctrine of the Trinity, the proper theological language employed to safeguard our creedal affirmations, and more often than not creative ideas on how to integrate the doctrine into our everyday experiences, relationships, and communities. If we wish to know why different theological decisions were made throughout the history of the church, we find a book on church history to fill in the details. The contrast is striking: Augustine sought exegesis, scriptural comment, God's Word; we seek theological summary and church history. We seek this in part because this is what scholars make available to us. Why is that the case? Why has the location of this doctrine shifted from commentaries to systematic theologies?

MODERN SCRIPTURAL INTERPRETATION

Many biblical scholars today associate responsible exegesis with the intended meaning of a text's original author and audience. Meaning emerges from discerning authorial intention, shaped, so it is assumed, by the immediate historical and social factors of the author's world, and determined by the audience's conceptual horizon. Scrutiny of the author's words, with the proper historical context in view, particularly its limitations, yields a sanitized meaning free of dogmatic prejudice and theological subjectivity.[8] The advantage of this approach for some is that it skirts the pressing questions of the Bible's historicity, its facticity, apart from the faith of the reader. Two examples from two very different scholars show this approach to the Bible's meaning. Elaine Wainwright,

---

6. Martin Chemnitz, *Loci Theologici*, trans. J. A. O. Preus (St. Louis: Concordia Publishing House, 2008), 1:87.

7. Already during the sixteenth century Protestants were removing the Trinity from their readings of the Old Testament. Luther's *The Last Words of David* (1543) responds to this trend among the "new Hebraists" in his day. From that perspective Luther can assert "we pay the commentaries no heed" (AE 15:319; WA 54:71.26). The commentaries he has in mind are those that read the Scriptures apart from the Trinity.

8. Cf. R. R. Reno's use of Benjamin Jowett in his series preface to the Brazos Theological Commentary on the Bible. Ephraim Radner, *Leviticus*, Brazos Theological Commentary on the Bible (Grand Rapids: Brazos, 2008), 10–11.

a critical scholar, discussing her approach to the New Testament, writes, "The interpreter tries to stand with the first-century readers/hearers *behind the text*, as it were, or *in relation to the text* to hear, initially, the text in its context of origin and not through the lens of later theology."[9] Ben Witherington, a prominent evangelical scholar, writes, "What the text could not have possibly meant to the original inspired biblical author, it cannot possibly mean today."[10] Witherington's position is echoed by a popular textbook on biblical interpretation used at evangelical seminaries: "The early church had the tendency—one continued by Protestants after the Reformation—to read New Testament theological concepts into Old Testament passages. We must avoid this error; our first task is always to understand each text on its own terms—as its writer and readers would have understood it."[11] Wainwright emphasizes the audience and Witherington the author because of their different positions on the historicity of the Bible. The Bible becomes the Word of God for Wainwright in its reception. The question she must pursue, however, is what that meaning could be given the historical context of such hearing/reading. In other words, what is available apart from the text—either behind it or in relation to it—to construct meaning? Witherington's higher view of what the Bible is as God's Word allows him to emphasize the author, not the audience, in determining authentic meaning. He goes too far, however, in limiting meaning to what the human author meant. The textbook brings both concerns together, the writer and reader.

For the scholars above the historical context or context of origin shared by the human author and the original audience is decisive for determining the authentic and accepted meaning of the text. Despite their differing emphases and theological commitments, all three embrace a flat understanding of meaning because of their narrow view of context. By emphasizing the human author, his intentions, and the conceptual limits of the audience, they remove the text from its sacred history, from its place in the spiritual life of the believing community, and from its home within the liturgy. They further marginalize the subsequent reception of these Scriptures in the history of the church, the theological reflection upon them by the faithful, the Fathers and reformers. These sorts of scholars view this later theology as misleading and substitute instead their own retelling of the authentic meaning of the text—one tradition for another. They accomplish this by embracing a more restrictive view of context than that held by the Fathers and reformers and by privileging modern notions of the self as subject. Both of these moves proceed from theological judgments bequeathed by modernity.[12]

---

9. Elaine Wainwright, "Exploring the Trinity in/and the New Testament," *The Cambridge Companion to the Trinity*, ed. Peter Phan (Cambridge: Cambridge University Press, 2011), 35.

10. Ben Witherington, *The Problem with Evangelical Theology* (Waco, TX: Baylor University Press, 2005), x.

11. William W. Klein, Craig L. Blomberg, and Robert L. Hubbard Jr., eds., *Introduction to Biblical Interpretation* (Dallas, TX: Word Publishing, 1993), 171.

12. Cf. Robert Jenson, "The Trinity in the Bible," Concordia Theological Quarterly

Trinity and the Bible

There are good reasons to lament the state of biblical scholarship in the academy. Francis Watson, a noted New Testament scholar, also worries that the average biblical scholar today permits no place for the Trinity in the Bible. In his estimation, such scholars think that "the doctrine of the Trinity should be left to church historians and systematic theologians; it has no place in 'our' field."[13] Watson continues:

> To present a paper even on so useful a topic as 'the doctrine of the Trinity and the Old Testament' would be regarded as an outrage and a provocation at most gatherings of scholars of the so-called 'Hebrew Bible' . . . In the field of New Testament scholarship, one is expected to distinguish sharply between the non-trinitarian or at best proto-trinitarian conceptuality of the New Testament writings and a later patristic theology whose Platonizing tendencies are said to lead to systematic misreading of the scriptural texts.[14]

The view described by Watson undermines the exegesis of the Fathers and reformers, questions the perfection and unity of the Scriptures, and explicitly divides God against Himself. Our Lutheran dogmaticians observed this problem in their own day. Johann Gerhard points his readers to Psalm 81: "There shall be no strange god [*Vulg.*, 'recent god'] among you; you shall not bow down to a foreign god." Gerhard explains, "If the mystery of the Trinity had been completely unknown in the Old Testament, surely a 'recent god' would be introduced in the New Testament through the worship of the Son and of the Holy Spirit." Likewise, we read in Isaiah, "Before me no god was formed, nor shall there be any after me" (Is 43:10).[15] Gerhard writes, "If the Son of God became God in the New Testament . . . and if He began to receive divine

---

68 (2004): 195–206.

13. Francis Watson, "Trinity and Community: A Reading of John 17," *International Journal of Systematic Theology* (1999): 168. Watson is criticizing the attitude of scholars in his field on the Trinity; he does not share these convictions.

14. Watson, "Trinity and Community," 168. The designation of the Old Testament as Hebrew Bible proceeds from liberal Protestant concerns over supersessionism. Jewish scholars are rightfully suspicious of the term. For the liberal scholar, the "Hebrew Bible" belongs to Jews, not Christians. Joseph Webb, one such liberal scholar, argues further that any Christological reading of the Old Testament is illegitimate. Amy-Jill Levine, a Jewish New Testament scholar, argues on the other hand that "terms like Hebrew Bible and Jewish Scriptures serve ultimately either to erase Judaism (since 'Jews' are not 'Hebrews' and the synagogue reads not the 'Hebrew Bible' but the Tanakh) or to deny Christians their own canon." Joseph M. Webb, "A Revolution in Christian Preaching: From the 'Old Testament' to the 'Hebrew Bible,'" *Quarterly Review* 20 (2000): 256–57; A.-J. Levine, "Jewish-Christian Relations from the 'Other Side,'" *Quarterly Review* 20 (2000): 298. For a discussion of both essays see Richard Hays, "Can the Gospels Teach Us How to Read the Old Testament?" *Pro Ecclesia* 11 (2002): 403–4.

The most vigorous argument against Christian supersessionism may be found in the works of R. Kendall Soulen. He identifies three types of supersessionism: economic, structural, and punitive. Classical trinitarianism, as confessed in the ecumenical creeds and defended by the Fathers and reformers, argues Soulen, must be rejected. See R. Kendall Soulen, *The God of Israel and Christian Theology* (Minneapolis: Fortress Press, 1996), 25–56; Soulen, "YHWH the Triune God," *Modern Theology* 15:1 (1999): 25–54.

15. Gregory of Nyssa makes a very similar point with this same text. Gregory of Nyssa *Contra Eunomium* 3.3 (GNO 1:110–11).

worship in the New Testament, then surely another god was formed after God the Father."[16] If the Trinity may not be found in the Old Testament, then, for Gerhard, Scripture contradicts itself and presents to us multiple gods.

Consider the following contrast. On the one hand most biblical scholars today avoid discussion of the Trinity in their commentaries because this "doctrine" belongs to the history of the church, not to the authentic meaning of the Bible. Can we really demonstrate, for example, that Isaiah and his historical audience professed the Trinity? If not, then offering a trinitarian reading of Isaiah, illumined by the rest of Scripture, produces irresponsible exegesis, guided more by later theology than the accepted norms for meaning in our day. On the other hand, Augustine researched what the church had to say about the Trinity by reading commentaries on the Old and New Testaments. What accounts for the difference? Quite obviously, modern scholars and the Fathers read the Scriptures in methodologically and therefore theologically opposed ways. Raymond Brown, one of the most distinguished biblical scholars of the twentieth century, acknowledged this fact and concluded, "I think we must recognize that the exegetical method of the Fathers is irrelevant to the study of the Bible today."[17] And with that move the Trinity loses. Exchanging one method for another necessarily affects doctrine. As Gerhard observes above, different exegesis results in different theology. The Fathers couldn't read the Bible without the Trinity; modern scholars can't read the Bible with the Trinity.[18]

The real problem, strange as it sounds, has to do with the place of God in our world. Most historical scholarship, including a great deal of biblical scholarship, removes God altogether from its understanding of history. Economic, political, and social forces, among other things, affect history and account for the things that happen. God does not. This a-theistic view of history, which is contrary to Scripture and Christian conviction, infects modern biblical exegesis. Brian Daley, a Jesuit patristic scholar, discussing the exegetical differences between the Fathers and that which prevails in our day, explains,

> Modern historical criticism—including the criticism of Biblical texts—is *methodologically* atheistic, even if what it studies is some form or facet of religious belief, and even if it is practiced by believers. Only "natural," inner-worldly explanations of why or how things happen, explanations that could be acceptable to believers and unbelievers alike, are taken as historically admissible. So God

---

16. Johann Gerhard, *Theological Commonplaces: On the Nature of God and On the Trinity*, trans. Richard Dinda (St. Louis: Concordia Publishing House, 2007), Exegesis III, §20, 279.

17. R. E. Brown, "The Problems with the *Sensus Plenior*," *Ephemerides Theologica Lovanienses* 43 (1967): 463.

18. Frances Young, after quoting the troparion for Epiphany used by the Eastern Orthodox, which emphasizes the revelation of the Trinity at the baptism of Jesus, writes, "But in scholarly circles no one has imagined for a very long time that such a revelation might have been in the minds of any of the Gospel writers as they told the story of the baptism. The modern consciousness of historical difference has excluded such dogmatic readings." Frances Young, "The Trinity and the New Testament," *The Nature of New Testament Theology*, ed. Christopher Rowland and Christopher Tuckett (Oxford: Blackwell, 2006), 286.

is not normally understood to count as an actor on the stage of history; God's providence in history, the divine inspiration of Scriptural authors and texts, even the miracles narrated in the Bible, are assumed to be private human interpretations of events, interior and non-demonstrable, rather than events or historical forces in themselves.[19]

This atheistic tendency, among both believers and unbelievers, renders the Scriptures a historical artifact, shaped by the vagaries of history, and limited in meaning to what particular authors and audiences intend and know. God's removal from history also requires His removal as author of Scripture. By rejecting or marginalizing the divine authorship of Scripture, modern biblical scholars reject the unity and perfection of Scripture in either theory or practice.[20] Since authentic meaning rests with human authors and audiences, the historical context of discrete books and, even further, sections of books, demands the attention of the responsible exegete. The canonical shape of the Bible plays only a secondary role in interpretation, if that. This means the Bible will not be read as the Bible, Genesis to Revelation, authored by the triune God. Such a reading would be historically irresponsible, informed by faith, not reason, by the church, not the academy. Scripture will not interpret Scripture; history will interpret Scripture. Therefore the Bible must be divided into discrete literary sections (Matthew apart from Mark; First Isaiah from Second Isaiah; Genesis 1 from Genesis 2) and meaning constructed by uncovering the social and historical contexts in which these pieces were written, heard, and read. When literary division fails to convince, scholars posit historical documents that do not exist, have no history, and rest purely on the reasoned faith of the scholar.[21] Such moves, however, are seen not as fideistic but as the best ideas of the day. For the modern biblical scholar, the constructed meaning of a text becomes not only the so-called literal or historical sense of Scripture but also the limit and extent of acceptable meaning.[22] Anything beyond this belongs to dogmatic prejudice.

---

19. Brian Daley, "Is Patristic Exegesis Still Usable? Reflections on Early Christian Interpretation of the Psalms," *Communio* 29 (2002): 191.

20. Cf. Hays, "Can the Gospels Teach Us," 404: "I propose that one reason we have lost our grip on reading the Bible is that we have forfeited our understanding of it as a single coherent story—a story in which the Old Testament and New Testament together bear complementary witness to the saving action of the one God, a *true* story into which we find ourselves taken up."

21. The scandal of Q, a text derived from the faith of academics, is the total absence of the crucifixion and resurrection of Christ. To suggest that such a proposed document could inform the Gospels shows a total misunderstanding of the gospel, of that which is first and most important ($\dot{\epsilon}\nu$ πρώτοις). Paul's words to the Corinthians stand directly opposed to this scholarly Q: "Now I would remind you, brothers, of the gospel I preached to you, which you received, in which you stand, and by which you are being saved, if you hold fast to the word I preached to you—unless you believed in vain. For I delivered to you as of first importance what I also received: that Christ died for our sins in accordance with the Scriptures, that he was buried, that he was raised on the third day in accordance with the Scriptures" (1 Cor 15:1-4). To believe in Q is to believe in vain.

22. Cf. Jenson, "Trinity in the Bible," 196: "Historicism is the belief that understanding something's history and understanding the thing itself are the same."

For the above reasons, the Trinity in our day has been rendered a doctrine apart from Scripture and assigned to the systematic theologian and church historian. A multitude of problems arise. The Fathers confessed the Trinity because of their commitment to the Scriptures. The doctrine rested for them upon exegesis and found expression in their prayers and liturgy. When modern biblical scholars reject the exegesis of the Fathers, they threaten the confession of the Trinity that proceeds from that exegesis. Many biblical scholars recognize this reality and for that reason hand over the "doctrine" to the historians and theologians. The result today is a doctrine that all orthodox Christians acknowledge, but they haven't a clue how it informs their reading of Scripture or the practice of their faith. We embrace the tradition of a doctrine but not the doctrine's tradition of exegesis, and therefore have no sense how it informs Christian identity.

The Fathers and reformers read differently. Although aware that the different books of the Bible were written at a different time than their own, and that this history provided important insights, nonetheless for them the history was only a place to begin, never the limit of meaning for the Scriptures. As Robert Wilken puts it, historical study was propaedeutic, a necessary first step but one that takes you only so far.[23] Decisive for the Fathers and reformers was God's authorship of Scripture. The implications of that divine authorship ranged from an affirmation of the unity and inerrancy of Scripture to the posture of humility and prayer for the reader of Scripture.[24] Although the divergent methods used for interpreting Scripture stand out when looking at modern and premodern exegetes, another significant difference, and likely what accounts for their opposing methods, has to do with the location of their interpretive efforts. The modern scholar works in the university classroom; the Fathers and reformers labored in and for the church, surrounded by font, pulpit, and altar. The point is simple: if you remove the church from your exegesis, a new grammar emerges, a new theology prevails.[25] Robert Wilken, responding to the historical concerns of the modern biblical scholar, describes the approach taken by the Fathers. The same could be said for the Lutheran reformers. He writes:

> Interpretation requires context, a framework of meaning created by the events, persons, ideas and experiences to which one relates the text. In which context is the Bible to be interpreted? The classical Christian commentators believed that the context was provided by the church, its creeds and conciliar decrees, its worship and sacraments, by Christian history and experience. They knew as well as we do that the books of the Bible were written in a different time than their own and

---

23. Robert Louis Wilken, "Wilken's Response to Hays," *Communio* 25 (1998): 529.
24. Frances Young, *Biblical Exegesis and the Formation of Christian Culture* (Grand Rapids: Baker Academic, 2002), 10: "Thus, the unity and inerrancy of the Bible, however problematic for modern scholars, have been taken to be, for the early Church, unsurprising dogmas."
25. Cf. Jenson, "The Trinity in the Bible," 197: "The church has her own way of reading Scripture."

that this history had to be understood and respected. But it was never definitive for interpretation. The history that was the key to the scripture was the history of Christ.[26]

When you read and interpret the Scriptures within the church, your reading habits are shaped by the church's liturgies, lectionaries, creeds, hymns, and life of prayer. Christ's person and work, His history, as made known in the Law, Prophets, and Writings, serves as the key to responsible exegesis for the Fathers and reformers. No one understood this point better than Luther. For him, "The whole of scripture is about Christ alone" and finds its "meaning" in Christ.[27] Elsewhere Luther insists that the whole of Scripture, the Old and New Testaments, all of it, points to the Son.[28] Scholars today dismiss Luther's strong Christological reading of the Scriptures as something not "originally" intended by the text.[29] This is true of both liberal and evangelical scholars. And yet, asks Luther, if you remove Christ from the Scriptures, what more will you find in them?[30] We must join Luther in asking this question. What is the "more" achieved by modern biblical scholarship—liberal or evangelical? The "more" always results in less—less Trinity, less gospel, less sacraments. The "more" becomes ambiguous divinity, often of our own liking, and confusion of law and gospel, again to our own liking.

Luther read Scripture Christologically and with ecclesial and liturgical presuppositions. He proceeded with the conviction that God is the author of Scripture and active in human history. For Luther a unity existed between the Old and New Testaments because it was God's Word, a unity that required him to read the Old Testament in the light of Christ. The "in the light of" reading was for Luther a historical-grammatical reading grounded in the incarnation and proclaimed in the church's prayers, hymns, and creeds. It proceeded from the clear statements of Christ Himself, who declared and taught that Moses, the Prophets, and the Psalms—all of Scripture—spoke of Him (Lk 24:25–27, 44–47; Jn 5:39–40, 46). Further, according to Christ, no one knows the Father nor comes to the Father apart from the Son (Mt 11:27; Jn 14:6–7; 8:19, 55). The one who proceeds with a Christocentric reading of Scripture will know both the Father and the Son and this by the Holy Spirit; the one who exchanges a Christocentric reading for a theocentric one puts aside Christ and "does not have God" (2 Jn 9). Again, for Luther, Scripture demanded this Christocentric reading.[31]

---

26. Wilken, "Wilken's Response to Hays," 529–30.

27. *Lectures on Romans*, 1515–16 (AE 25:405; WA 57:207.22, 208.1), my translation; cf. *On the Last Words of David*, 1543 (AE 15:268; WA 54:29.3–6).

28. *On the Last Words of David*, 1543 (AE 15:338; WA 54:88.10–11).

29. Raymond Surburg, "The Presuppositions of the Historical-Grammatical Method as Employed by Historic Lutheranism," *The Springfielder* 38:4 (1974): 285.

30. *The Bondage of the Will*, 1525 (AE 33:26; WA 18:606.29): "Tolle Christum e scripturis, quid amplius in illis invenies?"

31. For a helpful discussion of the theocentric reading by modern exegetes, liberal and evangelical, see Charles Gieschen, "The Real Presence of the Son Before Christ: Revisiting an

The Old Testament gave abundant witness to prophecy about Christ and to numerous appearances of Christ. He appeared to Abraham, bringing him great joy (Jn 8:56–59); Isaiah saw His glory and spoke of Him (Jn 12:41); He was with Israel in the wilderness (1 Cor 10:1–10) and led them out of Egypt (Jude 5). To remove Christ, to focus on the theocentric character of the Old Testament as opposed to its Christocentric character, muddles the witness of Scripture and reveals yourself, in Luther's words, as the "unspiritual" or natural man described by Paul (1 Cor 2:11–14).[32] Luther brings the above texts together with his usual rhetorical confidence. He writes:

> It follows cogently and incontrovertibly that the God who led the children of Israel from Egypt and through the Red Sea, who guided them in the wilderness by means of the pillar of cloud and the pillar of fire, who nourished them with bread from heaven, who performed all the miracles recorded by Moses in his books, again, who brought them into the land of Canaan and there gave them kings and priests and everything, is the very same God, and none other than Jesus of Nazareth, the Son of the Virgin Mary, whom we Christians call our Lord and God. . . . Likewise, it is He who gave Moses the Ten Commandments on Mount Sinai, saying (Ex. 20:2, 3): "I am the Lord your God, who brought you out of the land of Egypt . . . You shall have no other gods before Me." Yes, Jesus of Nazareth, who died for us on the cross, is the God who says in the First Commandment: "I am the Lord your God." How the Jews and Mohammed would rant if they heard that! Nevertheless, it is true and will eternally remain true. And he who disbelieves this will tremble before this truth and burn forever.[33]

Luther read Scripture in this way not because he was premodern but because he was faithful to the pattern of sound teaching given in Scripture. His reading proceeded from his faith in the Trinity which God is. Luther writes, "Thus all of Scripture, as already said, is pure Christ, God's and Mary's Son. Everything is focused on this Son, so that we might know Him distinctively and in that way see the Father and the Holy Spirit eternally as one God. To him who has the Son Scripture is an open book; and the stronger his faith in Christ becomes, the more brightly will the light of Scripture shine for him."[34] For Luther, the whole of Scripture, Old and New Testaments, points to Christ; indeed, Scripture is pure Christ, and by grasping this we grasp the meaning of Scripture, seeing the one true God, Father, Son, and Holy Spirit. A right confession of the Trinity begins with Christ. Luther was well aware that many in his day did not agree with his interpretation of Scripture. To them he simply responded: "If it [my exegesis] pleases no one else, it is sufficient that it pleases me."[35] That too must be our response today to those who wish to reject the unity and perfection of Scripture, Genesis to Revelation, in an effort to remove Christ

---

Old Approach to Old Testament Christology," *Concordia Theological Quarterly* 68 (2004): 110–14.
  32. *On the Last Words of David*, 1543 (AE 15:337; WA 54:87.3–5); see also AE 15:277 (WA 54:37.3) and AE 15:279 (WA 54:38.8) for other examples of this for Luther.
  33. *On the Last Words of David*, 1543 (AE 15:313–14; WA 54:67.1–16).
  34. *On the Last Words of David*, 1543 (AE 15:339; WA 54:88.38–89.4).
  35. *On the Last Words of David*, 1543 (AE 15:320; WA 54:73.2–3).

from the center of Scripture, thus marginalizing, if not rejecting altogether, the Blessed Trinity.

Lutherans today who give a *quia* subscription to the Book of Concord avoid many of the pitfalls plaguing modern biblical exegesis. We do so because we remain committed to the theological labors of Luther and the Concordists, confessing with them the authority of Scripture and the Christological center of God's revelation to us. That we fare better than others is not an opportunity for boasting but for thankfulness and continued diligence. To some extent we have been spared those pitfalls by a happy coincidence of history. Our confessional commitments bind us to a sixteenth-century collection of theological writings faithfully penned by so-called premodern exegetes. To share their theological convictions is to share their exegetical commitments. A later history will decide this for us, but one of the chief blessings of the Book of Concord for confessional Lutherans today may prove to be its resistance to the theologically destructive tendencies of modernity.

TWO MISLEADING IDEAS

The modern convictions discussed above have produced two misleading ideas that inform a great deal of the exegetical and theological scholarship on the Trinity in our day. The first misleading idea concerns the Fathers and their theological efforts on behalf of the Trinity. Many scholars today charge the Fathers with hellenizing the Christian faith by importing metaphysical categories into the faith and securing the doctrine of the Trinity with Greek ways of thinking. This charge of hellenization or platonizing, so popularly voiced in our day, has less to do with the Fathers and more to do with nineteenth-century theological interests. The derogatory phrase "the hellenization of Christianity" accomplishes two things at once: it judges early Christian theological reflection as a Greek defection from Scripture, and for this reason allows a person to dismiss the Fathers without engaging their commentaries and theological works.

The second misleading idea alleges that the New Testament shows little interest in the ontological status of Jesus and focuses primarily on the things He does. New Testament scholars advance a distinction between an ontological Christology—the interest of the Fathers and the product of their hellenizing tendencies—and a functional Christology—the interest of the New Testament writers. Like the charge of hellenization, the distinction between ontology and function, between who someone is in terms of substance, nature, essence, identity, or however else we might put it, and what sorts of things that person does, accomplishes two things at once: it tables all discussion of Christ's ontological identity as foreign to the interests of New Testament writers, and for this reason frees the exegete from taking up questions concerning the eternal relationship between the Father and the Son or the Son and the Spirit.

In other words, an exegete can focus on what Christ does without ever asking if the "what" has anything to do with who He is. The distinction is not only philosophically suspect but also opposed by Scripture. I deliberately refer to these ideas as misleading. There is some truth to both observations but not in the way alleged by many scholars today.

The Fathers and the Trinity: The First Misleading Idea
The triune identity of God as Father, Son, and Holy Spirit has been revealed by God Himself in the Scriptures, clarified by the exegesis and pious reasoning of the Fathers, and guarded for the faithful by the church's creedal statements and ecclesiastical terminology. The foundation of our faith in the Trinity is God's revelation of Himself; upon this foundation stands the exegesis of the Fathers who defended the scriptural identity of God against false teachers; and finally, at the top of this edifice rests the concise and technical trinitarian creeds of the church. All too often those discussing the trinitarian faith of the Fathers reduce their insights and concerns to the formal creeds produced during the so-called Arian controversy. These creeds were carefully crafted theological statements, shaped by the apologetic and polemical concerns of the Fathers, employing the conceptual idiom of the day to mark out the identity of the triune God whom they worshipped and in whom alone their salvation was found. Privileging creeds makes a person's task easier, to be sure, as he may avoid the lengthy exegetical works of the Fathers and focus instead on summary. But this gives the wrong impression of what the Fathers were doing in these debates, which in turn makes the misleading charge of hellenization easier.

The creed most familiar to Christians today is the Nicene Creed. This statement of faith, begun at Nicaea in 325 and completed, with slight revision, at Constantinople in 381, was not written by the Fathers gathered at the council. They modified an already existing creed, adding the controversial phrases that the Son was "from the *ousia*" of the Father and *homoousios* or consubstantial with the Father. The great creeds of the early church were baptismal confessions. Their provenance was the liturgy and most churches had their own baptismal creed. The fourth-century controversy over the Trinity involved both the proper exegesis of Scripture on the identity of God and the legitimacy of the church's liturgy and baptismal faith. An objection voiced frequently by the Nicene theologians concerns their baptism and the new life received in the sacrament of salvation. If the Arians are right that Christ is an exalted being but nonetheless created and not God in the same sense that the Father is God, then what does that mean for baptism, for salvation? How can salvation be found in a creature? How can the new life received in baptism mean anything if God is mingled with creatures in the baptismal formula?[36] The "what" and the "who" or the work and the worker always went together for the Fathers.

---

36. See Hilary of Poitiers *De Trinitate* 2.1–2; Athanasius *Letters to Serapion* 1.29–30, 2.6–8; Gregory of Nazianzus *Or.* 31.4 (salvation) and 31.6 (baptism).

Despite the ordinary textbook summary of the fourth-century trinitarian debates, the Fathers exhibit a notable hesitancy in appealing to the authority of Nicaea, its creed, and its technical language (*homoousios*). The instincts of the Fathers should be our instincts. If we start reflexively with the creeds of the early church or the technical theological vocabulary used to secure and clarify the church's judgment of the scriptural identity of the Trinity, we begin where the Fathers ended rather than where they began. This very issue arose during the Reformation. Luther accused Johann Eck and Johann Cochlaeus of taking this approach.[37] In Luther's estimation the Roman theologians establish the doctrine of the Trinity on the authority of the Fathers and the pope and not on the Scriptures. That approach ran contrary to the convictions of the Lutherans and, by extension, to the practice of the Fathers.

Although theologians today may wish to locate the doctrine of the Trinity in the authoritative statements of the Fathers and their theological insights, the Fathers appealed to Scripture in their arguments with the Arians. For example, Athanasius, who resolutely stood, as the story goes, *contra mundum* in his defense of the coequality and coeternity of the Father, Son, and Holy Spirit, composed three orations against the Arians in the early 340s without a single mention of the creed from Nicaea and only passing references to the language of *homoousios*. It was not until the 350s, twenty-five years after the council, that Athanasius invoked the authority of Nicaea and its terminology, and this only after considerable effort on his part to demonstrate the scriptural identity of the Trinity. The foundation for the church's confession was not a creed from Nicaea but the witness of God Himself in the Scriptures. The Fathers understood this and devoted their efforts to exegesis. We too must follow their lead and establish the eternal identity of the Father, Son, and Holy Spirit upon God's revelation and not upon creeds and the church's theological judgments against those who undermine this scriptural witness. These creeds are indispensable, to be sure, but they rest upon exegesis, upon the Scriptures, and it is this that we must relearn.[38] More will be said below on the charge of hellenization. At this point, the fact that the Fathers focused on the interpretation of Scripture to establish the triune identity of God should be enough to create serious doubt about how many characterize their efforts today.

Identity and Activity: The Second Misleading Idea
Many New Testament scholars make a distinction between functional Christology and ontological Christology. The former focuses on the activities or

---

37. *Die Promotionsdisputation von Georg Major und Johannes Faber*, 1544 (WA 39/2:305.24–26). Johann Gerhard provides numerous quotes from Roman theologians declaring that the Trinity cannot be believed from Scripture alone but requires tradition. Gerhard, *Theological Commonplaces*, Exegesis III, §19, 278.

38. For a fuller discussion of our commitment to Scripture in establishing the Trinity and how that commitment relates to the faithful labors of the Fathers, see Chemnitz, *Loci Theologici* 1:88–117; Gerhard, *Theological Commonplaces*, Exegesis III, §15–18, 274–77.

functions performed by Christ, and the latter assigns metaphysical categories to the person and nature of Christ. This latter approach was taken, it is argued, by the Fathers. According to Oscar Cullmann, the Fathers were concerned "almost exclusively" with the relation between the nature of the Son and the Father or the relation that exists between Christ's divine and human natures. Their interest in Christ's divine nature belongs to "the Hellenizing of the Christian faith."[39] These concerns, argues Cullmann, must be avoided in our reading of the New Testament.

Problems abound with this distinction. The first pertains to the characterization of patristic exegesis. A chief argument used by the Fathers to show the coequality of the Father, Son, and Holy Spirit centered on the relationship between nature and activity. For them, we rightly understand "who" someone or something is when we grasp "what" they do. The activity reveals the identity of the doer. Furthermore, for the Fathers, common works indicate common nature. This insight stands at the center of patristic trinitarian thought, and it is an insight owing to Scripture, not philosophy. Simply put, Scripture demanded the correlation of activity and identity or function and ontology. The Fathers observed how questions of identity routinely arose when Jesus did things belonging either to God alone or at the very least to some being greater than a mere man. When He forgave the sins of the woman with the alabaster jar, those who witnessed this began to say among themselves, "Who is this, who even forgives sins?" (Lk 7:49). When He forgave the sins of the paralytic, the scribes declared in their hearts, "He is blaspheming! Who can forgive sins but God alone?" (Mk 2:7). When He rebuked the wind and calmed the sea, the disciples, filled with fear, said to one another, "Who then is this, that even wind and sea obey him?" (Mk 4:41). Jesus' actions, His activities, raised questions of identity for those around Him. The Fathers pursued this insight, gleaned from Scripture, to argue that if Jesus does things belonging only to God, like forgiving sins or exercising power over nature, then He must be God. Activity and identity inform one another.

The Fathers also saw the Scriptures aligning activity and identity in God's delivery of His gifts to us. For example, St. Paul ends his second letter to the Corinthians commending "the love of God" to the Christians at Corinth (2 Cor 13:14). The love Paul commends to them, the Trinity grants and sustains. Jesus explains, "Whoever has my commandments and keeps them, he it is who loves me. And he who loves me will be loved by my Father, and I will love him

---

39. Oscar Cullmann, *The Christology of the New Testament* (Philadelphia: Westminster, 1963), 3. For a correct response to Adolf von Harnack's charge of the hellenization of Christianity, which Cullmann here echoes, see Robert Louis Wilken, *The Spirit of Early Christianity* (New Haven, CT: Yale University Press, 2003), xvi et passim. Wilken argues that the better phrase would be "the Christianization of Hellenism." Similarly, Robert Jenson suggests "Gospelizing of Hellenism." Robert Jenson, "Ipse Pater Non Est Impassibilis," in *Divine Impassibility and the Mystery of Human Suffering*, ed. James F. Keating and Thomas Joseph White (Grand Rapids: Eerdmans, 2009), 118 n. 1.

and manifest myself to him" (Jn 14:21). Jesus' love with which He loves is not different from the Father's love, who loves in order to save: "For God so loved the world, that he gave his only Son, that whoever believes in him should not perish but have eternal life" (Jn 3:16). The love with which we love is the fruit of the Holy Spirit (Gal 5:22), and this love is poured into our hearts by the Holy Spirit (Rom 5:5). This trinitarian pattern recurs throughout the Scriptures. The Father gives life to all things (1 Tm 6:13), Christ, our Good Shepherd, gives eternal life (Jn 10:27–28), and this life comes to us through the Holy Spirit (Rom 8:11). Again, God is the "only-wise" (Rom 16:27), the Son "the wisdom of God" (1 Cor 1:24), and the Holy Spirit the "Spirit of Wisdom" (Dt 34:9). Again, God is holy (Lv 11:44; 1 Pt 1:16), Christ Jesus is our sanctification, our holiness (1 Cor 1:30), and the Holy Spirit the one who sanctifies us (1 Cor 6:11) because He is the "Spirit of holiness" (Rom 1:4). The Fathers used the shared activities of the Father, Son, and Holy Spirit to demonstrate their coequality and inseparable working on our behalf. The scriptural correlation of activity and identity led the Fathers to express the relationship between the Father, Son, and Holy Spirit in the terms of their day—essence, substance, nature, person, etc. Platonism did not demand this of them. Scripture demanded it.

Although New Testament scholars recognize the above activities, many resist correlating activity and identity or activity and nature. They cite the distinction between a functional and ontological Christology in order to argue that the New Testament, in its original context and according to the intention of the human author, shows interest only in the type of activities or functions performed by Christ, not in the ontological implications of that action. This distinction is misleading. As the various figures in the New Testament understood, if Jesus creates all things, exercises power over the forces of nature, forgives sin, raises the dead by His own power, and so on, He must be God. The confusion of the disciples, the anger of the scribes, the violence of the Pharisees all evidence the connection between activity and identity observed by the Fathers. The point is simple: functions are never mere functions but reveal the identity and, yes, the very being, essence, or nature of the one accomplishing the activity.[40] For many New Testament scholars, the Gospel of John and its famous prologue are not concerned with metaphysical speculation on the eternal relationship between the Word and God or even on "how" the Word was in the beginning. Francis Watson explains, "Even in the case of the Gospel of John, a non-incarnational, non-trinitarian reading of this text has been available to New Testament scholarship at least since Schleiermacher. According to this reading, the Johannine concept of the 'sending' of Jesus by the Father implies a purely 'functional' rather than an 'ontological' understanding of his sonship."[41] What then is the point of John's prologue? According to Raymond Brown,

---

40. Cf. Richard Bauckham, "The Divinity of Jesus in the Letter to the Hebrews," in *Jesus and the God of Israel* (Grand Rapids: Eerdmans, 2008), 235.
41. Watson, "Trinity and Community," 168.

the important thing conveyed is what the Word does.[42] The Word creates and redeems. Here we land upon the problem with the distinction between function and ontology. What the Word does can be discussed apart from who the Word is. John's point in the prologue, however, is just the opposite: what the Word does (creation and redemption) is grounded in the ontological claim made about Him (the Word was with God and was God). The Word is not a modality of divine action. Functions are never mere functions. Scripture repeatedly declares that the activity of creating and redeeming belong to the unique identity of God. He alone creates, and He alone saves. Both of these activities or functions are assigned to the Word because the Word is *essentially* God—which is to say, whatever it means *to be* God, this the Word is. Rather than beginning with what the Word does in order to show who He is, John begins the prologue with an ontological claim about the Word and then proceeds to what the Word does. It is John's confession of the Word's coeternity and coequality with God the Father that makes sense of the Word's work as creator and redeemer. Indeed, since the purpose of John's prologue is to emphasize that salvation has come to us and is found in the Word, Jesus Christ, who has taken flesh and tabernacled among us, it is of great significance that he begins with identity and the chief activity that shows that identity (creation) before moving to the purpose of the prologue and the rest of the Gospel (redemption in Christ). Simply stated, ontological conditions attach to these scripturally specific divine functions.[43] If Jesus creates, if Jesus redeems, Jesus is God. That's how the Bible patterns our speech.

CONCLUSION

The next few chapters examine the scriptural identity of God. The question pursued is straightforward: how does God present His own eternal identity to us in the Scriptures? We proceed with the conviction that God is the author of Scripture and the best interpreter of His own Word. The interpretive insight practiced by the Fathers and reformers, and the one that will guide us, is that Scripture interprets Scripture. By approaching Scripture in this way, we will learn from God's Word how He reveals Himself to us as Father, Son, and Holy Spirit. We do this by taking seriously the revelation given to us in the Old Testament and observing how the New Testament clarifies and determines that revelation for us.

In addition to showing the scriptural identity of the Trinity, the next few chapters also aim to assist the reader in teaching and preaching the Trinity. With this in mind I present the material of Scripture by looking at both ordinary,

---

42. Raymond Brown, *The Gospel According to John I-XII*, The Anchor Bible (New York: Doubleday, 1966), 24.
43. Bauckham, "The Divinity of Jesus," 235, and "God Crucified," 30, in *Jesus and the God of Israel*.

narrative presentations of the Trinity and what are often thought of as the more precise dogmatic presentations. The distinction is mine; Scripture places both types of material side by side. My purpose in using this distinction is to show how the Trinity may be preached fruitfully by attending to both types of material. Toward that end I have incorporated many readings from the lectionary to assist both pastors and laypeople.

7

THE TRINITY AND THE OLD TESTAMENT: YHWH, OUR ELOHIM

Given the state of biblical interpretation in our day, the charm of natural theology, and the various cultural opinions on who God most fittingly ought to be, it is fair to ask how a person goes about demonstrating the identity of our triune God from the Scriptures. From the outset we must avoid unhelpful instincts and false assumptions. We cannot reduce the Trinity to a few isolated pericopes or verses of Scripture. Neither should we begin with texts exhibiting a threefold character of reference (e.g., Gn 18:1–15; Is 6:3; Rom 11:36) or texts employing plural verbs with a single referent (e.g., Gn 1:26). Although significant on the far side of the exegetical work required to render these enigmatic expressions telling and instructive of God's triune identity, and although these texts beautifully illumine and adorn our confession of the Trinity, they do not establish our scriptural understanding of Father, Son, and Holy Spirit.[1] We also cannot firstly concern ourselves with creedal expressions or liturgical formulae (1 Cor 8:6; 2 Cor 13:14; Mt 28:19). These brief statements, profoundly significant for any scriptural discussion of the Trinity, more appropriately belong to the end of the discussion. They resemble in purpose the creeds of the early church; they are concluding summaries, liturgical elements, resting upon the fuller disclosure of Father, Son, and Holy Spirit throughout the Scriptures.

At a very basic level, we need to recognize that God's self-revelation is trinitarian because YHWH, our Elohim, is triune, eternally distinct as Father, Son, and Holy Spirit, and yet inseparably and indivisibly one God. There is no scriptural warrant for reading the Old Testament as if the Son and Spirit aren't there. Similarly, we cannot read the New Testament as if something radical has happened to biblical monotheism. The plural identity of the one true God as Father, Son, and Holy Spirit is neither a Gentile, pagan corruption of biblical monotheism nor the result of years of development away from early Jewish commitments on monotheism.[2] The apostles were devout Jews who embraced a

---

1. *Lectures on Genesis*, 1535–45 (AE 3:190–91; WA 43:11.18–12.11); Johann Gerhard, *Theological Commonplaces: On the Nature of God and On the Trinity*, trans. Richard Dinda (St. Louis: Concordia Publishing House, 2007), Exegesis III, §29, 287. The Fathers made great use of texts such as these and offered intriguing allegories that further adorned and taught their trinitarian faith. Luther's comment on these allegories exudes generosity. Gerhard, on the other hand, finds them amusing and takes great delight in recounting some of the more extravagant examples from the Fathers.

2. For a survey of the various issues involved with Jewish monotheism and the principal scholarly works on this topic, see Richard Bauckham, "Biblical Theology and the Problems of

strict monotheism that included Jesus and the Holy Spirit in the unique identity of the one God of Israel. The New Testament consistently points us to the law and the prophets, to the Old Testament, to understand rightly the identity of Christ as the Son of God, the one sent by the Father, who in turn, with the Father, sends the Holy Spirit as promised by the prophets. The conviction of the apostles is that the triune identity of God is known according to the Scriptures, the Old Testament.

The approach taken in the next few chapters follows the instincts of the New Testament writers themselves. They confessed the triune identity of God based on their reception and interpretation of the Old Testament. The Fathers and Lutheran reformers shared this instinct. The exegesis of the Fathers focuses at length on the Old Testament. Johann Gerhard insists, "The mystery of the Trinity can and should be confirmed not only from the New Testament but also from the Old."[3] Brevard Childs, commenting on the labors of the early church, writes, "The church's struggle with the Trinity was not a battle *against* the Old Testament, but rather a battle *for* the Old Testament."[4] The testimony of the apostles proceeds from their commitment to the Old Testament as the sole authoritative witness to the work and identity of God. They unhesitatingly believed that *their* Scriptures, the Scriptures of Israel, described God as He is and that there was no other available source to speak rightly about God.[5] For this reason, writes Christopher Seitz, "YHWH, the Holy One of Israel, is the Father, and the Son, and the Holy Spirit not because such was required for a proper estimate of Jesus Christ as God or of the Spirit as God, but because this was held to be what the literal sense of the Old Testament required when its deliverances were properly grasped, in the light of Christ, as conveyed by the Holy Spirit."[6] There is no rival to God's self-revelation, self-presentation, of His divine identity. If we are to know, confess, and worship the triune YHWH, our Elohim, we require God and His revelation of who He is. No matter how surprising and peculiar that revealed identity might be, no matter how much it might offend our philosophical commitments, cultural allegiances, or moral expectations (1 Cor 1:18–2:16), faith receives this testimony of the only true God.

By allowing God to disclose His triune identity on His own terms, we will accomplish two important things. First, we will enter into the historical narrative God delivers to us through the patriarchs and prophets. Second, we

---

Monotheism," in *Jesus and the God of Israel* (Grand Rapids: Eerdmans, 2008), 60–106; Nathan MacDonald, *Deuteronomy and the Meaning of 'Monotheism'* (Tübingen: Mohr Siebeck, 2003). MacDonald shows the pervasiveness of an Enlightenment understanding of monotheism on biblical scholarship.

3. Gerhard, *Theological Commonplaces*, Exegesis III, §20, 279. For Gerhard's extensive demonstration of this point, see *De Tribus Elohim*, Locus 4/1, §3 (ed. Cotta, 185–223).

4. Brevard Childs, *Biblical Theology of the Old and New Testaments: Theological Reflection on the Christian Bible* (Minneapolis: Fortress Press, 1992), 376.

5. Christopher Seitz, "The Trinity in the Old Testament," *The Oxford Handbook of the Trinity* (Oxford: Oxford University Press, 2011), 31.

6. Seitz, "Trinity in the Old Testament," 38.

will arrive at a description of biblical monotheism and its essential features based solely on a reading of the Old Testament. Whatever constitutes *biblical monotheism* must be derived from the witness of Scripture itself and not from the lingering assumptions of what we think it must mean. The term should serve only as a placeholder to mark out the unique identity of God *according to the Scriptures*. Christopher Seitz explains:

> The pressure toward accounting for the eternal life of God as 'Trinitarian' emerges because of the character of claims made about God in the scriptures of Israel, to which one frequently assigns the term 'monotheistic'. The problem here is that the term 'monotheism', when used in reference to the Old Testament, is nothing but a placeholder serving to rule out some obvious alternatives (Israel did not worship multiple gods in a pantheon) but in itself it is imprecise. At issue is the *kind* of monotheism said to mark the life of God with his people Israel.[7]

When we turn to the New Testament, we observe a deliberate effort on the part of the apostles to locate Jesus and the Holy Spirit in this Old Testament description of the unique identity of God, of the monotheism of Israel. The Christology of the New Testament does not slowly accommodate Jesus into a novel understanding of monotheism any more than its pneumatology slowly incorporates the Holy Spirit. Larry Hurtado and Richard Bauckham have each in their own way demonstrated how the New Testament presents the Son and the Holy Spirit as intrinsic to the identity of God from the very beginning.[8] These divine persons belong eternally within that which marks out God's identity—and this *according to the Scriptures*.

NARRATIVE DESCRIPTION OF GOD

Pious Jews recited the Shema twice daily, morning and evening: "Hear, O Israel: The Lord [YHWH/κύριος] our God, the Lord [YHWH/κύριος] is one" (Dt 6:4). This God of morning and evening prayer had a name and a relationship with His people. The God whose name is YHWH (κύριος in the LXX) is the God of Abraham, Isaac, and Jacob (Exodus 3). He is the God who delivered His people from Egypt; He is the one and only God: "I am the Lord [YHWH/κύριος] your God [Elohim/θεός], who brought you out of the land of Egypt, out of the house of slavery. You shall have no other gods before me" (Ex 20:2–3). God's absolute uniqueness, His oneness, involved both confession and worship: "You shall worship no other god, for the Lord, whose name is Jealous, is a jealous God" (Ex 34:14; 20:5; cf. Dt 6:13–15). To confess the one true God meant to worship the one true God. To worship anything or anyone other than the Lord (YHWH/κύριος) meant idolatry. The first commandment of the Decalogue emphasizes the necessity and importance of both of these points (Ex 20:2–5; Dt 5:6–9). The

---

7. Seitz, "Trinity in the Old Testament," 30.
8. Larry Hurtado, *One God, One Lord: Early Christian Devotion and Ancient Jewish Monotheism*, 2d ed. (Edinburgh: T&T Clark, 1998); Bauckham, *Jesus and the God of Israel*.

prophets continue this emphasis: "I am the Lord [YHWH]; that is my name; my glory I give to no other, nor my praise to carved idols" (Is 42:8).

The one and only Lord God encountered in the Old Testament has a distinct and recognizable identity. We know Him by the things He does, the relationships He establishes, and the promises He makes. The opening verse of the Bible declares: "In the beginning God created the heavens and the earth" (Gn 1:1). He is the God who created all things (Is 40:26, 28; Psalm 104) and rules all things (Dn 4:34–35; Psalm 105). He is the God who delivered Israel from bondage in Egypt and made them His people. Moses is to declare to Pharaoh, "Thus says the Lord, 'Let *my* people go'" (Ex 5:1). Moses is to say to the people that the God of Abraham, Isaac, and Jacob, the God who established a covenant with their fathers, God Almighty, will deliver them from Egypt. He is to say to them, "I will take you to be my people, and I will be your God, and you shall know that I am YHWH your Elohim, who has brought you out from under the burdens of the Egyptians" (Ex 6:7). It is on Sinai that God reveals His most characteristic features to Moses, characteristics repeated throughout the Old Testament. The God who creates and rules His creation, the God who elects a people for Himself and puts His love upon them, the God who protects and delivers, the God who multiplies and blesses both the fruit of the womb and the fruit of the field, this God and no other is to be worshipped and glorified, this Lord God of Israel is "merciful and gracious, slow to anger, and abounding in steadfast love and faithfulness" (Ex 34:6; cf. Nm 14:18; Neh 9:17; Ps 103:8, Jl 2:13; Jon 4:2). God's grace and mercy establish the context in which He is known, confessed, and worshipped by His people.

Murmuring began as soon as the people set out from Sinai. They remembered not God's deliverance from Egypt but instead the fish that cost nothing, the cucumbers, the melons, the leeks, the onions, and the garlic (Nm 11:4–5). Israel sought her fill elsewhere than God: "I am the Lord your God, who brought you up out of the land of Egypt. Open your mouth wide, and I will fill it" (Ps 81:10). God promised to multiply His people and protect them against their enemies, more numerous and mightier though they be (Dt 7:1). The people were to be a blessing to the idolatrous and wayward nations; instead they longed to be like the other nations. They were not to intermarry but they did (Dt 7:3; Jos 23:12–13). They were not to pursue strange and foreign gods but they did. YHWH was never enough; the people wanted the Baals and Ashtaroth too (Jgs 2:13). The nations had kings; the people had only a King in heaven (1 Sm 8:5–9). The people wanted to be like the nations; they wanted to increase like them and become mighty like them. They forsook God, sinned against Him, and pursued the best ideas of the day, the ways of the nations: "They did not believe in God and did not trust his saving power" (Ps 78:22). When Israel rebelled, they "grieved his Holy Spirit" (Is 63:10).

The God who created all things and rules all things is the God who redeems and recreates. The God who delivered Israel from the Egyptians, who guided them through the wilderness, who spoke truth to Moses is also the very God who alone brings salvation. The Old Testament gives witness to who God is not principally in terms of Sinai and the Law but principally in terms of His steadfast love and mercy. YHWH our Elohim is known chiefly not by His might against the nations and against Pharaoh, but by His salvation and redemption of the nations through a people He elected, a people He protected and provided for, a people who chose strange gods over Him and the way of the nations over His way, their truth over His truth. The faithful remnant living among an unfaithful and unclean people witness this truth by their cry of faith: "Restore us again, O God of our salvation, and put away your indignation toward us" (Ps 85:4); "Cast me not off, forsake me not, O God of my salvation" (Ps 27:9); "Let your steadfast love come to me, O YHWH, your salvation according to your promise" (Ps 119:41); "But this I call to mind, and therefore I have hope: The steadfast love of YHWH never ceases; his mercies never come to an end; they are new every morning; great is your faithfulness" (Lam 3:21–23).

YHWH our Elohim is truth and His way is life. The Psalms never tire of confessing this: "Make me to know your ways, O Lord; teach me your paths. Lead me in your truth and teach me, for you are the God of my salvation; for you I wait all the day long" (Ps 25:4–5). Again, "Teach me your way, O Lord, that I may walk in your truth" (Ps 86:11). To walk in God's truth is to take refuge in Him, to find deliverance in His righteousness (Ps 31:1), for He alone is the way, the truth, and the life, and this life is the "everlasting light" of men (Is 60:19). The prayer of David (Psalm 51) and the prayer of Daniel (Daniel 9) seek salvation, the forgiveness of sins, from God, because against Him we sin and by Him we are freed from that sin (Is 43:25). To God alone belongs righteousness, to us shame (Dn 9:7); to God alone "mercy and forgiveness," to us transgression and "the curse" written in the Law of Moses (Dn 9:9–11). The one forgiven, whose sin is not counted, is blessed (Ps 32:1) and rejoices in the Lord, shouting for joy and bearing the name "righteous" (Ps 32:11; 33:1). The righteousness here spoken of is a borrowed righteousness. Just as we confess "in your Light shall we see light" (Ps 36:9) and that YHWH will be our "everlasting light" (Is 60:19), a light that is ours not by nature but by faith, a borrowed light, so too we bear the name "righteous" not by nature but by faith: "Only in YHWH, it shall be said of me, are righteousness and strength" (Is 45:24), for "YHWH is our Righteousness" (Jer 23:6). The faithful confess their sin to YHWH because from YHWH alone comes forgiveness: "I acknowledged my sin to you, and I did not cover my iniquity; I said, 'I will confess my transgressions to YHWH,' and you forgave the iniquity of my sin" (Ps 32:5). Again we read, "Out of the depths I cry to you, O YHWH! O Lord, hear my voice! Let your ears be attentive to the voice of my pleas for mercy! If you, O YHWH, should mark iniquities, O Lord, who could stand? But with you there is forgiveness, that you may be feared" (Ps 130:1–4). The faithful of all generations have cried out to God from depths of woe, confessing and singing, "Thy love and grace alone avail to blot out my transgression." Our hope

The Trinity and the Old Testament

rests not in ourselves and our merit (Jb 15:14; Is 64:6) but in the Lord, in His faithful Word and promise: "Turn thou us unto thee, O Lord, and we shall be turned" (Lam 5:21 KJV). The final stanza of Luther's well-known hymn captures the confession of Psalm 130, the pleas of David and Daniel, and that faithful remnant of Israel.

> Though great our sins and sore our woes,
>   His grace much more aboundeth;
> His helping love no limit knows,
>   Our utmost need it soundeth.
> Our Shepherd good and true is He,
> Who will at last His Israel free
>   From all their sin and sorrow. (TLH 329:5)

How will YHWH bring about this salvation? How will He deliver to us the forgiveness of our sins? The question raised and then answered throughout the prophets is how this salvation will come about and when it will occur.

Daniel confesses his sins and the sins of the people to God, seeking forgiveness not because of any presumed righteousness on their part but only because of God's great mercy (Dn 9:18). While making this confession, the angel Gabriel appears to Daniel and reveals to him when God will accomplish His salvation. A time will come ("seventy weeks are decreed") when the transgression will be finished, sin ended, iniquity atoned for, and everlasting righteousness brought in (Dn 9:24). These seventy weeks correspond to the time when "the God of heaven will set up a kingdom that shall never be destroyed, nor shall the kingdom be left to another people" (Dn 2:44). This kingdom that shall stand forever will be ushered in by the "stone" cut from a mountain "without human hand" (Dn 2:45). This stone is later identified as the Son of Man who is presented before the Ancient of Days: "And to him was given dominion and glory and a kingdom, that all peoples, nations, and languages should serve him; his dominion is an everlasting dominion, which shall not pass away, and his kingdom one that shall not be destroyed" (Dn 7:14). This Son of Man is the Messiah (KJV), the Christ (LXX), who shall be cut off, which is to say, suffer death (Dn 9:26). This is the Son promised to David, whom YHWH will raise up, whose kingdom shall be established and whose throne will be forever (1 Chr 17:11–12). Indeed, declares YHWH, "I will be his father, and he shall be my son" (2 Sm 7:14; 1 Chr 17:13 KJV).

All of this shall happen "in the latter days" (Is 2:2; Mi 4:1; Hos 3:5; cf. Acts 2). As noted above, forgiveness comes from YHWH alone. His "salvation will be forever" and His "righteousness will be forever" (Is 51:6, 8). According to the prophet Daniel, this salvation, forgiveness, and everlasting righteousness will be accomplished by the Messiah, the Son of Man, whose dominion is everlasting, whose kingdom shall not be destroyed, whose throne will be forever. The Old Testament emphatically states that salvation and righteousness belong to YHWH alone and to one distinct yet inseparable from YHWH, as a father is distinct and yet inseparable from his son. For this reason, YHWH says not only that "my salvation" and "my righteousness" are forever but that "my salvation has gone out" and "my righteousness draws near" (Is 51:5–8). The one who has gone out, the one who draws near, is the Son of Man, the Messiah, the Christ.

The prophecy of the Christ given to Daniel is found throughout the prophets. For Isaiah, the stone cut from the mountain without human hand is the Son born of the Virgin and called Immanuel, God with us (Is 7:14). The time when salvation will be accomplished and everlasting righteousness brought in is the day when the Lord will raise up a shoot from the stump of Jesse, a Branch, upon whom shall rest the Spirit of YHWH (Is 11:1–2; cf. 61:1). Likewise, in Jeremiah we read that YHWH will raise up for David "a righteous Branch" who shall reign as King and execute justice and righteousness in the land (Jer 23:5). Indeed, this Messiah, this Christ (Ps 2:2 LXX), declares YHWH, shall be "my King" (Ps 2:6) and "my Son" (Ps 2:7). This promised offspring, this Branch, this Son, is the promised "seed" of the woman (Gn 3:15), the "seed" of Abraham (Gn 22:18), the "seed" of David (1 Chr 17:11), whose Name is "YHWH our Righteousness" (Jer 23:5). We pray with David, "Hear my prayer, O YHWH, give ear to my supplications: in thy faithfulness answer me, and in thy righteousness. And enter not into judgment with thy servant: for in thy sight shall no man living be justified" (Ps 143:2 KJV). And we rejoice with Jeremiah, "YHWH is our Righteousness!"[9] Zechariah likewise tells us that this Branch is the Servant of God who will bring about the redemption of the world (Zec 3:8), who will be both King and Priest (Zec 6:13; Psalm 110), and who shall build the temple of the Lord (Zec 6:12).

This Righteous Branch, this Servant, this Son, this Christ, will not just build the temple but will Himself be the temple/tabernacle that dwells in the midst of His people. The Lord declares through Zechariah, "Sing and rejoice, O daughter of Zion, for behold, I come and I will dwell in your midst [κατασκηνώσω ἐν μέσῳ σου], and you shall know that YHWH Sabaoth has sent me to you" (Zec 2:10–11). The coming of the tabernacle to be in the midst of the people signals the "covenant of peace" and the "everlasting covenant" between God and His people (Ez 37:26). God declares through Ezekiel, "My tabernacle shall be with them; indeed I will be their Elohim, and they shall be my people. Then the nations will know that I, YHWH, sanctify Israel, when my sanctuary is in their midst forevermore" (Ez 37:27–28 NKJV).

This Righteous Branch, this Servant, this Savior and Redeemer, who will tabernacle with God's people forever, whose kingdom and throne shall be established forever, will come in the latter days. When He comes, He will bring comfort and pardon iniquity (Is 40:1–2). His way will be prepared by a messenger crying in the wilderness, "Prepare the way of YHWH; make straight in the desert a highway for our Elohim" (Is 40:3). When this day arrives, "the

---

9. For a helpful reflection on this divine name see Theodore Laetsch, *Jeremiah* (St. Louis: Concordia Publishing House, 1952), 189–90.

Glory of YHWH shall be revealed, and all flesh shall see it together, for the mouth of YHWH has spoken" (Is 40:5). YHWH's Glory will be revealed, all will see it, because "the Lord whom you seek will suddenly come to his temple" (Mal 3:1). "The day of YHWH" (Mal 4:1; Is 13:6, 9; Jer 46:10; Jl 1:15; 2:1, 11; Ob 15) is a day of judgment, a day of sifting, for the one to come is "like a refiner's fire and fullers' soap" (Mal 3:2). When this day comes, "you shall see the distinction between the righteous and the wicked, between one who serves God and one who does not serve him" (Mal 3:18). The children of Zion, the faithful, fear not this day but are glad and rejoice, for YHWH our Elohim will send "the Teacher of Righteousness" (Jl 2:23), who is our abundance and treasure (Jl 2:24–26).[10] And it shall come to pass afterward that the Spirit will be poured out (Jl 2:28; Ez 39:29) and "everyone who calls on the name of YHWH shall be saved" (Jl 2:32).

The prophets further clarify the identity of this Righteous Branch and the role of the Spirit in YHWH's saving work. The Righteous Branch is the one born of the Virgin, called Immanuel (Is 7:9), upon whom the Spirit of the Lord shall rest (Is 11:2; 42:1; 61:1; cf. Lk 4:18). He who is Righteousness (Jer 23:6) shall judge with righteousness (Is 11:4), imputing others with righteousness (Is 53:11) and ushering in peace (Is 11:5–9). In that day the faithful will declare, "Behold, God is my salvation; I will trust, and will not be afraid; for the LORD GOD is my strength and my song, and he has become my salvation" (Is 12:2). These themes of the Servant and YHWH alone as savior become intertwined the further into Isaiah's prophecy we read. The one upon whom the Spirit of YHWH shall rest, the same Spirit who shall be poured out following the Servant's work, will be "my Servant" and He will bring justice to the nations (Is 42:1; 62:1). The one who created is the one who will redeem:

> But now thus says YHWH, he who created you, O Jacob, he who formed you, O Israel: "Fear not, for I have redeemed you; I have called you by name, you are mine. . . . For I am YHWH your Elohim, the Holy One of Israel, your Savior. . . . You are my witnesses," declares YHWH, "and my Servant whom I have chosen, that you may know and believe me and understand that I am he. Before me no god was formed, nor shall there be any after me. I, I am YHWH, and besides me there is no savior. I declared and saved and proclaimed, when there was no strange god among you; and you are my witnesses," declares YHWH, "and I am God. Also henceforth I am he; there is none who can deliver from my hand; I work, and who can turn it back?" Thus says YHWH, your Redeemer, the Holy One of Israel." (Is 43:1–14)

The refrain continues in Isaiah that this YHWH who saves, this Holy One, is unlike any other. He alone created His people and will redeem them. He alone declares what is to come and what will happen. He is the first and the last. He is the Rock.

> Thus says YHWH, the King of Israel and his Redeemer, the Lord of hosts: "I am the first and I am the last; besides me there is no god. Who is like me? Let him proclaim

---

10. For a discussion of "Teacher of Righteousness" see Theodore Laetsch, *The Minor Prophets* (St. Louis: Concordia Publishing House, 1956), 125–26.

> it. Let him declare and set it before me, since I appointed an ancient people. Let them declare what is to come, and what will happen. Fear not, nor be afraid; have I not told you from of old and declared it? And you are my witnesses! Is there a God besides me? There is no Rock; I know not any." (Is 44:6–8)

Lest the point be missed, YHWH again declares, "For thus says YHWH, who created the heavens (he is Elohim!), who formed the earth and made it (he established it; he did not create it empty, he formed it to be inhabited!): 'I am YHWH, and there is no other'" (Is 45:18). The Lord who saves is the Lord who created the heavens and the earth. He alone is God who speaks "the truth" and declares what is right (Is 45:19). Again, YHWH declares, "there is no other god besides me, a righteous God, and a Savior; there is none besides me. . . . Only in YHWH, it shall be said of me, are righteousness and strength; to him shall come and be ashamed all who were incensed against him. In YHWH all the offspring of Israel shall be justified and shall glory" (Is 45:21–25).

At this point Isaiah returns to the Servant upon whom the Spirit shall rest. This Servant "shall be high and lifted up, and shall be exalted" (Is 52:13; cf. Jn 8:28; 12:32). Isaiah uses the same language for this Servant that he used to describe YHWH Sabaoth whom he beheld high on a lofty throne in splendor bright: "I saw the Lord sitting upon a throne, high and lifted up; and the train of his robe filled the temple" (Is 6:1; Jn 12:41). The Servant "high and lifted up" shares the throne of God. Later on Isaiah describes the Servant "high and lifted up" as the one "who inhabits eternity, whose name is Holy" (Is 57:15; cf. Lk 1:35). The Servant described by Isaiah is the eternal Lord who shall be high and lifted up and exalted to the right hand of God (Ps 110:1; cf. Acts 2:33; Rv 5:13–14). That is to say, the one who eternally shares the throne of God will be exalted. But how can one who eternally shares the throne be exalted? This is the question that St. Paul answers in Philippians 2. Exaltation assumes humiliation, the incarnation of the Servant called Holy (Lk 1:35, 49).[11]

Isaiah directs his attention to the humiliation of the Servant. The Servant will be despised and rejected by men, a man of sorrows, who will bear our griefs and carry our sorrows (Is 53:2–3). He will be wounded for our transgressions, crushed for our iniquities, for "YHWH has laid on him the iniquity of us all" (Is 53:5–6). He who bears our iniquities is the Righteous One who will justify us (Is 53:11). When this occurs, YHWH declares, I will pour out the Spirit of grace and mercy and the people "*shall look upon me whom they have pierced*, and they shall mourn *for him*, as one mourneth for his only son, and shall be in bitterness for him, as one that is in bitterness for his firstborn" (Zec 12:10 KJV; Jn 19:37; Rv 1:7). YHWH says they shall look upon "me" whom they have pierced, and at the same time they shall mourn "for him." The one pierced will be "a fountain opened for the house of David and the inhabitants of Jerusalem, to cleanse them from sin and uncleanness" (Zec 13:1). The one wounded for our transgressions, the one pierced for us, corresponds to the Christ described to Daniel who will

---

11. Bauckham, "God Crucified," in *Jesus and the God of Israel*, 35–36.

atone for sins, usher in everlasting righteousness, and be cut off (Dn 9:24, 26), the Righteous Branch, Immanuel, named by Jeremiah YHWH our Righteousness.

This high and lifted up Servant upon whom rests the Spirit of God will bring good news to the poor, bind up the brokenhearted, proclaim liberty to the captives, and comfort all who mourn (Is 61:1–2). He will open the eyes of the blind, unstop the ears of the deaf, and loosen the string of the mute (Is 35:4–6). This Servant, who is both King and Shepherd (Ez 34:23–24), will enter triumphantly into Jerusalem (Zec 9:9), bear our iniquities, and bring everlasting peace (Mi 5:2–5) and salvation to all (Isaiah 55–56). All of this will be done by the one YHWH Sabaoth calls "my Companion" (Zec 13:7 NKJV), "the Man who stands next to me" (Zec 13:7 ESV). Following the work of the Servant, the Christ, the one who is the eternal Son at the right hand of the eternal Father (Ps 110:1), the Spirit shall be poured out (Jl 2:28; Ez 39:29) and "everyone who calls on the name of YHWH shall be saved" (Jl 2:32). And finally, when the times are accomplished, the books shall be opened, and "those who sleep in the dust of the earth shall awake, some to everlasting life and some to shame and everlasting contempt" (Dn 12:1–2; Rv 20:12–13).

THE SEEN AND UNSEEN YHWH

YHWH declared to Moses, "You cannot see my face, for man shall not see me and live" (Ex 33:20). And yet YHWH has been seen by some, who initially express surprise that this could be happening only to be overcome with fear that this is happening. Hagar saw God and was surprised to live (Gn 16:13). Jacob declared, "For I have seen God face to face, and yet my life has been delivered" (Gn 32:30). Gideon saw the Angel of YHWH face to face and was overcome with fear for his life: "'Alas, O Lord God! For now I have seen the Angel of YHWH face to face.' But YHWH said to him, 'Peace be to you. Do not fear; you shall not die'" (Jgs 6:22–23). Likewise, Manoah, the father of Samson, said to his wife, after their encounter with the Angel of YHWH, "We shall surely die, for we have seen Elohim" (Jgs 13:22). Isaiah panics when he sees YHWH: "In the year that King Uzziah died I saw the Lord sitting upon a throne, high and lifted up; and the train of his robe filled the temple. . . . And I said: 'Woe is me! For I am lost; for I am a man of unclean lips, and I dwell in the midst of a people of unclean lips; for my eyes have seen the King, YHWH of hosts!'" (Is 6:1, 5).

Charles Gieschen has written extensively on these Old Testament theophanies. He asks, "If one cannot see YHWH and live, and yet people are seeing YHWH and not dying, then who is this visible image of YHWH that is being seen?"[12] The Old Testament variously identifies this visible YHWH as the

---

12. Charles Gieschen, "The Real Presence of the Son Before Christ: Revisiting an Old Approach to Old Testament Christology," *Concordia Theological Quarterly* 68 (2004): 115. The following discussion leans heavily on this article and Gieschen's more extensive treatment in *Angelomorphic Christology: Antecedents and Early Evidence* (Leiden: Brill, 1998).

Angel of YHWH, the Name of YHWH, the Glory of YHWH, or the Word of YHWH. Scripture also interchangeably makes use of Elohim and YHWH speaking also of the Angel of Elohim or designating the Glory of YHWH as the Elohim of Israel, the God of Israel. Gideon for example sees the "Angel of YHWH" but the one who speaks to him is YHWH. Manoah sees the Angel of YHWH and says that he and his wife will die because they have seen Elohim. Since Scripture declares only that those who see YHWH will die, we see here with Gideon and Manoah the semantic range available to them to designate YHWH. If Manoah had thought the Elohim or the Angel of YHWH he saw was not YHWH Himself, he never would have declared that he should surely die. His response is a variation of the activity/identity pattern of Scripture discussed in the previous chapter. We know the person he sees (however he might designate that person) based on the activity or consequence assigned by him for seeing such a person.

The difficulty with these theophanies rests not with determining the identity of the one seen or encountered by Hagar, Abraham, Jacob, Moses, and the rest. That point is made evident based on their reactions and a careful reading of the text. The difficulty has more to do with the fact that these texts make a distinction between the visible form of YHWH, who in some sense stands apart from the unseen YHWH, and yet at the same time both belong to the unique identity of YHWH. They are distinct but inseparable, two and yet one. The Old Testament shows no interest in resolving how we should understand this plurality within the unique identity of YHWH, the one true God of Israel. Rather than expressing angst over this question, the New Testament with remarkable consistency assigns these various appearances to Jesus Christ, the Son of God, the *Word* made flesh (Jn 1:14), the one who has come in the Father's *Name* (Jn 5:43), a Name the Father will glorify (Jn 12:28) with the *Glory* the Son had with the Father before the world began (Jn 17:5). The New Testament writers press even further, declaring that Jesus was present at various times to the patriarchs and prophets. Christ appeared to Abraham, bringing him great joy (Jn 8:56–59); Isaiah saw His glory and spoke of Him (Jn 12:41); Jesus led the people out of Egypt (Jude 5), Christ was with Israel in the wilderness (1 Cor 10:1–10). The Son is "the image of the invisible God" (Col 1:15) who is at the Father's side and who has made the unseen Father known to us (Jn 1:18). To look upon the Son is to see the Father (Jn 14:9–11). Who is the YHWH seen in the Old Testament making known the unseen YHWH? The New Testament never hesitates to make this identification. There only ever has been one upon whom you might look to see the Father: "For God, who said, 'Let light shine out of darkness,' has shone in our hearts to give the light of the knowledge of the glory of God in the face of Jesus Christ" (2 Cor 4:6). Jesus puts it simply: "Whoever has seen me has seen the Father" (Jn 14:9).

The Old Testament testifies both to prophecy about the coming Christ and to His true presence with the patriarchs and prophets. Although this chapter's purpose is to present the Old Testament identity of God, there is only so much that can be said about these theophanies without recourse to the New Testament. Here the unity and perfection of Scripture prove indispensable for sorting out these suggestive and ambiguous encounters between God and His people in the Old Testament. From the perspective of the New Testament, the one who assumed flesh and tabernacled among His people is also the one who appeared to the patriarchs and prophets. It is He who wrestled with Jacob, spoke to Moses from the burning bush, and led Israel through the wilderness; the same who conversed with Gideon and with Samson's parents, who showed His glory to Isaiah and Ezekiel, and who touched Jeremiah's mouth. Rather than correlating these various theophanies with the New Testament, the purpose below aims to establish a more basic point: YHWH manifests Himself in visible form to His people. That same YHWH upon whom no one may look and live also makes Himself known to His people and they live. Scripture accounts for this by distinguishing between the unseen YHWH and the seen YHWH, but not in such a manner as to compromise the unique oneness of YHWH.

The Angel of YHWH

Genesis presents a number of intriguing appearances of the Angel of YHWH/Elohim.[13] In the first the Angel of YHWH finds Hagar and speaks to her (Gn 16:7-11). The Angel of YHWH says, "I will surely multiply your offspring so that they cannot be numbered for multitude" (16:10). The Angel continues by explaining this at greater length and says this will happen because "YHWH has listened to her affliction" (16:11). Upon hearing this Hagar calls the "Name of YHWH" the "God of seeing," and then immediately wonders if she has really seen Him who sees her (16:13). In the next chapter God speaks to Abraham and tells him what He has said to Hagar about Ishmael: "Behold, I have blessed him and will make him fruitful and multiply him greatly" (17:20). In the discourse with Abraham no distinction is made between God and the Angel. Similarly, the Angel of YHWH speaks in the first person to Hagar, "*I* will multiply your offspring." When the Angel explains why, He shifts to the third person, saying that YHWH is the one doing this for her. Hagar for her part understands that she has come into the presence of God and questions whether this can really be the case. According to the pattern established here by Scripture, the Angel of YHWH remains distinct from YHWH and yet they both do that which belongs to YHWH alone.

Two chapters later we encounter one of the most puzzling theophanies in Scripture. We read that YHWH appears to Abraham by the oaks of Mamre (Gn 18:1). When Abraham lifts his eyes, he beholds three men (18:2) and feeds them (18:8). Things only become more difficult from here. The three men are referred

---

13. For a more detailed discussion of these Angel of YHWH appearances, see Gieschen, *Angelomorphic Christology*, 53-69. For a summary of them and their implication for trinitarian thinking, see Robert Jenson, "The Bible and the Trinity," *Pro Ecclesia* 11/3 (2002): 329-39; Jenson, "The Trinity in the Bible," *Concordia Theological Quarterly* 68 (2004): 195-206.

to as YHWH, and eventually two of them are called angels (19:1). YHWH speaks to Abraham in both the singular (18:10, 13) and the plural (18:9). Abraham stands before YHWH and pleads on behalf of Sodom and Gomorrah (18:22–32). In the account of the destruction of Sodom and Gomorrah the details become more puzzling: two of the men are identified as angels and continue to be seen as men (19:1, 5, 8). These two angels/men rescue Lot from the men of Sodom and strike some of them with blindness (19:10–11). They tell Lot to gather his family and leave Sodom. After they do this we read, "YHWH rained on Sodom and Gomorrah sulfur and fire from YHWH out of heaven" (19:24). This is a cryptic verse, to be sure.[14] Clarity could have been achieved if the verse said, "The Angel of YHWH rained on Sodom and Gomorrah sulfur and fire from YHWH out of heaven." That meaning seems to be implied by Gn 19:21, where the angel speaking to Lot identifies himself as the one who has the power to overthrow these cities. That sort of phrasing also would have fit well with the larger pattern we encounter in Genesis 16 and 22. And yet, if that is how the verse is to be understood, the omission of "Angel" only further emphasizes the unique identity exhibited by the Angel of YHWH and YHWH.[15] The Fathers followed the New Testament and identified the first YHWH with Jesus. He is the one who destroyed "those who did not believe" in the wilderness (cf. Numbers 14 and 16; 1 Cor 10:10) and those at Sodom and Gomorrah (Jude 5–7). The Fathers saw this text and the larger theophany as a revelation of the Trinity. Abraham sees the unseen, speaks to Him, and lives. YHWH speaks in both the singular and plural. The Scriptures further suggest diversity within the unity of YHWH in the destruction of Sodom and Gomorrah.[16]

---

14. For a similar doubling see Ex 35:5 and Hos 1:7. Johann Gerhard takes all three of these examples as speaking of the Father and the Son. See Gerhard, *Theological Commonplaces*, Exegesis III, §150, 399; Gerhard, *De Tribus Elohim*, Locus 4/1, § 8 (ed. Cotta, 188–89).

Luther follows the Fathers in understanding Gn 19:24 as a reference to the Trinity (AE 3:296–97; WA 43:87.25–40 and AE 15:280; WA 54:39.11–17). Hilary of Poitiers writes, "*The Lord rained brimstone and fire from the Lord*. It is *The Lord from the Lord*; scripture makes no distinction by difference of name between their natures, but discriminates between themselves. . . . Thus what the Lord gave the Lord had received from the Lord" (*De Trinitate*, 4.29; NPNF, ii, vol. 9, 80). Cf. Ambrose of Milan, *De Fide*, I.23 (NPNF, ii, vol. 10, 204).

Martin Chemnitz quotes Luther's rule: "Whenever in Scripture you find God speaking about God, as if there were two persons, you may boldly assume that three Persons of the Godhead are there indicated" (AE 15:280; WA 54:39.8–10). On Gn 19:24 he then writes, "'The Lord rained fire and brimstone from the Lord,' that is, the Son from the Father, with the Spirit acting as witness." Martin Chemnitz, *Loci Theologici*, trans. J. A. O. Preus (St. Louis: Concordia Publishing House, 2008), 1:91. For similar interpretations of this text by Lutherans see David Chytraeus, *In Genesin Enarratio* (Wittenberg, 1576), 376–77; Aegidius Hunnius, *Calvinus Iudaizans* (Wittenberg, 1604), 15–16; Matthias Hafenreffer, *Loci Theologici* (Tübingen, 1603), 32, 52.

15. Jarl E. Fossum, *The Image of the Invisible God* (Göttingen: Vandenhoek & Ruprecht, 1995), 51, 55–57.

16. The modern reading of Gn 19:27 departs from the ancient Jewish and Christian reading. Modern interpreters find literary emphasis—the YHWH who destroyed is the YHWH from heaven. The ancient rabbis recognized the grammatical distinction between YHWH the destroyer and the YHWH from heaven. They suggested the first was an angelic intermediary, perhaps Gabriel. The Fathers, as mentioned, saw the first YHWH as the Son and the second as the Father. For a

The Trinity and the Old Testament

A few chapters later God tells Abraham to offer Isaac as a burnt offering. When Abraham prepares the altar and places Isaac upon it, he reaches out his hand and takes the knife. At that moment, "the Angel of YHWH called to him from heaven . . . Do not lay your hand on the boy or do anything to him, for now *I know* you fear Elohim, seeing you have not withheld your son, your only son, *from me*" (22:11–12). As with Hagar above, there is both distinction and no distinction between the Angel of YHWH and God. On the one hand the Angel says, "I know you fear God," and on the other hand, "You have not withheld your son, your only son, from *me*." The Angel's words indicate that He is both distinct from God and is God.

The various appearances of the Angel of YHWH in the rest of the Old Testament are as suggestive and as ambiguous as the ones in Genesis. The Angel of YHWH appears to Moses in the flame of fire out of the midst of a bush that is not consumed (Ex 3:2). YHWH sees Moses turn toward the bush and Elohim calls out to him that the place on which he stands is holy ground (3:3–6). The voice from the bush declares, "I am the Elohim of your father, the Elohim of Abraham, the Elohim of Isaac, and the Elohim of Jacob" (3:6). Moses turns away "for he was afraid to look at God" (3:6). The voice from the bush continues to speak to Moses and the text identifies this voice as YHWH (3:7). We continue to see here with Moses what we saw with Hagar and Abraham: a distinction exists between the Angel of YHWH and YHWH, and yet the two are woven inseparably into the same text. For example, according to the text, who is in the burning bush? The answer is the Angel of YHWH. Again, according to the text, who speaks from the burning bush? The answer is YHWH.

Similar appearances happen with Gideon and with Manoah and his wife, the parents of Samson. The Angel of YHWH comes to Gideon, who fails to recognize the one before him. Only after offering his sacrifice, only in the act of worship, does Gideon understand. He then declares, "'For now I have seen the Angel of YHWH face to face.' But YHWH said to him, 'Peace be to you. Do not fear; you shall not die'" (Jgs 6:22–23). Manoah and his wife encounter one variously referred to as the Angel of YHWH (Jgs 13:3, 13, 15, 16, 18, 20, 21), the Angel of Elohim (13:6), a man of Elohim (13:6, 8), Elohim (13:9, 22), or simply as the man (13:10, 11), whose name is "wonderful" (13:18; Is 9:6). At the end of their exchange we read, "Then Manoah knew that he was the Angel of YHWH. And Manoah said to his wife, 'We shall surely die, for we have seen Elohim'" (Jgs 13:21–22).

Despite the numerous difficulties attending each example above, what the text asserts unambiguously, however difficult it might be to conceptualize or explain, is that real distinction avails between YHWH and the Angel *of* YHWH, and yet once that distinction establishes itself the Angel of YHWH speaks and acts as God in the first person. There is both distinction and identity between YHWH and the Angel of YHWH. Further, a point that will become more

---

thorough discussion of this text see Fossum, *Image of the Invisible God*, 41–51.

pronounced in the theophanies discussed below, the seen YHWH may also be called "the man of Elohim" or simply "the man" whose name is Wonderful. Following the pattern of Scripture, the one named Wonderful is the child born of the Virgin, Immanuel, whose name shall be called "Wonderful Counselor" (Is 9:6).[17]

The Name of YHWH

The Old Testament continues this pattern of alternating between one identified as YHWH and yet distinct from YHWH with the equally suggestive designations of the Name of YHWH, the Glory of YHWH, or the Word of YHWH.[18] For example, YHWH declares to Moses, "Behold, I send an Angel before you to guard you on the way and to bring you to the place that I have prepared. Pay careful attention to him and obey his voice; do not rebel against him, for he will not pardon your transgression, for my Name is in him. But if you carefully obey his voice and do all that I say, then I will be an enemy to your enemies and an adversary to your adversaries" (Ex 23:20–22). The Angel who will guard the people and in whom rests the power to absolve and retain sin possesses the "Name" of YHWH. The Name of YHWH is distinct from YHWH and yet also inseparable from YHWH. The people are to listen to the voice of the Angel who bears the Name of YHWH, and in doing this they listen to YHWH. As Gieschen succinctly puts it, "One cannot separate the name YHWH from the reality of YHWH."[19] In the same way a person cannot separate the voice of the Angel bearing the Name of YHWH from YHWH. To hear one is to hear the other. They are distinct but inseparable.

A few chapters later YHWH commands Moses to come upon Mount Sinai. Moses does as YHWH commands him. We then read, "YHWH descended in the cloud and stood with him there and proclaimed the Name of YHWH. YHWH passed before him and proclaimed, 'YHWH, YHWH, a God merciful and gracious, slow to anger, and abounding in steadfast love and faithfulness, keeping steadfast love for thousands, forgiving iniquity and transgression and sin'" (Ex 34:6–7). Again YHWH proclaims the Name of YHWH to Moses (distinction) and the proclamation is "YHWH, YHWH" (identity). That which describes YHWH, which marks out His identity—namely, that He is merciful, gracious, abounding in steadfast love and faithfulness, keeping steadfast love, and forgiving iniquity, transgression, and sin—is true of both YHWH and the Name of YHWH as proclaimed by YHWH.[20]

---

17. Although cryptic, Dn 8:13–14 identifies two angels. The reformers understood the first angel as Christ and the second as Gabriel. The text further names the first angel in the LXX as Palmoni (φελμουνι), an indeclinable noun that lacks definition. Most of the reformers elected to leave this name as is and argued that it was a title for Christ. Melanchthon argued that if it were to be translated it would be rendered "something or someone wonderful" and correspond to "Wonderful Counselor" in Is 9:6. See Philipp Melanchthon, *In Danielem Prophetam Commentarius* (Leipzig, 1543), 137.

18. On the Name of YHWH see further Gieschen, *Angelomorphic Christology*, 70–78.

19. Gieschen, "Real Presence of the Son Before Christ," 116.

20. A similar example, although not dealing with the Name of YHWH, occurs with Hosea.

The relationship between YHWH and the Name of YHWH becomes even more striking with the temple, the house built by Solomon where the Name of YHWH dwells: "And so I [Solomon] intend to build a house for the Name of YHWH my Elohim, as YHWH said to David my father, 'Your son, whom I will set on your throne in your place, shall build the house for my Name'" (1 Kgs 5:5). God had declared to Moses that His Name would dwell at His chosen place of worship when the people inherited the land that the Lord would provide for them across the Jordan. Then YHWH would give them rest from their enemies and a place to worship (Dt 12:9–10): "Then to the place that YHWH your Elohim will choose, to make his Name dwell there, there you shall bring all that I command you: your burnt offerings and your sacrifices, your tithes and the contribution that you present, and all your finest vow offerings that you vow to YHWH. And you shall rejoice before YHWH your Elohim" (Dt 12:11–12). All of this comes to pass with Solomon: "Blessed be YHWH who has given rest to his people Israel, according to all that he promised. Not one word has failed of all his good promise, which he spoke by Moses his servant" (1 Kgs 8:56). Solomon reflects at length on the presence of YHWH and His dwelling in the temple. YHWH who dwells in thick darkness (8:12) declared that His Name would dwell in the temple (8:16). But how, asks Solomon, will God dwell on earth as He has promised to do in the temple (8:27)? Solomon understands YHWH's promise to Moses and to David as describing His real presence in the temple. There is no figure of speech here, no Zwinglian alloeosis at his disposal. Solomon states reason's conundrum: "Behold, the heaven and the highest heaven cannot contain you; how much less this house that I have built" (8:27). And yet for Solomon God's promise stands and means what it says. YHWH declares, "My name shall be there," and so indeed it shall (8:29). Faith lays hold of the promise, justifying God in His words despite the difficulties of reason. The YHWH who dwells in heaven dwells too on earth, in His temple, where His Name is. As with all the examples above, there is again distinction between YHWH and the Name of YHWH, and yet the two are inseparable.

The Glory of YHWH

Aaron instructed the people to come before YHWH for He had heard their grumbling: "And as soon as Aaron spoke to the whole congregation of the people of Israel, they looked toward the wilderness, and behold, the Glory of YHWH appeared in the cloud" (Ex 16:10).[21] The cloud and pillar of fire routinely

---

YHWH declares to Hosea, "I will have mercy on the house of Judah, and I will save them by [or through] YHWH their Elohim" (Hos 1:7). The repetition, like that found in Gn 19:24 and Ex 34:6–7, is peculiar. YHWH does not say "I will save them" but "I will save them *by* or *through* YHWH their Elohim." Many would simply follow John Calvin and see only an *emphatica repetitio* in these texts. Martin Luther and Johann Gerhard saw them as trinitarian.

21. For a more detailed discussion of the texts that follow see Gieschen, *Angelomorphic Christology*, 78–88.

reveal the Glory of YHWH. We see this with Moses on Sinai and with the tabernacle/temple.

> Then Moses went up on the mountain, and the cloud covered the mountain. The Glory of YHWH dwelt on Mount Sinai, and the cloud covered it six days. And on the seventh day he called to Moses out of the midst of the cloud. Now the appearance of the Glory of YHWH was like a devouring fire on the top of the mountain in the sight of the people of Israel. Moses entered the cloud and went up on the mountain. And Moses was on the mountain forty days and forty nights. (Ex 24:15–18)

> Then the cloud covered the tent of meeting, and the Glory of YHWH filled the tabernacle. And Moses was not able to enter the tent of meeting because the cloud settled on it, and the Glory of YHWH filled the tabernacle. Throughout all their journeys, whenever the cloud was taken up from over the tabernacle, the people of Israel would set out. But if the cloud was not taken up, then they did not set out till the day that it was taken up. For the cloud of YHWH was on the tabernacle by day, and fire was in it by night, in the sight of all the house of Israel throughout all their journeys. (Ex 40:34–38)

The designation of the Glory of YHWH with the cloud merges with the Name of YHWH dwelling in the temple. Immediately before Solomon's blessing, quoted in part above, we read, "And when the priests came out of the Holy Place, a cloud filled the house of YHWH, so that the priests could not stand to minister because of the cloud, for the Glory of YHWH filled the house of YHWH" (1 Kgs 8:10). If we bring all of this together, we discover, as we have above, distinction and common identity between YHWH and the Glory of YHWH. The people came before YHWH, and that which was before them was the Glory of YHWH in the cloud; Moses entered the cloud, the Glory of YHWH, and was in the presence of YHWH. Likewise, the Glory of YHWH, the Name of YHWH, dwells in the temple, marking the real presence of YHWH with His people.

The most striking revelation of God's presence as the Glory of YHWH appears with Ezekiel's opening vision of four living creatures, their wheels, and the throne-chariot. As perplexing and startling as the first part of Ezekiel's vision might be, things only become more difficult at the end of the vision.

> And above the firmament that was over their heads was the likeness of a throne, as the appearance of a sapphire stone: and upon the likeness of the throne was the likeness as the appearance of a Man above upon it. And I saw as the colour of amber, as the appearance of fire round about within it, from the appearance of his loins even upward, and from the appearance of his loins even downward, I saw as it were the appearance of fire, and it had brightness round about. As the appearance of the bow that is in the cloud in the day of rain, so was the appearance of the brightness round about. This was the appearance of the likeness of the Glory of YHWH. And when I saw it, I fell upon my face, and I heard a voice of one that spake. (Ez 1:26–28 KJV)

Ezekiel sees the throne of God occupied by the Glory of YHWH. He describes the Glory of YHWH seated upon the throne as bearing the likeness of a Man. When Ezekiel sees this he falls upon his face. At this point the Man, the Glory of YHWH, speaks to Ezekiel, and as He does "the Spirit entered into me [Ezekiel] and set me on my feet, and I heard him speaking to me." For Ezekiel to hear the Man, the Glory of YHWH, the Spirit was needed that the Man's words would be received into Ezekiel's heart and heard with his ears (Ez 3:10). After Ezekiel hears these words from the Man by the Spirit, there is the sound of a great earthquake from behind him. Ezekiel hears, "Blessed be the Glory of YHWH from its place" (Ez 3:13)! Ezekiel understands that the hand of YHWH had been upon him (Ez 3:14).

After seven days the Glory of YHWH, the Man, comes again to the prophet, but this time Ezekiel says, "The Word of YHWH came to me" (Ez 3:16). Again, Ezekiel understands that the hand of YHWH is upon him: "And the hand of YHWH was upon me there. And he said to me, 'Arise, go out into the valley, and there I will speak with you.' So I arose and went out into the valley, and behold, the Glory of YHWH stood there, like the glory that I had seen by the Chebar canal, and I fell on my face. But the Spirit entered into me and set me on my feet, and he spoke with me and said to me . . . " (Ez 3:22–24). Ezekiel again sees the Glory of YHWH as he had in his earlier vision, which is to say in the likeness of the appearance of a Man. He again falls to the ground on his face and the Spirit enters into him and lifts him to his feet. The Glory of YHWH, the Man, speaks to Ezekiel as He had earlier. Despite these similarities, the difference between the two visions with respect to the Glory of YHWH, the Man, bears emphasis. The Glory now stands apart from the throne upon which He sat in the first chapter. Both truths should remain together. On the one hand Ezekiel sees the Glory of YHWH upon the divine throne, and what he sees has the appearance of Man. On the other hand, the Glory of YHWH, the one in the appearance of Man, leaves the throne and comes to Ezekiel, laying His hand upon him.

A second vision of the living creatures, whom Ezekiel now names as cherubim, occurs in the tenth chapter. When the man clothed in linen enters the sanctuary, a cloud fills the inner court: "And the Glory of YHWH went up from the cherub to the threshold of the house, and the house was filled with the cloud, and the court was filled with the brightness of the Glory of YHWH" (Ez 10:4). Ezekiel continues with a description of the cherubim and their wheels, emphasizing that these cherubim are the living creatures he saw by the Chebar canal in the first chapter (Ez 10:15, 20, 22). He ends by returning to the Glory of YHWH: "Then the Glory of YHWH went out from the threshold of the house, and stood over the cherubim. . . . And they [the cherubim] stood at the entrance of the east gate of the house of YHWH and the Glory of the Elohim of Israel was over them. These were the living creatures that I saw underneath the Elohim of Israel by the Chebar canal; and I knew that they were cherubim" (Ez 10:18–20). For Ezekiel, the one having the likeness of the appearance of Man is the Glory of YHWH that both sits upon the divine throne and comes to him. This Glory of YHWH speaks to Ezekiel, and Ezekiel hears His words by the Spirit.

The Glory of YHWH is the Elohim of Israel, the God of Israel (Ez 10:19–20). Ezekiel had described the Glory of YHWH, the one in the likeness of Man, as sitting upon a throne "in appearance like sapphire" (Ez 1:26). Ezekiel sees this one in the likeness of Man again in chapter 8 and describes Him as "like the appearance of brightness, like gleaming metal" (Ez 8:2). A similar description of the God of Israel appears in Exodus: "Then Moses and Aaron, Nadab and Abihu, and seventy of the elders of Israel went up, and they saw the Elohim of Israel. There was under his feet as it were a pavement of sapphire stone, like the very heaven for clearness. And he did not lay his hand on the chief men of the people of Israel; they beheld God, and ate and drank" (Ex 24:9–11). If we follow the pattern of Scripture, the chief men of Israel saw the Glory of YHWH, the Elohim of Israel, the very one seen by Ezekiel. Both search for words to describe what they saw and use similar expressions: "like sapphire" (Ez 1:26), "pavement of sapphire stone" (Ex 24:10), "appearance of brightness" (Ez 8:2), "like the very heaven for clearness" (Ex 24:10). Moses ends his description by simply stating, "They beheld God" (Ex 24:11).

The distinction and unity between the Glory of YHWH and YHWH, between the one in the likeness of the appearance of Man and the unseen YHWH, is expressed in different ways elsewhere in the Scriptures. Daniel for example sees the Ancient of Days upon His throne and "one like a Son of Man" (Dn 7:9, 13).

> I saw in the night visions, and behold, with the clouds of heaven there came one like a Son of Man, and he came to the Ancient of Days and was presented before him. And to him was given dominion and glory and a kingdom, that all peoples, nations, and languages should serve him; his dominion is an everlasting dominion, which shall not pass away, and his kingdom one that shall not be destroyed. (Dn 7:3–14)

The one like a Son of Man corresponds to the one in the likeness of the appearance of Man seen by Ezekiel. What Daniel sees then is the Glory of YHWH seated next to the Ancient of Days upon the divine throne. King David sees this and simply declares, "The Lord says to my Lord: 'Sit at my right hand, until I make your enemies your footstool'" (Ps 110:1).

Although it is striking that Ezekiel sees the Glory of YHWH in the appearance of a Man, what is more striking is how often God appears in the Old Testament in the appearance of Man. We have already noted how Ezekiel sees YHWH in the appearance of a Man in a manner quite similar to how Moses, Aaron, Nadab, Abihu, and the seventy elders of Israel do. Daniel sees Him variously as the Man clothed in linen and as one like the Son of Man. Abraham meets three men and feeds them, yet the three speak as one, designated, according to the Scriptures, as YHWH. Jacob wrestles with "a man," but so too wrestles with God. Joshua beholds "a man" before him with a drawn sword, whose name is "the Commander of the Army of YHWH" (Jos 5:14). Joshua's actions leave no doubt as to the identity of this Man: "Joshua fell on his face to the earth and worshiped" (Jos 5:14). For him to worship anyone or anything other than the one true God of Israel would be the height of blasphemy. The one he worships then, like the various other appearances of the Man in the Old Testament, is both distinct from YHWH and yet at the same time inseparable from YHWH, such that to see Him is to see YHWH and to worship Him is to worship YHWH. When Moses approaches the burning bush YHWH says, "Do not come near; take your sandals off your feet, for the place on which you are standing is holy ground" (Ex 3:5). So too when Joshua falls before the Man, the Commander of YHWH's army, and worships Him, the Man says, "Take off your sandals from your feet, for the place where you are standing is holy" (Jos 5:15). Joshua does so because he knows without doubt that He was before the God of his fathers, the God of Abraham, the God of Isaac, the God of Jacob (Ex 3:6).

The Word of YHWH

Finally, YHWH reveals His identity to His people with the designation Word of YHWH.[22] In the call of Jeremiah we read:

> Now the Word of YHWH came to me saying, "Before I formed you in the womb I knew you, and before you were born I consecrated you; I appointed you a prophet to the nations." Then I said, "Ah, Elohim Adonai! Behold, I do not know how to speak, for I am only a youth." But YHWH said to me, "Do not say, 'I am only a youth'; for to all to whom I send you, you shall go, and whatever I command you, you shall speak. Do not be afraid of them, for I am with you to deliver you, declares YHWH." Then YHWH put out his hand and touched my mouth. And YHWH said to me, "Behold, I have put my words in your mouth." (Jer 1:4-9)

The Word of YHWH comes to Jeremiah and declares that He created Jeremiah and knew him before he was born. Jeremiah, rightly discerning that such a thing could be said only of God, declares, Elohim Adonai! The text continues with YHWH speaking to Jeremiah. YHWH then reaches out His hand, touches Jeremiah's mouth, and places His words in his mouth. Like the various examples above, we see distinction between the Word of YHWH and YHWH, and once that distinction is established the Word of YHWH speaks as YHWH. Distinction and unity are both emphasized.

Another significant example of the Word of YHWH occurs with the prophet Zechariah. The Word of YHWH comes to Zechariah and shows him numerous visions, especially visions concerning the Christ, the Branch, who is YHWH, the one pierced for the transgressions of the people (Zec 12:9–13:1). In the third chapter Zechariah sees a vision of Joshua, the high priest, before the Angel of YHWH and Satan. The setting is that of a court room with Satan, the accuser, accusing Joshua, oppressing his conscience because of his sins. YHWH rebukes Satan: "And YHWH said to Satan, 'YHWH rebuke you, O Satan!'" (Zec 3:2). Joshua stands before the Angel of YHWH, but the one who speaks is YHWH. The vision continues: "Now Joshua was standing before the Angel, clothed with filthy garments. And the Angel said to those who were standing before him,

---

22. See further Gieschen, *Angelomorphic Christology*, 103–14.

'Remove the filthy garments from him.' And to him he said, 'Behold, I have taken your iniquity away from you, and I will clothe you with pure vestments'" (Zec 3:3–4). Within the context of Zechariah's book the sins of Joshua, his filthy garments, represent Israel. As the high priest he appears before the Angel of YHWH as Israel, filthy with sin, accused by Satan. The Angel of YHWH who is YHWH rebukes Satan and declares to Joshua, to Israel, that his sin will be removed and he will be clothed by the Angel of YHWH ("*I* will clothe you") with pure vestments. Joshua's sin is removed and he is clothed with the pureness of another. It is an alien pureness given to Joshua (cf. 1 Jn 3:2–3). That Joshua represents Israel and that the Angel of YHWH will put away the iniquity of Israel, clothing them in an alien pureness, the vision now makes explicit: "And the Angel of YHWH solemnly assured Joshua, 'Thus says YHWH Sabaoth . . . Behold, I will bring my Servant, the Branch. For behold, on the stone that I have set before Joshua, on a single stone with seven eyes, I will engrave its inscription, declares YHWH Sabaoth, and I will remove the iniquity of this land in a single day'" (Zec 3:6–9). Zechariah continues the language of the prophets here. The one in whom salvation is found is "my" Servant (Is 42:1; 52:13), the Branch (Is 4:2; Jer 33:15), and the Stone (Ps 118:22; Is 8:14; 28:16). In a single day YHWH's Servant, the Branch, the Stone, will remove all iniquity. The atonement here described is perfect and all-sufficient, and results in peace: "In that day, declares YHWH Sabaoth, every one of you will invite his neighbor to come under his vine and under his fig tree" (Zec 3:10).

Despite the obvious ambiguity attending most of the texts about the Angel, Name, Glory, and Word of YHWH, they all demonstrate how YHWH, the one true God of Israel, may never be seen and yet has been seen. Further, they show the attentive reader that within the unique identity of YHWH there is plurality. The Angel of YHWH stands apart from YHWH but is YHWH. The same applies to the Name, Glory, and Word. The point is further made that the Word of YHWH and the Glory of YHWH is understood only by the Spirit, who routinely is designated as the Spirit of YHWH or the Spirit of Elohim. When we put together the narrative summary of the Old Testament and the various texts about the seen and unseen YHWH, we unmistakably discover plurality within common identity. We discover that YHWH is triune.

DOGMATIC SUMMARY OF YHWH'S SCRIPTURAL IDENTITY

According to the Old Testament, who is God? The most direct answer to this question comes at the burning bush. God says to Moses, "I AM WHO I AM." When Moses goes to the Israelites, he is to say, "I AM" has sent him (Ex 3:14). God further tells Moses, "Say this to the people of Israel, 'YHWH, the Elohim of your ancestors, the Elohim of Abraham, the Elohim of Isaac, and the Elohim of Jacob, has sent me to you.' This is my name forever, and thus I am to be

The Trinity and the Old Testament

remembered throughout all generations" (Ex 3:15). Two mutually informing answers are here given. God is "I AM WHO I AM," and this reality may be expressed with the name YHWH, the Elohim of Abraham, Isaac, and Jacob. The two answers differ in terms of the context in which we know or understand the name. In the first, "I AM WHO I AM," we have a tautology. Who is this "I AM"? He is the "I AM" who spoke the first "I AM." Confusing as that might sound, the point made takes us to the heart of Scripture: God declares His identity on His own terms. The second, the name that shall forever be remembered, is YHWH, the Elohim of your ancestors, of Abraham, Isaac, and Jacob. The unique YHWH stands in a relationship to the people He created and elected. They have a history. Knowing YHWH involves remembering what He has done and what He promises to do for His people. Both of these responses to Moses go together, inform one another, and delimit how the God of the Bible is known by us.

The revelation given to Moses at the burning bush informs the rest of the Old Testament and stands at the liturgical center of Israel's worship. We see this especially in Deuteronomy. Again we ask, who is God? He is "YHWH, the Elohim of Israel" (Dt 6:4). His name is YHWH and He is the God "of Israel." He alone makes known His identity to us. He is YHWH; we receive Him as He is, as He declares to us. The point bears repeating: YHWH is never susceptible to our intellectual idolatries, our fitting arguments, or our shifting cultural allegiances—I AM WHO I AM, not who we want Him to be, not what we want Him to be. Further, this I AM, this YHWH, stands in relation to a people *He* created and elected and is known in terms of that *divinely* established relationship. This means the divine economy, the work of God toward creation and on behalf of His people, becomes the principal context in which we know, confess, and worship the only true God of the Bible. Right knowing involves true confession and true worship, which requires faith and therefore the means of grace. We cannot rightly know God apart from God, apart from the divinely established relationship with Him, apart from His grace, mercy, steadfast love, and righteousness—all of which we have, according to the Scriptures, in Christ alone by the Holy Spirit.

Scripture patterns our thoughts about *this* God by marking out His unique identity through the things He does and the promises He makes. YHWH declares, "When your son asks you in time to come, 'What is the meaning of the testimonies and the statutes and the rules that YHWH our Elohim has commanded you?' then you shall say to your son, 'We were Pharaoh's slaves in Egypt. And YHWH brought us out of Egypt with a mighty hand'" (Dt 6:20–21). YHWH's answer continues at length: you are to tell your son YHWH delivered us from slavery, elected us as His people, guided us through the wilderness, blessed us and sustained us, feeding us when there was no food and giving us drink when we were thirsty, all the while teaching us that "man does not live by bread alone, but man lives by every word that comes from the mouth of YHWH" (Dt 8:3). To know YHWH, who He is, you must remember what He has done, how He has acted in history, and the promises He has made. You may not abstract Him from His active involvement in history and on behalf of His people. Those who wish to undermine the historicity of the Scriptures, their facticity, alienate themselves from God's disclosure of Himself, retreating to philosophical pleasantries and intellectual idolatries. To know God according to the Scriptures is to recognize that God is subject, not object, that His work, particularly His proper work of salvation, determines our right knowing and understanding of Him, indeed makes it possible.

By remembering the scriptural telling of YHWH and His involvement, promises, and appearances to His people, you know what it means to say that He alone is Truth and Life. To forget YHWH your Elohim is to pursue other gods, false gods, and to serve and worship them (Dt 8:19). To forget is to pursue falsehood and death, despite the affirmation of the multitudes. The language of remembering YHWH—His works and His promises—in order to know Him finds its home in worship and the ordering of the believer's life. The narrative description of God given above is the basic way in which the faithful confess and worship the plural identity of the one true God, YHWH our Elohim. The New Testament clarifies this in more familiar terms: we worship and glorify the Father through the Son by the Holy Spirit. The New Testament allows us to parse the somewhat ambiguous language encountered throughout the Old Testament. The YHWH who appears to the patriarchs and prophets, who shows His glory to Isaiah and Ezekiel, the YHWH who is pierced for the sins of all, who is variously called Son of Man, Servant, Branch, Man, upon whom the Spirit of YHWH rests, is Jesus Christ, the Word made flesh, the only-begotten Son sent by the Father, who in turn, with the Father, sends the Holy Spirit as promised by the prophets. The ambiguity of the theophanies narrated above dissolves upon the witness of the New Testament. The point here is that the historical retelling, the remembering, of God's works and promises, His active involvement in our history, is how we chiefly know the God of the Bible. This retelling forms the content of our prayers and hymns, our sermons and liturgy. It gives meaning to our lives as God's people and informs both our living and dying as His redeemed children. Only when someone comes along and seeks to undermine this retelling, seeks to compromise the unique identity of YHWH, His works and promises, must the gathered faithful move from narrative confession to dogmatic pronouncement.

What can we say then about the dogmatic presentation of God based on the Old Testament? The Old Testament without ambiguity identifies the unique characteristics that mark out and set apart the Lord God of Israel from all false gods, all idols, and indeed all created reality. The above narrative presentation of God, the remembering of His deeds and promises, His active involvement with His people, can be summarized as follows:

1) He is the creator of the heavens and the earth. He alone creates and He creates without external assistance and without anything prior to His free act of creation.
2) As the sole creator of the heavens and the earth, He alone is the supreme ruler of all, who does not stand apart from His creation but is actively involved in it, determining its history, and especially electing and caring for His people.
3) As the one true God who has created all things, rules all things, who has called His people to be His people, establishing an everlasting covenant with them, redeeming them from bondage in Egypt, preserving them in the wilderness, bringing them into their own land, and so on, He is also, despite their sin and idolatry, merciful and gracious, slow to anger, and abounding in steadfast love and faithfulness toward them.
4) The God who creates and rules, the God who is merciful and gracious, will redeem His people from their sins, from their estrangement, from their ungodliness. He will be their savior, their righteousness, their justifier. He will send His Servant, high and lifted up, to bear their iniquities. The Servant, the Righteous Branch, shall be their King and the people shall take refuge in Him of whom YHWH says, "You are my Son; today I have begotten you" (Ps 2:7).
5) The Spirit of YHWH will rest upon this Servant, this Son, and this same Spirit will be poured out upon all following the exaltation of the Servant to the right hand of God.

The pressing question raised by this dogmatic summary is whether the Servant and the Spirit belong to YHWH's unique identity or if they are agents of His creating and redeeming work. If they are agents or intermediaries, they belong to the angelic host at best. It is at this very point that the question of how the Bible presents its monotheism becomes most pressing and the dogmatic conclusion insisted upon by the New Testament becomes most necessary. A concept of what monotheism must have entailed cannot be brought to bear on the witness of Scripture; rather what constitutes biblical monotheism must be gathered from the witness of Scripture itself.

We answer the question about the Servant and Spirit by returning to the narrative summary of YHWH. Simply put, there are things that belong to God alone and to none other. These things unambiguously mark out YHWH's identity for us. Richard Bauckham, who has written extensively on the question of divine identity and particularly the high Christology of the New Testament, argues that at the very least three characteristics constitute Second Temple Judaism's understanding of God: He is the sole creator of all things, He is the sole ruler of all things, and therefore He alone receives exclusive worship.[23] Bauckham's

---

23. Bauckham, "God Crucified," 1–17. Bauckham uses the qualification of Second Temple Judaism because this is the historical context of the New Testament and its Christology, which is the subject of his essay.

argument follows a similar narrative as that given above. Second Temple Jews were self-consciously monotheistic. They prayed the Shema twice daily and were well aware of their exclusive allegiance to the one true God. Their monotheism was not merely intellectual but involved their exclusive worship of God and their exclusive obedience to Him. Bauckham writes:

> To our question, "In what did Second Temple Judaism consider the uniqueness of the one God to consist, what distinguished God as unique from all other reality, including beings worshipped as gods by Gentiles?", the answer given again and again, in a wide variety of Second Temple Jewish literature, is that the only true God, YHWH, the God of Israel, is sole Creator of all things and sole Ruler of all things. While these characteristics are by no means *sufficient* to identify God (since they say nothing, for example, about his goodness or his justice), they are the features which most readily distinguish God absolutely from all other reality.... These ways of distinguishing God as unique formed a very easily intelligible way of defining the uniqueness of the God they worshipped which every Jew in every synagogue in the late Second Temple period would certainly have known. However diverse Judaism may have been in many other respects, this was common: only the God of Israel is worthy of worship because he is sole Creator of all things and sole Ruler of all things. Other beings who might otherwise be thought divine are by these criteria God's creatures and subjects.[24]

In our narrative presentation of God we highlighted these three characteristics of God as creator, ruler, and the one to whom worship alone is given. What we did not emphasize, however, is that Scripture continues the pattern of plurality within the unique identity of God in describing these three defining marks of identity. It is precisely here that Scripture resolves the above question about the Servant and Spirit.

First, God alone is creator. Irenaeus succinctly summarizes Scripture's teaching on this point: "God makes; man is made."[25] God had no helper, servant, or intermediary to assist Him in the act of creation. God declares repeatedly that He alone stretched out the heavens and spread out the earth (Is 44:24; cf. Ps 115:15; 121:2; 124:8). Scripture, however, variously assigns the one act of creation to YHWH, Elohim, the Word of YHWH, the Spirit of God, Wisdom, and the Father. In the first chapter of Genesis we read that God created, that He did this by speaking all things into existence, which is to say by His Word, and that the Spirit of God participated as well. Although three were involved, Scripture rejects the idea of three creations, one by the Speaker, one by the Word spoken, and one by the Spirit of God, telling only of a single creation. As Scripture stands, we have three involved in the one act of creation.

When Scripture elsewhere recounts God's creative activity, it says that the Word of YHWH and the Spirit or Breath of God created, sometimes with distinguishable roles, other times interchangeably. Psalm 33:6 reads, "By the

---

24. Bauckham, "God Crucified," 9. Cf. Bauckham's footnotes 8 and 9 for an extensive list of texts referring to God alone as creator and ruler.
25. Irenaeus, *Against Heresies*, 1.11.2 (ANF, 1, 474).

Word of YHWH the heavens were made, and by the breath [*rûach*] of his mouth all their host." The psalm continues that when YHWH "spoke" all things came to be (Ps 33:8–9).[26] The Word of YHWH made the heavens. Elsewhere Scripture declares, "YHWH made the heavens" (Ps 96:5). As seen with the theophanies above, the Word of YHWH is YHWH and yet also distinct from YHWH. In Jeremiah we read, "The Word of YHWH came to me, saying, 'Before I formed you in the womb I knew you'" (Jer 1:4–5). Again, the Word of YHWH is the Word spoken in Genesis 1, the Word of Psalm 33, who made the heavens, the Word who created Jeremiah, and indeed knew him before He created him. The second half of Ps 33:6 is intriguing: the "breath [*rûach*] of his mouth" is certainly a reference to the Spirit of God, and indeed may be translated just as easily as such, making the intertextual relationship with the Spirit (*rûach*) of God in Genesis 1 explicit. If the phrase "the breath of His mouth" is retained, it indicates nothing other than what Elihu declares to Job: "The Spirit of God has made me, and the breath of the Almighty gives me life" (Jb 33:4). The Spirit of God made Elihu, the Spirit who is the breath (*nishmat*) of the Almighty.

Scripture assigns creation not only to the Word of YHWH and the Spirit of God but also to Wisdom and the Father. We read for example that God "established the world by his wisdom" (Jer 10:12; 51:15); that He made all things "in wisdom" (Ps 104:24); that "the Lord by wisdom founded the earth" (Prv 3:19; 8:27–30).[27] Malachi asks, "Have we not all one Father? Has not one God created us?" (Mal 2:10). Although designating God as Father occurs less often than one might expect, it is not unknown to the Old Testament and almost always appears in the context of God's work as creator. In Isaiah we read, "But now, O YHWH, you are our Father; we are the clay, and you are the potter; we are all the work of your hand" (Is 64:8). Again Moses sings forth, "Do you thus repay YHWH, you foolish and senseless people? Is not he your Father, who created you, who made you and established you?" (Dt 32:6).

What are we to make of Scripture variously identifying the sole creator of the heavens and the earth as YHWH, Elohim, Word, Spirit, Wisdom, and Father? The answer must be that the scriptural understanding of monotheism encompasses both Is 44:24 ("Thus says YHWH, your Redeemer, who formed you from the womb: I am YHWH, who made all things, who alone stretched out the heavens, who spread out the earth *by myself*") and Gn 1:1, Dt 32:6, and Ps 33:6. Scripture declares that YHWH by Himself made all things, stretched out the heavens, and made us from the womb. According to Scripture, however, the same may be said of the Father, the Word/Wisdom, and the Spirit. Further,

---

26. Cf. Ps 148:5 (LXX): "Let them [i.e., all of creation] praise the Name of the Lord [YHWH]; for He spoke and they were made; He commanded and they were created."

27. Cf. Athanasius *Orations Against the Arians* 2.31 in *Athanasius*, trans. Khaled Anatolios (New York: Routledge, 2004), 126: "And the phrase, 'God said,' itself implies 'in the Word'; for it says, 'He made all things in Wisdom' (Ps 104:24), and 'by the Word of the Lord the heavens were established' (Ps 33:6) and 'one Lord Jesus Christ, through whom all things are and through whom we exist' (1 Cor 8:6)."

Scripture insists that we have one creation, not three, and that these three created, not that they contributed a part here and a part there. Their work of creation is one. The only responsible conclusion according to the Scriptures is to confess the correlative and coequal working of Father, Word/Wisdom, and Spirit, and to locate all three—equally and eternally—within the unique identity of YHWH, our Elohim.

Although some might wish to argue that we should not distinguish between Father, Word, and Spirit but allow them to stand as synonyms, as poetic expressions of YHWH, to allow for some version of Sabellianism, Scripture rejects this false conclusion. As we will see in the next chapter, the New Testament is particularly sensitive to this sort of misreading, emphasizing especially the unity and eternal distinction of Father, Son, and Holy Spirit. The Old Testament in its own way does something quite similar. In the previous section we saw the distinction and inseparability of YHWH and the Angel, Glory, Name, and Word of YHWH. The same emphasis appears with creation. Genesis 1:1 marks out three who create: the Speaker, the Word, and the Spirit. If we identify the Father with the Speaker, following the pattern of the New Testament, then we have in Genesis an attempt to distinguish the Father from His Word and His Spirit and yet to emphasize their unity in the act of creation.[28] Again, we have one creation, not three. The language used to describe the three with respect to creation highlights their interdependency and intimacy with one another. For example, you cannot be a Speaker without a Word and you cannot be a Word without a Speaker, which is to say the One who speaks is never apart from the Word He speaks. Their eternal relationship requires both distinction and inseparability. Further, the Speaker who speaks forth His Word does so by the "breath of his mouth," and we call this His voice. When Scripture declares, "The voice of YHWH is over the waters" (Ps 29:3), the faithful recall the Spirit of God, who enigmatically moved over the face of the waters (Gn 1:1). Similar language appears with Ps 33:6, "By the Word of YHWH the heavens were made, and by the breath/Spirit of his mouth all their host." Again, at a very basic level we understand that our words are expressed by passing breath, air, over our vocal chords. Where there is no breath, there can be no words. The two are necessarily dependent upon one another, and yet by that same necessity distinct from one another. The Spirit of *His* mouth, the mouth of the Word of YHWH, conveys the same intimacy as the Speaker and His Word from Gn 1:1 and further underscores for us the inseparable working of Speaker/Father, Word/Son, and Voice/Spirit. All of this highlights the crucial point made above: Father, Word, and Spirit are intrinsic to the identity, reality, being, and essence of YHWH, according to the Scriptures. A faithful and careful reading of the Scriptures demands the confession that YHWH is triune: He is Father, Word,

---

28. Cf. Augustine *The City of God* XI.24 (WSA I/7, 24–25): "For the Father of the Word is understood to be the one who said, 'Let it be made.' And what was made when he said this was undoubtedly made by his Word."

and Spirit, three who are one, coequal and coeternal, inseparably united and yet eternally distinct.

Second, God is ruler. As regularly as Scripture declares that God alone created all things, so too it emphasizes that He alone rules all things. He rules all of creation (Job 26, 28; Psalm 148) and all therein (Psalm 139), forever and ever: "YHWH will reign forever and ever" (Ex 15:18; Ps 146:10); "YHWH is king forever and ever" (Ps 10:16); "YHWH sits enthroned as king forever" (Ps 29:10); "Your throne, O God, is forever and ever" (Ps 45:6). YHWH's kingdom is an everlasting kingdom (Ps 145:13); His dominion is an everlasting dominion (Dn 4:34). The same is said of the Son of Man: "His dominion is an everlasting dominion, which shall not pass away, and his kingdom one that shall not be destroyed" (Dn 7:14). The eternal dominion and eternal kingdom will be set up by "the God of heaven" and accomplished by the "stone" cut without human hand, which as noted above is Daniel's way of designating the Messiah, the Righteous Branch upon whom rests the Spirit of YHWH (Is 11:1–20), the one born of the Virgin, called Immanuel (Is 7:14). This Son of Man corresponds to the only-begotten Son of Psalm 2. YHWH calls Him "my King" and "my Son" who possesses the ends of the earth and in whom all who take refuge are blessed (Ps 2:6–8, 12). The New Testament clarifies this distinction and unity for us. The kingdom and rule in question is "of our Lord and his Christ," and it shall be forever (Rv 11:15; 12:10). Again, "The Lord God will give to him [Jesus, the Son of the Most High, the one born of the Virgin] the throne of his father David, and he will reign over the house of Jacob forever, and of his kingdom there will be no end" (Lk 1:32–33).

Particular care is taken in Scripture to distinguish between God as sole ruler and the various angelic intermediaries used by God to execute His rule. They rule in His name, on His behalf, and not by their own power. These angels are God's servants who carry out His governance of the world (Dn 10:20; Rv 7:2–3; 15:1; 16:1).[29] Richard Bauckham shows how the Scriptures make this distinction between God and His angelic servants obvious by repeatedly drawing on the metaphor of height and the posture of the servants in relation to God.[30] For example, God alone sits upon His throne, far above the inhabitants of the earth (Ps 33:13–14), high and lifted up (Is 6:1). Again Isaiah records, "For thus says the High and Lofty One Who inhabits eternity, whose name is Holy: 'I dwell in the high and holy place'" (Is 57:15 NKJV). God alone sits on the throne; His ministering angels stand before Him. Daniel writes, "A thousand thousands served him, and ten thousand times ten thousand stood before him" (Dn 7:10). Similarly, Gabriel identifies himself in this way to Zechariah: "I am Gabriel, who stands in the presence of God, and I was sent to speak to you and to bring you

---

29. Cf. *Preface to the Prophet Daniel*, 1530 (AE 35:305; WADB 11/2:30.11–14): "Daniel writes something special about the angels, the like of which we find nowhere else in the Scriptures, namely, that the good angels do battle with the evil angels in defense of men."
30. Bauckham, "God Crucified," 10, 35–36.

this good news" (Lk 1:18). John reports, "Then I saw the seven angels who stand before God, and seven trumpets were given to them" (Rv 8:3).

Third, God alone is worshipped. Those who stand before God, who sits on His throne, high and lifted up, serve on His behalf. The confession of God as creator and ruler further entailed the practice of worshipping God alone: "I am YHWH; that is my name; my glory I give to no other, nor my praise to carved idols" (Is 42:8). The angels who serve God, no matter how exalted, never sit with God but always stand before Him and explicitly reject any worship given to them. Bauckham offers a number of examples from Second Temple pseudepigraphical and apocryphal works to show this.[31] The same practice is seen in Revelation, however. Twice John falls down before the angel and is vehemently told to stand: "Then I fell down at his feet to worship him, but he said to me, 'You must not do that! I am a fellow servant with you and your brothers who hold to the testimony of Jesus. Worship God'" (Rv 19:9–10; cf. Rv 22:8–9). The prophets and apostles act in a similar way (Dn 2:46 KJV; Acts 10:26). That the angels never hesitate to prevent fellow creatures from worshipping them resolves some of the ambiguity found with the theophanies discussed above. When Joshua and Ezekiel fall down to worship the one in the appearance of a Man, the Commander of YHWH's army, the Glory of YHWH, the one who both sits upon the throne and comes near, they are not rebuked and told to stand because they are in the presence of YHWH.

CONCLUSION

The Old Testament presents God as the sole creator and ruler of the world who alone sits upon His throne and to whom alone belongs worship. This unique identity of God as creator of the heavens and the earth includes Father, Word/Wisdom, and Spirit. These three are intrinsic to YHWH's unique identity. When we ask who God is according to the Old Testament, our response must be God "is" the one who created all things, rules all things, sits upon His throne, and alone receives worship. This God is the one who spoke in the beginning; this God is the spoken Word who created all things, the Word of YHWH; this God is the Spirit of God present at the beginning with the one speaking and the Word spoken, the Spirit of His mouth, the voice over the waters. This God who is indivisibly one is also irreducibly three. This is the one God who said, "Let *us* make man in *our* image" (Gn 1:26).

At the heart of YHWH's triune identity stands His promise to redeem His people from their sins. He will be pierced by them and will tabernacle with them forever. The one who accomplishes this salvation, this atonement, is both YHWH and sent by YHWH. The one sent, who is YHWH our Righteousness, is the one upon whom the Spirit of YHWH rests. The Scriptures never tire of assigning various names to this promised Savior. In addition to being the Angel, the Glory,

---

31. Bauckham, "God Crucified," 15.

the Name, the Word, and the Elohim of Israel, He is also Adonai (Ps 110:1), Elohim (Ps 45:6; Is 35:4), YHWH (Jer 23:6; 33:14; Hos 1:7), YHWH Saboath (Is 44:6; Zec 12:5), the Son of God (Ps 2:7; Prv 30:4; Is 9:6), the Son of Man (Dn 7:13), David's Lord and son (Ps 110:1; Mt 22:42–45). He is Shiloh (Gn 49:10 KJV), the Commander of the Army of YHWH (Jos 5:14), Wonderful (Jgs 13:18; Is 9:6), the Rock (Is 30:29), the Cornerstone (Ps 118:22), our Refuge (Ps 46:1) and Hiding Place (Ps 32:7), our Fortress (Ps 91:2) and Stronghold (Ps 18:2), our Shield (Ps 3:3; 18:30) and Strength (Ps 22:19). He is King (Ps 2:6; Is 6:5) and Shepherd (Ez 34:23–24). He is Christ (Ps 2:2; Dn 9:26), the Holy One (Ps 71:22; Is 40:25; 43:3; 48:17), and the Savior of all (Is 45:15).

The Scriptures not only locate this Christ in the unique identity of YHWH, but further, indeed crucially, specify how this one born of the Virgin will be known. Lest any ambiguity arise, the Scriptures explicitly mark out the things this one true Savior will do. He will be high and lifted up, the Spirit of YHWH will rest upon Him, and He will bring good news to the poor, bind up the brokenhearted, proclaim liberty to the captives, and comfort all who mourn (Is 61:1–2). He will open the eyes of the blind, unstop the ears of the deaf, and loosen the string of the mute (Is 35:4–6). He will enter triumphantly into Jerusalem (Zec 9:9), be wounded for our transgressions and crushed for our iniquities (Is 53:11), atone for sins and usher in everlasting righteousness (Dn 9:24, 26), bringing justification (Is 53:11), everlasting peace (Mi 5:2–5), and salvation to all (Isaiah 55–56). He is the Redeemer who lives and who shall raise the dead (Jb 19:25). All peoples of the earth are to serve Him (Ps 2:11; 72:11; Dn 7:14), to trust Him (Ps 2:12; Is 28:16), to fear Him (Ps 2:11), to hope in Him (Is 11:10; 14:32), and to worship and call upon Him (Ps 22:27; 45:11; 72:11; 97:7). The New Testament clarifies in crucial ways all of this which God has foretold through the patriarchs and prophets. It does so in terms of Jesus Christ. Christology always occupies the center of our trinitarian thinking because it is only through Christ by the Spirit that a right understanding of YHWH's triune identity is known, confessed, and worshipped.

8

FATHER AND SON: THE ORDINARY LANGUAGE OF THE NEW TESTAMENT

The writers of the New Testament mark out Jesus' divine identity through detailed and careful exegesis of the Old Testament. They assign to Him the divine name and the unique characteristics of YHWH highlighted in the previous chapter. By doing this, the New Testament writers identify and establish for us the normative naming of God. The ambiguity present in the Old Testament for naming the seen and unseen YHWH—the plurality within the unique identity of YHWH as noted in the distinction between YHWH and the Angel, Name, Glory, or Word of YHWH, who is YHWH and distinct from YHWH, or between the Man, the Servant, the Righteous One who is YHWH and distinct from YHWH—becomes intelligible, in the light of the New Testament, as the distinction and inseparability of the Father and Son. They are coeternally and coequally God but also eternally distinct as Father and Son. According to the New Testament, these names are normative and stand at the center of the ontological identity of God. Further, this relationship is known and confessed by us through the Holy Spirit whom the Father and the Son both send. The Spirit points us to the Son, speaking His words to us, anchoring us in His saving work, and it is in knowing the saving work of the Son, being clothed in His righteousness, that we know the Father and call on Him as *our* Father.

The person at the center of this proper naming, knowing, and worshipping of the triune God is Jesus Christ, the Son of God. Trinity begins with Christ. These two points, the normative naming of God and Christ at the center, are at the heart of the New Testament witness. They are not a theological extrapolation belonging to the dogmatic reflection of the church but are basic to Scripture's presentation of the identity of the one true God of Israel. The New Testament establishes these mutually informing points in two distinct ways—through historical narratives and in more robustly dogmatic sections. Although I have separated these two presentations in my chapters, the distinction is artificial: the New Testament presents them side by side. Too often, however, theologians gravitate to the more robustly dogmatic sections and overlook the more ordinary and basic presentation of His divine identity in the New Testament. Both are important; both pattern the speech of the faithful to talk about the triune God they worship and glorify.

According to the New Testament the Father is known and worshipped through the Son in the Spirit (Eph 2:18), and this always in the context of the salvation accomplished by Christ. Here we see the pattern of sound words used in Christian discourse about the saving work of the Trinity and the normative naming of God as Father, Son, and Holy Spirit. I refer to this as the ordinary language of faith—ordinary on the one hand because it is so prevalent throughout the New Testament, but also because so much is assumed by the New Testament writer and left unexplained. Both Paul and the four evangelists teach us this ordinary language of faith. Below I will demonstrate this principally with Paul's greetings and final blessings. When he reflects upon the salvation we receive from God, the unity we have in God, or the structure of the Christian life, he does so with a trinitarian grammar or pattern of speech. Although it may seem strange to analyze Paul's presentation in this way, it represents for us the most basic way in which the faithful talk about the Trinity according to the Scriptures. There is no extended theological reflection on the implications of this language about the Father, Son, and Holy Spirit, no consideration of the immanent and economic life of the Trinity, much less any urgency to justify this confession with faith in the one and only God of Israel. There is simply the exuberant language of faith shaped deeply by Scripture.

After establishing the normative naming of God, the New Testament writers show the correlative working of Father and Son in the acts belonging to God alone. The Scriptures are clear that God alone creates and rules the heavens and the earth, that He gives life and forgives sins, and that therefore He and no other is to be worshipped and glorified. All of these things said about YHWH in the Old Testament are said about Jesus in the New Testament. The writers of the New Testament call Jesus Lord and God and Savior, all titles, according to the Scriptures, that belong to YHWH alone. They do not hesitate to quote Old Testament texts about YHWH and use them to refer to Jesus. He is truly God and truly man. Jesus is YHWH in the same sense that the Father is YHWH. They both create and they both redeem, but there is only one creation and one redemption. They both receive worship, for they both occupy the divine throne belonging exclusively and only to the one true God. Further, and this is perhaps the most significant part of the New Testament's witness to God's identity, Father and Son entail one another. Although eternally distinct in who they are as Father and Son, they are at the same time one in who they are as God. As the Scriptures put it, the Father is in the Son and the Son is in the Father, but the Father is not the Son and the Son is not the Father. Each is intrinsic to the identity of the other and therefore to the ontological reality of God.

The above divine characteristics are emphasized especially in the dogmatic texts discussed in the next chapter. They are also found in subtle ways in the historical presentation of the Gospels. Just as Paul's seemingly insignificant greetings and final blessings yield rich trinitarian insight, the highly structured narratives of the Gospels provide similar insight in unexpected places. The Gospel writers pursue, almost relentlessly, the question of Jesus' identity. We see this in the questions of the disciples, the crowds, and the opponents of Jesus.

It is in this way, through the historical narrative of the life and work of Jesus, particularly in His interaction with others, that the Gospels present His identity as true God and true man, both David's Lord and son. The Gospels further highlight the continuity of Jesus' words and actions with the Old Testament. To fully appreciate what Jesus is saying about Himself or the point He aims to make by the things He does, the reader must always bear in mind the witness of the Old Testament. The New Testament writers locate Jesus explicitly and without hesitation in the scriptural identity of YHWH by assigning to Him the divine name or substituting His name for YHWH in Old Testament texts used in the New Testament. What should be clear from our reading of the New Testament is that the apostles, led by the Holy Spirit, were well aware of what they were confessing about the Son.

PAUL'S TRINITARIAN GRAMMAR

Although Paul's epistolary greetings and final doxologies may seem like an unexpected resource for trinitarian theology, they contribute significantly to the formal theological work of Paul's epistles, and for our purposes to the ordinary language of faith as expressed in Christian greeting, benediction, and prayer. Paul shows no interest in clarifying his exuberant language in these sections; the rest of the letter accomplishes that for him. These sections reflect for us the language of faith and prayer, the proper way of speaking forth the sound pattern of words concerning the triune God we worship. Something similar to this way of speaking appears in other parts of Paul's letters when he reflects, somewhat summarily, on God's saving work for us and how that work shapes the Christian life. In what follows we will look at examples from these areas of Paul's letters to see the pattern of sound words in confessing the eternal identity of the Trinity.

Paul's greetings confess the triune identity of God and show how Paul's own identity and authority are caught up in who God is. Paul presents himself in the context of the God who set him apart, who called him, and who redeemed him. What elicits our attention, however, is the flexibility with which Paul does this. For example, he can designate himself as either a servant of Christ Jesus (δοῦλος Χριστοῦ Ἰησοῦ, Rom 1:1), or a servant of God the Father (δοῦλος θεοῦ, Ti 1:1). Paul's correlation of Jesus and the Father makes sense only if they are both God. If they are not, then his statement borders on blasphemy. He would be saying that he serves both one who is true God and one who is not true God. You cannot serve both God and that which is not God without compromising the faithfulness of your service to God: "You cannot serve God and mammon" (Mt 6:24 NKJV). Paul serves both the Father and Jesus. James makes the same point but with greater clarity at the beginning of his letter: "James, a servant of God and of the Lord Jesus Christ" (Ἰάκωβος θεοῦ καὶ κυρίου Ἰησοῦ Χριστοῦ δοῦλος, Jas 1:1). James's more precise way of putting this is surely what Paul means.

Father and Son: Ordinary Language

Paul's identity is caught up in the identity of Jesus and the Father. To know Paul requires knowing the one he serves. He has been set apart by the will of God the Father (Rom 1:1; 1 Cor 1:1; 2 Cor 1:1; Col 1:1; 1 Tm 1:1), who promised through the prophets to send His Son (Rom 1:2-3; Ti 1:2-3). Here we have our first indication of the centrality of the Father and Son relationship to the ontological reality of God, a point emphasized so consistently throughout the New Testament. Paul always places the Father in relation to His Son. As Athanasius has taught the church, the names require this. You cannot be Father without Son, and therefore to say Son always involves Father. And yet there is more to this. God the Father is neither known nor named as Father apart from Jesus Christ, the incarnate Son. There is no reality named "God" apart from the Father and His Son.

This Son is Jesus Christ our Lord (Rom 1:4; 1 Cor 1:2) and our Savior (Ti 1:4; 2 Tm 1:10). And yet Paul can also confess that God the Father is our Savior (1 Tm 1:1; Ti 1:3). The salvation we have from the Father is of course the same as that accomplished by the Son. Paul's language highlights for us the correlative work of Father and Son for our salvation. Although less clear, he also confesses the work of the Holy Spirit in our salvation. In the greeting from Romans Paul refers to the Spirit as the Spirit of holiness (πνεῦμα ἁγιωσύνης, Rom 1:4; cf. Rom 15:16). And yet in the greeting from 1 Corinthians, the saints are sanctified, rendered holy, in Christ Jesus (1 Cor 1:2; cf Heb 10:10-14), who is both our righteousness and holiness (δικαιοσύνη τε καὶ ἁγιασμὸς, 1 Cor 1:30). These saints are sanctified in Christ by calling upon the name of our Lord Jesus Christ, acknowledging Him to be their Lord (1 Cor 1:2). Although not said in the greeting, Paul emphasizes further in the letter that this is the work of the Holy Spirit: "No one can say 'Jesus is Lord' except in the Holy Spirit" (1 Cor 12:3). The sanctification or holiness of the saints in Christ is the work of the Spirit of holiness (cf. 1 Cor 6:11). The salvation promised by the Father and accomplished by the Son becomes ours through the working of the Holy Spirit, who brings us to Christ, who in turn reconciles us to the Father. Our salvation is the work of the Trinity.

The point made most often by Paul is that grace and peace are from God the Father and the Lord Jesus Christ (Rom 1:7; 1 Cor 1:3; 2 Cor 1:2; Gal 1:3; Eph 1:2; Phil 1:2; Col 1:2; 2 Thes 1:2; 1 Tm 1:1; 2 Tm 1:2; Ti 1:4; Phlm 3). Grace and peace come to us from the Father and the Son together. Put another way, apart from either the Father or the Son there is no grace and peace. The grace and peace of the Father is the grace and peace of the Son. We do not receive one grace and one peace from the Father and another from the Son any more than calling the Father Savior and the Son Savior indicates two salvations. Paul's single preposition (ἀπὸ) governs both nouns and indicates for us the correlative work of redemption by the Father and the Son. They are both the source of our salvation. Similarly, in his doxology at the end of Romans Paul prays "to the only wise God be glory forevermore through Jesus Christ! Amen" (διὰ ᾽Ιησοῦ

Χριστου, Rom 16:27). We glorify the Father only through Jesus Christ (cf. Phil 2:11). Apart from Christ there is no glorifying the Father, for apart from Christ there is no grace, peace, or salvation. At the center of our lives of faith stands the Son, the one sent by the Father as foretold through prophets, who gave Himself for our sins (Gal 1:4), who was raised from the dead (Rom 1:4), and whose name we call upon by the power of the Spirit for our salvation (1 Cor 1:2).

When Paul qualifies the glory of the Father as rightly given only "through" the Son, he draws us away from ourselves and into the life and work of God. We may not glorify the Father however we want and in whatever way might please us or those around us. We rightly glorify Him only through the Son. So too, according to Paul, we may only find ourselves in Christ by the Holy Spirit. Those who call upon His name and no other are those who receive the salvation accomplished in Christ and those who are sanctified in Him by the Spirit of holiness. Paul emphasizes the same pattern of speech for our Christian lives. We love others not with some abstract love informed by the cultural expectations of our day. We love our neighbor rightly when we love "in Christ Jesus" (ἐν Χριστῷ Ἰησοῦ, 1 Cor 16:24). We love our neighbor rightly when we love apart from ourselves and according to the love of God in Christ Jesus which has been poured into our hearts by the Holy Spirit (Rom 5:5). Just as Paul directs the reader away from Paul to the Trinity in order to know Paul, he likewise directs us away from ourselves to both know God and serve our neighbor. In both cases Christ Jesus occupies the center, the pivot, or hinge of this right knowing and serving. We may glorify the Father only through the Son because only in the Son do we rightly come to know the glory of the Father *as He has revealed it*. Likewise, we may love one another only in Christ, for only in Him are we set free from the law to freely serve and love others. Therefore, the fellowship that avails among the faithful both in their worship and in their service of neighbor is one always anchored in Christ. Paul expresses this in his doxology at the end of 2 Corinthians: "The grace of our Lord Jesus Christ and the love of God and the fellowship of the Holy Spirit be with you all" (2 Cor 13:14).

Another doxology that offers a striking confession of Christ's identity is found at the end of 2 Thessalonians. Paul writes, "Now may the Lord of peace himself give you peace at all times in every way. The Lord be with you all.... The grace of our Lord Jesus Christ be with you all" (2 Thes 3:16, 18). As seen with the greetings, Paul very often designates Jesus as Lord (*kyrios*), which is his preferred way of assigning the divine name, YHWH, to Jesus.[1] When Paul confesses that Jesus Christ is our Lord, he is unmistakably assigning to Him the divine name and locating Him within the unique identity of YHWH. In the benediction at the end of 2 Thessalonians there is some ambiguity. Although Paul clearly designates Jesus Christ as Lord (*kyrios*) in verse 18, it is less clear

---

1. Larry Hurtado, *Lord Jesus Christ: Devotion to Jesus in Earliest Christianity* (Grand Rapids: Eerdmans, 2003), 112. We will discuss this point at greater length in the next chapter.

to whom he refers as Lord in verse 16. Paul's first use of Lord in verse 16 paraphrases the Aaronic blessing.[2] In the Old Testament we read,

> YHWH spoke to Moses, saying, "Speak to Aaron and his sons, saying, Thus you shall bless the people of Israel: you shall say to them, YHWH bless you and keep you; YHWH make his face to shine upon you and be gracious to you; YHWH lift up his countenance upon you and give you peace. So shall they put my name upon the people of Israel, and I will bless them." (Nm 6:22-27)

Peace comes from YHWH. The New Testament writers consistently link Father and Son together when talking about peace. We have already seen this with Paul's greetings above. Both Peter and John do something similar. Peter writes, "May grace and peace be multiplied to you in the knowledge of God and of Jesus our Lord" (2 Pt 1:2). Like Paul, Peter here designates the Father simply as God. John writes more fully, "Grace, mercy, and peace will be with us, from God the Father and from Jesus Christ the Father's Son, in truth and love" (2 Jn 1:3). With all this in mind, Paul either closes his letter by commending the peace and grace of the Father and the Son or he is referring to Jesus in both cases.[3] Either option is telling. If the Father (v. 16) and the Son (v. 18) are in mind, then it is significant that Paul ends by designating both Lord, and yet distinct as Father and Son. If Jesus is in mind with both references (vv. 16 and 18), then Paul is explicitly locating Jesus in the unique identity of YHWH, something we see him doing elsewhere in his letters. Either option yields significant trinitarian conclusions.

The trinitarian pattern of speech employed by Paul in his greetings and doxologies recurs throughout his letters. Again, we are here interested in those sections of his letters that offer seemingly incidental confessions of God's triune identity in the context of some other point Paul aims to establish. Observing the pattern of Paul's speech in such places allows us to see the normative language of faith and also how the Trinity informs all the articles of faith. For example, in Romans 5 the intelligibility of the reconciling work of God for us demands confession of Father, Son, and Holy Spirit. After Paul has thoroughly explained the justification we have in Christ alone, he turns in the first part of this chapter to the result of this justification. Paul writes, "Therefore, since we have been justified by faith, we have peace with God through our Lord Jesus Christ" (Rom 5:1). The justification we have by faith in Jesus Christ, who is Lord, means we have peace with God the Father. We stand in this grace and rejoice, knowing that such joy involves suffering, because "God's love has been poured into our hearts through the Holy Spirit who has been given to us" (Rom 5:5). Once again we see the governing centrality of Christ in the life of the faithful. Those who are in Christ, clothed with His righteousness, have peace with the Father, and

---

2. Cf. Martin Luther, *Der Sagen* (Nm 6:22-27), 1532 (WA 30/3:574-82). For a discussion of Luther's sermon see Nathan MacDonald, "A Trinitarian Palimpsest: Luther's Reading of the Priestly Blessing (Numbers 6.24-26)," *Pro Ecclesia* 11:3 (2012): 299-313.

3. Most scholars think both references are to Jesus. Abraham Malherbe, *The Letters to the Thessalonians* (New York: Doubleday, 2000), 461.

through Christ rejoice as people of faith, despite the difficulties entailed by such faith, because of the gift of the Holy Spirit. We may coordinate this work of salvation in the following way: the peace and love of the Father are ours through Christ and in Christ by the Holy Spirit. Paul does little to clarify this language and the possible incongruity of confessing the single work of salvation brought about by Father, Son, and Holy Spirit.

A very similar example of the Trinity's saving work and the ordinary language of the faithful to convey this appears in Paul's letter to Titus. We noted above that Paul names both the Father Savior and the Son Savior at the beginning of his letter to Titus (1:3–4). In the Greek this dual confession of the Father and the Son as both Savior appears in the same sentence. Paul makes this a point of emphasis throughout his letter. In the second chapter Paul mentions the doctrine of "God our Savior" (Ti 2:10), and then in the very next sentence refers to Jesus Christ as "our great God and Savior" who gave Himself for our redemption (Ti 2:13–14). Finally, Paul brings the letter to a close with a one-sentence summary of God's saving work for us:

> But when the goodness and loving kindness of God our Savior appeared, he saved us, not because of works done by us in righteousness, but according to his own mercy, by the washing of regeneration and renewal of the Holy Spirit, whom he poured out on us richly through Jesus Christ our Savior, so that being justified by his grace we might become heirs according to the hope of eternal life. (Ti 3:4–7)

For the third time Paul identifies both God the Father and God the Son as Savior. In this final summary sentence Paul draws together the central themes from his longer epistles to the Romans and Galatians. The salvation we have from the Father derives not from our works, not from our own proper righteousness, but from the imputed righteousness of Jesus Christ our Savior, and therefore by grace. We receive this salvation in Christ by the washing of regeneration and renewal of the Holy Spirit. The salvation of the Father brought about by the Son is ours by grace through the work of the Holy Spirit in our baptism.

To talk about salvation according to the Scriptures requires the person of faith to confess the correlative working of Father, Son, and Holy Spirit. The Trinity saves. Although Paul shows little interest in clarifying the language he uses for God and the salvation we have from Him alone, his language is not occasional but normative. Indeed, in the larger context of his letter to Titus Paul's trinitarian confession of our salvation stands at the heart of sound doctrine. The emphasis of Paul's letter to Titus, like his letters to Timothy, concerns sound or healthy doctrine (Ti 1:9; 2:1; 1 Tm 1:10; 6:3; 2 Tm 4:3). The man who wishes to preach and teach God's Word to God's people must "hold firm to the trustworthy word as taught, so that he may be able to give instruction in sound doctrine and also to rebuke those who contradict it" (Ti 1:9). Those who teach false doctrine are not sound in faith (Ti 1:13). They have turned away from the truth and defiled themselves (Ti 1:15–16). Paul urges Titus to teach only what accords with sound doctrine (Ti 2:1). By teaching sound doctrine we show forth our good faith and in everything adorn "the doctrine of God our Savior" (Ti 2:10). Doctrine and life go together. The doctrine Paul is here talking about concerns the salvation we have from the Trinity and the life that proceeds from that salvation. To depart from this sound doctrine is to depart from truth and to defile yourself.

Given the emphasis upon sound doctrine in Paul's letter to Titus, what are we to make of his correlation of the Father and the Son as Savior? Once again we cannot retreat to any idea that suggests poetic license or careless language. That conclusion stands opposed to the very point of Paul's letter. The only other conclusion is that Paul assigns to both the Father and the Son the salvation claimed exclusively by YHWH in the Old Testament: "I, I am YHWH, and besides me there is no Savior" (Is 43:11). The God of Israel is Savior (Is 45:15). Again, "There is no other god besides me, a righteous God and a Savior; there is none besides me" (Is 45:21). Paul does not hesitate to identify Jesus as our Savior and righteousness, as that which belongs exclusively to YHWH. Nor, we must note again, does Paul sense any need to clarify this language for Titus.

Although Paul's identification of Jesus with that which belongs to the unique identity of YHWH is clear in Titus, Paul can be even more explicit elsewhere.[4] In Romans 10 Paul writes, "If you confess with your mouth that Jesus is Lord [*kyrios*] and believe in your heart that God raised him from the dead, you will be saved" (Rom 10:9). Paul continues, "For the Scripture says, 'Everyone who believes in him will not be put to shame'" (Rom 10:11). Paul's reference is to Is 28:16, which he also uses at 9:33: "Behold, I am laying in Zion a stone of stumbling, and a rock of offense; and whoever believes in him will not be put to shame." Jesus is the stone of stumbling, the rock of offense, laid in Zion, and whoever believes in Him will not be put to shame. Paul links this text from Isaiah with Joel by way of the shared term "shame."[5] In the second chapter of Joel YHWH promises to restore His people and they shall never again be put to shame: "You shall know that I am in the midst of Israel, and that I am YHWH your Elohim and there is none else. And my people shall never again be put to shame" (Jl 2:27). When this salvation of Israel comes to pass, YHWH will pour out His Spirit upon all flesh (Jl 2:28), and "everyone who calls on the name of YHWH [κύριος] shall be saved" (Jl 2:32). Paul cites this text in Romans 10 but changes the referent from YHWH to Jesus. Paul writes: "For there is no distinction between Jew and Greek; the same Lord is Lord of all, bestowing

---

4. In addition to the following example see Rom 14:11; 1 Cor 1:31 and 2 Cor 10:17; 1 Cor 2:16; 1 Cor 10:26; and 2 Tm 2:19. For discussion of these texts see David Capes, *Old Testament Yahweh Texts in Paul's Christology* (Tübingen: Mohr/Siebeck, 1992), 115–49. For a lengthier list see Richard Bauckham, *Jesus and the God of Israel* (Grand Rapids: Eerdmans, 2008), 186–90, 219–21.

5. Paul often makes this exegetical move (*gezera shawa*) when interpreting the Old Testament. A classic example is Romans 4. Paul links Gn 15:6 (Rom 4:3) and Ps 32:1–2 (Rom 4:8) by means of the Greek word λογίζομαι. This intertextual linking uses Scripture to interpret Scripture. This exegetical approach was especially popular with the early church fathers, and as can be seen here it is an exegetical insight derived from Scripture.

riches on all who call on him. For everyone who calls on the name of the Lord [τὸ ὄνομα κυρίου] will be saved" (Rom 10:12–13). In the context of Romans 10, Jesus is the subject. Jesus is Lord of all, and everyone who calls on His name will be saved. The name that saves according to Joel is YHWH, and that YHWH, Paul says, is the man Jesus. All who believe in Jesus will avoid eternal shame and will be saved. He is Lord of all; He is YHWH.[6]

Paul never hesitates to talk of the salvation we have from God alone or the Christian life that follows upon that salvation in trinitarian terms. His letters are thoroughly trinitarian, and this trinitarian confession finds its center in Christ crucified. When Paul addresses the divisions in Corinth, he begins with the folly of the cross. Christ is the power and wisdom of God. Although a stumbling block to Jews and folly to Greeks, we preach Christ crucified (1 Cor 1:23–24). Paul continues, "I decided to know nothing among you except Jesus Christ and him crucified" (1 Cor 2:2). Those who preach Christ crucified do so by the power of the Spirit, and this preaching brings about a faith that rests in the power of God the Father and not the wisdom of the world (1 Cor 2:4–5). The natural man scoffs at those who preach the crucifixion of the Lord of Glory (1 Cor 2:8), but those of faith confess the crucified Christ. Paul's answer to divisions in Corinth begins with the Trinity and Christ crucified. The response of the faithful, as shown throughout Paul's letters, is to say, "I have been crucified with Christ. It is no longer I who live, but Christ who lives in me" (Gal 2:19–20). The one who lives in Christ is the one adopted by God through the Spirit: "And because you are sons, God has sent the Spirit of his Son into our hearts, crying, 'Abba! Father!'" (Gal 4:6). Those who live by the Spirit (Gal 5:25) are the ones born again by water and Spirit, cleansed by the washing of water with the Word (Eph 5:26).

Those who remember their baptism confess Christ crucified by the power of the Holy Spirit and cry out to the Father made known to them in Christ. Baptism always stands at the center of the Christian life and, rightly understood, heals all division. Here, in baptism, we are reborn as the children of God—not by the will of man but by God (Jn 1:13). Buried in baptism with Christ, joined to His death and resurrection, we are freed in Him from sin, death, and the devil, from the curse of the law and from ourselves, to walk in newness of life according to the Spirit (Romans 6–8; Col 2:12–15). As Paul puts it elsewhere, "You were washed, you were sanctified, you were justified in the name of the Lord Jesus Christ and by the Spirit of our God" (1 Cor 6:11). The Father who chose us in Christ before the foundation of the world blessed us in Christ (Eph 1:3–4), redeemed us through the blood of Christ, and forgave us our sins (Eph 1:7; 4:32). This salvation comes to us by grace through faith apart from works (Eph 2:8–9). We who once were far off have been brought near by the blood of Christ, who is our peace and reconciliation with the Father (Eph 2:13–16)

---

6. For a detailed discussion of Romans 10 see C. Kavin Rowe, "Romans 10:13: What Is the Name of the Lord?" *Horizons in Biblical Theology* 22 (2000): 135–73.

and with all others (Eph 4:32; 5:21; 1 Thes 5:9–13). Through Christ alone we have access to the Father in the Spirit (Eph 2:18).

Paul never seeks to justify his trinitarian language. He simply uses it and assumes the shared convictions of his audience. Moreover, he greets, blesses, prays, and talks about our salvation and Christian life in trinitarian terms. The ordinary language of faith, deeply shaped by the Scriptures, knows no other way.

THE IDENTITY OF CHRIST IN THE GOSPELS

Who Is Jesus?

The most basic way in which the question of Jesus' identity arises in the Gospels is with the general expectation of the promised Messiah, the one who is coming, and whether Jesus is that Messiah. John the Baptist, voicing the concerns of many, sends messengers to Jesus, asking, "Are you the one who is to come, or shall we look for another?" (Mt 11:3). The Samaritan woman confesses, "I know that Messiah is coming (he who is called Christ). When he comes, he will tell us all things" (Jn 4:25). Others who were looking for the Messiah rejoice that He has come. Andrew, finding his brother Simon Peter, says, "We have found the Messiah" (Jn 1:41). Likewise, Philip finds Nathanael and says to him, "We have found him of whom Moses in the Law and also the prophets wrote, Jesus of Nazareth, the son of Joseph" (Jn 1:45). The disciples on the road to Emmaus express surprise that Jesus, whom they did not yet recognize, knew nothing about the things that had occurred in Jerusalem.

> Then one of them, named Cleopas, answered him, "Are you the only visitor to Jerusalem who does not know the things that have happened there in these days?" And he said to them, "What things?" And they said to him, "Concerning Jesus of Nazareth, a man who was a prophet mighty in deed and word before God and all the people, and how our chief priests and rulers delivered him up to be condemned to death, and crucified him. But we had hoped that he was the one to redeem Israel. Yes, and besides all this, it is now the third day since these things happened. (Lk 24:18–21)

They had hoped, along with many others, that this Jesus was the one to come, the one to redeem Israel. The above examples show the common concern of ordinary believers in the New Testament steeped in the promises of the Old Testament. They were eagerly awaiting the promised Messiah, and some were actively searching for Him. Jesus comes under scrutiny precisely for this reason. Are *you* the Messiah? The question of Jesus' identity forms the backdrop of the historical presentation of the Gospels.

The Gospels answer the question of Jesus' identity in both obvious and subtle ways. When He does things belonging either to God alone or at the very least to some being greater than a mere man, those around Him wonder about His identity. When He forgives the sins of the woman with the alabaster jar, those who witness this begin to say among themselves, "Who is this, who even forgives sins?" (Lk 7:49). When He forgives the sins of the paralytic, the scribes declare in their hearts, "He is blaspheming! Who can forgive sins but God alone?" (Mk 2:7). When He rebukes the wind and calms the sea, the disciples, filled with fear, say to one another, "Who then is this, that even wind and sea obey him?" (Mk 4:41). Jesus' actions, His activities, raise questions of identity for those around Him.

Jesus often uses the confusion arising over the things He does to encourage questions of identity. To understand who He is we should look at what He does and consider it in the light of what the Old Testament says about these things. Jesus responds to the messengers sent by John the Baptist in this way: "Go and tell John what you have seen and heard: the blind receive their sight, the lame walk, lepers are cleansed, and the deaf hear, the dead are raised up, the poor have good news preached to them" (Lk 7:22; cf. 1 Jn 1:1–3). Jesus' answer establishes two important points. First, we discern the identity of the Messiah not only by what He declares about Himself but also by the things He does, by the power He exercises. His works, His activities, His functions, however we wish to put it, "reveal" His identity as the Messiah. Furthermore, these activities are done by His own power, not by the power of another. He forgives the sins of the paralytic and tells Him to rise and walk on His own authority (ἐξουσία, Lk 5:20–24). He commands Lazarus to come out by the power of His own voice (Jn 11:43), because "the Son gives life to whom he will" (Jn 5:21). By contrast, Elijah raises the widow of Zarephath's son by praying that God would accomplish this: "'O Lord my God, let this child's life come into him again.' And the Lord listened to the voice of Elijah. And the life of the child came into him again, and he revived" (1 Kgs 17:21–22). Although the prayer has been omitted, Paul imitates Elijah's actions in raising Eutychus (Acts 20:10). Another example, although of a different sort, occurs in the valley of the dry bones. Life returns to these bones through Ezekiel as an agent of God's power: "Thus says the Lord God to these bones: Behold, I will cause breath to enter you, and you shall live" (Ez 37:5). Elijah, Ezekiel, and Paul grant life by the power of another; Jesus gives life by His own power.

The second important thing shown by Jesus' response identifies for us the authority by which we rightly judge matters of activity and identity. We know the Messiah by what He does because Scripture establishes the things He will do. We are not left guessing if this or that action indicates His identity; we are to search the Scriptures, to rely upon God's witness about Himself. Jesus' response points especially to what God declared through the prophets about the Messiah. According to the Scriptures, the Messiah will bring good news to the poor, bind up the brokenhearted, proclaim liberty to the captives, and comfort all who mourn (Is 61:1–2). He will open the eyes of the blind, unstop the ears of the deaf, heal the lame, and loosen the string of the mute (Is 35:4–6). Further, He will be wounded for our transgressions

(Is 53:5–6), bear our iniquities (Mi 5:2–5), be pierced for us (Zec 12:10), and be a fountain that cleanses us from all sin (Zec 13:1).

Although typically the question of Jesus' identity centers on the things He does and the reaction others give to Him, the Gospels also present Jesus' identity in more subtle ways through the actions of others. In the well-known reading appointed for Epiphany, the Magi arrive in Jerusalem looking for the king of the Jews. They report that they have followed His star and "have come to worship him" (Mt 2:2).[7] Immediately we learn that both Herod and the people of Jerusalem were troubled. Were they troubled because the Magi sought another king, a rival to Herod, and therefore made a threat to Herod's throne and power? Were the people troubled because of what Herod would do to rid himself of this rival king? Although this may have had something to do with their fear, Scripture indicates another reason. The only thing reported to Herod by the Magi was that they came to worship the king of the Jews. Without hesitation Herod turned to the chief priests and scribes to inquire where the Christ, the Messiah, was to be born—a recurring identity question in the New Testament. Herod's reaction should give us pause. What could the Magi have

---

7. An exegetical puzzle that occupied the minds of sixteenth- and seventeenth-century Lutherans concerned how the Magi knew the Christ Child. The New Testament tells us only that the Magi were guided by "his star" to Jerusalem and to Herod (Mt 2:1). The question asked by Luther, Chemnitz, and Gerhard is if the Magi knew the Christ Child and worshipped Him because of their natural reason and the natural light of this star. For all of them, this was an impossible and profane conclusion. Johann Gerhard comments, "One thing is for sure, they would not have been able to recognize the birth of Christ from the appearance of the star alone" (*Postilla*, trans. Elmer Hohle [Malone, TX: Repristination Press, 2003], 1:138). The answer for both Chemnitz and Gerhard stretches back to Daniel and the Babylonian captivity, an insight Chemnitz gleaned from Veit Deitrich (Martin Chemnitz, *Harmoniae Evangelicae* [Geneva, 1628], 94). Gerhard thinks it beyond doubt that Daniel, who was made chief of the Magi (Dn 5:11), would have entrusted to the Babylonian wise men something about the promises of the Christ and that these teachings would have been retained continuously by them.

Somewhat less conclusively, Martin Chemnitz surmises, "It will not be absurd if some knowledge of the promises concerning the Messiah of the Jews—whose salvation extended also to the Gentiles—came to the magi either from remnants of Daniel's teachings, from the Israelite exiles remaining in Babylon, or from readings of the prophets" (*Harmoniae Evangelicae*, 95). What must not be believed is that the Magi arrived at this knowledge of Christ as their savior "from natural principles and knowledge" (*Harmoniae Evangelicae*, 94). Chemnitz grants a certain amount of exegetical freedom in solving this question, as long as a person's interpretation remains consistent with the analogy of faith. He writes, "The analogy of faith must be observed by not opposing the foundation of these Scriptures—Rom 10:17, 1 Cor 2:8, 1 Cor 2:14—which maintain that reason by its own natural light cannot attain the knowledge of Christ. Such knowledge is given by the Holy Spirit through the Word" (*Harmoniae Evangelicae*, 95). He insists that there is no such knowledge of Christ *sine verbo et revelatione divina*.

Luther preached on the Magi in a similar way. In a sermon for Epiphany he asks how the Magi found the Christ Child. It was not by natural reason or some natural occurrence, such as the star that guided their journey. The Magi, like all people, found Him, explains Luther, "solely because of the prophet, the written word . . . in order that all natural knowledge and all human reason might be rejected and every enlightenment repudiated except that which comes through the Spirit and grace" (*The Gospel for the Festival of the Epiphany*, 1522 [AE 52:194; WA 10/1, 1:609.5–9]). Although the star served the purpose of guiding the Magi to their destination, they sought the king of the Jews because He was the Christ, their savior, and this they knew from the Word.

said to indicate to Herod they were seeking the Messiah? To this point in the text no one had mentioned the Christ other than Herod. The answer lies in what they were seeking to do—to worship the king of the Jews. Only God receives worship. The Magi were seeking the God who blots out transgressions, who alone saves His people from their sins, whose dominion is an everlasting dominion. This Herod understood and this caused great fear for him and the people. Either "the day of the Lord" (Mal 4:1; Is 13:6, 9; Jer 46:10; Jl 1:15; 2:1; 2:11; Ob 15) was upon them or these Magi were blaspheming in the extreme, seeking to offer the worship owed to God alone to another, whom they regarded as the true king of the Jews (cf. 1 Sm 8:7). Either possibility would have brought fear to both Herod and the people. Herod's reaction, however, makes it quite clear how he understood their request. Activity (worship) reveals identity (God). These Magi were looking "to worship" the God who has come to tabernacle among His people, as promised by the prophets.

Finally, Jesus introduces the question of His own identity on a number of occasions. He asks the disciples directly, "Who do people say that I am?" (Mk 8:27). The people gave different answers. Some said John the Baptist, others said Elijah, and still others said one of the prophets (Mk 8:28) or even Jeremiah (Mt 16:14). John records an example of the crowds puzzling over Jesus' identity as reported here by the disciples. When Jesus is at the Feast of Booths, He teaches in the temple and the Jews marvel over His learning. The people wonder why the Pharisees do not seize Him since they were seeking to kill Him. Could it be, they wonder, that "the authorities really know that this is the Christ?" (Jn 7:26). The people continue, "But we know where this man comes from, and when the Christ appears, no one will know where he comes from" (Jn 7:27). The final point made by the crowd is not held by all. As seen above, Herod and his chief priests knew where the Christ would be born. Some in the crowd share Herod's position. On the last day of the feast Jesus begins teaching about the Spirit who will be given when He is glorified. The people again take up the question of Jesus' identity.

> When they heard these words, some of the people said, "This really is the Prophet." Others said, "This is the Christ." But some said, "Is the Christ to come from Galilee? Has not the Scripture said that the Christ comes from the offspring of David, and comes from Bethlehem, the village where David was?" So there was a division among the people over him. (Jn 7:40–43)

The division among the people concerns His identity as the Christ and what the Scriptures say about the Christ. The disagreement among the people extends even to the question of whether we would know where the Christ comes from. Those who know that the Christ comes from Bethlehem emphasize the clear testimony of Micah (5:2; cf. Mt 2:6). Those who suggest He will just appear and no one will know where He comes from offer a peculiar interpretation of Malachi (3:1; cf. Lk 2:25–35), who tells of the Lord suddenly coming to His temple. The significant point here is that the identity of the Christ depends upon the Scriptures and was a pressing topic of conversation among the crowds.

After the disciples answer Jesus' question by reporting the different responses from the people, Jesus asks them, "Who do you say that I am?" (Mk 8:29). Matthew records the fullest answer. Simon Peter replies, "You are the Christ, the Son of the living God" (Mt 16:16; cf. Jn 11:27; 20:31). The identity of Jesus is known by His saving work as the Christ and by His eternal relationship to the living God, the Father. Both statements reveal who Jesus is. This confession of Jesus' identity comes not from man, not from the plausible words of wisdom, but from the Father through the teaching of Christ (Mt 16:17).

Jesus queries not only His disciples but also His opponents about His identity. He asks the Pharisees, "What do you think about the Christ? Whose son is he?" (Mt 22:42). They respond that the Christ is the son of David. Jesus then asks, "How is it then that David, in the Spirit, calls him Lord?" (Mt 22:43). Jesus quotes Ps 110:1 and asks again how David can call Him both Lord and son. No one is able to answer (Mt 22:46). Two things are of note. To rightly understand the identity of Jesus a person must know the Scriptures. We know who the Christ is not by recourse to our best ideas but only and always by returning to the Word of God. Second, to know who Christ is, as seen with the disciples above and here with the Pharisees, requires God. David knew the Christ as both Lord and son by the Spirit; Peter knew from the Father through Christ's teaching.

The Identity of Jesus and the Trinity

The above examples show the importance of answering rightly the question of Jesus' identity and the importance of that question to the New Testament. From this perspective the Gospels may be seen as extended presentations of Christ's identity. Although the four Gospels present the same identity of Christ as true God and true man, they proceed in different but complementary ways. All of the Gospels take up the question of identity from the very beginning. Matthew records that Jesus Christ is the son of David and son of Abraham (Mt 1:1). Mark simply declares that Jesus is the Son of God (Mk 1:1). John opens with the lofty confession of Jesus as the eternal Word of God who became flesh and tabernacled among us (Jn 1:1, 14). Luke aims to provide an orderly account for his readers and more slowly builds to the question of Jesus' identity. His opening, however, refers to Jesus as the Word. Luke tells us he is passing on what was delivered to the faithful by the eyewitnesses and ministers "of the Word" (τοῦ λόγου, Lk 1:3).[8]

Both Luke and Matthew explicitly present Jesus' identity in trinitarian terms. In Luke's telling of the annunciation the angel declares to the Virgin Mary, "The Holy Spirit will come upon you, and the power of the Most High will

---

8. Arthur Just, Jr., *Luke 1:1–9:50*, Concordia Commentary (St. Louis: Concordia Publishing House, 1996), 36.

overshadow you; therefore the child to be born will be called holy—the Son of God" (Lk 1:35). Luke further underscores Jesus' divine identity by assigning the divine name (ΥΗWΗ/κύριος) to Him. Zechariah and Elizabeth walk blamelessly in the commandments and statutes "of the Lord" (Lk 1:6). Zechariah enters "the temple of the Lord" (Lk 1:9), and before him appears "an angel of the Lord" (Lk 1:11). Zechariah is told that Elizabeth will bear a son named John and he will turn many "to the Lord their God" (Lk 1:16). Similarly, Gabriel comes to the Virgin Mary and declares that "the Lord God" will give to Jesus, the Son of the Most High, the throne of His father David (Lk 1:32), and Mary eventually responds, "Behold, I am the servant of the Lord" (Lk 1:38). In all of these instances, Lord (κύριος) clearly refers to ΥΗWΗ.[9] Following the exchange with Gabriel, Mary visits Elizabeth: "And Elizabeth was filled with the Holy Spirit, and she exclaimed with a loud cry, 'Blessed are you among women, and blessed is the fruit of your womb! And why is this granted to me that the mother of my Lord [ἡ μήτηρ τοῦ κυρίου μου] should come to me?'" (Lk 1:41–43). Here Luke identifies Jesus with the divine name, ΥΗWΗ, and Elizabeth confesses this by the Holy Spirit.

In Matthew, the angel Gabriel comes to Joseph and tells him to take Mary as his wife, "for that which is conceived in her is from the Holy Spirit" (Mt 1:20). Jesus is born of Mary by the Holy Spirit. He has no human father. Matthew stresses the point with grammatical precision in his genealogy (ἐξ ἧς, Mt 1:16) and by appealing to Is 7:14 (Mt 1:23). The name Jesus means He will save His people from their sins (Mt 1:21). Salvation belongs to God alone, to His unique identity. There is no Savior other than ΥΗWΗ. Matthew here makes clear the divine identity of Jesus, who is both God and man. He saves, and He saves *His* people. They belong to Him as He is their God. Lest any ambiguity remain Matthew states Jesus' identity absolutely: He is Immanuel, God with us.

Although Matthew declares Jesus' identity as God in absolute terms, the Gospels more often present His identity in relative terms. He is the Son *of* the Father. Mark and John proceed in this way from the beginning. For Mark He is the Son *of* God and for John He is the Word *of* God. Luke does something similar. Gabriel declares to Mary that she will conceive and bear a son, and His name will be Jesus. Gabriel continues, "He will be great and will be called the Son of the Most High" (Lk 1:32). All four Gospels report that at Jesus' baptism the Holy Spirit descended on Him and a voice from above declared, "You are my beloved Son; with you I am well pleased" (Mt 3:16–17; Mk 1:10–11; Lk 3:22; cf. Jn 1:33–34). Jesus is the Son of God sent into the world by His Father. As shown in the previous chapter, the names Father and Son, their distinction and unity, were known in the Old Testament. Only with the revelation of Jesus' identity in the New Testament, however, can we say these names are normative for our right speaking and worshipping of the one true God of Israel.

---

9. C. Kavin Rowe, "Luke and the Trinity: An Essay in Ecclesial Biblical Theology," *Scottish Journal of Theology* 56/1 (2003): 13–14.

These scripturally normative names, Father and Son, are constitutive of God's eternal identity. The Father is the Father and eternally so. The Son is the Son and eternally so. Further, there is no reality prior to God *as Father* or God *as Son*.[10] The Son stands in an eternal relationship with the Father, and the Father in an eternal relationship with the Son. The Father is Father always in relation to His Son; the Son is Son always in relation to His Father. Each entails the other; each belongs to the identity of the one true God. For this reason the Scriptures further declare that to know the Son is to know the Father. Matthew, Luke, and John emphasize this point. In Matthew and Luke Jesus declares, "No one knows the Son except the Father, and no one knows the Father except the Son and anyone to whom the Son chooses to reveal him" (Mt 11:27; Lk 10:22). David Scaer observes that Father and Son have an exclusive knowledge of one another and relate to believers through revelation.[11] We grasp that revelation by the Holy Spirit (1 Cor 2:11 KJV). Further, access to the Father is through the Son, a point emphasized above with Paul, but one especially made clear by John.

John teaches that it is through the Son alone that we know, see, and honor the Father: "Whoever does not honor the Son does not honor the Father who sent him" (Jn 5:23). To honor the Father is to worship the Father. Therefore, whoever does not worship the Son does not worship the Father. We can see the Father only through the Son (Jn 12:45; 14:9) because it is through the Son that we come to know the Father (Jn 14:6–7). And yet it is also the case that the Father bears witness to the Son (Jn 5:37; 8:18) and no one comes to know the Son, who alone reveals and makes known the Father, unless the Father draws him (Jn 6:37, 44, 65). It is the will of the Father that all who seek eternal life should look upon the Son (Jn 6:40). To know the Son is to know the Father; to deny the Son is to deny the Father (1 Jn 2:23). Jesus declares, "Whoever hates me hates my Father also" (Jn 15:23). Similarly, John writes elsewhere, "Whoever transgresses and does not abide in the doctrine of Christ does not have God. He who abides in the doctrine has both the Father and the Son" (2 Jn 9 NKJV).

When the Jews accuse Jesus of making Himself equal to God by calling Him Father, He responds by showing the correlative working of them both. The Son does nothing of His own accord, only what He sees the Father doing. Jesus explains, "Whatever the Father does, that the Son does likewise" (Jn 5:19). They are distinct in who they are as Father and Son, but one in the work they do for us (*opera ad extra*). Jesus continues by explaining this correlative working: "For as the Father raises the dead and gives them life, so also the Son gives life to whom he will. The Father judges no one, but has given all judgment to the Son, that all may honor the Son, just as they honor the Father" (Jn 5:21–23).

---

10. William Weinrich, "Trinitarian Reality as Christian Truth: Reflections on Greek Patristic Discussion," *Concordia Theological Quarterly* 67:3/4 (2003): 338: "There is no reality that we might call 'God' that is prior to God *as God the Father*; there is no reality that we might call 'God' that is prior to God *as God the Son*."

11. David Scaer, "The Doctrine of the Trinity in Biblical Perspective," *Concordia Theological Quarterly* 67:3/4 (2003): 332.

To give life, to judge, these are divine prerogatives, belonging to the unique identity of God.

If we know and worship the Father through the Son alone, then how do we know and worship the Son? John addresses this very question. That we might know the Son and the Father, both send the Holy Spirit, the Comforter and Spirit of Truth (Jn 14:26; 15:26). The Spirit bears witness to the Son (Jn 15:26) by directing us to what Christ Himself has said (Jn 14:26). He will convict the world concerning "sin and righteousness and judgment" (Jn 16:8), and will declare to us what belongs to the Son and the Father (Jn 15:15). Finally, the Spirit of Truth will guide us into the Truth (Jn 15:13). No one comes to the Father except through the Son because He is "the way, and the truth, and the life" (Jn 14:6). The Spirit guides us into the Truth, speaking to us the words of Truth, and the Son, who is the Truth, is the way to the Father and eternal life. Jesus brings all of this together in His discourse with the woman from Samaria about right worship. True worshippers, He explains, "worship the Father in Spirit and Truth" (Jn 4:23).[12]

The above examples establish two important points. First, the question of Jesus' identity stands behind the historical presentation of His life, works, and teachings by the four evangelists. People were looking eagerly for the Messiah. Whether friend, foe, or bystander, when they are confronted by Christ, they all wonder about His identity. The evangelists present the answer to that question by telling of the life of Christ, His deeds and His words. Second, the question of Jesus' identity cannot be answered, according to the Scriptures, apart from the Father and the Spirit. To proclaim Christ, to speak of Him and to worship Him, is to confess the Trinity who God is, as seen from Paul and the evangelists. Furthermore, at the heart of God's identity stands the Father/Son relationship, a relationship made known to us by their Spirit whom they send to us.

Jesus and the Old Testament

The Gospel writers present Jesus' identity from the beginning by declaring Him the son of David and Abraham, the Son of God, the Son of the Most High, or the Word of God—all designations derived from the Old Testament. The evangelists then proceed, in their particular ways, to retell the events of His life and how these further reveal who He is. We should not, however, think of the Gospels as mere depositories of historical facts about Jesus. Nor should we think that they—the Gospel writers themselves—declare for us Jesus' identity as the eternal Son of God. Rather they present highly structured narratives of Jesus' life that show who Jesus is through faithful exegesis of the Old Testament. It is the Old Testament that declares Jesus' identity. The Gospel writers remind us of

---

12. Although most translations leave spirit and truth lowercase (προσκυνήσουσιν τῷ πατρὶ ἐν πνεύματι καὶ ἀληθείᾳ), the Fathers read "spirit" as a reference to the Holy Spirit and "truth" as a reference to the Son. See among others Athanasius *Letters to Serapion* 1.33 and Gregory of Nazianzus *Or.* 31.12.

this throughout. For example, all four evangelists use Isaiah 40 to establish the identity of the one about whom they write. Mark does this immediately. After he declares Jesus the Son of God, he quotes the prophet Isaiah: "Behold, I send my messenger before your face, who will prepare your way, the voice of one crying in the wilderness: Prepare the way of the Lord [YHWH/κύριος], make his paths straight" (Mk 1:2–3). Isaiah and Malachi make clear that the messenger will prepare the way for YHWH (Is 40:3; Mal 3:1). John the Baptist identifies himself as the voice crying in the wilderness (Jn 1:23), and Jesus confirms this (Lk 7:27). As with Paul above, the evangelists all cite an Old Testament text that refers explicitly to YHWH and assign it to Jesus. John the Baptist prepares the way for YHWH, the man Jesus. The Gospel writers also use the Old Testament in more subtle ways to mark off Jesus' identity.

Late in his reforming career Luther returned over and over again to the Old Testament. As noted in chapter 5, the Old Testament was being ignored by Christian exegetes in his day. In his *Preface to the Old Testament* Luther urges the faithful to take up the Old Testament that they might see Christ and understand the New Testament. He writes,

> There are some who have little regard for the Old Testament. They think of it as a book that was given to the Jewish people only and is now out of date, containing only stories of past times. They think they have enough in the New Testament and assert that only a spiritual sense is to be sought in the Old Testament. . . . But Christ says in John 5, "Search the Scriptures, for it is they that bear witness to me" (Jn 5:39). St. Paul bids Timothy attend to the reading of the Scriptures (1 Tm 4:13), and in Romans 1 he declares that the gospel was promised by God in the Scriptures (Rom 1:2), while in 1 Corinthians 15 he says that in accordance with the Scriptures Christ came of the seed of David, died, and was raised from the dead. St. Peter, too, points us back, more than once, to the Scriptures.[13]

Jesus and the New Testament writers point us back to the Old Testament. They do this that we might diligently study the Old Testament to better understand the New Testament. Since the Old Testament is the ground and proof of the New Testament, we must not despise it, writes Luther. He continues, "What is the New Testament but a public preaching and proclamation of Christ, set forth through the sayings of the Old Testament and fulfilled through Christ?"[14] What shall we expect to find in the Old Testament? Luther does not hesitate to answer: "Here you will find the swaddling cloths and the manger in which Christ lies, and to which the angel points the shepherds (Lk 2:12). Simple and lowly are these swaddling cloths, but dear is the treasure, Christ, who lies in them."[15]

The witness of the Gospels to Jesus as true God and true man rests upon the Old Testament and the knowledge of what God has declared through the patriarchs and prophets. We see this in two ways. On the one hand, each Gospel, taken as a whole, presents a carefully structured narrative that leads to

---

13. *Preface to the Old Testament*, 1545 (AE 35:235; WADB 8:11.1–12).
14. *Preface to the Old Testament*, 1545 (AE 35:235; WADB 8:11.19–21).
15. *Preface to the Old Testament*, 1545 (AE 35:235; WADB 8:13.6–8).

the same conclusion: Jesus is the Son of God, and this is rightly understood at the cross and with His death for us. That very point, as seen in the last chapter, is made known with great clarity in the Old Testament and gets to the heart of the unique identity of YHWH. Below I will show briefly how Mark presents this in his Gospel. Second, the issue of Jesus' identity and the Old Testament stands behind many of the familiar texts of the New Testament. Three examples will be given below. Too often these sorts of texts are skipped over and the more obviously dogmatic texts, like the prologue to the Gospel of John or the Christological hymn from Philippians 2, are favored. This is certainly understandable. Those dogmatic texts state unambiguously the divine identity of Jesus. The texts below are more subtle and require greater familiarity with the Old Testament. They may be described as homiletical examples of Jesus' divine identity. These sorts of texts litter our lectionaries and occupy the attention of our preaching and teaching.

Narrative Structure of Mark

The Gospel writers all make literary decisions in their presentation of Jesus' divine identity. In Mark's Gospel the phrase "Son of God" plays an instrumental role in disclosing who Jesus is. Mark opens his Gospel by declaring that Jesus is the Son of God and then proceeds with his Gospel to show us what this means. Jesus teaches with authority, unlike the scribes (Mk 1:22), which confuses the people but not the unclean spirit, who declares, "I know who you are—the Holy One of God" (Mk 1:24). Jesus rebukes the unclean spirit and frees the man from it. The people are further astonished: "What is this? A new teaching with authority! He commands even the unclean spirits, and they obey him" (Mk 1:27). The people know the unclean spirit but not the one with power over the unclean spirit. Jesus proceeds to heal many, cleanse a leper, and forgive the sins of the paralytic. He does this by His own authority and power. After Jesus declares to the paralytic, in the presence of the scribes, "My son, your sins are forgiven," the scribes begin to question: "Why does this man speak like that? He is blaspheming! Who can forgive sins but God alone?" (Mk 2:6–7). Although the scribes fail to believe who Jesus is, their own conclusion, based on what Jesus is doing, correctly identifies Him. He is God.

The confusion of the scribes corresponds to that of the disciples. When Jesus calms the storm the disciples say to one another, "Who then is this, that even wind and sea obey him?" (Mk 4:41). The one who stretched forth the heavens and the earth, the one who commanded the waves to go no further (Jb 38:11) is the one who does such things. The God who made all things and rules all things is also the God to whom we cry in our distress. The Psalmist records this very episode: "Then they cried to YHWH in their trouble, and he delivered them from their distress. He made the storm be still, and the waves of the sea were hushed. Then they were glad that the waters were quiet, and he brought them to their desired haven. Let them thank YHWH for his steadfast love, for his wondrous works to the children of men!" (Ps 107:28–31). God delivers His people in their distress; they rejoice and thank YHWH for His steadfast love. The disciples fear for their lives as the waves toss the boat and water comes over the side. Jesus awakes and rebukes the wind, and there is a great calm. He then says to them, "'Why are you so afraid? Have you still no faith?' They did not respond but instead wondered who this is that even sea and wind obey him" (Mk 4:40–41). The answer, given in their observation but not yet grasped and confessed, is that Jesus is the Son of God.

Mark begins his Gospel by declaring that Jesus is the Son of God. The unclean spirits acknowledge that He is the Holy One of God (Mk 1:24), the Son of God (Mk 3:11), and Son of the Most High God (Mk 5:7). Although the people, the scribes, and the disciples recognize that according to the Scriptures the things Jesus does are done by God alone, no human until the centurion at the cross confesses that Jesus is the Son of God (Mk 15:39). Although this should have been known to the scribes when He forgave the sins of the paralytic and the disciples when He rebuked the wind and calmed the storm, it was not. We need not look far for the reason. After Peter confesses that Jesus is the Christ (Mk 8:29) he proceeds to deny what that means, relying on the best ideas of man (Mk 8:32–33). God is not known if He is regarded only as the creator and ruler of His creation. He is known at the cross. Why? Here we get to the basic purpose of what Jesus has done in Mark's Gospel. His actions throughout are not gratuitous displays of divine power; rather, He is waging war on sin, death, and the devil. He drives out the demons, the unclean spirits. He heals the sicknesses brought about by sin and the Fall. He raises the dead, thwarting death's hold on them. He rebukes the wind and calms the storm, turning back the destructive forces of nature brought about by the Fall. The kingdom of God is at hand (Mk 1:15). The final defeat of sin, death, and devil, the final blow, comes at the cross. The centurion, of all people, understands this. He confesses that Jesus is the Son of God, and this at the death of Jesus. After Peter's confession Jesus explains this very truth to the disciples; Peter rebukes Him. The point made by Mark, and indeed the other Gospel writers as well, is that God is known on His own terms and not ours. This God of the Bible comes among us not simply to display His divine power over creation but to defeat Satan, to conquer sin, and to vanquish death. For this reason the triune God of the Bible is known in the death and resurrection of the man Jesus, the eternal Son of God.

The Disciples on the Road to Emmaus
When Jesus says to the disciples on the road to Emmaus that "everything written about me in the Law of Moses and the Prophets and the Psalms must be fulfilled" and proceeds to summarize what those Scriptures proclaim, namely "that the Christ should suffer and on the third day rise from the dead, and that repentance and forgiveness of sins should be proclaimed in his name to all nations" (Lk 24:44–46), He makes clear to them the proper Christological

sense in which we are to read the Scriptures. Two points of significance occur in this exchange with the Emmaus disciples. The first point, made with insistence throughout the New Testament and echoed by Luther above, emphasizes the authoritative and definitive source for knowing God and His works: the Scriptures. Jesus offers here no new visions, no unwritten insights or traditions to be guarded by the few. Jesus points the disciples to the Old Testament, to the Scriptures alone. To fail to understand what is written here is to be foolish and without sense (ὦ ἀνόητοι, Lk 24:25). Jesus further clarifies the content of the Scriptures: "And beginning with Moses and all the Prophets, he interpreted to them in all the Scriptures the things concerning himself" (Lk 24:27). The Old Testament proclaims Christ. Further, it does so not in isolated proof texts but "in all the Scriptures," from Genesis to Malachi. When Paul arrived in Rome he taught the Jews "about Jesus from the Law of Moses and from the Prophets" (Acts 28:23). If we are to know Christ rightly, we too must direct ourselves to the Old Testament. Christ tells the rich man, "If they do not hear Moses and the Prophets, neither will they be convinced if someone should rise from the dead" (Lk 16:31). To hear Moses and the prophets, to listen to them and heed their word requires that our ears be unstopped. It requires Jesus to place His fingers in our ears and declare, "Ephphatha" (Mk 7:34), which He does in our baptism.[16]

The second point made by Jesus concerns our understanding. We know God and His works by reading the Scriptures. We understand what we read when God opens our eyes and ears to grasp His Word. The disciples listened to Jesus expound the Scriptures to them, but their moment of understanding came later.

> So they drew near to the village to which they were going. He acted as if he were going farther, but they urged him strongly, saying, "Stay with us, for it is toward evening and the day is now far spent." So he went in to stay with them. When he was at table with them, he took the bread and blessed and broke it and gave it to them. And their eyes were opened, and they recognized him. And he vanished from their sight. They said to each other, "Did not our hearts burn within us while he talked to us on the road, while he opened to us the Scriptures?" And they rose that same hour and returned to Jerusalem. And they found the eleven and those who were with them gathered together, saying, "The Lord has risen indeed, and has appeared to Simon!" Then they told what had happened on the road, and how he was known to them in the breaking of the bread.

After Adam and Eve ate of the forbidden fruit their eyes were opened by the law as they saw their sin and their rejection of God. Their eyes were opened to evil by communing with the serpent and his false teaching. On the road to Emmaus, after the crucifixion and resurrection, the eyes of the two disciples were opened by communing with the risen Christ. When He took the bread,

---

16. In the Latin West, Mk 7:34 was used in the "opening" of the baptismal liturgy. The bishop would touch the candidate's ears while saying, "Ephphatha, that is, Be opened." See Ambrose *On the Mysteries* 1.3 (NPNF, ii, 10, 317). Luther retained this in his order of baptism (*The Order of Baptism*, 1523 [AE 53:99; WA 12:45.11–13]).

blessed it, and gave it to them, the veil was lifted, their eyes opened, their ears unstopped; they saw Jesus and understood the Scriptures.

Rightly knowing the Christological sense of Scripture entails the liturgical gathering of the baptized people of God around the Lord's Supper. Our right understanding of Scripture requires divine illumination, which for the disciples on the road to Emmaus was accomplished by Christ Himself, for Peter by the Father through Christ's teaching (Mt 16:17), and for all believers by the Holy Spirit (Mt 22:43; 1 Cor 2:10; 1 Pt 1:12). Apart from this illumination, the things about Christ's suffering and resurrection as proclaimed throughout the Scriptures, especially by the prophets, are neither understood nor grasped, indeed remain hidden from us (Lk 18:34). When we come to know these things and believe them we are said to be reborn as the children of God, "not of blood nor of the will of the flesh nor of the will of man, but of God" (Jn 1:13).

Two further points need to be emphasized. Our knowing about God comes only from God—Father, Son, and Holy Spirit. Moreover, this sort of knowing is identity-altering and regenerative. The natural man does not just fail to understand the things of the Spirit of God (1 Cor 2:14) but further regards them as folly and absurd. There is no neutral "theological" space: "Whoever is not with me is against me" (Lk 11:23). The light of the gospel remains veiled for this person, whose back is to the Lord (2 Cor 3:16; 4:3–4). When told he must be reborn, he can respond only with the absurd: "How can a man be born when he is old? Can he enter a second time into his mother's womb and be born?" The answer given by Jesus is that you must be born of water and the Spirit (Jn 3:4–5). Paul continued to preach this folly of baptismal regeneration and renewal by the Holy Spirit, emphasizing that this same Spirit is the one poured out richly upon us through Jesus Christ, our Savior, "that being justified by his grace we might become heirs according to the hope of eternal life" (Ti 3:5–6). This Spirit of regeneration and renewal is described elsewhere as the Spirit of Truth, who guides us in all truth, who speaks not on His own authority but only what He has heard from the Son, who sent Him to us (Jn 16:7). The source of right knowledge of God is from God, and the location of that knowledge is baptism.[17]

The centrality of Christ to the Scriptures and to the proper knowledge of the Trinity is emphasized throughout the New Testament. Jesus says to the Jews, "You search the Scriptures because you think that in them you have eternal life;

---

17. The Fathers often refer to baptism (βάπτισμα) as illumination (φωτισμος or φώτισμα). Gregory of Nazianzus writes, "Illumination is the splendor of souls, the conversion of life, the conscience's appeal to God. Illumination is help for our weakness, the renunciation of the flesh, the following of the Spirit, communion with the Word, the improvement of the creature, the destruction of sin, participation in light, the dissolution of darkness. It is the carriage that leads to God, dying with Christ, the perfecting of the mind, the bulwark of faith, the key of the kingdom of heaven, a change of life, the removal of slavery, the loosing of chains, the renewal of our complex being. Why should I go into further detail? Illumination is the greatest and most magnificent of the gifts of God." Gregory of Nazianzus *Or.* 40.3, translated in Christopher Beeley, *Gregory of Nazianzus on the Trinity and the Knowledge of God* (Oxford: Oxford University Press, 2008), 108.

and it is they that bear witness about me, yet you refuse to come to me that you may have life" (Jn 5:39–40). The Scriptures, the Old Testament, point to Christ and bear witness about His person and work (cf. Lk 24:25–27). Jesus continues, "If you believed Moses, you would believe me; for he wrote of me" (Jn 5:46). If we search the Scriptures for someone or something other than Christ, we search for what is not intended and fail to grasp the meaning and proper sense of God's Word—the Word given by and belonging to God. Moreover, if you fail to understand that the Old Testament reveals Christ, then according to the New Testament you also fail to understand God the Father. The Scriptures are the words of eternal life because they are Christ's words (Jn 6:68–69). And yet, explains Jesus, "The word that you hear is not mine but the Father's who sent me" (Jn 14:24; cf. Jn 12:49–50).

Jesus and the Disciples

Above we noted the narrative structure of Mark and how the disciples fail to understand Jesus' identity in the calming of the storm. The exchange between Jesus and the disciples rests upon a deeper understanding of the Old Testament. They should have known Jesus' identity not simply because He calmed the storm but because the Scriptures revealed this. Another example occurs when Jesus walks on water. After the feeding of the five thousand the disciples gather into a boat and set out from land to Bethsaida of Galilee (Mk 6:45; cf. Jn 12:21). The disciples are again struggling against sea and wind when Jesus comes to them. Mark writes, "And about the fourth watch of the night he came to them, walking on the sea. He meant to pass by them, but when they saw him walking on the sea they thought it was a ghost, and cried out, for they all saw him and were terrified. But immediately he spoke to them and said, 'Take heart; it is I. Do not be afraid'" (Mk 6:48–50). According to the Old Testament the one who walks on water is the one who created all things and rules and governs His creation. Job praises God as wise in heart and mighty in strength, the one who removes mountains and shakes the earth, who commands the sun and seals up the stars. God is the one "who alone stretched out the heavens and trampled the waves of the sea" (Jb 9:8). The LXX makes the parallel more explicit: God alone stretches out the heavens and "walks upon the sea as upon the ground" (περιπατῶν ὡς ἐπ'ἐδάφους ἐπὶ θαλάσσης).[18] On the one hand, Jesus' walking on the sea indicates His identity as the one through whom and by whom the sea was made. There is, however, a further point to observe.

Mark notes that Jesus meant to pass by the disciples. He intends, in other words, to come within view of the disciples but to pass by and not enter the boat. Why? Jesus' actions are explained by returning to the passage from Job. After Job recounts the mighty works of God, His power and rule over the things He has made and how these things elude our understanding, He confesses that

---

18. On this point see Richard Hays, "Can the Gospels Teach Us How to Read the Old Testament," *Pro Ecclesia* XI:4 (2002): 409–11.

Father and Son: Ordinary Language

this providence of God over the things He has made, including man, remains unseen and yet is known by Job. He writes, it is God "who does great things beyond searching out, and marvelous things beyond number. Behold, he passes by me, and I see him not; he moves on, but I do not perceive him" (Jb 9:10–11). The God who created all things and governs and rules all things eludes our vision but not our faith.

The disciples have been battling the wind and sea all night. They are exhausted in mind and body. They have forgotten that the Lord Himself sent them across the sea. Immediately prior to this they were with Jesus when He fed five thousand. A little context will help us see why this is significant. The twelve disciples had been sent out on a missionary trip and returned to tell Jesus what they had done and taught (Mk 6:7, 30). Jesus saw that they were exhausted and hungry (Mk 6:31) and told them to come away to a desolate place and rest a while. In the meantime a great multitude saw Jesus and the disciples gather into a boat and ran ahead by foot, collecting more people as they went (Mk 6:33). When Jesus saw the crowd, He had compassion on them and began to teach (Mk 6:34). The exhausted disciples, who needed rest and food, who were promised such things by Jesus Himself, arrive instead to find the crowds. As the hour grows late the frustration of the tired and hungry disciples takes over. They say to Jesus, "This is a desolate place, and the hour is now late. Send them away to go into the surrounding countryside and villages and buy themselves something to eat" (Mk 6:36). The disciples want rest and they want to eat the small amount of food they brought with them. They do not want Jesus to keep teaching; they do not want anything to do with the crowds. They are annoyed with them, and they want Jesus to send them away. Jesus responds, "Give ye them to eat" (δότε αὐτοῖς ὑμεῖς φαγεῖν, Mk 6:37 KJV). That is to say, you who have just returned from a missionary trip, you who are tired and haven't had a chance to eat, you take the little you have and give it to them. They are hungry. Feed them. Jesus' words are difficult not because of the little they have to give but because they have already given so much and He wants them to give more, even the little that remains.

The disciples yield and ask if they should purchase food. Instead Jesus displays before them His divine power. He takes the five loaves and two fish, gives thanks to the Father, breaks the bread, and gives it to the disciples to distribute to the people (Mk 6:41). All eat and are satisfied. Immediately after this Jesus sends the disciples to the boat and across the sea. Mark explicitly links these two events. When Jesus gets into the boat, the wind ceases. Mark then records, "And they were utterly astounded, for they did not understand about the loaves" (Mk 6:52). The connection between these two events has to do with the fact that Jesus intended not to get into the boat but to pass them by (Mk 6:48). As Job related, God's hidden providence over us and all creation passes us by without our seeing it. Jesus, who demonstrates His power over creation with the feeding of the five thousand and walking upon the sea, intends to pass by the disciples and assure them of His power over the things He has made, and of His care for them amidst the difficulties of life and their pastoral care of His people. In other words, Jesus feeds the five thousand in part to demonstrate His care for the disciples. They are tired, hungry, and frustrated *because of* their work on His behalf, work according to their calling, and He asks for more in order to show them they are to rely on Him and trust Him even when resources look bleak, even when the people become burdensome, even when physically it seems they can do no more. Jesus sends them out to sea, knowing the storm that lies ahead, and again aims to demonstrate His continued care for them as they heed His word and go where He sends them, all according to their calling. He will pass by and they will see. Job did not see God pass by. Moses saw only the back parts of God. The disciples will see God in the flesh pass by.

When the disciples see Jesus they are terrified. Jesus says to them, "Take heart; it is I [ἐγώ εἰμι]. Do not be afraid" (Mk 6:50). More literally Jesus says to them, "Be courageous, I AM. Do not be afraid." Jesus' words make explicit His divine identity, which is what the disciples should have understood from the feeding of the five thousand and the walking upon the sea. Further, their courage and strength come from Him. When they pursue their divine call, they are to go forth with boldness, with courage, with the assurance that the one sending them continues to provide for them. The foundation of their comfort is Christ, who is Immanuel, the Word made flesh, who created all things and rules over all things. That divine identity becomes clear to us, as it did for the disciples, when we contextualize the activities of Christ with the identity of God made known throughout the Scriptures. YHWH, I AM WHO I AM, tramples the waves under foot; Jesus walks on water and declares to them, "Be courageous, I AM." Matthew ends his account with this very realization by the disciples: "Those in the boat worshiped Him, saying, 'Truly you are the Son of God'" (Mt 14:32).

John and the I AM Sayings

In the above exchange between Jesus and the disciples, He comforts and encourages them by referring to Himself as I AM. This designation appears with regularity and purpose in the Gospel of John. The narrative structure of John's Gospel revolves around sets of seven. There are seven signs or miracles performed by Jesus (2:1–11; 4:46–54; 5:1–15; 6:1–15; 6:16–21; 9:1–41; 11:1–44); there are seven metaphorical I AM statements that correspond in part to the seven signs; and, finally, there are seven absolute I AM statements unambiguously marking out Jesus' divine identity in the terms established by the Old Testament.[19] The number seven indicates completeness. The first set of I AM statements uses predicate nominatives to provide a verbal picture of the salvation Christ brings. Some of them correspond to the signs. After the

---

19. Richard Bauckham, *The Testimony of the Beloved Disciple* (Grand Rapids: Baker Academic, 2007), 243–44.

feeding of the five thousand Jesus declares, "I AM the bread of life" (Jn 6:35, 48). After Jesus opens the eyes of the blind man He declares, "I AM the light of the world" (Jn 8:12). After Jesus raises Lazarus from the dead He declares, "I AM the resurrection and the life" (Jn 11:25). Jesus further refers to Himself, with the I AM formula, as the Gate (Jn 10:7, 9), the Good Shepherd (Jn 10:11, 14), the Way, Truth, and Life (Jn 14:6), and the True Vine (Jn 15:1, 5). All of these statements underscore the salvation we have in Christ. He is the source (vine, life, resurrection) and means (way, gate) of this salvation. He alone brings this about (shepherd) and He is completely sufficient (bread).

Jesus' explanation of Himself as the Good Shepherd illustrates the correlation between activity and identity and the importance of the Old Testament for understanding these I AM statements. After Jesus declares that He gives eternal life to His sheep (Jn 10:28) and that He and the Father are one (Jn 10:30), the Jews pick up stones to stone Him. Jesus responds, "I have shown you many good works from the Father; for which of them are you going to stone me?" (Jn 10:32). The Jews respond in a rather odd way. They wish to stone Him not for any good work He has done but for blasphemy, for making Himself God (Jn 10:33). Jesus responds by telling them not to believe that He is the Son of God because He has said that He is, but rather to look to the works He is doing and understand by this His identity: "If I am not doing the works of my Father, then do not believe me; but if I do them, even though you do not believe me, believe the works, that you may know and understand that the Father is in me and I am in the Father" (Jn 10:37–38). The Jews wish to separate activity and identity. They claim not to be offended by the works but by the conclusion drawn from the works. Their approach, it seems, is to recognize Jesus only as an agent of God's work. Jesus' response points out the obvious: activity and identity necessarily inform one another. Functions are never mere functions. They indicate identity; they indicate a subject who possesses the power to do the sorts of things being done. In this case Jesus is granting eternal life to His sheep, the sheep He knows by name, the sheep who hear His voice and follow Him (Jn 10:3, 27–28). God alone saves and grants eternal life. Jesus saves and grants eternal life because He is the Son of God (Jn 5:21, 26). He and the Father are one; the Father is in Him and He in the Father; but the Son is not the Father and the Father is not the Son.

The theological richness of these predicates comes from the Old Testament either by way of contrast or by way of fulfillment. The most obvious example is again that of Christ as the Good Shepherd. In Ezekiel the Lord declares that He will be the Shepherd of His people. He will seek the lost, bring back the strayed, bind up the injured, strengthen the weak, and destroy the fat and the strong (Ez 34:15–16). The Lord will be the Good Shepherd, and yet in the same passage we read, "I will set up over them one shepherd, my servant David, and he shall feed them" (Ez 34:23). The same pattern of distinction and unity observed throughout the Old Testament and discussed at length in the previous chapter appears here as well. Through Zechariah YHWH declares, "My shepherd, the Man who stands next to me" will be struck and the sheep will scatter (Zec 13:7). Jesus applies this text to Himself. He is the Shepherd, the Man who stands next to YHWH, and the disciples are the sheep who will be scattered (Mt 26:31). Jesus is Lord, the Great Shepherd of the sheep (Heb 13:20), who feeds us with the bread of life and through whom alone we have salvation.

The seven absolute I AM statements declare unambiguously Jesus' divine identity. Jesus discusses the true worship of the Father in Spirit and Truth with the Samaritan woman at the well. The woman responds to Jesus by confessing that she believes the Messiah, the Christ, is coming and He will tell us all things. He responds to her, "I AM, the one speaking to you" (ἐγώ εἰμι, ὁ λαλῶν σοι, Jn 4:26).[20] Jesus' response affirms both that He is the Messiah and that He belongs to the unique identity of YHWH. Similarly, Jesus twice uses I AM with the disciples. When He comes walking on water to the disciples being tossed in the boat He declares to them, "I AM; fear not" (ἐγώ εἰμι· μὴ φοβεῖσθε, Jn 6:20). After washing the disciples' feet Jesus foretells His betrayal by Judas. He then says, "I am telling you this now, before it takes place, that when it does take place you may believe that I AM" (Jn 13:19). Jesus' words to the disciples are meant to bring comfort by emphasizing His divine identity. YHWH alone tramples the waves underfoot. Jesus comes to the disciples, walking upon water, doing that which belongs to YHWH, and seeks to comfort them by declaring "I AM." Similarly, YHWH declares, "I am God, and there is no other; I am God, and there is none like me, declaring the end from the beginning and from ancient times things not yet done" (Is 46:9–10). And so too Jesus declares Judas' betrayal before it happens that they might know Jesus is I AM. Two times after this Jesus will emphasize that He declares things before they happen for the same reason (Jn 14:29; 16:4). That which belongs to God alone, those unique divine prerogatives, belong to Jesus, the Son of God.

Chapters 7 and 8 of John's Gospel take up directly the question of Jesus' identity. We have already seen above how this issue presents itself in chapter 7 with the crowds. In chapter 8 Jesus' opponents meet His use of I AM with confusion and violence. At first they do not know what to make of His use of the phrase I AM. Jesus tells the Pharisees that they are from below but He is from above; they are of this world but He is not of this world. He then says, "For indeed, unless you believe that I AM, you will die in your sins" (Jn 8:24). Jesus' language confuses the Pharisees and they ask Him, "Who are you?" (Jn 8:25). His second response creates even more confusion. Finally Jesus says, "When you have lifted up the Son of Man, then you will know that I AM" (Jn 8:28). Jesus' identity as I AM will be known at the cross. Despite His repeated claim to being I AM, the Pharisees do not understand until the conversation turns to Abraham. The Pharisees claim that Abraham is their father; Jesus tells

---

20. Too often English translations obscure Jesus' response. For this reason His responses are given more literally according the Greek.

Father and Son: Ordinary Language

them the devil is their father. Jesus then tells them that anyone who keeps His word will never see death (Jn 8:51). The Jews accuse Him of having a demon and ask Him if He is greater than Abraham and the prophets who died. They then ask, "Who do you make yourself out to be?" (Jn 8:53). Throughout this chapter the Pharisees accuse Jesus of bearing witness about Himself (Jn 8:13, 53), and each time Jesus responds by emphasizing His relationship with the Father. You cannot know the Father apart from the Son or the Son apart from the Father (Jn 8:14–19; 8:54–56). Those who know God as Father love the Son, whom He sent for our salvation (Jn 8:42). Abraham knew this. Jesus explains, "Your father Abraham rejoiced that he would see my day. He saw it and was glad" (Jn 8:56). The Pharisees object. It isn't possible that Abraham knew Jesus. Jesus responds, "Truly, truly, I say to you, before Abraham was, I AM" (πρὶν Ἀβραὰμ γενέσθαι ἐγὼ εἰμί, Jn 8:58). Confusion gives way to violence as the Pharisees now understand very clearly that Jesus locates Himself in the unique identity of YHWH.

The final absolute I AM statement appears at the end of the Gospel with Jesus' arrest. The band of soldiers, Judas, and officers from the chief priests and Pharisees approach Jesus. He asks them, "Whom do you seek?" (Jn 18:4). They say Jesus of Nazareth, and He responds, I AM (Jn 18:5). When He says this they draw back and fall to the ground (cf. Is 45:23). Although a good deal more can be said with Jesus' I AM declaration in the other instances, this one provides a subtler point. The significance rests with the audience. The earlier statements were made to the Samaritan woman, to the disciples, and to the Pharisees. That is to say, Jesus declares His divine identity to a religious outsider (Samaritan), to the disciples, and to religious insiders (Pharisees). The final constituency appears with the guards who come to arrest Jesus. These Gentiles represent the rest of humanity not already included in the other groups to whom He has appeared. The point made by John in assembling these particular examples of Jesus declaring His divine identity is that all people, the whole world, both Jew and Gentile, religious insider and outsider, believer and unbeliever are represented. The outsiders and unbelievers, whatever they think of Jesus, will still confront Him and come before Him as judge. Following the crucifixion and resurrection, following Jesus' exaltation to the right hand of God in glory, every knee will bend, in heaven and on earth and under the earth (Phil 2:10; Rom 14:10–11), and "every eye will see him, even those who pierced him, and all tribes of the earth will wail on account of him" (Rv 1:7; Jn 19:34–37).

The I AM phrase used by Jesus in John's Gospel but also in the other Gospels derives from the Old Testament.[21] The phrase appears in two

---

21. The absolute I AM statements in John also appear, albeit less frequently, in the other Gospels. We have already seen one example above with Jesus walking on water (Mk 6:50; Mt 14:27). There is also His warning that in the last days many will come in His name, saying "I AM" (ἐγώ εἰμι), and they will lead many astray (Mk 13:6; Lk 21:8). Perhaps the clearest example outside of John is found in Mark. When Jesus is asked by the high priest if He is the Christ, the Son of the Blessed, He responds, "I AM, and you will see the Son of Man seated at the right

related places. The first is the divine name revealed to Moses at the burning bush.

> Then Moses said to God, "If I come to the people of Israel and say to them, 'The God of your fathers has sent me to you,' and they ask me, 'What is his name?' what shall I say to them?" God said to Moses, "I AM WHO I AM." And he said, "Say this to the people of Israel, 'I AM has sent me to you.'" (Ex 3:13-14)

The English translation, based on the Hebrew, makes the connection with the I AM phrase more obvious than the Greek allows. The LXX reads, "God said to Moses, 'I AM the one who is' [ἐγώ εἰμι ὁ ὤν]. And thus you shall say to the sons of Israel, 'The one who is [ὁ ὤν] has sent me to you.'" Although ἐγώ εἰμι appears, it is joined with ὁ ὤν, which is then repeated without the ἐγώ εἰμι. Despite this difficulty the subsequent use of ἐγώ εἰμι throughout the rest of the Old Testament makes clear that the divine name is meant by the phrase.

The phrase ἐγώ εἰμι regularly appears in emphatically monotheistic sections of the Old Testament.[22] Richard Bauckham observes that these sections appear in either a set of seven (Greek) or nine (Hebrew), which corresponds to John's use, which may be counted as either seven or nine, depending on how one tallies the final I AM in John 18.[23] All of these examples come from Isaiah except the first. In Deuteronomy we read, "'See now that I, even I, am he, and there is no god beside me'" (32:39). The LXX makes this emphatic: "See! See! I AM [ἐγώ εἰμι] and there is no other god except me." The use of I AM becomes explicit in Isaiah. On the one hand the divine name is used to declare that YHWH is the first and the last: "I, YHWH, the first, and with the last; I AM" (Is 41:4), and "I AM; I am the first, and I am the last" (Is 48:12). As will be noted in the next chapter, these texts figure prominently in John's Revelation. There are also emphatic uses of I AM in Isaiah. YHWH declares, "I AM, I AM [אָנֹכִי אָנֹכִי הוּא; ἐγώ εἰμι ἐγώ εἰμι] who blots out your transgressions for my own sake, and I will not remember your sins" (Is 43:25; cf. 51:12). These few examples show clearly that I AM marks out the unique divine identity of YHWH. There is no other I AM than YHWH. That fact alone explains the violence toward Jesus when His enemies understand Him to be using I AM to mark out His identity.

The significance of Jesus' use of I AM extends beyond the name itself. When the Jews attempt to stone Him, Jesus tells them not to believe that He is the Son of God because He has said that He is, but rather look to the works He is doing

---

hand of Power, and coming with the clouds of heaven" (Mk 14:61-62). Upon hearing this the high priest tears his garment and declares Jesus' response blasphemy. Others spit upon Him and strike Him. The anger of the council stems from how Jesus answered the question. He is asked if He is the Christ. Jesus' response identifies Himself as God (I AM, ἐγώ εἰμι). YHWH saves; there is no other Savior than YHWH. Jesus' clear identification of Himself as God, by means of the divine name I AM, results in the charge of blasphemy and the violence against Him.

22. For a fuller discussion of the following texts see Bauckham, *Testimony of the Beloved Disciple*, 246–50.

23. Bauckham gives the following lists: in Hebrew Dt 32:39; Is 41:4; 43:10, 13, 25; 46:4; 48:12; 51:12; 52:6; and in LXX Dt 32:39; Is 4:14; 43:10; 43:25; 45:18; 46:4; 51:12. Bauckham, *The Testimony of the Beloved Disciple*, 247.

and understand by this His identity: "If I am not doing the works of my Father, then do not believe me; but if I do them, even though you do not believe me, believe the works, that you may know and understand that the Father is in me and I am in the Father" (Jn 10:37–38). The I AM statements in the Old Testament never appear apart from some activity belonging to God alone. After YHWH declares in Deuteronomy, "I AM and there is no god beside me," He proceeds to mark off His unique identity, declaring, "I kill and I make alive; I wound and I heal; and there is none that can deliver out of my hand" (Dt 32:39). I AM is the one who gives life and takes it away; He is the one who judges the living and the dead. This text is echoed in Isaiah. After YHWH declares I AM in Isaiah 43, He continues, "'Before me no god was formed, nor shall there be any after me. I, I am YHWH, and besides me there is no savior. I declared and saved and proclaimed, when there was no strange god among you; and you are my witnesses,' declares YHWH, 'and I am God. Also henceforth I AM; there is none who can deliver from my hand; I work, and who can turn it back?'" (Is 43:11–13). This I AM is the first and the last (Is 41:4; 48:12). He is the one who saves, for there is no other savior. He is judge and no one can deliver from His hand. He declares things before they happen: "For I am God, and there is no other; I am God, and there is none like me, declaring the end from the beginning and from ancient times things not yet done" (Is 46:9–10).

When Jesus uses the I AM formula in the Gospel of John He emphasizes precisely these divine prerogatives.[24] He is the first and the last, the eternal one: "Before Abraham was, I AM" (Jn 8:58). He gives life to Lazarus by His own power and authority: "I AM the resurrection and the life" (Jn 11:25). He is the Messiah (Jn 4:26), the one who saves: "For indeed, unless you believe that I AM, you will die in your sins" (Jn 8:24). He is the one who declares things before they happen that His disciples might know and believe that Jesus is I AM (Jn 13:19; 14:29; 16:4). The I AM statements using a predicate nominative show with great depth and clarity the perfect and complete saving work of Christ. The absolute I AM statements complement these by showing the divine identity of Jesus both by the name itself but also the divine prerogatives uniquely attached to the name. The one who accomplishes this salvation is God in the flesh, I AM, the seen YHWH.

CONCLUSION

The New Testament writers offer an unambiguous confession of Christ's divine identity. He is the true Son of God, coequal and coeternal with the Father. The New Testament norms for the faithful the proper naming of the triune God as Father, Son, and Holy Spirit. Christ stands at the center of that confession. We know the Father only through the Son and the Son only by the Holy Spirit, whom He and the Father send to us. Further, we know who Christ is through

---

24. Bauckham, *Testimony of the Beloved Disciple*, 242–43.

the law and the prophets. By anchoring our confession of Christ in the Old Testament we allow God to disclose His triune identity to us. There is no such thing as "Christian" monotheism or "Jewish" monotheism; there is only biblical monotheism. We do not posit that which is appropriate for God; rather, we conform our expectations to what God has revealed about Himself. God alone creates, rules His creation, forgives sins, and raises the dead, among other things. Jesus does these things because He is God.

In the above material Jesus' identity was made known through historical narratives of the Gospels and in the passing comments of Paul's letters. In these sections we see the ordinary language of faith expressed in our prayers, hymns, and sermons. In the next chapter we will look at the dogmatic sections of the New Testament that present the identity of Jesus. The conclusions will be the same; the difference rests in the type of presentation we will observe. These more technical discussions appear alongside the more ordinary texts emphasized above. Our distinction between the two is just that, a distinction, that usefully shows the different ways in which the New Testament writers confessed the divine identity of Jesus. The two belong together and neither should be privileged in our confession of the divine identity of Jesus Christ, the eternal Son of God.

9

FATHER AND SON: THE DOGMATIC COMMITMENTS OF THE NEW TESTAMENT

In chapter 8 we showed that the whole New Testament concerns the scriptural identity of Jesus and that His identity stands at the heart of knowing and worshipping the Trinity. The writers of the New Testament repeatedly emphasize that no one knows the Father apart from the Son and no one knows the Son apart from the Holy Spirit. Our access to the Father is by the Son in the Holy Spirit. At the center of Scripture's witness to the unique identity of God who is Trinity is the man Jesus, the crucified and risen Lord. Christology stands at the heart of trinitarian theology. This dogmatic point is made explicitly in the New Testament; it is not a conclusion drawn by the church but a point established by Scripture. A number of rich theological texts in the New Testament unambiguously establish Jesus' divine identity and His centrality to our confession of the Trinity. In the following chapter we will look in detail at these texts, which individually and collectively show that the apostles were well aware of the various questions involved in identifying Jesus as the true Son of God, who is eternally distinct and yet inseparably united to the Father and the Holy Spirit.

GOSPEL OF JOHN

The prologue to the Gospel of John provides a good example of how the apostles understood the unique identity of God, the eternal relationship between the Father and the Son, and the context in which God is known. John's prologue establishes a number of crucial points: he shows how Scripture is to be read and how the author of Scripture is to be known; he demonstrates how the person and work of Jesus, the incarnate Son of God, belong to the unique identity of God and determine our proper knowledge of God; and finally, he emphasizes the centrality of the cross for rightly knowing the glory of God. John's points of emphasis are found throughout the New Testament. Jesus' suffering, death, and resurrection establish the context in which the Trinity is to be known, worshipped, and glorified. Apart from Jesus' person and work there is no true knowledge of God; apart from the cross there is no true knowledge of God's love and the eternal relationship between Father, Son, and Holy Spirit.

Although systematic theologians often separate formal discussions of Christ from the Trinity, the Scriptures know nothing of this distinction. This is also true for a discussion of soteriology and the means of grace. To know our triune God is to know Christ crucified, and this only by the regenerative and renewing work of the Holy Spirit through the means of grace. We boldly preach the pure gospel of Jesus Christ because there is no other way to know, worship, and glorify the Holy Trinity. Indeed, apart from the gospel the triune God of Holy Scripture remains unknown. For this reason our Confessions rightly insist that "the chief worship of God is the preaching of the Gospel."[1]

The Eternal Word

"In the beginning," the same words used to open the book of Genesis, open the Gospel of John (Jn 1:1). For Luther the prologue to the Gospel of John serves as the scriptural lens through which we understand the opening chapter of Genesis.[2] John shows in a striking way how Scripture interprets Scripture. This simply means that God is His own interpreter. This point needs to be emphasized at all times. John's prologue provides one of the most concise statements in Scripture on the eternal identity of God. John, however, begins the prologue in such a way that the first statement concerns not the identity of God but rather *how* we achieve such knowledge of God, namely through the proper exegesis of Scripture by Scripture (*scriptura ex scriptura explicanda est*).[3] John starts as Moses started. To know the identity of Jesus, the purpose of John's prologue, we must return to Genesis and that which was first delivered to Moses. These two texts unfold the identity of God and exhibit for the reader the proper approach to knowledge of God.

The phrase "in the beginning" points not to the beginning of creation, not to the first moment of the creative act, but to that which, as Paul puts it, was "before the foundation of the world" (Eph 1:4). Our language struggles to express this pre-temporal period without recourse to temporal language. Paul's words are the best we can do, but even they involve obscurity. "Before" is a marker of time, but time belongs to creation. "In the beginning," like "before" the foundation of the world, retreats to circumlocution to designate eternity. In this sense, "eternity" accomplishes less than might be expected. Eternity means not temporal, not belonging to the limits of time, not that which is conceptually placed in the category of creation. Of course it also means more than this. There is a positive value to eternity, but the fullness of that word presently eludes us. As created beings we have no access to thinking or speaking about something absent of time and place. Scripture accommodates itself to our condition, our limitations, by stretching the conceptual possibilities of our temporal and spatial words.

---

1. Ap. XV.42 (Tappert, 221).
2. *Complete Sermons of Martin Luther*, trans. John Lenker (Grand Rapids: Baker Books, 2000), 1.1:174–79.
3. Francis Pieper, *Christian Dogmatics* (St. Louis: Concordia Publishing House, 1950), 1:362.

John locates the Word in this eternity. When John declares, "In the beginning *was* the Word," he uses an established scriptural idiom from Genesis to say, "From eternity *was* the Word," or as John puts it at the beginning of his first epistle, "That which *was* from the beginning" (Ὁ ἦν ἀπ' ἀρχῆς, 1 Jn 1:1). The Word "was" (ἦν) marks a period prior to and before all of creation. We might clumsily put it this way: whenever creation occurred, at whatever point it all started, there *was* already an eternal past, a history, in reference to its beginning. Hilary of Poitiers thinks the word "was" (*erat*) functions as the key theological term in John's opening verse. The force of *erat* means that the Word existed already *in principio* since it is incompatible with the meaning of "was" for something not to have existed already.[4] Creation marks the beginning of time, not existence. The pre-temporal Word, as the creator of time, stands apart from time. Since He "was" in the beginning, He Himself has no beginning. The expression *was the Word* is equivalent to *the Word is* and corresponds to the absolute I AM sayings found throughout John's Gospel.

The Word Eternally "with" God

After establishing the eternal existence of the Word, John immediately emphasizes that the Word *was with God* (πρὸς τὸν θεόν) *and was God* (καὶ θεὸς ἦν ὁ λόγος).[5] The Word stands in relation to another, to God. The Word is both eternally distinct from God and equally God. At the end of the prologue John will clarify this ambiguous language and pattern our speech to say that the Word, who is the Son of God, is eternally distinct from God the Father. In this sense John's prologue demonstrates the movement from Old Testament to New Testament in the normative naming of the triune God. The opening of the prologue, using the established idiom of the Old Testament, reflects the distinction and inseparability of the Word of YHWH and YHWH. For John this is expressed simply as the Word and God. They are distinct yet inseparable, coequal yet coeternal. The end of the prologue clarifies. The Word, the Word of YHWH, is the Son of God, and God, in distinction from His Word, is the Father.

John emphasizes the eternal distinction between God the Father and His Word a second time: "He was in the beginning with God" (πρὸς τὸν θεόν, Jn 1:2). Luther thinks John used the word "with" to gainsay natural reason and future heretics.[6] To speak of God abstractly, the preferred method of natural reason, speaks of God apart from His Word, apart from His eternal relationship with the Word (ὁ λόγος). An abstract "god" is a non-personal "god," an unreasonable or irrational (ἄλογος) "god." To speak of God as prior to His Word would be to read John as saying the Word was "in" God rather than "with" God. This approach appealed to both Arians (Asterius the Sophist)

---

4. Hilary of Poitiers *De Trinitate* 2.17. See also Basil of Caesarea *Against Eunomius* 2.14-15.
5. For a discussion of the anarthous use of theos see Raymond Brown, *The Gospel According to John I-XII* (New York: Doubleday, 1966), 5.
6. *Complete Sermons of Martin Luther*, 1.1:181.

and adoptionists (Photinus of Sirmium). John's πρὸς vanquishes both false teachings. Luther's point is that an eternal relationship avails between the Son and the Father such that one is never without the other. This means you cannot know the Father without the Son and you cannot know the Son apart from the Father. The Father is always the Father of the Son; the Son is always the Son of the Father. They entail one another.

From all eternity, God the Father existed with His Word. They are one as God but not one another. The Father is God; the Son is God; but the Father is not the Son and the Son is not the Father. As the church will later express this, God the Father and God the Word, although one, remain personally distinct from one another. John emphasizes this very point in his opening verses. Twice John says the Word was "with" God. John's concern appears to be false understandings of God's unique identity that either collapse the Father and His Word into one person or separate the Father from His coeternal and coequal Word. In the history of the church the first problem occurs with Sabellius and the second with Arius. Another way of expressing John's concern would be to say that a falsely constructed vision of biblical monotheism that excludes eternal distinctions within the unique identity of the one true God is opposed to God's self-revelation of Himself in Scripture. Here we begin to appreciate John's deliberate opening to his Gospel. We are not just to read Genesis in the light of the clearer revelation given to us in the prologue. We are to be reminded that the God who spoke to Moses, who entrusted His revelation to him, is the God who spoke all of creation into existence through His coequal and eternally distinct Word. Moses, like John, prayed the Shema twice daily; Moses, like John, records that in the beginning was God and the Word through whom all things were made.

A principal characteristic of God's unique identity is that He alone creates. Genesis declares, "In the beginning God created the heavens and the earth" (Gn 1:1). Scripture never tires of making this point. Isaiah proclaims that the work of creation belongs exclusively to God and none other: "For thus says YHWH, who created the heavens (he is God!), who formed the earth and made it (he established it; he did not create it empty, he formed it to be inhabited!): 'I am YHWH, and there is no other'" (Is 45:18). When John declares that all things came into being through the Word, who was *with* God and *is* God, he unequivocally locates the person of Jesus in the unique identity of YHWH. Lest the full weight of his point be missed John repeats himself: "All things were made through him and without him was not any thing made that was made" (Jn 1:3). The Word that created all things is the Word of YHWH: "By the Word of YHWH the heavens were made" (Ps 33:6). Again Jeremiah declares, "The Word of YHWH came to me, saying, 'Before I formed you in the womb I knew you'" (Jer 1:4–5). The Word of YHWH, the Word spoken in Genesis 1, is the very Word here confessed by John, the Word that he looked upon with his own eyes and touched with his own hands (1 Jn 1:1).

Salvation in the Divine Name

The work of creation points to the work of redemption. The Word who became flesh, who is the Son of God, is the one by whom we are created and in whom we have life. Salvation is found "in his name" (Jn 1:12). What "name" is this? Charles Gieschen argues it is the divine name.[7] We have seen in the previous two chapters that the divine name marks out God's unique identity, who He is and what He does. It belongs to Him alone and points especially to His work of judgment and salvation. In Ezekiel, for example, God pronounces judgment on the nations and Jerusalem that "they will know I am YHWH."[8] God brings salvation for the sake of His holy name (Ez 36:21–22). When he vindicates His holy name, the nations will know that YHWH alone is Lord (Ez 36:23). This salvation will come to the people. God will "sprinkle clean water" upon them, they will be cleansed of their iniquities and their idols, and a "new heart" and a "new spirit" will be given them (Ez 36:25). God declares, "I will put my Spirit within you ... and you shall be my people, and I will be your God" (Ez 36:28).

Scripture consistently emphasizes that salvation is the work of YHWH alone and that forgiveness of sins is found in His name. God declares through Isaiah, "I, I am he who blots out your transgressions for my own sake, and I will not remember your sins" (Is 43:25). The LXX makes the point more emphatically: "I AM I AM who blots out your transgressions" (ἐγώ εἰμι ἐγώ εἰμι).[9] As shown in the previous chapter, Jesus uses the divine name for these same purposes in the Gospel of John: "Unless you believe that I AM [ἐγώ εἰμι] you will die in your sins" (Jn 8:24) and "When you have lifted up the Son of Man, then you will know that I AM" (ἐγώ εἰμι, Jn 8:28). This second text is what YHWH declares to Isaiah: "'You are my witnesses,' declares YHWH, 'and my servant whom I have chosen, that you may know and believe me and understand that I AM" (ἐγώ εἰμι, Is 43:10). Jesus' audience understood His use of the divine name. When He declares, "Before Abraham was, I AM" (ἐγώ εἰμι, Jn 8:58), the Jews attempt to stone Him. When the soldiers, chief priests, and Pharisees come to arrest Him they ask for Jesus of Nazareth; He declares "I AM" (Jn 18:5, ἐγώ εἰμι), and those who hear it fall to the ground.

In the prologue the Word, who created the heavens and the earth, comes into the world, bringing salvation to all who believe in His name. As prophesied by Ezekiel, the Spirit delivers this salvation through holy baptism. Those reborn of water and the Spirit (Jn 3:5) are cleansed of their iniquities and given new hearts. This Spirit gives us a new spirit and "bears witness with our spirit that we are children of God" (Rom 8:16). That this salvation, this help, is from YHWH would not have been missed by those in John's audience versed in the Scriptures. When he opens his prologue in the same manner as Genesis, proceeds to clarify the meaning of Genesis in terms of the person of Jesus, and declares that the

---

7. Charles Gieschen, *Angelomorphic Christology* (Leiden: Brill, 1998), 272.
8. Ez 25:11, 17; 26:6; 28:24; 29:9; 30:8; 30:19; 33:29 et passim.
9. Brown, *Gospel According to John I–XII*, 536.

Word who was with God and is God created all things, the Word of YHWH, his audience would have known that it is YHWH who does these things: "Our help is in the Name of YHWH who made heaven and earth" (Ps 124:8; Ps 121:2). John does not stop here. The one who created heaven and earth and in whose name salvation is found is also the one who became flesh and tabernacled among us (ὁ λόγος σὰρξ ἐγένετο καὶ ἐσκήνωσεν ἐν ἡμῖν, Jn 1:14).

The Word Tabernacles

Although the New Testament typically uses activity to show identity, there are some important examples of identity preceding activity. John's prologue is one such example. The prologue begins with an ontological claim about the Word and then proceeds to the activity of this Word, who is coeternal and coequal with God the Father. For John it is the confession of the Word's identity that informs His work as creator and redeemer. Indeed, since the purpose of John's prologue is to show that salvation has come to us in the person and work of Jesus Christ, the Word made flesh, it is of great significance that he begins with identity and the chief activity marking that identity (creation) before moving to the purpose of the prologue and the rest of the Gospel (redemption). Just as he did at the beginning of the prologue, John moves in verse fourteen from identity to work: the God-man tabernacled among us (ἐσκήνωσεν ἐν ἡμῖν). Tabernacling designates the activity. In the Old Testament the tabernacle marked the place where the omnipresent God particularly dwelled and where atonement for sins occurred. Furthermore, the prophets increasingly emphasize that the promised Messiah, the Servant, the Righteous Branch, the Man, will tabernacle in the midst of the people, in time and forevermore. Jesus, true God and true man, is the true and perfect tabernacle, God with us (Immanuel), the atonement for our sins.

John's use of the verbal form of tabernacle should not be obscured in translation, lest the intertextual links with the prophets, seen clearly in the Greek, become obscured by the English. This verbal form occurs once in John's prologue and twice in Revelation. John tell us that the one who tabernacles is the one who sits on the throne (Rv 7:15). In his vision of the new heaven and the new earth John writes, "I heard a loud voice from the throne saying, 'Behold, the tabernacle of God [ἡ σκηνὴ τοῦ θεοῦ] is with man. He will tabernacle [σκηνώσει] with them, and they will be his people, and God Himself will be with them as their God'" (Rv 21:3). The language used throughout Revelation hearkens back to Ezekiel: "My tabernacle [ἡ κατασκήνωσίς μου] shall be with them; indeed I will be their God, and they shall be my people. Then the nations will know that I, the Lord, sanctify Israel, when my sanctuary is in their midst forevermore" (Ez 37:27–28 NKJV). As emphasized in chapter 7 the Messiah, the Righteous Branch, will be the one who tabernacles in the midst of the people: "Sing and rejoice, O daughter of Zion, for behold, I come and I will tabernacle in your midst [κατασκηνώσω ἐν μέσῳ σου], and you shall know that the Lord of hosts has sent me to you" (Zec 2:10–11). In the context of John's prologue Ez 43:7 (LXX) is especially striking: "My Name shall tabernacle in the midst of the house of Israel forever." The Name in which salvation is found, the Name that belongs to the Word, who was with God and is God, shall become flesh and tabernacle among His people.

Father and Son

John closes his prologue by introducing the language of Father and Son to clarify what has been said throughout the prologue concerning the relationship between the Word and God. Because the Word was made flesh, the glory of God the Son has been seen: "We have seen his glory, glory as of the only Son from the Father, full of grace and truth" (Jn 1:14). John's phrase asserts three significant things. First, the Son's glory is the divinity He shares with the Father. As it is said elsewhere in the New Testament, the Son is the "radiance of the glory of God and the exact imprint of his nature" (Heb 1:3). The Son's glory is His eternal being. It is the glory that the Son had with the Father "before the world existed" (Jn 17:5). This glory has become visible because the Word became flesh. It is seen not only in His teachings and miracles, as Luther observes, but also in His suffering, death, and resurrection (Jn 12:23; 12:27).[10] This is the Glory of YHWH that Isaiah and Ezekiel saw and prophesied about (Jn 12:41; Isaiah 6; Isaiah 53; Ez 1:26–28; 3:22–24). Finally, the saving work of the cross reveals the mutual glorification of the Father and the Son (Jn 17:1; cf. 13:31–32).

Second, John describes the Son with the elusive term *monogenes* (μονογενής). The Greek word communicates that this Word made flesh is the unique, one-of-a-kind Son from the Father. Jerome rendered *monogenes* as *unigenitus* in the Vulgate: the only-begotten Son. Although New Testament scholars worry about this translation, Jerome's *unigenitus* communicates the substance of what John has confessed in this prologue, especially against those with Arianizing tendencies. Only-begotten, like unique or only, expresses the exclusive and one-of-a-kind ontological relationship that avails between the Father and the Son. Moreover, it distinguishes the Son, who is so by nature, from those who are reborn children of God, not by nature but by grace (Jn 1:13) through baptism (Jn 3:5).

This leads to John's third point. The phrase "the only-begotten Son *from the Father*" (παρὰ πατρός) underscores the eternal relation of the Son and the Father, the only-begotten and the unbegotten. The phrase refers to the Son's eternal generation from the Father. Later in the Gospel Jesus uses the same expression to describe His pre-temporal (eternal) relationship with the Father: "I came from the Father [παρὰ τοῦ πατρὸς] and have come into the world, and now I am leaving the world and going to the Father" (Jn 16:28). Similarly, Jesus uses this expression to describe the temporal mission and eternal procession of the Spirit from the Father: "But when the Helper comes, whom I will send

---

10. *Complete Sermons of Martin Luther*, 1.1:221.

to you from the Father [παρὰ τοῦ πατρός], the Spirit of truth, who proceeds from the Father [παρὰ τοῦ πατρὸς], he will bear witness about me" (Jn 15:26). Much will be said about this verse in the chapter on the procession of the Holy Spirit, but for our purposes here it is sufficient to note the use of the phrase "from the Father" in these passages discussing the eternal relationship that avails between the Father and the Son (Jn 1:14; 16:28) and the Father and the Holy Spirit (Jn 15:26).

For the most part John has emphasized the eternal distinction between the Father and the Son in the prologue. He ends by underscoring their unity. The Father and the Son are eternally distinct and intimately one: "No one has ever seen God; the only begotten Son, who is in the bosom of the Father, he has made him known" (Jn 1:18).[11] The Son makes the Father known (distinction) because He is in the bosom of the Father (unity). As Jesus later expresses it, "Whoever has seen me has seen the Father" (Jn 14:9) because "I am in the Father and the Father is in me" (Jn 14:10). Arguably the clearest and most concise expression of unity and distinction is Jn 10:30: "I and the Father are one" (ἐγὼ καὶ ὁ πατὴρ ἕν ἐσμεν, Jn 10:30). In this verse we have distinction (ἐσμεν) and unity (ἕν). The neuter ἕν emphasizes the divine essence. Their oneness is found not in person (distinction) but in nature (unity).[12] John Bengal quips that ἐσμεν refutes Sabellius and ἕν Arius.[13] Similarly, Johann Gerhard says "one" strikes down Arius and "are" flattens Sabellius.[14] This eternal distinction and unity of the Father and the Son was not lost on Jesus' enemies. After He said that He and the Father are one the Jews picked up stones to stone Him. When He asked why, they responded, "For blasphemy, because you, being a man, make yourself God" (Jn 10:33). This was not the first time Jesus' enemies understood the significance of what He was doing and saying. Earlier in the Gospel we read, "The Jews were seeking all the more to kill him, because not only was he breaking the Sabbath, but he was even calling God his own Father, making himself equal to God" (Jn 5:18). Augustine remarks that Jesus' enemies understood very clearly what the Arians could not.[15]

John ends the prologue by emphasizing the same point with which he began: God alone reveals Himself to us, and God alone determines His identity. The Son came to us that we might come to know the Father. Two related points

---

11. For the textual witnesses on this verse and the different ways of rendering it see Brown, *Gospel According to John I–XII*, 17. The translation offered here is my own.

12. Cf. Abraham Calov, *Systema Locorum Theologicorum* (Wittenberg, 1659), 3:109: "I and the Father are one (*unum*). Christ did not say, I and the Father are *unus*, but *unum*, lest the distinction of the persons be undermined."

13. John Bengel, *Bengel's New Testament Commentary* (Grand Rapids: Kregel, 1981), 1:651.

14. Johann Gerhard, *Theological Commonplaces: On the Nature of God and On the Trinity*, trans. Richard Dinda (St. Louis: Concordia Publishing House, 2007), Exegesis III, §51, 307; cf. Augustine *On Heresies* 7 (WSA I/18); Thomas Aquinas, *Commentary on the Gospel of John*, trans. Fabian R. Larcher, 1451 (Lander, WY: Aquinas Institute for the Study of Sacred Doctrine, 2013), 2:63.

15. Augustine *In Johannis Evangelium Tractatus* 48.8 (PL 35, 1744); cf. Thomas Aquinas, *Gospel of John*, 1456, 2:67; Johann Gerhard, *De Tribus Elohim*, Locus 4/1, §22 (ed. Cotta, 373).

follow. First, if we seek to know the Father apart from the Son, whatever our motivations might be, it is "not according to knowledge" but ignorance (Rom 10:2; cf. Jn 16:2-3). Second, God is His own interpreter and determines His own identity. The key to rightly knowing and speaking about the triune God is found in the person and work of Christ, the eternal Son of God, distinct from the Father in person, one with the Father in nature. When the Council of Chalcedon (451) confessed that Jesus is true God and true man, perfect in Godhead and perfect in manhood, consubstantial with the Father in Godhead and consubstantial with us in manhood, it was saying nothing more than what John records in his prologue: the Word became flesh (ὁ λόγος σὰρξ ἐγένετο). The Word is God, and this God assumed flesh, becoming truly man. The difference lies in the idiom used to express the identity of God. The judgment regarding the identity of this God, however, remains the same for John as for those gathered at Nicaea, Constantinople, Ephesus, and Chalcedon.[16]

PSALM 110 AS NEW TESTAMENT TEXT

In John's prologue the principal themes marking off Jesus' divine identity are creation and salvation. The New Testament writers used Psalm 110, the most frequently cited Old Testament text in the New Testament, to show Jesus' eschatological lordship over all things. Psalm 110:1 reads:

> The Lord said to my Lord:
> "Sit at my right hand,
> until I make your enemies your footstool."

Twenty-one quotations or allusions to this psalm appear in the New Testament.[17] His lordship, His rule, extends over all things. The apostles show this by echoing what was said of God in the Old Testament. God "made all things" (Is 44:24), "formed all things" (Jer 10:16), and "cares for all things" (Wis 12:13). In the New Testament we are told that "all things" were made through Jesus (Jn 1:3; 1 Cor 8:6) and for Him (Col 1:16). As the creator of all things He is also "before all things" (Col 1:17). The one through whom all things were created is also the one through whom "all things hold together" (Col 1:17) and "exist" (1 Cor 8:6). The apostles bring this together by expressing Christ's eschatological lordship with Psalm 110. He is the Lord of all (Acts 10:36), for "all things" are put under His feet (Eph 1:22) and are subject to Him (Phil 3:21).

Since God could make use of angelic intermediaries to execute His rule, the New Testament writers further use Psalm 110 to emphasize that Jesus' rule and

---

16. David Yeago, "The New Testament and Nicene Dogma: A Contribution to the Recovery of Theological Exegesis," *Pro Ecclesia* 3 (1994): 152-64.
17. Richard Bauckham, "God Crucified," in *Jesus and the God of Israel* (Grand Rapids: Eerdmans, 2008), 22: Mt 22:44; 26:64; Mk 12:36; 14:62; 16:19; Lk 20:42-43; 22:69; Acts 2:33-35; 5:31; 7:55-56; Rom 8:34; 1 Cor 15:25; Eph 1:20; 2:6; Col 3:1; Heb 1:3, 13; 8:1; 10:12-13; 12:2; 1 Pt 3:22; Rv 3:21. See also Martin Hengel, *Studies in Early Christology* (Edinburgh: T&T Clark, 1995), 133-34.

authority stand apart from, indeed are altogether transcendent of, that which belongs to the angels. In Ephesians for example we read that the exalted Jesus, who is seated at the right hand of God and has all things under His feet, is "far above" everything that can be named or imagined (Eph 1:20–21).[18] He who descended has ascended "far above all the heavens" that He might fill "all things" (Eph 4:10). The metaphor of height used in the Old Testament to demonstrate God's transcendence over the angels and indeed over all things is used here to depict the lordship of Christ.

The frequent use of Psalm 110 in the New Testament likely stems from Jesus' own endorsement and use of this text to show His identity as David's Lord and son. All three synoptic Gospels record the following conversation between Jesus and some of the Pharisees.

> "What do you think about the Christ? Whose son is he?" They said to him, "The son of David." He said to them, "How is it then that David, in the Spirit, calls him Lord, saying, 'The Lord said to my Lord, Sit at my right hand, until I put your enemies under your feet'? If then David calls him Lord, how is he his son?'" (Mt 22:42–45; cf. Mk 12:35–37 and Lk 20:41–44)

The one whose rule and authority altogether transcends the angels and whose lordship extends over all things is the one who tabernacled among us, Jesus Christ, true God and true man, both David's Lord and son, all of which the Holy Spirit has caused to be recorded for us in Psalm 110.

The further point made by Jesus concerns right understanding and interpretation. The Old Testament teaches us how to understand the New Testament, and at the same time the New Testament teaches us how to understand the Old Testament. Both are mutually informing and further underscore the unity and perfection of the Scriptures. We saw this above with John's prologue and his retelling of Genesis in the light of Christ. Here Jesus' use of Psalm 110 and interpretation of it shows us the proper way in which to read *according to the Scriptures*. Christ nowhere indicates the presence of a layered meaning, such that we are encouraged to read Psalm 110 apart from the New Testament and Christ's words. David meant what Jesus says He meant. The proper understanding of Psalm 110 reveals Jesus, David's Lord and David's son.

EPISTLE TO THE HEBREWS

The Divinity of Christ

In a manner similar to the prologue to the Gospel of John, the first two chapters of Hebrews demonstrate that Jesus is true God and true man, sharing the unique identity of God and assuming true humanity for our salvation. The author of Hebrews especially emphasizes the distinction between Jesus and the angels.

---

18. Richard Bauckham, "The Throne of God and the Worship of Jesus," in *Jesus and the God of Israel*, 177–78.

Jesus is not a mere divine agent and must never be confused with the angels. Hebrews rereads various texts from the Old Testament in the light of the person and work of Jesus Christ in order to fill out a proper understanding of Psalm 110. Hebrews 1:1–4 reads:

> Long ago, at many times and in many ways, God spoke to our fathers by the prophets, but in these last days he has spoken to us by his Son, whom he appointed the heir of all things, through whom also he created the world. He is the radiance of the glory of God and the exact imprint of his nature, and he upholds the universe by the word of his power. After making purification for sins, he sat down at the right hand of the Majesty on high, having become as much superior to angels as the name he has inherited is more excellent than theirs.

The epistle approaches the question of Jesus' identity in a way similar to John's prologue. The opening verse concerns God's revelation and the way in which God communicates Himself and His work to us (1:1). Although a contrast exists between the many and various ways God spoke through the prophets of old and the decisive and final revelation given in the last days through the Son, continuity prevails in that it is the same God who speaks and the same message of salvation delivered (Heb 4:2; 11:30).[19]

Following the opening verse we encounter a clear statement of the full and eternal deity of the Son (1:2–4). These opening verses concisely state the Son's pre-existence, incarnation, death, and exaltation and concisely assign seven characteristics to Him that belong to the unique identity of God.[20] (1) As the heir of all things He has rule over all and all are subject to Him. (2) As the one through whom the world was created He is creator and therefore stands apart from all created reality and anything that is not God. (3) As the radiance of God's glory and exact imprint of His nature (χαρακτὴρ τῆς ὑποστάσεως αὐτοῦ) He is coequal and coeternal with God. (4) As the one who upholds the universe by the word of His power He providentially governs and rules all things. (5) As the one who makes purification for sins He is both priest and all-sufficient sacrifice for our eternal redemption. (6) As the one who "sat down" at the right hand of the Majesty "on high" He occupies the transcendent throne of God and is to be worshipped. (7) As the one who inherited "the name" He is much superior to the angels for He bears the divine name which is the name above every other name.

After this opening description of the full deity of the Son the author of Hebrews appeals to seven Old Testament texts demonstrating the superiority of Christ over the angelic host. The number seven, as we have seen elsewhere, underscores the completeness and all-sufficiency of what follows. The Son is

---

19. Harold Attridge, *The Epistle to the Hebrews* (Philadelphia: Fortress Press, 1989), 37–39.
20. Richard Bauckham refers to this as the sevenfold narrative identity of God's Son. Bauckham, "Monotheism and Christology in Hebrews 1," *Early Jewish and Christian Monotheism*, ed. Loren T. Stuckenbuch and Wendy E. S. North (Edinburgh: T&T Clark, 2004), 173. For what follows see Bauckham, "The Divinity of Jesus in the Letter to the Hebrews," in *Jesus and the God of Israel*, 237–39.

superior to the angels (Ps 2:7 and 2 Sm 7:14) and worshipped by them (Dt 32:43). Indeed, the angels are created by Him whom they worship (Ps 104:4). The one who created them and the one they worship reigns with God the Father on the throne (Ps 45:6–7). The Son is eternal, the same from eternity to eternity, while the creation which He made *is made* and changing (Ps 102:25–27). The catena of Old Testament texts ends with Ps 110:1, which has been said only ever of the Son, who is exalted to the throne of God to rule forever. This opening chapter establishes an absolute distinction between the Son and His angels. The angels are "ministering spirits" sent out to serve. They are servants of God and stand before the throne. Christ sits at the right hand of God (Heb 1:13; Ps 110:1). He occupies the throne of God and rules with God (Heb 1:8–9; Ps 45:6–7). He laid the foundation of the earth, created all that is, and is eternal (Heb 1:10–12; Ps 102:25–27). Christ created the angels and they serve Him.

Why does the author of Hebrews emphasize so decisively Christ's superiority to angels? The reason seems to be twofold. First, God made use of angels as divine agents to carry out His rule and governance of the world. Could it be that Jesus belongs to this angelic host and was one of these intermediaries used by God? This opening chapter unambiguously says no to that question. The second issue has to do with showing how Christ is both higher and lower than the angels. Richard Bauckham argues that the angels function as measures of ontological status.[21] The exalted Christ, who shares His Father's throne on high, is far above the angels and indeed all of created reality as He shares in the transcendent reality of God. This is the point of the first chapter in Hebrews. The second chapter shows the humiliation of the Son. When the Son assumed human flesh He was made for a little while lower than the angels (Ps 8:4–6; Heb 2:6–8). The angels mark this distinction for us. Bauckham explains, "To be above the angels is to be God, to be below the angels is to be human. Above the angels, Jesus transcends all creation, sharing the divine identity as Creator and Ruler even of the angels. Below the angels, Jesus shares the common identity of earthly humans in birth, suffering, and death."[22]

The Humanity of Christ

The opening chapter of Hebrews establishes the divinity of Christ, the one who is far above all angels, sitting at the right hand of God. The second chapter by contrast establishes the humanity of Christ, the one made a little lower than the angels, who shares in flesh and blood with all humans (Heb 2:7, 14; Ps 8:4–6). The Son of God assumes a true humanity to bring about our salvation. He tastes death for everyone (Heb 2:9), destroying through His death the one who has the power of death, the devil (Heb 2:14). As the captain of our salvation (Heb 2:10) He is our great high priest (Heb 4:14).

---

21. Bauckham, "Divinity of Jesus," 241.
22. Bauckham, "Divinity of Jesus," 241.

The purpose of the incarnation, the assumption of true humanity by the Son, occupies the rest of Hebrews. By being made a little lower than the angels Christ offered Himself as a sacrifice for the sins of all. The one for whom and through whom all things exist (Heb 2:10) becomes the Son of Man and is appointed our high priest (Heb 5:5). Again, the Psalms show this. Psalm 8 declares the incarnation, humiliation, and eschatological lordship of Christ (Heb 2:6–8). Psalms 2 and 110, which were used already in the opening chapter of Hebrews, appear again to emphasize that Christ did not elevate Himself to be made a high priest but was appointed so by the Father (Heb 5:5–6). Because of this the throne of glory, shared by Father and Son in all eternity, is also the throne of grace that sinners may approach now with confidence, seeking help in time of need and receiving mercy (Heb 4:16).

Psalm 110:1 demonstrates the coequality of the Son and the Father and their shared lordship. This point appears throughout the New Testament. Unique to Hebrews, however, is the further appeal to Ps 110:4, "You are a priest forever, after the order of Melchizedek." The author of Hebrews reads this obscure text through the lens of another equally obscure text, Gn 14:18 (Heb 7:1–2). This Melchizedek is both priest and king. The use of Melchizedek to describe Christ's high priesthood arises from Psalm 110. Again, no other text occurs more frequently in the New Testament than this psalm. Christ's lordship, His coeternity and coequality with the Father, has no clearer reference. What then are we to make of Ps 110:4 and the description of the Son's priesthood? For the author of Hebrews, Genesis 14 and Psalm 110 emphasize the eternity of the Son. Melchizedek is "without father or mother or genealogy, having neither beginning of days nor end of life" (Heb 7:3). In the context of Hebrews, Ps 110:4 underscores the divine identity of Christ, our eternal high priest. In this sense the reflection upon the all-sufficient and perfect atoning work of Christ, which will follow now in Hebrews, is grounded firmly in the true divinity and humanity of the Son, our Lord, Jesus Christ.[23]

After establishing the identity of the Son as true God and true man the author of Hebrews turns to a detailed reflection on the Son's saving work as high priest. Christ is the great high priest, "the greater and more perfect tabernacle, not made with human hands, that is, not of this creation" (Heb 9:11; cf. Dn 2:45), who entered once and for all into the holy places by means of His own blood, securing an eternal redemption (Heb 9:12). He is our mediator who appears in the presence of God on our behalf (Heb 9:24), making intercession for us (Heb 7:25). The author of Hebrews brings this lengthy reflection upon Christ's atoning work to a close by bringing together His priesthood and lordship: "But when Christ had offered for all time a single sacrifice for sins, He sat down

---

23. The titles used in Hebrews for Christ are varied and interchangeable. See for example Son (1:2; 1:5; 1:8; 5:5; 7:28), Son of God (4:14; 6:6; 7:3; 10:29), Jesus (2:9; 3:1; 6:20; 7:22; 10:19; 12:2; 12:24; 13:12; 13:20), Christ (3:6; 5:5; 6:1; 9:11; 9:14; 9:24; 9:28; 11:26), Jesus Christ (10:10; 13:8; 13:21), and Lord (2:3; 7:14; 13:20).

at the right hand of God, waiting from that time until his enemies should be made a footstool for his feet" (Heb 10:12). He appeared once for all to put away sin by the sacrifice of Himself (Heb 9:26). His work of atonement is complete and all-sufficient. He sits down upon the throne at the right hand of the Father.

If we are to understand rightly the scriptural identity of God we must give consideration to both creation and redemption. The God who alone creates is the same God who alone saves. Christ's high-priestly role expresses itself in the context of His messianic lordship. That is to say, we fail to understand Christ's lordship, God's unique lordship, apart from His atoning sacrifice and death. Again we find ourselves at the cross and all it entails in rightly knowing the scriptural identity of our triune God.

Holy Spirit

Another important feature of Hebrews concerns the role of the Holy Spirit. To some extent the author of Hebrews frames the entire consideration of the Son's atoning work by reference to the Trinity. The relationship between Father and Son in the atoning work of our high priest is evident throughout. Less obvious but just as important is the role played by the Holy Spirit in this saving work.

After establishing the identity of the Son in the first chapter, the second chapter begins with a warning. We are not to forget "our great salvation" which was declared by the Son (who is designated as Lord, using the language of Psalm 110), given witness by God the Father, and delivered by the gift of the Holy Spirit (Heb 2:3–4). From this point forward the Holy Spirit plays an instrumental role in the saving work of the Son. The prophetic witness given to this salvation belongs to the working of the Holy Spirit who announced these things long ago through the prophets (Heb 3:7; 10:15). Jesus, made lower than the angels, suffered death that He might taste death for everyone. This He did "by the grace of God" (Heb 2:9). That this is a reference to the Holy Spirit accords with the rest of Hebrews. At the high point of stating Christ's atoning work the author of the Hebrews declares that the eternal redemption secured for us was accomplished by "the blood of Christ, who through the eternal Spirit offered himself without blemish to God" (Heb 9:14). What was said about the "grace of God" in Heb 2:9 is referred here to the eternal Spirit. In the very next chapter the author of Hebrews declares that those who spurn the Son of God (identity) and profane His saving work (activity) outrage "the Spirit of grace" (Heb 10:29). The Spirit of grace is the God of grace from Hebrews 2 and the eternal Spirit of Hebrews 9. Since the work of salvation is the work of both the Son and the Spirit, inseparably united in their work for us, the author of Hebrews can claim that to share in the gift of salvation brought about by the Son is to share in the gift of the Spirit (Heb 6:4).

PHILIPPIANS 2:5-11

Many scholars think that Phil 2:5-11 originated as an early hymn that Paul either wrote or adapted for his epistle.[24] N. T. Wright considers this hymn one of the most remarkable passages in all of the New Testament.[25] The hymn makes explicit the unique identity of YHWH as presented in the Old Testament and clarifies in significant ways the naming of the triune YHWH. At the center of YHWH's identity stands Christ. Despite these lofty themes, Paul shows little urgency in explaining or justifying the Christological content of the hymn. He writes:

5 Have this mind among yourselves, which is yours in Christ Jesus,
6 who, being in the form of God, did not regard equality with God as something to be used for His own advantage,
7 but rather made Himself of no reputation, taking the form of a servant, being born in the likeness of men. And being found in human form,
8 He humbled Himself, becoming obedient to the point of death, even death on a cross.
9 Therefore God exalted Him to the highest place and bestowed on Him the name that is above every name,
10 so that at the name of Jesus every knee should bend, in heaven and on earth and under the earth,
11 and every tongue confess that Jesus Christ is Lord, to the glory of God the Father.[26]

In chapter 7 I listed both the Hebrew and Greek of the divine name to indicate the standard way in which the LXX renders YHWH. For example: "Hear, O Israel: The Lord [YHWH/κύριος] our God, the Lord [YHWH/κύριος] is one" (Dt 6:4). Although the New Testament never uses the Hebrew YHWH, it consistently employs the LXX rendering, *kyrios*, to indicate the divine name. In Romans alone numerous examples of this may be seen: Rom 4:8 (Ps 32:2); Rom 9:28 (Is 10:22); Rom 9:29 (Is 1:9); Rom 10:16 (Is 53:1); Rom 11:34 (Is 40:13); and Rom 15:11 (Ps 117:1). In all of these cases Paul substitutes *kyrios* for YHWH. At the very least this tells us that in Paul's theological vocabulary *kyrios* functions as the proper Greek substitute for YHWH.[27] What are we to make of Paul's use of *kyrios* for Jesus? What are we to make of Paul assigning Old Testament YHWH texts to

---

24. Ralph Martin, *Carmen Christi: Philippians 2:5-11 in Recent Interpretation and in the Setting of Early Christian Worship* (Grand Rapids: Eerdmans, 1983); N. T. Wright, *The Climax of the Covenant* (Minneapolis: Fortress Press, 1992), 56-98. On Pauline authorship of the hymn see Bauckham, "God Crucified," 41; Arthur W. Wainwright, *The Trinity in the New Testament* (Eugene, OR: Wipf and Stock, 2001), 87.
25. Wright, *Climax of the Covenant*, 56.
26. This is my own translation. It reflects the arguments of Wright and Bauckham. Wright, *Climax of the Covenant*, 62-90; Richard Bauckham, "Paul's Christology of Divine Identity," in *Jesus and the God of Israel*, 197-210.
27. Hurtado, *Lord Jesus Christ*, 112. Hurtado provides a number of other Pauline passages to substantiate this point further.

Jesus? The answer in both cases is that Paul unmistakably confesses that Christ belongs to the unique identity of YHWH.

The hymn begins by establishing the identity of Jesus Christ. Although in the form of God (v. 6), He humbled Himself and was born as man (v. 7). The pre-existent Christ, coequal with God the Father, does not regard His equality with the Father as something to be used for His own advantage. As N. T. Wright observes, you cannot take advantage of something you do not already possess.[28] Further, the conclusion of the hymn depends upon the coequality of the pre-existent Christ with the Father. Whatever we wish to say about the Father as God we must also say about the pre-existent Christ. The hymn, in almost the same breath, adds that this pre-existent Christ, coequal and coeternal with the Father, who did not regard His equality something to be taken advantage of (v. 6), humbled Himself to be born as man (v. 7). The issue expressed in these verses has nothing to do with gaining or losing what the pre-existent Christ eternally possesses. The hymn does not envision a divesting of essence or nature but rather a self-giving of Christ for the redemption of man.[29] This self-giving, this incarnation of God, leads to death upon the cross (v. 8). The remarkable confession of the hymn reveals with clarity what the prophets more obscurely confessed: constitutive of God's unique identity is suffering and the cross. N. T. Wright states, "The real humiliation of the incarnation and the cross is that one who was himself God, and who never during the whole process stopped being God, could embrace such a vocation."[30] At Calvary we see the truth of God's identity. Whatever we wish to say about God and whatever we think it means to be God, according to Scripture we must place at the heart of that description the cross and Christ crucified.

The hymn opens by confessing without ambiguity the coequality and coeternity of Christ and the Father, and that this Christ became man for our salvation, suffering death upon the cross. Therefore, for this reason, because of the suffering on the cross, the Father exalted *Him* to the highest place and conferred upon *Him* the Name that is above every name (v. 9). The Name that is above every name is a reference to the divine name, to YHWH.[31] To whom or to what does the exaltation refer? The answer, of course, is to Jesus (vv. 10–11), but that doesn't really answer the question. In what sense does this refer to Jesus? The exaltation refers not to the divine nature of Christ but to the honor and worship accorded the assumed humanity of Christ, the man Jesus, as Lord, as YHWH. God the Father exalted the *man* Jesus Christ. Here the Father publicly declares and acknowledges the completed and all-sufficient atoning work of Jesus, true God and true man. Moreover He directs all honor and worship of

---

28. Wright, *Climax of the Covenant*, 82.
29. Wright, *Climax of the Covenant*, 83–84.
30. Wright, *Climax of the Covenant*, 84.
31. Cf. Bauckham, "Paul's Christology of Divine Identity," 199: "There can be no doubt that 'the name that is above every name' (v. 9) is YHWH: it is inconceivable that any Jewish writer could use this phrase for a name other than God's own unique name."

Father and Son: Dogmatic Commitments

the Father to the crucified Christ. For this all-sufficient atoning work, at the name of Jesus every knee should bend (v. 10) and every tongue confess that Jesus Christ is Lord and this to the glory of the Father (v. 11; cf. Jn 5:23). The hymn begins by distinguishing the pre-existent Christ from the Father. The hymn ends by identifying the man Jesus with the Father. We know the man Jesus as Lord to the glory of the Father and this only, as Paul emphasizes elsewhere, by the Holy Spirit (1 Cor 12:3). Once again Christ stands at the center of our trinitarian confession.

Three things are particularly noteworthy about the end of this hymn. First, the eschatological lordship of Christ means that all people at the end of time, whether believers or unbelievers, will bend the knee at the name of Jesus, acknowledging Him to be the Lord to the glory of God the Father. A further point is made for believers. The worship of Jesus by the faithful involves the cross and crucifixion. The Father bestows the divine name on His Son, Jesus, who in eternity is God but in time humbles Himself, being born as a man and suffering death upon a cross, and all believers confess that He is Lord by the power of the Holy Spirit (Phil 2:1; 1 Cor 12:3). To worship the Father is to worship the crucified Jesus and this by the Spirit. Further, there is no worship of the Father apart from the man Jesus and His cross. In the same way there can be no understanding of the identity of YHWH apart from the incarnation and crucifixion of Jesus.

Second, understanding the hymn requires a thorough understanding of the prophets. The content of the hymn relies upon God's revelation of Himself and His unique identity to the prophets. The hymn does not give us a "new" way of thinking about God; rather it clarifies for us what God had already declared about Himself in the Old Testament. In chapter 7 we highlighted especially "the high and lifted up" Servant who was to be exalted to the right hand of God. We asked how the Servant, who shares the eternal throne of God, could be exalted. The answer is that exaltation assumes humiliation, the incarnation of the Servant. The prophets describe this humiliation at length. The Servant will be despised and rejected by men; He will be a man of sorrows who will bear our griefs and carry our sorrows (Is 53:2–3). He will be wounded for our transgressions and crushed for iniquities, for "YHWH has laid on him the iniquity of us all" (Is 53:5–6). He who bears our iniquities is "YHWH our Righteousness" (Jer 23:5), and He will justify us (Is 53:11). When this occurs, YHWH declares, I will pour out the Spirit of grace and mercy and the people "shall look upon me whom they have pierced, and they shall mourn for him, as one mourneth for his only son, and shall be in bitterness for him, as one that is in bitterness for his firstborn" (Zec 12:10 KJV; Jn 19:37; Rv 1:7). YHWH says they shall look upon "me" whom they have pierced, and at the same time they shall mourn "for him." The YHWH pierced remains distinct from the YHWH who sent Him. The one wounded for our transgressions, the one pierced for us, who is sent by YHWH and is YHWH, who shares the eternal throne, who shall be exalted after His humiliation, is Christ Jesus, who being coequal with the Father assumed true humanity in time and suffered and died upon the cross for us. Following this the Father exalted the man Christ Jesus, bestowing on Him the name above every name, and every knee shall bend and every tongue confess that He is Lord to the glory of the Father.

Third, the end of the hymn explicitly construes the identity of the man Jesus with Isaiah 45. In this chapter YHWH repeatedly declares His unique and exclusive identity. He alone is God. He alone created the heavens and earth. He alone saves. YHWH says through Isaiah:

> And there is no god besides me, a righteous God and a Savior; there is none besides me. Turn to me and be saved, all the ends of the earth! For I am God, and there is no other. By myself I have sworn; from my mouth has gone out in righteousness a word that shall not return: "To me every knee shall bow, every tongue shall swear." Only in YHWH, it shall be said of me, are righteousness and strength; to him shall come and be ashamed all who were incensed against him. In YHWH all the offspring of Israel shall be justified and shall glory. (Is 45:21–25)

YHWH repeatedly declares that He is the one and only God. He alone saves, for in Him alone are righteousness and strength. Justification is in Him alone. Moreover, His unique divine identity will be acknowledged universally in the context of His salvation. When this happens His identity shall be known rightly. Paul's use of these verses in the hymn means unambiguously that the exaltation of the man Jesus following the crucifixion is the fulfillment of what YHWH declares about Himself in Isaiah 45. Moreover, Is 42:8 remains: "I am YHWH; that is my Name; my glory I give to no other, nor my praise to carved idols." At the center of the explicit monotheism of Isaiah and the universal worship of YHWH is Christ crucified. To bend the knee and confess with the tongue that Jesus is Lord, possessing the name above every name, is to acknowledge YHWH's triune identity. The Father bestows the name upon the Son, and the faithful confess Him as Lord by the power of the Holy Spirit. All of this revolves around the cross. Constitutive of YHWH's identity, of the Blessed Trinity, is the cross, Christ crucified, the man Jesus.

FIRST CORINTHIANS 8:6

Twice a day faithful Jews prayed the Shema: "Hear, O Israel: The Lord [YHWH/κύριος] our God, the Lord [YHWH/κύριος] is one" (Dt 6:4). Confession of YHWH's unique identity also entailed worship and faithful living or ethics: "You shall love the Lord your God with all your heart and with all your soul and with all your might" (Dt 6:5). By this daily prayer faithful Jews confessed their allegiance to YHWH alone and ordered their lives. They loved the Lord because He loved them first. They loved their neighbors as themselves because of who the Lord is and because of His love for them (Leviticus 19). All of this bears on what Paul writes to the Corinthians. In his first letter to them he restates the Shema by explicitly and unambiguously including Jesus in the unique identity of YHWH.

The larger context of Paul's confession heightens the significance of what he says. He addresses concerns about eating meat offered to idols and how this might be understood by some as participating in polytheistic worship. Paul suggests that weaker brothers may be confused over the existence of idols and may think that eating meat offered to them defiles a person. Stronger brothers should avoid eating such meat lest they make their weaker brother stumble and defile himself (1 Cor 8:7-13). In the midst of recognizing this problem and giving his answer Paul raises the issue of idols and pagan gods. Despite the fact that they have no existence (1 Cor 8:4) the Greek and Roman imagination populates the heavens and earth with them (1 Cor 8:5). In this sense there are many "gods" and many "lords" surrounding us (1 Cor 8:5). At this point Paul writes, "For us there is one God, the Father, from whom are all things and for whom we exist, and one Lord, Jesus Christ, through whom are all things and through whom we exist" (1 Cor 8:6).

The issue at the center of Paul's restatement of the Shema concerns monotheism, the proper worship of the one true God, and faithful living. We emphasized in chapter 7 and throughout part 1 that confession, worship, and ethics go together. The Bible does not conceive of the confession of either God or an idol apart from the worship of God or that idol and the ethical behavior that follows. Paul's response underscores the exclusive divinity of YHWH. He alone is God and there is no other. God is one (1 Cor 8:4). In the light of the person and work of Christ Paul restates the Shema, rearranging in a sense the very words of the Shema.[32] The one God of the Shema is the Father; the one Lord of the Shema is Christ. They are distinct—the Father is the Father and not Jesus in the same way Jesus is Jesus and not the Father—but also one. N. T. Wright and Richard Bauckham call this Christological monotheism.[33] Paul includes Jesus in the unique divine identity expressed by the Shema. He does not "add" Jesus to the identity confessed in the Shema. Such an addition, notes Bauckham, would undermine the very point of the Shema as Paul has stated it.[34]

Paul further clarifies the divine identity of Christ by appealing to creation as a mark of His divine identity. Scripture states many times over that God alone creates. All things exist from the Father; all things exist through the Son. This divine prerogative of creation belongs to the Father and the Son equally and eternally. There is nothing that exists or has existed apart from the Father and the Son. The divine act of creation necessarily involves both Father and Son. There is no conceptual space given to a consideration of creation apart from either. They are distinct and yet inseparable in their correlative

---

32. Bauckham, "God Crucified," 27-28.
33. Wright, *Climax of the Covenant*, 132; Bauckham, "God Crucified," 28.
34. Bauckham, "Paul's Christology of Divine Identity," 212-13.

work of creation. All that exists is both "from" the Father and "through" the Son.

Finally, Paul states that "we" exist for the Father through the Son. Paul began his discussion of the food offered to idols by making a distinction between knowledge which puffs up and that which proceeds from the love of God. The former lacks humility and reposes in spiritual arrogance. The latter loves God, is known by God, and therefore loves neighbor. This person knows the love of God in Christ Jesus, knows the salvation won for us by Him who humbled Himself, enduring suffering and the cross. This person does not exploit his Christian freedom at the expense of others (cf. 1 Corinthians 9). On the contrary, though this person is free from all, he makes himself a servant to all (1 Cor 9:19).[35] It is this person who knows he exists for the Father through the Son. Paul's final declaration pertains to the humble knowledge of the faithful who know not only that there is one God and one Lord, from whom and through whom are all things, but also that this one God and one Lord have brought us to know, worship, and confess them as Father and Son. Our life is through the Son for the Father. The proud and arrogant, the ones who flaunt their freedom at the expense of their brothers, think they exist for themselves and through themselves.

REVELATION

The closing book of the New Testament presents a highly structured and precise presentation of the Trinity and especially Jesus' identity as true God and true man. All that John sees and records is by the Spirit (Rv 1:10; 4:2; 17:3; 21:10). The Spirit of prophecy prevalent throughout the Old Testament and present in Revelation points to Christ, His saving work, and the context in which we know Him and the Father. Revelation makes clear the identity of Christ and His relationship to the Father by assigning to Christ the same divine name assigned to God the Father, by locating Christ, the Lamb of God, in the midst of the divine throne receiving worship with the Father, and finally by using a peculiar grammar to convey the unique divine identity of God and Christ.

God the Father speaks on only two occasions in Revelation. Immediately before John's vision we read, "'I am the Alpha and the Omega,' says the Lord God, 'who is and who was and who is to come, the Almighty'" (Rv 1:8). In the vision of the new heaven and new earth the Father declares from the throne, "I am the Alpha and the Omega, the beginning and the end" (Rv 21:6). God declares three things about Himself: He is the Alpha and the Omega, the beginning and the end, the one who is, was, and is to come. The first two statements are synonymous. Alpha and Omega are the first and last letters of

---

35. The exegetical background to Luther's *Freedom of a Christian* is Paul's discussion in 1 Corinthians 8 and 9. The descriptive ethic Paul establishes here is what Luther expresses fully in his treatise.

the Greek alphabet. The final statement glosses the divine name, YHWH, I AM WHO I AM, or as the Septuagint has it, I AM the one who is.

The first two statements underscore the absolute uniqueness of God. He is the beginning without beginning and the end without end. He is the creator of all and ruler of all. These things God alone is. Through the prophet Isaiah YHWH declared, "I am the first and I am the last; besides me there is no god" (Is 44:6). Again He declares, "I, YHWH, the first, and with the last; I AM" (Is 41:4) and "I AM; I am the first, and I am the last" (Is 48:12). These three texts from Isaiah emphasize the exclusive divinity of YHWH. He alone is God and there is no other. He is first and last; He is incomparable to all. Indeed He is the context in which all else finds its meaning and life. He precedes all as Creator and He completes all, brings all to fulfillment, as Lord. None of this is particularly surprising, of course. The Scriptures throughout affirm that God alone creates and rules, that He alone and none other is God. What captures the reader's attention in Revelation is that Christ uses the same titles to describe Himself on two separate occasions. In the opening vision John sees "one like a son of man" and falls at His feet. The description of this one like the son of man resembles the one seen by Ezekiel and Daniel. The son of man touches Him and says, "Fear not, I AM the first and the last [ἐγώ εἰμι ὁ πρῶτος καὶ ὁ ἔσχατος], and the living one. I died, and behold I am alive forevermore, and I have the keys of Death and Hades" (Rv 1:17–19). Jesus leads with the same response to John as He did to the disciples when He came walking on water (Jn 6:20). Here, however, He adds to the divine name the further description given in Isaiah and used by the Father immediately before this vision. At the end of Revelation Jesus similarly declares, "I am the Alpha and Omega, the first and the last, the beginning and the end" (Rv 22:13).

These four statements, two for the Father and two for Christ, appear in the opening and closing of John's vision. The statements made by the Father and Christ derive from YHWH's declarations about Himself in Isaiah. Both belong to the unique identity of God. Whatever it means for the Father to be the Alpha and the Omega or the beginning and the end, it means the same for Christ and these things are only and ever said of YHWH. They are both *this* and yet also eternally distinct as Father and Son. Furthermore, Christ, who is God, also became man. The living one died and lives forevermore. This one like the son of man is the Messiah promised of old, who is both YHWH and distinct from YHWH. Elsewhere in Revelation Christ further describes Himself in messianic terms as the Lion of Judah, the Root and offspring of David, the bright morning star (Rv 5:5; 22:16).

The Father declares that He is the one who is, who was, and who is to come. Although the other titles appear with Christ, this one does not in so many words. And yet the same thing is affirmed about Christ. He is the living one; He is the first and the last; and He is, by His own promise, the one coming soon (Rv 22:7, 12). In this sense what the Father says about Himself is said also about the Son. There is however a further and more significant point. The Father's statement is a gloss on the divine name, YHWH. What is noteworthy is that He does not say, "I am the one who is, was, and *will be*."[36] Had God said this He would have placed the emphasis on His eternity as He is in Himself. The Father says instead, "I am the one who is, who was, and who is to come." He shifts from the verb "to be" to the verb "to come." The future of God is expressed here by His relationship with His people. God's future does not stand apart from the redemptive work of Christ, the slain Lamb of God, the living one who died and rose again. The final phrase used by the Father places emphasis upon salvation, judgment, and God's eschatological fulfillment of His purposes. He is the Alpha and the Omega, the first and the last, not simply apart from creation but very much active in that creation in claiming His children as His own. God's future lies with His people. Likewise, our future lies in the one to come.

The final declaration made by the Father includes the Son and the Spirit. The end of Revelation makes this clear by using the common titles that belong to the Father and the Son, as established from the outset of John's vision. In chapter 21 John sees the new heaven and the new earth, the holy city, new Jerusalem. A loud voice, the voice of the Father from the throne, declares, "Behold, the tabernacle of God is with man. He will dwell with them, and they will be His people, and God Himself will be with them as their God. He will wipe away every tear from their eyes, and death shall be no more, neither shall there be mourning nor crying nor pain anymore, for the former things have passed away" (Rv 21:3–4). The one sitting on the throne, the one who says these things, tells John He is making all things new. He then says to him, "It is done! I am the Alpha and the Omega, the beginning and the end" (Rv 21:6). The faithful will receive these things as sons and daughters; the faithless will receive the lake that burns with fire and sulfur, the second death (Rv 21:8). God's future lies with His people; their future, where death is no more, where there is neither mourning nor pain, is with God.

John continues with a description of the New Jerusalem and especially highlights the inseparability of God and the Lamb. He sees no temple, for the temple is the Lord God the Almighty and the Lamb (Rv 21:22). In this city where there is no night John sees no sun, for the glory of God gives it light and its lamp is the Lamb (Rv 21:23). John sees the river of the water of life, which is the Holy Spirit, proceeding from the throne of God and of the Lamb (Rv 22:1). Following this vision John hears, "And behold, I am coming soon" (Rv 22:7). Again Jesus declares, "Behold, I am coming soon, bringing my recompense with me, to repay everyone for what he has done. I am the Alpha and the Omega, the first and the last, the beginning and the end" (Rv 22:12). When Christ returns there is judgment and the completion of the Lamb's saving work. For a third time Christ declares, "Surely, I am coming soon" (Rv 22:20). The Father's future

---

36. Cf. Richard Bauckham, *The Theology of the Book of Revelation* (Cambridge: Cambridge University Press, 1993), 28–29.

never stands apart from the Son's saving work and their mutual dwelling with the faithful, the Bride of Christ, who, led by the Spirit, thirst for the water of life without price (Rv 22:17) and cry out, "Amen. Come, Lord Jesus!" (Rv 22:20).[37]

The context in which God is rightly known is worship. Here the final two points made by John can be observed. First, the faithful gather around the throne to worship God and the Lamb (Rv 22:3). John's initial vision of heaven describes the heavenly scene of worship around the throne of God. The twenty-four elders and the four living creatures cry out, "Holy, holy, holy, is the Lord God Almighty, who was and is and is to come!" (Rv 4:8). When the four living creatures give glory and honor and thanks to the Father, the twenty-four elders fall down before Him and worship Him. They cast their golden crowns before the throne and cry out, "Worthy are you, our Lord and God, to receive glory and honor and power, for you created all things and by your will they existed and were created" (Rv 4:11). John's description echoes that given by Isaiah and Ezekiel. The theological point, made throughout the Scriptures, is that God alone receives worship. Those who serve or rule on His behalf, the twenty-four elders, fall down before Him in worship, casting their golden crowns before the throne. God alone creates, He alone rules, and He alone receives worship.

Above John assigns the same divine name to God the Father and to Christ. He first records the Father's declaration about Himself and then Christ's statement. They are both the Alpha and the Omega, the first and the last, the beginning and the end because they are both God and yet they are distinct as Father and Son. In a similar way John first sees the Father on His throne, and then in the next chapter sees the Lamb. The same divine prerogatives observed in chapter 4 are observed in chapter 5 but this time with the Lamb, the Lion of Judah, the Root of David (Rv 5:5). John sees a scroll in the hand of the one seated on the throne. When the Lamb takes the scroll from the one seated on the throne the four living creatures and the twenty-four elders fall down before the Lamb (Rv 5:8). John then hears the four living creatures, the twenty-four elders, and angels numbering myriads of myriads, thousands of thousands, say with a loud voice, "Worthy is the Lamb who was slain, to receive power and wealth and wisdom and might and honor and glory and blessing!" (Rv 5:12). The whole heavenly host, the whole hierarchy of heaven, falls down before the Lamb in worship. They not only worship the Lamb as they had the Father but also give glory and honor to the Lamb as they had the Father. The same divine worship, the same glory and honor given to the Father in chapter 4 is given to the Lamb in chapter 5. Finally John hears every creature in heaven and on earth and under the earth and in the sea, and all that is in them, say, "To him who sits on the throne and to the Lamb be blessing and honor and glory and might

---

37. Cf. TLH 343:7: "Oh, joy to know that Thou, my Friend / Art Lord, Beginning without end / The First and Last, Eternal! / And Thou at length—O glorious grace!— / Wilt take me to that holy place / The home of joys supernal. / Amen, Amen! / Come and meet me! Quickly greet me! / With deep yearning / Lord, I look for Thy returning."

forever and ever!" (Rv 5:13). To this the four living creatures say "Amen" and the elders fall down and worship (Rv 5:14). The Lamb who is "in the midst of the throne" (Rv 7:17) receives the same worship given the Father, for both are the Alpha and the Omega, the first and the last.

The exclusive worship given to YHWH, to the one true God of Israel, belongs to both God and the Lamb. The same worship given by the four living creatures and the elders to the Father is given to the Lamb. In chapter 7 we observed that the Old Testament marks out the unique identity of YHWH by emphasizing the characteristics and prerogatives that belong to Him alone and to none other. YHWH alone creates and rules His creation, He alone sits upon the throne and receives worship, He alone redeems His people from their sins. The New Testament never hesitates to assign these divine prerogatives to Jesus, the true Son of God. We have seen already the emphasis upon Christ as creator and ruler, the one who receives worship from all, but it is chiefly in Revelation that we see the emphasis upon the divine throne. Both God and the Lamb are upon the throne and receive the worship reserved for YHWH alone.

Finally, a peculiarity with John's vision concerns the reluctance to refer to God and Christ with plural verbs or pronouns.[38] In the above example of the New Jerusalem John sees the throne of God and the Lamb. He writes, "No longer will there be anything accursed, but the throne of God and of the Lamb will be in it, and *his* [αὐτοῦ] servants will worship *him* [αὐτῷ]" (Rv 22:3). John deliberately uses the singular pronoun to refer to both God and Christ. He does the same thing elsewhere in Revelation. For example, he hears a loud voice in heaven saying, "The kingdom of the world has become the kingdom of our Lord and his Christ, and *he shall reign* [βασιλεύσει] forever and ever" (Rv 11:15). Here the singular verb refers to both our Lord and His Christ. John's language avoids any hint of polytheism and underscores the unity of God and Christ as the one true God who is eternally distinct as Father and Son. Both share the same glory and receive the same worship. Both sit upon the divine throne and are known by the Spirit in the context of worship, which is to say in the church's divine service.

CONCLUSION

In the last chapter we saw that the New Testament writers unambiguously confess Christ's divine identity through the historical narratives of the Gospels and the seemingly insignificant sections of Paul's letters. The ordinary language of faith, as I called it, confesses, prays, and sings forth the coequality and coeternity of the Father and the Son. In this chapter we focused on the more dogmatic and concise presentations of Christ's identity. These texts, like those in the previous chapter, place Christ at the center of our confession of God's scriptural identity. We know the Father only through the Son; we know the Son

---

38. Bauckham, *Theology of the Book of Revelation*, 60–61.

by the Holy Spirit, whom both the Father and the Son send to us. Moreover, the texts in this chapter emphasize again the necessity of the Old Testament for our understanding of the person and work of Christ. God alone determines His identity, and this He providentially preserves for us in His Scriptures. Finally, the New Testament makes clear that God's identity is fully revealed at the cross. It is at this very point that we come to know the glory of God in the crucified Christ, seeing our reconciliation with the Father through the saving work of the Son. This we know, confess, sing, and pray by the power of the Holy Spirit.

10

THE HOLY SPIRIT

Our previous chapters have shown the plural identity of YHWH our Elohim, the normative naming of YHWH as Father, Son, and Holy Spirit, the centrality of Christ for our confession of the Trinity, and the inseparable working of Father and Son in our creation and redemption. Scripture does not isolate its presentation of the eternal identity of the Trinity into discrete sections on the individual persons. We do not look to the Old Testament for the Father, the Gospels for the Son, and the Acts of the Apostles and their Epistles for the Holy Spirit.[1] All of Scripture testifies to the Trinity. For that reason we have had occasion already to comment on the Holy Spirit in our discussion of the scriptural identity of YHWH in the Old Testament and in our discussion of the Father and the Son in the New Testament. The following chapter aims to build on what has been said already, focusing especially on the New Testament and the role of the Spirit in the church.

Our discussion of the Holy Spirit's scriptural identity involves two issues: the divine identity of the Holy Spirit and the eternal origin of the Holy Spirit. In the Nicene Creed we confess that the Holy Spirit, the Lord and giver of life, proceeds from the Father and the Son. The language of "procession" points to the eternal origin of the Spirit from the Father and the Son. The additional phrase "and the Son," which in Latin is *filioque*, was added subsequently to the Creed from Constantinople (381) and sparked what is called the *filioque* controversy. Since Lutherans confess and teach the *filioque* because of their commitment to Scripture, this question belongs for us in the discussion of the Holy Spirit's scriptural identity. And yet to have that discussion we must avail ourselves of technical terms and patterns of speech used by the church that we have not yet introduced. Despite that difficulty we will address the *filioque* in the next chapter before turning in part 3 to how the faithful throughout the

---

1. Gregory of Nazianzus famously asserted that God progressively discloses His triune identity throughout the Scriptures. The Father is best made known in the Old Testament, the Son in the New Testament, and the Holy Spirit in the history of the church. Gregory of Nazianzus *Or.* 31.26 (PPS, 137). A similar sentiment can be found with Martin Chemnitz. He writes, "The person and deity of the Father are often and clearly witnessed in the Old Testament. Concerning the person and deity of the Son the Old Testament passages are rather obscure. But in the New Testament the deity of the Son is most clearly demonstrated by more and clearer passages than is the deity of the Holy Spirit." Chemnitz, *Loci Theologici*, trans. J. A. O. Preus (St. Louis: Concordia Publishing House, 2008), 1:237. Comments such as these often are taken in the wrong way. Both Gregory and Martin Chemnitz provide significant examples of the Son and the Spirit in the Old Testament.

The Holy Spirit

history of the church have confessed, defended, and guarded the scriptural identity of the Trinity.

In this chapter we will show the divine identity of the Holy Spirit by focusing on some of the same things we did with the Son. We will discuss how Scripture assigns the divine name to the Holy Spirit, calls Him God, and attributes to Him works belonging exclusively to God. These sorts of things are only ever done for the one true God of Scripture. Before we turn to these things, however, we will address an issue not found with the Father and the Son—the peculiar name Holy Spirit. Augustine long ago commented that the Holy Spirit lacks a personal name.[2] We call Him Holy Spirit because this is what Scripture gives us, but that name is shared in different ways with the Father and the Son and also created things. Scripture uses the word Spirit, *rûach* or *pneuma*, to refer to God, to the person of the Holy Spirit, to the gifts of the Holy Spirit, or even to the created spirits—angelic, demonic, and human.[3] Some people have used this ambiguity to undermine the Spirit's distinct and eternal identity. Others have exploited this ambiguity in translation to limit the visibility of the Spirit in the Bible.

A further issue requiring our attention concerns the way God reveals Himself to us and delivers His salvation to us. A point repeated throughout the Scriptures is that the Father will be known only in His Son. And so it is that when we cast our eyes upon Jesus we see the Father (Jn 14:8–9). A recurring problem throughout the history of the church is that people have sought God on their own terms. Scripture makes clear to us that only by the Holy Spirit may we know God and the things of God (1 Cor 2:11–12). If not for the Spirit we could neither confess Christ as Lord (1 Cor 12:3) to the glory of the Father (Phil 2:11) nor access the Father through the Son (Eph 3:18). The chief gift of the Spirit, the chief charism among the faithful, is confessing Christ as Lord, as the Son of the Father, in whom alone we have redemption and life. Without the Spirit the Son remains unknown and so too the Father (Jn 15:23; 2 Jn 9 NKJV). This gift of the Spirit gives everything: proper knowledge of the Trinity and of ourselves, the salvation worked for us by the Trinity, freedom in Christ to love and serve neighbor (Galatians 5; Romans 8), the words to confess the Trinity and the gospel (Mt 10:20; 28:20), the words to pray, and indeed prayers too deep for words (Rom 8:26). The Spirit delivers this gift through the divinely appointed means of grace, through God's Word and sacraments, that we might know and be known by God (Gal 4:9). When we bring this all together, we learn that only by the working of the Holy Spirit through the means of grace may we know the Trinity and the salvation won for us. The Bible knows no exceptions to this. Those who seek God apart from His Word and sacraments are no different than those wanting to see the Father apart from the man Jesus.

---

2. Augustine *The Trinity* V.12 (WSA I/5, 197–98).
3. On this point see LC II.35–36 (Tappert, 415).

The following chapter will demonstrate the scriptural identity of the Holy Spirit but will focus especially on the work of the Spirit in creating and sustaining saving faith through the means of grace in the church. It is this final point that will make clear for us that a proper understanding of the Holy Spirit and His works makes us Christ-centered in both doctrine and life. Lutherans emphasize Christology for this reason. Christ stands at the center of the Trinity, our salvation, and baptismal living.

THE NAME HOLY SPIRIT

The proper name given by Scripture to the Third Person of the Trinity presents difficulties not encountered with the Father and the Son. The Holy Spirit is spirit, but so too the Father and the Son are spirit: "God is spirit" (Jn 4:24). Scripture also declares that the Father and the Son are holy as the Spirit is holy: "Holy, holy, holy is YHWH Sabaoth" (Is 6:4).[4] Jesus prays, "Holy Father, keep them in your Name, which you have given to me, that they may be one, even as we are one" (Jn 17:11). The angel Gabriel tells the Virgin Mary that "the Holy One to be born will be called the Son of God" (Lk 1:35 NKJV; cf. Jn 6:69; Acts 3:14).[5] Even the unclean spirits declare this truth: "What have you to do with us, Jesus of Nazareth? Have you come to destroy us? I know who you are—the Holy One of God" (Mk 1:24–25). It is said throughout the Old and New Testaments that God is holy and will work His holiness in us: "You shall be holy, for I the Lord [YHWH] am holy" (Lv 19:2; 1 Pt 1:15–16). This holiness comes to us by the Holy Spirit (Rom 1:4; 1 Pt 1:2) but also by Christ, who is our holiness, our sanctification (1 Cor 1:30). Scripture emphasizes both the Spirit and Christ in this work: "But you were washed, you were sanctified, you were justified in the name of the Lord Jesus Christ and by the Spirit of our God" (1 Cor 6:11). The name Holy Spirit belongs uniquely to the Third Person of the Trinity, but not in such a way that the Father and the Son are not also rightly said to be "holy" and "spirit."

Why does any of the above present a problem? An issue we will explore in depth in the next few chapters concerns the way in which we confess what Scripture reveals about Father, Son, and Holy Spirit. Certain words of Scripture talk about the essence of our triune God and other words talk about the eternally distinct persons of the Trinity. The Fathers and reformers distinguished these ways of talking by saying that Scripture predicates some things in terms of substance (substantive predication) and other things in terms of person (relative predication). Father and Son are the personal names of the First and Second Persons of the Trinity. The Father is Father and never Son; the

---

4. Ambrose *On the Holy Spirit* I.9 (Fathers of the Church, 73–74); Augustine *The Trinity* V.12 (WSA I/5, 197–98); Johann Gerhard, *De Spiritu Sancto*, Locus 4/3, §20 (ed. Cotta, 302).

5. The ESV translates this verse in the following way: "The child to be born will be called holy—the Son of God." Both translations make the point but NKJV follows the text more closely.

Son is Son and never Father. Both are God in the same sense. When we use the name Holy Spirit as a personal name, we use it in the same way as Father and Son. The Father is never the Holy Spirit; the Holy Spirit is never the Son. Since all three are God but not three gods, Scripture further patterns us to say that the Father is almighty, the Son is almighty, and the Holy Spirit is almighty, but they are not three almighties but one almighty. Whatever it means to be God is true of the Father, the Son, and the Holy Spirit who are the one true God. All of this will be explained further in subsequent chapters, but with this brief summary we detect a problem already. The Holy Spirit is both holy and spirit in the same way the Father and the Son are but the Father and the Son are not *the* Holy Spirit. Two very different things are being said here with the same words. All three are holy and spirit in terms of essence; only the Holy Spirit is Holy Spirit in terms of person. When we depart from this pattern of speaking, from rightly distinguishing between substantive and relative predication, confusion and false statements about the Trinity arise. This confusion led some in the early church and again some during the Reformation to assert that the Holy Spirit was not a distinct and separate person (*hypostasis*) but merely an influence or manifestation of God. For this reason it was and still is important to show how Scripture proclaims the eternally distinct and separate *hypostasis* or person of the Holy Spirit from the Father and the Son.

Rûach and *Pneuma*

Another difficulty rests with the broad range of meaning for the Hebrew word *rûach* and Greek word *pneuma*.[6] The Hebrew *rûach* may mean spirit, wind, or breath, among other things. Scripture uses the same term to designate the "four winds" of heaven (Dn 8:8; 11:4; Zec 2:6), YHWH's angels who are "winds" (Ps 104:4; Heb 1:7 ESV), and "spirits" (KJV). Again the term may refer to the judgment of God as a "scorching wind" (Ps 11:6), the "spirit" of man (Ps 51:10, 12), or "the Holy Spirit" (Ps 51:11) who moved upon the face of the waters (Gn 1:2). The term may refer to the "breath" of man (Ps 146:4; Jb 12:10) or the "breath" of YHWH (Ps 33:6). We read of "the Spirit of God" who creates (Jb 33:4) and of the "spirit of man," the "spirit of beasts" (Eccl 3:21), and the "spirits of all flesh" which are created (Nm 16:22). Man may have either "the Spirit of YHWH" within him or "an evil spirit" (1 Sm 16:14). The "spirit of whoredom" leads God's people into idolatry (Hos 4:12) and they no longer know the Lord (Hos 5:4). The same word may describe our emotions: "A joyful heart is good medicine, but a crushed spirit dries up the bones" (Prv 17:22); "He that is slow to wrath is of great understanding: but he that is hasty of spirit exalteth folly" (Prv 14:29 KJV). The "spirit" in man may be haughty (Prv 16:18) or humble (Prv 16:19), cool (Prv 17:27) or crushed (Prv 18:14). Finally, Scripture sometimes uses this word to refer to the gifts of the Spirit rather than the person of the Spirit. Elisha pleads with Elijah, "Please let there be a double portion of your spirit upon me"

---

6. Cf. Didymus the Blind *On the Holy Spirit* 236–56 (PPS, 216–22).

(2 Kgs 2:9). Similarly, YHWH tells Moses to gather together seventy elders from the people. When he has done this, YHWH "will take some of the Spirit that is on you and put it on them, and they shall bear the burden of the people with you, so that you may not bear it yourself alone" (Nm 11:17).

A similar diversity may be found in the New Testament with the Greek *pneuma*. Often the term designates "the Holy Spirit" (Mt 1:18 et passim) or "the Spirit of God" (Mt 3:16 et passim). This latter designation is the title used most frequently throughout the Scriptures. The Spirit of God encountered in the New Testament is the same Spirit who created in the beginning with the Father and His Word (Gn 1:3), who inspired the patriarchs and prophets (1 Sm 11:6; 2 Chr 24:20; Ez 11:24 et passim), and who would rest upon the Christ, the promised Messiah (Is 11:2; 42:1; 61:1). The Gospel writers record that indeed the Spirit of God descended upon Christ at His baptism (Mt 3:16), drove Him into the wilderness (Mt 4:1), returned Him to Galilee (Lk 4:14), and was upon Him throughout His ministry (Lk 4:18). It is this same Holy Spirit that Christ breathed upon the disciples, instituting the office of ministry (Jn 20:22). Paul tells us that the Spirit of God dwells in all believers, and this Spirit of God is the Spirit of Christ (Rom 8:9). When Israel rebelled against YHWH, they "grieved his Holy Spirit" (Is 63:10). Likewise, Paul warns believers not to "grieve the Holy Spirit of God" (Eph 4:30).

Pneuma may refer just as frequently to something other than the Holy Spirit. The same term applies to those who are "poor in spirit" (Mt 5:3) or "fervent in spirit" (Rom 12:11). A great deal is said about the spirit of man in Scripture. His spirit rejoices (Lk 1:47) and stands in need of refreshment (2 Cor 7:13) or renewal (Eph 4:23). His spirit contends with the flesh (Mt 26:41). A person may have a spirit of fear (2 Tm 1:7) or a gentle and quiet spirit (1 Pt 3:4). Sometimes Scripture uses the same word to designate the Holy Spirit and the spirit of man in the same verse: "The Spirit himself bears witness with our spirit that we are children of God" (Rom 8:16). Occasionally this word may mean breath (2 Thes 2:8) or wind (Jn 3:8), but normally Greek uses other words for these meanings.[7] The word also may refer to "an unclean spirit" (Mk 1:23) or may be used in the sense of "ghost" (Lk 24:37, 39). The term contrasts the Holy

---

7. John 3:8 is especially difficult on this point. The New Testament prefers ὁ ἄνεμος (Mk 4:39-41; Mt 11:7) and less frequently ἡ πνοή (Acts 2:2) for wind. John 3 uses *pneuma* and this creates ambiguity. English readers can see this especially with the Vulgate, since our word Spirit comes from the Latin. Jesus is talking about the Spirit. He tells Nicodemus that which is born of the Spirit is spirit ("quod natum est ex Spiritu spiritus est"). Although Nicodemus marvels over this, he should not. Jesus explains, "Spiritus ubi vult spirat." The KJV and ESV translate this as the wind blowing or listing where it pleases. Douay-Rheims, which is a translation of the Vulgate, reads, "The Spirit breatheth where he will." Jesus ends His example by saying that so it is with "every one that is born of the Spirit" ("qui natus ex Spiritu"). Latin, like Greek, prefers other words for wind (e.g. *ventus* and less commonly *flatus*). All of this is not to argue for the translation of Spirit throughout Jn 3:8 but merely to show the difficulty of translating *pneuma* or *Spiritus*. In Jn 3:6-8 the KJV and ESV move back and forth between "Spirit" and "wind," but in the Greek and Latin the same word is being used throughout. All of this is obscured for those accessing the Scriptures only in English.

Spirit with evil spirits or the spirit of antichrist. There is the Spirit of truth and the spirit of error (1 Jn 4:6). John writes, "By this you know the Spirit of God: every spirit that confesses that Jesus Christ has come in the flesh is from God, and every spirit that does not confess Jesus is not from God. This is the spirit of the antichrist, which you heard was coming and now is in the world already" (1 Jn 4:2–3). It is this evil spirit that is at work in the sons of disobedience (Eph 2:2).

The difficulty with the above examples is obvious. The word used to designate the Holy Spirit may be used to describe angels, people, demons, emotions, gifts, and even wind or breath. The history of the church shows that many have stumbled because of this ambiguity. False teachers in the early church (Macedonians or pneumatomachians) and during the Reformation (Socinians) contended that the Holy Spirit was not a self-subsistent person, separate and distinct from the Father and the Son, but rather a created influence or some impersonal means used by God. The ambiguity in language allowed them to make this false argument. Translators today capitalize on this ambiguity of language to offer interpretations that obscure the text's plain meaning and further confuse unsuspecting readers. Those unfamiliar with Hebrew or Greek may be misled because of this or may fail to see Scripture's sound pattern of words and intertextual links.

Since the same word may be translated in a number of ways it is especially important to allow Scripture to interpret Scripture in determining whether the word means the Holy Spirit, a created spirit, wind, or breath. A well-known example is the beginning of Genesis. The ESV and KJV both have the Spirit of God moving over the face of the waters; the NRSV translates this as a wind from God (Gn 1:2). Those dependent upon the NRSV will not see the presence of the Holy Spirit in the creation of the world. The same word from Genesis 1, which the ESV and KJV translate as Spirit, is rendered "breath" in Psalm 33: "By the Word of the Lord the heavens were made, and by the breath of his mouth all their host" (Ps 33:6; cf. Is 40:7–8). The Fathers and reformers all read this verse as referring to the Word and Spirit (breath).[8] Retaining breath in the translation is perfectly acceptable as long as we understand that this psalm, as Aegidius Hunnius argues, is a summary or transcript of creation by Father, Son, and Holy Spirit.[9] Elsewhere the Scriptures state plainly that the Holy Spirit gives life (2 Cor 3:6; Jn 6:63). Similarly, Elihu declares to Job: "The Spirit of God has made me, and the breath of the Almighty gives me life" (Jb 33:4). Both Genesis

---

8. For the patristic reading of this verse see Irenaeus *Against Heresies* 1.22.1 and 3.8.3; Irenaeus *Proof of the Apostolic Preaching* 11; Athanasius *Orations Against the Arians* 2.31; Basil of Caesarea *Letter* 8.11 and *On the Spirit* 38 and 49; Gregory of Nazianzus *Or.* 41.14; and Augustine *Exposition of Psalm 32(33)*, verse 6, exposition 1 and 3. The Lutheran reformers continue the patristic and medieval tradition of interpretation for this verse. See *On the Last Words of David*, 1543 (AE 15:301; WA 54:56.29–57.8); Melanchthon, *Loci Communes*, 40; Chemnitz, *Loci Theologici* 1:89, 91. This interpretation is continued throughout the seventeenth century by the Lutheran dogmaticians.

9. Aegidius Hunnius, *Calvinus Iudaizans* (Wittenberg, 1604), 24–29; cf. AE 15:301; WA 54:57.9–25.

1 and Psalm 33 describe creation and both involve the Holy Spirit. Translators may obscure this fact by their choice of words or use of the lowercase for spirit or breath. Such moves are interpretive and make dogmatic claims—as does of course the insistence that these texts refer to the Spirit. Again, Scripture must interpret Scripture in these matters.

A similar ambiguity may be found in the Gospel of John. That we might know the Son and the Father both send the Holy Spirit, the Comforter, the Spirit of Truth (Jn 14:26; 15:26). The Spirit bears witness to the Son (Jn 15:26) by directing us to what Christ Himself has said (Jn 14:26). He will convict the world concerning "sin and righteousness and judgment" (Jn 16:8), and He will declare to us what belongs to the Son and the Father (Jn 15:15). Further, the Spirit of Truth will guide us into the Truth (Jn 15:13), which is to say the Spirit of the Son will guide us to the Son. No one comes to the Father except through the Son because He is "the way, and the truth, and the life" (Jn 14:6). The Spirit guides us into the Truth, speaking to us the words of Truth, and the Son, who is the Truth, is the way to the Father and eternal life. All of this is conveyed by Jesus in His discourse with the woman from Samaria about the manner of right worship. True worshippers, He explains, "worship the Father in Spirit and Truth" (Jn 4:23). Although most translations leave spirit and truth lowercase (προσκυνήσουσιν τῷ πατρὶ ἐν πνεύματι καὶ ἀληθείᾳ), the Fathers read "spirit" as a reference to the Holy Spirit and "truth" as a reference to the Son.[10] For Athanasius our worship of the Father is determined by the Father; we worship Him rightly when we are led by the faith given to us by the Holy Spirit, a faith that places its gaze always and ever upon the Son, the Truth, and this to the delight of the Father. There is no other worship of the Father except by the Spirit through the Son (Eph 2:18). For Athanasius this way of translating Jn 4:23–24 emphasizes the inseparability of the Son and the Spirit. The Spirit, sent by the Father and the Son, always points us back to the Son, the Truth, that we might worship and glorify the Father.[11]

The Fathers and reformers resolve the above difficulties by attending to context and grammar. When Scripture modifies *rûach* or *pneuma* with "Holy," or qualifies it with "of God" or "of the Father" or "of the Son" or "of Christ" or "of Truth," then in all of these cases there is no question that the Spirit being discussed is the Holy Spirit. When the modifier is absent, when there is no qualifier marking off the meaning for us, then context becomes our guide.[12]

---

10. According to Raymond Brown, most exegetes today agree that the spirit spoken of by Jesus is the Holy Spirit. He does not think "truth" refers to the Son but suggests that "Spirit and truth" act as hendiadys and is equivalent to Spirit of Truth, a common expression in John (cf. Jn 14:17; 15:26; 16:13). See Raymond Brown, *The Gospel According to John I-XII* (New York: Doubleday, 1966), 180.

11. Athanasius *Letters to Serapion* 1.33.3–5 (PPS, 104); cf. Gregory of Nazianzus *Or.* 31.12 (PPS, 125).

12. Athanasius and Didymus the Blind further observe that most of the time—there are exceptions—Scripture distinguishes the Holy Spirit from the gifts of the Spirit or from created spirits by using the definite article. When Scripture talks about "the Spirit" it is referring to the

The Fathers and reformers looked especially at what was being said about the "spirit" and from there determined if Scripture was talking about the person of the Spirit, the gifts of the Spirit, or a created spirit. Didymus the Blind explains, "We should consider the manner in which the term is used in each instance, lest perhaps through ignorance we fall into the pit of error."[13] A further difficulty, and one we will look at more closely, concerns the ambiguity mentioned above with Father, Son, and Holy Spirit. Since all three are spirit and holy, it is sometimes difficult to know if Scripture's reference to "Spirit" indicates the Holy Spirit, the Father, or the Son. This may be seen especially with the divine name.

THE DIVINE NAME

St. Matthew and the Baptismal Formula

As we have seen in our previous chapters, the divine name marks out God's unique identity, who He is and what He does. It belongs to Him alone and points especially to His work of creation, judgment, and salvation. In the previous chapters we have shown the importance of the divine name in the Old Testament and how the New Testament assigns this name to Jesus. The New Testament writers also assign the divine name to the Holy Spirit, locating Him unambiguously in the divine identity of YHWH. This fact alone demonstrates the consubstantiality and coequality of the Holy Spirit with the Father and the Son and His hypostatic or personal distinction from them. The baptismal formula from Matthew's Gospel is a good example of this. Jesus instructs the disciples to baptize "in the name of the Father and of the Son and of the Holy Spirit" (Mt 28:19). This name, the divine name, belongs to Father, Son, and Holy Spirit equally and eternally. The Holy Spirit delivers through holy baptism the salvation of the Father achieved by the Son (cf. Ti 3:4–6); here we become children of God, children of the Father, Son, and Holy Spirit (Jn 1:12–13; Rom 8:16–17). The Trinity saves, and in this name which belongs exclusively to the Trinity we find our life, our salvation: "Save us, O YHWH, our Elohim, and gather us from among the nations, that we may give thanks to your holy name and glory in your praise" (Ps 106:47; 1 Chr 16:35).[14] We worship and glorify Father, Son, and Holy Spirit in the context of our baptism, where we become children of God.

When we view Jesus' words at the end of Matthew's Gospel in the context of the whole Gospel, we discover the richness of the trinitarian formula. Matthew's

---

Holy Spirit; when Scripture leaves the article out and refers to "spirit," it is usually talking about a created spirit. For many examples of this see Athanasius *Letters to Serapion* 1.5.1–1.6.13 (PPS, 57–65) and Didymus the Blind *On the Holy Spirit* 8, 73 (PPS, 145–46; 165–66). Martin Chemnitz praises this observation and finds it useful. See Chemnitz, *Loci Theologici* 1:221.

13. Didymus the Blind *On the Holy Spirit* 256 (PPS, 222).

14. Correlating Mt 28:19, Ps 106:47, and 1 Chr 16:35 yields the following equivalencies: Father, Son, and Holy Spirit equal YHWH our Elohim, which may be confessed more simply as the God of our salvation. This final way of expressing the Trinity corresponds to Mary's song: "My soul magnifies the Lord and my spirit rejoices in God my Savior" (Lk 1:46–47).

Gospel, like all of Scripture, is thoroughly trinitarian. The counterpart to the concluding baptismal formula is the beginning of the Gospel and the baptism of Jesus. These trinitarian bookends form the broad context for all that Matthew says. Following the opening genealogy Matthew turns directly to the birth of Christ. Mary is found to be with child "from the Holy Spirit" (Mt 1:19). When Joseph becomes concerned, an angel of the Lord appears to him:

> But as he considered these things, behold, an angel of the Lord appeared to him in a dream, saying, "Joseph, son of David, do not fear to take Mary as your wife, for that which is conceived in her is from the Holy Spirit. She will bear a son, and you shall call his name Jesus, for he will save his people from their sins." (Mt 1:20–22)

Matthew immediately directs the reader to the prophecy of Is 7:14, "'Behold, the virgin shall conceive and bear a son, and they shall call his name Immanuel' (which means, God with us)" (Mt 1:23). The one born of Mary is the Son of God, God with us, Immanuel. Mary conceives this child by the Holy Spirit. The angel of the Lord, given the context of what is said here, must be understood to be the angel of the Father. This is confirmed a few verses later (though chronologically a good bit later) when the same angel of the Lord appears to Joseph. The angel directs him to take the child to Egypt and remain there until the angel summons him back. This was to fulfill what the Lord had spoken through Hosea: "Out of Egypt I called my Son" (Mt 2:15). The Father announces to Joseph that Mary will bear the very Son of God by the Holy Spirit for the salvation of all people. From the very opening of the Gospel Matthew proclaims the Trinity and the Trinity's work of salvation for us.

Matthew deliberately frames his Gospel with these two explicitly trinitarian texts. The work of the Spirit in these two pericopes demands emphasis. David Scaer writes, "The Spirit in whose name Baptism is given is responsible for the incarnation of the Son."[15] The Spirit who gives human life to the Son is the same Spirit who regenerates and renews us through baptism (Ti 3:4–7), making us sons of God and coheirs with Christ (Rom 8:14–17; cf. Jn 1:12–14). The Spirit who brings us to Christ and His salvation makes known to us the Father through the Son, allowing us cry out "Abba, Father" and to pray boldly "Our Father." This point becomes explicit for Matthew in the baptism of Jesus. Immediately when Jesus is baptized the heavens are opened, the Spirit of God descends upon Him, and a loud voice declares, "This is my beloved Son, with whom I am well pleased" (Mt 3:17). The Spirit who comes upon Jesus in His baptism to fulfill all righteousness (Mt 3:15) is the same Holy Spirit with whom He will baptize us (Mt 3:11).

We need to dwell here for a moment. The Spirit's descent upon Jesus illustrates the proper work of the Spirit; He concludes always with Jesus. When the Spirit descends upon Jesus for us, which is to say when we by faith see Jesus

---

15. David Scaer, *Baptism*, vol. 11 of Confessional Lutheran Dogmatics (St. Louis: Luther Academy, 1999), 75.

as the very Son of God, something possible only by the Holy Spirit, then we hear the voice of the Father declaring this to be His beloved Son. Christology stands at the center of a proper understanding of the Spirit and the Father; indeed, a proper Christology alone guarantees a proper understanding of the Trinity. We see this with the name Immanuel as well. The child Mary conceives by the Holy Spirit, the one in whom the Father is well pleased, will be called Immanuel, God with us. This name frames Matthew's Gospel and stands at the center of the two trinitarian pericopes at the beginning and the end of the Gospel (Mt 1:23; 28:20). Christ is with us unto the ages by the working of the Holy Spirit through Word and sacrament; when we abide in Christ we know the Father and delight in the freedom of the Spirit to love and serve our neighbors.

Matthew moves from Epiphany to Lent, from baptism to temptation, from new life to the life of the baptized. Following His baptism "Jesus was led up by the Spirit into the wilderness to be tempted by the devil" (Mt 4:1). Jesus and the Spirit remain together in bringing about the work of salvation. This too, as Matthew later reminds us, is to fulfill what was spoken by Isaiah: "Behold, my servant whom I have chosen, my beloved with whom my soul is well pleased. I will put my Spirit upon him, and he will proclaim justice to the Gentiles. . . . and in his name the Gentiles will hope" (Mt 12:18, 21; Is 42:1–3; 42:4 LXX [Rom 15:12]). The Father declares His great pleasure with the Son at the baptism and puts His Spirit upon Him. The Trinity's work of salvation for us foretold by Isaiah is explained now with great clarity by Matthew.[16]

Two further points are made by Matthew before we arrive at the baptismal formula and the Name that belongs uniquely and exclusively to Father, Son, and Holy Spirit, to YHWH our Elohim, to God our Savior. Jesus declares, "All things have been handed over to me by my Father, and no one knows the Son except the Father, and no one knows the Father except the Son and anyone to whom the Son chooses to reveal him" (Mt 11:27). This point has been made already with some force by Matthew. At the baptism of Jesus we hear the Father declare that Jesus is His beloved Son, with whom He is well pleased. Again at the Transfiguration the Father declares, "This is my beloved Son, with whom I am well pleased; listen to him" (Mt 17:5). Those who wish to know the Father must know the Son. The Father directs all to His Son: "Listen to him." In the Sermon on the Mount Jesus speaks at length about the Father. By listening to Jesus and doing what He tells us to do, we will be sons of the Father (Mt 5:43–45). Those who love and serve their neighbors without seeking attention and reward but do so because of their lively and active faith—a faith given and nourished by the Holy Spirit through the means of grace—will receive their reward from the Father (Mt 6:1) who sees all things (Mt 6:4, 6, 18). We are to pray to the Father

---

16. The connection here is even more explicit in Luke. When Jesus returns from the wilderness he comes to Nazareth and goes into the synagogue on the Sabbath day. He takes the scroll of Isaiah, unrolls it, and reads from Is 61:1–2 (Lk 4:16–19). He then says to those gathered, "Today this Scripture has been fulfilled in your hearing" (Lk 4:21).

(Mt 6:6) who knows our needs before we ask Him (Mt 6:9, 32). Through the Son we call upon Him as "our Father" (Mt 6:9) and from Him we have forgiveness (Mt 6:14). Our Father who feeds the birds of the air and clothes the grass of the field (Mt 6:26–28) knows our needs and will give good things to those who ask (Mt 7:11).

Scripture emphasizes at length that it is the Spirit who uses the Word to bring us to faith. The Spirit who inspired the patriarchs, prophets, and apostles uses His inspired Word to bring us to the Son and the Father. We confess and know the Son, and if the Son then also the Father, by the working of the Holy Spirit through the Word. David knew the Father as Lord and the Son as Lord and this, according to Jesus, "in the Spirit" (Mt 22:43). The same Spirit who spoke the good confession through David continues to speak through the faithful. Jesus tells the disciples they will be delivered over to the courts and flogged because of Him. In that hour they need not fear what they will say. Jesus explains, "For it is not you who speak, but the Spirit of your Father speaking through you" (Mt 10:20). We see this confession spoken by the Spirit of the Father in Peter's great confession: "You are the Christ, the Son of the living God" (Mt 16:16). That sort of confession, Jesus emphasizes, comes not from flesh and blood but from "my Father who is in heaven" (Mt 16:17) through the teaching of Christ by the Holy Spirit. It is by that same Spirit that the disciples will teach all that Christ has commanded (Mt 28:20). We see this stated also by John. He records what he does in his Gospel in order that "you might believe that Jesus is the Christ, the Son of God, and that by believing you may have life in his name" (Jn 20:31). Peter's confession is the confession made by the faithful. As Martha puts it, by the Holy Spirit we confess, "Yes, Lord; I believe that you are the Christ, the Son of God" (Jn 11:27).

Matthew makes a further point with the Holy Spirit. When Jesus casts out demons He is accused by the Pharisees of doing this by Beelzebul. Jesus tells them that He casts out demons by the Spirit of God (Mt 12:28), the very Spirit of God who descended upon Him at His baptism (Mt 3:16) and led Him into the wilderness (Mt 4:1). Further, that this happens means the kingdom of God has come upon us (Mt 12:29). Jesus then says something that has perplexed interpreters throughout the history of the church:

> Therefore I tell you, every sin and blasphemy will be forgiven people, but the blasphemy against the Spirit will not be forgiven. And whoever speaks a word against the Son of Man will be forgiven, but whoever speaks against the Holy Spirit will not be forgiven, either in this age or in the age to come. (Mt 12:31–32)

In Matthew's Gospel the word blasphemy is only ever used with reference to the work of God. Jesus' enemies know that the works He does belong only to God. Rather than confessing His divine identity because of these works, they accuse Him of blasphemy (Mt 26:65). Jesus tells us that out of the heart come evil thoughts and blasphemies, which means slander or abusive speech (Mt 15:19). This is how Jesus uses the word elsewhere in Matthew's Gospel. When

Jesus forgives the sins of the paralytic the scribes accuse Him of blaspheming. Jesus responds, "Why do you think evil in your hearts?" (Mt 9:2–4).

Blasphemy against the Holy Spirit is active rejection of the work of God that slanders God. In the context of Matthew 12 the Pharisees slander Jesus' work of healing the demon-oppressed man who was blind and mute. This particular work belongs to the Messiah upon whom the Spirit of YHWH rests (Is 35:5), a messianic text Jesus applies to Himself when John the Baptist's disciples come to Him with their questions about His identity (Mt 11:4–6). Rather than confessing this as the work of the Messiah by the Spirit of God, Jesus' opponents say it comes from Beelzebul. They not only resist the work of the Spirit among themselves (Acts 7:51) but also slander the saving work of God. They actively reject God and His work, assigning it to the devil. This is blasphemy, and these wicked thoughts and accusations, which harm not only the person uttering them but potentially those hearing them as well, are against the Holy Spirit and will not be forgiven. Mark calls this "an eternal sin" (Mk 3:29).

What troubles so many people with this text is that Jesus says this sort of sin will not be forgiven. Why would Jesus isolate this particular sin and say it could not be forgiven? A broader interpretation will shed light on this. Jesus makes a distinction between those who speak against the Son of Man and those who speak against the Holy Spirit.[17] What is the difference? A person could speak against the Son of Man by seeing Him only as a carpenter's son (Mt 13:55; Lk 4:22) or a mere Nazarene (Mk 14:67; Jn 1:46). To stumble upon the Son's humility, seeing only His humanity lacking the expected majesty and beauty (Is 53:2) that appeals to the theologian of glory, has led many throughout the centuries to avoid the manger and the cross, the lowly places of God. That doubt proceeds from discontent with the ordinary and the scandal of preaching Christ crucified. When the Holy Spirit brings us to faith, He frees us from these doubts, these false constructions of what seems reasonable and fitting for God. These sorts of doubts, according to Jesus, are of a different character than speaking against the Holy Spirit.

When a person expresses discontent with the ordinary water of baptism or the ordinary bread and wine of the Lord's Supper, or with the perfect salvation accomplished by Christ apart from us and our works, or other such matters that pertain to the way in which God saves us and has determined to deliver that salvation to us, something else is being said than the doubts above. We have no access to the salvation purchased for us by the Son except by the Holy Spirit. Ordinarily this comes through the divinely appointed means of grace, Word and sacrament. A person can no more see the Father apart from the Son (Jn 14:8–11) than confess the Son as Lord apart from the Holy Spirit (1 Cor 14:3). Our salvation was accomplished by God and will be delivered by God through

---

17. For Abraham Calov, Jesus' distinction between a sin against the Holy Spirit or against the Son of Man highlights the hypostatic distinction of the Spirit from the Son and by extension the Father. Calov, *Systema Locorum Theologicorum* (Wittenberg, 1659), 3:727, 752–53.

His appointed means. There is no way around this. The Pharisees grumble about the work of the Spirit of God in Christ. They dislike the manner in which God works so much that they accuse Christ of working on behalf of the devil. They don't want God's work of salvation in the manner He accomplishes it. They want to see and speak apart from Christ and the Spirit. They further wish to separate the Son from the Spirit and remove God from the ordinary and lowly. They blaspheme the Holy Spirit in this way, rejecting God and His work for us. Those who wish to know the Father apart from the Son, the Son apart from the Spirit, or the salvation of God apart from the Spirit's work through Word, baptism, and the Lord's Supper reject who God is and the way in which He works and delivers His saving benefits to us. Their active rejection harms themselves and those around them. That slander, that blasphemy, resists the Holy Spirit. Such blasphemy cannot be forgiven because it is a total rejection of the triune God and His salvation.[18]

Matthew consistently shows the identity and work of the Trinity. The baptismal formula at the end of the Gospel concisely states the trinitarian structure of the whole Gospel. Jesus is Immanuel, He is God with us, the beloved Son of the Father. The Spirit is the Spirit of the Father, the Spirit of God, who rests upon Jesus and works intimately with Him. What the ending of Matthew reveals with exceptional clarity is that Father, Son, and Holy Spirit belong to the unique identity of YHWH. Further, the divine name, in which salvation is found, stands at the heart of baptism, and it is here that God comes to us, baptizing us and delivering to us His salvation. As our Confessions put it, "To be baptized in God's name is to be baptized not by men but by God himself."[19] There, in holy baptism, we become children of God, our sins forgiven, our salvation delivered. Our identity, our existence, our life is grounded firmly in baptism. This is why Luther and the Lutheran tradition never tire of extolling the virtue of baptism. In the Large Catechism Luther calls baptism a treasure that God gives us (LC IV.37), a medicine that swallows up death and keeps us alive (LC IV.43), our daily source of strength and comfort (LC IV.44), a great jewel that adorns our body and soul (LC IV.46), our daily garment (LC IV.84). The Christian life is nothing else than a daily baptism (LC IV.65). "In baptism," writes Luther, "every Christian has enough to study and practice all his life" (LC IV.41). Here, in baptism, we know ourselves and the Trinity who saves, here we worship and glorify the Father with the Son and with the Holy Spirit. From this baptism we never graduate as Christians; we return daily, living and dying in our baptism.

The Holy Spirit Is Lord (YHWH)

St. Paul also identifies the Holy Spirit with the divine name. In the previous chapters we have shown that in Paul's theological vocabulary *kyrios* functioned

---

18. For a somewhat similar interpretation, see Ambrose of Milan *On the Holy Spirit* I.54 (Fathers of the Church, 55).

19. LC IV.10 (Tappert, 437).

as the proper Greek substitute for YHWH. What then are we to make of his use of *kyrios* for the Holy Spirit? What are we to make of him assigning Old Testament YHWH texts to the Holy Spirit? We asked these same questions about Paul assigning YHWH texts to Jesus. The answer is that Paul unmistakably confesses that the Holy Spirit, like Jesus, belongs to the unique identity of YHWH. The text in question comes from his second letter to the Corinthians. In this letter Paul opposes a group of false teachers questioning his proclamation of the gospel and his authority. He tells us that these opponents peddle and tamper with God's Word (2 Cor 2:17; 4:2). These "superapostles" preach another Jesus and another gospel (2 Cor 11:4-5). They mislead through their eloquence (2 Cor 11:6) and by boasting of their Jewishness (2 Cor 11:22). They produce "letters of recommendation," and in turn question Paul's authority and apostolic credentials (2 Cor 3:1-2). It is difficult to know precisely what these opponents were arguing. At the very least it had to do with a false understanding of Moses and the law that undermined Christ and the freedom of the Spirit. Their false teaching raised questions about how we read and interpret the Scriptures (hermeneutics), and further how that reading informs Christian living (ethics). This is the issue taken up by Paul in the third chapter of his letter.

Paul draws a contrast between the letter and the Spirit, between the ministry of death carved in stones and the ministry of the Spirit written on human hearts, between the ministry of condemnation and the ministry of righteousness (2 Cor 3:3-9). Each contrast made by Paul is between a lesser glory that has come to have no glory and one more glorious that surpasses it (2 Cor 3:10). Paul then turns to Moses and Christ (2 Cor 3:12-18). His argument stems from Ex 34:29-35, and a contrast between the glory of the old covenant (death and condemnation) and the greater glory of the new covenant (Spirit and righteousness).[20] Paul explains this contrast by appealing to Moses' use of a veil. Moses veiled his face, he explains, "so that the Israelites might not gaze at the outcome of what was being brought to an end" (2 Cor 3:13). This veil remains for those who read the old covenant apart from Christ. Paul is emphatic: "Only through Christ is the veil taken away" (2 Cor 3:14). He then paraphrases Ex 34:34. "But when one turns to the Lord, the veil is removed" (2 Cor 3:16). When Moses went in before the Lord (YHWH), he removed the veil. How do we pass from the lesser glory of the old covenant that is no glory to the greater glory of the new covenant? Paul's answer is through Christ by turning to the Lord. Who is the Lord in question? He continues, "Now the Lord is the Spirit" (ὁ δὲ κύριος τὸ πνεῦμά ἐστιν, 2 Cor 3:17). This is the same Spirit Paul has already mentioned: the Spirit of the living God (2 Cor 3:3), the Spirit who gives life (2

---

20. On what follows see especially J. D. G. Dunn, "2 Corinthians III.17—The Lord Is the Spirit," *Journal of Theological Studies*, N.S., 21:2 (1970): 309-20; Richard B. Hays, *Echoes of Scripture in the Letters of Paul* (New Haven, CT: Yale University Press, 1989), 125-53; and C. Kavin Rowe, "Biblical Pressure and Trinitarian Hermeneutics," *Pro Ecclesia* 11/3 (2002): 303-4.

Cor 3:6). The veil of the old covenant of death is removed by turning to the Spirit of life who delivers to us the saving work of Christ. Paul explains, "Where the Spirit of the Lord is, there is freedom" (2 Cor 3:17). Only by the Spirit through Christ do we have freedom from the death and condemnation of the law, the old covenant. This Spirit of life frees us in Christ from ourselves to love and serve our neighbors (2 Cor 5:14–15).

Those who have turned to the Spirit will behold the glory of the Lord in the face of Jesus Christ, who is Lord (2 Cor 3:18; 4:5–6), and this "from the Lord who is the Spirit" (2 Cor 3:18). Paul in the space of only a few verses assigns the divine name to God the Father, Jesus, and the Spirit. The Father is Lord, Jesus is Lord, the Holy Spirit is Lord but they are not three lords but one Lord. All of this is said by Paul in the context of our salvation, which he summarizes in his closing doxology: "The grace of the Lord Jesus Christ and the love of God and the fellowship of the Holy Spirit be with you all" (2 Cor 13:14).[21]

THE HOLY SPIRIT IS GOD

The baptismal formula at the end of Matthew's Gospel and Paul's identification of the Holy Spirit as Lord clearly and unambiguously locate the Holy Spirit in the unique identity of YHWH. The New Testament also identifies the divine status of the Holy Spirit by either calling Him God or describing Him in the same way as God. Ananias and Sapphira refuse to share their possessions with the other disciples and instead secretly and with the intent to deceive keep back a portion (Acts 5:2). Peter confronts Ananias: "Ananias, why has Satan filled your heart to lie to the Holy Spirit and to keep back for yourself part of the proceeds of the land?" (Acts 5:3).[22] Ananias's lie to the disciples was a lie against the Holy Spirit. Peter continues, making it very clear who the Holy Spirit is: "You have not lied to men but to God" (Acts 5:4). To lie to the Holy Spirit is to lie to God because the Holy Spirit is God.

The New Testament also confesses the divine identity of the Spirit by assigning to Him the same activity as that assigned to the Father and the Son. In the Nicene Creed the church confesses that the Spirit is the Lord and giver of life (2 Cor 3:17–18). There is some intentional ambiguity here. The Spirit gives both life in terms of existence, which is especially emphasized in the Old Testament, and also eternal life. Both points are made in the New Testament. God alone gives life; He alone creates and redeems. A chief way in which the Scriptures mark off the unique identity of God is by assigning this work to the Father, the Son, and the Holy Spirit alone. There is no one else who creates and no one else who saves.

---

21. Paul routinely uses trinitarian formulae. In addition to this one see Rom 1:1–4; 1 Cor 12:4–6; Gal 4:4–6; Eph 1:3–13; 4:4–6; Ti 3:4–7.

22. On the exegetical issue of Satan filling the heart see Didymus the Blind *On the Holy Spirit* 257–67 (PPS, 222–25).

The prologue to the Gospel of John emphasizes creation and redemption in order to show the coequality and eternal distinction of the Father and the Son. So too we find this same concern with the Father and the Spirit in the New Testament. Paul writes, "The Spirit gives life" (2 Cor 3:6). Elsewhere he uses the same expression for the Father. He writes to Timothy: "I charge you in the presence of God, who gives life to all things, and of Christ Jesus, who in his testimony before Pontius Pilate made the good confession" (1 Tm 6:13). Here Paul refers to God the Father who gives life. Elsewhere he confesses that the Son created all things and sustains all things (Col 1:16–17). Elsewhere still he simply confesses that YHWH calls all things into existence and gives life and breath (Rom 4:17; Acts 17:25). As we have seen, the Old Testament variously says that YHWH alone creates, the Word of YHWH creates, and the Spirit of YHWH, who is the breath of the Almighty, creates. The same diversity found in the Old Testament is found in the New Testament. For Paul the life given by the Spirit is the life given by the Father and the Son. There is distinction and unity: God the Father, God the Son, and God the Holy Spirit give life, and the life they give is one.

In John's Gospel the focus is on the work of the Holy Spirit delivering eternal life to us. Jesus says, "He [the Spirit] will glorify me, for he will take what is mine and declare it to you. All that the Father has is mine; therefore I said that he will take what is mine and declare it to you" (Jn 16:14–15). Jesus has already explained that whatever the Father does the Son does (Jn 5:19). The Father gives life; the Son gives life. The same honor the Father receives from us the Son receives. Whoever does not honor the Son does not honor the Father. This coequality of the Father and the Son is then expressed in terms of consubstantiality: "For as the Father has life in himself, so he has granted the Son also to have life in himself" (Jn 5:26). What the Father has by nature (here stated as "life"), the Son has by nature from the Father. Moreover, since what the Father is as God He is so eternally (Ps 102:27; Mal 3:6; Jas 1:17) and the Son has "all" that the Father has, the Father and Son are coeternal. Thus when Jesus declares, "All that the Father has is mine," He is speaking in terms of their coequal and coeternal divine nature, which the church has confessed throughout the centuries with the word *homoousios*. They are both "life" itself. This "life" is what the Spirit also has from the Father and the Son: "It is the Spirit who gives life" (Jn 6:63). This "life," eternal life, is the life of the Trinity shared with us in holy baptism. The Father is life, the Son is life, the Holy Spirit is life. They are not three "lives" such that we receive three different gifts of eternal life, one from the Father, one from the Son, and one from the Holy Spirit. The life they give is one because they are one. We share in the life of the Father through the Son by the Holy Spirit.

Father, Son, and Holy Spirit create and give life. In the chapters on the Father and the Son we also noted texts where they bring the dead back to life. This power belongs to God alone and serves to mark off His identity from all others. Scripture also assigns this divine prerogative to the Holy Spirit. Scripture most frequently states that God the Father raised Jesus from the dead (Acts 2:24, 32; 3:15; Rom 4:24; 6:4; 10:9; 2 Cor 4:14; Gal 1:1; Eph 1:20). The same thing also is said for Jesus and the Holy Spirit. Jesus says, "I lay down my life that I may take it up again. No one takes it from me, but I lay it down of my accord. I have authority to lay it down, and I have authority to take it up again. This charge I have received from my Father" (Jn 10:17–18). Jesus' statement corresponds to His enigmatic response to the Jews about the temple: "Destroy this temple, and in three days I will raise it up" (Jn 2:19). The Jews were confused by this. The disciples understood Jesus' words only following the resurrection: "He was speaking about the temple of his body" (Jn 2:21). Although less clearly, Scripture also says that the Spirit of God raised Jesus: "If the Spirit of him who raised Jesus from the dead dwells in you ..." (2 Cor 8:11). According to Scripture the power that raised Jesus from the dead belongs to Father, Son, and Holy Spirit. All three may be said, in different contexts, to have raised the man Jesus from the dead. Their power, however, is one as they are one. The unique divine prerogative to create and sustain life, to give life back to the dead, belongs to God alone, to Father, Son, and Holy Spirit.

WORK OF THE HOLY SPIRIT

In our earlier chapters we have emphasized the unique work of God in creation, in the governance of His creation, in judgment, and in salvation. The Old Testament establishes the work of the Spirit in all of these things and the New Testament further confesses it. As we have seen above, the Spirit of God created all things in the beginning with the Father and His Word (Gn 1:3). Overcome with the grandeur and beauty of creation, David sings forth praises to God for His creation of all things in Psalm 104. YHWH stretched out the heavens, set the earth upon its foundations, raised the mountains, and pressed down the valleys. He made the springs gush forth to give drink to animals, planted trees with branches for the birds, grew grass for the livestock and plants for man to cultivate. He gave wine to gladden the heart of man and bread for strength. How did He create all these things? David writes, "When you send forth your Spirit, they are created, and you renew the face of the ground" (Ps 104:30).[23] Moreover, the Spirit who creates, the Spirit of YHWH, abides in man and sustains His life (Gn 6:3). As we have seen, the New Testament continues this emphasis on the Spirit as the giver of life and eternal life.

The creative Spirit who brings all things into existence also directs human history. He is the one who spoke through the prophets, declaring the things of God to us. The Spirit who creates rests in the patriarchs, judges, prophets, and servants of God (Gn 41:38; Nm 11:17, 29; Jgs 6:34; 14:6; 1 Sm 10:6; 11:6; 2 Chr 24:20; Ez 11:24 et passim). The New Testament never tires of emphasizing the

---

23. Athanasius *Letters to Serapion* 1.24.5 (PPS, 91) and 1.9.6 (PPS, 67).

work of the Holy Spirit in the prophets. Their prophecies came not from them, not from their will, but "from God as they were carried along by the Holy Spirit" (2 Pt 1:21; cf. Acts 28:25). Peter further says that the Holy Spirit, the Spirit of Christ, was sent from heaven to declare these prophecies about the Christ and our salvation to the prophets of old. They declared these things by the Spirit for us (1 Pt 1:10–12; cf. Heb 10:15–18). The Spirit continues to speak forth God's truth through the people of faith. No one may say that Jesus is Lord except by the Holy Spirit (1 Cor 12:3); those of faith speak in the Spirit of God, for no one comprehends the things of God except the Spirit of God (1 Cor 2:11). Peter says that those who are insulted for the name of Christ are blessed because "the Spirit of Glory and of God" rests upon them (1 Pt 4:14).

The prophets further emphasize that the Spirit will rest upon the Christ, the promised Messiah (Is 11:1–2; 42:1; 61:1). In the day of YHWH, after the Teacher of Righteousness (Jl 2:23) has come, this Spirit will be poured out (Jl 2:28; Ez 39:29; Zec 12:10) and "everyone who calls on the name of YHWH shall be saved" (Jl 2:32). The New Testament repeatedly emphasizes the pouring out of the Holy Spirit upon the people of God. When the Spirit fills believers He brings them faith, love, joy, wisdom, grace, power, and confidence to speak the Word of God. John the Baptist is "filled with the Holy Spirit, even from his mother's womb" (Lk 1:15). His mother Elizabeth, when she hears Mary's greeting, "was filled with the Holy Spirit, and she exclaimed with a loud cry, 'Blessed are you among women; and blessed is the fruit of your womb!'" (Lk 1:41–42). Filled with the Holy Spirit, Elizabeth rejoices that the mother of her Lord has come to her (Lk 1:43). Zechariah too is "filled with the Holy Spirit and prophesied, saying, 'Blessed be the Lord God of Israel; for he hath visited and redeemed his people and hath raised up an horn of salvation for us in the house of his servant David'" (Lk 1:67–69 KJV). Following Christ's ascension, when the day of Pentecost arrives, the disciples are gathered and are all "filled with the Holy Spirit" and go forth proclaiming the gospel in various languages (Acts 2:1–4). As with Elizabeth and Zechariah, when the disciples are filled with the Holy Spirit, they go forth proclaiming the salvation we have in Christ.

In Acts, after the disciples are filled with the Spirit, they proclaim the gospel in the various languages of the day, overcoming the confusion of Babel. Their preaching, by the power of the Holy Spirit, is thoroughly Christological. This point must be stressed. In the previous two chapters we showed how Jesus makes clear to us the Christological sense in which we are to read the Scriptures. The preaching of the apostles shows this very thing. In Solomon's portico after Pentecost Peter preaches about the risen Jesus, "the Holy and Righteous One" who is the "Author of life" raised from the dead by the Father (Acts 3:14). All that God had declared "by the mouth of all the prophets, that his Christ would suffer, he thus fulfilled" (Acts 3:18, 21). Both Moses and Samuel spoke about Him (Acts 3:22, 24). He is the blessing promised to the nations from the seed of Abraham who has come and been raised from the dead (Acts 3:26–27). Similarly, in his great sermon at Pentecost Peter begins by directing his hearers to what the prophets of old proclaimed. The sermon is thoroughly trinitarian. It is the Spirit that points us to the Son and the Son who reveals to us the Father. Peter follows this pattern in his sermon by beginning with the Spirit and ending with the Father. He starts with an introductory verse from Isaiah and then a lengthy quote from Joel: "And in the last days it shall be, God declares, that I will pour out my Spirit on all flesh, and your sons and your daughters shall prophesy, and your young men shall see visions, and your old men shall dream dreams . . . And it shall come to pass that everyone who calls upon the name of the Lord shall be saved" (Acts 2:17–21; Is 2:2; Mi 4:1; Jl 2:28–32). The Spirit points to the Son, in whose name all who believe have eternal life (Jn 3:16–18; 1 Jn 5:13).

Lest we read too quickly through Peter's sermon, we need to recall the context from Joel for what Peter is saying. This context allows us to appreciate more fully the force of Peter's sermon and how three thousand souls could be saved by this one sermon (Acts 2:41). The one speaking in Joel is YHWH. He promises salvation to His people. YHWH our Elohim will send "the Teacher of Righteousness" (Jl 2:23), who is our abundance and treasure (Jl 2:24–26).[24] And it shall come to pass afterward that the Spirit of YHWH will be poured out (Jl 2:28; cf. Ez 39:29; Zec 12:10), and "everyone who calls on the name of YHWH shall be saved" (Jl 2:32). According to the prophets, the last days are the days of the coming Messiah (Isaiah 2; Micah 4). The Spirit of YHWH will be poured out in those days, and by Him people will call upon the "name" of YHWH and be saved. Peter's point is that these days have arrived. The Spirit of YHWH has been sent, and the name of YHWH that the people are to call upon is Jesus in whom forgiveness of sins and salvation alone is found (Acts 2:38; cf. Acts 4:12; Rom 10:9–13).

In his Pentecost sermon Peter moves from the Holy Spirit to the Son and then to the Father. The patriarch and prophet King David declared:

> I saw the Lord always before me, for he is at my right hand that I may not be shaken; therefore my heart was glad, and my tongue rejoiced; my flesh also will dwell in hope. For you will not abandon my soul to Hades, or let your Holy One see corruption. You have made known to me the paths of life; you will make me full of gladness with your presence. (Acts 2:25–28; Ps 16:8–11)

As Peter points out, David both died and was buried (Acts 2:29). These words were given by David as prophecy. They are about Christ. He is the Holy One (Lk 1:35; Mk 1:24–25; Jn 6:69; Acts 3:14) whose flesh saw no corruption. Moreover, after He was exalted by the Father "the promise of the Holy Spirit" was poured out (Acts 2:33; cf. Gal 3:14). Once again Peter appeals to the Psalms and the words of David: "The Lord said to my Lord, Sit at my right hand, until I make your enemies your footstool" (Acts 2:34; Ps 110:1). God the Father has made Jesus, the one crucified, both Lord and Christ. The Father is Lord; the

---

24. For a discussion of "Teacher of Righteousness," see Theodore Laetsch, *The Minor Prophets* (St. Louis: Concordia Publishing House, 1956), 125–26.

Son is Lord. They are both Lord and this we know by the Spirit who is Lord (2 Cor 3:17–18).

Throughout Acts the disciples, filled with the Holy Spirit, proclaim the salvation we have in Christ alone. Peter appears before the Sanhedrin and they ask him by what power or by what name he preaches. Peter, "filled with the Holy Spirit" (Acts 4:8), points to Christ crucified, the cornerstone, in whom alone there is salvation, "for there is no other name under heaven given among men by which we must be saved" (Acts 4:12). The Spirit points to Christ; those filled with the Spirit proclaim the salvation we have in Christ. When Stephen is filled with the Holy Spirit, he sees the glory of God and Jesus at His right hand (Acts 7:55). With Stephen especially we see that those filled with the Holy Spirit have the gifts of the Spirit. Stephen is "filled with wisdom and the Holy Spirit" (Acts 6:3); he is a man "filled with faith and the Holy Spirit" (Acts 6:5); again, he is a man "filled with grace and power" (Acts 6:8), and the people who argue with Him "could not withstand the wisdom and the Spirit with which he was speaking" (Acts 6:11). Later in Acts we read that "the disciples were filled with joy and with the Holy Spirit" (Acts 13:52).

When the Holy Spirit is poured forth upon the people of God, when He fills a believer, He brings to them faith, love, joy, wisdom, grace, power, and confidence to speak the Word of God. These gifts of God come to us from the Holy Spirit. Paul writes, "God's love has been poured into our hearts through the Holy Spirit who has been given us" (Rom 5:5). The Father pours out His Spirit, the Spirit of the Father, through Jesus Christ our Savior. Again Paul writes:

> But when the goodness and loving kindness of God our Savior appeared, he saved us, not because of works done by us in righteousness, but according to his own mercy, by the washing of regeneration and renewal of the Holy Spirit, whom he poured out on us richly through Jesus Christ our Savior, so that being justified by his grace we might become heirs according to the hope of eternal life. (Ti 3:4–7)

As seen in chapter 8, Paul refers to both the Father and the Son as Savior in his short letter to Titus. Their salvation we receive through holy baptism by the regenerating and renewing working of the Holy Spirit, whom the Father pours out upon us through Jesus Christ our Savior. As Luther succinctly puts it, the Trinity saves.

The work of creation and redemption involves the Spirit as much as the Father and the Son. The three are distinct but inseparable. A consistent feature of the Spirit's work is that He points all people to the Son. He rests upon the patriarchs and prophets, that they might proclaim the promises of the Father that find fulfillment in the Son. He rests upon the Christ in His economic work and is sent by the Father and the Son following Christ's saving work, that all might call upon the name of YHWH, the name of Jesus, and be saved. Likewise, when the people of God rebel, when they turn to their own ways and forget what God has done for them and promised to them, they are said to "grieve" the Holy Spirit (Is 63:10; Eph 4:30). When the faithful see their sin and know that sin to be against God (Ps 51:4), they repent, pray that their sins be washed away and that a clean heart be created within them, that the Holy Spirit not be taken from them (Ps 51:11). To have the Holy Spirit, as David continues in his psalm, is to have the joy of salvation (v. 12), to teach sinners about God's way and His salvation (v. 13), to sing aloud of His righteousness (v. 14), to declare His praise (v. 15). All of this proceeds from the Holy Spirit who rests within. The same Holy Spirit who filled David fills Elizabeth, Zechariah, and John the Baptist, fills Peter, Stephen, and the disciples, and indeed fills all believers who confess that Jesus is the Christ, the Son of God, and who proclaim salvation in Him alone, delighting in the joy, love, grace, and power of God that is ours through the working of the Holy Spirit in us.

THE HOLY SPIRIT AND THE CHURCH

We said above that we cannot know the Father or the Son apart from the Spirit. For this reason both the Father and the Son send the Holy Spirit to us (Jn 14:26; 15:26). We have access to the Father through the Son in the Spirit (Eph 3:18). The Spirit works faith in our hearts to confess Christ as Lord to the glory of the Father. The Spirit works this faith in the church through Word and sacrament, making sinners pure and holy (1 Cor 6:11). Here, in the ordered means of grace, the Spirit is present and at work. Those who look elsewhere for the Spirit seek that which is not the Holy Spirit. The Lutheran Confessions state this clearly: "The Father will not [draw us to Christ] without means, and he has ordained Word and sacraments as the ordinary means or instruments to accomplish this end."[25] Scripture knows of no separation between Word and Spirit, nor do our Confessions. Where the Word is proclaimed, the Spirit is with certainty at work. Luther writes, "We should and must constantly maintain that God will not deal with us except through His external Word and sacrament. Whatever is attributed to the Spirit apart from such Word and sacrament is of the devil."[26] The Father and the Son send the Spirit to us to bring us to faith through Word and sacrament. The Spirit takes the words of Christ and speaks them to us, pointing us always to Christ (Jn 14:26; 15:26) and working faith in our hearts (Rom 10:17). These words of faith, of doctrine, nourish us (1 Tm 4:6 KJV); they are our pure spiritual milk (1 Pt 2:2). The Spirit uses the Word to nourish us and enlighten us (Ps 119:105), the Word He gave to the prophets of old (2 Pt 1:21) who proclaimed the saving work of Christ by the Spirit (1 Pt 1:11–12). This is why the Spirit, the Lord and giver of life, remains linked inseparably to the proclamation of the gospel.

Paul proclaims the gospel not according to his own cleverness but according to the Spirit. And this he does so that our faith may repose in God and not man. Paul writes, "My speech and my message were not in plausible words of

---

25. SD XI.76 (Tappert, 628).
26. SA III.viii.10 (Tappert, 313).

wisdom, but in demonstration of the Spirit and of power, that your faith might not rest in the wisdom of men but in the power of God" (1 Cor 2:4-5). To the Thessalonians he writes, "Our Gospel came to you not only in word, but also in power and in the Holy Spirit and with full conviction" (1 Thes 1:5). The gospel preached by Paul in power and in the Holy Spirit brings to us "the joy of the Holy Spirit" (1 Thes 1:6). As God makes use of water, wine, and bread to convey His grace and forgiveness, He makes use of Paul, and, in our day, His called and ordained servants of the Word, to proclaim His gospel and administer His sacraments to His people. Here the Holy Spirit creates and sustains the faith of those who belong to the Body of Christ.

Paul emphasizes that it is by the gospel that we receive the Holy Spirit. After proclaiming that we are justified not by works of the law but through faith in Jesus Christ, which means we have died to the law and live to God, indeed that Christ lives in us (Gal 2:15-21), Paul asks the Galatians, "Did you receive the Spirit by works of the law or by hearing with faith?" (Gal 3:2). He asks the question again, and this time brings Abraham into the conversation. Abraham believed God and his faith was counted to him as righteousness (Gal 3:6). Those of faith are sons of Abraham, the man of faith. The same gospel that justified Abraham justifies the Gentiles by faith (Gal 3:8-9). Paul emphasizes this point in Romans: "The words 'it was counted to him' were not written for his sake alone, but for ours also" (Rom 4:23-24). God promised Abraham that all nations would be blessed in him. Paul tells us this has happened with Christ. Our interest is how he connects this to the Spirit. He writes, "In Christ Jesus the blessing of Abraham [came] to the Gentiles, so that we might receive the promised Spirit through faith" (Gal 3:14). Above we noted how Peter emphasizes the promise of the Spirit from the Father (Acts 2:33). Here Paul too directs the Galatians to the Father's promise of the Spirit which they receive by faith in Christ. Only when we confess Christ as Lord, recognizing Him as the only-begotten Son of the Father, do we also come to know and rejoice in the Spirit of Christ that dwells within us. A proper understanding of the Spirit always places Christ at the center.

The chief gift or charism of the Spirit is faith in the saving work of Christ. This He brings about through the hearing of the Word and baptism. When we come to faith, we recognize and know Jesus, the true Son of God, and through Him we know the Father and the Spirit. The Spirit who brings us to faith and sustains us in that faith is the Spirit of Christ who dwells in us and intercedes for us. It is through Him that we become "sons of God, through faith" (Gal 3:26). Elsewhere Paul explains that those who are sons of God are coheirs with Christ and live "by the Spirit of God" (Rom 8:14). We are set free in Christ by the Spirit and "walk not according to the flesh but according to the Spirit" (Rom 8:4; Gal 3:29). This freedom is joy and life and Paul connects it with baptism. Those who have "put on Christ," which as seen above occurs by the working of the Holy Spirit, are those who "were baptized into Christ" (Gal 3:27). When we are baptized into Christ, we are "baptized into his death" (Rom 6:3). What does this mean? Paul explains, "We were buried therefore with him by baptism into death, in order that, just as Christ was raised from the dead by the glory of the Father, we too might walk in newness of life" (Rom 6:4). At the heart of our baptism we find the death and resurrection of Christ, we find our death to sin and our freedom to live in Christ, loving and serving our neighbor in the ordinary places of our vocations. The shorthand expression for this death and new life is the forgiveness of sins. Where there is forgiveness there is also life and salvation. That life comes to us by the Holy Spirit, the Lord and giver of life, who dwells in us richly and unites us to Christ. Paul writes,

> You . . . are not in the flesh but in the Spirit, if in fact the Spirit of God dwells in you. Anyone who does not have the Spirit of Christ does not belong to him. But if Christ is in you, although the body is dead because of sin, the Spirit is life because of righteousness. If the Spirit of him who raised Jesus from the dead dwells in you, he who raised Christ Jesus from the dead will also give life to your mortal bodies through his Spirit who dwells in you. (Rom 8:9–11)

The Spirit who dwells in us is the Spirit of God the Father, the Spirit of Christ. He regenerates and renews us in holy baptism (Ti 3:5), which means He buries us by baptism into Christ's death, putting to death our sin and imputing to us Christ's righteousness, that we might walk in newness of life as sons of God, coheirs with Christ, crying out "Abba, Father" (Rom 8:12–17). Paul never tires of summarizing this teaching on baptism. In addition to Titus 3 he also writes, "You were washed [i.e., baptized], you were sanctified, you were justified in the name of the Lord Jesus Christ and by the Spirit of our God" (1 Cor 6:11). God alone recreates us and makes us new through baptism. For this reason Luther framed the Christian day and indeed the whole Christian life around baptismal dying and living: "Thus a Christian life is nothing else than a daily baptism, once begun and ever continued."[27] Luther continues by describing how the believer "daily" plunges into his baptism, putting the old Adam to death and rising in Christ. He aligns penance with baptism. If you live in repentance, you walk in baptism. And this, explains Luther, produces and promotes the "new life" brought about by the power and grace of the Holy Spirit.[28] The life of sanctification involves the daily remembrance of one's baptism. Apart from baptism the life of sanctification, the Christian walk, dislodges itself from justification and the righteousness of Christ.

Paul further connects baptism with the church, the Body of Christ. Paul expresses this in the context of his reflection on husbands and wives. He writes,

> Husbands, love your wives, as Christ loved the church and gave himself up for her, that he might sanctify her, having cleansed her by the washing of water with

---

27. LC IV.65 (Tappert, 445).
28. LC IV.71–76 (Tappert, 445–46). No one in the history of the church has a more robust theology of baptism than Luther. In my opinion, the closest theologian to Luther on baptism is Gregory of Nazianzus.

the word, so that he might present the church to himself in splendor, without spot or wrinkle or any such thing, that she might be holy and without blemish. (Eph 5:25–27)

Christ and the church serve as the image of marriage between husband and wife. Christ, the head of the church, gave Himself up for her, purchased her with His own blood (Acts 20:28 KJV), and cleansed her through the washing of baptism by the Word that He might present His Bride, the church, to Himself without spot or blemish. Sanctification and baptism go together. Further, the Body of Christ is the household of God, built on the foundation of the apostles and prophets, Christ the cornerstone, and this by the Spirit (Eph 2:18–22). When Paul says that we access the Father through the Son in the Spirit (Eph 2:18), he speaks concretely about the place where that happens: the church. The Spirit who is our guarantee (Eph 1:14; 2 Cor 1:22; 5:5) is the Spirit of the Father, the Spirit of the Son, sent to us to create and sustain faith through Word and sacrament, and these are the marks of the church. The Spirit works through the divinely appointed office of ministry (Jn 20:21–23) to bring us to the Son and His saving benefits, and herein we find our access to the Father. There is no enthusiasm or disorder envisioned by Paul. The Spirit is a Spirit of order, bestowing a diversity of gifts, to be sure, but the chief gift, the chief charism, is new life in Christ to the glory of the Father (1 Cor 12:1–31). In faithfulness to Scripture we insist that the Father sends His Spirit to us through Word and sacrament to draw us to Christ and to keep us in Him. Our Confessions insist upon this when they emphasize that the Holy Spirit brings us to faith through the Word and sacrament as through means.[29] The Word is the means used by the Holy Spirit to bring about conversion;[30] apart from the Word, apart from means, the Holy Spirit does not bring about conversion.[31]

CONCLUSION

Two statements occur with regularity in the literature on the Trinity today. Routinely we are told by biblical scholars and some theologians that the doctrine of the Trinity cannot be found in the Bible.[32] For them it belongs to the history of the church and the labors of the church Fathers. Orthodox writers will grant that the Fathers used Scripture to confess the Trinity, but whatever form the Trinity has in Scripture, it is at best rudimentary.[33] Although the Fathers assembled the

---

29. AC V (Tappert, 31); cf. AC XVIII (Tappert, 39).
30. Ep. II.19 (Tappert, 472).
31. Ep. II.4 (Tappert, 470).
32. Donald Juel, "The Trinity in the New Testament," *Theology Today* 54 (1997): 313: "The New Testament contains no doctrine of the Trinity." Emil Brunner, *The Christian Doctrine of God: Dogmatics*, trans. Olive Wyon (Philadelphia: The Westminster Press, 1950), 1:236: "The doctrine of the Trinity itself, however, is not a Biblical doctrine, and this indeed not by accident but of necessity." Cf. Robert Jenson, "The Bible and the Trinity," *Pro Ecclesia* XI:3 (2002): 329.
33. Robert Jenson, "The Trinity in the Bible," *Concordia Theological Quarterly* 68 (2004): 196: "Some historicists take the supposed post-biblical status of the doctrine of Trinity as

witness of Scripture in such a way as to confess the consubstantial Trinity, the suggestion, it seems, is that something else could have been confessed.[34] This position further implies that no trinitarian consciousness can be found among the biblical writers. Second, we are told that the Holy Spirit is the unknown God or forgotten God among Western Christians.[35] Pentecostals and charismatics emphasize the "Spirit," but the other more institutional and sacramental Christians lack an awareness of the Spirit's gifts and activity among the faithful.

Those who think the doctrine of the Trinity belongs to the history of the church and not to the Bible use the word "doctrine" in a peculiar way. Likewise, those who think Pentecostals and charismatics emphasize the "Spirit" and others do not have a peculiar way of understanding the person and work of the Holy Spirit. If doctrine means technical theological terms and precise formulae, along the lines of the later creeds, then the Bible does not offer such a thing. If doctrine means teaching, then without doubt the Bible teaches the triune identity of the one true God as Father, Son, and Holy Spirit. If having the "spirit" means ecstatic experience removed from Christ and apart from Word and sacrament, then the "spirit" had is not that promised in the Scriptures as the Holy Spirit. In both cases, the above two statements appearing with regularity in our day proceed with judgments not derived from Scripture but with expectations conforming to our best ideas or desires.

A faulty view of the Spirit always results in a defective Christology, which by necessity results in a rejection of the Trinity. Oneness Pentecostals are evidence of this. Although they speak at length about Jesus and the Spirit, they reject the Trinity and therefore deny the God of the Bible. The history of the church has shown us that when the Trinity is rejected, so too is the gospel. In all cases legalism alone prevails. We live in a day when many Bible scholars, not a few of whom still claim Christianity, assert that the Bible does not teach the doctrine of the Trinity. To make that claim is no different than saying the Bible does not teach Christianity. To deny the Trinity is to deny Christianity. We also live in a world in which the fastest-growing "denomination" is Pentecostalism, which either denies or distorts the Trinity. To separate the Spirit and the Son is to advance ideas about God unknown to Scripture. To remove the Spirit from the means of grace, from the very things given to create, nourish, and sustain

---

liberation from what they anyway regard as an absurd doctrine. Others will say things like I used to, that while the doctrine of the Trinity is indeed not in Scripture, it is a proper development from things that are in Scripture—and indeed I might still say this in certain contexts, but have come to see that it is but a small part of the truth."

34. Juel, "The Trinity in the New Testament," 313: "Full-blown trinitarian faith is a later, creative interpretation of the biblical witness by the church."

35. Cf. Robert Jenson, *Systematic Theology* (Oxford: Oxford University Press, 1997), 1:153; Walter Kaspar, *The God of Jesus Christ* (New York, NY: Crossroad, 1984), 198. Pope Francis's apostolic exhortation *Evangelii Gaudium* received the following praise in a review: "The emphasis upon the Trinity's most neglected member—the Holy Spirit—in the Church's life is especially inspiring." Samuel Gregg, "Pope Francis and Poverty," in The Corner, *National Review Online*, 26 November 2013.

faith in us, is to reject the Body of Christ, the church. The battle in our day over the Bible and the Spirit go to the heart of Christianity. We must relearn the exegesis of the Fathers and the reformers, the voice of the church, and continue to preach, teach, pray, sing, and live according to our baptismal faith. Gregory of Nyssa exhorts us to do this very thing. He writes:

> Hence we are baptized as it has been handed down to us, into *Father and Son and Holy Spirit*, and we believe as we are baptized—for it is fitting that our confession be of one voice with our faith—and we give glory as we believe, for it is not natural that worship make war against faith, but as we believe, so also we give glory. Now since our faith is in *Father and Son and Holy Spirit*, faith, worship, and baptism accord with each other.[36]

Many centuries later Luther would say very similar things. As we have had occasion to see, Luther frames the Christian life around baptism. A right understanding of baptism preserves the gospel and the salvation of the Trinity. We should join our voices to Luther's and declare, "I am baptized, instructed with the word alone, absolved, and partake of the Lord's Supper. But with the word and through the word the Holy Spirit is present, and the whole Trinity works salvation, as the words of baptism declare."[37] Both Gregory and Luther spoke in this way because they knew the Bible was thoroughly trinitarian, that our salvation was accomplished and worked in us by the Trinity through the divinely appointed means of grace, and that all of this was rightly contemplated and lived in our baptism.

---

36. Gregory of Nyssa *Letter* 24.8 in *Gregory of Nyssa: The Letters*, trans. Anna M. Silvas (Leiden: Brill, 2007), 194.

37. Martin Luther, *Lectures on Genesis*, 1535–45 (AE 8:264; WA 44:773.4–6).

11

THE PROCESSION OF THE HOLY SPIRIT

In the previous chapter we showed how Scripture reveals the divine identity of the Holy Spirit. He is Lord and God in the same way the Father and Son are Lord and God. He creates and judges, He directs human history, and He delivers to us the salvation of the Father accomplished in the Son through the divinely instituted office of ministry and the ordered means of grace. Apart from the Holy Spirit there is no salvation, for apart from Him no one can call upon the name of Jesus in whom alone we have reconciliation with the Father and the righteousness that avails for eternal life. It is by that same Spirit that we go forth in Christian freedom, loving and serving our neighbors in the places God has called us and proclaiming in word and deed the salvation of the Lord our God.

We also have emphasized in the previous few chapters the inseparability of the Son and the Spirit. Every significant event in the human life of Jesus involves the Holy Spirit. From birth to baptism, from temptation to trial, the Holy Spirit is upon Jesus and at work with Him for our salvation. Following the resurrection the Son breathes the Spirit upon the disciples, instituting the ministry of the Word; following the ascension of our Lord the Holy Spirit is poured out upon all believers. Although this same Spirit worked in the Old Testament through the patriarchs, judges, and prophets, and worked during the life of Christ by filling Zechariah, Elizabeth, John the Baptist, and Simeon among others, that they might point to the Christ and proclaim His salvation, something decisive occurs with Pentecost. Both the Father and the Son had promised to send the Spirit to us, to take the words of Christ, which are the words of the Father, and to speak them to us, creating and sustaining faith within us—in short, turning us from our sin to our life in Christ, and all of this to the delight of the Father.

A pressing theological question that arises in the early church concerns the eternal relationship that avails between Father, Son, and Holy Spirit. How are they one? How are they three? How might we distinguish these three persons without compromising their unity? How might we talk about their unity without collapsing their diversity? They are eternally distinct from one another as three and yet inseparably united as one. Scripture makes this clear throughout both testaments. Although we will take up the theological reasoning of the church on these questions in the next few chapters, we need to address in this chapter the origin of the Spirit and whether He proceeds from the Father alone or from the Father *and the Son* (*filioque*). Our convictions compel us to address this question here, in our chapters on scriptural identity, and not as part of the dogmatic history of the church. The Lutheran position on the *filioque* stands on Scripture.

The later Orthodox objection against the *filioque* derives from controversy and a particular theological judgment. They posit a sharp distinction between eternal procession and temporal mission that was not widely held in the early church and was understood differently by the theologians of the West, including our Lutheran fathers. That objection becomes central to the Orthodox argument only at the beginning of the medieval period, when the controversy emerges, and therefore belongs to a later period of the church than the initial teaching found among the Fathers on how the Spirit eternally relates to the Son.[1] It is vitally important to recognize this fact. The commitments of the Latin church, early and medieval, to the *filioque*, the very commitments embraced by our Lutheran fathers and confessed in the Book of Concord, arose first from their reading of Scripture and not in response to the later controversy.[2] Before there was such a thing as the *filioque* controversy, the theologians and creeds of the Western church had long established the scriptural teaching of the Spirit's procession from the Father and the Son.

A BRIEF HISTORY OF THE *FILIOQUE*

The addition of the *filioque* to the Western Nicene Creed has a long and complicated history.[3] It becomes fixed in the Western liturgy as a whole only

---

1. David Bentley Hart, an Orthodox theologian, writes, "Since the time of Vladimir Lossky, various modern Orthodox theologians have, in their assault on 'filioquism', adopted an exaggerated 'Photianism', and argued that between God's acts in the economy of salvation and God's eternal life of generation and procession there is not an exact correspondence of order.... This, however, is a theologically disastrous course to tread, and one that leads away from the genuine Orthodox tradition altogether. One might note, to begin with, that were this claim sound, the arguments by which the Cappadocians defended the full Trinitarian theology against Arian and Eunomian theology—in works like Basil's *De Spiritu Sancto* and Gregory's *Adversus Macedonianos*—would entirely fall apart; more terribly, however, behind such a severance of the *ordines* of the economic and immanent Trinities from one another lies the quite unexorcisable spectre of nominalism ... all of which is quite repugnant to patristic tradition." David Bentley Hart, "The Mirror of the Infinite: Gregory of Nyssa on the *Vestigia Trinitatis*," *Modern Theology* 18:4 (2002): 559 n. 11.

2. Apart from the Nicene Creed and the Athanasian Creed, the Book of Concord mentions the *filioque* only twice: SA I.2 (Tappert, 291) and SD VIII.73 (Tappert, 605). Luther merely mentions it. The Formula briefly reflects upon it: "Since Christ according to his Godhead is the second person in the holy Trinity and the Holy Spirit proceeds from him as well as from the Father (and therefore he is and remains to all eternity his and the Father's own Spirit, who is never separated from the Son), it follows that through the personal union the entire fullness of the Spirit (as the ancient Fathers say) is communicated to Christ according to the flesh that is personally united with the Son of God."

3. For a review of the history of the *filioque* see A. Edward Siecienski, *The Filioque: A History of a Doctrinal Controversy* (Oxford: Oxford University Press, 2010); Brian Daley, "Revisiting the *Filioque*: Roots and Branches of an Old Debate," *Pro Ecclesia* 10 (2001): 31–62; Brian Daley, "Revisiting the *Filioque*: Contemporary Catholic Approaches," *Pro Ecclesia* 10 (2001): 195–212; J. N. D. Kelly, *Early Christian Creeds*, 3d ed. (London: Longman, 1972), 358–67. See also Bernard Lonergan, *The Triune God: Doctrines* (Toronto: University of Toronto Press, 2009), 517–31.

during the eleventh century. Two centuries before this Charlemagne had inserted the *filioque* into the creed for the Franks, and that altered creed was used in the liturgy at Aachen and by Frankish missionaries to Bulgaria. The presence of these missionaries in lands under the jurisdiction of the Orthodox created problems; their use of the *filioque* added fuel to the fire. The pope at the time, Leo III, refused to change the wording of the Nicene Creed in the Roman liturgy, as Charlemagne had done in the north, but agreed with the teaching.

The use of the *filioque* does not originate with Charlemagne. Although the so-called *filioque* controversy owes much to Charlemagne's antipathy toward the Orthodox, the teaching itself goes back long before him. Apart from the altered Nicene Creed, the procession of the Spirit from the Father and the Son had been confessed already in local creeds in the West. The most famous of these creeds is the fifth-century Athanasian Creed, which states, "The Holy Ghost is of the Father and the Son, neither made nor created nor begotten, but proceeding."[4] Somewhat similarly, a creed dating from the late fourth century confesses, "We believe . . . in the Holy Spirit, not begotten nor unbegotten, not created nor made, but proceeding from the Father and the Son."[5] The first association of the *filioque* with the Nicene Creed occurs at the Third Council of Toledo (589). The bishops at this council taught the *filioque* as a part of the Nicene Creed and condemned any who did not teach that the Spirit proceeds from the Father and the Son (*a Patre et Filio procedere*).[6]

Creeds summarize long-held beliefs. They may use unfamiliar language to do this (e.g., *homoousios*) but their dogmatic content derives from the liturgy of the people and long-held understandings of Scripture. We find this pattern with the *filioque*. Both Greek and Latin fathers taught it long before any creed confessed it. Hilary of Poitiers, like many of his Greek contemporaries, assumes something like the *filioque* without using the exact expression. Ambrose and Augustine taught it explicitly; Fulgentius of Ruspe thought it genuinely apostolic.[7] From this perspective the addition of the *filioque* into the Nicene Creed by the later Western church should be seen more in terms of aligning the theology of the Creed with long-held dogmatic and liturgical commitments, expressed by theologians, councils, and earlier creeds. Given this brief sketch of the history, we can understand why Charlemagne's theologians thought the *filioque* must have been a part of the original Nicene Creed and was subsequently removed by the Greeks.[8]

The *filioque* has two very different histories. On the one hand there is the heated debate between the Latin and Greek churches beginning in the eighth

---

4. TLH, p. 53.
5. Kelly, *Early Christian Creeds*, 360.
6. Kelly, *Early Christian Creeds*, 361-62.
7. For Hilary, Ambrose, and Augustine see the discussion below. For Fulgentius see Siecienski, *The Filioque*, 67-68.
8. *Opus Caroli regis contra synodum* (= Libri Carolini), 3.3, ed. Ann Freeman (Hanover, Germany: Hahnsche Buchhandlung, 1998); Siecienski, *The Filioque*, 91-93.

and ninth centuries, continuing throughout the medieval and Reformation periods, and remaining to this day. Much of this history is regrettable and full of caricature. On the other hand, there is the affirmation, variously stated by the Fathers, both Greek and Latin, that the Spirit in some way proceeds from the Son, derives from the Son, depends upon the Son, or flows forth from the Son. These various expressions were guided by Scripture and aimed to say something significant about the Holy Spirit and His eternal relation to the Father and the Son. These different ways of stating what Scripture reveals had nothing to do with compromising the Nicene Creed (which neither affirmed nor denied the Spirit's procession from the Son) or with agreeing or disagreeing with the later *filioque* controversy.[9] It is necessary to free the Fathers from the later theological judgments of this controversy. Unfortunately most of the literature on the Fathers remains stubbornly committed to these later judgments. In what follows we will lay out the scriptural argument for the procession of the Spirit from both the Father and the Son, show the way in which the Fathers expressed this scriptural teaching, and end with a comment on the theological significance of the *filioque*.

SCRIPTURAL TEACHING ON THE SPIRIT'S PROCESSION

Scripture distinguishes Father, Son, and Holy Spirit from one another by emphasizing their different ways of existing. The Fathers use the phrase mode or manner of existence (τρόπος τῆς ὑπάρξεως) to express this. For example, Scripture states that the Son is the only-begotten (Ps 2:7 [Heb 1:5]; Jn 1:14, 18; 3:16, 18 KJV). Only-begotten is a term expressing relation; it is said about the Son with reference to the Father. If it were used to describe His essence, that the Son was "only-begotten-ness" in His substance, then either the Father and the Holy Spirit would have to be described in the same way or it would follow that the Son was not God in the same way as the Father and Holy Spirit. The Son alone is only-begotten, and this term expresses His relation to the Father. By implication the Father is unbegotten, which is to say nothing more than not-begotten or not the Son. If the Son was begotten of the Father, what about the Holy Spirit? Although Scripture has less to say here, it is not entirely silent on the question. John tells us that the Holy Spirit proceeds from the Father (Jn 15:26). The Son is begotten and the Spirit proceeds. Procession belongs to the Spirit and expresses His relation to the Father. This way of distinguishing the persons, which derives from Scripture, becomes standard for the Fathers and

---

9. The original Creed said merely that the Spirit proceeds from the Father, using the language of Jn 15:26. It did not say, nor did it imply, that the Spirit proceeds from the Father alone and apart from the Son. Even the Greek theologians of the fourth and fifth centuries emphasized that the Spirit proceeds from the Father through the Son, which meant that the Spirit's procession involves the Son and should never be conceived of as apart from the Son. Cf. Gregory of Nyssa *Letter* 35, 4d in *Gregory of Nyssa: The Letters*, trans. Anna M. Silvas (Leiden: Brill, 2007), 253.

finds a home in the Nicene and Athanasian Creeds. The Son is begotten of the Father, and the Spirit proceeds from the Father.

In chapter 9 we drew attention to John's language for expressing the eternal relationship between the Father and the Son and the Father and the Spirit. In the prologue John refers to Christ as "the only-begotten Son *from the Father*" (παρὰ πατρός). As mentioned above, the language of "only-begotten" is relational. John makes that plain here by adding the phrase "from the Father." He underscores the eternal relation between the Son and the Father, the only-begotten and the unbegotten. Later in the Gospel Jesus uses the same expression to describe His eternal relationship with the Father: "I came from the Father [παρὰ τοῦ πατρὸς] and have come into the world, and now I am leaving the world and going to the Father" (Jn 16:28). We find this same phrasing with the Holy Spirit. Jesus says, "But when the Helper comes, whom I will send to you from the Father [παρὰ τοῦ πατρός], the Spirit of truth, who proceeds from the Father [παρὰ τοῦ πατρὸς], he will bear witness about me" (Jn 15:26). The same phrasing used to describe the eternal relationship between the Father and the Son is used by Jesus to describe the relationship between the Father and the Spirit. The church later will describe these relationships as the eternal generation of the Son from the Father and the eternal procession of the Spirit from the Father.

The language used by Jesus bears directly on the question of the *filioque*. When Scripture speaks about the divine persons, the language of being from someone corresponds to being sent by that same person. For example, Scripture states that the Son and the Spirit are both from the Father and sent by the Father. There is congruence here. We may say, according to Scripture, that the Son is from the Father or that the Father sends the Son. Although the order of times differs—from the Father refers to the eternal generation of the Son and being sent by the Father refers to the Son's temporal mission—both expressions correspond to one another and reflect the eternal order, the interior order, of the Father to the Son. Similarly, we may say that the Spirit is from the Father and the Father sends the Spirit. Both expressions reveal to us something real and true concerning the eternal relation of the Father and the Spirit. The language of "sending" pertains to the economic or temporal mission of the Son or the Spirit, and corresponds to the eternal origin of that person "from" the Father. Why should that be the case? The answer is rather simple. We may know God only insofar as He reveals Himself, shows Himself, to us. Therefore, whatever we may say about the Trinity either in time or eternity, economically or immanently, must be learned from God's history with us. There is no way of getting beyond or behind this history. This means that what the Father, Son, and Holy Spirit do in time for our salvation also reveals to us their eternal relations apart from creation and salvation. This insight is at the heart of Latin trinitarian thinking and bears directly on how Lutherans think about the church and the means of grace.

The Fathers and the later dogmatic tradition of the medieval and Reformation periods further appeal to the order of persons (τάξις, *taxis*) confessed in Scripture. The First Person of the Trinity is the Father, the Second Person is the Son, and the Third Person is the Holy Spirit. This order has significance for how we think about the persons and corresponds to what we have charted above. The Father sends the Son; the Son is from the Father. Those expressions reflect the order of the persons made known to us throughout the Scriptures and bears on the question of origin. We read about the Son of the Father and the Spirit of the Father but never the Father of the Spirit. What about the Son and the Spirit? Do we find a similar use of language with them? Here we need to work backwards. By looking at the language of "sending" and at the order of persons we will learn about the eternal relation that avails between the Son and the Spirit. When we further ask why it matters that the Spirit's person and life are derived from the Father and the Son (*filioque*), we find ourselves at the heart of the issue.

On three occasions Jesus refers to the Holy Spirit as sent by the Father and by Him. Jesus says, "These things I have spoken to you while I am still with you. But the Helper, the Holy Spirit, whom the Father will send in my name, he [ἐκεῖνος] will teach you all things and bring to your remembrance all that I have said to you" (Jn 14:25–26). Jesus emphasizes the mutual sending of the Holy Spirit from the Father and Himself. Although Spirit in Greek is neuter and requires neuter pronouns, we find here the deliberate use of the masculine pronoun for the Spirit, underscoring the distinct and separate hypostatic existence of the Holy Spirit from the Father and the Son. Jesus' second mention of the mutual sending of the Spirit occurs in Jn 15:26, where, as quoted above, He further states that the Spirit proceeds from the Father. Immediately after this He mentions the sending of the Spirit for a third time: "Nevertheless, I tell you the truth: it is to your advantage that I go away, for if I do not go away, the Helper will not come to you. But if I go, I will send him to you" (Jn 16:7). Here Jesus alone says that He will send the Spirit. The language is interchangeable. We may say the Father sends the Spirit, the Son sends the Spirit, or both send the Spirit. The sending of the Spirit involves both Father and Son even if only one is mentioned. And yet we are not talking about two sendings, two missions, but one. In that sense we could restrict our language further and say that the Father of the Son principally (*principaliter*) sends the Spirit. Since Scripture nowhere locates the sending of the Spirit from the Son as something the Son receives in time, it follows that the sending belongs to Him eternally as the Son and therefore was given to Him by the Father in His begetting.

In the above three passages from the Gospel of John two things are stated: the Father and the Son "send" the Holy Spirit and the Spirit "proceeds" from the Father. It is almost impossible for the reader today to see these two statements apart from the *filioque* controversy. We must, however, attempt this. Our chief problem is that we attach theological significance to the word "procession" and think of it only in the technical terms of the later creeds which contrast it with the Son's "generation" from the Father. Without taking anything away from that technical use and creedal history, we need to explore the wider sense of the term in Scripture. In the Vulgate the phrase "who proceeds from the Father" (Jn 15:26) is rendered *qui a Patre procedit*. Here the Latin *procedere* translates the Greek ἐκπορεύομαι. These words are used widely in the Bible and translated variously in our English Bibles. Although most English Bibles translate Jn 15:26 with the word "proceeds," a more literal translation would be "comes forth." The Spirit "comes forth" from the Father. Most of the other uses of this word in the New Testament have to do with what "comes forth" or "comes out of" the mouth. Jesus tells Satan, "Man shall not live by bread alone, but by every word that *comes from* the mouth of God" (Mt 4:4). Again Jesus says, "It is not what goes into the mouth that defiles a person, but what *comes out* of the mouth; this defiles a person" (Mt 15:11). Paul exhorts, "Let no corrupting talk *come out* of your mouths" (Eph 4:29).

The word used in John's Gospel to describe the relationship of the Spirit to the Father would have reminded both Greek and Latin readers of that which comes out of the mouth. This in turn would have reminded them of the Old Testament image of the Spirit as the breath of the Almighty or the breath of the mouth of YHWH. By now we have become quite familiar with these texts. Elihu declared to Job: "The Spirit of God has made me, and the breath of the Almighty gives me life" (Jb 33:4). In Psalm 33 we read, "By the Word of YHWH the heavens were made, and by the Breath of his mouth all their host" (Ps 33:6). The Father speaks all of creation into existence by His Word through His Spirit, the Breath of His mouth. This is the image of the Holy Spirit we encounter in Jn 15:26. The Spirit of YHWH, the breath of the Almighty Father, "comes forth" from Him but never apart from His Son, the Word of the Father. This way of putting it corresponds to what we discussed in our earlier chapters on the Father and the Son. Since the Father is always Father *of the Son* and the Son is always Son *of the Father*, to say either Father or Son always involves the other. For that reason the procession from the Father should be understood minimally as the procession from the Father of the Son. No matter what position you take on the *filioque*, the Scriptures never envision a separation of the Father and the Son.

Does that mean the Spirit comes forth only from the Father and not also from the Son? Before answering this question we need to look further at the use of *procedere* in the Bible. This same Latin word also may be used to translate the Greek word ἐξέρχομαι, which also may mean to come out from or proceed from.[10] This Greek word also denotes generation. The author of Hebrews uses this word to describe those who are descended or proceed from the loins of Abraham (Heb 7:5). A similar use may be found to describe the eternal generation of the Son from the Father. Jesus says, "If God were your

---

10. Although the Orthodox will not align these two Greek words, Scripture does. James 3:10, "From the same mouth come [ἐξέρχεται, *procedit*] blessing and cursing."

The Procession of the Holy Spirit

Father, ye would love me: for I proceeded forth [ἐξῆλθον] and came from [ἥκω] God; neither came I of myself, but he sent me" (Jn 8:42 KJV). A few chapters later Jesus says again: "I came forth [ἐξῆλθον] from the Father and am come into the world" (Jn 16:28 KJV). Because of texts such as these, the theologians of the medieval and Reformation periods used the language of procession in both a wide and narrow sense.[11] In its wider sense this language can be used for both the Son and the Spirit. Our hymns reflect this. About the Son we sing, "Glorious Lord, Thyself impart / Light of Light, from God proceeding; / Open Thou our ears and heart / Help us by Thy Spirit's pleading" (TLH 16:3). About the Spirit we sing in Paul Gerhardt's hymn on the Trinity ("The Mystery Hidden from the Eyes"):

> The Father hath the Son begot,
>   First-born of every creature;
> The Son took our weak flesh, but not
>   Our sinfulness of nature;
> Both from the Father and the Son
>   The Holy Ghost proceedeth
> From all eternity; yet none
>   In might and pow'r exceedeth;
> All equal, coeternal. (ELH 405:3; ELHB 264:3)

The term "procession" is commonly applied, states Thomas Aquinas, to anything denoting origin of any kind.[12] The Son's procession from the Father is properly called generation; the Spirit's procession is properly called spiration. Here we encounter a fundamental difference between East and West. For the medieval Byzantine theologians and for Fathers like Gregory of Nazianzus and Gregory of Nyssa, procession is a technical term applied only to the Spirit; for the Latin theologians of the medieval and Reformation periods the term lacks that sort of precision. Although the language may be a bit confusing, it arises from their reading of the Scriptures.[13]

For our purposes we need to observe the pattern set here by the Scriptures. The Son, begotten of the Father in all eternity, proceeds from Him and is sent by Him. That is to say, the Son proceeds in eternity from the Father and is sent in time by the Father. The two expressions stand next to one another and inform one another. The one sent by the Father is the one who proceeds eternally from Him as His only-begotten Son: "You are my Son; today I have begotten you" (Ps 2:7).[14] With all of this in mind we return to Jn 15:26 and see that the Spirit who proceeds or comes forth from the Father will be sent by the Son. Although we

---

11. See for example Thomas Aquinas *ST* I.27.1-4.
12. Thomas Aquinas *ST* I.36.2c.
13. The argument that our return to the Greek of the New Testament alleviates this problem does not suffice. The Vulgate translation indicates for us how these Greek words were understood by the Fathers. The later technical distinctions assigned these words are also attempts at translation. Recognizing this fact means only that the task of exegesis requires more than dictionaries.
14. Cf Ps 109:3 (Vulg.), "From the womb before the Daystar I begot you."

rightly distinguish here between the eternal origin of the Spirit and the sending in time of the Spirit, what warrant do we have to conclude further that the two are mutually exclusive? What prevents us from concluding, as the Latin tradition has done, that the sending of the Spirit in time reveals to us something about the eternal relationship of the Son and the Spirit?[15] This conclusion would be in keeping with the pattern set by Scripture, which consistently informs us of the eternal relationship between the Father and the Son by using language of the Son's origin from the Father or the temporal sending of the Son from the Father. Could not the same be indicated with the Son and the Spirit? For example, Jesus tells us that He will send the Holy Spirit. This occurs following the resurrection. In Jn 20:22 Jesus "breathes" on the disciples and says to them, "Receive [λάβετε, *accipite*] the Holy Spirit." The Spirit who comes forth from the Son is none other than the Spirit of the Son, who "receives" all that He is from the Son. Jesus explains, "All that the Father has is mine; therefore I said he will receive [λαμβάνει, *accipite*] what is mine and make it known to you" (Jn 16:15). Hilary of Poitiers aligns the above texts with Jn 15:26. He writes:

> Accordingly he "receives" from the Son, [this Spirit] who is both sent by him and proceeds from the Father (Jn 15:26, 16:14–15). Now I ask whether to receive from the Son is the same thing as to proceed from the Father. But if one believes that there is a difference between receiving from the Son and proceeding from the Father, surely to receive from the Son and to receive from the Father will be regarded as one and the same thing. . . . Such a unity admits no difference, nor does it make any difference from whom that is received, which, given by the Father is described as given by the Son.[16]

Although Hilary does not pursue the initial question he raises, it did not seem obvious to him that a sharp distinction should be drawn between "receiving" from the Son and "proceeding" from the Father. Elsewhere Hilary could simply state, "We must confess him [the Spirit] as having the Father and the Son as his source."[17]

Latin theologians found the eternal relationship of the Spirit to the Father and to the Son further taught in the way Scripture patterns our speech for the Spirit. The Holy Spirit is called the Spirit of God consistently throughout the Scriptures. This same Spirit is further identified as the Spirit of the Father (Mt 10:20), the Spirit of the Son (Gal 4:6), the Spirit of Christ (Phil 1:19; 1 Pt 1:11), and the Spirit of Jesus (Acts 16:7). At one point Paul refers to the Spirit as the

---

15. Johann Andreas Quenstedt, *Systema Theologicum* I, 9 (Wittenberg, 1691), 331: "The mission of the Holy Spirit in time upon and to the Apostles and other believers is the manifestation or consequence and effect of the eternal procession." Cf. Martin Luther, *The Three Symbols or Creeds of the Christian Faith*, 1538 (AE 34:217; WA 50:274.9-10): "The Holy Spirit proceeds from the Father and is sent by the Son. One who is sent, however, is also said to 'proceed from.'"

16. Hilary of Poitiers *De Trinitate* 8.20 (SC 448, p. 408), quoted in Daley, "Revisiting the *Filioque*: Roots and Branches," 38.

17. Hilary of Poitiers *De Trinitate* 2.29 (SC 443, p. 322). For this translation see Daley, "Revisiting the *Filioque*: Roots and Branches," 38. Also see Kelly, *Early Christian Creeds*, 358.

Spirit of God and the Spirit of Christ in the same verse (Rom 8:9). What do these genitives indicate? Certainly the relationship of the Spirit to the Father and the Son is indicated in some way with these expressions. What sort of relationship is that? These expressions correspond to the order of the persons in Scripture: the Father is the First Person, the Son the Second Person, and the Holy Spirit the Third Person of the Trinity. The genitives throughout the New Testament further teach this order of the persons. For example, Jesus is "the Son of the Most High" (Lk 1:32), the only-begotten Son of the Father (Jn 1:18), or, simply put, "the Son of the Father" (2 Jn 1:3 KJV). The relationship expressed with these genitives points to the origin of the Son; He is begotten of the Father in all eternity. The same conclusion reasonably follows for the expressions dealing with the Holy Spirit.[18] In the same way that the Spirit is the Spirit of God and the Spirit of the Father, He is also the Spirit of the Son and the Spirit of Christ. The Spirit who belongs to the Father proceeds from Him and is sent by Him. This Spirit also belongs to the Son, to Jesus Christ, and receives from Him and is sent by Him. Any objection to this understanding of the genitives would further entail an objection to the expressions about the Son of the Father and the Spirit of the Father. If Spirit of the Son does not point to the origin of the Spirit, then the Spirit of the Father cannot either. That these expressions should be taken to express origin accounts for why we never see them reversed. As Augustine points out, Scripture never says "Son of the Spirit" or "Christ of the Spirit."[19]

We see this order of the persons further expressed in Scripture with the dependence of one person on another. Jesus tells us that the Spirit "will not speak on his own authority" but will speak whatever He hears (Jn 16:13–14). The Spirit, who is the Spirit of the Son and the Spirit of the Father, depends upon the Father and the Son in His speaking. Similarly, the Son depends upon the Father: "The Son can do nothing of his own accord, but only what he sees the Father doing" (Jn 5:19). The language of dependence in no way diminishes the coequality and coeternity of the persons.[20] Rather this language points to the origin of the Son from the Father and the Spirit from the Father and the Son and corresponds to the deliberate use of genitives in Scripture for the persons: Son of the Father, Spirit of the Father, and Spirit of the Son. When we put these expressions together with the texts about the Son sending the Spirit, the broader sense of *procedere* as seen throughout Scripture, and the dependence of the Spirit upon the Son, we begin to understand why the fathers, both Greek and Latin, would either explicitly state that the Spirit proceeds from the Son or teach, without recourse to the term, the dependence of the Spirit upon the Son.

If all the above is true, why does Scripture never explicitly say the Spirit proceeds from the Son? Although many modern readers of Scripture might

---

18. Augustine *The Trinity* V.13 (WSA I/5, 197–98); Gerhard, *De Spiritu Sancto*, Locus 4/3, §20 (ed. Cotta, 302).
19. Augustine *The Trinity* V.12 (WSA I/5, 198).
20. For an extended discussion of dependence see Lonergan, *Triune God: Doctrines*, 534–47.

think this, premodern exegetes would not. For them Scripture does use the language of procession for the Spirit from the Father and the Son. On the last day of the Feast of Booths Jesus stands up and cries out, "If anyone thirsts, let him come to me and drink. Whoever believes in me, as the Scripture has said, 'Out of his heart will flow rivers of living water'" (Jn 7:37–38). What does that mean? John tells us: "Now this he said about the Spirit, whom those who believed in him were to receive, for as yet the Spirit had not been given, because Jesus was not yet glorified" (Jn 7:39). Jesus refers to a main idea of Scripture rather than to a particular verse. The river of living water reminds us of a number of texts in the Old Testament. We will take just one. In Ezekiel 47 the prophet sees the eschatological temple of God and the river of living water proceeding from it. This river gives life. Where this river is, life is found; apart from this river there is no life (Ez 47:9). This river issues from the temple. John has already informed us that Jesus spoke of the Holy Spirit. Where the Spirit is, life is; where life is, the Holy Spirit is.[21] Further, John identifies Jesus as the tabernacle/temple that dwells in the midst of us (cf. Zec 2:10–11; Ez 37:26–28). It is no stretch then to see the reference to the river of living water that proceeds from the temple as the Holy Spirit who gives and sustains life. John removes any doubt about this reading with what he sees in Revelation 22.

> Then the angel showed me the river of the water of life, bright as crystal, flowing from the throne of God and of the Lamb through the middle of the street of the city; also, on either side of the river, the tree of life with its twelve kinds of fruit, yielding its fruit each month. (Rv 22:1–2)

John's vision of the New Jerusalem focuses on the salvation accomplished for us by the Son and delivered to us by the Holy Spirit. The river of the water of life is as bright as crystal, indicating its pureness and holiness. This river brings life and flows from God and the Lamb. The river brings us to the tree of life that yields fruit continuously. The fruit of this tree is perfect, all-sufficient, and never-ending. That tree of life is the cross. We come to the cross and the benefits there won for us through the life-giving waters of baptism in which works the Holy Spirit, the Lord and giver of life. What is expressed here is not all that different from what Paul says in Titus. God our Father mercifully saved us by the washing of regeneration and renewal of the Holy Spirit, whom He poured out richly upon us through Jesus Christ our Savior. And this means we are justified by His grace (Ti 3:4–8). The life and holiness and righteousness given by the Holy Spirit through baptism is the life, righteousness, and holiness of Christ purchased for all upon the cross, the tree of life.

The Fathers did not hesitate to read Revelation 22 in this way. Ambrose focuses especially on the river that goes forth from God. The Holy Spirit is the river proceeding from the throne of God that the believer in Christ drinks,

---

21. Ambrose *On the Holy Spirit* I.15 (Fathers of the Church, 90).

The Procession of the Holy Spirit

as Christ Himself said in John 7.²² For Ambrose this text demonstrates the coequality of Father, Son, and Holy Spirit. It shows that the Spirit brings about the kingdom of God and reigns with Christ. Our Lutheran fathers continued this sort of reading but especially noted the language used by John. The word for "flowing" (ἐκπορευόμενον) is the same word used to describe the procession of the Spirit from the Father in John's Gospel (Jn 15:26). In Latin this text from Revelation reads "procedentem de throno Dei et agni."²³ We could just as easily translate as follows: "the river of the water of life, bright as crystal, proceeding from the throne of God and of the Lamb." The river of the water of life is the Spirit proceeding (ἐκπορευόμενον) from God the Father and the Lamb, Jesus Christ.²⁴ The Spirit, the river of life, is the Lord and giver of life, who delivers to us the merits of the Lamb to the glory of the Father, and all the benefits and graces of life. In the sixteenth century Georg Nigrinus made these points in his sermon on Revelation 22. He writes,

> That the Holy Spirit is this river of living water which proceeds from the Father and the Son (*vom Vater und Sohn ausgehet*) as the essential love and joy of the eternal Godhead (*Gottheit*), whereby the faithful become closely attached, joined and united to God the Father and God the Son and live in them, Christ, the Lord himself, attested in John 7, saying, "If any one thirsts, let him come to me and drink. He that believes in me, as Scripture has said, 'Out of his heart will flow rivers of living water.'" But this he spoke of the Spirit, says John, whom they that believe in him should receive.²⁵

For our Lutheran fathers this text on the river of living water, the river of life that proceeds from God and the Lamb, was a central text for demonstrating the

---

22. Ambrose of Milan *On the Holy Spirit* III, 20 (Fathers of the Church, 208-9).
23. Our Lutheran fathers give witness to a number of variations for this text. Gerhard sometimes substitutes "de throno" (throne) for "de sede" (seat). Calov and Quenstedt, as far as I can tell, use only "de throno." David Hollaz offers a different reading than all of them. He quotes the text in Greek and then in Latin. His Latin text reads "exeuntem e throno Dei et Agni," which may be his own translation. Although the Greek functions authoritatively for them all, Hollaz has the further task of showing that *exire* means *procedere*. For references to these texts see the next note.
24. Both Abraham Calov and David Hollaz list Revelation 22 as one of the chief proofs for the procession of the Spirit from the Father and the Son. This interpretation is widely attested among the dogmaticians and in the dogmatic handbooks of the nineteenth and twentieth centuries. See Calov, *Systema Locorum Theologicorum* (Wittenberg, 1659), 3:809, 811; Hollaz, *Examen Theologicum Acroamaticum*, I, 2, Q. 50 (Leipzig, 1763), 337-38; cf. Johann Gerhard, *De Morte*, Locus 29, §476.17 (Jena, 1621), 909; Johann Gerhard, *De Vita Aeterna*, Locus 34, §24 (Jena, 1622), 761-62; Johann Andreas Quenstedt, *Systema Theologicum*, I, 9 (Wittenberg, 1691), 405.

For more recent use of this text see Heinrich Schmid, *The Doctrinal Theology of the Evangelical Lutheran Church*, 3d ed. (Philadelphia: United Lutheran Publication House, 1899), 155; Henry Eyster Jacobs, *A Summary of the Christian Faith* (Philadelphia: United Lutheran Publication House, 1905), 55; G. Gösswein, *Schriftgemässe und erbauliche Erklärung der Offenbarung St. Johannis* (St. Louis: Concordia Publishing House, 1900), 301. For the use of this text in Roman Catholic dogmatic works see the discussion and notes in Lonergan, *The Triune God: Doctrines*, 550-55.

25. Georg Nigrinus, *Apocalypsis: Die Offenbarunge Sanct Johanniss des Apostels und Evangelisten* (Ursel, 1573), 600.

procession of the Holy Spirit from the Father and the Son. If the ἐκπορεύομαι of Jn 15:26 carries a technical meaning, which the church both East and West has always thought it did, then so too does the same word by the same John in Revelation 22.

TEMPORAL MISSION AND ETERNAL PROCESSION

The Orthodox often object that Latin theologians fail to distinguish sufficiently between eternal procession and temporal mission. The Orthodox argue that the sending of the Spirit by the Father and the Son refers to the temporal mission of the Spirit. The procession of the Spirit, on the other hand, refers to the eternal origin of the Spirit from the Father. The Father eternally begets the Son and eternally spirates the Spirit. The Father is the source and origin of the Spirit in eternity; the Father and the Son send the Spirit in time. This distinction corresponds to the distinction between the immanent and the economic Trinity. The immanent Trinity concerns God in Himself in all eternity. The economic Trinity concerns the way in which God reveals Himself to us in creation and salvation.

The distinction between eternal origin and temporal mission or between immanent and economic Trinity is important, widely acknowledged, and used by our Lutheran dogmaticians. What is not agreed upon—and this is really quite crucial for the whole *filioque* debate—is what the distinction amounts to. Orthodox theologians since the late patristic and early medieval period argue that the economic order is distinct from the eternal to such an extent that we may not draw any conclusions from the economic manifestation of God to the eternal being of God.[26] In other words, the temporal sending of the Spirit by the Father and the Son reveals nothing about the eternal relations between the persons. Mission posits nothing real in God.[27] Our Lutheran fathers, in keeping with the Latin tradition, particularly Augustine, draw an entirely different conclusion.[28] For them, we know God only through the economy and His

---

26. John Meyendorff, *A Study of Gregory Palamas* (Crestwood, NY: St. Vladimir's Seminary Press, 1998), 232. See also Vladimir Lossky, *In the Image and Likeness of God* (Crestwood, NY: St. Vladimir's Seminary Press, 1985), 71–96. Amphilokios Radovic writes, "On the basis of the manifestation of the Trinity in the world, we cannot come to any conclusions about God's mode of eternal existence." A. Radovic, "Le 'Filioque' et l'énergie incréée de la Sainte Trinité selon la doctrine de S. Grégoire Palamas," *Le Messager de l'Exarchat du patriarche russe en Europe occidentale*, 89–90 (1975), 19, quoted in Yves Congar, *I Believe in the Holy Spirit*, trans. David Smith (New York: Crossroad, 2013), 3:17. See also n. 1 above.

27. The Orthodox demonstrate this point by saying that Scripture also assigns to the Spirit the sending of the Son (Is 61:1 LXX). It is the Spirit who is put upon the Son at His baptism, drives Him into the wilderness, and returns Him to Galilee (Mt 3:16; 4:1; Lk 4:14). If sending and proceeding align with one another, we also would be able to say that the Son proceeds from the Spirit. Latin theologians have responded that the Son is both God and man. The sending of the Son by the Spirit pertains to His humanity and corresponds to the Spirit's indwelling of all believers.

28. Lewis Ayres, *Augustine and the Trinity* (Cambridge: Cambridge University

revelation to us of Himself. This means in part that the temporal missions of the Son and the Spirit reveal to us the way they relate eternally to one another. Abraham Calov expresses this succinctly: "A divine person is not sent in time except by one from whom that person eternally comes forth [*procedit*]."[29] There is nothing misleading about the Son sending the Spirit. Both the Father and the Son send the Spirit in time because of the eternal order that avails between the persons, an order that reflects their unique mode of existence, which in turn allows us to distinguish the persons. Further, this bears on how we come to know God. It is the Spirit of Christ that brings us to Christ, who in turn makes known to us the persons of the Father and the Holy Spirit.

Many of the Fathers did not distinguish eternal origin and temporal mission in the way later Orthodox theologians would. To parse their statements according to the immanent and economic Trinity or that which belongs to God in eternity or God in time is to read them deliberately through the lens of later theological categories and judgments.[30] Unfortunately, this happens routinely. This is not the place to offer an extensive reading of how the Fathers expressed the eternal relation of the Son and the Spirit, but we must offer at least a small sample. Two examples will suffice to show how the Fathers moved back and forth from what later would be distinguished as economic and immanent expressions. Since we have said already this is true of the Latin tradition, we will use two examples from Greek writers.

Athanasius connects the procession of the Spirit from the Father with the sending of the Spirit from the Son: "[The Spirit] is said to proceed from the Father, because the Spirit shines forth [ἐκλάμπει], and is sent, and is given from the Word, who is confessed to be from the Father."[31] Athanasius then says the Son is sent from the Father and the Spirit from the Son, and this corresponds to the Son glorifying the Father (Jn 17:4) and the Spirit glorifying the Son (Jn 16:14), the Son declaring what He heard from the Father (Jn 8:26) and the Spirit receiving from the Son (Jn 16:14), and the Son coming in the name of the Father (cf. Jn 5:43) and the Spirit coming in the name of the Son (Jn 14:26). Athanasius will say later that just as the Son is proper to the Father's substance because He is from Him, the Spirit, who is from God, is proper to the Son's substance.[32] Athanasius belongs to neither party of the *filioque* controversy.

Press, 2010), 183, 247.

29. Calov, *Systema Locorum Theologicorum* (Wittenberg, 1659), 3:813, quoted in Bruce Marshall, "The Defense of the *Filioque* in Classical Lutheran Theology," *Neue Zeitschrift für systematische Theologie und Religionsphilosophie* 44:2 (2002): 164.

30. André de Halleux, "Towards an Ecumenical Agreement on the Procession of the Holy Spirit and the Addition of the *Filioque* to the Creed," in *Spirit of God, Spirit of Christ: Ecumenical Reflections on the "Filioque" Controversy*, ed. Lukas Vischer (London: SPCK, 1981), 80. After reviewing statements by the Greek fathers Halleux concludes: "To limit these and other affirmations of the same tenor to the mission and to leave out the eternal source and essential roots of the economy in the immanent Trinity would be tantamount to foisting on the standpoint of the fourth and fifth century Fathers a dichotomy still alien to them."

31. Athanasius *Letters to Serapion* 1.20.5 (PPS, 85).

32. Athanasius *Letters to Serapion* 1.25.2 (PPS, 92).

ON THE TRINITY

He is a scriptural theologian who uses the language and pattern of Scripture to confess the coequality and consubstantiality of Father, Son, and Holy Spirit. For this reason he moves back and forth between expressions the church will later divide between theology proper and economy, between God in Himself and God revealed to us in creation and redemption. For Athanasius, these inform one another. When later patristic scholars discount Athanasius's language by saying that he is concerned chiefly with our salvation and therefore speaks in terms of the economic Trinity, they offer an interpretation of Athanasius grounded in a later theological distinction.

Epiphanius of Salamis, another fourth-century Greek theologian, writes, "The Holy Spirit, whom the sacred Scripture calls the Paraclete, owes his being to the Father through the Son."[33] When he turns to a discussion of the Spirit's eternal origin, he combines Jn 15:26 (the Spirit "proceeds from" the Father) with Jn 16:14-15 (the Spirit "receives" from the Son) when speaking about the relation of the Spirit to the Father and the Son: "If it is believed that Christ, as 'God of God,' is of the Father, and his Spirit is of Christ or of both—as Christ says, 'who proceedeth from the Father' (Jn 15:26), and, 'He shall receive of me' (Jn 16:14) ... then I know the Mystery that redeems me by faith."[34] For Epiphanius, these texts indicate that "the Holy Spirit is from both (παρ' ἀμφοτέρων), as Spirit of Spirit."[35] The objection is soon raised: does this mean there are two Sons? Epiphanius says no and then clarifies his point:

> If God calls the One who is from him, the Son, and the One who is of Both, the Holy Spirit—things understood by saints alone, by faith—things which are light, which give light, which have the power to enlighten, and create a harmony of light with the Father himself! [If this is so], Sir, hear with faith that the Father is the Father of a true Son and is all light, and that <the> Son is the <Son> of a true Father and is light of light, [and] not merely in name, as artifacts or created things are. And the Holy Spirit is the Spirit of truth, a third light, from the Father and the Son.[36]

Epiphanius returns again to Jn 15:26 and Jn 16:14. He continues to place them side by side and seems to understand them as pointing to the same reality. He writes:

> Now if the Spirit proceeds from the Father and, as the Lord says, is to receive "of mine," I will venture to say that, just as "No man knoweth the Father save the Son, nor the Son save the Father," so no one knows the Spirit except the Son from whom he receives and the Father from whom he proceeds. And no one knows the Son and the Father except the Holy Spirit who truly glorifies them, who teaches all things, who testifies of the Son, is from the Father, is of the Son, is the only guide

---

33. Epiphanius *Panarion* 73.16; *The Panarion of Epiphanius of Salamis*, trans. Frank Williams (Leiden: Brill, 1994), 450.
34. Epiphanius *Panarion* 74, 4 (Williams, 476).
35. Epiphanius *Panarion* 74, 7 (Williams, 482). For further examples of this expression see Epiphanius *Ancoratus* 8, 9, 67, 70-72, and 75.
36. Epiphanius *Panarion* 74, 8 (Williams, 482).

to truth, the expounder of holy laws, instructor in the spiritual law, preceptor of the prophets, teacher of the apostles, enlightener with the Gospel's doctrines, elector of the saints, true light of true light.[37]

The difficulty with Epiphanius's teaching on the origin of the Spirit, the reason it strikes many later students of theology as confusing, is that he fails to distinguish the temporal missions of the Son and the Spirit from their eternal origins in the manner advocated by many today. For Epiphanius as for the Latin fathers, temporal mission, the manner in which God reveals Himself to us in bringing about our salvation, informs our understanding of the eternal origin of the persons. This does not mean we collapse the two together but it also does not mean we reject the congruence between them.

THE MONARCHY OF THE FATHER

If we say that the Holy Spirit proceeds from the Father and the Son, are we positing two sources or causes in the Godhead? This is the great worry of the Orthodox. The scriptural teaching on the mode of existence was expressed further by the Greek fathers in terms of cause. Although this language of causality may sound overly philosophical to some, it proceeds from piety and aims to express the eternal relation of the Father, Son, and Holy Spirit. For our purposes, it will shed considerable light on why the *filioque* offends Orthodox Christians so deeply to this day. With the unique mode of existence for the three persons of the Trinity in mind, we may say that the Father, who is unbegotten, has no cause. He is the source without source, principle without principle. The Son is begotten of the Father and the Spirit proceeds from the Father. This means that the Father is the cause or principle of the Son and the Holy Spirit. When the Orthodox hear Western Christians confess in the Nicene Creed that the Holy Spirit "proceeds from the Father *and the Son*," they think we mean that there are two sources or principles of divinity in the Trinity, the Father and the Son. In other words, the Father is the source of the Spirit's divinity, but so too is the Son. Therefore, there must be two sources or principles, and this means two gods and may also mean two Spirits, one from the Father and one from the Son. From their perspective the *filioque* necessarily denies the Trinity and inevitably falls into absurdity and blasphemy. Of course no Western Christian using the *filioque* thinks this. Further, the Latin tradition and our Lutheran fathers have always alleviated this concern—if that is even the right way of putting it since Augustine said this before any such controversy existed—by emphasizing that the Spirit proceeds *principaliter* from the Father.

Augustine bases his argument for the *filioque* on Scripture's insistence that the Spirit is the Spirit of the Father and the Spirit of the Son. Further, the Father and the Son both send the Holy Spirit.[38] For Augustine, the economy

---

37. Epiphanius *Panarion* 74, 10 (Williams, 485).
38. Augustine *The Trinity* IV.29 (WSA I/5, 174).

discloses the order of persons and their eternal relations.[39] Because the Father has given all things to the Son, the Spirit proceeds from both. Does this mean there are two sources of origin for the Spirit? Augustine says no: "The source of all Godhead, or if you prefer it, of all deity, is the Father. So the Spirit who proceeds from the Father and the Son is traced back, on both counts, to him of whom the Son is born."[40] The Spirit proceeds from the Father and the Son, or as Augustine suggests here from the Father of the Son. There are not two sources of deity but only one, the Father. Augustine places emphasis on this point by saying that the Spirit proceeds *principaliter* from the Father. He writes:

> And yet it is not without point that in this triad only the Son is called the Word of God, and only the Holy Spirit is called the gift of God, and only the Father is called the one from whom the Word is born and from whom the Holy Spirit principally proceeds. I added "principally," because we have found that the Holy Spirit also proceeds from the Son. But this too was given to the Son by the Father—not given to him when he already existed and did not yet have it; but whatever the Father gave to his only-begotten Word he gave by begetting him. He so begot him then that their common gift would proceed from him too, and the Holy Spirit would be the Spirit of them both.[41]

These few sentences from Augustine lay out the Latin position on the *filioque*. The Spirit is the Spirit of the Father and of the Son, the Spirit of both. All that the Father has the Son has. The Spirit proceeds principally from the Father but also from the Son, who has been given this as the only-begotten of the Father. Augustine states this succinctly toward the end of his work: "The Holy Spirit proceeds from the Father principally, and by the Father's wholly timeless gift from both of them (the Father and the Son) jointly."[42] The concern of the later Greek theologians is here addressed by Augustine. The Father is the principal source of the Son and the Holy Spirit. Augustine's language of the Father as the source is repeated throughout the Western tradition and particularly by our Lutheran fathers. Luther writes, "The Father is the source (*ursprung*), or the fountainhead (*quelle*) (if we may use that term as the fathers do) of the Godhead (*Gottheit*), that the Son derives it from Him and that the Holy Spirit derives it from Him and the Son, and not vice versa."[43] This same sort of language appears throughout the writings of the dogmaticians.[44]

---

39. Augustine *The Trinity* books II–IV. Cf. Joseph Lienhard, "Augustine and the *Filioque*," in *Tolle et Lege: Essays on Augustine and Medieval Philosophy in Honor of Roland J. Teske, S.J.*, ed. Richard C. Taylor, David Twetten, and Michael Wreen (Marquette, WI: Marquette University Press, 2011), 137–54.
40. Augustine *The Trinity* IV.29 (WSA I/5, 174).
41. Augustine *The Trinity* XV.29 (WSA I/5, 419).
42. Augustine *The Trinity* XV.47 (WSA I/5, 433).
43. *On the Last Words of David*, 1543 (AE 15:309; WA 54:64.4–5). See also AE 15:316; WA 54:69.20–21.
44. Johann Gerhard, *De Deo Patre*, Locus 4/2, §2 (ed. Cotta, 223): the Father is "the origin of the Trinity (*origo Trinitatis*), begetting the Son and with the Son spirating one Holy Spirit." Gerhard uses similar expressions elsewhere. The Father is the *fons Trinitatis* (4/2, §4, 224); the Father is the *fons et origo Trinitatis* (4/2, § 9, 225). Similarly, Quenstedt, *Systema Theologicum*,

The point made by Augustine and our Lutheran fathers may also be found in Gregory of Nyssa. Once again we encounter the difficulty of the patristic witness on the question of the *filioque* and how later categories prove insufficient for describing their efforts. Although Gregory clearly affirms the monarchy of the Father, he also emphasizes the role of the Son in the procession of the Spirit and the dependence of the Spirit upon the Son. In his debate with Eunomius Gregory acknowledges the order of the persons in Scripture and says this bears on how we think of the Spirit's relation to the Son. He writes, "As the Son is joined to the Father, and having his being from him does not come afterwards in existence, so in turn the Holy Spirit holds close also to the only-begotten, who only in terms of causation is thought of as prior to the *hypostasis* of the Spirit . . . So with the exception of the idea of cause, the Holy Trinity has no variation in itself at all."[45] Gregory explains the distinction with respect to causality elsewhere. He especially emphasizes the dependence of the Spirit upon the Son, which says nothing more than that the Spirit proceeds from the Father but never apart from the Son. He writes:

> Although we acknowledge the nature is undifferentiated, we do not deny a distinction with respect to causality. That is the only way by which we distinguish one Person from the other, by believing, that is, that one is the cause and the other depends on the cause. Again, we recognize another distinction with regard to that which depends on the cause. There is that which depends on the first cause and that which is derived from what immediately depends on the first cause. Thus the attribute of being only-begotten without doubt remains with the Son, and we do not question that the Spirit is derived from the Father. For the mediation of the Son, while it guards his prerogative of being only-begotten, does not exclude the relation which the Spirit has by nature to the Father.[46]

For Gregory, the Son depends upon the Father, and the Spirit is derived from the Father and the Son. For this reason Gregory also can say that "the Holy Spirit . . . depends [ἤρτηται] on the Son with whom he is indivisibly apprehended." Further the Spirit is known only "after the Son and with him."[47] John Behr, an Orthodox theologian, commenting on these texts, writes, "Gregory clearly affirms the Son's mediation in the procession of the Spirit, for the Spirit proceeds not simply from God, but from the Father of the Son, and therefore always in relation to the Son."[48]

I, 9 (Wittenberg, 1691), 327: the Father is *fons et principium*.

45. Gregory of Nyssa *Contra Eunomium* I.691 (PG 45, 464), trans. Stuart G. Hall, *El 'Contra Eunomium I'* (Pamplona: Universidad de Navarra, 1988), 135.

46. Gregory of Nyssa, *An Answer to Ablabius*, trans. E. R. Hardy, *The Christology of the Later Fathers* (Philadelphia: Westminster, 1954), 266. Both of these texts from Gregory are commented on in Brian Daley, "Revisiting the *Filioque*: Roots and Branches," 43–44.

47. Gregory of Nyssa *Letter* 35, 4d (Silvas, 253). I have used John Behr's translation of this text (*The Nicene Faith* [Crestwood, NY: St. Vladimir's Seminary Press, 2004], vol. 2, part 2, 419). Cf. Khaled Anatolios, *Retrieving Nicaea* (Grand Rapids: Baker Academic, 2011), 223.

48. Behr, *Nicene Faith*, vol. 2, part 2, 434.

WHY TEACH THE *FILIOQUE*?

We need to be careful in answering this question. We teach the *filioque* because Scripture teaches it. We do not teach it because we find it confessed in the Athanasian Creed and the Nicene Creed. Nor do we teach it because of some later theological rationalization that makes sense of the *filioque*. Should we be convinced that Scripture does not teach the *filioque*, we would be compelled to stop teaching it and to remove it from our creeds, hymns, and prayers. The ground for our arguments must always be Scripture. There's a better way of expressing this question: why does Scripture reveal to us that the Spirit's person and life proceed from both the Father and the Son? Why does Scripture make a point of identifying the Spirit as the Spirit of the Father and the Spirit of the Son? Indeed, even further declaring, the Spirit is the Spirit of Christ, the Spirit of Jesus, and this is the same Spirit that bears witness with our spirit that we are children of God and coheirs with Christ (Rom 8:16–17).

The necessity of the *filioque* and its theological significance lies with the relation that avails between Christ and the Spirit and the place of the church in delivering the salvation of our triune God to us. The Father will have us know Him only in the man Jesus; Jesus will have us know Him, confess Him, and lay hold of the salvation purchased by Him only by the Holy Spirit. Further, the Holy Spirit comes to us through Word and sacrament, through the divinely appointed means of grace. We know this Spirit as the Holy Spirit by first knowing Him as the Spirit of Christ, the Spirit who drives us always and ever to Christ and sustains us in Christ throughout our lives. The "spirit" that takes us away from Christ, even piously trying to get us to the Father apart from His Son, is the spirit of *anti*-Christ. The spirit opposed to Christ is always opposed to the Father, whom we know only in Christ, and opposed to the Spirit of the Father and the Son who send to us their Spirit that we might know and delight in Christ alone to the glory of the Father. David Scaer explains:

> Since the Father, the Son, and the Holy Spirit are present and working in the means of grace, they reflect the eternal relationship of one divine person to the other. The Father eternally begets the Son who makes believers His children in baptism (Jn 1:12–13) and coheirs with Jesus (Rom 8:17). Regeneration is completed and accomplished by the Spirit (Jn 3:8) who proceeds from and is sent into the world by the Father and the Son. Just as the Father is the eternal origin within the Trinity, the Spirit is its eternal completion. What is begun by the Father and accomplished by the Son's redemption is brought to completion by the Spirit's engendering faith in believers. Things and human words and actions, which are the outward forms of the means of grace, are coverings for the Trinity in which He comes to forgive sinners and declare them righteous. Sacramental theology is not an independent or autonomous section in dogmatics but flows out of a prior understanding of God as Father, Son, and Holy Spirit who is at work in His creation for the salvation of man.[49]

---

49. David Scaer, *Law and Gospel and the Means of Grace*, vol. 8 of Confessional Lutheran Dogmatics (St. Louis: Luther Academy, 2008), 144–45; for his whole discussion of the Spirit and

Trinity and salvation go together. The Trinity saves. It did not occur to the Fathers to separate the so-called imminent Trinity from the economic Trinity because it never occurred to them to talk about the God of the Bible apart from His creation and redemption.

We end our unit on the scriptural identity of Father, Son, and Holy Spirit with a discussion of the *filioque*. There is something fitting in that. At the very least, the *filioque* shows us that Father, Son, and Holy Spirit are never parted from one another; they not only mutually indwell one another but also make themselves known to us in such a way that our thoughts always move from one person to the other in a never-ending figure eight. Gregory of Nyssa captures this well. He writes:

> We are not to think of the Father as ever parted from the Son, nor to look for the Son as separate from the Holy Spirit. As it is impossible to mount to the Father, unless our thoughts are exalted thither through the Son, so it is impossible also to say that Jesus is Lord except by the Holy Spirit. Therefore, Father, Son, and Holy Spirit are to be known only in a perfect Trinity, in closest consequence and union with each other, before all creation, before all the ages, before anything whatever of which we can form an idea. The Father is always Father, and in Him the Son, and with the Son the Holy Spirit.[50]

Part 3, to which we now turn, will show how the Fathers and reformers confessed, clarified, and guarded the scriptural identity of the Trinity. What we must not lose sight of, however, is their commitment to the Scriptures, to the salvation accomplished for us by the Trinity, and to the liturgical context of our knowing and confessing the Trinity.

---

the sacraments see 143–55.
50. Gregory of Nyssa *On the Holy Spirit* (NPNF, second series, V, 319).

PART THREE

DOGMATIC REFLECTION OF THE CHURCH

The faithful confess that three eternally distinct persons—Father, Son, and Holy Spirit—are united inseparably in one essence. Most of the trinitarian problems that arise throughout the history of the church stem from this way of speaking. When the faithful confess that the Father is God, the Son is God, and the Holy Spirit is God, but there is one God and not three gods, they must find some way of expressing how Father, Son, and Holy Spirit are the same and not the same. Otherwise they will be asked why they count Father, Son, and Holy Spirit as three but count the repetition of God with Father, Son, and Holy Spirit as one. Why not also say three gods? Alternatively, why insist that Father, Son, and Holy Spirit are real persons, eternally distinct from one another, rather than three expressions of the one God? Our answers to these questions never begin with creeds or persuasive argument. Rather, we do not say three gods because Scripture does not say three gods. Our confession of three persons who share equally and indivisibly one essence—indeed, who are one essence—proceeds from the sound or healthy doctrine handed down to us in the Scriptures. We speak in the way we do about the Trinity because Scripture alone determines our confession.

The Fathers reflected at length on this question of threeness and oneness in their confession and defense of the scriptural identity of God. Along the way they developed appropriate language to express what was common among the three and what distinguished the three from one another. We count Father, Son, and Holy Spirit as three when talking in terms of person, subsistence, or *hypostasis*, but count only one when talking in terms of nature, essence, substance, or *ousia*. The Father is neither the Son nor the Spirit; the Son is neither the Father nor the Spirit; the Spirit is neither the Father nor the Son. But Father, Son, and Holy Spirit are one God. The terminology proved useful for conveying how Scripture presents the divine persons as essentially identical but personally distinct.

Rightly distinguishing Father, Son, and Holy Spirit, rightly expressing the unique threeness of God, must always find its complement in affirming the inseparable and indivisible unity of the three, the unique oneness of the three. Another difficulty faced by the church pertains to the essential oneness of the divine persons. The problem has to do with their acts or works toward creation.

We rightly confess that the Father creates, the Son creates, and the Holy Spirit creates. Does that mean the Father creates apart from the Son and the Spirit, the Son apart from the Father and the Spirit, and the Spirit apart from the Father and the Son? If we argue that they create apart from one another or that each contributes a part to the act of creation, we compromise our confession of their unity and simplicity. The church has explained this knotty issue by saying that the works of the Trinity toward creation are indivisible (*opera Trinitatis ad extra indivisa sunt*). This means every action of the three persons *ad extra* is numerically one and proceeds from their unity of will and power. When the Father works, the Son and the Holy Spirit work also in the same act.

The above two problems were worked out together by the Fathers, medieval theologians, and reformers. For the sake of clarity we will separate them. Our first two chapters of part 3 will discuss the first problem and show how the church's theologians distinguished the persons of the Trinity. Following these two chapters we will take up the second problem charted above. There we will show how these same theologians discussed the works of the Trinity toward creation and how certain titles or names may be assigned to one of the persons. At this point we also will address more explicitly the divine attributes. Although we have discussed the divine attributes throughout the chapters of this book, we have avoided some of the more vexing questions related to them. When we take up the question of the Trinity's works *ad extra*, we will be in a position to discuss them more properly.

12

DISTINGUISHING THE PERSONS: PATRISTIC INSIGHTS

When Gregory of Nyssa defended the divinity of the Holy Spirit against the so-called Spirit haters of his day (Pneumatomachians), he focused at length on how we form theological ideas and express them. Gregory observed that people use the word "God" differently. His opponents, who considered themselves Christians, operated with an elastic concept of God. They could distinguish between one called God and another called true God.[1] Their language derives not from Scripture but from their own peculiar ideas. For Gregory, Scripture not only norms sound doctrine but also establishes our grammar of faith, the patterns of speech we use to confess God. He explains,

> We do not consider it right to make the custom that prevails among them [the Pneumatomachians] the law and rule of sound doctrine. For if custom is valid as a proof of soundness, surely we too may put forward in our defense the custom that prevails among us, and if they reject this, we surely do not have to follow theirs. Let the God-inspired Scriptures therefore decide between us, and the verdict of truth will surely go to those whose teachings are found to be in harmony with the divine words.[2]

The rule here is a simple one: Scripture both warrants and determines the church's talk about God.[3] We have made this point in different ways throughout parts 1 and 2 of this book. In part 3 we will focus especially on how the church proclaims and guards the sure deposit of faith given to us in the Scriptures on the identity of Father, Son, and Holy Spirit.

---

1. A parallel would be the sixteenth-century Eucharistic controversies, where talk of Christ's body in the Lord's Supper was different from talk of Christ's *true* body in the Lord's Supper, which in turn became different from talk of Christ's *true* and *essential* body in the Lord's Supper. Calvin's real presence is *really* different from Luther's real presence. SD VII.2–11 (Tappert, 569–71).

2. Gregory of Nyssa *Letter 33 (Ad Eustathium de Sancta Trinitate)* 3b in *Gregory of Nyssa: The Letters*, trans. Anna M. Silvas (Leiden: Brill, 2007), 238; GNO 3.1, 5–6.

3. Martin Chemnitz, *Loci Theologici*, trans. J. A. O. Preus (St. Louis: Concordia Publishing House, 2008), 1:100. Chemnitz reflects on the use of theological language in the church and acknowledges that many of these words are taken from the common language of the people and not from Scripture. The church uses these common terms but in a scripturally responsible way. In that sense the church adjusts the meaning of these common terms to reflect the truth of Scripture. He writes, "The church for good and sufficient reasons from time to time must adopt certain terms and make changes in their meaning ... [B]ecause the church speaks about things which are unknown to our reason, it uses these words in a somewhat different sense." Chemnitz has in mind the trinitarian terms "essence" and "person."

DOGMATIC REFLECTION OF THE CHURCH

When we preach the gospel, we preach the Trinity because salvation comes to us from Father, Son, and Holy Spirit. Preaching this salvation elicits questions and concerns from the faithful about the Trinity's revealed identity and raises objections by those outside the faith. The response of the church's faithful to these questions and objections forms the grammar of faith preserved for us in the church's creeds and dogmatic works. An important point needs to be stressed here. The formal ways of talking about the Trinity, the finer points of trinitarian doctrine handed down by the church, proceed from the church's unwavering certainty that rightly confessing the scriptural identity of the triune God has to do with our salvation, our baptism, our liturgy, our prayers, our Christian life. This practical way of thinking about the Trinity may be seen in the way the Fathers always connect their confession of the Trinity to baptism and salvation. Francis Pieper observed this very concern with the Nicene Creed. The Fathers confess the Trinity in a baptismal creed that underscores the salvation accomplished by Christ and delivered by the Holy Spirit in the church.[4] Confessing the Trinity never stands apart from confessing salvation.

The following chapters discuss the ecclesiastical terminology and preferred patterns of speech used throughout the history of the church to convey Scripture's revelation of the Trinity. Although such language is not absolutely necessary for rightly confessing the triune identity of God, it should not be carelessly dismissed nor too easily departed from.[5] When we confess that God is one *ousia* and three *hypostases*,[6] that Father, Son, and Holy Spirit are consubstantial, and that the divine persons are distinguished by their personal properties and relations of opposition, we are not just borrowing theological language from the history of the church. We are joining our voices to the language and labors of the faithful. Our warrant for speaking this way about the

---

4. Francis Pieper, *Christian Dogmatics* (St. Louis: Concordia Publishing House, 1950), 1:406.

5. Philipp Melanchthon, *Loci Communes*, trans. J. A. O. Preus, 2d ed. (St. Louis: Concordia Publishing House, 2011), 16: "We shall omit all arguments about words and simply retain the meaning of the church and use those words which have been already used and accepted in the church without any ambiguity." Again, p. 28: "Care behooves the pious, for the sake of harmony, to speak in line with the church. And it was not without good reasons that the ancient church approved some ways of speaking and rejected others. Let us then avoid zeal for caviling and retain the forms received with weighty and true authority." For a similar sentiment see Pieper, *Christian Dogmatics* 1:417-18, "This terminology is not meaningless jargon, but necessary theological apparatus.... [This terminology] is in full accord with the teaching of Scripture.... In reality this terminology expresses the simple faith which every Christian believes on the basis of clear Scripture passages even though he has never heard of these terms. Every Christian believes that the Son is the Only-Begotten of the Father and that the Holy Ghost is the Spirit of the Father and of the Son. Therefore he believes implicitly the *actus personales* (generation and spiration), the *proprietates personales* (paternity, etc.), and the allegedly meaningless *notiones personales* (innascibility, etc.)."

6. Scholars often refer to the phrase "one *ousia*, three *hypostases*" (μία οὐσια τρεῖς ὑποστάσεις) as the Cappadocian settlement. This exact phrase never occurs in the writings of the Cappadocian fathers. It is found in Augustine's *The Trinity* 5.8.10 (CCSL 50.216-17): "Dicunt quidem et illi ὑποστάσιν, sed nescio quid volunt interesse inter οὐσίαν et ὑποστάσιν ita ut plerique nostri qui haec graeco tractant eloquio dicere consuerint μία οὐσια τρεῖς ὑποστάσεις, quod est latine, unam essentiam, tres substantias." Cf. Basil of Caesarea *Letter* 214 (LCL, 3:234).

Trinity proceeds from Scripture and finds its continuing relevance in the liturgy, prayers, and hymns of the church. If the language and grammar encountered in the next few chapters sounds unfamiliar, the desire of the faithful should be catechesis not retreat. The Fathers and reformers used this language in worship and preaching. We should as well. Such use, however, requires relearning the church's way of confessing the scriptural identity of the Trinity and the value of that shared language, that churchly vernacular, among the faithful from generation to generation.

KNOWING GOD

When we talk about God, we must be clear from the start about what we can know and not know. Basil, Gregory of Nazianzus, and Gregory of Nyssa, the Cappadocians as they are called collectively, argued that we know God by the things He does, by His works or activities in the world, from creation to salvation to His providential ordering and care of our lives. They made a distinction between knowing God in Himself (*theologia*) and knowing God through His acts (*oikonomia*). Although we certainly know things about God's essence, about God in Himself, we cannot in this life know Him fully or completely. That sort of knowledge eludes us. God's essence is infinite and therefore beyond our created, finite intelligence and capabilities.[7] God's essence exceeds our conceptualizations, including the concept of being, because He is not any particular kind of being that we can point to. This is why the Fathers and all orthodox theologians after them insisted that God was beyond being, which meant beyond definition, beyond the limits of our human concepts, transcending every category available to our minds and speech.

We have seen already in earlier chapters how Gregory of Nyssa regards it as idle speculation to assign any discrete concept to what is above all concept.[8] Likewise, Augustine famously declares to his congregation: "We are talking about God; so why be surprised if you cannot grasp it? I mean, if you can grasp it, it isn't God. Let us rather make a devout confession of ignorance, instead of a brash profession of knowledge."[9] Again Augustine preaches, "So what are we to say, brothers, about God? For if you have fully grasped what you want to say, it isn't God. If you have been able to comprehend it, you have comprehended something else instead of God. If you think you have been able to comprehend, your thoughts have deceived you."[10] Luther's Reformation breakthrough freed

---

7. For a similar discussion of this see Calov, *Systema Locorum Theologicorum* (Wittenberg, 1655), 2:191–95.

8. Gregory of Nyssa *Letter* 35, 3e (Silvas, 252); cf. *Letter* 24, 5: "But their substance, whatever this is—for it is inexpressible in words and cannot be grasped in thought" (Silvas, 193).

9. Augustine *Sermon* 117.5 (WSA III/4, 211).

10. Augustine *Sermon* 52.6 (WSA III/3, 57). Cf. Athanasian Creed: "The Father incomprehensible, the Son incomprehensible, and the Holy Ghost incomprehensible. . . . As there are not three Uncreated nor three Incomprehensibles, but one Uncreated and one Incomprehensible" (TLH, p. 53).

God from our incessant attempt to conceptualize Him, to limit His possibilities, and to mold Him after our best ideas. Luther's insistence that we let God be God means we no longer seek to storm heaven to know the God of Scripture but we receive Him by faith as He comes to us in Word and sacrament.[11] This basic point made in different ways by the Cappadocians, Augustine, and Luther rejects all attempts at theism by reposing in Scripture, in God's revelation of Himself.

We must pause here lest misunderstanding arise. When the Fathers and reformers assert the incomprehensibility of God, they are not saying we do not know God. Rather they are saying that we cannot reduce God to a single concept or definition above which we stand. To offer a definition of something is to delimit that thing, to mark out completely and therefore to state unambiguously what that thing is. We may do that only with something finite, something susceptible to limit, to definition. We may rightly and coherently define a book. A book may be described under the categories of shape, size, weight, color, etc. We may also say that a book contains front and back covers and a spine joining the pages between the covers. We may discuss a book's purpose or use; we also could extrapolate things about the maker of a book, the skills required and the resources needed to produce such a thing. We similarly describe chairs, tables, and the various things we encounter with our senses. A definition may state both what a thing is and what a thing is not. A book is not a chair and we can give many reasons for this. Those reasons will be expressed either positively or negatively; for example, a book is 'x' or a book is not 'x'.

Not everything we encounter with the senses has a known limit or defined boundary. We know there is wind because we feel it, we hear it rustling the leaves, and we see it moving the branches of trees. And yet we do not know the limits of the wind; we do not know, as Jesus reminds us, "where it comes from or where it goes" (Jn 3:8). There is an aspect of wind incomprehensible to us. Yes, we know a good deal about it; we can profitably describe it but there remain aspects of it that elude us. We know it with certainty, not because we can actually see something called wind, but because we see the effects or activities of the wind. In this sense we know the wind only when it comes to us, when it does something to us or around us, when it makes itself known to our senses.

When the Fathers and reformers assert the incomprehensibility of God, when they say He is beyond every definition and exceeds our conceptualizations, they are not saying we cannot know God or rightly talk about Him. The triune God of Scripture is not the wholly other of Platonism. The incomprehensible one has made Himself known truly and really in the person of Christ and by

---

11. Cf. Martin Luther, "First Christmas Sermon: Christmas Eve Service (Titus 2:11–15)," in *The Complete Sermons of Martin Luther*, trans. John Nicholas Lenker (Grand Rapids: Baker Books, 2000), vol. 3.2, 116–17; *Disputation on Scholastic Theology*, 1517 (AE 31:10, thesis 17; WA 1:225.1–2); Robert Kolb, "Luther on the Theology of the Cross," *Lutheran Quarterly* 16 (2002): 455, 459.

the actions or operations of the Trinity in the world. We know God and talk about God as He has revealed Himself to us. No one knows the Father apart from the Son and no one knows the Son apart from the Holy Spirit. Part 2 of this book showed at length how Scripture makes known to us the one true God of Israel who is three eternally distinct persons, Father, Son, and Holy Spirit. God *is* Father, Son, and Holy Spirit.

Johann Gerhard in the space of only a few pages states that God is both beyond definition and yet also perfectly known by us. If we seek to know the essence of God, to define it, we seek what is unavailable to us. Gerhard writes, "In this life we cannot look upon the essence of God with our eyes, grasp it with our minds, or speak of it with our lips. How, then, would we be able to define it perfectly?"[12] And yet God has made Himself known to us in Scripture. Gerhard further declares that the knowledge of God we have from Scripture may be said to be perfect because it is sufficient for salvation and because it comes from God.[13] Therefore, when asked who God is, we proclaim the one revealed to us in Scripture. Gerhard writes:

> [God is] the Father, who from eternity begot His Son, His image, and who created and preserves all things through the Son in the Holy Spirit; the Son, who was begotten of the Father from eternity, who in the fullness of time assumed human nature and in it carried out the work of redemption; the Holy Spirit, who proceeds ineffably from the Father and the Son from eternity, who was poured out visibly upon the apostles and still today is sent invisibly into the hearts of believers, and who through the preaching of the Gospel gathers the Church from the whole human race and sanctifies it to the glory of God's name and the eternal salvation of those who believe.[14]

Gerhard's proclamation of who God is follows the instincts of the Fathers. He confesses the identity of the triune God in the context of the church and the salvation proclaimed therein. Gerhard's description of God is far removed from the philosophers and delights of reason; it is a churchly confession that humbly follows the sound words of Scripture.

DISTINGUISHING THE PERSONS

Cappadocians

The pressing concern of the early church was how to distinguish rightly the three divine persons from one another without undermining their essential unity. The two great heresies of the early church failed to do this. Sabellianism asserted the unity of God at the expense of three coequal and eternally distinct persons. Arianism argued that the true God was the Father alone and not the Son or the Spirit. The Arians thought there was a time when the Son was not, that He was

---

12. Johann Gerhard, *Theological Commonplaces: On the Nature of God and On the Trinity*, trans. Richard Dinda (St. Louis: Concordia Publishing House, 2007), Exegesis II, §89, 93.
13. Gerhard, *Theological Commonplaces*, Exegesis II, §90, 95.
14. Gerhard, *Theological Commonplaces*, Exegesis II, §94, 98.

created by the Father in order to create all other things, including the Spirit. For the Arians the Son ranked higher than the angels but lower than God. In the words of the Athanasian Creed, the Sabellians confounded the persons; the Arians divided the essence.[15] The Fathers rejected and condemned both Sabellianism and Arianism. They focused their efforts on finding appropriate ways of expressing the distinction of persons and the unity of essence without succumbing to the errors of either.

The Cappadocians used the language of "distinguishing properties" or "distinguishing marks" to talk about the divine persons. This language proceeded from a distinction between what is said of God in terms of His essence and what is said of God in reference to another. When things are said of God in terms of His essence, they are said of all three divine persons, equally and indivisibly. When things are said of God in terms of relation, they are said with reference to another. For example, when we say God is eternal, we are talking about an essential property that Father, Son, and Holy Spirit share indivisibly as one God. When we say Father or Son, we are using relational terms. We rightly use the word "eternal" with Father, Son, and Holy Spirit interchangeably. We do not use the terms Father and Son interchangeably. The Father is always Father and never Son; the Son is always Son and never Father. What about such terms as unbegotten and begotten? Do these terms refer to God as He is in His eternal being or do they refer to relations? When we say the Father is unbegotten or unoriginate and the Son is begotten or originate, are we talking in terms of essence or relation? That question perplexed many in the early church and stands behind many of the fourth-century debates on the Trinity. The answer to that question by both the Greek and Latin fathers yielded rich trinitarian distinctions that helpfully pattern the language of our faith, liturgy, and prayers.

Eunomius of Cyzicus thought we knew as much about God's essence as God does. The name for God's essence, he argued, was unbegotten. If God's essence is unbegotten, then clearly the Son could not be God in the same way the Father is God because Scripture says He is begotten. Therefore, thought Eunomius, when Scripture declares that Jesus is the only-begotten Son of God, it clearly differentiates the essence of the Son from the Father. Eunomius was not alone in thinking this way; Asterius the Sophist thought something quite similar. Both were convinced that unbegotten or unoriginate indicated the essence of God, and therefore the Son was necessarily unlike the Father in essence. The orthodox theologians of the fourth and fifth centuries argued that "unbegotten" or "unoriginate" are not substance terms, words describing God's essence, but relational terms, terms marking off the Father from something or someone else. Their agreement consists in seeing these terms as relational. What that relation was, however, they express differently.

---

15. Cf. Thomas Aquinas, *Commentary on the Gospel of John*, 1451 (Lander, WY: The Aquinas Institute, 2013), 2:63.

Athanasius argues that "unoriginate" is used for God to mark Him off from the rest of creation. The term is used not in reference to the Son, indeed has nothing to do with the Son, but of those things created by the Father through the Son.[16] The term "Father," on the other hand, is used with reference to the Son and distinguishes the First Person of the Trinity from the Second Person. Moreover, the term Father properly indicates the coeternity and coequality of the Son. When people refer to God as unoriginate, they mark Him off from the perspective of creation, from His works. God is unoriginate, which means He is un-made, un-created. When people refer to God as Father, they distinguish Him from the perspective of the Son through whom alone they know the Father. Although both designations are true, Scripture prefers the language of Father and Son. Athanasius writes: "'Unoriginated' was discovered by the Greeks, who do not know the Son. But 'Father' was known by our Lord, and he rejoiced in it."[17] Athanasius points out that Jesus did not teach us to pray "Our unoriginate" but "Our Father." Likewise, we were not commanded to baptize into the name of the unoriginate but into the name of Father, Son, and Holy Spirit.

Basil of Caesarea takes a more nuanced approach to arrive at a similar point. He argues that "unbegottenness" when applied to the Father does not indicate for us "what He is" but rather "how He is."[18] Basil makes this distinction to counter Eunomius's claim that "unbegotten" is a term indicating essence. Basil argues that the term does not work that way. "Unbegotten" tells us not what God is but rather how He is "from no one" or "from no source."[19] The term describes not God's essence but God's origin. When we talk about human beings and say that this person comes from that person, we indicate not "what that person is" but "from where that person comes." Basil appeals to Luke's genealogy. When Luke says that Seth came from Adam, he tells us where Seth comes from, not what Seth is in terms of essence. Being "from someone" indicates source and relation. Seth's source is Adam. Therefore Seth stands in relation to Adam as the one from whom he comes, or as we would put it, as son to father or child to parent.

Basil further shows how we use proper names to distinguish one person from another. We do not use proper names to distinguish essences or "humanities" but to distinguish persons. Seth is distinguished from Adam by his name as a separate person but not as a different essence. So too Peter is distinguished from Paul by his name. Basil presses this point to make an

---

16. Athanasius *Orations Against the Arians* I.33, in William Rusch, *The Trinitarian Controversy*, Sources in Early Christian Thought (Philadelphia: Fortress Press, 1980), 96. Athanasius shows how the Son may also be called unoriginate when the word is used to mark the Son off from the rest of creation: *Orations Against the Arians* I.31; *De Decretis* 29–30. A similar point is made by Gregory of Nazianzus *Or.* 39, 12 in *Gregory of Nazianzus*, trans. Brian Daley (New York: Routledge, 2006), 133.

17. Athanasius *Orations Against the Arians* I.34 (Rusch, 97); cf. *De Decretis* 31.

18. Basil of Caesarea *Against Eunomius* 1.15 (Fathers of the Church, 114).

19. Basil of Caesarea *Against Eunomius* 1.15 (Fathers of the Church, 114). Cf. Gregory of Nazianzus *Or.* 29.11 (PPS, 79): "Unbegotten means that he has no parent. It does not state his nature, but simply the fact that he was not begotten."

important distinction for our theological language. We identify Peter by his distinguishing marks: he is the son of Jonah, the man from Bethsaida, the brother of Andrew.[20] The single name "Peter" expresses all these things for us. Similarly, we identify Paul as the man from Tarsus, who was a disciple of Gamaliel and who became the apostle to the Gentiles. The single name "Paul" encompasses all of these things and marks him off as the particular person possessing these distinguishing marks. We would never use the name Peter to mark off the one from Tarsus who studied under Gamaliel and who became the apostle to the Gentiles. That's not Peter, we would say, but Paul. When we discuss their distinguishing marks or properties, the names are not interchangeable or intersubstitutable.

Similar reasoning applies to the names of Father and Son. Basil writes, "In the case of both 'Father' and 'Son' the names do not communicate substance but instead are revelatory of the distinguishing marks."[21] This means that their unity pertains to what they are in common, and their difference resides in number and in the distinctive features that characterize each.[22] A distinctive feature of the Father is that He is "unbegotten," which means He is without source. When we say the Son is begotten, we confess that He is begotten *of the Father*. The source of His divinity is the Father. When we say that the Father is the source of the Son, we are marking off their distinctive relations. The Father has no source; He is unbegotten. The Son comes from the Father in eternity; He is eternally begotten.

Does this mean that there is "order" (τάξις) in God? If we say yes, does that mean that the one ordered (in this case the Son) stands at a later point in time than the orderer (in this case the Father)? The Arians thought any discussion of order meant this. They argued that order is secondary to the one who orders, and therefore the Son is secondary to the Father and is not God in the same way the Father is God.[23] For Basil there are different ways in which we may think of order. There is an order that is natural and another that comes about by deliberation. Natural order may be seen in such things as numbers: one precedes two and both precede three. That order or sequence is natural and can never be undone without lapsing into nonsense. We may also say that the order is relational. One implies two and two assumes one. But we would never reverse the order and count two, one, three. We may also say that one is the cause of two. Without one, the order is disrupted and we do not arrive at two. What is not the case, however, is that one and two differ in what they are. It may sound a little odd to put it this way, but one is no more a number than two and two is no less a number than one, despite the natural order and sequence that eternally avails between them.

---

20. Basil of Caesarea *Against Eunomius* 2.4 (Fathers of the Church, 134–35).
21. Basil of Caesarea *Against Eunomius* 2.5 (Fathers of the Church, 136).
22. Basil of Caesarea *Against Eunomius* 1.19 (Fathers of the Church, 120).
23. Basil of Caesarea *Against Eunomius* 1.20 (Fathers of the Church, 121).

The Persons: Patristic Insights

The second kind of order comes from us and our deliberation upon things. We impose an order and distinction between two things that are naturally ordered or sequenced. Basil gives the example of fire and light. There is a natural order between fire and light established by our minds. First there is fire, so we think, and then there is light. We assume an "interval" between the fire and the light, but no such interval exists in the natural order. As soon as there is fire, there is light. Basil takes these insights and applies them to the Father and the Son. He writes: "We say the Father is ranked prior to the Son in terms of the relation that causes have with what comes from them, not in terms of a difference of nature or a pre-eminence based on time."[24] The difference in terms of causality touches not on the question of essence or time but of relation. The Son is related to the Father in a way similar to how the number two is related to the number one. There is a natural sequence or order that distinguishes one from the other, but not in the sense of nature or time. There is no difference in nature and there is no interval or interstice between them.

Basil brings the above points together by considering a favorite proof-text of the Arians, Jn 14:28, "The Father is greater than I." What does Christ mean when He says this? The answer rests with Christ's carefully chosen words. Since Christ says Father and not God, He means to say only that "the Father" is greater "insofar as he is Father."[25] What does Father mean? Basil explains, "He is the cause and the principle of the one begotten from him."[26] Basil understands Christ's words in terms of relation. When Christ says, "The Father is greater than I," He points us to the eternal relation that avails between the Father and Himself. Basil is not alone in this exegetical insight. Athanasius already had interpreted this text to refer to the Son's eternal generation from the Father.[27] Gregory of Nazianzus acknowledges that some take this text to refer to the Son's economy: the Father is greater than the Son considered as man. That interpretation is true but trivial. As Gregory puts it, everyone knows that God is greater than man. The point Christ wishes to make points to the Father as His cause. The language of "greater" points us to the Father as the principle and cause of the Son.[28]

We need to dwell for a moment on this language of cause. Many people today worry that the language of causality stands apart from the Scriptures and retreats to philosophy. Although it is the case that this language derives from the philosophical schools, the need for it comes from Scripture. The language and logic of the Scriptures led the Fathers to distinguish the persons in terms of their mode or manner of existence (τρόπος τῆς ὑπάρξεως). A statement repeated throughout the Scriptures is that Son is the only-begotten (Ps 2:7 [Heb 1:5]; Jn 1:14, 18; Jn 3:16, 18 KJV). The significance of this language may be seen in

---

24. Basil of Caesarea *Against Eunomius* 1.20 (Fathers of the Church, 121).
25. Basil of Caesarea *Against Eunomius* 1.25 (Fathers of the Church, 127).
26. Basil of Caesarea *Against Eunomius* 1.25 (Fathers of the Church, 127).
27. Athanasius *Orations Against the Arians* I.58.
28. Basil of Caesarea *Against Eunomius* 1.25 (Fathers of the Church, 127).

the Nicene Creed, where the one Lord Jesus Christ is qualified in the following way: "The only-begotten Son of God, begotten of His Father before all worlds ... begotten, not made, being of one substance with the Father." Although Scripture does not say explicitly that the Father is unbegotten, this was implied for the Fathers (and their opponents) from the way Scripture patterns us to think of the Son. If the Son was begotten of the Father, what about the Spirit? According to the language of the Gospel of John, the Holy Spirit proceeds from the Father (Jn 15:26). The Son is begotten and the Spirit proceeds. This way of distinguishing the persons becomes standard for the Fathers. John of Damascus puts the matter succinctly:

> For the Father is uncaused and unbegotten, because He is not from anything, but has His being from Himself and does not have from any other anything whatsoever He has. Rather, He himself is the principle and cause by which all things naturally exist as they do. And the Son is begotten of the Father, while the Holy Ghost is Himself also of the Father—although not by begetting, but by procession. Now, we have learned that there is a difference between begetting and procession, but what the manner of this difference is we have not learned at all. However, the begetting of the Son and the procession of the Holy Ghost from the Father are simultaneous.[29]

The Father is unbegotten, the Son the only-begotten, and the Holy Spirit the one who proceeds from the Father and the Son. These three modes of existence, expressed in terms of causality, are derived from the witness of Scripture. It is this insight that allows the Fathers to answer the problem of how we differentiate the persons when the nature they share is undifferentiated. Gregory of Nyssa explains, "Although we acknowledge the nature is undifferentiated, we do not deny a distinction with respect to causality."[30] We distinguish the divine persons by understanding that one is the cause and the other depends upon that cause. In putting it in this way we begin to see that the language of cause expresses itself in terms of relation not essence. The Father is the cause or principle of the Son and the Holy Spirit. The Son's mode of existence (τρόπος τῆς ὑπάρξεως) is that He is begotten of the Father. The Holy Spirit's mode of existence is that He proceeds from the Father and the Son. The Father's mode of existence is that He is unbegotten, He has no source or principle of His divinity. Lest misunderstanding arise at this point Gregory of Nyssa clarifies his terms. He writes:

> When we speak of a cause and that which depends upon it, we do not by these words refer to nature. For no one would hold that cause and nature are identical. Rather do we indicate a difference in manner of existence [τὸ πῶς εἶναι]. For

---

29. John of Damascus *An Exact Exposition of the Orthodox Faith* 1.8 (Fathers of the Church, 184). John's final point about the difference between being begotten and proceeding comes from Gregory of Nazianzus. See Gregory *Or.* 31.8. See also Pieper, *Christian Dogmatics*, 1:418, "Every wise theologian will confess: '*Quid sit nasci, quid processus, me nescire sum professus.*'"

30. Gregory of Nyssa *An Answer to Ablabius* in *Christology of the Later Fathers*, ed. Edward R. Hardy (Philadelphia: Westminster, 1954), 266.

in saying the one is caused and the other uncaused, we do not divide the nature by the principle of causality, but only explain that the Son does not exist without generation, nor the Father by generation.[31]

Gregory's language is precise. To say that something exists is one thing and to say how something exists is another. To say that something exists without generation is to say only how that thing exists; it is not to say anything about what that thing is. Gregory offers the example of a tree. If you see a tree and ask the owner if it was planted or grew wild and he responds that it had been planted, all you have learned is the manner or mode of existence for that tree. You have yet to learn what kind of tree it is.[32] In a similar way, to say that the Father is unbegotten, the Son begotten, and that the Spirit proceeds indicates for us their mode of existence. The Father depends upon no source or principle; the Son depends upon the Father; and the Spirit depends upon the Father and the Son.

A further point needs to be made here: the order of the Trinity follows their mode of existence. For this reason, we say Father, Son, and Holy Spirit. We do not confuse the order, saying Son, Father, Spirit or Spirit, Father, Son. The order of the persons—Father, Son, and Holy Spirit—reveals to us their distinctive features, their distinguishing marks. The name Father expresses His distinctive feature of being unbegotten and possessing fatherhood; the name Son expresses His distinctive feature of being begotten and possessing sonship. Basil explains:

> The distinctive features, which are like certain characters and forms observed in the substance, differentiate what is common by means of the distinguishing characters and do not sunder the substance's sameness in nature. For example, the divinity is common, whereas the fatherhood and sonship are distinguishing marks: from the combination of both, that is, of the common and the unique, we arrive at comprehension of the truth.[33]

The Father is eternally distinguished from the Son by His fatherhood; the Son is eternally distinguished from the Father by His sonship. Gregory of Nyssa will add to Basil's statement that the Holy Spirit is distinguished from the Father and the Son by His procession. Although he does not say that the Holy Spirit proceeds from the Father and the Son, Gregory does insist that the Spirit never proceeds from the Father apart from the Son.[34] Later Greek writers would

---

31. Gregory of Nyssa *An Answer to Ablabius*, 266.
32. Gregory of Nyssa *An Answer to Ablabius*, 267.
33. Basil of Caesarea *Against Eunomius* 2.28 (Fathers of the Church, 174). This passage from Basil is quoted by nearly all medieval and Reformation writers discussing the distinction of persons.
34. For Gregory, the procession of the Spirit from the Father intimately involves the Son. The Spirit depends (ἤρτηται) on the Son and is known after the Son and with Son. See Gregory of Nyssa *Letter* 35, 4d (Silvas, 253). Cf. John Behr, *The Nicene Faith* (Crestwood, NY: St. Vladimir's Seminary Press, 2004), vol. 2, part 2, 434: "Gregory clearly affirms the Son's mediation in the procession of the Spirit, for the Spirit proceeds not simply from God, but from the Father of the Son, and therefore always in relation to the Son."

express the inseparability of the Son and the Spirit by saying the Spirit proceeds from the Father through the Son.

Gregory of Nazianzus warns the faithful not to show so much devotion to the Father that they rob Him of His fatherhood or so much devotion to Christ that they neglect His sonship.[35] God the Father stands eternally in relation to God the Son and therefore can never be separated from Him. As Basil had put it, fatherhood is coextensive with the Father's eternity.[36] The Father is not Father without the Son; the Son is not Son without the Father. The eternal identities of Father and Son demand one another. Similarly, the faithful must not separate the Son from the Spirit. The Son sends the Spirit, who proceeds from the Father, to us that we might know the Son. The Spirit sent to us by the Son points us always to the Son, who in turn reveals the Father to us. Basil explains: "Never do we separate the Paraclete from His union with the Father and the Son. For our mind being enlightened by the Spirit looks up at the Son, and in Him as in an image beholds the Father."[37] As soon as we behold the Father our minds go to the Son and their Spirit. Gregory of Nyssa writes, "One who has given thought to the Father and given thought to him as he is in Himself, has also embraced the Son in his understanding, and one who has received him does not portion off the Spirit from the Son."[38] Anyone who mentions the Spirit confesses the one of whom He is the Spirit. Since He is, notes Gregory, the Spirit of Christ (Rom 8:9) and the Spirit of God the Father (1 Cor 2:12), then to think of the Spirit is also to think of the Son and the Father.[39] Likewise, to think of the Father is to think also of His Son and Spirit.[40]

Basil of Caesarea and Gregory of Nyssa both argue that there is no interval or interstice ($\delta\iota\acute{\alpha}\sigma\tau\eta\mu\alpha$) between Father, Son, and Holy Spirit.[41] Although distinct and known to us by their distinguishing properties, they are also intimately in one another: "I am in the Father and the Father is in me" (Jn 14:10). The inseparability of the Father and the Son is true also of the Son and the Spirit. The persons abide and rest in one another. Fulgentius of Ruspe expresses this with particular clarity: "The whole of the Father is in the Son and the Holy Spirit, and the whole of the Son is in the Father and the Holy Spirit, and, as well, the whole of the Holy Spirit in the Father and the Son."[42] The church would later call this *perichoresis* or *circumcessio*, the mutual interpenetration or coinherence of the persons. The persons are intimately united without confusion and mutually indwell one another without any blending or mingling, without change

---

35. Gregory of Nazianzus *Or.* 2, 38 (NPNF, ii, VII, 212).
36. Basil of Caesarea *Against Eunomius* 2.12 (Fathers of the Church, 146).
37. Basil of Caesarea *Letter* 226 (LCL, 3:339).
38. Gregory of Nyssa *Letter* 35, 4j (Silvas, 254).
39. Gregory of Nyssa *Letter* 35, 4k (Silvas, 254).
40. Gregory of Nyssa *Letter* 35, 4m (Silvas, 255).
41. Cf. Basil of Caesarea *Against Eunomius* 2.12 (Fathers of the Church, 146); Gregory of Nyssa *Letter* 35, 4i (Silvas, 254).
42. Fulgentius of Ruspe *To Peter on the Faith* 4 (Fathers of the Church, 62).

or division.⁴³ As John of Damascus would later put it, the Son is in the Father and the Spirit, the Spirit is in the Father and the Son, and the Father is in the Son and the Spirit, and this without merging, blending, or confusion.⁴⁴

Augustine

Augustine echoes much of the language introduced above, and through Augustine the Latin West continues this way of speaking during the medieval and Reformation periods. Augustine thinks of the term "unbegotten" differently than Athanasius and Basil and prefers the "trivial" interpretation of Jn 14:28 dismissed by Gregory of Nazianzus.⁴⁵ Despite these differences the conclusions drawn by Augustine on the points we are discussing coincide with the Greek theologians above and should be seen as complementary. Augustine begins by stating a number of crucial points that both establish difference between the Father and the Son and emphasize their unity. He does this in terms of "rules" that should govern our reading of Scripture and therefore also our speaking. After dwelling on the point that the works of the Father and the Son *ad extra* are inseparable, Augustine states that the Son's working is "from the Father" just as He Himself is "from the Father."⁴⁶ He then writes:

> This then is the rule which governs many scriptural texts, intended to show not that one person is less than the other, but only that one is from the other. Yet some people have extracted from it the sense that the Son is less than the Father. . . . [This rule] tells us not that the Son is less than the Father, but that he is from the Father. This does not imply any dearth of inequality, but only his birth in eternity.⁴⁷

Augustine turns to the scriptural texts that indicate for us that the Son is the only-begotten of the Father and that the Spirit proceeds from the Father.⁴⁸ He makes the further point that "the source of all godhead, or if you prefer it, of all deity, is the Father."⁴⁹ This we acknowledge and confess when we say that the Son is begotten of the Father and that the Holy Spirit proceeds from the

---

43. John of Damascus *An Exact Exposition of the Orthodox Faith* 1.8 (Fathers of the Church, 187).

44. John of Damascus *An Exact Exposition of the Orthodox Faith* 1.14 (Fathers of the Church, 202).

45. For Augustine's discussion of Jn 14:28 see *The Trinity* 1.15 (WSA I/5, 75); 2.3 (WSA I/5, 98). An important exegetical reason for his interpretation may be seen at *The Trinity* 2.11 (WSA I/5, 104). Cf. also *The Trinity* 6.5 (WSA I/5, 208). Hilary of Poitiers favors the Greek interpretation. Thomas Aquinas prefers Augustine's exegesis but recognizes the legitimacy of Hilary's interpretation and therefore also of the Greek fathers. Thomas Aquinas, *Gospel of John*, 1970-71, 2:273-74. The Lutherans follow Augustine. Cf. Melanchthon, *Loci Communes*, 29; Chemnitz, *Loci Theologici* 1:159. Chemnitz is aware of Gregory of Nazianzus's exegesis and regards it as too subtle and departing from the simplicity of the faith. For a modern Western interpretation of this text that favors the Greek reading see Bernard Lonergan, *The Triune God: Doctrines* (Toronto: University of Toronto Press, 2009), 489.

46. Augustine *The Trinity* 2.3 (WSA I/5, 99).

47. Augustine *The Trinity* 2.4-5 (WSA I/5, 99-100).

48. Augustine *The Trinity* 4.29 (WSA I/5, 174).

49. Augustine *The Trinity* 4.29 (WSA I/5, 174).

Father and the Son. Such language does not indicate "any inequality, disparity, or dissimilarity of substance between the divine persons" but rather makes the point that "the Father is the source and origin of all deity."[50] Further, such language rightly distinguishes the persons for us: "The Father has begotten the Son, and therefore he who is the Father is not the Son; and the Son is begotten by the Father, and therefore he who is the Son is not the Father."[51]

Augustine deliberately avoids the language of unbegotten until he has established all of the above. Only after showing how we distinguish the persons without implying inequality of substance does he raise the question of how we understand the terms unbegotten and begotten. The Arians, he tells us, claim these are substance words. Therefore, the Father and Son are of different substances because one is unbegotten and the other begotten.[52] Augustine directs his attention to how the Arians read Scripture. They fail to understand how Scripture assigns things to God; they do not understand the grammar of Scripture. Scripture says some things in terms of substance and some things in terms of relation. When it comes to things or people other than God, Scripture also says things in terms of modification, reflecting changes in that thing or person. Since God does not change in the sense that He becomes something He was not, Scripture never speaks of God in terms of modification. That leaves us with only two ways in which Scripture talks about God: in terms of substance or in terms of relation.[53] The words Father and Son are said in terms of relation. Father is said with reference to the Son and Son with reference to the Father. Since there is no modification in God, these relational terms indicate eternal relationships. The Father is always Father and the Son is always Son. There was never a time when the Father was not Father of the Son nor a time when the Son was not Son of the Father.[54]

What about the terms "unbegotten" and "begotten"? Augustine notes that the two terms operate differently. A person can be father without being unbegotten in the same way that one may be unbegotten without being father. The two terms do not require one another.[55] One, however, cannot be son without being begotten. These two terms require one another. Further, while unbegotten does not require a relation (the unbegotten need not beget), begotten

---

50. Augustine *The Trinity* 4.32 (WSA I/5, 177).
51. Augustine *The Trinity* 1.7 (WSA I/5, 69). Augustine makes this comment at the beginning of his work, indicating what he will demonstrate.
52. Augustine *The Trinity* 5.4 (WSA I/5, 191).
53. Augustine *The Trinity* 5.6 (WSA I/5, 192).
54. Cf. John of Damascus *An Exact Exposition of the Orthodox Faith* 1.8 (Fathers of the Church, 178): "For the Father never was when the Son was not, but the Father and the Son begotten of Him exist together simultaneously, because the Father could not be so called without a Son. Now, if He was not Father when He did not have the Son, and then later became Father without having been Father before, then He was changed from not being Father to being Father, which is the worst of all blasphemies."
55. Cf. Gregory of Nazianzus *Or.* 29.3 (PPS, 71): "'Being unoriginate' necessarily implies 'being eternal,' but 'being eternal' does not entail 'being unoriginate,' so long as the Father is referred to as origin."

The Persons: Patristic Insights

assumes begetter and therefore assumes relation.[56] Augustine concludes: "Two distinct notions are conveyed by 'begetter' and 'unbegotten.' Both indeed are said of God the Father."[57] What then do these terms mean? When Scripture says that the Son is begotten, it uses redundancy. Begotten and son mean the same thing. Being son is a consequence of being begotten. The word unbegotten, the privative form of begotten, grammatically means nothing more than "not son."[58] We may say either "unbegotten" or "not begotten" and mean the same thing. The rules of language, laments Augustine, will not allow us to say "unson" (*infilius*), but that is what "unbegotten" or "not begotten" means.[59]

Augustine has shown already that Father and Son are relational terms. Begotten and son designate the same reality, and both are used relationally. Unbegotten and not begotten deny a particular relationship, and in that sense both are also used relationally. Augustine explains:

> I affirm relationship-wise when I say "son," since I refer it to father; I deny relationship-wise when I say "He is not a son," since I am referring the negation to parent, in wishing to declare that he has not got a parent. But if what is meant by saying "son" can be said just as well by saying "begotten" as I remarked above, then one can say "not son" just as well by saying "not begotten." Now we deny relationship-wise when we say "not son"; therefore we deny relationship-wise when we say "not begotten." And what does unbegotten mean but not begotten? So we do not leave the predication of relationship when we say unbegotten.... And what is stated relationship-wise does not designate substance. So although begotten differs from unbegotten, it does not indicate a different substance, because just as son refers to father, and 'not son' to 'not father', so begotten must refer to begetter, and 'not begotten' to 'not begetter'.[60]

We should not think that Augustine's emphasis on relation amounts to only a particular way of talking about the divine persons. The language has ontological significance. The Father really *is* Father, and this always on account of the Son; the Son always *is* Son, and this on account of the Father. In his tractates on John Augustine addresses these very points. He writes:

> The Father is life, not by "being born" [*non nascendo*]; the Son is life by "being born" [*nascendo*]. The Father is not from any father, the Son is from God the Father. The Father, that he is, is from no one; but that he is Father he is on account of the Son [*propter Filium*]. But for the Son both that he is the Son is on account of the Father [*propter Patrem*] and that he is, he is from the Father [*a Patre*].[61]

Here we see that Augustine's language for relation amounts to far more than a logical way of talking about the Father and the Son. It pertains to who they

---

56. Augustine *The Trinity* 5.7 (WSA I/5, 192).
57. Augustine *The Trinity* 5.7 (WSA I/5, 192).
58. Augustine *The Trinity* 5.8 (WSA I/5, 193).
59. Augustine *The Trinity* 5.8 (WSA I/5, 193).
60. Augustine *The Trinity* 5.8 (WSA I/5, 194).
61. Augustine *In Johannis Evangelium Tractatus* 19.13 (PL 35, 1550); cf. Augustine *Homilies on the Gospel of John* 19.13 (WSA III/12, 346–47).

eternally are. This means that even apart from our speaking and thinking, these relations are real. The Father is Father, *propter Filium*; the Son is Son, and this toward the Father.[62] Again Augustine writes, "But truly God the Father is Father toward another [*ad aliquid*], that is, to the Son; and God the Son is Son toward another [*ad aliquid*], that is, to the Father."[63]

Augustine's distinction between substantive and relative predication in our talk about God becomes his most significant contribution to trinitarian theology and trinitarian logic. Luther and the Lutheran dogmaticians never tire of using it. Although Augustine takes a different route than the Greek theologians to get to his conclusion, they both press the distinction between substance and relation in Scripture's language about God. Moreover, they all appeal to mode of existence or causality to distinguish the persons. The Father is the cause or origin of the Son and the Holy Spirit. Augustine writes, "He is called Father relationship-wise, and he is also called origin relationship-wise."[64] The Father is the origin with reference to the Son because He begets Him and with reference to the Spirit because He gives Him. It may also be said, continues Augustine, that the Father and the Son are both the origin of the Holy Spirit, but not in such a way that they are two origins.[65] The Cappadocians and Augustine employ the language of cause or origin to express the mode of existence unique to each person. That unique mode distinguishes the persons from one another and reveals their personal properties for us.

TERMINOLOGY

The Fathers labored to arrive at terms that would adequately convey the oneness and threeness of God. The church's technical language, which finds a home in the great creeds of the church, aimed to bring clarity of expression to Scripture's witness to the Trinity, and at the same time to expose all heretics and false teachers who sought to undermine that witness. The continued use of this technical language in the liturgy, especially in the prayers and proper preface for Trinity season, joins the voices of the faithful together from generation to generation. Since this language serves to preserve the meaning of Scripture, there is no graduating from it. To do so exposes a person to the ever-present danger of obscuring the scriptural witness guarded by this language.

At the Council of Nicaea (325) the bishops declared that the Son was "from the *ousia*" of the Father (ἐκ τῆς οὐσίας), the Son was *homoousios* (consubstantial) with the Father, and, in the anathemas attached to the Creed, the council condemned anyone who taught that the Son was "of a different

---

62. On this point see Lewis Ayres, *Augustine and the Trinity* (Cambridge: Cambridge University Press, 2010), 245–47.
63. Augustine *In Johannis Evangelium Tractatus* 20.9 (PL 35, 1683); cf. Augustine *Homilies on the Gospel of John* 39.4 (WSA III/12, 588).
64. Augustine *The Trinity* 5.14 (WSA I/5, 198); cf. *The Trinity* 6.3 (WSA I/5, 206).
65. Augustine *The Trinity* 5.15 (WSA I/5, 199).

hypostasis or *ousia* from the Father."⁶⁶ Those familiar with the church's way of speaking will find this anathema surprising and confusing. The anathema serves as a useful reminder that language is fluid and the meaning of words changes. At the Council of Nicaea, *hypostasis* and *ousia* were synonyms. To say that the Son's *hypostasis* was eternally distinct from the Father's *hypostasis* was anathema; following the Council of Constantinople (381), *not* to say this was anathema. The key terms from Nicaea (*ousia*, *homoousios*, *hypostasis*) occupied the attention of all theologians throughout the fourth and well into the fifth century. The terms were confusing for both Greek and Latin theologians. Some Greek writers continued to think of *hypostasis* and *ousia* as synonyms, refusing to say that there was more than one *hypostasis* in God; others distinguished the terms in such a way that God was one *ousia* and three *hypostases*. Rendering these Greek words into Latin proved nearly impossible. Even thirty years after the Council of Constantinople Augustine expresses confusion and frustration. The Greek phrase "one *ousia* and three *hypostases*" is rendered into Latin as "one *essentia* and three *substantiae*."⁶⁷ The word *ousia* means being, and Augustine can use *essentia* to translate it but the more typical way, he tells us, would be to use *substantia*.⁶⁸ To hear someone say God is "one substance and three substances" borders on nonsense and risks heresy.⁶⁹ Augustine did not fare much better with the word *hypostasis* or *person*. He famously declares, "When you ask, 'Three what?' human speech labors under a great dearth of words. So we say three persons, not in order to say that precisely, but in order not to be reduced to silence."⁷⁰

The Fathers did not begin their discussions of the Trinity with technical terms but ended with them. The terms served as markers of what had been demonstrated from the Scriptures and explained according to their pious reasoning. Although this point is somewhat obvious, it bears emphasis. The terms deployed did not already possess sufficient meaning for confessing the Trinity. The terms had to be christianized, to be redefined and properly

---

66. For the Greek of the Creed and a good discussion of its terms see T. Herbert Bindley, *The Oecumenical Documents of the Faith*, rev. F. W. Green (Oxford: Oxford University Press, 1950), 26-49. See also J. N. D. Kelly, *Early Christian Creeds*, 3d ed. (London: Longman, 1972), 231-62; and R. P. C. Hanson, *The Search for the Christian Doctrine of God* (Grand Rapids: Baker Academic, 2005), 181-207.

67. Augustine *The Trinity* 5.10 (WSA I/5, 196).

68. Augustine *The Trinity* 5.9 (WSA I/5, 196).

69. Cf. William Alston, "Substance and the Trinity," in *The Trinity*, ed. Steven T. Davis, Daniel Kendall, and Gerald O'Collins (Oxford: Oxford University Press, 1999), 179-201, especially 181-89; H. A. Wolfson, *The Philosophy of the Church Fathers* (Cambridge, MA: Harvard University Press, 1956), 317-22. The language of *ousia* derives from Aristotle. He distinguished between primary *ousia* and secondary *ousia*. Primary *ousia* referred to the individual bearer of an essence, and secondary *ousia* referred to the essence that makes the individual what it is. With this in mind, it would be possible for someone familiar with Aristotle to say that the Trinity is "three *ousiai* and one *ousia*," and mean by that "three *hypostases* and one *ousia*," as the formula would eventually be stated. Origen is an example of someone who spoke like this.

70. Augustine *The Trinity* 5.9 (WSA I/5, 196). Cf. Augustine *Homilies on the Gospel of John* 39.3 (WSA III/12, 588).

deployed according the witness of Scripture. Even if we may trace the pedigree of these terms to ancient philosophical schools, we will fail to understand their use by pro-Nicene theologians if we restrict their meaning to these ancient schools. Further, technical terms work only when we agree to use them in the same way. If some use *hypostasis* as *ousia* and others use these terms to refer to two different things, confusion necessarily arises and Scripture becomes distorted. As Lutherans we are very good at conveying the scriptural meaning of such words as sin, grace, faith, and justification. Our ears are trained to detect the slightest deviation from the meaning of Scripture in the use of these words. When confusion arises, we do not hesitate to further clarify these words, even if it means departing from the exact phrasing of Scripture (e.g., justified by faith *alone* or distinguishing objective and subjective justification). Despite the confusion that resulted, the Fathers gathered at Nicaea attempted to do the same thing with the word *homoousios*. Athanasius explains:

> But since the generation of the Son from the Father is other than that which pertains to the nature of human beings and he is not only like [*homoios*] but also inseparable from the essence [*ousia*] of the Father and he and the Father are one, as he himself said (Jn 10:30), and the Word is always in the Father and the Father in the Word (Jn 10:38)—as is the radiance in relation to the light (for this is what the phrase means)—the council, understanding all this, aptly wrote "one in essence" [*homoousion*].[71]

The bishops gathered at Nicaea used the word *homoousios* or consubstantial to convey the meaning of Scripture. The Father and Son, who are eternally distinct from one another, are of the same substance. Whatever it means for the Father to be God, it means this for the Son as well.[72] Every scriptural word used and every text produced to convey this meaning was distorted by those who rejected the coequality and coeternity of the Father and the Son. The word that exposed their false teaching was *homoousios*, and so it was used.[73] Should we be concerned that this word does not come from Scripture? Athanasius responds:

> Nevertheless, let it be known to anyone who wishes to learn, that even if the words are not as such in the Scriptures, yet, as has been said before, they contain the sense (*dianoian*) of the Scriptures and they express this sense and communicate it to those who have ears that are whole and hearken unto piety.[74]

---

71. Athanasius *De Decretis* 20 (Anatolios, 198). Cf. Basil of Caesarea *Letter* 52 (LCL, 1:327–37).

72. Basil of Caesarea *Letter* 226 (LCL, 3:337): "That holy and God-beloved synod . . . [held] that whatever the Father is in substance this should be understood of the Son also. For thus those very men have explained it when they said: 'Light of Light.'"

73. Scholars continue to argue about how this word emerged in the debates at Nicaea. One possibility may be found with Ambrose of Milan. According to him, at the Council Eusebius of Nicomedia asserted, "If we do indeed call the Son of God 'uncreated' as well, we are on the way to confessing that he is *homoousios* with the Father." The bishops may have gravitated to this word because of the strong dislike of it by those rallying around the theological position of Arius. For this argument and the Ambrose quote see Rowan Williams, *Arius: A Heresy and Tradition*, 2d ed. (London: SCM, 2001), 68–70.

74. Athanasius *De Decretis* 21 (Anatolios, 199). Cf. Martin Luther, *On the Councils and the*

As a general rule, the best words available to convey the meaning of Scripture come from Scripture. The persistence of false teaching, however, requires the faithful to clarify the meaning of Scripture by appealing to other expressions or words like objective justification or *homoousios*.[75]

Above we saw how Basil of Caesarea expressed the identity and distinction of the persons by reflecting on the teaching of Scripture. Basil further advocated *ousia* and *hypostasis* to express what the persons held in common and what distinguished them.[76] We rightly confess the persons of the Trinity when we add the particular, the distinguishing property, to what is common. For example, when we understand the *ousia* as common and distinguish paternity as the particular, we combine these and confess "I believe in God the Father." Likewise, when we distinguish sonship as the particular, we confess "I believe in God the Son."[77] Gregory of Nyssa elaborated upon Basil's insight in a brief letter to their brother Peter. He starts with an example from our everyday affairs and rehearses the insights we observed above. When we use the general term "man," we use it to indicate the common nature of all people. The term no more indicates Peter than it does Andrew, John, or James. Peter is "man" in the same way Andrew is "man." Both are human, and one is not more human than the other. The names Peter and Andrew, on the other hand, signify not the common nature but an individual expression of that nature. We distinguish Peter from Andrew by identifying certain individual properties that belong to one and not the other. Gregory applies technical terms to what he here observes. We use the word *hypostasis* to indicate what is spoken of individually.[78] The word "man" designates something general, something abstract. In this case, "man" marks out what kind of being (*ousia*) we are talking about but not any particular instance of that being. *Hypostasis* serves this purpose. *Hypostasis* expresses the individual properties, the particulars of Peter, Andrew, John, or James.

At this point Gregory turns to the Trinity. If we take this basic understanding of what is common and what is particular in our affairs and apply these insights to Father, Son, and Holy Spirit, we will better express our faith in the Trinity.[79] Whatever we think of the Father's *ousia*, we must think also of the Son and the Holy Spirit. Since we can never arrive at a "concept" or exhaustive knowledge of God's being, Gregory deliberately uses negative terms to illustrate his point. The principle of the "incomprehensible" and "uncreated" remains one and

---

Church, 1539 (AE 41:83; WA 50:572.20–26): "It is certainly true that one should teach nothing outside of Scripture pertaining to divine matters, as St. Hilary writes in *On the Trinity*, Book I[.18], which means only that one should teach nothing that is at variance with Scripture. But that one should not use more or other words than those contained in Scripture—this cannot be adhered to, especially in a controversy and when heretics want to falsify things with trickery and distort the words of Scripture."

75. Cf. Chemnitz, *Loci Theologici* 1:96–98.
76. Basil of Caesarea *Letter 246* (LCL, 3:401).
77. Basil of Caesarea *Letter 246* (LCL, 3:403).
78. Gregory of Nyssa *Letter 35*, 3a (Silvas, 251).
79. Gregory of Nyssa *Letter 35*, 3e (Silvas, 252).

the same, whether we regard Father, Son, or Holy Spirit.[80] One is not more incomprehensible and uncreated and another less so.[81] Gregory turns next to the distinction of persons as presented by Scripture.[82] He uses the example of how good things come to us by God. Scripture says that the Holy Spirit "works all things in all" and distributes to each as He wills (1 Cor 12:6, 11). If we further ask if these good things come from the Holy Spirit alone, Scripture directs us to the Son, "the only-begotten God" (Jn 1:18), through whom all things came to be (Jn 1:3). Further, this Son who is only-begotten is from the Father, who is without generation and origin. This means that the good things distributed by the Holy Spirit are from the Father through the Son.

Gregory makes two points from the way Scripture describes the activities of the three persons. First, we distinguish the persons by the way Scripture reveals their origin. The Spirit proceeds from the Father, but not in such a way that excludes the Son; the only-begotten Son is from the Father; the Father alone has no cause.[83] These distinguishing marks identify the three persons for us, and the word *hypostasis* designates that which possesses the distinguishing mark. Second, we know the Son only by the Holy Spirit and the Father only by the Son. And yet, continues Gregory, you cannot think of the Father without immediately embracing the Son and the Spirit.[84] We know the persons according to their order (*taxis*), the order of how they are in relation to one another (order of being) and the order by which they bring us to know them and share in their divine life (order of knowing).[85]

Gregory of Nazianzus follows a similar course but with a different emphasis. He stresses the importance of recognizing what is one in God and what is three: "The divinity is one in three, and the three are one—those three in whom the divinity exists, or to put it more accurately who are the divinity."[86] Scripture makes clear to us that the Father is Father and without source; the Son is Son and from the Father by generation; the Spirit is truly Spirit and comes forth from the Father by procession.[87] Further, the Father is always Father, the Son always Son, and the Spirit always Spirit. Their distinguishing properties are

---

80. Gregory of Nyssa *Letter* 35, 3f (Silvas, 252).
81. The Athanasian Creed incorporates this point by Gregory. After declaring the Godhead of Father, Son, and Holy Spirit one, the glory equal and the majesty coeternal, the Creed declares (TLH, p. 53): "Such as the Father is, such is the Son, and such is the Holy Ghost. The Father uncreate, the Son uncreate, and the Holy Ghost uncreate. The Father incomprehensible, the Son incomprehensible, and the Holy Ghost incomprehensible. And yet not three Eternals, but one Eternal. As there are not three Uncreated nor three Incomprehensibles, but one Uncreated and one Incomprehensible."
82. Gregory of Nyssa *Letter* 35, 4 (Silvas, 252).
83. Gregory of Nyssa *Letter* 35, 4 (Silvas, 253).
84. Cf. Augustine *The Trinity* VI.9 (WSA I/5, 211): "Admittedly it is not easy to see how you can talk of the Father alone or the Son alone, since the Father is always and inseparably with the Son and the Son with the Father; not that both are Father or both Son, but that they are always in each other and neither is alone."
85. Gregory of Nyssa *Letter* 35, 4 (Silvas, 254).
86. Gregory of Nazianzus *Or.* 39, 11 (Daley, 133).
87. Gregory of Nazianzus *Or.* 39, 12 (Daley, 133).

unalterable and incommunicable. The Father's paternity belongs to Him alone; the Son's sonship to Him alone; and the Spirit's procession to Him alone. What is important for the faithful is that they rightly grasp this oneness and threeness. Gregory writes,

> When I speak of God, let yourselves be surrounded with a flash of that light which is both one and three: three in properties, or indeed in hypostases, if one wants to call them that, or indeed in "persons"—for we will not become involved in a battle over names, as long as the syllables point towards the same notion—and one with regard to the concept of substance, or indeed divinity.[88]

Gregory expresses all of this in an oration on baptism. Here the faithful learn the grammar of the church's faith, the way in which we may confess and pray the truth of God's scriptural identity as we come to share in His triune life. The faithful come to know the Son by the Holy Spirit, and in knowing the Son know the Father. These three are distinguished, according to Scripture, by their personal properties, and we express this with the word *hypostasis* or person, whichever word best expresses for us God's revelation of Himself.

The three Cappadocians sought to standardize the way in which the church confessed its faith in the Trinity in order to express the witness of Scripture and to guard that truth from false teachings. They employed *ousia* to mark out that which was common to the three and *hypostasis* to mark off the properties that distinguished the three. With God there was a single, infinite reality, substance, or nature, and at the heart of this single reality three irreducible *hypostases*.[89] The church would incorporate this vocabulary into its dogmatic works and creeds. The faithful would pattern their speech in worship and prayer with these terms, and pastors would preach accordingly. With the Athanasian Creed they confessed the unity in Trinity and Trinity in unity; they confessed three persons and one God and Lord, neither confounding the persons nor dividing the substance.

What about the confusion expressed by Augustine above? Although the church's way of talking about the Trinity seeks to express the common and particular in a manner faithful to Scripture, the language still remains obscure and strained. The terms have a unique use and meaning when applied to the Trinity.[90] Although "essence," "substance," and "nature" may be used of both God and man, they have different meanings. The same is true for *hypostasis* or person. In ordinary speech, three persons are three separate human beings, and each individually has three of everything that pertains to being human, for example power, will, work, etc. Here we enter upon the mystery that is the Trinity. Father, Son, and Holy Spirit are three persons with one essence, one power, one will, and one in work toward creation. Their essence is one, and that one essence belongs wholly and completely, truly and really, without division

---

88. Gregory of Nazianzus *Or.* 39, 11 (Daley, 132).
89. Brian Daley, "Introduction," *Gregory of Nazianzus* (New York: Routledge, 2006), 46.
90. Pieper, *Christian Dogmatics* 1:410–13; Chemnitz, *Loci Theologici* 1:100–103.

and separation, to Father, Son, and Holy Spirit. The word "person" works differently too. Modern notions of personhood emphasize self-consciousness and self-determination. The freedom to assert the self and one's own individuality stand at the heart of what many think it means to be an authentic person today.[91] When this modern understanding of person is applied to the Trinity, we end up with something resembling tritheism. For this reason our Confessions state explicitly that the word "person" is to be used as the Fathers used it and not as the prevailing culture does.[92]

Above we noted that Augustine used this word "person" not so much because it expressed the mystery of the three but in order not to remain silent. Luther says something quite similar. He writes:

> Because Christ is born of the Father, he must be a Person distinct from the Father. You may use whatever term you will, we use the term *person*. We realize, of course, that our terminology is inadequate and is really only a stammering. But we cannot do justice to this truth, for we have no better term.[93]

The technical language of the church aimed to mark out what Scripture said about the oneness and threeness of God. Never did the Fathers or reformers think the language wholly satisfactory, but they also never thought the language dispensable. The Emperor Gratian said to Ambrose, "We speak about these things not in the way we ought but in the way we can."[94] We acknowledge the same when we use these terms, and with Augustine and Luther continue to use them lest we remain silent and confusion arise.

The insights of the Fathers on how we distinguish the persons, the distinction between essence and relation, and the technical terminology used to mark off Father, Son, and Holy Spirit as both one and three come to our Lutheran fathers by way of the medieval theologians. Although we rightly critique elements of this medieval heritage, there is no way to understand the trinitarian commitments of our Lutheran fathers apart from the pious labors of the schoolmen. The next chapter will show these two things: the traditional patterns of speech used to discuss the Trinity by our Lutheran fathers and their indebtedness to the medieval theologians.

---

91. For a further discussion of modern notions of person in contemporary trinitarian thinking see the Conclusion.

92. AC I.3–4 (Tappert, 28).

93. "On Trinity Sunday, first sermon, 1535," 11 in *Luthers Sämtliche Schriften*, ed. J. G. Walch (St. Louis: Concordia Publishing House, 1904), 669; quoted in Francis Pieper, *Christian Dogmatics* 1:409.

94. This is Chemnitz's paraphrase of Gratian's comment to Ambrose. Chemnitz, *Loci Theologici* 1:102. Cf. Ambrose, *Ep.* 1, in *Saint Ambrose Letters* (Fathers of the Church, 5): "You [Gratian] have remarked in addition that, being weak and frail, you cannot so praise Him as to exalt the Godhead by your words. But you will preach Him according to your ability, not according to what the Godhead warrants."

13

DISTINGUISHING THE PERSONS: MEDIEVAL AND REFORMATION REFLECTIONS

The grammar and pattern of trinitarian speech shown in the previous chapter comes to Lutheranism by way of the medieval schoolmen. The Lutheran engagement with medieval trinitarian thought exhibits both a debt to and critical distance from medieval patterns of speech and ways of conceiving the Trinity. Luther and our dogmaticians knew the rules of logic and semantic patterns explored by the schoolmen. They moved easily within this intellectual environment and deployed the technical insights of the schoolmen when necessary and useful. Luther never wavered from teaching these insights in the classroom. The Lutheran dogmaticians and the dogmatic textbooks of the nineteenth and twentieth centuries retained these medieval insights in their own discussions of the Trinity.[1] From this perspective, Lutheran trinitarian theology remains firmly committed to the church's way of confessing the Trinity.

Although Lutheran trinitarian theology owes much to the schoolmen, the Lutherans received this tradition critically. Two questions discussed at length during the medieval period illustrate well the balanced reception by Luther and the dogmaticians: whether relations of opposition (*relationes oppositiae*) distinguish the persons of the Trinity and whether in God the essence generates essence (*essentia generet essentiam*)? Although these questions are technical, they shed considerable light on how to speak and think rightly about the scriptural identity of God. Our Lutheran dogmaticians, especially Johann Gerhard and Abraham Calov, found the teaching on *relationes oppositiae* useful for distinguishing the persons of the Trinity and for explaining the scriptural teaching on the *filioque*. After presenting what the medieval writers had to say about relations of opposition, I will turn to Gerhard and Calov and show how they incorporated these insights into their discussions of the Trinity, looking particularly at the issue of the *filioque*.

The second question on whether the essence generates presents problems. Lateran IV (1215) answered "no" to this question and condemned any who would say otherwise. From this perspective, the question was decided for the medieval church. Luther was aware of this history and rejected the decision

---

1. For example, John William Baier, *Compendium Theologiae Positivae*, ed. C. F. W. Walther (St. Louis: Concordia Publishing House, 1879), I, §29–47; Francis Pieper, *Christian Dogmatics* (St. Louis: Concordia Publishing House, 1950), 1:406–63; Adolf Hoenecke, *Evangelical Lutheran Dogmatics*, trans. James Langebartels and Richard Krause (Milwaukee: Northwestern Publishing House, 2009), 2:49–209.

of the council. His rejection of Lateran IV only further fueled the Roman polemics of the sixteenth and seventeenth centuries against his trinitarian doctrine.[2] Below I will briefly review the issue at Lateran IV and then turn to Luther's surprising affirmation of *essentia generet essentiam*.[3] Luther's answer focuses especially on how language works and the way in which our words refer. Semantic arguments play an important role in trinitarian theology. As the Athanasian Creed impresses upon us, we need to know what we can and cannot say about the Trinity. Luther's discussion of this particular issue, something that comes out of the Wittenberg classroom and therefore something rehearsed by Luther for future pastors, teaches us important lessons for how we proclaim in worship and prayer the scriptural identity of the Trinity.

RELATIONS OF OPPOSITION

The greatest divide among the late medieval thinkers on the Trinity had to do with whether the persons were distinguished because of emanation or relation.[4] They asked, for example, whether the Father is Father because He generates or whether He generates because He is the Father.[5] If you say He is Father because He generates, you place the emphasis on generation and hold to the emanation account of personal distinction.[6] Bonaventure defended this view, and it became associated with the Franciscan way of conceiving the Trinity. The other view stems from Augustine and was defended by Thomas Aquinas. For Thomas, the Father generates because He is the Father. This way of conceiving the Trinity became associated with the Dominicans. The disagreement between the Dominicans and the Franciscans proceeded from a great deal of agreement on the basic structure of trinitarian thought.[7] They agreed, for example, that

---

2. For some criticisms brought against Luther's trinitarian commitments by Roman Catholics, see Johann Gerhard, *De Tribus Elohim*, Locus 4/1, §3 (ed. Cotta, 185); Gerhard, *Confessionis Catholicae* (Jena, 1634), II, 501.

3. Luther's affirmation forced the dogmaticians to explain what Luther meant when he affirmed *essentia generet*. See Johann Gerhard, *De Deo Patre*, Locus 4/2, §176-78 (ed. Cotta, 291); Leonard Hutter, *Loci Communes Theologici* (Wittenberg, 1619), 104-5; and Jesper Rasmussen Brochmand, *Universae Theologiae Systema* (Ulm, 1638), I, 144.

4. The clearest presentation of these two ways of conceiving the Trinity is by Russell Friedman, *Medieval Trinitarian Thought from Aquinas to Ockham* (Cambridge: Cambridge University Press, 2010). For a more detailed discussion see Russell Friedman, *Intellectual Traditions at the Medieval University*, 2 vols. (Leiden: Brill, 2012).

5. Bonaventure, *Commentarius in I Librum Sentiarum*, d. 27, p. 1, a.un., q. 2 in *Opera Omnia*, (Quaracchi, 1882), 1:468-69; Thomas Aquinas, *Scriptum super libros Sententiarum*, lib. 1, d. 27, q. 1, a. 2, ed. R. P. Mandonnet (Paris: P. Lethielleux, 1929), 650-52.

6. The term "emanation" could be used for all three persons in the following sense. The Father is innascible, which means unemanated; the Son's emanation is generation; the Spirit's emanation is spiration. The three persons are emanationally distinct but essentially identical. See Friedman, *Medieval Trinitarian Thought*, 17.

7. Friedman emphasizes that the dispute between Bonaventure and Thomas had to do with the way they "conceived" of the personal properties, as either emanations or relations, and not about what the properties are. They agreed on the properties. See Friedman, *Medieval Trinitarian Thought*, 19-20.

there were two emanations in God (generation and spiration), three hypostases (Father, Son, and Holy Spirit), and three personal properties (paternity, sonship, and procession).[8] The disagreement was over how to organize these truths logically. Bonaventure thinks it makes more sense to move from emanation to person to relation, which is to say, generation, Father, paternity.[9] Generation establishes the Father as Father and the Son as a person distinct from the Father. Only after this do we have the opposing relations of paternity and filiation, relations dependent upon the persons, who are in turn dependent upon emanation, the one generating and the other being generated. Thomas thought this way of thinking made no sense. Actors act. You cannot have the "act" of generation preceding the actor, or in this case the divine person. That way of thinking has everything backwards, conceptually speaking.

Although the Dominicans and the Franciscans argued at length about how we should conceive of the persons being constituted, whether by relation or emanation, and this eventually led them to positions that were not so easily reconcilable,[10] they were in agreement that the personal properties properly distinguish the persons from each other.[11] Our Lutheran fathers showed little interest in the debate on relation versus emanation. Gerhard thought the schoolmen troubled themselves too much with this question and could not come to any agreement among themselves.[12] Our Lutheran fathers, however, welcomed the insight that personal properties stand in opposition to one another and provide a meaningful way for us to distinguish the persons. Three names frequently appear in the discussion of this issue by the dogmaticians: Boethius, Anselm, and Thomas Aquinas.

---

8. Cf. Bonaventure, *Breviloquium*, I, 3, in *Works of St. Bonaventure*, vol. 9, ed. Dominic Monti (St. Bonaventure, NY: The Franciscan Institute, 2005), 33–36. For Thomas, see the references below. To this list they would also add four relations and five notions or characteristics.

9. Bonaventure, *Disputed Questions on the Mystery of the Trinity*, in *Works of Saint Bonaventure*, vol. 3, ed. Zachary Hayes (St. Bonaventure, NY: The Franciscan Institute, 2000), 39–43; Friedman, *Medieval Trinitarian Thought*, 25.

10. The Franciscans merged their emanation account of personal distinction with a strong view of the psychological model of the Trinity. The second half of Augustine's *The Trinity* probed the architecture and activities of the human mind in order to clarify the threeness and oneness of the Trinity. The Franciscans and even the Dominicans to a lesser extent used the psychological model to explain the distinction of the divine persons. For example, the Son as Word was identified with intellect and the Holy Spirit was identified with will. The emanation of the Son was by nature or intellect and the Spirit's emanation was by will. The strong form of the psychological model fails in significant ways. It closely construes emanation with the divine attributes and thus compromises what the church has always affirmed about divine simplicity. Second, it retains only with difficulty the scriptural teaching on the *filioque* and the inseparability of the Son and the Spirit. Neither the strong nor weak form of this way of thinking about the Trinity offers much. Although Luther and the Lutheran dogmaticians will occasionally make reference to it, they hesitate to use it in any constructive manner. For a detailed explanation of the psychological model as used by the Franciscans and the Dominicans see Friedman, *Medieval Trinitarian Thought*, 50–132.

11. Bonaventure, *Disputed Questions*, 42–43.

12. Gerhard, *De Tribus Elohim*, Locus 4/1, §42 (ed. Cotta, 201). Gerhard gives an accurate summary of what Bonaventure and Thomas thought on this question. It is telling, I think, that this is the only time, as far as I can tell, that Gerhard mentions Bonaventure in his three-part work on the Trinity (Locus 4/1, 4/2, 4/3). On the other hand, he quotes Thomas extensively throughout.

In his *De Trinitate* Boethius clarifies the way in which relation should be understood when used of God. He argues that "relationship" predicates the circumstances of a thing.[13] When two people stand next each other, we say that one person stands to the left of the other and one to the right of the other. The standing to the left or right describes the circumstance of their relationship to one another. The circumstance indicates a "real" relation but does not affect the essence of the two people. When understood in this way, relation says something real without altering, changing, or disturbing essence in any way.[14] Relations, then, are not accidents, not something added to essence or inhering in the essence (contra Aristotle). Boethius uses this insight to understand better what Scripture proclaims about the three divine persons, their personal relations, and the essential unity of the one true God. The church confesses that the Father is related to the Son by His relation of paternity and the Son to the Father by filiation. Paternity and filiation are the personal properties or distinguishing marks that set apart the Father and the Son personally, not essentially.[15] Scripture tells us these are real relations: the Father is always Father; the Son is always Son; the Father is never Son and the Son is never Father. They are distinguished relationally but united essentially. Boethius puts this succinctly: "Substance preserves the unity, relation multiplies the Trinity."[16] The medieval theologians and our Lutheran dogmaticians never tire of using this statement by Boethius.

An equally influential statement or rule comes from Anselm. In his treatise on the procession of the Holy Spirit Anselm rehearses a number of ways in which the faithful talk about the Trinity. We say that the Father is God, the Son is God, and the Holy Spirit is God. We do not say, however, that the same thing is designated by God as by Father or Son or Holy Spirit. In the above expressions God refers to their shared essence; the names refer to their relations.[17] We also say that the Son is God from God the Father by generation; the Holy Spirit is God from God the Father by procession. Anselm pushes this point. We say that the Son is from His Father, from God who is Father, but we do not say it this way for the Holy Spirit. The Holy Spirit is not from God as *His* Father (the Spirit is not another son) but from God who is Father.[18] Anselm continues with many more examples of what we may say and what we may not say. His point is that the speech of the faithful must reflect what God is as one and who God is as three, rightly distinguishing between the what and the who in the way our words refer. The faithful diligently distinguish between the essence and persons

---

13. Boethius *De Trinitate* V (LCL, 25–27).
14. Boethius *De Trinitate* V (LCL, 27).
15. Boethius *Utrum Pater et Filius* (LCL, 37).
16. Boethius *De Trinitate* VI (LCL, 28, 30): "Ita igitur substantia continent unitatem, relatio multiplicat trinitatem."
17. Anselm, *On the Procession of the Holy Spirit*, in *Anselm of Canterbury: The Major Works*, ed. Brian Davies and G. R. Evans (Oxford: Oxford University Press, 1998), 390.
18. Anselm, *Procession of the Holy Spirit*, 391.

in their speech, lest they divide the unity or confuse the persons. Anselm summarizes this insight: "The unity should never lose its consequence except when a relational opposition stands in the way."[19] The church would shorten Anselm's statement into the following rule: "In God all is one where there is no opposition of relation."[20] The persons of the Trinity are rightly distinguished by these opposing relations, and this is what governs the speech of the faithful.

Thomas Aquinas uses these insights from Boethius and Anselm in his own presentation of the divine persons. Thomas emphasizes that these relations are real. They are not something accidental, something inhering in the divine substance. Nor are they merely logical and according to our manner of speaking and understanding. Nor are they dependent upon something outside of God. These real relations are intrinsic to the divine persons and therefore eternal. Thomas especially wishes to avoid any suggestion of Sabellianism in his discussion of divine relations.[21] In order to do this to his own satisfaction and in order to avoid the pitfalls of Aristotle's insistence that relations are accidental, Thomas argues that relation and essence do not differ from each other when discussing a particular person. Thomas's point is subtle. There are two ways of considering relation in the divine. When relation is said in comparison to the essence, no real distinction exists as we are comparing the relation to itself. That is to say, no distinction exists between the Son as Son and the Son as God when we are talking only about the Son. The only distinction would be a logical one made by us to facilitate discussion of the Son. Thomas presses this point lest we think of relations as inhering in the essence. There is no composition of relation and essence. This is why we should say, argues Thomas, "in God relation and essence do not differ from each other, but are one and the same."[22]

When relation is said toward another, which is the particular characteristic of relation, these real relations distinguish the persons for us. When relation is expressed in this way, argues Thomas, "no respect to essence is signified, but rather to its opposite term."[23] Depending on our perspective, relation

---

19. Anselm, *Procession of the Holy Spirit*, 393.

20. The fifteenth-century Council of Florence quotes the rule in this way. See *Decrees of the Ecumenical Councils*, ed. Norman P. Tanner (Washington, D. C.: Georgetown University Press, 1990), 1:571.1–2.

21. Cf. Thomas Aquinas *ST* I.28.1 sed contra and *ST* I.28.3 sed contra.

22. Thomas Aquinas *ST* I.28.2c. Thomas's point expands upon Augustine's observation: "It is not one thing for God to be and another for him to be person, but [they are both] altogether the same" (*The Trinity*, VII.11, WSA I/5, 228). Cf. Johann Gerhard, *Theological Commonplaces: On the Nature of God and On the Trinity*, trans. Richard Dinda (St. Louis: Concordia Publishing House, 2007), Exegesis II, §134, 137–38: "We do not claim that the divine essence is distinguished really from the persons . . . Rather, we assert that the essence of God and the three persons of the Godhead are really and simply one. Therefore there is no composition here. The personal properties do not multiply the divine essence nor are they compounded because one and the same divine essence is in the Father, Son, and Holy Spirit—in the Father as unbegotten, in the Son as begotten, in the Holy Spirit as proceeding. . . . The person of the Father is not a composite of essence and personal property as of two things really diverse, but essence and unbegottenness are really one in the Father." See also Johann Andreas Quenstedt, *Systema Theologicum*, I, 9 (Wittenberg, 1691), 326.

23. Thomas Aquinas *ST* I.28.2c. On this point see further Friedman, *Medieval Trinitarian*

and essence do not differ and yet these relations are distinguished from each other.[24] At this point Thomas turns to Boethius and quotes his statement above: "Relation multiplies the Trinity." Thomas continues, "If the relations were not really distinguished from each other, there would be no real trinity in God, but only an ideal trinity, which is the error of Sabellius."[25] From here Thomas shows that in the divine persons these real relations involve opposition and constitute the persons.[26]

As shown by Boethius and Aristotle before him, relation is always expressed toward another (*ad aliquid* or πρός τι). In this sense we can say that every relation is really distinguished from that to which it refers. Thomas expresses this with the language of "principle" and "what is from the principle," or more simply put, subject and term.[27] Opposed relations mark off and distinguish the persons for us when subject and term correlate in such a way that no one person is both subject and term.[28] For example, the Father is always Father and never Son; the Son is always Son and never Father. The property that identifies the Father is *paternitas*; the property that identifies the Son is *filiatio*. As we say the Father is always Father and never Son, so we also say the Father always possesses *paternitas* and never *filiatio*; the Son always possesses *filiatio* and never *paternitas*. The eternal generation of the Son from the Father shows these opposed and complementary relations. When the Father is subject, the Son is the term of paternity. When the Son is subject, the Father is the term of filiation. These relations are basic. The Father always involves the Son; the Son always involves the Father. Further, these relations irreducibly distinguish Father and Son and show their mutual interdependence. The Father is never the Son; the Father is never the subject of filiation but always the term. The Son is never the Father; the Son is never the subject of paternity but always the term. So too the Father is never apart from His Son; the Son is never apart from His Father: always Father, always Son. The same framework applies to the Holy Spirit. The

---

Thought, 13-14.

24. On this point see also Thomas Aquinas *ST* I.39.1c: "It follows that in God essence is not really distinct from person; and yet that the persons are really distinguished from each other. For person, as above stated (*ST* I.29.4), signifies relation as subsisting in the divine nature. But relation as referred to the essence does not differ therefrom really, but only in our way of thinking; while as referred to an opposite relation, it has a real distinction by virtue of that opposition. Thus there are one essence and three persons." Cf. Gerhard, *De Tribus Elohim*, Locus 4/1, §60-61 (ed. Cotta, 205-6).

25. Thomas Aquinas *ST* I.28.3 sed contra.

26. Thomas Aquinas *ST* I.28.3-4 and *ST* I.30.2 ad 1. Thomas further adds that there are five notions or notional acts that make known the persons: innascibility, paternity, filiation, spiration, and procession (*ST* I.32.2-3). All of these distinctions were known and used by the Lutheran dogmaticians. For a particularly clear example see Gerhard, *De Tribus Elohim*, Locus 4/1 §46 (ed. Cotta, 202).

27. Thomas Aquinas *ST* I.28.4c and *ST* I.36.2c. Thomas explains this more fully at *Summa Contra Gentiles* IV.24.7-11.

28. Thomas Aquinas *ST* I.30.2c and *ST* I.32.2c. On this point and for what follows see Bruce Marshall, "The Defense of the *Filioque* in Classical Lutheran Theology," *Neue Zeitschrift für systematische Theologie und Religionsphilosophie* 44:2 (2002): 160-61.

Spirit proceeds from the Father and the Son, who both spirate the Holy Spirit. The passive spiration of the Spirit is opposed to the active spiration of the Father and the Son. For Thomas, relative opposition usefully expresses the distinction between the subsisting persons.[29]

The Lutheran dogmaticians and the dogmatic textbooks of the nineteenth and twentieth centuries incorporate into their discussions of the Trinity the above insights from Boethius, Anselm, and Thomas Aquinas. Johann Gerhard deploys the above terminology from the Fathers and schoolmen in his three works on the Trinity: *On the Three Elohim, On God the Father and His Eternal Son*, and *On the Holy Spirit*. Gerhard uses the grammar of the Athanasian Creed to express the distinction of persons: "The Father is *alius*, the Son is *alius*, and the Holy Spirit is *alius* but the Father is neither the Son nor the Holy Spirit."[30] Father, Son, and Holy Spirit are one in essence but not in person. The Father is neither the Son nor the Holy Spirit. What accounts for their distinction? Gerhard directs his reader to the personal properties:

> The reason for these personal distinctions depends upon distinguishing properties, notions, or relations of origin, by which one person is truly and really distinguished from another. The personal property of the Father is unbegottenness or innascibility; *the Father is made of none, neither created nor begotten*. The personal property of the Son is begottenness; *the Son is of the Father alone, not made nor created, but begotten*. The personal property of the Holy Spirit is procession; *the Holy Spirit is of the Father and of the Son, neither made nor created nor begotten, but proceeding*.[31]

The personal property of the Father is unbegottenness or ingeneracy, which the schoolmen call innascibility.[32] What does unbegotten mean? Gerhard quotes Basil's definition in *Against Eunomius*: "Unbegotten signifies not having any other source" (*principium*).[33] The term "unbegotten" designates the Father's

---

29. Thomas Aquinas *ST* I.30.2c. For a very clear discussion of relative opposition and the Spirit's procession from the Father and the Son, see Thomas Aquinas, *Gospel of John*, 2062–65 (Lander, WY: The Aquinas Institute, 2013), 2:311–13.

30. Gerhard, *De Tribus Elohim*, Locus 4/1, §46 (ed. Cotta, 202). Gerhard is well aware of the patristic lineage of this distinction. He points the reader to two texts from Augustine and Gregory of Nazianzus. Augustine writes, "Now the Spirit is other (*alius*) than the Father and the Son, for it is neither the Father nor the Son. But I said 'other' (*alius*) not 'something other' (*aliud*), because it is equally simple and is equally the immutable and coeternal good." Augustine *De Civitate Dei* 11.10 (WSA I/7, 11; CCSL 47, 330). Gregory of Nazianzus used the Greek terms to show how Christ is one thing and another (ἄλλο καὶ ἄλλο) but not one subject and another (ἄλλος καὶ ἄλλος). The persons of the Trinity are (ἄλλος καὶ ἄλλος καὶ ἄλλος). Gregory of Nazianzus *Ep.* 101 (PG 37, 180). Similarly, Lateran IV wrote, "Although therefore the Father is one person (*alius*), the Son another (*alius*), and the Holy Spirit another (*alius*), they are not *aliud* (different realities)." *Decrees of the Ecumenical Councils*, 1:232, 14–15. On all of this see Gerhard, *De Tribus Elohim*, Locus 4/1, §63 (ed. Cotta, 206–7).

31. Gerhard, *De Tribus Elohim*, Locus 4/1, §46 (ed. Cotta, 202). The italicized words are from the Athanasian Creed.

32. Gerhard, *De Deo Patre*, Locus 4/2, §5 (ed. Cotta, 224).

33. Gerhard, *De Deo Patre*, Locus 4/2, §5 (ed. Cotta, 224); Basil *Against Eunomius* 1.15 (Fathers of the Church, 114).

unique mode of existence. It does not, as Eunomius thought, designate His substance.[34] This personal property of the Father belongs neither to the Son, who is begotten from the Father, nor to the Holy Spirit, who proceeds from the Father and the Son.[35] The Son's personal property is begottenness or generation; He is eternally generated from the Father.[36] The Spirit's personal property is procession; He ineffably proceeds from the Father and the Son.[37] The personal properties distinguish the persons from one another in the intimate unity of their essence.[38] Again Gerhard writes:

> The Father is another person [*alia persona*], who begets, and the Son is another person [*alia persona*], who is begotten. The same may be said with the Holy Spirit who proceeds from the Son. Therefore, the Holy Spirit is another person [*alia persona*] than the Son, who with the Father, in one spiration, spirates the Holy Spirit. Thus, the Holy Spirit is truly another person [*alia persona*] who proceeds from the Father and the Son.[39]

The personal properties and relations of origin truly and really distinguish the persons from one another: the Father begets, the Son is begotten, the Spirit proceeds from the Father and the Son.

What about relations of opposition? For Gerhard, they demonstrate that Father, Son, and Holy Spirit are "truly and really distinct persons."[40] Gerhard frequently quotes Boethius when discussing relative opposition. Boethius said, "Relation alone multiplies the persons of the Trinity."[41] Boethius's statement should be understood in the following sense: "The property of the Father—unbegottenness—and the relation—paternity and spiration—are really in the Father and in this sense the Father is distinguished from the other persons by relation."[42] Gerhard then quotes Thomas: "There is no real distinction unless there is relative opposition" (*ST* I.30.2c). Gerhard writes, "*Paternitas* and *filiatio*

---

34. Gerhard, *De Deo Patre*, Locus 4/2, §5 (ed. Cotta, 225).
35. Gerhard, *De Deo Patre*, Locus 4/2, §5 (ed. Cotta, 224–25).
36. Gerhard, *De Deo Patre*, Locus 4/2, §153 (ed. Cotta, 283).
37. Gerhard, *De Spiritu Sancto*, Locus 4/3, §59 (ed. Cotta, 319). Gerhard discusses the procession of the Spirit from the Father and the Son at length. At stake in affirming the procession of the Spirit is the order of the persons and the distinction of the Spirit from the Son: "If it is denied that the Holy Spirit proceeds from the Son, the order of the persons of the Trinity would be uncertain and any relation of the Son to the Holy Spirit would be absurd" (Locus 4/3, §82, 326).
38. Gerhard, *De Deo Patre*, Locus 4/2, §153 (ed. Cotta, 283).
39. Gerhard, *De Deo Patre*, Locus, 4/2, §182 (ed. Cotta, 292).
40. Gerhard, *De Deo Patre*, Locus, 4/2, §182 (ed. Cotta, 293). Gerhard had already briefly raised the issue of opposed relations in his discussion of how the persons are distinct but intimately present in the other. See *De Tribus Elohim*, Locus 4/1, §29 (ed. Cotta, 197). For similar discussions see Quenstedt, *Systema Theologicum*, I, 9 (Wittenberg, 1691), 336–37; Baier-Walther, *Compendium Theologiae Positivae*, I, §43. Abraham Calov frequently appeals to opposed relations. See for example *Systema Locorum Theologicorum* (Wittenberg, 1659), 3:108 (with reference to Father and Son); 3:161 (with reference to the Trinity); 3:836 (with reference to the *filioque*); 3:862 (with reference to the Son and the Spirit).
41. Gerhard, *De Tribus Elohim*, Locus 4/1, §51 (ed. Cotta, 203). Although he does not always do this, Gerhard here adds the word "alone" to Boethius's statement. He likely gets this wording from Thomas Aquinas *ST* I.40.2 sed contra.
42. Gerhard, *De Tribus Elohim*, Locus 4/1, §51 (ed. Cotta, 203).

are opposed relations; *spiratio* and *processio* are opposed relations; therefore they refer to two persons."⁴³ Personal properties belong only to one person, constitute that person, and distinguish that person from another. We maintain the unity of God and the distinction of persons when we follow Anselm's rule: "In God all is one where there is no opposition of relation" (*relationis oppositio*).⁴⁴

Gerhard and the other dogmaticians appeal to relations of opposition as a helpful way of distinguishing the persons and also as a way of explaining what Scripture says about the *filioque*. As our chapter on the Holy Spirit's procession showed, the church's teaching on the *filioque* derives from Scripture. Our Lutheran dogmaticians dwell on the scriptural teaching before turning to the opposition of relations as a way of thinking about the order of the persons and the *filioque*.⁴⁵ The dogmaticians emphasize that the Spirit is called the Spirit of the Father, the Spirit of God, the Spirit of the Son, and the Spirit of Christ. Never do we see Scripture saying the Christ of the Spirit or the Son of the Spirit. Why would Scripture not reverse this relationship? Our dogmaticians all conclude that it has to do with the order of the persons and their eternal relationship to one another. Abraham Calov writes:

> Just as he is called "the Spirit of the Father" (Mt 10:20) ... and the Spirit "of God" (Is 44:3; Rom 8:9) because he is breathed by the Father and is from the Father by eternal procession, so also he is equally named the Spirit "of the Son" (Gal 4:6) and the Spirit "of Christ" (Rom 8:9; Phil 1:19) ... because he is equally from the Son by eternal procession, and is breathed by the Son of God, just as by the Father.⁴⁶

If the scriptural language "of the Father" means something, then so too must the language "of the Son" and "of Christ." The same must be true of the way Scripture patterns our language for expressing the order of the persons. We see this especially with baptism: the Father is first, the Son second, and the Holy Spirit third. Calov explains:

> Since the Father is from no one, he is the first person; the Son, who is from the Father, is second; and therefore the Holy Spirit is the third person of the Godhead insofar as he is from the Father and the Son. If the Holy Spirit were not from the Father and the Son, there would be no reason why he ought to be called the third person of the Holy Trinity.⁴⁷

---

43. Gerhard, *De Tribus Elohim*, Locus 4/1, §51 (ed. Cotta, 203).

44. Gerhard, *De Tribus Elohim*, Locus 4/1, §51 (ed. Cotta, 203). Gerhard first introduces Anselm's rule at Locus 4/1 §43 (ed. Cotta, 201). The dogmaticians do not always credit Anselm with this rule. Abraham Calov simply calls it the rule of the schoolmen and Baier the rule of the theologians. See Calov, *De Spiritu Sancto*, in *Systema Locorum Theologicorum* 3:836; Baier-Walther, *Compendium Theologiae Positivae*, I, §43.

45. The standard arguments by the dogmaticians are scriptural. Cf. Calov, *De Spiritu Sancto*, in *Systema*, 3:811. Calov says the procession of the Spirit is proved by accepting the scriptural witness that the Spirit is from the Son, He is called the Spirit of the Son, the Son is consubstantial with the Father (thus whatever the Father has the Son has, Jn 16:14–15), by the order of the trinitarian persons, from the river "proceeding" from the throne of the Lamb (Rv 22:1), by the mission of the Holy Spirit from the Son, and the unanimous judgment of the ancient church. Except for this final comment, Calov's proofs all come from Scripture.

46. Calov, *De Spiritu Sancto*, in *Systema*, 3:812. Cf. Marshall, "Defense of the *Filioque*," 158.

47. Calov, *De Spiritu Sancto*, in *Systema*, 3:813.

The scriptural use of genitives in presenting the persons and the scriptural order of the persons further reveals the eternal relationship that avails between the persons, allowing us to distinguish them from one another. As soon as Calov points this out, he anticipates an objection. What does order mean? Does it imply subordination? Calov addresses this concern in a manner similar to the Fathers. He writes, "If you consider essence and nature in themselves, then, no, there is no order of before and after."[48] And yet Scripture presents an order of the persons. Again, Scripture says "Spirit of the Father" or "Spirit of the Son," but never "Father of the Spirit" or "Son of the Spirit." How should we understand this order? It clearly does not apply to their shared essence. Here there is the greatest unity, the greatest oneness, indeed, as Calov says elsewhere, their oneness is as Luther cleverly put it, "unissima," which would be translated "one-est" or "most single singleness."[49] There is no unity more unified or no oneness more one than theirs. If the order does not pertain to their nature or essence, which is one, it must point to their relations. Calov explains, "Therefore, the order must be found in the persons because of their personal or hypostatic characters."[50]

If the order pertains to relations, how should we understand the order of persons? It means, explains Calov, the Father is the First Person of the Trinity because He is the "principium fons," the principle source of the Son and the Spirit.[51] The Son is the Second Person because of origin—but not, emphasizes Calov, because He is after the Father or before the Spirit temporally. The Spirit is the Third Person because He has His origin from both the Father and the Son. Although the Son is from the Father, He is neither less than the Father in essence nor later than the Father in time. The Father and the Son are coequal and coeternal. The same applies when talking about the Son and the Spirit. The Spirit is not less than the Son in nature, majesty, dignity, time, or anything else.[52] The only difference is that of origin and personal property. Calov appeals to Gregory of Nyssa to make his point: "Since the Holy Spirit ... depends on the Son with whom he is comprehended inseparably, and has his being from the Father as cause [*ut principio*], from whom he proceeds [*procedit*], the distinguishing mark of his hypostasis is that he is known after the Son [i.e., in terms of order] and with him [*post Filium et cum ipso*]."[53]

---

48. Calov, *De Spiritu Sancto*, in *Systema*, 3:813.
49. Calov, *De Sancta Trinitate*, in *Systema Locorum Theologicorum* 3:139. Cf. Martin Luther, *Lectures on Genesis*, 1535-45, "most perfect unity" (AE 1:12; WA 42:10.20–22), and "most single singleness" (AE 1:17; WA 42:14.10–11),
50. Calov, *De Spiritu Sancto*, in *Systema*, 3:813.
51. Calov, *De Spiritu Sancto*, in *Systema*, 3:837.
52. Calov, *De Spiritu Sancto*, in *Systema*, 3:837.
53. Calov, *De Spiritu Sancto*, in *Systema*, 3:837–38; Gregory of Nyssa Letter 35.4 in *Gregory of Nyssa: The Letters*, trans. Anna M. Silvas (Leiden: Brill, 2007), 253. Calov attributes the letter to Basil but most scholars now assign it to Gregory.

Johann Gerhard had offered a similar argument as that given by Calov. Gerhard emphasized the order of the persons and what that order means and does not mean. Gerhard writes, "The Father is the first person not by reason of time (the three persons are coeternal), nor by reason of nature or essence (they are *homoousios*), nor by reason of dignity (they are of equal glory and majesty) but by reason of origin or production."[54] The Son and the Holy Spirit exist from the Father but not after Him. The Father is the First Person of the Trinity "because he is from no one and because he is the origin of the Trinity [*origo Trinitatis*], begetting the Son and with the Son spirating one Holy Spirit."[55] The order of the persons does not indicate time, nature, or majesty.[56] As we confess in the Athanasian Creed, "None is before or after another, none is greater or less than another."[57] The order among the persons is according to origin, not nature. For Gerhard, all of this bears especially on the procession of the Spirit. He writes, "If it is denied that the Holy Spirit proceeds from the Son, the order of the persons of the Trinity would be uncertain and any relation of the Son to the Holy Spirit would be absurd."[58] Similarly, Calov, using the words of Thomas Aquinas, states, "If the Holy Spirit had not proceeded from the Son, he would not be distinguished from him, which would be contrary to faith."[59]

It is at this very point that both Gerhard and Calov appeal to the relations of opposition as put forward by Thomas. If the Holy Spirit does not proceed from the Son, He could not be distinguished from Him. The persons are not distinguished in any absolute sense since everything said absolutely belongs to the unity of essence. Gerhard continues, paraphrasing Thomas: "Therefore, the persons are distinguished only by relations and relations are distinguished only

---

54. Gerhard, *De Deo Patre*, Locus 4/2, §1 (ed. Cotta, 223).

55. Gerhard, *De Deo Patre*, Locus 4/2, §2 (ed. Cotta, 223). Gerhard uses similar expressions elsewhere. The Father is the *fons Trinitatis* (4/2, §4, 224); the Father is the *fons et origo Trinitatis* (4/2, §9, 225). Cf. David Chytraeus, *In Genesin Enarratio* (Wittenberg, 1576), 25-26: "Pater est principium et fons totius divinitatis."

56. Cf. Quenstedt, *Systema Theologicum*, I, 9 (Wittenberg, 1691), 327, theses 17 and 18: "The real distinction of the divine persons arises from their order, both in subsistence and in activity. And yet we must distinguish between order of nature, order of time, order of dignity, and order of origin and relation [*originis et relationis*]. We ascribe no order of nature to the divine persons because they are *homoousios*, of the same nature and essence. Nor do we ascribe an order of time because they are consubstantial and coeternal, nor an order of dignity because they are of the same honor. But we do ascribe to them an order of origin and relation because the Father is from no one, the Son is from the Father, and the Holy Spirit is from both.

"The order of subsisting among the divine persons is demonstrated only by way of procession or emanation of one person from another. If the Father proceeds from no one, but has his essence of himself, as the fountain and source [*fons et principium*] of the Holy Trinity, if the Son has his essence from the Father through eternal generation, if the Holy Spirit has his essence from the Father and the Son through eternal spiration, then it follows that the Father is first, the Son second, and the Holy Spirit the third person and this order is immutably fixed in their nature and clearly shown in the baptismal formula (Mt 28:19; 1 Jn 5:7)."

57. Gerhard, *De Deo Patre*, Locus 4/2, §2 (ed. Cotta, 223).

58. Gerhard, *De Spiritu Sancto*, Locus 4/3, §82 (ed. Cotta, 326).

59. Calov, *De Spiritu Sancto*, in *Systema*, 3:844. Calov is paraphrasing Thomas Aquinas *Summa Contra Gentiles* IV.24.

as they are opposed."⁶⁰ Thomas argues that a pair of opposed relations must avail between the Son and the Spirit in order for them to be distinct from one another. Here the Lutheran dogmaticians followed Thomas. Bruce Marshall summarizes the logic of their position:

> Following Aquinas, the Lutheran theologians typically maintain that relations of opposition can only arise in God where there is an act which originates a person. So in order for the Spirit to be distinct from the Son, either the Spirit has to originate from the Son, or the Son has to originate from him. Given assumptions which both sides accept about the *taxis* or order of the divine persons, the Son cannot originate from the Spirit. Therefore *Filioque*: the Spirit has to originate from the Son in order to be a person distinct from the Son, just as he has to originate from the Father in order to be a person distinct from the Father.⁶¹

The argument for the *filioque* proceeds from Scripture. Our Lutheran dogmaticians show their commitment to Scripture throughout their lengthy discussions of the Trinity. The theological merit of the church's insight on relations of opposition is that it usefully expresses what Scripture reveals about the persons, their distinguishing properties, and how these properties oppose one another and mark off the divine persons from one another. The *filioque* accomplishes this very thing for the dogmaticians—it marks off the Holy Spirit as a distinct hypostasis from the Father *and the Son*. Far from indicating any inferiority of the Spirit to the Son, the scriptural teaching and the creedal affirmation shows both their distinction and inseparability. Those who fail to see this risk collapsing the Son and the Spirit together, confusing the distinction of persons made known in Scripture. Calov states it clearly:

> Those who deny the procession of the Holy Spirit from the Son are not able to preserve a real distinction [*realis distinctio*] of the Holy Spirit from the Son because the divine persons are not distinguished except by relative oppositions. There is no relative opposition between the Son and the Holy Spirit unless the Spirit proceeds from the Son for there are no other opposed relations in God except relations of origin.⁶²

For our Lutheran fathers the insights of the medieval writers on divine relations helped them carefully and clearly express the witness of Scripture on the divine persons and the manner in which they relate to one another.

MARTIN LUTHER AND *UTRUM ESSENTIA GENERET ESSENTIAM*

Anyone concerned with properly confessing the Trinity must at some point inquire into the meaning of the words we use to do this. Theologians cannot

---

60. Gerhard, *De Spiritu Sancto*, Locus 4/3, §83 (ed. Cotta, 326).
61. Marshall, "Defense of the *Filioque*," 161.
62. Calov, *De Spiritu Sancto*, in *Systema* 3:862. Note Calov's use of Anselm's rule in this quote. Cf. *De Spiritu Sancto*, in *Systema* 3:836–37.

restrict themselves only to talking about God; they must also talk about the words we use to talk about God. A very basic example would be the word "God." When we use the word God, are we talking about the essence or person? Are we talking about one person or all three persons? Is this word to be used substantively and relatively, or only substantively or only relatively? When we confess in the Nicene Creed that Jesus Christ is *Deum ex Deo*, God from God, how is the word God being used? Does it refer to substance, person, both? Only when we sort out what we mean by the words we use in particular cases can our trinitarian speech have meaning and avoid misunderstanding. The preoccupation of theologians with semantic matters and what certain linguistic circumstances allow us to say or not to say may strike the modern reader as trivial, as obscuring more than clarifying, or as trifling over words. The attention given by the medieval and Reformation theologians to how we faithfully and responsibly talk about God aim for the very opposite. Their attention to such questions exhibits a pious concern for the pattern of sound speech in our talk about God. These are not language games that arbitrarily stipulate the reference of terms in order to establish previously held commitments. They are efforts to understand why we say things one way and not another. All the faithful exhibit this kind of concern when they confess that the Father is God, the Son is God, and the Holy Spirit is God but they are not three gods.

Luther's provocative rejection of Lateran IV on the question of whether essence generates essence shows the importance of rightly understanding our theological words. Lateran IV condemned any who would say that essence generates essence. Following the council the medieval theologians focused their efforts on metaphysical and semantic arguments to show the correctness of the council's conclusion. Luther stands apart from this tradition. The earliest theological work we have from him already exhibits hesitancy with the council's authority and Peter Lombard's argument, which led to the council's decision. Toward the end of his life this hesitancy disappears. Luther explicitly rejects the decision of the council and Lombard's position against *essentia generat essentiam*. What follows is a very brief review of the question and a consideration of what Luther has to say and why he says what he does.

The question of whether the essence generates stems from book one of Peter Lombard's *Sentences*.[63] Peter asks whether the Father generates the divine essence, whether the divine essence generates the Son, or whether the essence generates essence.[64] It is this latter way of putting the question that becomes

---

63. On this question among the medieval theologians see Bruce Marshall, "*Utrum Essentia Generet*: Semantics and Metaphysics in Later Medieval Trinitarian Theology," in *Trinitarian Theology in the Medieval West*, ed. Pekka Kärkkäinen (Helsinki: Luther-Agricola-Society, 2004), 88–123. See also Bruce Marshall, "Aquinas the Augustinian? On the Uses of Augustine in Aquinas' Trinitarian Theology," in *Aquinas the Augustinian*, ed. Michael Dauphinais, Barry David, and Matthew Levering (Washington, D.C.: Catholic University of America Press, 2007), 41–61; Bruce Marshall, "In Search of an Analytic Aquinas: Grammar and the Trinity," in *Grammar and Grace*, ed. Robert MacSwain and Jeffrey Stout (London: SCM Press, 2004), 55–74.

64. Lombard *Sentences* I, 5, 1.1 in Peter Lombard, *The Sentences*, trans. Giulio Silano (Toronto:

standard throughout the medieval period. Lombard's answer to all of these questions is no. After taking the reader through his various arguments Lombard writes, "The divine essence did not generate an essence. Since the divine essence is one and the highest thing, if the divine essence generated an essence, then the same thing generated itself, which is not at all possible. But the Father alone begot the Son, and the Holy Spirit proceeds from the Father and the Son."[65] Lombard bases his conclusion on the metaphysical impossibility of the divine essence generating itself.

Joachim of Fiore rejected Lombard's conclusion and raised concerns about his trinitarian orthodoxy.[66] The Fourth Lateran Council in 1215, an ecumenical council for the Roman church, supported Lombard and condemned the opinion of Joachim. Lateran IV made two distinctions in answering this question that stem from Lombard's comments. First, there is one supreme reality (*una quaedam summa res*) which Father, Son, and Holy Spirit are.[67] Whether the persons are taken together or separately they are this one supreme reality, which is the divine substance, essence, or nature.[68] Second, that one supreme reality (*res*) neither begets nor is begotten nor proceeds.[69] For this reason we say "the Father begets, the Son is begotten, and the Holy Spirit proceeds, so that the distinction is in the persons and unity in the nature."[70] The decision by Lateran IV ended all debate during the medieval period on how the question is to be answered.

Theologians throughout the medieval period employed both metaphysical and semantic arguments to explain why it is wrong to say the essence generates. A number of problems confronted them. One difficulty stemmed from the Nicene Creed and what we mean by *Deum ex Deo*. If we can say "God from God" and mean God begets God, why not also essence begets essence? Even Augustine seems to have spoken in this way. After establishing the difference between substantive and relative predication in the Trinity, between what is said of God *ad se* and what is said *ad aliquid*, Augustine writes, "So Father and Son are together one wisdom because they are one essence [*una essentia*], and one by one they are wisdom from wisdom as they are essence from essence [*essentia de essentia*]."[71] Augustine's "essence from essence" seems to come quite close to what Lombard rejected and Lateran IV condemned. This was not lost

---

Pontifical Institute of Medieval Studies, 2007), 30.

65. Lombard *Sentences* I, 5, 1.6 (Silano, 31–32).

66. The work of Joachim against Lombard, if such a work ever existed, no longer survives. For a suggestion as to what his argument might have been, see Marshall, "*Utrum Essentia Generet*," 93–94.

67. *Decrees of the Ecumenical Councils*, 1:232, 6–8; cf. Bernard Lonergan, *The Triune God: Systematics* (Toronto: University of Toronto Press, 2007), 264–68.

68. *Decrees of the Ecumenical Councils*, 1:232, 10.

69. *Decrees of the Ecumenical Councils*, 1:232, 11–12.

70. *Decrees of the Ecumenical Councils*, 1:232, 12–14.

71. Augustine *The Trinity* 7.3 (WSA I/5, 221), translation slightly altered. Both Peter Lombard and Thomas Aquinas single out this text as particularly vexing. Lombard *Sentences* I, 5, 1.7 (Silano, 32); Thomas Aquinas *ST* I.39.5 obj. 1.

on Lombard. After giving his opinion on the question of whether the essence generates, he turned to a number of difficult passages from Hilary of Poitiers and Augustine that seem to say it does. After reviewing a number of these texts Lombard states simply, "These words disturb us strongly."[72] The medieval theologians found themselves in the awkward position of affirming Lateran IV and at the same time having to explain how Augustine's *essentia de essentia* did not contradict the council.

One way of answering the apparent contradiction between Lateran IV on the one hand and the Nicene Creed and Augustine on the other was to reflect on what the words God and essence meant. Thomas Aquinas addressed these concerns directly.[73] He began with the distinction between the mode of signification (*modus significandi*) and the thing signified (*res significata*). Different terms can refer to the same thing (*res significata*) but in different ways (*modus significandi*). Both God and essence signify the Godhead or divinity, but they do so in different ways. God signifies concretely and essence abstractly. As Thomas puts it, God signifies the divine essence "in Him that possesses it," but essence cannot stand for a divine person because it signifies essence "as an abstract form."[74] We reflect this distinction when we say God begets or God is begotten. The God that begets is the Father; the God that is begotten is the Son.[75] When the Creed confesses *Deum ex Deo*, it means that the Son is from the Father. The distinguishing properties of the persons may be expressed with the concrete word God in a way that they cannot be with the abstract term essence. Therefore, when we say God begets, we are talking about the divine person to whom belongs the personal property of begetting, namely the Father. If we were to say the essence begets, we would be speaking abstractly of the essence, apart from the persons. For Thomas that way of talking has no meaning or truth to it. What then do we make of Augustine's *essentia de essentia*? Thomas simply says Augustine spoke imprecisely and should not be imitated. Instead, his language should be explained in a proper manner.[76]

Luther penned his marginal notes on Peter Lombard's *Sentences* from 1509 to 1511.[77] Although he agrees with Lombard in these marginal notes, he already expresses hesitation with Lombard's conclusions. Luther agrees that God can be taken to refer to the divine persons but misunderstandings abound. If it is said that "God the Father begets God," a statement that can be rightly understood as shown by Pierre d'Ailly, some may take this to mean that God begets another God (*alium deum*) and begin to think there is more than one God.[78] For this

---

72. Lombard *Sentences* I, 5, 1.17 (Silano, 36).
73. The following is based on Thomas Aquinas *ST* I.39.4c and 39.5c. For a helpful and detailed analysis of Thomas's position see Marshall, "*Utrum Essentia Generet*," 103–9.
74. Thomas Aquinas *ST* I.39.5c.
75. Thomas Aquinas *ST* I.39.4 ad 3.
76. Thomas Aquinas *ST* I.39.5 ad 1.
77. Pekka Kärkkäinen, "Martin Luther," in *Mediaeval Commentaries on the Sentences of Peter Lombard*, ed. Philipp W. Rosemann (Leiden: Brill, 2010), 2:471–94.
78. *Zu den Sentenzen des Petrus Lombardus*, 1510 (WA 9:34.10–16).

reason the church avoids such language. Luther returns a second time to the question of whether God may be understood relatively. He notes that Lombard seems to say two different things. On the one hand Lombard affirms the legitimacy of confessing "true God from true God" in the Creed. Here we are to understand that God the Father generates God the Son. In that sense it is correct to say God generates God.[79] This puzzles Luther. If God may be taken relatively, as seen in the Creed and granted by Lombard, why not also essence? Why not take essence in the same way we take Light from Light?[80] At this point Luther says simply that the arguments against doing this are not conclusive but that the Holy Spirit has spoken to the church at Lateran IV. Therefore what the council has said is true.[81]

In December 1544 Luther presided over the doctoral disputation for Georg Major. The theses for Major's disputation concerned the Trinity. Of the twenty-six theses, the final eleven address the question of whether the essence generates.[82] We encounter a very different Luther in these theses—not so much in terms of theological substance but in the manner in which he now speaks about the tradition. Thesis 15 reads, "The Master of the Sentences [Peter Lombard] taught not rightly enough that the divine essence neither generates nor is generated."[83] Moreover, Lateran IV accomplished nothing with its canon on the Trinity (Thesis 17). The argument of the theses moves quickly. Since Augustine could say "substance from substance" and "wisdom from wisdom," the Lombard should have known essence could be said to generate essence in a similar way (Thesis 18–19). It is acknowledged in the theses that this way of speaking may give rise to the false idea that there are two or three essences (Thesis 21) or two or three gods (Thesis 22). But since both Hilary of Poitiers and Augustine use the terms substance (*substantia*), wisdom, and nature, among other terms, relatively (*relative*) in divine matters (Thesis 24), there is no reason Lombard could not have taken essence (*essentia*) relatively as well (Thesis 25).

The discussion of the theses begins by highlighting the dangers inherent in saying the essence generates.[84] Does this not suggest that the essence generates

---

79. Lombard *Sentences* I, 4, 1.1–2 (Silano, 27–28).
80. *Zu den Sentenzen des Petrus Lombardus*, 1510 (WA 9:34.35–35.2).
81. *Zu den Sentenzen des Petrus Lombardus*, 1510 (WA 9:35.3–5).
82. On the question of *essentia generat* in Luther, see Graham White, *Luther as Nominalist* (Helsinki: Luther-Agricola-Society, 1994), 181–91, but also 192–230 for Luther's use of Augustine, William Ockham, and Pierre d'Ailly on this question. Luther is particularly indebted to d'Ailly on this issue, as he indicates in the theses. Graham White is especially helpful in showing Luther's facility with semantic theory and rules of medieval logic. Too often Luther is thought to be removed from this sort of scholasticism; the later disputations show that he was not. On the question of *essentia generat* in Luther, see also Simo Knuuttila and Risto Saarinen, "Luther's Trinitarian Theology and Its Medieval Background," *Studia Theologica-Nordic Journal of Theology* 53:1 (1999): 3–12; and Dennis Bielfeldt, Mickey L. Mattox, and Paul R. Hinlicky, *The Substance of the Faith: Luther's Doctrinal Theology for Today* (Minneapolis: Fortress, 2008).
83. *Die Promotionsdisputation von Georg Major und Johannes Faber*, 1544 (WA 39/2:287.31).
84. For what follows, see *Die Promotionsdisputation von Georg Major und Johannes Faber*, 1544 (WA 39/2:291.10–18).

itself? Major says no. The divine essence does not generate itself but another, another person, the Son. This response leads to a second question: if God generates the Son, does it mean He generates another god (*alium deum*)? Again, Major says no. The one generated is His very image, the Son, who is one God with the Father. The questions to Major are reminiscent of the concerns expressed by Luther in his marginal notes on the *Sentences*. At this point Luther interrupts:

> This is the argument that disturbed the Master [Peter Lombard] so he denied this proposition . . . But he should not have denied that the essence relatively [*relative*] generates a person, especially when he saw Augustine say that God was generated from God, Light was generated from Light. Since he conceded these expressions, he should not have denied a similar expression using the essence.[85]

For Luther everything rests with how the "word" essence is used, how it is made to refer. If it is used absolutely (*absolute*), then it is wrong to say the essence generates. If it is used relatively (*relative*), then it is correct to say the essence generates. This was Lombard's problem. He wanted to use "essence" only "absolutely" and not "relatively," and therefore thought that affirming *essentia generat* meant affirming more than one god.[86] Luther continues: "Against the Master and pope we say that essence, wisdom, and light may be taken relatively."[87] Since Hilary and Augustine took these words relatively, we may as well.

Throughout the disputation Luther revisits the patristic evidence showing how these words can be taken relatively. At one point he restates the question from his earlier marginal notes on the *Sentences*. He asks, "If it can be said that wisdom generates wisdom, why not essence from essence?"[88] Although Luther acknowledged in his marginal notes that the arguments against this were weak, he stopped short of offering his own answer because of Lateran IV. Since the council and its decision on the matter no longer constrain him, he offers a response: "Essence, it is certain, does not generate absolutely [*absolute*] but taken relatively [*relative*], it certainly generates."[89] This sentiment emerges as the consensus at the disputation. In one particular exchange Johann Bugenhagen, Georg Major, and Luther all affirm the distinction between absolute and relative predication on this question.[90]

The usefulness of the rule used throughout the disputation brings greater clarity to how we distinguish the persons from one another without undermining their substantial unity. For example, Major is asked how the

---

85. *Die Promotionsdisputation von Georg Major und Johannes Faber*, 1544 (WA 39/2:291.19–292.2). Lombard makes these concessions at *Sentences*, I, 27, 5.2 (Silano, 150–51).
86. *Die Promotionsdisputation von Georg Major und Johannes Faber*, 1544 (WA 39/2:295.13–15).
87. *Die Promotionsdisputation von Georg Major und Johannes Faber*, 1544 (WA 39/2:295.15–16).
88. *Die Promotionsdisputation von Georg Major und Johannes Faber*, 1544 (WA 39/2:316.19–20).
89. *Die Promotionsdisputation von Georg Major und Johannes Faber*, 1544 (WA 39/2:316.20–21).
90. *Die Promotionsdisputation von Georg Major und Johannes Faber*, 1544 (WA 39/2: 312.18–313.29).

following statement is wrong: "If the divine essence is said to generate properly, it follows that all of the persons generate."[91] The question put to Major is far more difficult to answer than it might seem at first. If we say the essence generates, then we seem to be saying that a property of the essence is that it generates. If this is the case, then all those who possess the essence must be said to generate. If the Son possesses the same substance as the Father, then the Son too must generate; if the Spirit possesses the same substance as the Father and the Son, then He too must be said to generate. If that is the case, all three persons generate and there will be no end to the number of divine persons. The alternative would seem to be Arianism: the three persons do not possess the same substance. Both conclusions are contrary to the faith.[92] How then are we to understand the phrase "the essence generates" and the confession that Father, Son, and Holy Spirit are consubstantial without also admitting that "to generate" belongs to all three as all three are consubstantial? Major disposes of this concern by carefully stating the distinction between absolute and relative predication. He responds,

> Indeed, the essence [*essentia*] is common to all three persons, Father, Son, and Holy Spirit. But when we say 'to generate', we do not understand this 'absolutely' [*absolute*], but 'relatively' [*relative*], insofar as the Father is a person and Scripture only attributes generation to the Father and not to the Son and Holy Spirit.[93]

Major, like Luther and others throughout the disputation, presses the distinction between relative and absolute predication. The phrase *essentia generat* provides the occasion to explore this distinction and to show its usefulness in making true statements about the Trinity.

Luther's other disputations from the end of his life show us that this concern for proper speaking in discussing divine matters was integral to the teaching at Wittenberg. Two points need to be emphasized here. On the one hand, Luther recognized the ambiguity of language. If the speaker intends for a word to refer in a particular way but the hearer takes the reference differently, false ideas may be drawn from what a person says. This would be detrimental to the faith. In his marginal notes on the *Sentences* Luther hesitated to say the essence generates because he worried such language would be misunderstood by taking it absolutely when it was meant relatively. That worry remains for the late Luther, and it is a lesson he impressed upon his students. A few years before Major's doctoral disputation, Luther conducted a disputation on Jn 1:14. The disputation raised the question of the essence generating and allowed Luther to emphasize the need for care in our theological language. All of the standard questions were raised. How do we understand "God from God" and "Light

---

91. *Die Promotionsdisputation von Georg Major und Johannes Faber*, 1544 (WA 39/2:307.17–19).
92. This scenario is explored by Bugenhagen elsewhere in the disputation. He regards both options as blasphemy. See *Die Promotionsdisputation von Georg Major und Johannes Faber*, 1544 (WA 39/2:312.5–11).
93. *Die Promotionsdisputation von Georg Major und Johannes Faber*, 1544 (WA 39/2:307.20–23).

from Light"? Why did Lombard and the theologians who followed him reject the proposition that the essence generates? Luther takes a cautious approach. He warns that if we say the essence generates and use the word absolutely, we would be asserting more than one god. Luther continues, "Therefore, it is more appropriate, and both a safer and better theological confession, to say the Father generates rather than the essence or Trinity generates."[94] Luther still has in mind the distinction between absolute and relative predication, but expresses himself more clearly and cautiously by saying the Father generates.

The issue of theological language and how words refer arises again in the doctoral examination of Petrus Hegemon. Luther explores the distinction of the trinitarian persons and emphasizes the limits of our language and conceptual resources. He reflects especially on absolute and relative predication and the relationship between theology and philosophy. The issue of predication proceeds in the manner we have seen above. When the question is asked how we understand the word "God" in the phrase "God from God," Luther emphasizes how the words refer. He writes, "If we take God personally [i.e., relatively], then it is true that God generates God. If we take God essentially [i.e., absolutely], then God neither generates himself nor another God. The essence does not generate but a person does."[95] Luther briefly rehearses his earlier concerns and shows how our theological language properly talks about the Trinity.

Another issue pursued in the Hegemon disputation concerns the relationship between philosophy and theology. The basic point made by Luther is that theology and philosophy work differently and arrive at truth differently. What is true in philosophy is not necessarily true in theology. Faith receives God's truth (theology) whether it conforms to our way of reasoning or not (philosophy). We see this difference when it comes to the divine relations. Here theology accepts something that philosophy cannot. Theses 11, 12, and 13 press this issue.[96] A "relation" is different among creatures than among the divine persons (Thesis 11). Among creatures relation does not constitute the person; it does not subsist through itself but is accidental (Thesis 12). This works differently for the divine persons: "Thesis 13. In divine matters, relation is a *res*, that is, a hypostasis and subsistence. Truly, it is the same as divinity itself; for there are three persons, three hypostases and subsisting things."[97] The discussion of this thesis highlights the difficulties encountered above with Major: how do we distinguish the persons and maintain their unity of being?

The limits and difficulties of our human language emerge at this very point. If we say that the relation constitutes the person, we mark off two things belonging to each person: relation and essence. But as soon as we say this we want to assert that the relation is not something added to the essence. Luther

---

94. *Die Disputation de sententia: Verbum caro factum est*, 1539 (WA 39/2:18.6-8).
95. *Die Promotionsdisputation von Petrus Hegemon*, 1545 (WA 39/2:370.8-14).
96. *Die Promotionsdisputation von Petrus Hegemon*, 1545 (WA 39/2:339.26-340.5).
97. *Die Promotionsdisputation von Petrus Hegemon*, 1545 (WA 39/2:340.3-5).

responds in the disputation that there are two things in each person: "Two things come together to make a person. A person is constituted from the divine nature and a relation."[98] Language marks off two things, essence and relation, but the divine persons are not composite. Luther recognizes the difficulty here and the limits of our language, but lacks Thomas's subtlety. Although we say that the persons are constituted from essence and from relation, this way of speaking is inappropriate (*improprius*). And yet when we seek to explain the distinction of persons we must resort to this way of talking: "Relation is a thing, essence is a thing, [two things] constituting one person. That is said very inappropriately. But what can you do? We are not able to speak perfectly in these matters and nevertheless this is how we must speak. That is called believing."[99] Luther shows his frustration by going back and forth between Latin and German in his response.

The continuity between the marginal comments in the *Sentences* and Luther's statements in his later disputations, separated as they are by more than thirty years, shows the enduring significance of medieval logic and semantic theory for Luther and his teaching. It matters how we talk about God and how we understand the reference of our words. Attending to these issues determines the truth value of our propositions and the pattern of sound words to be used by the theologian. For this reason Luther emphasizes throughout the disputations that faith confesses the truth of what God reveals in the best language available. Our speech follows certain rules, and proper confession attends to those rules. The faithful know that the persons are three and the essence one, that the Father is Father and never the Son or the Spirit, that the Father alone is unbegotten, the Son begotten, and the Spirit proceeds. These things we know from Scripture. The language used to guard this truth must be well considered. We also recognize the limits and inappropriateness of our language but never at the expense of failing to confess what Scripture makes known.

CONCLUSION

Our Lutheran fathers knew well the history of trinitarian reflection from the early church through the medieval period. They knew the traditional exegesis of the church, the importance of technical terminology, and the patterns of speech used to discuss the Trinity in the classroom and to confess the Trinity in the liturgy, prayers, and hymns of the church. Although at times critical of the

---

98. *Die Promotionsdisputation von Petrus Hegemon*, 1545 (WA 39/2:363.16–18).

99. *Die Promotionsdisputation von Petrus Hegemon*, 1545 (WA 39/2:384.9–22). Cf. Robert Preus, *The Theology of Post-Reformation Lutheranism* (St. Louis: Concordia Publishing House, 1972), 2:123: "When we consider that the Three Persons of the Godhead differ from each other as persons *realiter* and yet remain one undivided divine essence, we realize the inadequacy of our stammering and of even the most careful terminology; for we are faced here with the ineffable and inscrutable mystery of the Trinity, and the church can only do the best she can in speaking of this on the basis of revelation and in avoiding all heresy."

Fathers and medieval schoolmen, they were at the same time deeply indebted to them, especially when it came to their reflections on the Trinity. There are no easy paths to thinking responsibly about the Trinity. Careful consideration of how the divine persons are to be distinguished or how we say what we say about the Trinity may strike many today as overly speculative and even superfluous. Our Lutheran fathers did not share these sentiments. They taught in the classroom and preached from the pulpit these insights from the church in an effort to clarify and guard the scriptural identity of the Trinity.

14

UNITY IN TRINITY:
OPERA AD EXTRA

Scripture affirms both the oneness of God and the threeness of God. The three divine persons, Father, Son, and Holy Spirit, are indivisibly one. In terms of essence, being, substance, nature, or God*ness*, however we wish to express it, Father and Son, along with the Holy Spirit, are indivisibly one. Their oneness is unlike any oneness we know; *unissima*, as Luther put it, oneest or a most single singleness.[1] Luther's *unissima* is no mere rhetorical nicety, no pious gesture to the mystery of the Trinity, but a real and necessary confession that proceeds from Scripture's presentation of the indivisible unity of the Trinity. This unity is always Trinity. God's unity is always known and confessed in three irreducible persons, Father, Son, and Holy Spirit—three irreducibly unique subsistences or hypostases, who are inseparable, mutually indwelling one another, and yet eternally distinct. Although three, they are not three gods but one God. Herein lies the chief difficulty of confessing the Trinity: we confess in our liturgy, prayers, and hymns that three irreducible divine persons are indivisibly one God.

This difficulty, this mystery, led the Fathers and reformers to reflect on scripturally appropriate and responsible patterns of speech for confessing the threeness and oneness of the Trinity. In our previous chapters we have noted the church's linguistic commitments for distinguishing Father, Son, and Holy Spirit from one another. In this chapter we will take up in greater detail the indivisible unity of the Trinity. The Fathers demonstrated the unity of the Trinity by reflecting on the acts and attributes of the divine persons. The acts, works, or activities of the Trinity toward creation demonstrated their unity, their shared power, and therefore their shared nature. The acknowledgment that the works of the Trinity toward creation (*ad extra*) are undivided, meaning they belong equally and inseparably to the three persons, constitutes one of the broadest points of consensus among the Fathers. This theological commonplace became a maxim of orthodox trinitarian thinking throughout the tradition and was dubbed Augustine's rule. At the same time, this scriptural acknowledgement raises potential problems.

The first problem has to do with the works themselves. If the works of the Trinity toward creation are numerically one but the persons of the Trinity

---

1. WA 42:10.20–22 (*Lectures on Genesis*, 1535–45, AE 1:12, "most perfect unity") and WA 42:14.10–11 (AE 1:17, "most single singleness").

are numerically three, then how are we to distinguish the divine persons in their works or even know that there are three persons to distinguish? If we cannot distinguish them in their works, it would seem that distinguishing them at all belongs to God's revelation of Himself as Trinity but has little meaning for us when considering the works or activities of God for us.[2] The Fathers and reformers resolved this difficulty by maintaining that the persons are distinguishable in their economic working in the same way that they are eternally distinguishable from one another. The distinguishing characteristics or unique personal properties of Father, Son, and Holy Spirit permit the reader of Scripture to see both mutuality and distinction in the actions of the Trinity toward creation. On this very point our Lutheran dogmaticians correct a potential misunderstanding of Augustine's rule, as formulated by the medieval schoolmen, and bring to bear the personal properties and order of the divine persons on the external works.

A related problem concerns the way the creeds and faithful confess the works of the Trinity. On the one hand, we say that the Father creates, the Son creates, and the Holy Spirit creates, and yet they are not three creators but one creator. Something similar occurs with all the essential attributes of God. We say the Father is wise, the Son is wise, and the Holy Spirit is wise, but they are not three wisdoms but one. So too they are not three powers but one power, not three eternals but one eternal, not three goods but one good, etc. And here we encounter questions. What does it mean for Scripture to refer to the Son as the "wisdom of God" and the "power of God"? Similarly, in the Large Catechism, Luther writes, "The Creed may be briefly comprised in these few words: 'I believe in God the Father, who created me; I believe in God the Son, who redeemed me; I believe in the Holy Spirit, who sanctifies me.'"[3] If Father, Son, and Holy Spirit all create, save, and sanctify, what does it mean to ascribe these works more particularly to the divine persons? Again, Luther writes, "As the Father is called Creator and the Son is called Redeemer, so on account of his work the Holy Spirit must be called Sanctifier, the One who makes holy."[4] If these acts (creation, redemption, sanctification) and attributes (wisdom, power) belong equally and indivisibly to the Father, the Son, and the Holy Spirit, why assign them more particularly to one person? The church refers to this as appropriation or attribution. The doctrine of appropriation assists us in conceiving the divine persons in their actions toward us. Luther will argue further that appropriation usefully informs our worship of Father, Son, and Holy Spirit.

Finally, the last major problem, and perhaps the issue lurking behind all of the above, concerns the church's confession of God's simplicity. The Fathers

---

2. Bruce Marshall, "Action and Person: Do Palamas and Aquinas Agree about the Spirit," *St. Vladimir's Theological Quarterly* 39/4 (1995): 394-95.
3. LC II.7 (Tappert, 411).
4. LC II.36 (Tappert, 415).

and reformers never hesitate to affirm the doctrine of divine simplicity. Here we encounter one of the great peculiarities of Scripture that is too often forgotten. God reveals Himself to us in the Scriptures by accommodating Himself to our fallen understanding and creaturely language. As finite beings our thoughts and words necessarily conform to our temporal and spatial context. Although we use words like eternal or infinite, they function chiefly as words marking off what something is not. That is to say, these words chiefly negate realities known and experienced by us. We are finite, we are limited creatures, but God is not. Thus we say He is *in*finite, not finite. Likewise, we are constrained by time in both our thoughts and words, but God is not. He is eternal, which is to say that He escapes the temporal constraints and limitations that affect us. With this in mind we also confess that God is simple. He is not made up of parts (AC I). He is not contained by space (1 Kgs 8:27) or time (Ps 90:2). He does not become something He is not; He does not change (Mal 3:6; Jas 1:17). And yet, that we might know God and confess things truly about Him, He has revealed Himself to us in such a way that accommodates Himself to our ways of thinking and speaking. Although God's essence and attributes are not separate, not two different things, such that we must not say that God is wise insofar as He participates in wisdom or good insofar as He participates in goodness, He has nonetheless revealed Himself to us in such a way that we can number His attributes and talk about them separately.

The three problems briefly laid out above will occupy us for the next two chapters. In what follows we will discuss at length the undivided works and inseparable working of the Trinity. Our conclusions here will inform our handling of the final two problems. In the next chapter we discuss appropriation, attributes, and simplicity.

THREENESS AND ONENESS

Before we turn to the external works of the Trinity, we need to say something briefly about the relationship between God's threeness and oneness, and whether one should necessarily and logically precede the other in our dogmatic presentations. Since the medieval period the Western theological tradition has preferred to begin with a discussion of the unity of God and His attributes (*de deo uno*), or what is common to the three persons, before moving to a discussion of the Trinity, or what is proper to the three persons (*de deo trino*). During the sixteenth century our Lutheran fathers departed from this medieval ordering and discussed the Trinity first. They offered no doctrine of God apart from their teaching on the Trinity, and considered the divine attributes in the context of discussing who God is (Trinity) and what God does (works). For various reasons this changed with Johann Gerhard in the seventeenth century.[5]

---

5. For a discussion and critique of this move by Gerhard see Robert Preus, *The Theology of Post-Reformation Lutheranism* (St. Louis: Concordia Publishing House, 1972), 2:15–17 and 2:54–55.

Gerhard returned to the medieval ordering of topics and discussed at length the essence and attributes of God in a separate locus before turning to the Trinity. The dogmaticians who followed Gerhard continued this medieval ordering of topics and defended it. Johannes Quenstedt explains:

> The consideration of God is twofold: one is absolute and the other is relative. The former is occupied with God considered essentially and without respect to the three persons of the Godhead; the latter is occupied with God viewed personally. The former sets forth both the essence and the essential attributes of God; the latter explains the persons of the Holy Trinity and the personal attributes of each.[6]

Gerhard's reason for following the medieval ordering of topics may have had more to do with defending God against the anti-Trinitarians and clarifying a proper understanding of the attributes against various Reformed ideas. Quenstedt, on the other hand, grounds his decision in logic and reason. For him, the most orderly and logical way to proceed begins with essence and attributes and proceeds to persons and works. The medieval schoolmen reasoned in a similar way. They thought you must first know something about divinity, what it is and what it entails, before discussing the divinity of Father, Son, and Holy Spirit. The schoolmen argued that, according to our way of thinking, what is proper presupposes what is common, and therefore we must first grasp "God" before we consider the proper characteristics of the divine persons. This distinction further allowed the schoolmen to comment on natural knowledge of God and what can be known about God by the philosophers or by human reason apart from His revelation as Trinity. Gerhard and the dogmaticians who followed him, including the Baier-Walther *Compendium*, pursue a very similar approach.[7] Francis Pieper departed from the order of presentation found in the later dogmaticians. He did this to emphasize the fundamental difference between Christian knowledge of God and natural knowledge—a difference, he thought, almost universally ignored in his day.[8]

Were the later dogmaticians wrong to follow the schoolmen in their presentation of the doctrine of God and of the Trinity? The answer is both yes and no. Any responsible confession of the Trinity requires confession of God's unique threeness and God's unique oneness. Scripture demands both ways of speaking without prejudicing one over the other. Neither the schoolmen nor the dogmaticians thought their discussion of God stood apart from their discussion of the Trinity.[9] Both discussions went together. From this perspective

---

6. Johann Andreas Quenstedt, *Systema Theologicum*, I, 8 (Wittenberg, 1691), 284.

7. Johann Gerhard's *De Natura Dei*, Locus 3 (ed. Cotta, 91–159) differs slightly from *Theological Commonplaces: On the Nature of God and on the Trinity*, trans. Richard Dinda (St. Louis: Concordia Publishing House, 2007), Exegesis II. Locus 3 begins with a consideration of the knowledge of God and natural knowledge arguments for God (91–98). Gerhard next considers the names of God (98–102) and key trinitarian terms (102–4). The rest of his discussion focuses on the unity of God and the divine attributes (105–59).

8. Francis Pieper, *Christian Dogmatics* (St. Louis: Concordia Publishing House, 1950), 1:428.

9. On the unity of the articles of faith see Abraham Calov, *De Articulis Fidei*, in *Systema*

it matters very little whether you discuss the unity of God before God as Trinity or God as Trinity before the unity of God. And yet how you do this matters quite a bit.

Our chapters discussing the way in which the Fathers and reformers distinguished the divine persons also dealt at length with the unity of the Trinity, the divine attributes, and the external works of the Trinity. So too our discussion of the unity of God will have constant reference to the divine persons. There is no way around this for the scriptural theologian. Scripture makes abundantly clear that the one true God is three eternal persons, Father, Son, and Holy Spirit. This means there is no reality prior to or apart from the Father who eternally begets His coequal and coeternal Son, and who along with the Son breathes forth their coequal and coeternal Spirit. Moreover, it is this very Spirit who searches the deep things of God and who brings us to know and share in the divine life of the Son, who alone in turn makes known to us the Father and the Spirit as the Spirit of the Father and the Spirit of the Son. There is no abstract divine essence that the faithful seek to contemplate or repose in. There is only—if such a word can even be profitably used here—the Father who is made known through the Son by the Holy Spirit.

Francis Pieper worried that the difference between natural knowledge of God and its generic notion of a supreme and perfect being and Scripture's revelation of the Holy Trinity was becoming increasingly blurred in his day. We have cause to worry that matters have only worsened in our day. Many wrongly think that Jews, Christians, and Muslims worship the same God, whom they identify as the God of Abraham. Philosophers endlessly debate in our day the existence of God, the doctrine of divine simplicity, and the attributes of God apart from the divine persons as if they are talking about the God revealed by Scripture and confessed by Christians. For these reasons, and others, it is especially irresponsible in our day for a Christian theologian to pursue a discussion of God, His essence and attributes, apart from His eternal identity as Father, Son, and Holy Spirit. It is irresponsible, on the one hand, because it is not scripturally possible, but even further, it is suspect to the highest degree because there may be no profitable understanding of God's attributes apart from the divine persons, who are these attributes, and their works.[10] And in this sense the later Lutheran dogmaticians should not have begun with the doctrine of God and His attributes before discussing the divine persons. We will return to this issue in our discussion of the divine attributes in the next chapter. With all of this in mind, it may be said without much exaggeration that this chapter and the next, more than any other in part 3, touch on some of the most misunderstood and disputed questions on the Trinity in our day, and

---

Locorum Theologicorum (Wittenberg, 1655), 1:773.

10. This is Martin Chemnitz's position and the way in which he discusses the Trinity. See especially Martin Chemnitz, *Loci Theologici*, trans. J. A. O. Preus (St. Louis: Concordia Publishing House, 2008), 1:68–69.

therefore a great deal is at stake in rightly thinking through the acts, attributes, and simplicity of the Trinity.

OPERA AD EXTRA

Rightly distinguishing Father, Son, and Holy Spirit, rightly expressing the unique and inseparable threeness of God, always entails the further affirmation of the indivisible unity of the three, the unique oneness of the three. In the early church the question was asked why we do not confess three gods. Since we say the Father is God, the Son is God, and the Holy Spirit is God, why do we not also say that these three are three gods? Why count Father, Son, and Holy Spirit as three but not the repetition of the word "God"? This question of names and numbers became so pressing during the fourth century that Basil of Caesarea in a moment of frustration declared, "When the Lord taught us the doctrine of Father, Son, and Holy Spirit, He did not make arithmetic a part of this gift!"[11] As Basil sees it, those who persist in this kind of questioning have turned our ability to count against the faith, honoring arithmetic more than the revealed divine nature. Basil continues, "There is one God and Father, one Only-Begotten Son, and one Holy Spirit. We declare each Person to be unique, and if we must use numbers, we will not let a stupid arithmetic lead us astray to the idea of many gods."[12] Many years later Augustine faced a similar problem. When people hear that the Father is not the Son, the Son is not the Father, and the Holy Spirit, the Spirit of the Father and the Spirit of the Son, is neither the Father nor the Son, they think they must say three gods because Father, Son, and Holy Spirit are three.[13] Again the problem has to do with counting. Augustine responds:

> If three, three what? Counting does not work. Thus God neither refuses to be counted, nor submits to being counted. Because they are three, it looks like counting; if you ask three what, counting does not work. That is why it says, *Great is our Lord and great is his strength, and there is no counting his wisdom* (Ps 146:5 Vulg.). When you start thinking about it, you begin counting; when you have counted, you cannot say what you have counted. The Father is the Father, the Son is the Son, the Holy Spirit is the Holy Spirit. . . . You see, this number three only creeps into their relation to each other, not into what each is to oneself.[14]

The difficulty that stands behind the question of whether we may say three gods and the sharp responses from Basil and Augustine have to do with the essential unity, the unique oneness, of the divine persons. It wasn't however just arithmetic that led to the question of whether or not we should say three gods. The problem has to do with the acts or works of the divine persons toward creation.

---

11. Basil of Caesarea *On the Holy Spirit* 18.44 (PPS, 71).
12. Basil of Caesarea *On the Holy Spirit* 18.44 (PPS, 72).
13. Augustine *Homilies on the Gospel of John* 39.2 (WSA III/12, 587).
14. Augustine *Homilies on the Gospel of John* 39.4 (WSA III/12, 588–89).

Scripture makes clear that the Father creates, the Son creates, and the Holy Spirit creates. How should we understand this? Does it mean that the Father creates apart from the Son and the Spirit, the Son apart from the Father and the Spirit, and the Spirit apart from the Father and the Son? Does it mean that each contributes to the work of creation such that one part is done by the Father, another part by the Son, and yet another part by the Holy Spirit? If either of these statements is true, then the church's confession of the unity and simplicity of the Trinity would be false, and indeed we should say three gods. The Fathers explained these difficult questions by showing from Scripture that the works of the Trinity toward creation are inseparable and indivisible. This theological conclusion became known during the medieval period as Augustine's rule: *opera Trinitatis ad extra indivisa sunt*. This rule states that every action of the three persons toward the outside (*ad extra*), which is to say every external work or every work toward creation, is numerically one and proceeds from their unity of will and power. When the Father works, the Son and the Holy Spirit work also in the same act by the same power of their common nature.

The Fathers demonstrated the indivisible unity of the Trinity by showing how Scripture assigns the same activity or work to Father, Son, and Holy Spirit. The church confesses that the Trinity is holy and perfect. This means, explains Athanasius, that the Trinity's nature is indivisible and "has one activity."[15] Here Athanasius voices a commonplace among the Fathers: activity and nature go together. Common activity indicates common nature, and common nature produces common activity. The argument follows a basic insight. Every nature possesses the power to do the things belonging to that nature. Since Father, Son, and Holy Spirit are one God, are one simple essence or nature, it follows that They are one power and that one power acts in creation from the Father through the Son in the Holy Spirit. This one nature, one power, one activity (ἐνεργία, *operatio*) theology is emphasized by all the orthodox writers of the early church. Before turning to Scripture Athanasius summarizes his point: "The Father does all things through the Word in the Holy Spirit. In this way is the unity of the Holy Trinity preserved, and in this way is the one God preached in the Church."[16]

We see the common work of the Trinity in the work of creation and also in the grace and gifts bestowed upon us by the Trinity. Scripture makes abundantly clear that creation is the work of the Father, the Son, and the Holy Spirit. John's prologue shows that the Father creates through the Word. The Psalms show that the Father creates by sending forth His Spirit (Ps 104:30), and further that the Word and the Spirit create inseparably (Ps 33:6).[17] These Scriptures teach that "the Father creates all things through the Word in the Spirit."[18] Similarly, Paul

---

15. Athanasius *Letters to Serapion* 1.28.2 (PPS, 97).
16. Athanasius *Letters to Serapion* 1.28.2 (PPS, 97).
17. Athanasius *Letters to Serapion* 2.13.4–14.1 (PPS, 123–24).
18. Athanasius *Letters to Serapion* 2.14.1 (PPS, 124); cf 1.24.5–6 (PPS, 91).

teaches the unity of the Trinity to the Corinthians when discussing spiritual gifts: "Now there are distributions of gifts, but the same Spirit; and there are distributions of service, but the same Lord; and there are distributions of activities, but it is the same God who works them all in everyone" (1 Cor 12:4–6). Athanasius explains, "The gifts which the Spirit distributes to each are bestowed by the Father through the Word. For all that the Father has is the Son's. Thus what is given by the Son in the Spirit is a gift of the Father."[19] What we receive from God the Father comes to us through the Son in the Spirit. Athanasius appeals to one of his favorite scriptural analogies to express this (cf. Heb 1:3). Where there is light, there is light's radiance, and where there is light's radiance, there is the activity and luminous grace of that radiance.[20] These three, like the activity of Father, Son, and Holy Spirit, are inseparable and yet distinct.

Athanasius observes the same pattern in Paul's second letter to the Corinthians: "The grace of the Lord Jesus Christ and the love of God and the fellowship of the Holy Spirit be with you all" (2 Cor 13:14). Athanasius writes, "This grace and gift given in the Trinity is given by the Father through the Son in the Holy Spirit. Just as the grace given through the Son is from the Father, so too we cannot have fellowship with the gift except in the Holy Spirit. For it is when we participate in the Spirit that we have the love of the Father and the grace of the Son and fellowship of the Spirit himself."[21] The grace and gift given is given by the Trinity. It is the same grace and same gift given to us from the Father through the Son in the Holy Spirit. When we participate in the Spirit, we have the grace of the Word, and when we have the grace of the Word by the Spirit, we have the love of the Father.[22] Here we see, concludes Athanasius, "there is one activity of the Trinity."[23] This one activity, one grace, shows the indivisibility of the Trinity.[24]

Athanasius's insistence on the one activity of the Trinity finds greater clarity with Didymus the Blind. Didymus uses the same passage from 2 Corinthians. Paul shows in this passage that there is "a single reception of the Trinity," for whoever receives the grace of Christ has it as much by the Father's administering as by the Spirit's bestowing.[25] We should never think that the grace given by the Father differs from that given by the Son. It is one and the same. Paul makes this explicit at the beginning of his letter to the Romans: "Grace to you and peace from God our Father and the Lord Jesus Christ" (Rom 1:7). Here Paul talks of a singular grace and a singular peace that we have from the Father and the Son. It is this same grace from the Father and the Son that is perfected by

---

19. Athanasius *Letters to Serapion* 1.30.4 (PPS, 100).
20. Athanasius *Letters to Serapion* 1.30.5 (PPS, 100). For a similar analogy in the context of the inseparable working of the Trinity see Augustine *Homilies on the Gospel of John* 20.13 (WSA III/12, 370).
21. Athanasius *Letters to Serapion* 1.30.6–7 (PPS, 100).
22. Athanasius *Letters to Serapion* 2.15.1 (PPS, 125).
23. Athanasius *Letters to Serapion* 1.31.1 (PPS, 100).
24. Athanasius *Letters to Serapion* 2.15.1 (PPS, 125).
25. Didymus the Blind *On the Holy Spirit* 75 (PPS, 166).

the Holy Spirit. Didymus explains, "It is not the case that the Father gives one grace and the Savior another, inasmuch as Paul writes that the grace given by both the Father and the Lord Jesus Christ is perfected by the communion of the Holy Spirit."[26] Lest we think the grace we receive from the Father through the Son stands apart from the Holy Spirit, Didymus immediately directs our attention to Scripture's insistence that this same grace comes to us by the Holy Spirit. According to Scripture those who spurn the Son of God, profaning the blood of the covenant, outrage "the Spirit of grace" (Heb 10:29). It is this same Spirit, proclaimed by the prophets, that would be poured out on God's people (Jl 2:28), the Spirit of YHWH (Ez 39:29), the Spirit of grace (Zec 12:10). Didymus explains, "Whenever anyone receives the grace of the Holy Spirit, he has it as a gift from God the Father and our Lord Jesus Christ. Therefore, the fact that there is a single grace of the Father and the Son perfected by the activity of the Holy Spirit demonstrates that the Trinity is of one substance."[27]

Didymus delights in showing how Scripture presents the unity of the Trinity in Their works for us. He returns to the passage from Paul's second letter to the Corinthians. Paul commends "the love of God" to the Christians at Corinth (2 Cor 13:14). The love Paul commends the Trinity grants and sustains. Jesus explains, "Whoever has my commandments and keeps them, he it is who loves me. And he who loves me will be loved by my Father, and I will love him and manifest myself to him" (Jn 14:21). Jesus' love with which He loves is not different from the Father's love, who loves in order to save: "For God so loved the world, that he gave his only Son, that whoever believes in him should not perish but have eternal life" (Jn 3:16). The love with which we love is the fruit of the Holy Spirit (Gal 5:22) poured into our hearts (Rom 5:5).[28] Similarly, notes Didymus, the grace of our Lord Jesus Christ and the love of God the Father—same grace and same love—bring about our fellowship in the Holy Spirit (2 Cor 13:14).[29] The fellowship brought about in the Holy Spirit is the same fellowship the Father calls us to in His Son: "God is faithful, by whom you were called into the fellowship of his Son, Jesus Christ our Lord" (1 Cor 1:9). Similarly, John writes that God is light, and if we walk in the light we have fellowship with Him (1 Jn 1:7), and that fellowship is the fellowship we have as believers "with the Father and with his Son Jesus Christ" (1 Jn 1:3). Didymus concludes:

> Therefore, since whoever has communion with the Holy Spirit immediately has communion with both the Father and the Son, whenever anyone has the love of the Father, he has it as a gift from the Son through the Holy Spirit. In addition, whenever anyone is a participant of the grace of Jesus Christ, he has the same grace as a gift from the Father through the Holy Spirit.[30]

---

26. Didymus the Blind *On the Holy Spirit* 75 (PPS, 166–67).
27. Didymus the Blind *On the Holy Spirit* 76 (PPS, 167).
28. Didymus the Blind *On the Holy Spirit* 77–78 (PPS, 167–68).
29. Didymus the Blind *On the Holy Spirit* 78–79 (PPS, 168).
30. Didymus the Blind *On the Holy Spirit* 80 (PPS, 168).

All of the above show that the activity of Father, Son, and Holy Spirit is numerically the same. And this, explains Didymus, is how Scripture presents the unity of the Trinity: "Those who have a single activity also have a single substance."[31]

The above Scriptures demonstrate for Athanasius and Didymus the shared activities of Father, Son, and Holy Spirit and the indivisibility of their substance. Athanasius concludes, "The Trinity is indivisible, and there is one divinity of the Trinity ... This is the faith of the Catholic church."[32] Similarly, Didymus writes, "From these texts we conclude that the substance of the Trinity is indivisible, and that the Father is truly the Father of the Son, and that the Son is truly the Son of the Father, and that the Holy Spirit is truly the Spirit of the Father and God, and especially the Spirit of Wisdom and Truth, that is, of the Son of God. So then, this is salvation for those who believe."[33] The unity of the Trinity proceeds from Scripture's presentation of the working of the divine persons for our creation and redemption. The Fathers began with Scripture, not with prior philosophical commitments on what unity or simplicity entailed, and showed the one nature, one power, and one activity of Father, Son, and Holy Spirit.

Although Scripture makes plain the shared activity of the divine persons in their works toward creation, questions continued to be raised about how we understand their actual working. When we say, for example, that the Father works through the Son in the Holy Spirit, are we parceling out the work among the three? Are we merely saying the Son and Holy Spirit are agents of the Father's activity? In what sense is their working equal and inseparable? These more specific questions are addressed by Gregory of Nyssa. From the outset Gregory insists that we not think about the common work of the Trinity in the way we think of human works. For example, we say that those who cultivate the land or raise animals are farmers. Although we use the plural for farmers, we refer to their common work in the singular—farming. What makes their work common? Although we may say that two farmers do the same work, we mean only that they engage in the same kind of work. We do not mean that they work inseparably in the very same work. The action of one farmer belongs to him alone and the action of another belongs to him alone. In that sense we may count the separate actions of these two farmers and still say that they belong to the common work of farming. This is not at all what Scripture teaches about the inseparable and mutual working of the Trinity. Gregory explains:

> With regard to the divine nature, on the other hand, it is otherwise. We do not learn that the Father does something on his own in which the Son does not cooperate. Or again, that the Son acts on his own without the Spirit. Rather does every operation which extends from God to creation and is designated according to our differing conceptions of it have its origin in the Father, proceed through the Son, and reach its completion by the Holy Spirit. It is for this reason that the word

---

31. Didymus the Blind *On the Holy Spirit* 81 (PPS, 168).
32. Athanasius *Letters to Serapion* 2.15.4 (PPS, 125).
33. Didymus the Blind *On the Holy Spirit* 103 (PPS, 175–76).

for the operation is not divided among the persons involved. For the action of each in any matter is not separate and individualized. But whatever occurs, whether in reference to God's providence for us or to the government and constitution of the universe, occurs through the three Persons, and is not three separate things.[34]

Gregory insists that you cannot divide the works of the Trinity "according to the number of *hypostases*."[35] No activity is distinguished among the divine persons (*hypostases*) as if it were done individually or separately by one person and not the other two.[36] Gregory gives the example of baptism and the gift of life we receive from Father, Son, and Holy Spirit in our baptism. According to Scripture this single gift comes to us from the three persons. We must not, however, count the work as we would the persons: "Though we take it for granted that there are three Persons and names, we do not imagine that three different lives are granted us—one from each of them."[37] This is why we do not call those who produce this single life "three life-givers." The same applies for all their other acts and attributes. The Father is good, the Son is good, and the Spirit is good, but we do not say they are "three goods."[38]

Gregory addresses one final question. If the Father works through the Son in the Holy Spirit "jointly, inseparably, and mutually," does that mean they also work simultaneously?[39] The answer is yes. Father, Son, and Holy Spirit are one simple and undivided essence, power, and will. Therefore, all that the Father does through the Son by the Holy Spirit occurs without sequence or interval. Their works are not serially related. We must not think of any delay, writes Gregory, "in the movement of the divine will from the Father through the Son and to the Holy Spirit."[40] The confession of the faithful is that the divine persons work inseparably and mutually without sequence or interval. Herein lies their unique unity, their *unissima*, as made known to us by Scripture and confessed by us through our liturgy, prayers, and hymns.

THE DISTINCTION OF PERSONS AND COMMON WORKS

The trinitarian insight shown above—basic to the tradition of the church—has come under scrutiny in our day. The problem has to do with how we maintain the significance of three persons when we insist that any action done by one is done by the other two as well. If God's actions remain undivided *ad extra*, how are we to distinguish the persons? Is there even a point to distinguishing the persons? Could it be that the eternal distinction of Father, Son, and Holy Spirit

---

34. Gregory of Nyssa *An Answer to Ablabius* in *Christology of the Later Fathers*, ed. Edward R. Hardy (Philadelphia: Westminster Press, 1954), 261–62 (GNO 3.1, 47.21–48.8).

35. Gregory of Nyssa *An Answer to Ablabius* 262 (GNO 3.1, 48.21–22). The English translation obscures the Greek.

36. Gregory of Nyssa *An Answer to Ablabius* 263 (GNO 3.1, 50.17–20).

37. Gregory of Nyssa *An Answer to Ablabius* 262 (GNO 3.1, 48.14–16).

38. Gregory of Nyssa *An Answer to Ablabius* 262 (GNO 3.1, 49.1–4).

39. Gregory of Nyssa *An Answer to Ablabius* 262 (GNO 3.1, 49.6–7).

40. Gregory of Nyssa *An Answer to Ablabius* 264 (GNO 3.1, 51.19–20).

is a truth revealed by God in Scripture but one that has no bearing on His work in the world and therefore no meaning for the faithful? Put in this way, it is no small matter that we affirm the following two things: the works of the Trinity *ad extra* are undivided and the eternal distinction of the three persons does not overturn the numerical identity of their actions.

A number of strategies have been deployed throughout the tradition of the church to explain in some sense the concerns of the previous paragraph. Understanding action and difference between what Father, Son, and Holy Spirit do in the completion of any single action by them proceeds from the *taxis* or order of the persons. As we have seen in our previous chapters, the faithful pattern their liturgy and prayers according to the order of the divine persons given to us in Scripture. Gregory of Nyssa writes:

> Hence we are baptized as it has been handed down to us, into *Father and Son and Holy Spirit*, and we believe as we are baptized—for it is fitting that our confession be of one voice with our faith—and we give glory as we believe, for it is not natural that worship make war against faith, but as we believe, so also we give glory. Now since our faith is in *Father and Son and Holy Spirit*, faith, worship, and baptism accord with each other.[41]

The order of the persons revealed in Scripture informs baptism, worship, and prayer. We baptize in the name of the Father, the Son, and the Holy Spirit; we sing the doxology to the Father and the Son and the Holy Spirit; we make the sign of the cross in the name of the Father, the Son, and the Holy Spirit. We never baptize in the name of the Spirit, the Father, and the Son; we never sing the doxology in the name of the Son and the Father and the Spirit; we never make the sign of the cross in the name of the Father and of the Spirit and of the Son. Why? Scripture patterns our speech, our worship, our prayers in a way that corresponds to the eternal relation and identity of the persons.

How does the order of the divine persons as revealed in Scripture inform their mutual working for us? To begin with, the order of the persons corresponds to their mode of origin and unique personal properties as revealed in Scripture. The Father alone is unbegotten, the Son the only-begotten, and the Spirit proceeds from the Father and the Son. In our previous two chapters we have shown how the Fathers and reformers distinguished the divine persons from one another by appealing to their distinctive properties (unbegotten, begotten, proceeding) and relative properties (paternity, filiation, procession).[42] Similarly, they used these same scriptural insights to understand the difference between the persons in their undivided works. The divine persons work in an ordered manner according to their personal properties and relations of origin.

---

41. Gregory of Nyssa *Letter 24*, 8–9 in *Gregory of Nyssa: The Letters*, trans. Anna M. Silvas (Leiden: Brill, 2007), 194.

42. These are not two sets of properties but rather two ways of viewing the unique personal properties of Father, Son, and Holy Spirit. Cf. Basil of Caesarea *Against Eunomius* 2.28 (Fathers of the Church, 174) and especially Gregory of Nazianzus *Or.* 39, 11–12 in *Gregory of Nazianzus*, trans. Brian Daley (New York: Routledge, 2006), 132–33.

For example, the Father is the principal source and origin of the Son and the Spirit. This means that the Son and the Spirit depend upon the Father for their being and for their acts and attributes. Jesus says, "Truly, truly, I say to you, the Son can do nothing of his own accord, but only what he sees the Father doing. For whatever the Father does, that the Son does likewise" (Jn 5:19). Jesus continues with examples. The Father gives life and so too the Son gives life (Jn 5:21). Likewise, the Holy Spirit "gives life" (Jn 6:63). Further, Jesus says, "the Spirit of Truth . . . will not speak on his own authority, but whatever he hears he will speak, and he will declare to you the things that are to come. He will glorify me, for he will take what is mine and declare it to you. All that the Father has is mine; therefore I said that he will take what is mine and declare it to you" (Jn 16:13–15). The ordered working of the divine persons pertains to their eternal relations to one another. The Son is from the Father and the Spirit is from the Father and the Son. This means the Father acts through the Son in the Holy Spirit. It belongs to the Father to act through the Son in the Holy Spirit; it belongs to the Son to be the one through whom the Father acts; and it belongs to the Holy Spirit to be the one in whom and by whom the Father and the Son act. These passages from John's Gospel show the inseparable working of Father, Son, and Holy Spirit according to their relations of origin. As shown in our previous chapter with Calov and Gerhard, this language of dependence refers only to the mode of origin as revealed in Scripture. Gerhard writes:

> The Father is the first person not by reason of time (the three persons are coeternal), nor by reason of nature or essence (they are *homoousios*), nor by reason of dignity (they are of equal glory and majesty) but by reason of origin or production.[43]

The Son and the Holy Spirit are from the Father but not after Him. The Father is the First Person of the Trinity "because he is from no one and because he is the origin of the Trinity (*origo Trinitatis*), begetting the Son and with the Son spirating one Holy Spirit."[44]

The Father is eternally distinguished from the Son by His fatherhood (*paternitas*); the Son is eternally distinguished from the Father by His sonship (*filiatio*); and the Holy Spirit is eternally distinguished from the Father and the Son by His procession (*processio*). These distinctive and relative properties not only distinguish the divine persons from one another but also inform their unique and inseparable working. For example, Athanasius states that the one divine will or power of the Trinity proceeds from the Father through the Son in the Holy Spirit. All that is done proceeds from the Father as principle or source, is mediated by the Son, and is manifested or perfected in the Spirit. Athanasius explains:

---

43. Johann Gerhard, *De Deo Patre*, Locus 4/2, §1 (ed. Cotta, 223).
44. Gerhard, *De Deo Patre*, Locus 4/2, §2 (ed. Cotta, 223). Cf. Baier-Walther, *Compendium Theologiae Positivae*, I, §44.

The Father does all things through the Word in the Holy Spirit. In this way is the unity of the Holy Trinity preserved, and in this way is the one God preached in the Church, *who is above all and through all and in all* [Eph 4:6]—*above all*, as Father, as beginning, as source; *through all*, through the Word; *in all*, in the Holy Spirit. It is not a Trinity in name alone and in linguistic expression, but in truth and actual existence.[45]

Likewise, Gregory of Nyssa says, "There is one motion and disposition of the good will which proceeds from the Father, through the Son, to the Spirit."[46] Martin Luther continues this way of speaking from the Fathers. Luther writes:

> The Scriptures teach us that all creation is the work of one God, or the whole Godhead; and yet, inasmuch as they make a distinction between the three persons of the one Godhead, we may properly say that everything had its origin, everything exists and continues, in the Father as the first person; through the Son, who is of the Father; and in the Holy Spirit, who proceeds from both the Father and the Son; which three, nevertheless, are comprehended in the one undivided essence.[47]

The work of creation is one, not three. We do not have one creation from the Father, another from the Son, and yet another from the Holy Spirit. The single work of creation proceeds from the Father as the First Person, through the Son of the Father, and in the Holy Spirit, who is from the Father and the Son.

Augustine

For the most part the above insights come to our Lutheran fathers by way of the Augustinian tradition. And yet, as we will see below, the dogmaticians express some unhappiness with the way in which the medieval schoolmen preserved Augustine's teaching on the inseparable working of the Trinity and therefore the insights of the Fathers. Augustine writes, "Although just as the Father and the Son and the Holy Spirit are inseparable, so do they work inseparably. This is also my faith inasmuch as it is the Catholic faith."[48] Augustine makes the inseparable works of the Trinity a principal feature of his trinitarian theology—so much so that the scholastic rule, *opera Trinitatis ad extra indivisa sunt*, repeated throughout the Western theological tradition as Augustine's rule, aimed to summarize his exegetical insights on the external works of the Trinity.

Augustine presents a similar argument as that found above with Athanasius, Didymus, and Gregory of Nyssa. Father, Son, and Holy Spirit are one indivisible Trinity. They are one God and not three gods: "One God in such a way that the Son is not the Father, that the Father is not the Son, that the Holy Spirit is neither the Father nor the Son, but the Spirit of the Father and of the Son."[49] These three work inseparably in every action toward creation according to

---

45. Athanasius *Letters to Serapion* 1.28.3 (PPS, 97).
46. Gregory of Nyssa *An Answer to Ablabius* 262 (GNO 3.1, 48.22–49.1).
47. Martin Luther, "Sermon for Trinity Sunday on Rom 11:33–36 (1537)," in *Complete Sermons of Martin Luther*, trans. John Lenker (Grand Rapids: Baker Books, 2000), 4.2:24.
48. Augustine *The Trinity* I.7 (WSA I/5, 70). See also Augustine *Sermon 52*, 2 (WSA III/3, 51).
49. Augustine *Sermon 52*, 2 (WSA III/3, 51).

their one divine will and power.⁵⁰ Further, their working corresponds to their eternal relationship to one another. Since the Son is from the Father, He exists and works from the Father; since the Holy Spirit is from the Father and the Son, He exists and works from the Father through the Son.⁵¹ Augustine uses the example of creation. He writes:

> What one has made, the other has made also. The Father made the world, the Son made the world, the Holy Spirit made the world. If three gods, three worlds; if one God—the Father, the Son, and the Holy Spirit—then one world was made by the Father through the Son in the Holy Spirit.⁵²

Augustine maintains two important points. On the one hand the Father, the Son, and the Holy Spirit are truly and fully one God. Whatever it means to be God is true of God the Father, God the Son, and God the Holy Spirit equally and indivisibly. On the other hand, the Father, the Son, and the Holy Spirit stand in an eternal relationship to one another. As we emphasized above and have stated throughout this book, there is no reality prior to or apart from the Father who eternally begets His coequal and coeternal Son, and who along with the Son breathes forth Their coequal and coeternal Spirit. These two points bear on Augustine's understanding of the Trinity's working *ad extra*.

Augustine demonstrates the above with Jn 5:26 ("For as the Father has life in himself, so he has granted the Son also to have life in himself").⁵³ The Father does not have His life from elsewhere, He does not derive it from another, He does not partake of it or borrow it, but has it from Himself.⁵⁴ Indeed, life itself is for Him the same as Himself. The Son, begotten of the Father, "is" life by being begotten. Augustine continues:

> The Father is life, not by "being born" [*non nascendo*]; the Son is life by "being born" [*nascendo*]. The Father is not from any father, the Son is from God the Father. The Father, that he is, is from no one; but that he is Father he is on account of the Son [*propter Filium*]. But for the Son both that he is the Son is on account of the Father [*propter Patrem*] and that he is, he is from the Father [*a Patre*]. . . . Therefore, the Father remains life and the Son remains life. The Father has life in himself [*semetipso*], not from the Son; the Son has life in himself [*semetipso*], but from the Father.⁵⁵

---

50. Augustine *Homilies on the Gospel of John* 20.4 (WSA III/12, 360–61).
51. Augustine *Homilies on the Gospel of John* 20.4 (WSA III/12, 361): "So then, because the Son's power is from the Father, that is why the Son's substance too is from the Father; and because the Son's substance is from the Father, that is why the Son's power too is from the Father." See also 20.8 (WSA III/12, 365).
52. Augustine *In Johannis Evangelium Tractatus* 20.9 (PL 35, 1561): "Quae ille, haec et ipse: mundum Pater, mundum Filius, mundum Spiritus sanctus. Si tres dii, tres mundi: si unus Deus Pater et Filius et Spiritus sanctus, unus mundus factus est a Patre per Filium in Spiritu sancto." Cf. Augustine *Homilies on the Gospel of John* 20.9 (WSA III/12, 366).
53. On what follows see Lewis Ayres, *Augustine and the Trinity* (Cambridge: Cambridge University Press, 2010), 245–46.
54. Augustine *Homilies on the Gospel of John* 19.11 (WSA III/12, 343). John 5:26 Vulg. reads: "Sicut enim Pater habet vitam in semetipso sic dedit et Filio vitam habere in semetipso" (PL 35, 1548).
55. Augustine *In Johannis Evangelium Tractatus* 19.13 (PL 35, 1550–51); cf. Augustine *Homilies*

The Father is always Father *of the Son* and the Son is always Son *of the Father*.[56] The Father of the Son is life in Himself toward the Son; the Son of the Father is life in Himself from the Father. Although we rightly confess the indivisible unity of the Father and the Son, we never do this at the expense of distinguishing the persons or neglecting the order of the persons as made known by Scripture. Their equality, their unique unity, never stands apart from their eternal reality as Father and Son. Augustine explains:

> For, while we indeed say and believe that the Son is equal to the Father, and that there is no difference of nature or substance between them, and that there was no interval of time interposed between begetter and begotten, all the same, with that being assured and maintained, we still say that one is the Father, the other is the Son. The one would not be the Father unless he had a Son; the other would not be the Son unless he had a Father. Nonetheless, the Son is God *from the Father*, while the Father is God, but not from the Son. The Father of the Son is not God from the Son, while the other, the Son of the Father, is also God from the Father. The Lord Christ, remember, is called [in the Nicene Creed] 'Light from Light.' So then there is Light which is not from Light [the Father], and an equal Light which is from Light [the Son], together one Light, not two Lights.[57]

When we are talking about the indivisible unity of God, we are, as Augustine here emphasizes, also always and only talking about Father, Son, and Holy Spirit. Likewise, when we are talking about the inseparable works of the Trinity *ad extra*, we are also always talking about their relations of origin and the order of the persons as revealed in Scripture. The Father is always the Father who eternally begets His coequal and coeternal Son, and who along with the Son breathes forth their coequal and coeternal Spirit. The Father is God, the Son is God, and the Holy Spirit is God. And yet, insists Augustine, "for all that, the Father is not who the Son is, nor is the Son who the Father is, nor is the Holy Spirit of the Father and the Spirit of the Son either the Father or the Son."[58] Again, the Father is from no one, the Son is from the Father, and the Holy Spirit is from the Father and the Son. These eternal relations, these irreducible eternal relationships, allow us to confess both the inseparability of their works and to recognize the distinction of those who work inseparably.

Martin Luther

Martin Luther's discussion of the inseparable working of the Trinity follows Augustine closely. He too uses the example of creation. Luther appeals to Psalm

---

on the Gospel of John 19.13 (WSA III/12, 346–47).

56. Augustine *Homilies on the Gospel of John* 39.4 (WSA III/12, 589). Here Augustine adds the Holy Spirit to the discussion. The Father is always in reference to the Son, the Son in reference to the Father, and the Holy Spirit in reference to both Father and Son as the Spirit of the Father and the Spirit of the Son.

57. Augustine *Homilies on the Gospel of John* 29.5 (WSA III/12, 492). See also *Homilies* 31.4 (WSA III/12, 506).

58. Augustine *Homilies on the Gospel of John* 39.3 (WSA III/12, 587).

33: "By the Word of the Lord the heavens were made, and all their host by the Breath of His mouth" (Ps 33:6).[59] This verse names three distinct persons—Lord, Word, and Breath—who do the same work. The Lord does not work apart from His Word, the Word does not work apart from His Breath. As the Lord creates, the Word creates, and the Breath creates: "It is one essence that creates, and it is one creation that all three Persons create."[60] This verse further teaches us not to mingle the persons into one person, nor to divide and separate the one divine essence into three persons. Luther explains,

> If I ascribe to each Person a distinct external work in creation and exclude the other two Persons from this, then I have divided the one Godhead and have fashioned three gods or creators. And that is wrong. Again, if I do not ascribe to each Person within the Godhead, or outside and beyond creation, a special distinction not appropriate to the other two, then I have mingled the Persons into one Person. And that is also wrong.[61]

When we discuss the external works of the Trinity we are talking about both the indivisible essence and the inseparable persons. At this point Luther makes reference to "the rule of St. Augustine," which states, according to Luther, that the works of the Trinity *ad extra* are undivided (*opera Trinitatis ad extra indivisa sunt*). Augustine's rule prevents us from dividing the external works of the Trinity and thus separating the persons.

Augustine's rule, as quoted by Luther, comes not from Augustine but from the medieval schoolmen. Although the rule, so far as it goes, represents Augustine's thought, it makes a subtle change to Augustine's Latin. Augustine prefers to say the works of the Trinity are inseparable (*opera inseparabilia sunt*).[62] The scholastic rule substitutes undivided (*indivisa sunt*). To say the works of the Trinity are undivided places emphasis on the essential unity of the Trinity. Augustine's *inseparabilia*, on the other hand, has the advantage of directing our attention to the mutual working of the persons. That is to say, rather than concentrating on the unity of action that proceeds from their common nature, Augustine's preferred language encourages us to consider how three agents—Father, Son, and Holy Spirit—work inseparably and equally in one action. In other words, how do three act in such a way that we know there are three working and yet there is only one action? To think about the external works of the Trinity in this way forces us to consider how the unique personal properties of the divine persons and their relations of origin inform their works. Luther seems to recognize this. After quoting Augustine's rule he continues his explanation by showing how we rightly understand the difference between Father, Son, and Holy Spirit in their inseparable working. Like the Greek Fathers above and like Augustine, Luther directs the reader's attention to the mode of

---

59. *On the Last Words of David*, 1543 (AE 15:301; WA 54:56.30–31). I have quoted Psalm 33 as it appears in AE.
60. *On the Last Words of David*, 1543 (AE 15:302; WA 54:57.20–21).
61. *On the Last Words of David*, 1543 (AE 15:302; WA 54:57.28–31).
62. Augustine *In Johannis Evangelium Tractatus* 20.3 (PL 35, 1557) et passim.

origin for the divine persons. Scripture teaches that Father, Son, and Holy Spirit are distinct within the one indivisible and eternal Godhead, and this distinction pertains to their relations of origin. Luther explains:

> The difference is that He is the Father and does not derive His Godhead from the Son or anyone else. The Son is a Person distinct from the Father in the same, one paternal Godhead. The difference is that He is the Son and that He does not have Godhead from Himself, nor from anyone else but the Father, since He was born of the Father from eternity. The Holy Spirit is a Person distinct from the Father and the Son in the same, one Godhead. The difference is that He is the Holy Spirit, who eternally proceeds both from the Father and from the Son, and who does not have the Godhead from Himself nor from anyone else but from both the Father and the Son, and all of this from eternity to eternity.[63]

The works of the Trinity toward creation are undivided and their mutual working accords with their unique personal properties. By keeping these two insights together we avoid dividing the substance or mingling the persons.[64] Luther applies this insight to their work of creation in terms that sound very close to Augustine above. We confess that the Father creates, the Son creates, and the Holy Spirit creates. Further, insists Luther, we speak of their mutual creation according to their relations of origin. This means, for example, that the Son is God and Creator, like the Father, but He is this *from the Father*. Luther continues:

> The Father does not owe the fact that He is God and Creator to the Son, but the Son owes the fact that He is God and Creator to the Father. And the fact that Father and Son are God and Creator they do not owe to the Holy Spirit; but the Holy Spirit owes the fact that He is God and Creator to the Father and to the Son. . . . The Father is the source, or the fountainhead (if we may use the term as the fathers do) of the Godhead, that the Son derives it from Him and that the Holy Spirit derives it from Him and the Son, and not vice versa.[65]

When it comes to the external works of the Trinity, we must always bear in mind that we are talking about Father, Son, and Holy Spirit. There is no prior reality called "God" apart from God the Father, God the Son, and God the Holy Spirit. Their unique mode of existence and their relations of origin allow us to rightly distinguish the persons and to rightly understand the indivisible unity of their external works. Put simply, this means the Father works or acts through the Son in the Holy Spirit; the Son is the one through whom the Father acts; the Holy Spirit is the one in whom and by whom the Father and the Son act. Because they mutually indwell one another, Father, Son, and Holy Spirit act inseparably and equally in one single action. Luther's insights become a point of emphasis for the Lutheran dogmaticians.

---

63. *On the Last Words of David*, 1543 (AE 15:303; WA 54:58.19–28).
64. *On the Last Words of David*, 1543 (AE 15:304; WA 54:59.9–10 and AE 15:309; WA 54:63.30–31).
65. *On the Last Words of David*, 1543 (AE 15:309–10; WA 54:63.35–64.7).

THE LUTHERAN ADDENDUM TO AUGUSTINE'S RULE

The scholastic rule attributed to Augustine is good as far as it goes. Luther recognized that the Fathers and particularly Augustine had more to say than what the rule says, and he incorporated those insights into his discussion of the external works of the Trinity. The Lutheran dogmaticians follow Luther closely and convey his insights by explicitly altering the scholastic rule attributed to Augustine. This begins with Melanchthon but becomes explicit with Chemnitz and Quenstedt among others. Melanchthon addresses the issue of the external works of the Trinity in his unfinished explanation of the Nicene Creed. At the end of his discussion of the Second Article of the Creed Melanchthon answers a number of Christological objections. Some have wondered if salvation is the common work of the Trinity or of Christ alone. He begins with a syllogism:

> The works of the Trinity *ad extra* are undivided.
>
> Salvation is a work *ad extra*.
>
> Therefore, the Father, Son, and Holy Spirit work in the same way [for our salvation] and it is said improperly concerning Christ, "he crushed the head of the serpent" (Gen 3:15).[66]

Since salvation is an external work and since all agree that the external works of the Trinity are undivided, it must be the case that Father, Son, and Holy Spirit work our salvation in the same way (*eodem modo*). This immediately presents a problem. The Son alone assumed human nature. He alone suffered and died on the cross. Neither the Father nor the Holy Spirit may be said to have done this. By stating the problem in this way Melanchthon aligns himself with Augustine, who had already discussed this very question on more than one occasion.[67]

Melanchthon begins by clarifying the scholastic rule. He writes, "The works of the Trinity *ad extra* are undivided, preserving, of course, the properties of each person."[68] Yes, the work of salvation is common to the Trinity as the rule itself states. But more needs to be said than this. Our understanding of that common work may not blur the distinction of persons, their unique personal properties, nor the order of the Trinity. In other words, we must not reduce the common work of the Trinity to their common essence and simply say these acts or these works are accomplished by the divine nature. There is only ever Father, Son, and Holy Spirit who act inseparably and equally by the common power of their nature. There is no common nature that acts apart from the divine persons. Further, these divine persons act as Father, Son, and Holy Spirit, as the Father who eternally begets His Son and breathes forth the Holy Spirit, as the Son who is eternally begotten of His Father and with His Father breathes forth the

---

66. Philipp Melanchthon, *Explicatio symboli Niceni*, CR 23:374.
67. Augustine *Sermon 52*, 6 (WSA III/3, 53). We will discuss this text in some detail in the next chapter.
68. Melanchthon, *Explicatio symboli Niceni*, CR 23:374: "Opera trinitatis ad extra sunt indivisa, scilicet servata cuiusque personae proprietate."

Holy Spirit, and the Holy Spirit who eternally proceeds from the Father and the Son. To make this clear Melanchthon adds the final clause to Augustine's rule: "preserving, of course, the properties of each person."

Melanchthon briefly explains how we should understand the addition to Augustine's rule. Three things must be remembered with the question at hand: the Son alone assumed human nature, the Father sent the Son and the Holy Spirit, and finally, "the Son acts not by himself but through himself" (*agit Filius non a se sed per se*).[69] Melanchthon adds a lot in a few words. All three statements are shorthand expressions pointing to larger trinitarian commitments. Yes, salvation is the common work of the Trinity but this scriptural truth does not ignore the distinction of persons. In the particular question at hand on the saving work of the Son, we must always bear in mind that He alone assumed human nature and not another person.[70] Further, the Father sent the Son and the Holy Spirit. That sending bears on their eternal relations with one another and the way in which we understand their mutual and inseparable working. This is the point we have emphasized above.

Melanchthon's final comment requires more explanation. The distinction between the Son working through Himself and not from Himself comes from Hilary of Poitiers. Hilary writes,

> The Son acts through himself in such a way that he does not act by himself, and that he does not act by himself in such a way that he acts through himself. Grasp the fact that the Son acts and the Father acts through him. He does not act by himself, since we have to make known how the Father remains in him. He acts through himself when he himself does the things that are pleasing to the Father in accordance with the nature of his birth as the Son.[71]

Peter Lombard incorporated Hilary's comment into his *Sentences*. Lombard is likely Melanchthon's source. Lombard observes that some use Hilary's statement to say "the Son acts through himself, but not by himself" (*Filius agit per se sed non a se*).[72] Some theologians used Hilary's distinction to explain what it means to say the Son is wise. The Son is not wise by Himself or from Himself; rather He is wise by the Father and from the Father. His wisdom, like His being and power, are eternally from the Father. Since the Father and the Son are one in essence, you cannot say that the Son is wise "by Himself" as that would divide the essence. Rather the Son is wise through His divine essence, which He eternally receives from the Father. As we have seen in our previous chapter, semantic arguments play an important role in the trinitarian discussions of the schoolmen and reformers. Here their speech is patterned according to the way

---

69. Melanchthon, *Explicatio symboli Niceni*, CR 23:374.
70. Melanchthon, *Explicatio symboli Niceni*, CR 23:374. Melanchthon does not further explain the relationship between the incarnation and the works of the Trinity. In the next chapter, we will see how Augustine and Luther address this issue.
71. Hilary of Poitiers *De Trinitate* 9.48 (Fathers of the Church, 370), altered.
72. Lombard *Sentences* I, 32, 3.3 in Peter Lombard, *The Sentences*, trans. Giulio Silvano (Toronto: Pontifical Institute of Medieval Studies, 2007) 177.

in which Scripture distinguishes the divine persons for us: the Father has His being from no one; the Son is not from Himself but from the Father; and the Holy Spirit is not from Himself but from the Father and the Son. This pattern informs how we understand the acts and attributes of the divine persons. The Father is the principal source and origin of the Son and the Spirit. This means that the Son and the Spirit depend upon the Father for their being, and therefore also their acts and attributes. As the Son eternally receives His being from the Father, so too He eternally receives His acts and attributes from the Father; as the Holy Spirit eternally receives His being from the Father and the Son, so too He eternally receives His acts and attributes from the Father and the Son. The Father works through the Son in the Holy Spirit, the Son is the one through whom the Father works, the Holy Spirit is the one in whom and by whom the Father and the Son work.

Melanchthon's statement that the Son acts not by Himself (*a se*) but through Himself (*per se*) alerts the reader to this broader scholastic and patristic commitment to rightly distinguishing the persons and observing their inseparable works. The Son never acts apart from the Father or the Holy Spirit. With this in mind, continues Melanchthon, we rightly say that the Father saves and makes alive through the Son (*per Filiium*).[73] This order of working, which corresponds to the order of the persons, preserves their personal properties, and informs our understanding of their mutual and inseparable working. Melanchthon ends with three texts from Scripture that demonstrate this for him. Paul writes, "But thanks be to God, who gives us victory through [*per*] our Lord Jesus Christ" (1 Cor 15:57). Again, Paul writes, "Christ was made for us by God [the Father], wisdom, righteousness, redemption" (1 Cor 1:30). Finally, the Lord Himself says, "No one comes to the Father except through me" (*per me*).[74]

When Melanchthon makes use of Augustine's rule, as handed down by the schoolmen, he always returns to the points above. He clarifies that the rule must be used in such a way that preserves the unique properties and order of the persons.[75] Further, he reminds the reader that the Son works not by Himself but through Himself.[76] As the Fathers routinely put it, the external works of the Trinity are from the Father through the Son in the Holy Spirit. Melanchthon's addition to Augustine's rule secures this scriptural understanding and becomes a fixture in the works of the dogmaticians.

Martin Chemnitz brings together the thoughts of Luther and Melanchthon and bequeaths to the dogmaticians the definitive statement on the external

---

73. Melanchthon, *Explicatio symboli Niceni*, CR 23:374.
74. Melanchthon, *Explicatio symboli Niceni*, CR 23:374. The Scripture verses are translated according to Melanchthon's text.
75. Melanchthon, *Explicatio symboli Niceni*, CR 23:511: "Servata cuiusque personae proprietate, vel servato ordine personarum."
76. Melanchthon, *Explicatio symboli Niceni*, CR 23:511: "Unde et regula Augustini tradita est: Agit Filius non a se, sed per se."

works of the Trinity.⁷⁷ Chemnitz states two rules from the tradition. The first is Augustine's rule that the Trinity's works *ad extra* are undivided. The second states that the internal works of the Trinity (*opera ad intra*) are divided. This second rule shows how the order of the persons and their personal properties distinguish the persons from one another. The Father alone begets the Son, the Son alone is begotten of the Father, and the Holy Spirit alone proceeds from the Father and the Son. After raising possible objections to these rules, Chemnitz summarizes why they are important for us.

> The persons are distinguished not only by internal differences, such as that one begets, another is begotten, the third proceeds, but also by external differences. . . . For in the external works [*opera ad extra*] the three persons are together and work together, and yet with a certain order and with the properties of each person preserved.⁷⁸

As we have seen above with the Fathers and with Luther, the distinguishing marks of the persons inform our understanding of their external works. Chemnitz states this truth by incorporating the clause from Melanchthon.⁷⁹ The scriptural warrant for this addendum comes from Rom 11:36, "For of Him and through Him and in Him are all things; to whom be glory and honor." Chemnitz explains:

> For because the apostle is speaking of external works, he mentions the one eternal essence, "To him be honor," not "to them." And yet, just as there is one essence without confusion of the persons, so this essence performs the external works in common for the three persons, without confusion, but hints at the difference of the persons—"of him, in him, and through him." . . . In summary, just as we believe in the unity of the essence and yet must not permit a confusion of the persons, so we must understand also this rule: the external works are common to the three persons, but in such a way that the differences and properties of the persons are not confused.⁸⁰

For Chemnitz these two rules complement one another and show us how to confess properly and responsibly our faith in the Trinity.⁸¹ Scripture patterns

---

77. Francis Pieper directs the reader to Chemnitz to understand the works *ad extra* and the Lutheran addendum. See Pieper, *Christian Dogmatics* 1:424 n. 57.

78. Chemnitz, *Loci Theologici* 1:107–8.

79. Chemnitz does not mention Melanchthon here. Instead, he credits Augustine with this language. Although the work cited by Chemnitz circulated under Augustine's name, it comes from Vigilius of Thapsus. See ps-Augustine (Vigilius of Thapsus), *Contra Felicianum* 3 (PL 42, 1159): "Nam dum utrumque unum dico, substantiam veri Patris ac veri Filii ex toto non separo: et dum non eumdem Patrem quem Filium predico, *utriusque personam servata uniuscuiusque proprietate discerno*. Itaque si substantiam quaeris, ipsa Trinitas unus est Deus; si personam, alter est Filius." Vigilius is not talking about the external works of the Trinity but rather the coequality of the Father and Son and their unique personal properties.

80. Chemnitz, *Loci Theologici* 1:108.

81. Johann Gerhard also emphasizes this addendum. Toward the end of his locus on the interpretation of Scripture Gerhard introduces a number of scriptural obscurities that touch on the articles of faith. One of these obscurities concerns a right understanding of the inseparable working of the Trinity. He writes, "In the article on God the following axiom must be observed: the

our language in such a way that we acknowledge the external works of the Trinity without dividing the substance or mingling the persons. And this we do when we rightly clarify Augustine's rule. Chemnitz ends his discussion by emphatically stating the importance of these rules for the faithful: "Do not get the notion that these observations are foolish subtleties. But because God wills to be known, invoked, and proclaimed by us as He has revealed Himself, therefore we must make every effort to believe in a godly way these great mysteries and speak reverently and soberly about them."[82]

Johann Andreas Quenstedt offers a concise summary of the argument made by Luther, Melanchthon, and Chemnitz. It is also through Quenstedt, as far as I can tell, that the addendum to Augustine's rule passes into the trinitarian discussions of the twentieth century.[83] Quenstedt emphasizes that the distinction of the divine persons pertains not only to their relation to one another, the order of the persons and their relations of opposition, but also to their external works: "The real difference of the divine persons arises from their order, both in subsistence and in activity."[84] As we have seen with Gerhard and Calov, Quenstedt immediately clarifies what he means by order. Among the divine persons there is no order of nature, time, or dignity but only an order of origin and relation: "The Father is from no one, the Son is from

---

works of the Trinity *ad extra* are indivisible, nevertheless preserving the order and distinction of the persons." Gerhard, *De Interpretatione Scripturae Sacrae*, Locus 2, §191 (ed. Cotta, 83). Gerhard makes the same point in his discussion of how Scripture distinguishes the persons of the Trinity: *De Tribus Elohim*, Locus 4/1, §52 (ed. Cotta, 203).

82. Chemnitz, *Loci Theologici* 1:109.

83. See for example Herman Bavinck, *Reformed Dogmatics*, ed. John Bolt (Grand Rapids: Baker Academic, 2004), 2:318: "God's works *ad extra* are indivisible, though the order and distinction of the persons is preserved." Bavinck offers this as a quote but no reference is given. The same wording is given by Emil Brunner and comes from Quenstedt. Emil Brunner, *The Christian Doctrine of God: Dogmatics*, trans. Olive Wyon (Philadelphia: Westminster Press, 1950), 1:234: "The statement which, from the point of view of Trinitarian theology has been laid down as a 'rule,' and which has been repeated countless times: *opera trinitatis ad extra sunt indivisa*, must therefore be used with extreme caution." Brunner argues this rule cannot be used "without the 'Augustinian Clause': *servato discrimine et ordine personarum*." Brunner references Luthardt's *Kopendium* and gives the impression that this statement comes from Luthardt. It does not. Luthardt is offering a long quote from Quenstedt. See Christoph Ernst Luthardt, *Kopendium der Dogmatik* (Leipzig, 1866), 80. Quenstedt by way of Luthardt seems to be the source for both Bavinck and Brunner. Both of them, of course, could have appealed to Reformed sources for this teaching. The closest Reformed example that I have found is Christoph Pezel, *Argumentorum et Obiectionum De Articulis Doctrinae Christianae* (Neustadt an der Weinstrasse, 1591), 100: "Augustine says, 'as the persons are inseparable so too they work inseparably.' Nevertheless, this restriction must be added: preserving the order of persons and their personal properties." Pezel taught at the University of Wittenberg and by 1569 was the leader of its theological faculty. Pezel taught a spiritualizing view of the Lord's Supper and aligned himself with the moderate Philippists. It seems likely that he learned this addendum from Melanchthon. For similar statements see the selections from Gulielmus Bucanus, Johannes Alstedius, and Johannes Marckius in Heinrich Heppe, *Reformed Dogmatics*, trans. G. T. Thompson (Grand Rapids: Baker Book House, 1950), 112, 116–18.

84. Quenstedt, *Systema Theologicum*, I, 9 (Wittenberg, 1691), 327, thesis 17.

Unity: Opera ad Extra

the Father, and the Holy Spirit is from both."[85] Scripture further reflects the order of activity according to the order of origin and relation. Quenstedt, as with Chemnitz above, appeals to Rom 11:36. Quenstedt explains, "According to the holy Fathers, the preposition 'from' refers to the Father, 'through' to the Son, and 'in' to the Holy Spirit. Nevertheless, these prepositions introduce no inequality among the divine persons in the work of creation, but rather reveal their order in working."[86]

For Quenstedt, Augustine's rule emphasizes the unity of the persons in their external works.[87] The rule, however, insufficiently conveys the fullness of the scriptural witness, and therefore we must say more than the rule does. Quenstedt writes, "We must add this clause to Augustine's rule: *the order and distinction of the persons is preserved.*" The works of the Trinity toward creation are one and accord with the order and personal properties of the persons. Quenstedt explains, "Since the Father has his essence from himself, he acts from himself, the Son acts and works from the Father, and the Holy Spirit acts and works from both."[88] Jesus reflects this truth when He says, "Truly, truly, I say to you, the Son can do nothing of his own accord, but only what he sees the Father doing. For whatever the Father does, that the Son does likewise" (Jn 5:19). The undivided works of the Trinity *ad extra* follow the mode of existence (τρόπος τῆς ὑπάρξεως). Quenstedt explains, "The Son, as he is not from himself, but has his essence from the Father through eternal generation, so also he has not the power of working from himself nor does he act from himself, but from the Father. In the same sense, as the Holy Spirit proceeds also from the Son, he speaks not from himself but speaks whatever he receives from Christ, as it is said in John 16:13–14."[89]

When Quenstedt turns to creation, he resumes his discussion of the *opera ad extra*. The works of the Trinity toward creation are one and this reflects their essential unity. Nevertheless, notes Quenstedt, "the mode and order of their working is distinct." That distinction pertains to the order of the divine persons and their personal properties. Quenstedt explains, "Insofar as the Father has his essence from himself, he acts from himself. Moreover, the Son acts and works from the Father and the Holy Spirit acts and works from the Father and the Son. The Father works through the Son and the Holy Spirit and not otherwise."[90] Quenstedt then offers Augustine's rule, but this time leaves Augustine's name out and includes the addendum as part of the rule. He writes, "That the Father, Son, and Holy Spirit created the world is proved by the common theological rule that 'the works of the Godhead *ad extra* are undivided and the order and distinction of the persons is preserved in the common work

---

85. Quenstedt, *Systema Theologicum*, I, 9 (Wittenberg, 1691), 327, thesis 18.
86. Quenstedt, *Systema Theologicum*, I, 9 (Wittenberg, 1691), 327, thesis 19.
87. Quenstedt, *Systema Theologicum*, I, 9 (Wittenberg, 1691), 328, thesis 21.
88. Quenstedt, *Systema Theologicum*, I, 9 (Wittenberg, 1691), 328, thesis 21.
89. Quenstedt, *Systema Theologicum*, I, 9 (Wittenberg, 1691), 328, thesis 21.
90. Quenstedt, *Systema Theologicum*, I, 10 (Wittenberg, 1691), 416, thesis 7.

of all three persons."'[91] The Lutheran addendum has now become part of the common theological rule.

CONCLUSION

The Fathers and reformers insisted that the works of the Trinity toward creation are undivided. If we are to count, then we must say that the actions are shared numerically. They are one as Father, Son, and Holy Spirit are one. Whatever the action, we count it as one, numerically one, just as we count Father, Son, and Holy Spirit as one God. The three divine persons possess one power, not three powers, in the same way they possess one essence, not three essences. For this reason the Father undertakes no action toward creation apart from the Son and the Spirit; the Son undertakes no action toward creation apart from the Father and the Spirit; the Spirit undertakes no action apart from the Father and the Son. Two important but difficult points follow. First, we cannot count actions by counting persons. Three persons do not equal three actions. Second, shared action does not collapse the distinction of the three persons. There is no getting behind the persons to some prior reality we might call God. The Father is God the Father, the Son is God the Son, and the Holy Spirit is God the Holy Spirit.

The Fathers and especially the Lutheran dogmaticians further argue that the action or work of the divine persons corresponds to the uniqueness of that person. Since the Father is always Father and never Son and the Son is always Son and never Father, it follows that the common work of the Father and the Son is accomplished in a way that corresponds to the distinguishing properties of that person. The Father works in a way distinguishable from the Son, but not in such a way that undermines the numerical identity of their work. This means that not only the order of the divine persons as revealed in Scripture bears on this question of works *ad extra* but so too does the incommunicable uniqueness of the divine persons themselves. And all of this aims to confess the unique oneness, Luther's *unissima*, of the divine persons. This unity is always Trinity.

The insights of the Fathers and reformers provide the necessary tools to understand better the works and attributes of the Trinity as made known in Scripture. Although their works are common, although they work inseparably, nevertheless Scripture ascribes certain works or attributes to certain persons. How do we rightly understand these two truths? Why does Scripture ascribe wisdom to the Son, calling Him the wisdom of God, when wisdom belongs equally and indivisibly to Father, Son, and Holy Spirit? Very much related to this is the broader question of how we understand the attributes of God. What is the relationship between God's essence and His attributes? What is the

---

91. Quenstedt, *Systema Theologicum*, I, 10 (Wittenberg, 1691), 416, thesis 10. For the modification to Augustine's rule in later dogmaticians, see David Hollaz, *Examen Theologicum Acroamaticum*, I, 3, Q. 4 (Leipzig, 1763), 351. Although Hollaz fails to mention Quenstedt, he quotes him almost word for word.

Unity: Opera ad Extra

relationship between one attribute and another? If God's essence is simple, as the tradition has always confessed, what does it mean to distinguish between God's mercy and God's justice or God's righteousness and God's holiness? If mercy is different from justice and both are different from righteousness and holiness, then what does it mean to affirm God's unity and simplicity? The labors of part 3 have prepared us to address these knotty questions.

15

UNITY IN TRINITY: APPROPRIATION, ATTRIBUTES, AND DIVINE SIMPLICITY

Augustine's rule states plainly that the external works of the Trinity are undivided. The church has confessed consistently that one must not ascribe an external work to one person to the exclusion of the other. We may not say that the Father creates apart from the Son and the Holy Spirit, nor that the Son redeems apart from the Father and the Holy Spirit, nor that the Holy Spirit sanctifies apart from the Father and the Son. And yet the Apostles' Creed does the very thing the church says should not happen. Luther writes, "The Creed may be briefly comprised in these few words: 'I believe in God the Father, who created me; I believe in God the Son, who redeemed me; I believe in the Holy Spirit, who sanctifies me.'"[1] Does Luther's summary of the Apostles' Creed divide the works of the Trinity? Why ascribe creation, redemption, and sanctification to particular persons when Scripture plainly states that these works belong equally and inseparably to Father, Son, and Holy Spirit?

Similarly, if God is one and the essential attributes of the Father belong to the Son and to the Holy Spirit equally and indivisibly, why does Scripture say that Christ is the power of God and the wisdom of God? What does it mean to identify the Holy Spirit as the Spirit of holiness or the Spirit of truth? If the essential attributes, like the external acts of the Trinity, belong equally and indivisibly to Father, Son, and Holy Spirit, as the church rightly confesses, why do Scripture and our creeds sometimes assign them more particularly to one person? The explanation given by the Fathers and reformers has been that the external acts and essential attributes of God may be appropriated or attributed more particularly to one person in order to more fully disclose the persons of the Trinity to our creaturely ways of thinking. This doctrine of appropriation assists us conceptually and aims to focus our prayers and worship on the divine persons. Below we will show the different ways in which the church has discussed this doctrine and highlight especially the practical importance of it.

Our discussion of appropriation will provide the proper context in which to discuss more formally the essential attributes of God. We will begin with a rather basic question. Where should a discussion of the essential attributes occur? Our Lutheran fathers were divided on this question. The early

---

1. LC II.7 (Tappert, 411).

dogmaticians did not designate any one area of their dogmatics for a discussion of the attributes. Instead they discussed them in the context of the works of God which involved the whole of their dogmatics. The later dogmaticians addressed the attributes in a separate locus on the nature of God before turning to a discussion of the Trinity. Although a host of reasons account for this shift with the later dogmaticians, our preference remains with the early dogmaticians. Any discussion of the essential attributes needs to attend to the subject of these attributes—God the Father, God the Son, and God the Holy Spirit— and to the works done by the Trinity that make known to us these attributes. By adopting this approach, which our sixteenth-century Lutheran fathers favored, the whole of dogmatics becomes a sustained reflection on Father, Son, and Holy Spirit.

Despite the difference among the dogmaticians on the placement of the attributes in their dogmatics, they stood in agreement on a number of difficult metaphysical and logical questions. What is the relationship between the attributes and the essence of God? What is the relationship between the multiple attributes of God? Are they different from one another? Does the difference lie with the attributes and therefore with God, or does it lie with us and our mode of conceiving and talking about "the simple multiplicity" of God's essence?[2] At a more basic level, how should we understand the correspondence between attributes ascribed to God by Scripture and our own possession of these attributes? God is love and we love. Does our love correspond to the love that God is? Do we understand God's love by first reflecting on our love? Similarly, God is and we are. Does our being correspond to God's being?

These questions present difficulties because the church's confession of the unity of the Trinity, the oneness of God, presupposes the simplicity of God. Many in our day avoid the difficult questions raised above by abandoning the church's traditional teaching on divine appropriations and divine simplicity. They argue that the teaching on simplicity, unknown to Scripture, is incoherent and reduces 'God' to a property.[3] In other words, the doctrine of divine simplicity, asserted throughout the Christian tradition from the Fathers to the reformers, is alien to Scripture and a proper Christian confession of God. We will argue below that this rejection of simplicity proceeds from a false understanding of the teaching as found with the Fathers and the reformers, and this false understanding leads to the seemingly insurmountable questions above.

---

2. Augustine *The Trinity* VI.6 (WSA I/5, 209).

3. Alvin Plantinga, *Does God Have a Nature?* (Milwaukee: Marquette University Press, 1980); Richard J. Plantinga, Thomas R. Thompson, and Matthew D. Lundberg, *An Introduction to Christian Theology* (Cambridge: Cambridge University Press, 2010), 104: The doctrine of divine simplicity has "no real biblical basis and has in fact worked to defeat the resources of a full-fledged trinitarianism." For a critique of Alvin Plantinga's argument that the doctrine of divine simplicity reduces God to a property see William Mann, "Divine Simplicity," *Religious Studies* 18 (1982): 451–71.

DIVINE APPROPRIATION

Why do Scripture and the Apostles' Creed ascribe certain attributes or works to the Father, the Son, or the Holy Spirit? The church's explanation of this practice is appropriation. Although this teaching goes back to the Fathers, the terminology is medieval. Thomas Aquinas defined appropriation as drawing an essential attribute common to all three persons toward what is unique to each person (*commune trahere ad proprium*), or toward that which has a greater similitude to the *propria* of one person more than the *propria* of another.[4] For example, power has the nature of a principle and the Father is the principle of the Godhead. Therefore, power has a certain likeness to the *propria* of the Father and is properly attributed to Him. Likewise, wisdom has likeness to the Son, who is the Word, and "word is nothing but the concept of wisdom."[5] So too goodness, as the nature and likeness of love, more fittingly may be ascribed to the Holy Spirit. In this sense the triad of power, wisdom, and goodness corresponds to the Father, the Son, and the Holy Spirit. These appropriations further illumine our understanding of the external works of the Trinity. Since we ascribe power to the Father and this power is chiefly shown in creation, "it is attributed to him to be the Creator."[6]

The schoolmen explored at length the appropriation of essential attributes by the divine persons. To the Father they ascribed eternity, unity, power; to the Son they ascribed form, equality, and wisdom; and to the Holy Spirit they ascribed use, concord, and goodness. They further showed how Paul's language of from Him, through Him, and in Him (Rom 11:36) corresponds to Father, Son, and Holy Spirit.[7] In each case they sought the underlying rationale for why an essential attribute more fittingly may be ascribed to one divine person over the other. Although their explanations often seem overly speculative and sometimes too clever, their aim was pious. They sought to manifest the truth of the Trinity.[8] The purpose of appropriation was to disclose the distinction of persons to our creaturely patterns of thought. The scholastic arguments for appropriation were never arbitrary. Rules were followed to demonstrate suitable appropriations. For example, their arguments consistently attend to the unique personal properties of the divine persons and the order and origin of the Father, the Son, and the Holy Spirit. This is an important point to emphasize. Divine appropriations are not the personal properties of Father, Son, and Holy Spirit. Although power is appropriated to the Father, this essential attribute is shared

---

4. Thomas Aquinas *De Veritate* 7, 3c.
5. Thomas Aquinas *ST* I, 39.8c.
6. Thomas Aquinas *ST* I, 45.6 ad 2.
7. The four traditional triads are presented in Peter Lombard *Sentences* I, 31, 2 (Silano, 166–69): eternity, form, use; I, 31, 2–3 (Silano, 169–70): unity, equality, concord; I, 34, 3–5 (Silano, 191–93): power, wisdom, goodness; I, 36, 3–5 (Silano, 200–202): from Him, through Him, in Him (Rom 11:36). *The Sentences*, trans. Giulio Silano (Toronto: Pontifical Institute of Medieval Studies, 2007).
8. Thomas Aquinas *ST* I, 39.7c and ad 1. Thomas follows Albert the Great on this point.

equally and indivisibly by Father, Son, and Holy Spirit. Hence the Father is almighty, the Son is almighty, and the Holy Spirit is almighty; they are not three almighties but one almighty. No appropriation ever is stated in such a way as to exclude the other two persons. The personal properties are real and eternally distinguish the persons for us. The divine appropriations, on the other hand, are conceptual markers assisting our creaturely understanding to better grasp the three divine persons and their essential unity.

Luther and our Lutheran dogmaticians belong to this scholastic tradition but exercise more reserve in discussing the various triads posited by the Fathers and the schoolmen. Although you may find the traditional triads in the works of our dogmaticians, their discussions tend only to summarize scholastic insights. Despite this reserve, our Lutheran fathers agree wholeheartedly with the schoolmen that divine appropriations help disclose the divine persons to us. The schoolmen tended to show this by appealing to essential attributes. Our Lutheran dogmaticians focus more on the external acts of creation, redemption, and sanctification. By doing this they concentrate their efforts on the language of Scripture and the Apostles' Creed, and by extension on Luther's comments on the Creed in the Large Catechism. As we have seen in our previous chapters, Luther's brief reflections on these trinitarian matters exercise considerable influence over the dogmaticians. We see again his influence on this question of appropriation and particularly his somewhat indirect way of showing divine appropriations.

Luther's insight on the purpose of divine appropriations proceeds from his reflection on the undivided external works of the Trinity. The baptism of Christ provided the scriptural basis for both discussions. Luther's choice of scriptural texts was not arbitrary. The baptism of Christ served as an important trinitarian proof text for the Fathers and the reformers. Johann Gerhard writes, "Just as the devout ancients say: 'If you do not believe the Trinity, accompany John to the Jordan and you will see it.'"[9] Although the baptism of Christ shows the Trinity clearly enough, it also presents difficulties for the attentive reader. At Christ's baptism Scripture distinguishes the Father, the Son, and the Holy Spirit doing three different things. The Father's voice from heaven is distinct from the Son being baptized by John, and both are distinct from the Holy Spirit bodily descending in the form of a dove. None other than Augustine, the very one credited with the church's rule on the undivided works of the Trinity, observes this difficulty in a sermon on the baptism of Christ: "I make bold to say (I say it timidly enough, but I still make bold to say it), we have the three apparently

---

9. Johann Gerhard, *Theological Commonplaces: On the Nature of God and On the Trinity*, trans. Richard Dinda (St. Louis: Concordia Publishing House, 2007), Exegesis III, §81, 338. This appears to be Gerhard's own paraphrase of a long quotation from Epiphanius as quoted by Martin Chemnitz in his own discussion of the baptism of Christ. Martin Chemnitz, *Harmoniae Evangelicae*, chap. 17 (Geneva, 1628), 190. Cf. Epiphanius, *Panarion*, 62, 5.1–6.5 (Against Sabellians) in *The Panarion of Epiphanius of Salamis, Books II and III De Fide*, trans. Frank Williams, 2d ed. (Leiden: Brill, 2013), 126–27.

separable.... These three are apparently separated by place, separated by function, separated by action."[10] As soon as Augustine says this, he anticipates strong objections from the congregation. They will say to him:

> Remember you're speaking as a Catholic, speaking to Catholics. Our faith, after all, that is to say the true faith, the right faith, the Catholic faith, which is not a bundle of opinions and prejudices but a summary of biblical testimonies, not riddled with heretical rashness, but founded on apostolic truth—our faith insists on this. This is what we know, this is what we believe; this, even if we don't see it with our eyes, nor even with our hearts as long as we are being purified by faith, this all the same we hold with the firmest and most orthodox faith, that Father, Son, and Holy Spirit are one inseparable trinity or triad; one God, not three gods; but one God in such a way that the Son is not the Father, that the Father is not the Son, that the Holy Spirit is neither the Father nor the Son, but the Spirit of the Father and of the Son.[11]

After positing this response from his congregation, after recognizing that Scripture seems to identify three as working separately and yet the faith constrains us to confess three who work inseparably, lest we divide the essence, Augustine simply asks, "So what are we to do?"[12]

Our previous chapter showed the church's commitment to the inseparable and indivisible external works of the Trinity. All external works of the Trinity are from the Father through the Son in the Holy Spirit. This is the first point made by Augustine in his sermon. He begins with what Scripture says about creation. We have seen in our previous chapters that creation belongs to God alone. Scripture marks off the unique identity of YHWH in the Old Testament by assigning creation to the Father, the Son/Word, and the Spirit/Breath. The New Testament unambiguously declares the divine identity of Christ by stating that "all things were made through him" (Jn 1:3) and "in him all things hold together" (Col 1:17). Augustine rehearses all of this and concludes: "Thus the Father does nothing without the Son, the Son nothing without the Father."[13] They work inseparably toward creation. And here problems arise. Does this mean we must also say that the Father was born of the Virgin Mary, suffered under Pontius Pilate, died, rose again, and ascended into heaven? Augustine replies, "Not at all. We don't say this because we don't believe this."[14] Augustine admits this sounds contradictory. On the one hand he has shown according to Scripture that the Father does nothing without the Son nor the Son without the Father. So too he has shown according to Scripture that the Son and not the Father was born of the Virgin Mary, suffered under Pontius Pilate, died, rose again, and ascended into heaven. So which is it? Do they work inseparably or not? The answer is not picking one over the other but rather rightly understanding what both mean. He explains:

---

10. Augustine *Sermon 52*, 2 (WSA III/3, 51).
11. Augustine *Sermon 52*, 2 (WSA III/3, 51).
12. Augustine *Sermon 52*, 3 (WSA III/3, 51).
13. Augustine *Sermon 52*, 5 (WSA III/3, 52).
14. Augustine *Sermon 52*, 6 (WSA III/3, 53).

> The Son, indeed, and not the Father, was born of the Virgin Mary; but this birth of the Son, not the Father, from the Virgin Mary was the work of both Father and Son. It was not the Father, but the Son who suffered; yet the suffering of the Son was the work of both Father and Son. It wasn't the Father who rose again, but the Son; yet the resurrection of the Son was the work of both Father and Son.[15]

Augustine immediately turns to Scripture to support these statements. According to Scripture, the birth of the Son was the work of the Father: "But when the fullness of time had come, God sent forth his Son, born of woman, born under the law, to redeem those who were under the law, so that we might receive adoption as sons" (Gal 4:4–5). So too Scripture assigns the birth of the Son to the Son: "Christ Jesus, who, though he was in the form of God ... emptied himself, by taking the form of a servant, being born in the likeness of men" (Phil 2:5–7). Likewise, when the Virgin Mary asked the angel Gabriel how she will bear a child, Gabriel responds, "The Holy Spirit will come upon you, and the power of the Most High will overshadow you; therefore the child to be born will be called holy—the Son of God" (Lk 1:35). Augustine shows how Scripture similarly talks about the Son's passion and resurrection.[16] By attending to Scripture we see the distinction of persons and their inseparable working. Only the Son and not the Father or the Spirit was born of the Virgin Mary, and yet the birth was the work of Father, Son, and Holy Spirit.

Martin Luther uses the baptism of Christ and the insights of Augustine to explain how the divine persons work inseparably but also remain distinct.[17] The Holy Spirit descended on Jesus in bodily form, like a dove, and the Father's voice was heard from heaven. The reader must understand that the Holy Spirit alone is the dove; the Father alone speaks from heaven; and the Son alone is the man baptized by John, upon whom the dove descends and about whom the voice declares, "This is my beloved Son." Luther rehearses a number of proper and improper statements regarding this truth. When it comes to the dove, you may not say that it is God the Father or God the Son. You may say only that it is God the Holy Spirit. Likewise, when it comes to the voice, you may not say that it is God the Son or God the Holy Spirit. You may say only that it is God the Father. Again, when it comes to the man, you may not say that it is God the Father or God the Holy Spirit. You may say only that it is God the Son. And yet, the works of the Trinity remain undivided. This means, explains Luther, the dove as a creature is created by Father, Son, and Holy Spirit. So too the voice as something created is created by Father, Son, and Holy Spirit, and likewise the humanity of Christ. Thus Gabriel says, "The Holy Spirit will come upon you, and the power of the Most High will overshadow you" (Lk 1:35). Here Gabriel names the Holy Spirit, the Father, who is the Most High, and the Son, the power of the Most High (1 Cor 1:24). Luther summarizes his point: "Thus the entire

---

15. Augustine *Sermon 52*, 8 (WSA III/3, 53–54).
16. Augustine *Sermon 52*, 12–13 (WSA III/3, 55–56).
17. On what follows see *On the Last Words of David*, 1543 (AE 15:304–5; WA 54:59.12–60.15).

Trinity is present here as one Creator and has created and made the one work, the humanity. And yet it was only the Person of the Son that united with the human nature and became incarnate, not the Father nor the Holy Spirit."[18]

The baptism of Christ demonstrates for both Augustine and Luther the distinction of persons and their inseparable working. Further, and to the point of this chapter, Scripture shows us how to discern rightly the common working of the Trinity and to distinguish the persons in that common working. If we fail on this score, we risk dividing the substance or mingling the persons. Luther returns to the baptism of Christ to show how Scripture ascribes certain acts to particular persons of the Trinity. He starts with a number of difficult questions: why does Scripture assign acts or works more particularly to one divine person when the church confesses that the acts and works of the Trinity are undivided? Why does the Apostles' Creed assign creation to the Father, redemption to the Son, and sanctification to the Holy Spirit? Why differentiate the external works of the Trinity, assigning them more particularly to one person, when the church confesses that these works are common and inseparable? Luther admits that the answer to these questions may be too subtle for simple Christians, but nevertheless the answer is necessary to protect the faith from false teaching.[19] The first thing to note, explains Luther, is that we may know God only through His own revelation. He instructs us by making Himself known to us: "God wants to be known by us, here on earth by faith, yonder by sight, that He is one God and yet three Persons. And according to John 17:3, this is our everlasting life."[20] God does this by accommodating Himself to our creaturely condition and revealing Himself through visible elements in His creation.

When we consider the creature, as used by God to reveal Himself to us, or the work, accomplished by God for us, we must view them in two distinct and complementary ways. We are to see these works both absolutely and relatively. When viewed absolutely, we understand that the creature or work is the single activity of all three persons.[21] When we consider the dove, voice, or humanity of Christ absolutely, we confess that they are creations of the Trinity. Here we find our confession of the inseparable works of the Trinity. On the other hand, when we view the creature or work relatively, in their relation to us, we observe the particular function of the created thing used by God. Luther explains this with the dove.

> Here God takes His creature, which all three Persons as one God have created, and uses it as an image, or form, or figure, in which He reveals Himself and in which He appears. Here distinctive images, forms, and revelations of the three separate Persons come into being. Thus God employs the dove to become an image or revelation of the Holy Spirit. This is a distinctive image, which does not portray the Father or the Son but only the Holy Spirit. The Father, the Son, and the Holy

---

18. *On the Last Words of David*, 1543 (AE 15:305; WA 54:60.12–15).
19. *On the Last Words of David*, 1543 (AE 15:306; WA 54:61.13–17).
20. *On the Last Words of David*, 1543 (AE 15:306; WA 54:61.17–19).
21. *On the Last Words of David*, 1543 (AE 15:307; WA 54:61.27–32).

Spirit want the dove to depict and reveal distinctively only the person of the Holy Spirit, to assure us that God's one essence is definitely three separate Persons from eternity. That is why Luke 3:22 states, "The Holy Spirit descended upon Him in bodily form, as a dove."[22]

The same insight applies to the humanity of Christ and to the Father's voice. Although the humanity of Christ is the single creation of Father, Son, and Holy Spirit, "it is the peculiar and special form and revelation of the Son alone."[23] Likewise, the Father alone is revealed to us in the voice. The voice as a created thing is the single work of the Trinity, but the voice reveals to us neither the Son nor the Holy Spirit but the Father alone. Again, the dove, humanity, and voice show us the inseparable work of the Trinity when viewed absolutely and their distinction as Father, Son, and Holy Spirit when viewed relatively.

After establishing what it means to view the activity of the Trinity absolutely and relatively, Luther moves to the more difficult questions raised by the Apostles' Creed. The unity and distinction of the divine persons, as seen with the dove, humanity of Christ, and the voice, show us how to understand the creed's ascription of creation to the Father, redemption to the Son, and sanctification to the Holy Spirit. When we reflect upon creation, redemption, and sanctification, we may do this either absolutely or relatively. Absolutely viewed, creation, redemption, and sanctification belong to the Trinity: the Father creates, the Son creates, the Holy Spirit creates; the Father saves, the Son saves, the Holy Spirit saves; the Father sanctifies, the Son sanctifies, and the Holy Spirit sanctifies. Relatively viewed, we confess with Scripture and the Apostles' Creed, which Luther calls the children's creed, the Father as creator, the Son as redeemer, and the Spirit as sanctifier.[24] Luther explains:

> When we confess in the children's Creed: "I believe in God the Father Almighty, Creator of heaven and earth," we do not mean to imply that only the Person of the Father is the almighty Creator and Father. No, the Son is likewise almighty, Creator, and Father. And the Holy Spirit is likewise almighty, Creator, and Father. And yet there are not three almighty creators and fathers but only one almighty Creator and Father of heaven and earth and of us all. Similarly, the Father is our Savior and Redeemer, the Son is our Savior and Redeemer, and the Holy Spirit is our Savior and Redeemer, and yet there are not three saviors and redeemers, but only one Savior and Redeemer. Likewise, the Father is our God, the Son is our God, and the Holy Spirit is our God, and yet there are not three gods, but only one God. Likewise, the Holy Ghost sanctifies Christendom, so does the Father, so does the Son, and still there are not three sanctifiers, but only one Sanctifier, etc.[25]

---

22. *On the Last Words of David*, 1543 (AE 15:307; WA 54:61.34–62.6).

23. *On the Last Words of David*, 1543 (AE 15:307; WA 54:62.11–12). The humanity is eternally assumed by the Son. The dove and the voice are not eternally assumed by the Spirit and the Father. On this point see AE 15:308–9; WA 54:63.8–13.

24. Cf. LC II.36 (Tappert, 415): "As the Father is called Creator and the Son is called Redeemer, so on account of his work the Holy Spirit must be called Sanctifier, the One who makes holy."

25. *On the Last Words of David*, 1543 (AE 15:309; WA 54:63.14–27). On the use of the name "father" for the divine essence, see further AE 15:310–12 (WA 54:64.22–65.37); Martin Chemnitz, *Loci Theologici*, trans. J. A. O. Preus (St. Louis: Concordia Publishing House, 2008), 1:109; Hollaz,

When we view the external activities or acts of God absolutely, we confess that Father, Son, and Holy Spirit create, redeem, and sanctify equally and inseparably; when we view these activities or acts relatively, we ascribe, following the pattern of Scripture, creation especially to the Father, redemption especially to the Son, and sanctification especially to the Holy Spirit. The Father creates through the Son (Col 1:15–16; Heb 1:2) and the Holy Spirit (Ps 33:6); the Son became man, redeemed us from the curse of the law, suffered, died, and rose again (Jn 1:14; 1 Tm 2:6; Gal 3:13; 1 Cor 15:3–5); and the Holy Spirit, the Spirit of holiness and adoption, convicts the world, glorifies Christ, and guides us into all truth (Rom 8:15–17; Jn 16:8–14).[26]

By attending to Scripture and the manner in which God reveals Himself to us, we learn with certainty what reason finds impossible and contradictory. Luther concludes his discussion of appropriations with this insight: "All of this has been said so that we may recognize and believe in three distinct Persons in the one Godhead and not jumble the Persons together nor divide the essence."[27] For Luther all of this pertains to our right understanding of who God is and our proper worship of Him.[28] Luther's point is reminiscent of the Fathers and their understanding of these appropriations. Leo the Great explains:

> The unchangeable divinity of this Blessed Trinity is one in substance, undivided in work, united in will, the same in power, equal in glory. When Holy Scripture speaks of it thus and gives in deeds or in words anything that seems to belong to separate Persons, Catholic faith is not disturbed but instructed. Through the proper signification of either the word or the action, the truth of the Trinity is brought home to us, and the mind does not divide what the hearing establishes. Certain things come to us under the name of the Father or the Son or the Holy Spirit, so that the acknowledgment of the faithful in the Trinity might not err. Although it is inseparable, it will never be known to be a Trinity if it is always mentioned without differentiation. This difficulty in expressing clearly by speech draws our hearts to the power of discerning, and, through our weakness, the heavenly doctrine helps us, that, because in the divinity of Father, Son, and Holy Spirit, neither singularity nor diversity is to be considered. The true unity and true Trinity can be apprehended 'at the same time' by the mind, but cannot be produced at the same time by the lips.[29]

By attending to the pattern of Scripture, as reflected in the creeds, the divine persons are seen by us according to their distinctive personal properties. Divine appropriations presuppose these distinctive properties and aim to manifest further the divine persons to us and focus our worship of Father, Son, and Holy Spirit. All of this is done by God, concludes Luther,

---

Examen Theologicum Acroamaticum, I, 2, Q. 21 (Leipzig, 1763), 301–2; and John Theodore Mueller, *Christian Dogmatics* (St. Louis: Concordia Publishing House, 1934), 157.

26. Francis Pieper, *Christian Dogmatics* (St. Louis: Concordia Publishing House, 1950), 1:422.
27. *On the Last Words of David*, 1543 (AE 15:309; WA 54:63.29–31).
28. *On the Last Words of David*, 1543 (AE 15:311; WA 54:65.23–24).
29. Leo the Great, *Sermon* 76.2 (Fathers of the Church, 335–36).

"to assure us that God's one essence is definitely three separate Persons from eternity."³⁰

Although the Lutheran dogmatic tradition continued to emphasize the points made by Luther, there is variety with them and this variety is itself instructive. Although Luther carefully shows how to understand the appropriation of certain works to the persons, as seen especially in the Apostles' Creed, Chemnitz does this only with reservation. He prefers to emphasize the mutual working of all three divine persons in creation, redemption, and sanctification, and only rarely uses the language of appropriation in discussing these external works. For example, the one time he introduces the Apostles' Creed and the ascription of creation to the Father, he immediately clarifies how we should understand this: "Thus in the Creed the Father is called the Creator, but not to the exclusion of the Son or the Holy Spirit." Chemnitz provides a number of Scripture texts showing the work of the Son and the Holy Spirit in creation. He concludes, "Thus providence and the sustaining and conservation of things are often attributed to one person, and yet it is the common work of the whole Trinity."³¹ Elsewhere he warns against looking too curiously into the difference of the persons in their external works: "Now we must not engage in arguments motivated merely by curiosity as to the difference of the persons in the work of creation, but rest content with that revelation that all things have been created by the eternal Father through the Son with the help of the Holy Spirit."³² Where Chemnitz is hesitant, Gerhard is bold. Gerhard discusses both the appropriation of external works to particular persons and the more speculative triads on the essential attributes explored by the medieval schoolmen.³³

Despite this variety in emphasis and content, there is much to learn from both Chemnitz and Gerhard. Chemnitz places his consideration of appropriation within the larger context of the scriptural teaching on the Trinity. Here we especially see his conservatism. Chemnitz identifies four points that must be understood and confessed by the faithful when discussing Father, Son, and Holy Spirit.³⁴ First, we acknowledge the consubstantiality of the persons and their order. The Father is the First Person, the Son the Second Person, and the Holy Spirit the Third Person of the Trinity. Second, each person has His own unique personal property by which He is distinguished from the other two persons. The property of the Father is to beget, of the Son to be begotten, and of the Holy Spirit to proceed from the Father and the Son. These first two points comprise the so-called Lutheran addendum to Augustine's rule discussed in our previous chapter. As Chemnitz puts it, "In the external works [*opera ad*

---

30. *On the Last Words of David*, 1543 (AE 15:307; WA 54:62.3–4).
31. Chemnitz, *Loci Theologici* 1:105.
32. Chemnitz, *Loci Theologici* 1:267.
33. Gerhard, *De Tribus Elohim*, Locus 4/1, §53 (ed. Cotta, 203–4).
34. Chemnitz, *Loci Theologici* 1:112–14.

extra] the three persons are together and work together, and yet with a certain order and with the properties of each person preserved."³⁵ We will recall that for Chemnitz the scriptural warrant for this addendum was Rom 11:36, "For of Him and through Him and in Him are all things; to whom be glory and honor." This text served as the fourth triad for divine appropriations in the discussions of the medieval schoolmen. Chemnitz passes over the other more speculative triads and focuses instead on this text from Scripture to show the appropriation of certain external works to the persons. This becomes his third main point in discussing the divine persons. Chemnitz writes, "Each person has certain properties in His external works [*opera ad extra*], as in the words, 'of Him, though Him, and in Him . . . to whom be glory and honor,' Rom 11:36."³⁶ The fourth and final point emphasizes the practical importance of appropriations. They assist us in identifying the benefits of each person toward the church.

After identifying the above four points, Chemnitz shows how they apply to Father, Son, and Holy Spirit.³⁷ Here we come upon an excellent dogmatic and pastoral summary of the main points of trinitarian thought. The Father (1) is the First Person of the Godhead; (2) who is neither begotten nor proceeding from another but who begets the Son and with the Son breathes forth the Holy Spirit; (3) who with the Son and the Holy Spirit creates, sustains, preserves, and governs all things; (4) and who, out of unspeakable love, sends the Son as the Redeemer and the Holy Spirit as the Sanctifier. The Son (1) is the Second Person of the Godhead; (2) eternally begotten of the Father; (3) through whom the Father creates, redeems, and sanctifies; (4) who became man for us, redeems us, and sends His Holy Spirit to us. The Holy Spirit (1) is the Third Person of the Godhead; (2) eternally proceeding from the Father and the Son; (3) in Him the Father, through the Son, creates, preserves, and governs all things; (4) and who was sent by the Father through the Son upon the apostles and into the hearts of believers to sanctify them through Word and sacrament.

Chemnitz's summary shows how the divine persons are eternally distinguished from each other and also how they work distinctively and yet inseparably toward creation and on behalf of the church. When we bear in mind (1) the order of persons, (2) their internal distinguishing properties, (3) their external distinguishing properties, (4) and the benefits of each person toward us, we rightly discern the persons and properly order our prayers and worship.

---

35. Chemnitz, *Loci Theologici* 1:108.
36. Cf. Chemnitz, *Loci Theologici* 1:267–68.
37. The importance of this section for Chemnitz cannot be overstated. He devotes two paragraphs each to Father, Son, and Holy Spirit. The first is in Latin and the second in German. The German paragraph is not a translation of the Latin but rather a longer restatement of its main points. My summary which follows combines the insights of both the Latin and German paragraphs. For what follows see Chemnitz, *Loci Theologici* 1:113–14. For the continuing significance of these paragraphs from Chemnitz see Leonard Hutter, *Compendium Locorum Theologicorum* (Berlin, 1855, 1st ed. 1610), 7–8. Hutter's presentation of Father, Son, and Holy Spirit paraphrases this section from Chemnitz.

Unity: Appropriation, Attributes, and Divine Simplicity

The first two points summarize how Scripture distinguishes the persons from each other. These eternal characteristics bear on our understanding of the external working of the Trinity. This is the point insisted on by Luther, Melanchthon, and the entirety of the Lutheran dogmatic tradition. The final two points show the way in which Chemnitz prefers to reflect on the doctrine of appropriation or the external acts of the Trinity. Scripture draws our minds to the Father as our creator who creates through the Son and in the Holy Spirit. Similarly, our minds are drawn to the Son, who was sent by the Father to redeem us and who with the Father sends the Holy Spirit to sanctify us through Word and sacrament. If we wish to ascribe creation to the Father, we may responsibly do this only by confessing the inseparable working of the Son and the Holy Spirit. It is the Father of the Son who creates through the Son and by the Spirit, the Spirit of the Father and the Spirit of the Son. The same pattern holds for redemption and sanctification. Chemnitz's emphasis rests always on seeing both the distinction and inseparability of the persons in their external works for us. Further, this external working always reflects the order of the persons and their unique personal properties.

Although Johann Gerhard emphasizes these same points, he also shows a greater willingness to explore the more speculative suggestions of the schoolmen on the appropriation of essential attributes. It would be misleading, however, to focus on Gerhard's interest in these speculative appropriations and his difference with Chemnitz. Gerhard begins his discussion in a manner similar to Luther. Scripture distinguishes the Father with the voice at the baptism of Christ and at the Transfiguration; the Son as the one who is baptized and transfigured; and the Holy Spirit who descends in the form of a dove and manifests Himself in the bright cloud at the Transfiguration.[38] Gerhard offers a number of other examples from Scripture that distinguish Father, Son, and Holy Spirit from one another. He then turns to their internal properties and shows how they are distinguished from each another by their incommunicable personal properties: the Father is unbegotten, the Son is begotten, and the Holy Spirit proceeds.[39] The persons also may be distinguished by their external personal properties. Here we arrive at Gerhard's discussion of appropriation. He explains, "The divine persons are distinguished not only by internal personal properties but also externally by their works and benefits toward creatures, especially toward the church."[40] This is why, explains Gerhard, creation is attributed (*tribuitur*) to the Father, redemption to the Son, and sanctification to the Holy Spirit. This does not mean that the Son and the Holy Spirit are excluded from the work of

---

38. Gerhard, *De Tribus Elohim*, Locus 4/1, §41 (ed. Cotta, 200). For an extensive discussion of the baptism of Christ see Gerhard, *Theological Commonplaces*, Exegesis III, §§75–84, 332–42. Gerhard's conflation of the baptism and Transfiguration derives from Chemnitz, *Harmoniae Evangelicae*, chap. 17 (Geneva, 1628), 189–94. For a somewhat similar patristic discussion see Fulgentius *To Peter on the Faith* 52 (Fathers of the Church, 92–93).
39. Gerhard, *De Tribus Elohim*, Locus 4/1, §§46–51 (ed. Cotta, 202–3).
40. Gerhard, *De Tribus Elohim*, Locus 4/1, §52 (ed. Cotta, 203).

creation. Gerhard appeals to the Lutheran addendum. The external works of the Trinity are undivided, and yet their personal properties and order of working are preserved.[41] Gerhard brings both truths together: "The Father creates and He creates and preserves all things through the Son in the Holy Spirit." The same may be said about redemption and sanctification. We are redeemed by the Son but this does not exclude the Father or the Holy Spirit; we are sanctified by the Holy Spirit but this does not exclude the Father or the Son. Gerhard expresses himself in terms that sound quite close to Chemnitz. He writes, "From the work of sanctification, neither the Father nor the Son are excluded. The Father sanctifies as he sends the Holy Spirit, in the name of the Son, into the hearts of believers through whom they are sanctified."[42] After establishing how we understand the external works of creation, redemption, and sanctification, Gerhard continues with a discussion of the essential attributes. He explains, "From here certain essential attributes are appropriated to each person by the ecclesiastical writers, nevertheless, the essential attributes are common to the three persons because of the identity of essence."[43] Gerhard shows the appropriation of the essential attributes by summarizing Thomas Aquinas's discussion.[44] Gerhard does not shy away from discussing the appropriation of essential attributes. For him appropriation usefully distinguishes the persons for us and orders our thoughts and worship. This may be seen with both the external acts and the essential attributes.

The medieval schoolmen reflected on the essential attributes of God to show how the doctrine of appropriation could help us distinguish the persons and better understand their unity. Although Luther and our Lutheran dogmaticians similarly reflect upon appropriation, they prefer for the most part to concentrate on the external acts of the Trinity, on creation, redemption, and sanctification. The Lutheran focus on the external works indicates better how we rightly know God. We know Him by His acts, by the things He does toward creation, as recorded for us in the Scriptures. A point made throughout part 1 of this book is that the Fathers sought to know God by the things God did. There is no other access to God. This means further that God's attributes are never known in the abstract, never known apart from the God who acts, and therefore never known apart from the activity of Father, Son, and Holy Spirit. When we reflect upon God, His acts and attributes, we can only ever reflect upon the God who reveals Himself to us in His Word, indeed, the one who shows and gives Himself to us. This God, the only true God, YHWH our Elohim, is Father, Son, and Holy Spirit. For this reason we cannot profitably discuss the divine attributes prior to a discussion of the divine persons. We may further argue that these divine attributes, shown in the external acts of the Trinity, may be rightly known only

---

41. Gerhard, *De Tribus Elohim*, Locus 4/1, §52 (ed. Cotta, 203).
42. Gerhard, *De Tribus Elohim*, Locus 4/1, §52 (ed. Cotta, 203).
43. Gerhard, *De Tribus Elohim*, Locus 4/1, §53 (ed. Cotta, 203).
44. Gerhard, *De Tribus Elohim*, Locus 4/1, §§53–54 (ed. Cotta, 203–4); Thomas Aquinas *ST* I.39.8.

DIVINE ATTRIBUTES AND LUTHERAN DOGMATICS

in the church, wherein we find the means of grace, the very means appointed and used by God to bring us to a proper knowledge of Him and a share in His divine life.

The Lutheran dogmatic tradition discussed the doctrine of God in two distinct ways. During the sixteenth century our Lutheran fathers departed from the ordering of theological topics used by the medieval schoolmen. The medieval schoolmen began with natural knowledge of God, proofs for God's existence, and a discussion of the essence and attributes of God. After this they discussed the revealed knowledge of God and the divine persons. Their logic was fairly straightforward. Many things may be known about God and His existence from human reason. After establishing these natural insights and after discussing that which is common to God (essence and attributes), they turned to the supernatural knowledge of God made known to us in Scripture (Trinity). Prior to Johann Gerhard our Lutheran dogmaticians departed from this order of topics.[45] For this reason they offer meager discussions of natural knowledge of God, often pass over a discussion of philosophical proofs for the existence of God, and combine their discussion of unity and Trinity, of what is common and proper to the one true God. Martin Chemnitz is a good example of this.

Chemnitz knew the schoolmen posited a distinction between what is common and what is proper to God, and ordered their discussions accordingly. He did not dispute the logical distinction between the common and the proper, between the essential and notional, as the schoolmen put it. Rather he disagreed with how they used this distinction to order their dogmatics. Chemnitz's preferred order is quite conservative and avoids the frivolous curiosities of human reason that burdened the medieval schoolmen. Chemnitz writes, "We should have no other thoughts about God than He has revealed to us in the Word which He has given us."[46] Scripture serves as our boundary and restrains us from needless speculation. More to the point, Scripture focuses on two things for us: who God is and what God does. If we are to make a distinction in our dogmatic discussions of God, it should be between the coeternity and coequality of Father, Son, and Holy Spirit (unity and Trinity) *and* the will of God as made known in His creation and preservation of all things, and especially in His special benefits for the sake of His church.[47] By following this insight, Chemnitz discusses both the Trinity and the works of the Trinity in his locus on God and throughout his entire dogmatics. Robert Preus explains, "To Chemnitz revealed theology should begin with the doctrine of the Trinity, which tells

---

45. Robert Preus, *The Theology of Post-Reformation Lutheranism* (St. Louis: Concordia Publishing House, 1972), 2:16.
46. Chemnitz, *Loci Theologici* 1:69.
47. Chemnitz, *Loci Theologici* 1:68.

us who the true God is and leads directly to what God has done."[48] Since the entire dogmatic enterprise involves these two points, Chemnitz's presentation throughout is centered on the Trinity. Again Preus writes, "To Chemnitz all articles of faith center in this article of the Trinity."[49]

Chemnitz's ordering of his discussion displays well the Lutheran approach to the Trinity and yields rich theological insights for our consideration of the divine attributes. To begin with, any discussion of the attributes must attend to the works of God. We cannot know who God is apart from His own revelation of Himself to us.[50] This means, as Preus explains, that "any discussion of divine attributes is subsumed under the *locus* on the Trinity or the works of God, which include the whole of dogmatics."[51] We could put the question this way: when do we talk about the attributes of God? The answer is when we talk about who God is and the things He does. In a work on dogmatics that ought to mean everywhere. This integrated approach is scriptural and privileges the Trinity in all of our dogmatic discussions. Chemnitz's approach further circumvents the arbitrary God-talk and perfect being theology that plagues modernity. If we are to talk about the essential attributes according to Scripture, we must talk about the Trinity, about Father, Son, and Holy Spirit who create, redeem, and sanctify. Here we rightly discern the power of God, the love of God, the holiness of God, the eternity of God, the truth of God, the grace and mercy of God, and so on.

Johann Gerhard departed from Chemnitz's approach and aligned himself more closely with the medieval schoolmen. He began, as they had, with natural knowledge of God and the various proofs for God's existence. From here Gerhard proceeded in an orderly and logical manner. He discussed the divine names of God as a way of better understanding the essence of God. He then offered a thorough consideration of the unity and attributes of God. After establishing what was common to God (unity and attributes), he turned in his next locus to a lengthy consideration of the Trinity. Gerhard's discussion of the Trinity is exceptional and has been used extensively throughout this book. Gerhard begins his discussion of the Trinity with a careful examination of the Old and New Testaments. He clearly and concisely presents the ways in which the church has guarded this scriptural witness, highlighting the church's grammar and salutary patterns of speech (Locus 4/1). He dedicates a separate locus to the Father and the Son (Locus 4/2), and another to the Holy Spirit (Locus 4/3).

Why should Gerhard's approach, which influences nearly all of the dogmaticians who follow him, be problematic? May we not simply see his approach as an alternative presentation of the same topic? It's not as if Gerhard and those who follow him say anything contrary to Scripture or neglect to

---

48. Preus, *Theology of Post-Reformation Lutheranism* 2:55.

49. Preus, *Theology of Post-Reformation Lutheranism* 2:55.

50. Chemnitz, *Loci Theologici* 1:71: "It is an absolute certainty that God wills to be known and invoked in the same way as He has revealed Himself."

51. Preus, *Theology of Post-Reformation Lutheranism* 2:55.

discuss the Trinity. We need to be careful at this point. Our concern with Gerhard, and for that matter the later dogmaticians that followed him, has less to do with what is said and more to do with how it is said. The problem is not, for example, with Gerhard's comments on the divine names or on the various attributes. Gerhard brings to bear a great deal of Scripture on these topics and always underscores the practical value and comfort of these teachings.[52] The problem with Gerhard's discussion on the unity of God and the divine attributes is that he separates it from his discussion of the Trinity. Gerhard distinguishes where Chemnitz says no distinction should exist.[53] Gerhard's ordering becomes the rule for the dogmaticians that follow him. Although we have already quoted Quenstedt's reasoning for doing this in the previous chapter, it bears repeating here. Quenstedt writes:

> The consideration of God is twofold: one is absolute and the other is relative. The former is occupied with God considered essentially and without respect to the three persons of the Godhead; the latter is occupied with God viewed personally. The former sets forth both the essence and the essential attributes of God; the latter explains the persons of the Holy Trinity and the personal attributes of each.[54]

As Robert Preus has observed, Quenstedt's logic runs counter to Chemnitz's instincts.[55] Quenstedt's separation of the essence and attributes of God from the divine persons, who are these attributes, while at home in the discussion of the schoolmen, betrays the commitments of Chemnitz and the scriptural approach of the early dogmaticians. The very idea that we may talk about God "without respect to the three persons" ought to make any scriptural theologian uneasy.

Quenstedt's distinction between an absolute and relative consideration of God shapes the way he distinguishes the attributes. Here we see the slippery slope of Gerhard's reordering of topics. For Quenstedt there are two categories of attributes. The first, the absolute or immanent attributes, are true of the divine essence apart from creation and God's external works. The second, the relative or operative attributes, describe the divine essence with reference to God's works.[56] Here we especially see the dangers of separating a discussion of God's essence and attributes from who God is (unity and Trinity) and His works. According to Quenstedt and the later dogmaticians there are attributes that belong to God in Himself, absolutely, and therefore apart from His engagement with creation. Robert Preus sharply criticizes this move. Preus thought it highly

---

52. See for example Johann Gerhard, *Schola Pietatis*, vol. 1, trans. Elmer Hohle (Malone, TX: Repristination Press, 2006), part 1. Gerhard offers a meditation on the divine attributes in order to encourage the believer in godliness.

53. Cf. Hutter, *Compendium Locorum Theologicorum*, 5: "Locus II. De Deo Uno et Trino." Hutter discusses both the unity of God and the Trinity of persons together. Hutter's *Compendium*, a popular manual of Lutheran theology, presents the articles of faith by emphasizing Scripture and the Lutheran Confessions. His brief discussion of the Trinity demonstrates well the commitments of Luther and Chemnitz and is a good example of the Lutheran approach to the doctrine of God.

54. Johann Andreas Quenstedt, *Systema Theologicum*, I, 8 (Wittenberg, 1691), 284.

55. Preus, *Theology of Post-Reformation Lutheranism* 2:55.

56. Quenstedt, *Systema Theologicum*, I, 8 (Wittenberg, 1691), 285.

questionable whether one should ever speak of absolute attributes in God apart from any relation to creatures, of *Deus per se* as distinct from *Deus ad hominem*.[57] The problem is twofold. The later dogmaticians make a distinction where no distinction may exist. Further, we only know about these so-called absolute attributes because God has revealed them to us. Preus concludes, "When the Lutheran theologians in their *locus de Deo* seek to speak of God apart from His works, they are attempting the impossible; and they are well aware of this and of the grotesque caricature which would result if they were to be successful in their attempt."[58]

The advantage of discussing the attributes in the context of the Trinity's external works means that the whole of dogmatics, not simply one or two loci, concern Father, Son, and Holy Spirit. By seeing this basic point we begin to free ourselves from the modern burden of reducing the Trinity to a doctrine or an article of faith and begin to see it as the horizon of all theology, all our speaking, praying, and signing about God the Father, God the Son, and God the Holy Spirit. With that said, we must make one further cautionary remark. Despite the shortcomings of the way in which Gerhard and Quenstedt, among others, ordered their doctrine of God, they addressed a number of difficult questions on the divine attributes that were left unanswered by Chemnitz and the earlier dogmaticians. We might say the early dogmaticians did not say enough about the divine attributes and the later dogmaticians said too much. This is why Robert Preus, who has studied this issue among the dogmaticians more than anyone else, writes, "All in all we must say that the doctrine of God as presented by evangelical orthodoxy is one of the least satisfactory."[59] It will not do simply to adopt the approach of either Chemnitz or Gerhard and Quenstedt. We need them all together. We need the insights of Chemnitz's order, Gerhard's pastoral instincts, and Quenstedt's thoroughness and rigor.

DIVINE ATTRIBUTES

We noted above a number of difficult questions that arise in any discussion of the divine attributes. What is the relationship between the attributes and the essence of God? What is the relationship between the multiple attributes of God? Are they different from one another? Before we address these difficult questions we must state two basic truths from the beginning that bear directly on how we think about the attributes. First, the attributes of God are the attributes *of* God. Scripture makes this abundantly clear. When we are talking about divine power, we are talking about the power of God. The same holds true for the wisdom of God, the love of God, the goodness of God, the righteousness of God, and every other essential attribute we might name. The same point is

---

57. Preus, *Theology of Post-Reformation Lutheranism* 2:63 and 2:17.
58. Preus, *Theology of Post-Reformation Lutheranism* 2:17.
59. Preus, *Theology of Post-Reformation Lutheranism* 2:16.

made by Scripture when it declares the Spirit as the Spirit of holiness or Christ as the Lord of glory. Holiness and glory belong to God; they are of God. Any responsible discussion of the divine attributes must bear this in mind. God is the subject of the divine attributes made known to us in Scripture. This means we may not abstract the divine attributes from the Trinity. We cannot discuss truth, life, love, righteousness, or any other essential attribute apart from the divine persons who are these attributes. Two insurmountable reasons preclude this. First, God does not participate in truth and life or any other essential attribute. God is His truth. God is His life. More to the point, Scripture says that the Father is truth; Jesus, the eternal Son of God, is truth; the Spirit is truth. Likewise, Scripture says the Father is life; the Son is life; and the Holy Spirit is life. The unique unity of God and the mutual indwelling of the divine persons mean they are not three truths or three lives but one truth and one life, equally and indivisibly.

Second, we may not abstract these attributes lest we reduce them to univocal concepts that belong to both God and man. Many have done this, and the result is always the answer to our greatest fears and anxieties. God becomes the biggest and best thing around. For example, we begin with love or justice, and determine from our collective wisdom and cultural allegiances what we think love and justice are. We then project these notions upon God. God's love becomes what we find lovable; God's justice becomes what we feel to be just. This reduces God to an idol, to a projection of the sort of "god" we wish ourselves to be. None of this accords with Scripture. Rather, God is *His* love; God is *His* truth; God is *His* righteousness. When our love is ordered by God's grace, it may be said to be analogous to God's love. Our love more naturally, however, is disordered by our sin and therefore evokes God's wrath and judgment. In truth, our loves are both ordered and disordered because we are both saint and sinner. We know God's love by what God has done for us in Christ Jesus, and this we know only by the Spirit's work of regeneration and renewal through the means of grace. When the Father pours forth His love into our hearts by the Holy Spirit, He brings us to faith in Christ Jesus, the true Son of God, in whom alone we are justified by faith and have peace. The Trinity saves, and in this salvation we know God's love, truth, and righteousness and we rightly proclaim and rejoice in His glory. Apart from that salvation, apart from the means of grace, we grope in a darkness of our own making and do the very thing that comes most naturally to us: we make idols (Ps 115:4–8).

Any understanding we are to have of God's essential attributes requires God's revelation, and more specifically His works toward us. It requires, very precisely, the manger, the cross, the font, and the altar. The deep things of God are known only by the Holy Spirit, the very Spirit poured into our hearts by the Father through the Son. The Spirit comes to us by Word and sacrament, speaking to us the words of Christ, which are the words of the Father. These words of eternal life bring repentance and new life. They free us from ourselves and our idols. In this freedom of the Spirit we find ourselves in Christ to the glory of the Father. And here, in this precise place, we gaze upon the manger and the cross and behold the love of God, the mercy of God, the power of God, indeed, the glory of God the Father, the Son, and the Holy Spirit. This is the wisdom from above. Anything less than this returns us to the factory of idols.

This way of knowing God reposes in the righteousness of Christ and the revelation of our triune God made known to us in Christ. Part 1 of this book argued these points at length, and they bear directly on our consideration of the divine attributes. Indeed, without much exaggeration we could say that it is precisely here, in a discussion of the attributes of God, that our Lutheran commitments are tested. For example, in part 1 we showed the necessity of the gospel and justification by faith as the proper lens through which we rightly know and confess the Trinity. We properly know God the Father, the Son, and the Holy Spirit by grace through faith, and that faith—saving faith—cannot be had apart from the imputation of Christ's righteousness by which we are reconciled to the Father. Justifying faith makes known to us the Son by the Holy Spirit, the Spirit of Christ, and through the Son we know the Father. What does this mean? In short, it means what Irenaeus long ago declared: *sine Deo non cognosci Deum*, without God no one knows God.[60] God has done this in unexpected places. In the estimation of human reason and human wisdom, the manger and the cross are unlikely places to find the Lord of glory, and yet it is in these places that faith beholds God. Luther writes, "Let us go to the child lying in the lap of His mother Mary and to the sacrificial victim suspended on the cross; there we shall really behold God, and there we shall look into His very heart."[61] Whether we are discussing natural knowledge of God, the essential attributes of God, or anything whatsoever to do with the God made known to us in Scripture, we may permit no wedge between knowing the Trinity and being clothed in the righteousness of Christ. The manger and the cross reveal two inseparable things: who God is and what God is. Again, as we have argued in part 1, if knowing the Father is knowing His glory, and His glory is known only through the peace brought about by the saving work of the Son and delivered by the Holy Spirit through the means of grace, then knowing the Father rightly always entails knowing the salvation wrought by Christ through His incarnation, suffering, death, resurrection, and ascension. And this knowing involves the divine persons, the essential attributes, and the external works that make them known to us. David Scaer writes:

> In the cross what God really is comes to its fullest and most complete expression. The Son is begotten of God who is eternal love and thus He fully shares in the Father's love. Out of this divine love the world was created and also because of it the Son was sent by the Father for the world's redemption. The crucifixion, more

---

60. Irenaeus *Adversus Haereses* IV, 6, 4; cf. Johann Gerhard, *De Natura Dei*, Locus 3, §6 (ed. Cotta, 92).

61. *Lectures on Genesis*, 1535–45 (AE 3:276–77; WA 43:73.4–6).

than any other moment in the history of the world, of Israel, or even of the life of Jesus, is the greatest manifestation of God's essence.[62]

The love of God in Christ Jesus may not be known apart from the cross and the faith that lays hold of that cross, a faith delivered by the Holy Spirit through the divinely appointed means of grace. Therefore to know God always requires God and His church. It requires the divinely instituted office of ministry; it requires Word and sacrament; it requires law and gospel; it requires repentance and faith, prayer and doxology; it requires, in short, the divine service.

ATTRIBUTES, ESSENCE, AND SIMPLICITY

What is the relationship between the attributes and the divine essence? When Scripture declares that God is love, what is the relationship between God and His love? Does saying God is love mean God's essence is love? If so, does the same hold true for righteousness or truth or any other essential attribute we might name? These questions lead us to yet another difficult question. What is the relationship between the different attributes? If God is love, righteousness, and truth, and these pertain to the essence of God such that God does not participate in something called love, righteousness, or truth that stands apart from Him, then how do we understand the relationship between the attributes themselves? Is there difference? Is there identity? If identity, does that mean that God's love is righteousness and both are truth?

The above questions present difficulties because the church's confession of the unity of the Trinity, the oneness of God, presupposes the simplicity of God. As our Lutheran Confessions put it, God is indivisible (*impartibilis*), or more literally without parts (*ohne Stücke*).[63] For this reason we cannot say God's essence is one thing and His attributes another. Augustine writes, "For God it is the same thing to be [*esse*] as to be powerful or just or wise or anything else that can be said about his simple . . . substance."[64] This means God's being is His attributes. There is no difference between what God is and what God is said to have: the divine nature is simple because "it is what it has" (*quod habet hoc est*).[65] If this is the case, why does Scripture distinguish for us God's greatness, God's power, God's goodness, and God's wisdom? Although Scripture distinguishes these attributes *for us*, and indeed they are according to Scripture in some sense distinct such that God's love is not God's wrath, the church nevertheless confesses that these attributes are neither distinct one from another nor distinct from God's essence. Why? Because God is indivisible and without parts. Does that mean we must also say, as Augustine does, that "greatness is the same as

---

62. David Scaer, *Christology*, vol. 6 of Confessional Lutheran Dogmatics (St. Louis: Luther Academy, 1989), 75.
63. AC I.2 (Tappert, 27); BSLK, 50; *Triglotta* (Bente, 42).
64. Augustine *The Trinity* VI.6 (WSA I/5, 209).
65. Augustine *The City of God* XI.10 (WSA, I/7, 11); Mann, "Divine Simplicity," 451.

power and goodness the same as wisdom"?[66] These thorny questions bring us once again to Luther's *unissima*, God's unique oneness that is unlike any oneness we know.

Both Gerhard and Quenstedt address these difficult questions by always returning to the faithful confession of the unique simplicity of God.[67] The essential attributes are really and completely one with the divine essence.[68] The attributes are neither accidents nor something superadded to the essence. God is not like angels or men or any other created thing for which attributes and qualities differ from essence.[69] The divine attributes exist inseparably in God.[70] This means both that God is life itself, light itself, and goodness itself, and also that God is His life, His light, and His goodness.[71] Why then does Scripture distinguish these attributes for us? Gerhard explains,

> Although the divine attributes are neither distinct in reality among themselves nor from the divine essence, nevertheless our intellectual weakness requires that we treat them separately. Augustine says, "God descends to us that we might ascend to him." Therefore, since we are men, God speaks to us in a human way.[72]

In reality the divine attributes are not divided from the divine essence. And yet God in His wisdom and mercy has revealed Himself to us in such a way that we may know Him in part (1 Cor 13:9) and therefore speak about Him. By bearing all of this in mind, we will not think wrongly about the attributes or the divine essence. Quenstedt, following Gerhard, emphasizes especially our intellectual limitations in grasping God. He writes:

> Attributes are nothing else than inadequate conceptions of the divine essence ... Since our finite intellect cannot adequately conceive of the infinite and absolutely simple essence of God by a single adequate conception, it therefore apprehends the same by distinct and inadequate conceptions which represent only inadequately the divine essence. These inadequate conceptions are called the properties and attributes of God, properties because they have to do with the divine essence and denote it, attributes because they are attributed to the same by our intellect.[73]

Quenstedt carefully emphasizes that the divine attributes are not merely names we give to the divine essence; they are real and belong to God apart from

---

66. Augustine *The Trinity* VII.1 (WSA I/5, 217).
67. Similarly, Abraham Calov writes, "From the unity of God proceeds the simplicity of God, according to which God is free from all real composition." Calov, *Systema Locorum Theologicorum* (Wittenberg, 1655), 2:284.
68. Gerhard, *De Natura Dei*, Locus 3, §47 (ed. Cotta, 108).
69. Gerhard, *De Natura Dei*, Locus 3, §47 (ed. Cotta, 108).
70. Quenstedt, *Systema Theologicum*, I, 8 (Wittenberg, 1691), 296–97.
71. Gerhard, *De Natura Dei*, Locus 3, §§48–49 (ed. Cotta, 108–9).
72. Gerhard, *De Natura Dei*, Locus 3, §51 (ed. Cotta, 109). See also Quenstedt, *Systema Theologicum*, I, 8 (Wittenberg, 1691), 300.
73. Quenstedt, *Systema Theologicum*, I, 8 (Wittenberg, 1691), 284; Quoted in Preus, *Theology of Post-Reformation Lutheranism* 2:56. Note especially Preus's comment about the sense of *inadaequatus*.

our own conceptualization of them.[74] Nonetheless we name as multiple what exists in God simply and unitedly, but among us, insofar as we too know these attributes in creatures, they are divided and multiplied.[75] To explain God's simplicity and attributes, without on the one hand collapsing the attributes together and on the other hand separating them from the essence, remains an impossibility for us. To borrow from Luther at this point, we confess that we are not able to speak perfectly in these matters, and nevertheless this is how we must speak. And this is what we call believing.[76]

CONCLUSION

This chapter has tackled some of the most vexing questions that confront anyone wishing to discuss the doctrine of God in our day. It is also true that this chapter remains somewhat inadequate and unsatisfying, as the subject matter itself will always elude our best words and thoughts. We know God in part and yet we seek to speak and think beyond this, beyond what is available to us as fallen, created beings. With our creaturely words and thoughts we seek to speak about the one who dwells in light inaccessible. The possibility of speaking about God, of describing God, stems from God's own mercy and grace. He discloses Himself to us, He comes near, He frees us from our idols and idolatries, from the bondage of our sin and the weakness of our thoughts, that we might become sharers and participants in His divine life, in His goodness and majesty, resting in Him and finding our joy in Him alone. From the humility of faith we confess as best we can the unique oneness and threeness of our God, a oneness unlike any oneness we know, a threeness unlike any threeness we know.

---

74. Quenstedt, *Systema Theologicum*, I, 8 (Wittenberg, 1691), 296.
75. Thomas Aquinas *ST* I.13.12c: "God ... is altogether one and simple, yet our intellect knows Him by different conceptions because it cannot see Him as He is in Himself. Nevertheless, although it understands Him under different conceptions, it knows that one and the same simple object corresponds to its conceptions." See also *ST* I.13.4c.
76. *Die Promotionsdisputation von Petrus Hegemon*, 1545 (WA 39/2:384.9–22).

CONCLUSION:
MODERN TRINITARIANISM

Systematic theologians typically describe the twentieth century as a period of renewed interest in the doctrine of the Trinity. Karl Barth and Karl Rahner are credited with returning the Trinity to the center of Christian life and thought for both Protestants and Roman Catholics. In the nineteenth century, Friedrich Schleiermacher had placed his formal discussion of the doctrine of the Trinity in the appendix to his massive dogmatic theology, *The Christian Faith*. Schleiermacher's point was clear: the church's doctrine of the Trinity had no relevance for the ordinary Christian. Experience proved this. Believers give little attention to the coequality and coeternity of the divine persons in their daily lives. Schleiermacher went further. He rejected the orthodox doctrine of the Trinity, declaring it incoherent and unknown to Scripture. Karl Barth responded both structurally and dogmatically. Barth began his even more massive *Church Dogmatics* with the Trinity. Where you would expect prolegomena, you get the Trinity. Barth's point was just as clear: the Trinity makes possible Christian theology. Every aspect of the Christian faith bears witness to this. Reject the Trinity and you reject Christianity.

Why did the Trinity fall on such difficult times during modernity? Karl Rahner thought part of the problem was a separation of the doctrine of God from the doctrine of the Trinity. His chief contribution to the renewed interest in the Trinity can be reduced to a guiding methodological insight. Rahner's rule, as it is often called, states, "The 'economic' Trinity is the 'immanent' Trinity and the 'immanent' Trinity is the 'economic' Trinity."[1] Rahner emphasized that the mystery of the Trinity is the mystery of salvation for us. By recovering this insight we avoid reducing the Trinity to a mere doctrine.[2] Rahner's correlation of the immanent Trinity and the economic Trinity has been both widely celebrated and strongly critiqued. Yves Congar regards Rahner's insight as "the most original contemporary contribution to the theology of the Trinity."[3] Alternatively, Bruce Marshall finds Rahner's formulation either trivial or

---

[1]. Karl Rahner, *The Trinity*, trans. Joseph Donceel (New York: Crossroad, 1997), 22.

[2]. The substance of Rahner's rule had been articulated by theologians before him. Karl Barth and Friedrich Schleiermacher both said something very similar. Karl Barth, *Church Dogmatics*, I/1, ed. G. W. Bromiley and T. F. Torrance (New York: T & T Clark, 2010), 548; Friedrich Schleiermacher, *The Christian Faith* (Edinburgh: T & T Clark, 1986), 748 (§172): "We have no formula for the being of God in himself as distinct from the being of God in the world." Schleiermacher shows us, at the very least, that Rahner's rule cannot guarantee orthodoxy.

[3]. Yves Congar, *I Believe in the Holy Spirit* (New York: Crossroad, 2013), 3:11. Although Congar accepts Rahner's rule, he limits its absolute character (3:13–17).

absurd.⁴ Marshall points out that no one ever has thought to deny that the immanent Trinity is the economic Trinity. No one, for example, posits six persons, three who make up the immanent Trinity and three who make up the economic Trinity.⁵ On the other hand, if this rule is taken to mean that a strict correspondence avails between the immanent and economic Trinity, then we are forced to say that "being incarnate belongs to the Son immanently and economically, being poured out on all flesh belongs to the Spirit immanently as well as economically, and so forth."⁶

However you evaluate the contributions made by Barth and Rahner, you cannot deny their considerable influence on the shape and interest of systematic theology in the twentieth century. Theologians as diverse as Wolfhart Pannenberg, Jürgen Moltmann, Walter Kaspar, Robert Jenson, Leonardo Boff, John Zizoulas, Catherine LaCugna, and many more authored significant works on the Trinity that both rejected long-held trinitarian commitments, especially as articulated in the Western tradition, and advanced new proposals for trinitarian thinking today.⁷ In doing this they continued the trajectory set by Barth and Rahner, both of whom sought to reconfigure certain aspects of the tradition. Scholars have been divided over the value of these recent trinitarian works. In our earlier chapters we have both agreed and disagreed with certain things said by the Fathers and by the schoolmen. That same approach is needed with contemporary trinitarian theology. We share the concern to place the Trinity at the center of Christian theology; we too worry that a discussion of God's essence and attributes apart from the divine persons who are those attributes is problematic. These concerns, as we have shown, are part of the tradition itself and hardly new with the twentieth century. Although we may share these more general positions, we do not accept the way in which they have been developed by many contemporary theologians. The point that must be insisted upon is that renewed interest in the Trinity does not count as a revival of the doctrine itself.

Although many works continue to be published on behalf of this so-called trinitarian renewal, there is an equally significant body of literature questioning the orthodoxy of this literature. Bruce Marshall has written a clear and concise account of the main points advanced by those contributing to the so-called

---

4. Bruce Marshall, *Trinity and Truth* (Cambridge: Cambridge University Press, 2000), 264.

5. Although, as Marshall notes, "Barth's odd remarks about the triune God making a 'copy' (*Nachbild*) of himself in the world do give one pause." Barth, *Church Dogmatics*, III/2, 218–19; Marshall, "Trinity," in *The Blackwell Companion to Theology*, ed. Gareth Jones (Oxford: Blackwell, 2004), 201 n. 21.

6. Marshall, *Trinity and Truth*, 265. For a similar critique see Miroslav Wolf, "'The Trinity Is Our Social Program': The Doctrine of the Trinity and the Shape of Social Engagement," *Modern Theology* 14:3 (1998): 407.

7. Summaries of these theologians abound. Ted Peters, *God as Trinity: Relationality and Temporality in Divine Life* (Louisville, KY: Westminster/John Knox, 1993); John Thompson, *Modern Trinitarian Perspectives* (Oxford: Oxford University Press, 1994); Stanley Grenz, *Rediscovering the Triune God: The Trinity in Contemporary Theology* (Minneapolis: Fortress Press, 2004).

trinitarian renewal of the twentieth century.[8] Marshall finds many of these ideas either lacking the novelty they claim or simply implausible. He concludes, "The past century's reflection on the Trinity arguably embodies not so much the renewal as the eclipse of trinitarian theology as an ongoing tradition of inquiry."[9] Stephen Holmes, once persuaded by the novelty of modern trinitarianism, has offered an even stronger critique.

> In our accounts of a Trinitarian revival, we wanted little or nothing to do with such strictures [i.e., patristic trinitarianism]. As a result, we set out on our own to offer a different, and we believed better, doctrine.... We called what we were doing a 'Trinitarian revival'; future historians might want to ask us why.[10]

In Holmes's estimation, the scholars aligning themselves with this so-called revival read Scripture like the Gnostics and Arians, think about the divine essence like Eunomius and Scotus, and reject divine simplicity like the anti-Trinitarians of the Reformation. Holmes's critique is devastating: those identifying with the "Trinitarian revival" of the twentieth century stand with the great heretics of the church and against the Fathers and reformers. Holmes is not alone in offering a strong critique of recent trinitarian theology. Kevin Giles argues that many of the most significant American Evangelical theologians of the twentieth century have reinvented the Trinity and embraced Arianism.[11] Francesca Murphy, for rather different reasons, argues that a great deal of recent trinitarian thinking is mired in method, narrative, and talk about talk. The diversity found among those contributing to the renewal of trinitarian theology is matched by the diversity of those critiquing it. It is especially here that we enter the confusing world of the present critique of recent trinitarian theology. Murphy thinks Robert Jenson is a "cinematic modalist"; George Hunsinger thinks Jenson is a tritheist.[12] How could such radically different evaluations be made of Jenson? Murphy has an answer: "The modern modalist looks like a tritheist to the modern Augustinian."[13]

The theological culture of the twentieth century owes much to modernity, and this has in decisive ways shaped the revival of scholarly interest in the Trinity. One of the most striking features of modern trinitarian thought is the pragmatic use of the doctrine of the Trinity. It is no longer sufficient to assert that the importance of the doctrine of the Trinity is the eternal being of the God made known to us in Scripture. In the twentieth century the doctrine of the Trinity has been put to work. The Trinity becomes the answer to political,

---

8. Marshall, "Trinity," 183–203.
9. Marshall, "Trinity," 200.
10. Stephen Holmes, *The Quest for the Trinity* (Downers Grove, IL: IVP Academic, 2012), 200.
11. Kevin Giles, *Jesus and the Father: Modern Evangelicals Reinvent the Doctrine of the Trinity* (Grand Rapids: Zondervan, 2006).
12. Francesca Murphy, *God Is Not a Story: Realism Revisited* (Oxford: Oxford University Press, 2007); George Hunsinger, "Robert Jenson's *Systematic Theology*: A Review Essay," *Scottish Journal of Theology* 55 (2002): 193–95.
13. Murphy, *God Is Not a Story*, 262.

economic, ethical, and social concerns.[14] The inclusive Trinity, we are told, helps us understand ourselves, our ecclesial communities, and our mission work. Some have gone so far as to suggest that the doctrine of the Trinity is our social program.[15] Aligning the Trinity with these pressing social and political concerns has led to the most significant development in modern trinitarian thought. The classical ontology embraced by the Fathers and reformers to secure a proper scriptural understanding of the Trinity has been reconfigured entirely. If there has been ecumenical achievement in the twentieth century, it has been on this very point. Protestant, Roman Catholic, and Orthodox theologians, of all stripes and political persuasions, insist that God must be reconceived in terms of relationality.[16] This concern is expressed among contemporary theologians under the name of either social trinitarianism or relational ontology.[17]

Social trinitarianism insists upon a different understanding of "person" when talking about the Trinity. Here we see especially the twentieth-century debt to modern assumptions. For modernity, personhood was reconceived in terms of freedom, dignity, and human rights.[18] To be an authentic person is to be self-determining, to be on your own terms, apart from political and moral constraint.[19] When we apply this modern notion of person to the Trinity, we end up with three distinct subjectivities, three authentic and self-determining persons, who freely and willingly coexist in unity. We end up with sophisticated sounding tritheism.[20] Many social trinitarians alleviate this result by insisting that "person" be understood chiefly in relational terms. An understanding of person that tends to extreme individualism is defective; a proper understanding of person involves the other, involves relationship. "I" and "Thou" require one another. In the words of Jürgen Moltmann, a person's social liberty is opened up through community.[21] Cornelius Plantinga brings these two concerns together.

---

14. Little consensus, of course, exists on how the Trinity informs politics and the economy. Some think the doctrine of the Trinity yields capitalism and others socialism. Michael Novak, *The Spirit of Democratic Capitalism* (New York: American Enterprise Institute, 1982); Leonardo Boff, *Trinity and Society*, trans. Paul Burns (Maryknoll, NY: Orbis Books, 1988).

15. The Russian Orthodox theologian Nicholas Fedorov has argued that "the dogma of the Trinity is our social program." Fedorov's proposal is discussed and critiqued by Wolf, "'The Trinity Is Our Social Program,' 403-23. Wolf distances himself from the language of social program and prefers to see the doctrine of the Trinity as shaping our social vision.

16. Peters, *God as Trinity*, 34.

17. For a survey of Protestant, Catholic, Orthodox, liberation, feminist, evangelical, and process theologians embracing a social model of the Trinity, see John Gresham, Jr., "The Social Model of the Trinity and Its Critics," *Scottish Journal of Theology* 46 (1993): 325-43.

18. Peters, *God as Trinity*, 35.

19. Karl Rahner, *Grundkurs des Glaubens* (Freiburg im Breisgau: Herder, 1976), 140. Rahner says that to be a person, different from another person, means "there is an independent, free, self-disposing centre of action in knowledge and freedom, different from others; and that the person is constituted by this very fact." Quoted in Jürgen Moltmann, *The Trinity and the Kingdom*, trans. Margaret Kohl (Minneapolis: Fortress Press, 1993), 145.

20. Peters, *God as Trinity*, 35.

21. Moltmann, *Trinity and the Kingdom*, 145. Cf. Boff, *Trinity and Society*, 89.

He thinks of the divine persons as a "perfect family" after whom we are to model our lives together. Plantinga explains:

> By "social analogy," or, alternatively, "strong trinitarianism," I mean any theory in which (1) Father, Son, and Spirit are conceived as persons in a full sense of "person" i.e., as distinct centers of love, will, knowledge, and purposeful action (all of which require consciousness) and (2) who are conceived as related to each other in some central ways analogous to, even if sublimely surpassing, relations among the members of a society of three human persons.[22]

For these theologians, the way we ideally think of ourselves as persons, in the full sense of that word, and how we think of our ideal communities inform our understanding of the Trinity. Father, Son, and Holy Spirit become for us what we wish to be for ourselves and others.

Social trinitarians generally locate their insights in the work of the Greek fathers, particularly Gregory of Nyssa. Readers are routinely told by systematic theologians that the Latin or Western tradition began discussions of the Trinity with the unity of God and then moved to the Trinity, while the Greek or Eastern tradition began with the divine persons and then moved to the unity of God. This Latin and Greek model can be seen especially with Augustine and the Cappadocians. Augustine starts with the unity of God and prefers psychological analogies; the Cappadocians start with the divine persons and prefer social analogies. Augustine, more than any other figure in the history of the church, has emerged as the source for nearly every unfortunate misstep associated with Western trinitarian thought.[23] Systematic theologians celebrate the insights of the Cappadocians and lament the blunders of Augustine.[24] Although the distinction between Latin and Greek theology has become commonplace in contemporary literature on the Trinity, it is historically indefensible.

The misreading of patristic trinitarian theology and particularly pro-Nicene theology has resulted in another major wave of trinitarian scholarship. Michel René Barnes, a patristic scholar, has shown the historical location of the so-called Latin and Greek or Western and Eastern trinitarian distinction. Théodore de Régnon, a nineteenth-century French Jesuit, first posited the existence of these two trinitarian paradigms.[25] Barnes has shown how de Régnon's thesis and proof texts have appeared in books and articles on the Trinity throughout the twentieth century, often without any attribution. The distinction between Latin and Greek trinitarian models made in most textbooks today cannot be supported by the writings of the Fathers. Patristic scholars have shown this by

---

22. Cornelius Plantinga, Jr., "Gregory of Nyssa and the Social Analogy of the Trinity," *The Thomist* 50 (1986): 325 n. 1. Cf. Cornelius Plantinga, Jr., "The Perfect Family: Our Model of Life Together Is Found in the Father, Son, and Holy Spirit," *Christianity Today* 32 (4 March 1988): 24-28.

23. Michel René Barnes, "Augustine in Contemporary Trinitarian Theology," *Theological Studies* 56 (1995): 237-50.

24. For a particularly clear example of this see Robert Jenson, *Systematic Theology* (Oxford: Oxford University Press, 1997), 1:110-14.

25. Michel René Barnes, "De Régnon Reconsidered," *Augustinian Studies* 26:2 (1995): 51-79.

producing a number of specialized studies on the fourth-century trinitarian debates.[26] These scholars have offered historically sensitive and responsible readings of the works by the Fathers that have bolstered our understanding of pro-Nicene theology and provided a needed critique of modern trinitarian assumptions.[27] For the Fathers, trinitarian reflection involves careful reading and contemplation of Scripture, sensitivity to human speech about God, prayer, and the liturgical life of the church.[28]

Our volume on the Trinity has participated in the above critique of modern trinitarianism by showing how the Fathers and reformers discussed the Trinity and guarded the scriptural teaching of Father, Son, and Holy Spirit. We have further demonstrated at length the trinitarian exegesis known and confessed by the Fathers and reformers in their commentaries and sermons. The Lutheran approach to the Trinity centers on Christ and His work. If we wish to know the Trinity, we must place our gaze upon Christ, who alone reveals the Father to us. We confess Christ by the Holy Spirit to the glory of the Father, and this especially as the gathered faithful in the divine service. Here, with Basil of Caesarea, "we offer the confession of our faith in accordance with our baptism, and also the doxology in accordance with our faith, glorifying the Holy Spirit with the Father and the Son."[29] The Trinity saves. This is why our Confessions insist that "the chief worship of God is the preaching of the Gospel."[30]

We live in a world that has a lot to say about God. We have shown throughout this book that whatever a person says about God bears directly on what that person thinks about himself and the world around him. This means at the very least that any discussion of the Trinity involves a whole lot more than a single article of faith. Scripture makes this clear by correlating right knowledge of God with both worship and ethics. Trinity, gospel, worship, and ethics all belong together. We are mistaken if we think that debates on worship and ethics have no bearing on the gospel and the Trinity. Gregory of Nyssa, like Basil, argued that our confession of the Trinity proceeds from our baptismal faith. This faith, Gregory further insisted, mirrors our worship: "It is not natural that worship make war against faith, but as we believe, so also we give glory. Now since our faith is in *Father and Son and Holy Spirit*, faith, worship, and baptism accord with each other."[31]

---

26. Among others see especially Lewis Ayres, *Nicaea and Its Legacy* (Oxford: Oxford University Press, 2004); Lewis Ayres, *Augustine and the Trinity* (Cambridge: Cambridge University Press, 2010); and Khaled Anatolios, *Retrieving Nicaea* (Grand Rapids: Baker Academic, 2011).

27. On this point see especially, Ayres, *Nicaea and Its Legacy*, 384–429; Anatolios, *Retrieving Nicaea*, 1–13 and ix–xiv (Brian Daley's foreword).

28. For one example of this see Carl L. Beckwith, *Hilary of Poitiers on the Trinity* (Oxford: Oxford University Press, 2008).

29. Basil of Caesarea, *Letter* 159 (LCC 2:395–97), translation slightly altered.

30. Ap. XV.42 (Tappert, 221). The Triglot adds: "Now, if this worship is omitted, how can there be knowledge of God, the doctrine of Christ, or the Gospel?"

31. Gregory of Nyssa *Letter* 24.8 in *Gregory of Nyssa: The Letters*, trans. Anna M. Silvas (Leiden: Brill, 2007), 194.

Conclusion: Modern Trinitarianism

We have followed the scriptural insights of the Fathers and reformers in our response to the broad questions and concerns of modernity. We have explained our epistemological and soteriological commitments for properly discussing and confessing the Trinity. We have demonstrated Scripture's revelation of the Trinity in both the Old and New Testaments. We have familiarized ourselves with the church's traditional patterns of speech for protecting and proclaiming those scriptural insights. We are the heirs and guardians of a rich tradition. With this inheritance in hand, we join our voices critically and constructively to the trinitarian conversations of our day. And we do this, first and foremost, by boldly preaching the pure gospel of Jesus Christ, because there is no other way to know, worship, and glorify the Holy Trinity.

SELECTED BIBLIOGRAPHY

PRIMARY SOURCES

Ambrose of Milan. *The Holy Spirit*. In *Theological and Dogmatic Works*. Translated by Roy Deferrari. Washington, D.C.: The Catholic University of America Press, 1963.
Anselm. *Proslogion*. Edited and translated by M. J. Charlesworth. Notre Dame, IN: University of Notre Dame Press, 1979.
Anselm of Canterbury: The Major Works. Edited by Brian Davies and G. R. Evans.Oxford: Oxford University Press, 1998.
Athanasius. *Athanasius*. Translated by Khaled Anatolios. New York: Routledge, 2004.
_____. *Contra Gentes* and *De Incarnatione*. Edited and translated by Robert W. Thomson. Oxford: Clarendon Press, 1971.
Athanasius the Great and Didymus the Blind. *Works on the Spirit*. Popular Patristics Series. Translated by Mark DelCogliano, Andrew Radde-Gallwitz, and Lewis Ayres. Yonkers, NY: St. Vladimir's Seminary Press, 2011.
Augustine. *Homilies on the Gospel of John 1–40*. Translated by Edmund Hill. Works of Saint Augustine III/12. Hyde Park, NY: New City Press, 2009.
_____. *The Trinity*. Translated by Edmund Hill. Works of Saint Augustine I/5. Hyde Park, NY: New City Press, 1991.
Baier, John William. *Compendium Theologiae Positivae*. Edited by C. F. W. Walther. 3 vols. St. Louis: Concordia Publishing House, 1879.
Basil of Caesarea. *Against Eunomius*. Translated by Mark DelCogliano and Andrew Radde-Gallwitz. Washington, D.C.: The Catholic University of America Press, 2011.
_____. *The Letters*. Translated by Roy Deferrari. Loeb Classical Library. 4 vols. Cambridge, MA: Harvard University Press, 1926–34.
_____. *On the Holy Spirit*. Popular Patristics Series. Translated by David Anderson. Crestwood, NY: St. Vladimir's Seminary Press, 1997.
Boethius. *Theological Tractates*. Loeb Classical Library. Translated by H. F. Stewart, E. K. Rand, and S. J. Tester. Cambridge, MA: Harvard University Press, 1973.
Bonaventure. *Breviloquium*. In *Works of St. Bonaventure*, vol. 9, edited by Dominic Monti. St. Bonaventure, NY: The Franciscan Institute, 2005.
_____. *Disputed Questions on the Mystery of the Trinity*. In *Works of Saint Bonaventure*, vol. 3, edited by Zachary Hayes. St. Bonaventure, NY: The Franciscan Institute, 2000.
The Book of Concord: The Confessions of the Evangelical Lutheran Church. Translated and edited by Theodore G. Tappert. Philadelphia: Fortress Press, 1959.
Calov, Abraham. *Systema Locorum Theologicorum*. 12 vols. Wittenberg, 1655–77.
Chemnitz, Martin. *Examen Concilii Tridentini*. Frankfurt, 1596.
_____. *Loci Theologici*. Translated by J. A. O. Preus. St. Louis: Concordia Publishing House, 2008.
Decrees of the Ecumenical Councils. Edited by Norman P. Tanner. 2 vols. Washington, D.C.: Georgetown University Press, 1990.

Epiphanius of Cyprus. *Ancoratus*. Translated by Young Richard Kim. Washington, D.C.: The Catholic University of America Press, 2014.

———. *The Panarion of Epiphanius of Salamis*. Translated by Frank Williams. Leiden: Brill, 1994.

Epistle to Diognetus. In *The Apostolic Fathers*, 2d ed., edited by Michael Holmes. Grand Rapids: Baker Academic, 1989.

Gerhard, Johann. *De Deo Patre et Aeterno Eius Filio*. Locus 4/2. Edited by Johann Friedrich Cotta. Tübingen, 1762.

———. *De Spiritu Sancto*. Locus 4/3. Edited by Johann Friedrich Cotta. Tübingen, 1762.

———. *De Tribus Elohim*. Locus 4/1. Edited by Johann Friedrich Cotta. Tübingen, 1762.

———. *Theological Commonplaces: On the Nature of God and on the Trinity*. Translated by Richard Dinda. St. Louis: Concordia Publishing House, 2007.

Gregory of Nazianzus. *Festal Orations*. Popular Patristics Series. Translated by Nonna Verna Harrison. Crestwood, New York, 2008.

———. *Gregory of Nazianzus*. Translated by Brian Daley. New York: Routledge, 2006.

———. *On God and Christ*. Popular Patristics Series. Translated by Frederick Williams and Lionel Wickham. Crestwood, NY: St. Vladimir's Seminary Press, 2002. This volume contains Gregory's *Five Theological Orations* (Orations 27–31).

———. *Select Orations*. Translated by Martha Vinson. Washington, D.C.: The Catholic University of America Press, 2003.

Gregory of Nyssa. *An Answer to Ablabius*. In *Christology of the Later Fathers*, edited by Edward R. Hardy, 256–67. Philadelphia: Westminster, 1954.

———. *Gregory of Nyssa: The Letters*. Translated by Anna M. Silvas. Leiden: Brill, 2007.

Hafenreffer, Matthias. *Loci Theologici*. Tübingen, 1603.

Hilary of Poitiers. *The Trinity*. Translated by Stephen McKenna. Washington, D.C.: The Catholic University of America Press, 1954.

Hollaz, David. *Examen Theologicum Acroamaticum*. Leipzig, 1763.

Holmes, Michael, ed. *The Apostolic Fathers*. 2d ed. Grand Rapids: Baker Academic, 1989.

Hunnius, Aegidius. *Calvinus Iudaizans*. Wittenberg, 1604.

Hutter, Leonard. *Compendium Locorum Theologicorum*. 1610. Reprint. Berlin: Wilhelm Hertz, 1855.

Irenaeus of Lyons. *Against the Heresies*. Translated by Dominic Unger and Matthew Steenberg. 3 vols. Ancient Christian Writers. Mahwah, NJ: Paulist Press, 1991, 2012.

John Chrysostom. *On the Incomprehensible Nature of God*. Translated by Paul W. Harkins. Washington, D.C.: The Catholic University of America Press, 1984.

John of Damascus. *An Exact Exposition of the Orthodox Faith*. In *Writings*. Translated by Frederic H. Chase, Jr. Washington, D.C.: The Catholic University of America Press, 1958.

John Duns Scotus. *Duns Scotus: Philosophical Writings*. Translated by Allan B. Wolter. Indianapolis: Hackett, 1987.

———. *God and Creatures: The Quodlibetal Questions*. Translated by Felix Alluntis and Allan B. Wolter. Princeton, NJ: Princeton University Press, 2015.

Luther, Martin. *D. Martin Luthers Werke: Kritische Gesamtausgabe*. 65 vols. Weimar: Hermann Böhlaus Nachfolger, 1883–1993.

———. *Luther's Works*. American Edition. 82 vols. Edited by Jaroslav Jan Pelikan, Hilton C. Oswald, Helmut T. Lehmann, and Christopher Boyd Brown. St. Louis: Concordia Publishing House, 1955–.

Melanchthon, Philipp. *Explicatio symboli Niceni*. Corpus Reformatorum, vol. 23, edited by Henricus Ernestus Bindseil, 347–584. Brunswick: C. A. Schwetschke and Sons, 1855.
———. *Loci Theologici*. Corpus Reformatorum, vol. 21, edited by Henricus Ernestus Bindseil. Brunswick: C. A. Schwetschke and Sons, 1854.
Peter Lombard. *The Sentences*. Translated by Giulio Silano. Toronto: Pontifical Institute of Medieval Studies, 2007.
Quenstedt, Johann Andreas. *Systema Theologicum*. Wittenberg, 1691.
The Trinitarian Controversy. Translated by William Rusch. Sources in Early Christian Thought. Philadelphia: Fortress Press, 1980.
Thomas Aquinas. *Commentary on the Gospel of John*. Translated by Fabian R. Larcher. 2 vols. Lander, WY: The Aquinas Institute for the Study of Sacred Doctrine, 2013.
———. *Summa Theologiae*. Translated by Laurence Shapcote. 8 vols. Lander, WY: The Aquinas Institute for the Study of Sacred Doctrine, 2012.
Vaggione, Richard. *Eunomius: The Extant Works*. Oxford: Oxford University Press, 1987.

SECONDARY SOURCES

Anatolios, Khaled. *Retrieving Nicaea*. Grand Rapids: Baker Academic, 2011.
Attridge, Harold. *The Epistle to the Hebrews*. Philadelphia: Fortress Press, 1989.
Ayres, Lewis. *Augustine and the Trinity*. Cambridge: Cambridge University Press, 2010.
———. *Nicaea and Its Legacy*. Oxford: Oxford University Press, 2004.
———. "'Remember that you are Catholic' (Serm. 52.2): Augustine on the Unity of the Triune God." *Journal of Early Christian Studies* 8 (2000): 39–82.
Barnes, Michel René. "Augustine in Contemporary Trinitarian Theology." *Theological Studies* 56 (1995): 237–50.
———. "De Régnon Reconsidered." *Augustinian Studies* 26 no. 2 (1995): 51–79.
———. "The Fourth Century as Trinitarian Canon." In *Christian Origins: Theology, Rhetoric and Community*, edited by Lewis Ayres and Gareth Jones, 47–67. New York: Routledge, 1998.
———. "Irenaeus's Trinitarian Theology." *Nova et Vetera* 7 (2009): 67–109.
———. *The Power of God: 'Dunamis' in Gregory of Nyssa's Trinitarian Theology*. Washington, D.C.: The Catholic University of America Press, 2001.
Bauckham, Richard. *Jesus and the God of Israel: 'God Crucified' and Other Studies on the New Testament's Christology of Divine Identity*. Grand Rapids: Eerdmans, 2008.
———. "Monotheism and Christology in Hebrews 1." In *Early Jewish and Christian Monotheism*, edited by Loren T. Stuckenbuch and Wendy E. S. North, 167–85. Edinburgh: T&T Clark, 2004.
———. *The Testimony of the Beloved Disciple*. Grand Rapids: Baker Academic, 2007.
———. *The Theology of the Book of Revelation*. Cambridge: Cambridge University Press, 1993.
Bayer, Oswald. *Martin Luther's Theology: A Contemporary Interpretation*. Translated by Thomas Trapp. Grand Rapids: Eerdmans, 2008.
———. *Theology the Lutheran Way*. Translated by Jeffrey Silcock and Mark Mattes. Grand Rapids: Eerdmans, 2007.
Beckwith, Carl L. *Hilary of Poitiers on the Trinity*. Oxford Early Christian Studies. Oxford: Oxford University Press, 2008.

Bibliography

Beeley, Christopher. *Gregory of Nazianzus on the Trinity and the Knowledge of God*. Oxford: Oxford University Press, 2008.
Behr, John. *The Nicene Faith*. Crestwood, NY: St. Vladimir's Seminary Press, 2004.
———. *The Way to Nicaea*. Crestwood, NY: St. Vladimir's Seminary Press, 2001.
Bielfeldt, Dennis, Mickey L. Mattox, and Paul R. Hinlicky. *The Substance of the Faith: Luther's Doctrinal Theology for Today*. Minneapolis: Fortress Press, 2008.
Bobrinskoy, Boris. *The Mystery of the Trinity: Trinitarian Experience and Vision in the Biblical and Patristic Tradition*. Crestwood, NY: St. Vladimir's Seminary Press, 1999.
Brown, Raymond. *The Gospel According to John 1–XII*. New York: Doubleday, 1966.
Brunner, Emil. *The Christian Doctrine of God: Dogmatics*. Translated by Olive Wyon. Philadelphia: Westminster Press, 1950.
Buckley, Michael J. *At the Origins of Modern Atheism*. New Haven, CT: Yale University Press, 1990.
Buckley, Michael, and David Yeago. *Knowing the Triune God: The Work of the Spirit in the Practices of the Church*. Grand Rapids: Eerdmans, 2001.
Burrell, David. "Analogy, Creation, and Theological Language." *Proceedings of the American Catholic Philosophical Association*. 74 (2000): 35–52.
———. *Aquinas: God and Action*. London: Routledge, 1979.
Bushur, Jim. "Worship: The Activity of the Trinity." *Logia: A Journal of Lutheran Theology* 3 no. 3 (1994): 3–12.
Byrne, James M. *Religion and the Enlightenment*. Louisville, KY: Westminster John Knox Press, 1996.
Capes, David. *Old Testament Yahweh Texts in Paul's Christology*. Tübingen: Mohr/Siebeck, 1992.
Congar, Yves. *I Believe in the Holy Spirit*. Translated by David Smith. 3 vols. New York: Crossroad, 2013.
Cross, Richard. *Duns Scotus*. Oxford: Oxford University Press, 1999.
———. *Duns Scotus on God*. Burlington, VT: Ashgate, 2005.
Daley, Brian. "Is Patristic Exegesis Still Usable? Reflections on Early Christian Interpretation of the Psalms." *Communio* 29 (2002): 185–216.
———."Revisiting the *Filioque*: Contemporary Catholic Approaches." *Pro Ecclesia* 10 no. 2 (2001): 195–212.
———. "Revisiting the *Filioque*: Roots and Branches of an Old Debate." *Pro Ecclesia* 10 no. 1 (2001): 31–62.
Davis, Stephen, Daniel Kendall, and Gerald O'Collins, eds. *The Trinity: An Interdisciplinary Symposium on the Trinity*. Oxford: Oxford University Press, 1999.
Dumont, Stephen. "Henry of Ghent and Duns Scotus." In *Medieval Philosophy: Routledge History of Philosophy*, edited by John Merenbon, vol. 3, 291–328. London: Routledge, 1998.
Emery, Gilles. *The Trinitarian Theology of Thomas Aquinas*. Translated by Francesca Murphy. Oxford: Oxford University Press, 2007.
———. *The Trinity: An Introduction to Catholic Doctrine on the Triune God*. Washington, D.C.: The Catholic University of America, 2011.
Emery, Gilles, and Matthew Levering, eds. *The Oxford Handbook of the Trinity*. Oxford: Oxford University Press, 2011.
Fagerberg, Holsten. *A New Look at the Lutheran Confessions 1529–1537*. Translated by Gene J. Lund. St. Louis: Concordia Publishing House, 1972.

Fossum, Jarl E. *The Image of the Invisible God*. Göttingen: Vandenhoek & Ruprecht, 1995.
Friedman, Russell. *Medieval Trinitarian Thought from Aquinas to Ockham*. Cambridge: Cambridge University Press, 2010.
Gathercole, Simon. *The Preexistent Son: Recovering the Christologies of Matthew, Mark, and Luke*. Grand Rapids: Eerdmans, 2006.
Gerrish, Brian. *Grace and Reason: A Study in the Theology of Luther*. Oxford: Oxford University Press, 1962.
Gieschen, Charles. *Angelomorphic Christology: Antecedents and Early Evidence*. Leiden: Brill, 1998.
_____. "The Divine Name in Ante-Nicene Christology." *Vigiliae Christianae* 57 no. 2 (2003): 115–58.
_____. "The Real Presence of the Son Before Christ: Revisiting an Old Approach to Old Testament Christology." *Concordia Theological Quarterly* 68 no. 2 (2004): 105–26.
Gilson, Etienne. *The Christian Philosophy of St. Thomas Aquinas*. Notre Dame, IN: Notre Dame University Press, 1956.
Hanson, R. P. C. *The Search for the Christian Doctrine of God*. Grand Rapids: Baker Academic, 2005.
Hart, David Bentley. *Atheist Delusions: The Christian Revolution and Its Fashionable Enemies*. New Haven, CT: Yale University Press, 2009.
_____. "The Destiny of Christian Metaphysics: Reflections on the *Analogia Entis*." In *The Analogy of Being: Invention of the Antichrist or the Wisdom of God?* edited by Thomas Joseph White, 395–410. Grand Rapids: Eerdmans, 2011.
_____. "The Mirror of the Infinite: Gregory of Nyssa on the *Vestigia Trinitatis*." *Modern Theology* 18 no. 4 (2002): 541–61.
Hays, Richard. "Can the Gospels Teach Us How to Read the Old Testament?" *Pro Ecclesia* 11 no. 4 (2002): 402–18.
_____. *Echoes of Scripture in the Letters of Paul*. New Haven, CT: Yale University Press, 1989.
_____. "Response to Robert Wilken, *In Dominico Eloquio*." *Communio* 25 (1998): 520–28.
Helmer, Christine. "Luther's Trinitarian Hermeneutic and the Old Testament." *Modern Theology* 18 no. 1 (2002): 49–73.
Hengel, Martin. *Studies in Early Christology*. Edinburgh: T&T Clark, 1998.
Hoenecke, Adolf. *Evangelical Lutheran Dogmatics*. 2 vols. Translated by James Langebartels and Richard Krause. Milwaukee: Northwestern Publishing House, 2009.
Holmes, Stephen. "The Attributes of God." In *The Blackwell Companion to Theology*, edited by Gareth Jones, 54–71. Oxford: Blackwell, 2004.
_____. "Divine Attributes." In *Mapping Modern Theology*, edited by Kelly Kapic and Bruce McCormack, 47–66. Grand Rapids: Baker Academic, 2012.
_____. *The Quest for the Trinity: The Doctrine of God in Scripture, History and Modernity*. Downers Grove, IL: IVP, 2012.
Hurtado, Larry. *Lord Jesus Christ: Devotion to Jesus in Earliest Christianity*. Grand Rapids: Eerdmans, 2003.
_____. *One God, One Lord: Early Christian Devotion and Ancient Jewish Monotheism*. 2d ed. Edinburgh: T&T Clark, 1998.
Jenson, Robert. "The Bible and the Trinity." *Pro Ecclesia* 11 no. 3 (2002): 329–39.

———. "Ipse Pater Non Est Impassibilis." In *Divine Impassibility and the Mystery of Human Suffering*, edited by James Keating and Thomas Joseph White, 117–26. Grand Rapids: Eerdmans, 2009.
———. *Systematic Theology*. 2 vols. Oxford: Oxford University Press, 1997.
———. "The Trinity in the Bible." *Concordia Theological Quarterly* 68 no. 3/4 (2004): 195–206.
———. *The Triune Identity*. Philadelphia: Fortress Press, 1982.
———. "You Wonder Where the Spirit Went." *Pro Ecclesia* 2 no. 3 (1993): 296–304.
Kasper, Walter. *The God of Jesus Christ*. New York: Crossroad, 1984.
Kelly, J. N. D. *Early Christian Creeds*. 3d ed. New York: Longman, 1972.
Kolb, Robert. "Luther on the Theology of the Cross." *Lutheran Quarterly* 16 (2002): 443–66.
———. "Luther's Theology of the Cross Fifteen Years after Heidelberg: Lectures on the Psalms of Ascent." *Journal of Ecclesiastical History* 61 no. 1 (2010): 69–85.
Laetsch, Theodore. *Jeremiah*. St. Louis: Concordia Publishing House, 1952.
———. *The Minor Prophets*. St. Louis: Concordia Publishing House, 1956.
Lash, Nicholas. *The Beginning and End of 'Religion'*. Cambridge: Cambridge University Press, 1996.
Lohse, Bernhard. *Martin Luther's Theology*. Translated by Roy A. Harrisville. Minneapolis: Fortress Press, 1999.
Lonergan, Bernard. *The Triune God: Doctrines*. Toronto: University of Toronto Press, 2009.
———. *The Triune God: Systematics*. Toronto: University of Toronto Press, 2007.
Louth, Andrew. *St. John Damascene: Tradition and Originality*. Oxford: Oxford University Press, 2005.
MacDonald, Nathan. "A Trinitarian Palimpsest: Luther's Reading of the Priestly Blessing (Numbers 6:24–26)." *Pro Ecclesia* 11 no. 3 (2012): 299–313.
McInerny, Ralph. *Aquinas and Analogy*. Washington, D.C.: Catholic University of America Press, 1996.
———. *Praeambula Fidei: Thomism and the God of the Philosophers*. Washington, D.C.: Catholic University of America Press, 2006.
Mann, William. "Divine Simplicity." *Religious Studies* 18 (1982): 451–71.
———. "Duns Scotus on Natural and Supernatural Knowledge of God." In *Cambridge Companion to Duns Scotus*, edited by Thomas Williams, 238–62. Cambridge: Cambridge University Press, 2002.
Marion, Jean-Luc. *God Without Being*. 2d ed. Translated by Thomas Carlson. Chicago: The University of Chicago Press, 2012.
———. "Is the Ontological Argument Ontological? The Argument According to Anselm and Its Metaphysical Interpretation According to Kant." In *Flight of the Gods: Philosophical Perspectives on Negative Theology*, edited by Ilse Bulhof and Laurens ten Kate, 78–99. New York: Fordham University Press, 2000.
Marshall, Bruce. "Action and Person: Do Palamas and Aquinas Agree about the Spirit?" *St. Vladimir's Theological Quarterly* 39 no. 4 (1995): 379–408.
———. "Aquinas the Augustinian? On the Uses of Augustine in Aquinas' Trinitarian Theology." In *Aquinas the Augustinian*, edited by Michael Dauphinais, Barry David, and Matthew Levering, 41–61. Washington, D.C.: Catholic University of America Press, 2007.

———. "Christ the End of Analogy." In *The Analogy of Being: Invention of the Antichrist or the Wisdom of God?* edited by Thomas Joseph White, 280–313. Grand Rapids: Eerdmans, 2011.

———. "The Defense of the *Filioque* in Classical Lutheran Theology." *Neue Zeitschrift für systematische Theologie und Religionsphilosophie* 44 no. 2 (2002): 154–73.

———. "Trinity." In *The Blackwell Companion to Theology*, edited by Gareth Jones, 183–203. Oxford: Blackwell, 2004.

———. *Trinity and Truth.* Cambridge: Cambridge University Press, 2000.

———. "*Utrum Essentia Generet*: Semantics and Metaphysics in Later Medieval Trinitarian Theology." In *Trinitarian Theology in the Medieval West*, edited by Pekka Kärkkäinen, 88–123. Helsinki: Luther-Agricola-Society, 2004.

Mayes, Benjamin T. G. "Post-Reformation Lutheran Attitudes Toward the Reformed Doctrine of God." *Concordia Theological Quarterly* 75 no. 1/2 (2011): 111–34.

Moltmann, Jürgen. *The Trinity and the Kingdom.* Translated by Margaret Kohl. Minneapolis: Fortress Press, 1993.

Mueller, John Theodore. *Christian Dogmatics.* St. Louis: Concordia Publishing House, 1934.

Oberman, Heiko A. *The Harvest of Medieval Theology.* Grand Rapids: Baker Academic, 2000.

———. "*Via Antiqua* and *Via Moderna*: Late Medieval Prolegomena to Early Reformation Thought." *Journal of the History of Ideas* 48 no. 1 (1987): 23–40.

Pesch, Otto Hermann. *The God Question in Thomas Aquinas and Martin Luther.* Translated by Gottfried G. Krodel. Philadelphia: Fortress Press, 1972.

Peters, Ted. *God as Trinity: Relationality and Temporality in Divine Life.* Louisville: Westminster John Knox Press, 1993.

Phan, Peter, ed. *The Cambridge Companion to the Trinity.* Cambridge: Cambridge University Press, 2011.

Pieper, Francis. *Christian Dogmatics.* 3 vols. St. Louis: Concordia Publishing House, 1950–53.

Placher, William. *The Domestication of Transcendence.* Louisville: Westminster John Knox Press, 1996.

———. *The Triune God: An Essay in Postliberal Theology.* Louisville: Westminster John Knox Press, 2007.

Pless, John. "Tracking the Trinity in Contemporary Theology." *Concordia Theological Quarterly* 69 no. 2 (2005): 99–118.

Prestige, G. L. *God in Patristic Thought.* London: SPCK, 1964.

Preus, Robert. *The Theology of Post-Reformation Lutheranism.* 2 vols. St. Louis: Concordia Publishing House, 1972.

Rahner, Karl. *The Trinity.* Translated by Joseph Donceel. New York: Crossroad, 1997.

Rowe, C. Kavin. "Biblical Pressure and Trinitarian Hermeneutics." *Pro Ecclesia* 11 no. 3 (2002): 295–312.

———. *Early Narrative Christology: The Lord in the Gospel of Luke.* Berlin: Walter de Gruyter, 2006.

———. "Luke and the Trinity: An Essay in Ecclesial Biblical Theology." *Scottish Journal of Theology* 56 no. 1 (2003): 1–26.

———. "Romans 10:13: What Is the Name of the Lord?" *Horizons in Biblical Theology* 22 (2000): 135–73.

Bibliography

Sasse, Hermann. "Tradition and Confession: A Response to Jaroslav Pelikan." *Lutheran World* 4 no. 1 (June 1957): 76–81.
Scaer, David P. *Baptism*. Confessional Lutheran Dogmatics, vol. 9. St. Louis: Luther Academy, 1999.
_____. *Christology*. Confessional Lutheran Dogmatics, vol. 6. St. Louis: Luther Academy, 1989.
_____. "*Cum Patre et Filio Adoratur*: The Holy Spirit Understood Christologically." *Concordia Theological Quarterly* 61 no. 1/2 (1997): 93–112.
_____. "The Doctrine of the Trinity in Biblical Perspective." *Concordia Theological Quarterly* 67 no. 3/4 (2003): 323–34.
_____. "God as Secondary Fundamental Doctrine in Missouri Synod Theology." *Concordia Theological Quarterly* 75 no. 1/2 (2011): 43–62.
_____. "The Holy Spirit, Sacraments, and Church Rites." *Concordia Theological Quarterly* 70 no. 3/4 (2006): 311–22.
_____. "*Homo Factus Est* as the Revelation of God." *Concordia Theological Quarterly* 65 no. 2 (2001): 111–26.
_____. "The Revelation of Matthew 28:16–20 to the Rest of the Gospel." *Concordia Theological Quarterly* 55 no. 4 (1991): 245–66.
Schlink, Edmund. *Theology of the Lutheran Confessions*. Translated by Paul F. Koehneke and Herbert J. A. Bouman. St. Louis: Concordia Publishing House, 1961.
Schneider, Carolyn. "Luther's Preface to Bugenhagen's Edition of Athanasius." *Lutheran Quarterly* 17 (2003): 226–30.
Seitz, Christopher. "The Trinity in the Old Testament." In *The Oxford Handbook of the Trinity*, edited by Gilles Emery and Matthew Levering, 28–40. Oxford: Oxford University Press, 2011.
Siecienski, A. Edward. *The Filioque: A History of a Doctrinal Controversy*. Oxford: Oxford University Press, 2010.
Soulen, R. Kendall. *The Divine Name(s) and the Holy Trinity: Distinguishing the Voices*. Louisville: Westminster John Knox Press, 2011.
_____. *The God of Israel and Christian Theology*. Minneapolis: Fortress Press, 1996.
_____. "YHWH the Triune God." *Modern Theology* 15 no. 1 (1999): 25–54.
Staniloe, Dumitru. *The Holy Trinity: In the Beginning There Was Love*. Translated by Roland Clark. Brookline, MA: Holy Cross Orthodox Press, 2012.
Stead, Christopher. *Divine Substance*. Oxford: Oxford University Press, 1977.
Steinmetz, David. "The Superiority of Pre-Critical Exegesis." *Theology Today* 37 no. 1 (1980): 27–38.
Thompson, John. *Modern Trinitarian Perspectives*. Oxford: Oxford University Press, 1994.
Wainwright, Arthur. *The Trinity in the New Testament*. London: SPCK, 1962.
Watson, Francis. "Trinity and Community: A Reading of John 17." *International Journal of Systematic Theology* 1 no. 2 (1999): 168–84.
Weinrich, William. "Father, Son, and Holy Spirit Is God: What Is the Point?" *Concordia Theological Quarterly* 75 no. 1/2 (2011): 27–42.
_____. "Patristic Exegesis as Ecclesial and Sacramental." *Concordia Theological Quarterly* 64 no. 1 (2000): 21–38.
_____. "Trinitarian Reality as Christian Truth: Reflections on Greek Patristic Discussion." *Concordia Theological Quarterly* 67 no. 3/4 (2003): 335–46.

White, Graham. *Luther as Nominalist*. Helsinki: Luther-Agricola-Society, 1994.
Wilken, Robert Louis. "*In Dominico Eloquio*: Learning the Lord's Style of Language." *Communio* 24 (1997): 846-66.
_____. *The Spirit of Early Christianity*. New Haven, CT: Yale University Press, 2003.
_____. "Wilken's Response to Hays." *Communio* 25 (1998): 529-31.
Wozniak, Robert, and Giulio Maspero, eds. *Rethinking Trinitarian Theology*. London: T&T Clark, 2012.
Wright, N. T. *The Climax of the Covenant*. Minneapolis: Fortress Press, 1992.
Yeago, David. "The New Testament and Nicene Dogma: A Contribution to the Recovery of Theological Exegesis." *Pro Ecclesia* 3 no. 2 (1994): 152-64.
Young, Frances. *Biblical Exegesis and the Formation of Christian Culture*. Grand Rapids: Baker Academic, 2002.
Ziegler, Roland. "Luther and Calvin on God: Origins of Lutheran and Reformed Differences." *Concordia Theological Quarterly* 75 no. 1/2 (2011): 63-90.
_____. "Natural Knowledge of God and the Trinity." *Concordia Theological Quarterly* 69 no. 2 (2005): 133-58.

SACRED SCRIPTURE INDEX

Genesis	194, 195, 196, 197, 202	Exodus		11:17	222, 234
1	121, 156, 157, 196, 223–24	3	134	14	144
		3:2	145	14:18	135
1:1	135, 158, 196	3:3–6	145	16	144
1:2	221, 223	3:5	151	16:22	221
1:3	222, 234	3:6	145, 151		
1:26	132, 160	3:7	145	Deuteronomy	
1:31	91n6	3:13–14	190	4:24	69n
2	121	3:14	152	5:6–9	134
3:15	138, 328	3:15	153	6:1	8
3:20	91n6	5:1	135	6:4	134, 153, 207, 210
6:3	234	6:7	135	6:5	210
6:5	26	15:18	159	6:7	35n
14	205	16:10	147	6:13–15	134
14:18	205	20:2	8	6:20–21	153
15:6	169n5	20:2–3	124, 134	7:1	135
16	144	20:2–5	134	7:3	135
16:7–11	143	20:5	134	8:3	154
16:10	143	23:20–22	146	8:19	154
16:11	143	24:9–11	150	12:9–10	147
16:13	141, 143	24:10	150	12:11–12	147
17:20	143	24:11	150	32:6	157
18:1	143	24:15–18	148	32:39	190, 190n23, 191
18:1–15	132	33:20	141	32:43	204
18:2	143	33:21–23	36n	32:52	91n6
18:8	143	34:6	135	34:9	129
18:9	144	34:6–7	146, 147n20		
18:10	144	34:14	134	Joshua	
18:13	144	34:29–35	231	5:14	150, 161
18:22–32	144	34:34	231	5:15	151
19:1	144	35:5	144n14	20:12–13	135
19:5	144	40:34–38	148		
19:8	144			Judges	
19:10–11	144	Leviticus		2:13	135
19:21	144	11:44	129	6:22–23	141, 145
19:24	144, 147n20	19	210	6:34	234
19:27	144n16	19:2	220	13:3	145
22	144			13:6	145
22:18	138	Numbers		13:8	145
32:30	141	6:22	221	13:9	145
41:38	234	6:22–27	167	13:10	145
49:10	161	11:4–5	135	13:11	145

Sacred Scripture Index

13:13	145	Job	184	33	157, 224, 326n
13:15	145	9:8	184	33:1	136
13:16	145	9:10–11	185	33:6	156, 157, 157n27,
13:18	145, 161	12:7–10	25		158, 196, 221, 223,
13:20	145	12:10	25, 221		250, 326, 344
13:21	145	15:14	137	33:8–9	157
13:21–22	145	19:25	161	33:13–14	159
13:22	141, 145	26	159	34:1	35n37
14:6	234	28	159	36:9	50, 136
		33:4	157, 221, 223, 250	39:5	79
1 Samuel		38:11	180	45:6	159, 161
8:5–9	135			45:6–7	204
8:7	174	Psalms		45:11	161
10:6	234	1:2	35n	46:1	161
11:6	222	2	159, 205	46:10	35, 51
16:14	221	2:2	138, 161	51	69, 71, 74n48, 136
		2:6	138, 161	51:4	71, 238
2 Samuel		2:6–8	159	51:10	221
7:14	137, 204	2:7	138, 155, 161, 204,	51:11	221, 238
			247, 251, 275	51:12	221, 238
1 Kings		2:11	161	51:13	238
5:1	91n	2:12	159, 161	51:14	238
5:5	147	3:3	161	51:15	238
8:10	148	8	47, 205	53:1	48
8:12	147	8:4–6	204	55:17	35n37
8:16	147	10:16	159	71:22	161
8:27	147, 312	11:6	221	72:11	161
8:29	147	14:1	27, 47, 49	78:22	135
8:56	147	16:8–11	236	81	119
12:28	77	18:2	161	81:10	135
17:21–22	172	18:30	161	85:4	136
		19:1	25	86:11	136
2 Kings		22:19	161	90:1	72
2:9	222	22:27	161	90:2	312
		24:1	30	91:2	161
1 Chronicles		25:4–5	136	92:6	48
16:35	225	27:9	136	96:5	48, 157
17:11–12	137	29:3	158	97:7	161
17:11	138	29:10	159	102:25–27	204
17:13	137	31:1	136	102:27	233
		32:1	136	103:8	135
2 Chronicles		32:1–2	169n5	104	47, 135, 234
24:20	222, 234	32:2	207	104:4	204, 221
		32:5	136	104:24	157
Nehemiah		32:6	316	104:30	234, 316
9:17	135	32:7	161	105	135
		32:11	136	106:47	225

377

Sacred Scripture Index

107:28–31	181	Isaiah	120, 121, 139, 140,	42:4	227		
109:3	251n14		190, 213, 215	42:8	135, 160, 210		
110	138, 201–2, 203,	1:9	207	43:1–14	139		
	205, 206	2	236	43:3	161		
110:1	140, 141, 150, 161,	2:2	137, 236	43:10	119, 190n23, 197		
	175, 201, 204,	4:2	152	43:11	169		
	205, 236	4:14	190n23	43:11–13	191		
110:4	205	5:20	27	43:13	190n23		
111	47	6	199	43:25	136, 190, 190n23,		
115:4–8	353	6:1	140, 141, 159		197		
115:8	19	6:3	132	44:3	297		
115:15	156	6:4	220	44:6	161, 213		
116:11	79	6:5	151, 161	44:6–8	140		
117:1	207	7:9	52, 139	44:24	156, 157, 201		
118:22	152, 161	7:14	138, 159, 176, 226	45	210		
119:41	136	8:14	152	45:15	161, 169		
119:105	238	9:6	145, 146, 161	45:18	140, 190n23, 196		
121	86	9:33	169	45:19	140		
121:2	156, 198	10:22	207	45:21	169		
124:8	156, 198	11:1–2	138, 235	45:21–25	140, 210		
130	137	11:1–20	159	45:23	189		
130:1–4	136	11:2	139, 222	45:24	136		
137:4	35n34	11:4	139	46:4	190n23		
139	159	11:5–9	139	46:9–10	188, 191		
143:2	138	11:10	161	48:12	91, 190, 190n23,		
145:13	159	12:2	139		191, 213		
146:4	221	13:6	139, 174	48:17	161		
146:5	315	13:9	174	49:15	94		
146:10	159	14:32	161	51:5–8	138		
148	159	28:16	152, 161, 169	51:6	137		
148:5	157n26	30:29	161	51:8	137		
150:6	25	35:4	161	51:12	190, 190n23		
		35:4–6	141, 161, 172	52:6	190n23		
Proverbs		35:5	229	52:13	140, 152		
3:19	157	40	179	53	199		
8:27–30	157	40:1–2	138	53:1	207		
14:29	221	40:3	138, 179	53:2	229		
16:18	221	40:5	139	53:2–3	140, 209		
16:19	221	40:7–8	223	53:4–6	172		
17:22	221	40:13	207	53:5–6	140, 173, 209		
17:27	221	40:25	161	53:11	139, 140, 161, 209		
18:14	221	40:26	135	55–56	141, 161		
30:4	161	40:28	135	57:15	140, 159		
		41:4	190, 190n23, 191,	60:19	136		
Ecclesiastes			213	61:1	138, 139, 222, 235,		
1:8	89	42:1	139, 152, 222, 235		256n27		
3:21	221	42:1–3	227	61:1–2	141, 161, 172, 227n		

Sacred Scripture Index

62:1	139	25:17	197n8	11:4	221
63:10	135, 222, 237	26:6	197n8	12:1–2	141
64:6	137	28:24	197n8	13	70n27
64:8	157	29:9	197n8	13:35	70
		30:8	197n8		
Jeremiah	138, 141, 151	30:19	197n8	Hosea	226
1:4–5	157, 196	33:29	197n8	1:7	147n14, 161
1:4–9	151	34:15–16	187	2:16	77
6:14	7	34:23	187	2:28	318
8:11	7	34:23–24	141, 161	3:5	137
9:8	7	36:21–22	197	4:12	221
10:12	157	36:23	197	5:4	221
10:16	201	36:25	197		
17:9	26	36:28	197	Joel	169, 170
23:5	138, 209	37:5	172	1:15	139, 174
23:6	136, 139, 161	37:26	138	2	169
33:14	161	37:26–28	254	2:1	139, 174
33:15	152	37:27–28	138, 198	2:11	139, 174
46:10	139, 174	39:29	139, 141, 235, 236, 318	2:13	135
51:15	157			2:23	139, 235, 236
		43:7	199	2:24–26	139, 236
Lamentations		47	254	2:27	169
3:21–23	136	47:9	254	2:28	139, 141, 169, 235, 236
3:34	38				
5:21	137	Daniel	137, 138	2:28–32	236
		2:44	137	2:32	139, 141, 169, 235, 236
Ezekiel	197, 215	2:45	137, 205		
1:26	150	2:46	160	Obadiah	
1:26–28	148, 199	4:34	159	15	139, 174
3:10	149	4:34–35	135		
3:13	149	5:11	173n	Jonah	76–77
3:14	149	5:23	25	1:5	76
3:16	149	6:23	70	4:2	135
3:22–24	149, 199	7:3–14	150		
8:2	150	7:9	150	Micah	
10:4	149	7:10	159	4	236
10:15	149	7:13	150, 161	5:2	174
10:18–20	149	7:14	137, 159, 161	5:2–5	173
10:19–20	150	8:8	221		
10:20	149	8:13–14	146n17	Zechariah	
10:22	149	9	136	2:6	221
11:24	222, 234	9:7	136	2:10–11	138, 199, 254
14:16	91n6	9:9–11	136	3:2	151
24:9–11	150	9:18	137	3:3–4	152
24:10	150	9:24	137, 141, 161	3:6–9	152
24:11	150	9:26	137, 141, 161	3:8	138
25:11	197n8	10:20	159		

379

Sacred Scripture Index

3:10	152	6:4	227	1:10–11	176
6:12	138	6:6	227, 228	1:15	181
6:13	138	6:9	228	1:22	180
9:9	141, 161	6:14	228	1:23	222
12:5	161	6:18	227	1:24	180, 181
12:9–13:1	151	6:24	164	1:24–25	220, 236
12:10	140, 173, 209, 235, 236	6:26–28	228	1:27	180
		6:32	228	2:6–7	180
13:1	140, 173	7:11	228	2:7	128, 172
13:7	141, 188	9:2–4	229	3:11	181
		10:20	219, 228, 252, 297	3:29	229
Malachi	182	11:3	171	4:39–41	222n7
2:10	157	11:4–6	229	4:40–41	181
3:1	139, 174, 179	11:7	222n	4:41	128, 172, 180
3:2	139	11:27	78n62, 105, 123, 177, 227	5:7	181
3:6	233, 312			6:7	185
3:18	139	12	229	6:30	185
4:1	139, 174	12:18	227	6:31	185
		12:28	228	6:33	185
Wisdom of Solomon		12:29	228	6:34	185
12:13	201	12:31–32	228	6:36	185
		13:55	229	6:37	185
Matthew	121, 175, 176, 177, 225–30	14:27	189n	6:41	185
		14:32	186	6:45	184
1:1	175	15:11	250	6:48	185
1:16	176	15:19	228	6:48–50	184
1:18	222	16:14	174	6:50	186, 189n
1:19	91n6, 226	16:16	175, 228	6:52	185
1:20	176	16:16–23	66	7:34	182
1:20–22	226	16:17	175, 183, 228	8:27	174
1:21	176	17:5	227	8:28	174
1:23	176, 226, 227	22:42	175	8:29	175, 181
2:1	173n	22:42–45	161, 202	8:32–33	181
2:2	173	22:43	175, 183, 228	12:35–37	202
2:6	174	22:44	201n17	12:36	201n17
2:15	226	22:46	175	13:6	189n
3:11	226	25:21	53	14:61–62	190n21
3:15	226	26:31	188	14:62	201n17
3:16	222, 228, 256n27	26:41	222	14:67	229
3:16–17	176	26:64	201n17	15:39	181
3:17	226	26:65	228	16:19	201n17
4:1	222, 227, 228, 256n27	28:19	132, 225, 299		
		28:20	219, 227, 228	Luke	175
4:4	250			1:3	175, 286
5:3	222	Mark	121, 176, 180–81, 184	1:6	176
5:43–45	227	1:1	175	1:9	176
6:1	227	1:2–3	179	1:11	176

Sacred Scripture Index

1:15	235	John	77–80, 129, 176,	5:21–23	177
1:16	176		177, 180, 186–91,	5:23	177, 179, 209
1:18	160, 286		193–201, 223	5:26	187, 233, 324
1:32	176, 253	1:1	175, 194	5:37	177
1:32–33	159	1:2	195	5:39	179
1:35	140, 176, 220,	1:3	196, 201, 340	5:39–40	123, 184
	236, 341	1:4	104n68	5:43	142, 257
1:38	176	1:9	86	5:46	xi, 123, 184
1:41–42	235	1:12	197	6:1–15	186
1:41–43	176	1:12–13	225, 262	6:16–21	186
1:43	235	1:12–14	226	6:20	188, 213
1:46–47	225	1:13	170, 183, 199	6:35	187
1:47	222	1:14	142, 175, 198, 199,	6:37	177
1:49	140		200, 247, 275,	6:40	177
1:67–69	235		306, 344	6:44	177
2:12	179	1:18	142, 200, 247,	6:48	187
2:25–35	174		253, 275	6:63	223, 233, 322
3:22	176, 343	1:23	179	6:65	177
4:14	222, 256n27	1:33–34	176	6:68–69	184
4:16–19	227	1:41	171	6:69	220, 236
4:18	139, 222	1:45	171	7	188, 255
4:21	227	1:46	229	7:26	174
4:22	229	2:1–11	186	7:27	174
5:20–24	172	2:19	234	7:37–38	254
7:22	172	2:21	234	7:39	254
7:27	179	3	222n	7:40–43	174
7:49	128, 172	3:4–5	183	8	78, 188
10:22	78n62, 177	3:5	86, 197, 199	8:12	86, 187
11:23	183	3:6–8	222n	8:13	189
16:31	182	3:8	222, 262, 270	8:14–19	189
18:31–34	66	3:16	91n6, 129, 247,	8:18	177
18:34	183		275, 318	8:19	123
20:41–44	202	3:16–18	236	8:24	188, 191, 197
20:42–43	201n17	3:18	247, 275	8:25	188
21:8	189n	3:19	86	8:26	257
22:69	201n17	4:2–3	223	8:28	140, 188, 197
24:13–35	181–84	4:23	178, 224	8:42	189, 251
24:18–21	171	4:23–24	224	8:51	189
24:25	182	4:24	220	8:52	104n68
24:25–27	xi, 123 184	4:25	171	8:53	189
24:27	182	4:26	188, 191	8:54–56	189
24:37	222	4:46–54	186	8:55	123
24:39	222	5:1–15	186	8:56	189
24:44–45	xi	5:18	200	8:56–59	124, 142
24:44–46	181	5:19	177, 233, 253, 322,	8:58	189, 191, 197
24:44–47	123		333	9	248
		5:21	172, 187, 322	9:1–41	186

381

Sacred Scripture Index

10:3	187	15:26	178, 200, 224,	3:14	220, 235, 236
10:7	187		224n10, 238, 247,	3:15	234
10:9	187		247n, 248, 249,	3:18	235
10:11	187		250, 251, 252, 255,	3:21	235
10:14	187		256, 258, 276	3:22	235
10:17–18	234	16:2–3	87, 201	3:24	235
10:27–28	129, 187	16:4	188, 191	3:26–27	235
10:28	187	16:7	183, 249	4:8	237
10:30	187, 200, 284	16:8	178, 224	4:12	236, 237
10:32	187	16:8–14	344	5:2	232
10:33	187, 200	16:12–13	109	5:3	232
10:37–38	187, 191	16:12–15	89	5:4	232
10:38	284	16:13	224n10	5:31	201n17
11:1–44	186	16:13–14	253, 333	6:3	237
11:25	104n68, 187, 191	16:13–15	322	6:5	237
11:27	175, 228	16:14	257, 258	6:8	237
11:43	172	16:14–15	233, 252, 258, 297	6:11	237
12:21	184	16:15	252	7:51	229
12:23	199	16:28	199, 200, 248, 251	7:55	237
12:27	199	17:1	199	7:55–56	201n17
12:28	142	17:3	342	10:26	160
12:32	140	17:4	257	10:36	201
12:41	124, 140, 142, 199	17:5	142, 199	13:52	237
12:45	87, 177	17:11	220	16:7	252
12:49–50	184	18	190	17:23	8
13:19	188, 191	18:4	189	17:25	233
13:31–32	199	18:5	189, 197	17:28	91n6, 104n68
14:6	178, 187, 224	19:34–37	189	20:10	172
14:6–7	123, 177	19:37	140, 209	20:28	241
14:8–9	219	20:21–23	241	28:23	182
14:8–11	229	20:22	222, 252	28:25	235
14:9	87, 142, 177, 200	20:31	175, 228		
14:9–11	142			Romans	77, 168
14:10	200, 278	Acts	235	1	25, 33, 54, 56, 76,
14:17	224n	2	137		80, 85
14:21	129, 318	2:1–4	235	1:1	164, 165
14:24	184	2:2	222n	1:1–4	232
14:25–26	249	2:17–21	236	1:2	179
14:26	178, 224, 238, 257	2:24	234	1:2–3	165
14:27	7	2:25–28	236	1:4	129, 165, 166, 220
14:28	275, 279	2:29	236	1:7	165, 317
14:29	188, 191	2:32	234	1:18	24, 25
15:1	187	2:33	140, 236, 239	1:18–3:20	23
15:5	187	2:33–35	201n17	1:19	24, 25
15:13	178, 224	2:34	236	1:19–20	22
15:15	178, 224	2:38	236	1:19–21	85
15:23	177, 219	2:41	236	1:19–23	77

Sacred Scripture Index

1:20	24, 25, 27, 91	9:33	169	7:13	222
1:21	24, 75, 81, 84	10	169, 170	7:15	7
1:22	24	10:2	87, 201	8	212n
1:23	24, 83	10:9	169, 234	8–9	212
1:24–32	24, 27	10:9–13	236	8:4	211
1:25	25, 53	10:11	169	8:5	211
1:26	83	10:12–13	170	8:6	210–12, 132, 157n27, 201, 211
1:28	85	10:16	207		
1:32	85	10:17	173n, 238	8:7–13	211
2	25, 26, 80	11:34	207	9	212
2:15	22, 78	11:36	132, 331, 333, 338, 346	9:19	212
3:20	69			10:1–10	124, 142
3:26	91	12:11	222	10:10	144
3:28	7	14:10–11	189	10:26	169n4
4	169n5	14:11	169n4	12:1–31	241
4:3	169n5	14:23	26	12:3	89, 165, 209, 219, 235
4:8	169n5, 207	15:11	207		
4:17	233	15:12	227	12:4–6	232n21, 317
4:23–24	239	15:16	165	12:6	286
4:24	234	16:27	129, 166	12:11	286
4:25	72n37			13:9	108, 356
5	167	**1 Corinthians**		14:3	229
5:1	7, 167	1:1	165	15	179
5:5	108, 129, 166, 167, 237, 318	1:2	165, 166	15:1–4	121n21
		1:3	165	15:3–5	344
6–8	170	1:9	318	15:25	201n17
6:3	240	1:18	92	15:57	330
6:4	234, 240	1:18–2:16	133	16:24	166
7:7	69	1:19	92		
8	219	1:23–24	170	**2 Corinthians**	
8:4	239	1:24	92, 129, 341	1:1	165
8:7	83	1:30	92, 129, 165, 220, 330	1:2	165
8:9	222, 253, 278, 297	1:31	169n4	1:22	241
8:9–11	240	2:2	170	2:12	278
8:11	129	2:4–5	170, 239	2:17	231
8:12–17	240	2:8	92, 170, 173n	3:1–2	231
8:14	239	2:9	107	3:3	231
8:14–17	226	2:10	105n73, 183	3:3–9	231
8:15–17	344	2:10–11	105, 108	3:6	223, 232, 233
8:16	197, 222	2:11	177, 235	3:10	231
8:16–17	225, 262	2:11–12	219	3:12–18	231
8:17	262	2:11–14	124	3:13	231
8:26	219	2:12	105n73, 278	3:14	231
8:34	201	2:14	173n, 183	3:16	183, 231
8:39	108	2:16	169n4	3:17	231, 232
9:28	207	6:11	129, 165, 170, 220, 238, 240	3:17–18	232, 237
9:29	207			3:18	232

Sacred Scripture Index

4:2	231	1:3–13	232	1:2	165
4:3–4	183	1:4	194	1:15	142
4:4	27, 86	1:7	170	1:15–16	344
4:5–6	232	1:14	241	1:16	201
4:6	142	1:20	201n17, 234	1:16–17	233
4:14	234	1:20–21	202	1:17	201, 340
5:5	241	1:22	201	2:9	24n3
5:14–15	232	2:2	223	2:12–15	170
6:14–15	86	2:6	201n17	3:1	201n17
8:11	234	2:8–9	170		
10:17	169n4	2:13–16	170	1 Thessalonians	
11:4–5	231	2:18	162, 171, 224, 241	1:5	239
11:6	231	2:18–22	241	1:6	239
11:22	231	3:18	219, 238	5:3	7
12:2–4	109	3:19	108	5:9–13	171
12:9	92	4:4–6	232	5:23	7
13:14	128, 132, 166, 232,	4:6	323		
	317, 318	4:10	202	2 Thessalonians	
		4:17	27	1:2	165
Galatians	168	4:18	27	2:8	222
1:1	234	4:23	222	3:16	7, 166
1:3	165	4:29	250	3:18	166
1:4	166	4:30	222, 237		
2:15–21	239	4:32	170, 171	1 Timothy	
2:19–20	170	5:21	171	1:1	165
3:2	239	5:25–27	241	1:10	168
3:6	239	5:26	170	2:6	344
3:8–9	239			4:6	238
3:13	344	Philippians		4:10	66
3:14	236, 239	1:2	165	4:13	179
3:26	239	1:19	252, 297	6:3	168
3:27	239	2	140, 180	6:13	129, 233
3:29	239	2:1	209	6:16	50
4:4–5	341	2:5–7	341		
4:4–6	232n21	2:5–11	207–10	2 Timothy	
4:6	170, 252, 297	2:6	208	1:2	165
4:9	219	2:7	208	1:7	222
5	219	2:8	208	1:10	165
5:13	21	2:9	208	2:19	169n4
5:17	83	2:10	189, 209	3:2	7
5:19–20	83	2:10–11	208	3:16	viii
5:22	7, 129, 318	2:11	166, 209, 219	4:3	168
5:25	170	3:21	201		
		4:7	105	Titus	169
Ephesians				1:1	164
1:2	165	Colossians		1:2–3	165
1:3–4	170	1:1	165	1:3	165

384

1:3–4	168	7:5	250	3:4	222	
1:4	165	7:14	205n	3:22	201n17	
1:9	168	7:22	205n	4:14	235	
1:13	168	7:25	205	5:14	7	
1:15–16	168	7:28	205n			
2:1	168, 169	8:1	201n17	2 Peter		
2:10	168, 169	9	206	1:2	167	
2:13–14	168	9:11	205, 205n	1:20–21	89	
3:4–6	225	9:12	205	1:21	7n15, 235, 238	
3:4–7	168, 226, 232n21, 237	9:14	205n, 206			
		9:24	205, 205n	1 John		
3:4–8	254	9:26	206	1:1	195, 196	
3:5	240	9:28	205n	1:1–3	172	
3:5–6	183	10:10	205n	1:3	318	
3:5–7	86	10:10–14	165	1:7	318	
		10:12	206	2:23	177	
Hebrews 202–6		10:12–13	201n17	3:1	7	
1:1–2	89	10:15	206	3:2–3	152	
1:2	71, 205n30, 344	10:15–18	235	3:16	7, 108	
1:3	199, 201n17, 317	10:19	205n	4:6	223	
1:5	205n, 247, 275	10:29	205n, 206, 318	5:7	299n56	
1:7	39, 221	10:32	86	5:13	236	
1:8–9	204	11:6	48, 54			
1:10–12	204	11:26	205n	2 John		
1:13	201n17, 204	11:30	203	1:3	167, 253	
2	206	12:2	201n17, 205n	9	123, 177, 219	
2:3	205n	12:24	205n			
2:3–4	206	13:8	205n	Jude		
2:6–8	204, 205	13:12	205n	5	124, 142	
2:7	204	13:20	188, 205n	5–7	144	
2:9	204, 205n, 206	13:21	205n			
2:10	204, 205			Revelation	190, 212–16	
2:14	204	James		1:7	140, 189, 209	
3:1	205n	1:1	164	1:8	212	
3:6	205n	1:17	233	1:10	212	
3:7	206	3:10	250n	1:17–19	213	
4:2	203			3:21	201n17	
4:14	204, 205n	1 Peter		4:2	212	
4:16	205	1:2	220	4:8	215	
5:5	205, 205n	1:10–12	89, 235	4:11	215	
5:5–6	205	1:11	252	5:5	213, 215	
6:1	205n	1:11–12	238	5:8	215	
6:4	86, 206	1:12	89, 183	5:12	215	
6:6	205n	1:15–16	220	5:13	216	
6:20	205n	1:16	129	5:13–14	140	
7:1–2	205	2:2	238	5:14	216	
7:3	205, 205n	2:9	86	7:2–3	159	

7:15	198	21:3	198	22:3	215, 216
7:17	216	21:3–4	214	22:7	213, 214
8:3	160	21:6	212, 214	22:8–9	160
11:15	159, 216	21:8	214	22:12	213, 214
12:10	159	21:10	212	22:13	213
15:1	159	21:22	214	22:16	213
16:1	159	21:23	214	22:17	215
17:3	212	22	254–56	22:20	214, 215
19:9–10	160	22:1	214, 297n45		
20:12–13	141	22:1–2	254		

LUTHERAN CONFESSIONS INDEX

Book of Concord
  ix, 1, 62, 65, 80–86, 125, 245, 245n

Ecumenical Creeds
  62, 119n14

Apostles' Creed
  62, 63, 63n, 65, 81, 82, 336, 338, 339, 342, 343, 345

Nicene Creed
  xiv, 62, 63, 126, 218, 232, 245–48, 259, 262, 268, 276, 301, 302, 303, 325, 328

Athanasian Creed
  xiv, 62, 63, 63n, 245n2, 246, 248, 262, 269n10, 272, 286n81, 287, 290, 295, 295n31, 299

Augsburg Confession 62
AC I 312
AC I.1–3 62n1
AC I.2 63n5, 355
AC I.3–4 288n92
AC V 241n29
AC XVIII 241n29

Apology of the Augsburg Confession
Ap. II.8 83n95
Ap. II.14 83n95
Ap. II.17–18 83n96

Ap. II.23 83n96
Ap. IV.184 26n6
Ap. IV.203–5 75n53
Ap. IV.351 83n96
Ap. XV.42 84n99, 194n1, 364n30

Smalcald Articles
SA I.2   245n2
SA I.4   xin2, 64n9
SA III.i.3 79n74
SA III.viii.10 238n26

Small Catechism 111
Creed
  para. 2 71n33
Lord's Prayer
  para. 4 72n39
Daily Prayers
  para. 1 5
  para. 4 5

Large Catechism 44
LC I.2–3 80n80
LC I.17 81n81
LC I.18–23 81n83
LC I.21 81n81
LC I.22–23 82n88
LC II.7 311n3, 336n
LC II.9 81n83
LC II.35–36 219n3
LC II.36 311n4, 343n24
LC II.38 65n16
LC II.63 81n86
LC II.63–69 81n84
LC II.65 66n17, 81n86
LC II.67 82n87
LC II.67–69 82n91

LC IV.10 230n19
LC IV.37 230
LC IV.41 230
LC IV.43 230
LC IV.44 230
LC IV.46 230
LC IV.65 230, 240n27
LC IV.71–76 240n28
LC IV.84 230

Formula of Concord
  ix, 62, 84

Formula of Concord Epitome
Ep. II.4 241n31
Ep. II.19 241n30

Formula of Concord Solid Declaration
SD II.5 84n102
SD II.7 85n103–5
SD II.9 81n83, 82n92, 85n106
SD II.10 85n107
SD II.15–16 86n108
SD II.16 83n96
SD II.17 83n94
SD V.22 84n98
SD VII.2–11 267
SD VIII.73 245n2
SD XI.76 238n25
SD XII.36–38 62n2

Formula of Concord Rule and Norm
SD RN.10 ix

NAME AND SUBJECT INDEX

Abelard 54
Abraham 1, 124, 134, 135, 138, 142–45, 150–53, 175, 178, 188, 189, 191, 197, 235, 239, 250, 314
Aetius 10
Agnosticism 28, 93n14
Ambrose of Milan 144n14, 182n16, 220n4, 230n18, 246, 254–55, 284n73, 288
Analogy 37, 90–92, 109, 317n20, 363
   among Lutheran dogmaticians 94n16
   Thomas Aquinas 94–197
   John Duns Scotus 97–102
Anatolios, Khaled 12n33, 261n47, 364n26
Anselm of Canterbury 43, 45, 46, 48–53, 61, 98, 101, 102n55, 291–93, 297, 300n62
Appropriation, doctrine of 311, 336–49
Aquinas. *See* Thomas Aquinas
Arians 9, 34, 62
Aristotle 30, 43, 92n11, 94n16, 98, 283n69, 292, 293, 294
Arius 10, 196, 200, 284n73
Asterius the Sophist 195, 272
Athanasius of Alexandria xi, 8n18, 9n22, 23, 29n15, 32–34, 40, 50, 60, 65, 111, 126n36, 127, 157n27, 165, 178n12, 223n8, 224, 225n12, 234n23, 257, 258, 273, 275, 279, 284, 316–19, 322–23
Atonement 29, 75n53, 152, 160, 198, 206
Augustine of Hippo 10n24, 16n49, 27, 32, 36n41, 53, 79n74, 82n87, 103, 103n62, 104n65, 106, 116–17, 120, 158n28, 200, 219, 220n4, 223n8, 246, 253, 256, 259–61, 268n6, 269–70, 279–82, 283, 286n84, 287, 288, 290, 291n10, 293n22, 295n30, 301n63, 302–5, 310, 315, 316, 323–26, 327, 328, 329n70, 332n83, 337n2, 339–42, 355–56, 363
Ayres, Lewis 256n28, 282n62, 324n53, 364n26, 364n27

Baier, John William 289n1, 296n40, 297n44, 313, 322n44
Baptism 5–6, 44n11, 60, 63, 83n96, 85–86, 90n3, 106, 111, 112, 120n18, 126, 168, 170, 176, 182, 183, 197, 199, 220, 222, 233, 237, 239–41, 243, 244, 254, 256n27, 262, 268, 287, 297, 320, 321, 339, 364
   baptism of Christ 339–43, 347
   baptismal formula 225–30, 299n56
Barnes, Michel René 363
Barth, Karl 359–60
Basil of Caesarea 284n72, 285, 315
Bauckham, Richard 129n40, 130n43, 132n2, 134, 140n11, 155, 156, 159, 160, 169n4, 186n19, 190, 191n24, 201n17, 202n18, 203n20, 204, 207n24, 208n31, 211, 214n36, 216n38
Bavinck, Herman 332n83
Bayer, Oswald 70, 76n56
Beeley, Christopher 38n53, 107, 183n17
Behr, John 30n17, 261, 277n34
Blasphemy 151, 164, 187, 190n21, 200, 228, 229, 230, 259, 306n92
Boethius 292, 293, 294, 295, 296
Bonaventure 70, 98n33, 290, 291
Brown, Raymond 120, 129–30, 195n5, 197n9, 200n11, 224n10
Brunner, Emil 115n2, 241n32, 332n83
Buckley, Michael 14n41, 18, 56
Bugenhagen, Johann xin3, 305, 306n92
Burrell, David 104n69

Calov, Abraham xii–xiv, 7n15, 8, 29n16, 54n44, 93n13, 94n16, 200n12, 229n17, 255n53, 255n24, 257, 269n7, 289, 296n40, 297–300, 313n9, 322, 332, 356n67
Calvin, John 147n20, 267n1
Capes, David 169n4
Charlemagne 246

Name and Subject Index

Chemnitz, Martin 7n15, 26n5, 45, 46, 48, 63, 116–17, 127n38, 144n14, 173n7, 218n1, 223n8, 225n12, 288n94, 314n10, 328, 330–32, 339n9, 343n25, 345–47, 349–50, 352, 267n3, 279n45, 285n75, 287n90, 288n94
Childs, Brevard 133
Chytraeus, David 144n14, 299n55
Cochlaeus, Johann 127
Congar, Yves 256n26, 359
Consubstantial 126, 201, 225, 233, 242, 258, 268, 282, 284, 297n45, 299n56, 306, 345
Councils
   Chalcedon 201
   Constantinople 7, 32, 34, 40, 126, 201, 218, 283
   Ephesus 201
   Lateran IV 91n5, 289–90, 295n30, 301–4
   Nicaea 7, 32, 40, 62, 126, 127, 201, 282–84
Cross, Richard 98, 101, 103n59
Cullmann, Oscar 128
Cyril of Jerusalem 36n41

Daley, Brian E. 120, 121n19, 245n3, 252n16, 252n17, 261n46, 273n16, 287n89, 364n27
Descartes, René 13–21, 28, 37, 50, 51, 111
Didymus the Blind 221n6, 224n12, 225, 232n22, 317–19, 323
Divine persons
   correlative working 158, 163, 165, 168, 177, 211–12
   distinguishing marks 272–77, 286, 292, 321–22, 331, 344
   mode of existence 257, 259, 276, 277, 282, 296, 327, 333
   order of divine persons 248–49, 253, 260, 261, 277, 286, 296n37, 297–300, 311, 321, 325, 328, 330–34, 346, 347, 348
   perichoresis 278
   personal properties 268n5, 277, 278, 285, 287, 291–94, 296, 321–22
   relations of opposition 277, 290–300, 322

Doxology xiv, 5, 90n3, 165, 166, 232, 321, 355, 364
Dumont, Stephen 98n33, 102

Eck, Johann 127
Enlightenment xii, 11, 14n41, 20
Epicureans 30, 31, 78
Epiphanius 258–59, 339n9
Epistemology 13, 44, 49
Epistle to Diognetus 28–29
Essentia 268n6, 283, 289–90, 300–306
   See also substantia
Eunomius of Cyzicus 10, 34, 97, 105, 109, 110, 261, 272, 273, 296, 361
Evangelical Lutheran Hymn-Book (ELHB) xin3, 108, 251
Evangelical Lutheran Hymnary (ELH) 108, 251

Fagerberg, Holsten 63n5, 82
Father
   as Creator 135, 139–40, 155–59, 316, 323, 336
   glorified through the Son 8, 154, 162, 166, 177, 212, 219, 224
   monarchy of Father 259–61, 274, 298, 299n55, 299n56, 322, 327
   unbegotten 34, 199, 246, 247, 248, 259, 272–81, 293n22, 295–96, 308, 321, 347
   See also Eunomius of Cyzicus
Feuerbach, Ludwig 18, 19, 37
Filioque 218, 244–63, 289, 291n10, 294n28, 296n40, 297, 300
Fossum, Jarl 144n15, 145n16
Friedman, Russell 290n4, 290n6, 290n7, 291n9, 291n10, 293n23
Fulgentius of Ruspe 246, 278, 347n38

Gerhard, Johann xii, 4n4, 8n19, 26n5, 26n7, 28n12, 29n16, 54n44, 54n46, 108, 119–20, 127n37, 127n38, 132n1, 133, 144n14, 147n20, 173n7, 200, 220n4, 253n18, 255n23, 255n24, 260n44, 271, 289, 290n2, 290n3, 291, 293n22, 294n24, 294n26, 295–97, 299, 312–13, 322, 331n81, 332, 339, 345, 347–49, 350–52, 354n60, 356

389

Name and Subject Index

Gerhardt, Paul 108, 251
Gieschen, Charles 123n31, 141, 143n13, 146, 147n21, 151n22, 197
Gilson, Etienne 49n25, 57, 58
Gnostics 9, 14n40, 361
Gnosticism 9, 93
God
   attributes of 56, 65, 72, 73, 90, 91, 93n12, 93n14, 94n15, 94n16, 96, 108n86, 109n89, 219, 291n10, 310, 311, 312–15, 320, 322, 330, 334, 336–37, 345, 347, 349–57, 360
   divine incomprehensibility 36, 38, 97, 107, 108n86, 269–70, 285–86
   divine infinity 15, 16, 51n33, 55, 91, 100–101, 106–7, 108n86, 109, 269, 287, 312, 356
   ethics xii, 5, 19, 24, 33, 43, 90, 210, 211, 231, 364
   proofs, a posteriori 23, 43, 54, 98
   proofs, a priori 23, 43, 54, 98, 108
   proofs for existence of 14–20, 23, 29n15, 45–58, 67–68, 349, 350
   simplicity 56, 291n10, 311–12, 314–15, 316, 319, 335, 337, 355–59
   See also language for God
Gospels 121n21, 163, 164, 171–92, 202, 216, 218
Graebner, August 24n3, 27
Gregory of Nazianzus 8n17, 23, 32, 34–40, 48, 53, 60, 65, 76n55, 106–10, 111, 126n36, 178n12, 183n17, 218n1, 223n8, 224n11, 240n28, 251, 269, 273n16, 273n19, 275, 276n29, 278, 279, 280n55, 286–87, 295n30, 321n42
Gregory of Nyssa 5–6, 20, 66, 106, 119, 243, 245n1, 247n9, 251, 261, 263, 267, 269, 276, 277, 278, 285–86, 298, 319, 320–21, 323, 363, 364

Hafenreffer, Matthias 4n1, 144n14
Hanson, R. P. C. 10n25, 283n66
Hart, David Bentley 103, 104n64, 245n1
Hays, Richard 119n14, 121n20, 122n23, 123n26, 184n18, 231n20
Hegel, G. W. F. 11, 12, 13, 14n40, 20
Hellenization of Christianity 10, 125–28

Hengel, Martin 201n17
Hilary of Poitiers 31–32, 116, 126n36, 144n14, 195, 246, 252, 279n45, 285n74, 303, 304, 305, 329
Hoenecke, Adolf 289n1
Hollaz, David 93n13, 94n16, 255n23, 255n24, 334n91, 343n25
Holy Spirit
   as Creator 156–59, 316, 323, 336
   as God 230–34
   blasphemy against 228–30
   name of 220–25
   work of 234–41
   See also YHWH
Homoousios 126, 127, 233, 246, 282, 283, 284, 285, 299, 322
   See also consubstantial
Hunnius, Aegidius 144n14, 223
Hurtado, Larry 134, 166n1, 207n27
Hutter, Leonard 290n3, 346n37, 351n53
Hypostasis 7, 221, 261, 265, 283–87, 298, 300, 307
   See also divine persons

Irenaeus of Lyon 63n4, 91n9, 156, 223n8, 354

Jenson, Robert 8–9, 11n26, 115n1, 118n12, 121n22, 122n25, 128n39, 143n13, 241n32, 241n33, 242n35, 360, 361, 363n24
Jesus
   baptism 120n18, 226, 227, 339–42, 347
   cross 18, 40, 62, 64, 66, 67, 69, 70–71, 111, 124, 170, 180, 181, 188, 193, 199, 206–10, 212, 217, 229, 254, 328, 353–55
   ascension 235, 244, 354
   See also Son
John Duns Scotus 1, 65, 84n100, 85, 89n1, 92, 93n12, 94, 97–105, 107, 110, 111, 361
John of Damascus 45–48, 61, 276, 279, 280n54
Juel, Donald 115n1, 241n32, 242n34
Justification 4, 62, 63, 67, 70, 72, 76, 82, 90n4, 161, 167, 210, 240, 284, 285, 354
Justin Martyr 1, 28–32, 40

Kant, Immanuel 11–15, 17n51, 19, 20, 48
Kasper, Walter 19n59
Kelly, J. N. D. 245n3, 246n5, 246n6, 252n17, 283n66
Kolb, Robert 87n111, 270n11

Laetsch, Theodore 138n9, 139n10, 236n24
Language for God 7–8, 10, 20, 21, 71, 89, 94–105, 162, 244, 263, 272, 280, 285, 292–93, 298, 301, 303, 307–8, 314, 325, 327, 337, 350–53, 362
  apophatic terms 37, 89
  limitations of our language 1, 35–38, 44, 106, 107, 194, 267–70, 287–88, 312
  substantive and relative predication 176, 220–21, 282, 299, 301–2, 304–7, 313, 342–44, 351
  univocal, equivocal, and analogical predication 92–94, 99–100
Lash, Nicholas 89, 90n2
Law and gospel 63, 78, 81–84, 123, 355
Leibnitz, Gottfried 14n41, 18, 19n62, 20n63
Leo the Great 344
Lessing, Gotthold xiii–xiv
Liturgy xiv, 3, 62, 90n3, 111–12, 118, 122, 126, 154, 182n16, 245, 246, 268, 269, 272, 282, 308, 310, 320, 321
Locke, John 20
Lohse, Bernard 43n6, 65, 76n54, 80n78, 83n93
Lonergan, Bernard 245n3, 253n20, 255n24, 279n45, 302n67
Lord's Supper 5, 70n25, 183, 229, 230, 243, 267n1, 332n83
Louth, Andrew 46n14
Lully, Raymond 54
Luther, Martin xi, 1, 4n1, 5, 6, 7, 28, 40, 43, 44, 45, 60, 61, 63, 65, 67–82, 85, 86, 90–92, 104n68, 110–11, 116, 117n7, 123–24, 127, 132n1, 137, 144n14, 147n20, 167n2, 173n7, 179, 182, 194–96, 199, 212n35, 230, 238, 240, 243, 245n2, 252n15, 260, 267n1, 269–70, 282, 284n74, 288, 289, 290, 298, 300–309, 310, 311, 323, 325–27, 334, 336, 339, 341–45, 347, 348, 354, 356, 357

MacDonald, Nathan 133n2, 167n2
McInerny, Ralph 57n59, 58n64, 97n31
Marion, Jean-Luc 49, 50, 51, 104n70
Marshall, Bruce 12n31, 13n36, 94n17, 95–97, 257n29, 294n28, 297n46, 300, 301n63, 302n66, 303n73, 311n2, 359–60, 361
Martin, Ralph 207n24
Melanchthon, Philipp 29n14, 45, 46, 48, 146n17, 223n8, 268n5, 279n45, 328–30, 332n83, 347
Modalism 3, 12
  See also Sabellianism
Moltmann, Jürgen 360, 362
Monotheism 132–34, 155–57, 192, 196, 210, 211
Mueller, John Theodore 93n12, 94n15, 344n25

Natural knowledge of God
  for Book of Concord 80–86
  for the Fathers 28–40, 44, 46, 48
  for John Duns Scotus 97–102
  for Martin Luther 74–80, 173n7
  for Thomas Aquinas 53–58
  Scripture's teaching of 22–28
  use of xiv, 1, 60, 64, 71, 87, 89, 90, 91, 313, 314, 349, 350, 354
Natural theology xii, 27, 87, 116
Neo-Platonism 9
Nigrinus, Georg 255
Nominalists 43–45, 58, 110

Oberman, Heiko 43n5, 59n68, 60, 110n92
Opera ad extra 177, 310–35, 346
  as Augustine's rule 310–11, 316, 323, 326, 336, 345
  Lutheran addendum 328–35, 345
Ousia 7, 126, 265, 268, 282–85, 287

Perichoresis 278
Peter Lombard 70, 301–5, 307, 329, 338n7
Philo of Alexandria 14n40

Name and Subject Index

Photinus of Sirmium 196
Pieper, Francis 26n5, 54n46, 75n53, 91n6, 108n86, 109n89, 194n3, 268, 268n5, 276n29, 287n90, 288n93, 289n1, 313, 314, 331n77, 344n26
Placher, William 13n39, 14n41
Plato 8, 30, 43, 54
Platonism 32, 129, 270
Pneumatomachians 223, 267
Preus, Robert 22n1, 26n5, 63, 94n16, 308n99, 312n5, 349, 350, 351, 352, 356n73

Quenstedt, Johann Andreas xii, 7n15, 54n46, 84n101, 93n13, 94n16, 252n15, 255n23, 255n24, 260n44, 293n22, 296n40, 299n56, 313, 328, 332–34, 351–52, 356–57

Rahner, Karl 4, 359, 360, 362n19
Reformation xii, 51n33, 63n5, 68, 70, 75, 110, 118, 127, 221, 223, 247, 249, 251, 269, 277n33, 279, 289–309, 361
Rowe, C. Kavin 170n6, 176n9, 231n20

Sabellianism 12n29, 158, 271, 272, 293
Sasse, Hermann xi, 56n58, 64
Satan 74n48, 151, 152, 181, 232, 250
Scaer, David 67, 177, 226, 262, 354, 355n62
Schleiermacher, Friedrich 11–13, 20, 129, 359
Schlink, Edmund ix, 64n7, 82n90, 83n97
Scholasticism 42, 45n13, 64, 69, 70, 73, 90n4, 304n82
Seitz, Christopher 133–34
Sin 4, 23, 27, 104n68, 129, 136, 137, 140, 146, 152, 155, 170, 173, 178, 181, 182, 183n, 206, 224, 228, 229, 237, 238, 240, 244, 284, 253, 357
and knowledge of God 67–73, 78–80, 83
original 79, 83, 84
problem of 33, 84–86, 90n4
Social trinitarianism 362–63
Socrates 21, 30

Son
as Creator 151, 156–59, 163, 196, 211–12, 271, 273, 316, 323, 336, 344, 345–48
exaltation 140, 155, 189, 203, 208–10
giver of Holy Spirit 247, 249, 250, 252, 253, 257, 258, 278
humiliation 140, 204, 205, 208–10
incarnation xin2, 23, 40, 46, 59, 60, 64n9, 67, 87, 123, 140, 203, 205, 208, 209, 226, 329n70, 354
only-begotten 34, 154, 159, 199, 239, 247–48, 251, 253, 260, 261, 268n5, 272, 275–76, 279, 286, 315, 321
Old Testament appearances 141–52
Old Testament prophecy 137–41
reveals the Father 29, 34, 66, 76, 86, 88, 89, 105, 162, 177–78, 189, 191, 193, 201, 216–17, 224, 226, 228, 229, 230, 233, 238, 241, 257, 271, 314, 354
See also YHWH
Stoeckhardt, George 26n6
Stoicism 30–31, 111
Subordinationism 3
Substantia 71n32, 73n41, 268n6, 283, 292n16, 304, 331n79

Tertullian 1, 28–32, 40, 57, 64, 111
The Lutheran Hymnal (TLH) 40, 93, 137, 215n37, 251
Thomas Aquinas 1, 6n12, 32, 43, 44, 45, 48, 53–61, 64, 67, 70, 80, 83, 84n100, 92, 93n13, 94–97, 98, 100, 103–4, 107, 111, 200n14, 251, 272n15, 279n45, 290–96, 299–300, 302n71, 303, 308, 338, 348, 357n75
Trinity
and Christology xi, 23, 60, 66, 70, 87, 124, 162, 166, 191, 193, 207, 209, 210, 216, 220, 227, 239, 360
de deo uno and *de deo trino* 54, 312
essentia generet essentiam 300–308
marginalization of xii, 11–14, 115
relation to Doctrine of God 44, 312–14, 349–52
See also divine persons
Tritheism 3, 288, 362

Unissima 298, 310, 320, 334, 356

Valentinus 14n40

Wainwright, Arthur 207n24
Wainwright, Elaine 117–18
Watson, Francis 119, 129
Weinrich, William 103, 177n10
White, Graham 304n82
Wilken, Robert Louis 10n23, 122, 123n26, 128n39
William of Ockham 43, 44, 45n13, 58–60, 84n100, 110, 304n82
Witherington, Ben 118
Word and sacrament 44, 62, 65, 85, 219, 227, 229, 238, 241, 242, 262, 270, 346, 347, 353, 355
Wright, N. T. 207, 208, 211

Yeago, David 201n16
YHWH 132–61
   Holy Spirit 230–32
   seen and unseen 141–52
   Son 144n14, 164, 166–67, 169–70, 176, 179, 180–81, 186–91, 207–12
Young, Frances 120n18, 122n24

Ziegler, Roland 24n4, 27, 76n54, 87
Zwingli, Ulrich 26

www.ingramcontent.com/pod-product-compliance
Lightning Source LLC
Chambersburg PA
CBHW020937180426

43194CB00038B/213